Counter-revolution of the Word

Counter-revolution of the Word

of the Word

THE CONSERVATIVE ATTACK

ON MODERN POETRY, 1945–1960

BY ALAN FILREIS

THE UNIVERSITY OF NORTH CAROLINA PRESS

CHAPEL HILL

© 2008
The University of North Carolina Press
All rights reserved
Set in Minion and The Sans types
by Keystone Typesetting, Inc.
Manufactured in the United States of America

The paper in this book meets the guidelines for
permanence and durability of the Committee
on Production Guidelines for Book Longevity
of the Council on Library Resources.

Library of Congress
Cataloging-in-Publication Data
Filreis, Alan, 1956–
Counter-revolution of the word : the
conservative attack on modern poetry, 1945–
1960 / by Alan Filreis.
    p. cm.
Includes bibliographical references and index.
ISBN 978-0-8078-3162-5 (cloth : alk. paper)
1. American poetry—20th century—History
and criticism. 2. Politics and literature—
United States—History—20th century.
3. Conservatism and literature—United
States—History—20th century. 4. Modernism
(Literature)—United States. I. Title. II. Variant
title: Counterrevolution of the word.
PS310.P6F56 2008
811'.5409—dc22   2007029357

Portions of this book are drawn from
previously published material: Several
revised paragraphs from "Modern Poetry and
Anticommunism," in *A Concise Companion to
Twentieth-Century American Poetry*, ed. Stephen
Fredman (Malden, Mass.: Blackwell, 2005), pp.
173–90. © 2005. Used by permission. Several
paragraphs from "What's Historical about
Historicism?," *Wallace Stevens Journal* 28, 2
(Fall 2004): pp. 210–18. © 2004 Wallace Stevens
Society. Used by permission. Revisions of
several pages from "Tests of Poetry," *American
Literary History* 15, 1 (Spring 2003): pp. 27–35.
© 2003 Oxford University Press. Used by
permission. Acknowledgment of permission to
reprint other copyrighted material appears in a
section preceding the index.

12 11 10 09 08   5 4 3 2 1

This book was published with the assistance
of the Anniversary Endowment Fund of the
University of North Carolina Press.

for Jane,
Ben, and Hannah

Contents

Illustrations

Preface

> Then they returned to America crying out, "God is dead! Long live
> grammar!"—Edward Dahlberg, "The Act of Concealment" (1952)

> The New Deal had sanctified the alphabet.
> —Ralph de Toledano, *Lament for a Generation* (1960)

Counter-revolution of the Word is about conservatives' attempt to destroy the
modernist avant-garde in the anticommunist period after World War II. The
antagonists readers will meet in these pages by no means constitute a monolithic force. They were not ideologically of a kind. But *aesthetically*? Well, yes,
aesthetically they were more or less unified; they knew what they formally
opposed, and the narrative of that surprising unity lies at the center of this
study. A few of these people did work together, such as the band of poets and
poetry editors—most of them reactionary antimodernists—that the prolific
Stanton Coblentz helped assemble under the banner of the League for Sanity in
Poetry. Others among Coblentz's colleagues, however, would not have recognized themselves as allies; quite aside from their hatred of modern poetry,
differences between them—academic, theoretical, personal—would have gotten
in the way. In this telling of the story of the attempt to roll back modernism, to
finalize "what might be called the divorce of the two avant-gardes" (aesthetic
and political),[1] we see bona fide conservatives joined by a variety of liberal
anticommunists who shared the anticommunist ground. The people whom I
dub "antimodernist anticommunists" came to the matter of poetry with the
real heterogeneity characteristic of the postwar right and so-called New Conservatives. Some of them, like Max Eastman, hardly an unknown—indeed, at one
time a major figure—had been both communists and supporters of modernism. Others, like the now-forgotten Read Bain, proudly stood to the *left* of
center on social issues and were willing to tolerate contemporary poets who
tended toward the traditional side of the modern idiomatic and metrical scale.[2]
Some, like E. Merrill Root, were lifelong radical individualists who were consistent in their beliefs, at least in the abstract, but organizationally made the
journey from the communist left to the extreme right—in Root's case, from
editorial posts at the *New Masses* to the poetry editorship of *American Opinion*,
the magazine of the John Birch Society. Other figures freely conceded that they
had moved from left to right: the Poetry Society of America's A. M. Sullivan, for

example, earlier had "wandered a trifle left of center," voting for socialist Norman Thomas despite registration as a Democrat, but by 1954 "certainly applaud[ed] [Joseph] McCarthy's clean-up of the U.S. Printing Office."[3] Many of them, like Welford Inge, actually feared the modernist conspiracy as a tactical aspect of the world domination of communism; these people—their views strange to us now—are of particular interest. Among this latter sort of conservative is Archer Milton Huntington, a personally modest although immensely wealthy person who saw the demise of the American poetic academy as "symptomatic": "The source of the trouble is *elsewhere*," Huntington wrote, and he meant generally the radical sensibility and specifically the economics of the New Deal and its destruction of traditional arts philanthropy.[4] Virginia Kent Cummins decried William Carlos Williams's commitment to the principle "that experimentation is necessary to the life of the language" and urged her readers to conclude that "it may all be a part of Communism, trying to undermine our most treasured traditions."[5] The querulous Battle Creek poet Jessie Wilmore Murton deemed communism in modern verse every bit as harmful as the (alleged) takeover by leftists of a Michigan denominational college or the wrecking of a manufacturing plant in Kalamazoo by a "motorcade of . . . radicals."[6] Others, such as Robert Hillyer, a figure known nationally for his role in the controversy stirred when Ezra Pound received the Bollingen Prize, probably did not believe any ultimate political conspiracy theory yet used and admired anticommunism as a means of striking hard at the cultural betrayal modernism seemed generally to represent. Some, such as Richard Weaver, were consistent, thoroughgoing, *true* reactionaries—remarkable minds, fine writers, brilliant in their theoretical absolutism. Still others, a troublesome vocal minority, were inconstant careerists, such as Ben Lucien Burman, whose salacious red-baiting tropes went logically and literarily awry.

All agreed, however, that modern poetic experimentalism was horrendous in a way that either was a form of communist subversion or was exactly *like* communism. Modernists' "attempt to destroy poetry," one of them wrote, "their enmity . . . their hostility . . . their zest . . . admit of no interpretation but that which, *in another field*, would be made of the attitude of an American who constantly applauded Russian actions, attitudes and ways of life while sneering at everything in our own from Washington to Truman."[7]

Is it right to say that modernism's detractors were indeed working "in *another* field"—or in the same? Perhaps *that* is the larger question raised and answered here. I began this study bearing the general expectation that I would discover and then conclude that antimodernists at midcentury shared the anticommunist field with economic, political, and sociological critics and commentators. To be sure, in the course of my research I did discern significant overlaps, and I came to understand that the logic, analytical tools, and theories critics in fields other than my own have used to interpret anticommunism would be helpful. Many poetic traditionalists who had long thought of themselves as apolitical found, especially in the late 1940s, that they were shifting quickly into politicized vocabularies and borrowing analyses from anticommunist colleagues in disciplines they had previously deemed irrelevant to poetry. Finally, though, this book concludes that the anticommunist antimodernists ultimately sought to change the aesthetic landscape and that this attempt caused as much damage to the art of poetry as if the campaign against modernism had been waged solely on the political grounds held by anticommunists in the practical fields of public policy, education, and the judiciary.

Anticommunist antimodernists sought to deny the assumption that aesthetic progress required formal experimentation, and they sought to find a way—any way, even a crude, straightforwardly political way—of dubbing the verse of formal experiment "bad poetry"; and finally, they sought to enact a permanent "restoration of the language," a heroic counter-revolutionary act that required suppression of the avant-garde and even the idea of an avant-garde. Restoration meant (somehow) taking poetic language "back" to a (fantasized) moment in literary history just prior to its affiliation with extrapoetic modes, an affiliation modernism's anticommunist detractors blamed on the way American poets—and intellectuals generally—of the 1930s had allegedly co-opted the free, unfettered, individualistic creative geniuses of the 1910s and 1920s. Anticommunism provided the most effective means by which modernism's enemies could set up a permanent opposition between, on one hand, writing that "utters the everlasting language of poetry" and, on the other hand, writing that cannot go "beyond experimentation" to poetic tradition and thus invited the reasonable American reader to wonder "if it utters *any language at all*."[8] Anticommunism offered an ideological mechanism by which the antimodernist could deny modern poetry its status as language. The second half of this book tells that story, which leads, in the final chapter, to a survey of the resistance against modernism put up by purveyors of the primary fetishism—namely, grammar—that operated by political analogy in reactionary language.

So antimodernism in the 1950s was really, at bottom, a fight against "liberals [who] tend to assume that only the left in politics, only the avant-garde in literature, are against conformity."[9] The anticommunist in the poetry world worked to undo this alleged association between the radical left and poetic avant-gardism. The project entailed—I am tempted to say *required*—an aggressive reinterpretation of the 1930s. Here Cold War antimodernists borrowed amply from the larger political-cultural critique; that critique is the topic of the first half of *Counter-revolution of the Word*.

The version of the "thirties" constructed in the "fifties" (actually, 1945–60) enabled *liberals* to claim that one could be "against conformity" while still hating avant-gardism. And hate it they did, with new reason.

To my knowledge, this is the first book written about the overall effects of actual anticommunism on modernist American poetry and poetics. Such a blank in our understanding of American art and artists has its specific causes. A main cause is the apparent disappearance of the evidence for links between and among disparate, truculent McCarthyite elements in the poetry world and their "communist poet" enemies *and* the modernist experimenters who have not been known to have connections to the communist movement. Other historians of the twentieth-century American literary left have perhaps beheld this evidence more systematically at the start, with keener initial intent, than I. My own story of starting out is more that of the accidental archival traveler, although permitting myself such veerings and branchings off as I could literally afford has led me to think self-consciously and more confidently than ever about the importance of the archive in the context of American intellectuals' politics, especially the politics of communism and anticommunism. An otherwise brilliant work about the 1950s such as Richard Hofstadter's *Anti-Intellectualism in American Life* (1963)[10]—the second half of which is really, I would say, a study of philistine antimodernism—is vulnerable to counterargument because Hofstadter disdained what historians call "primary research." The same problem besets Hofstadter's essay, "The Pseudo-Conservative Revolt —1954," which nonetheless influences this study, as does *The Authoritarian Personality* (1950), a theoretically but also experimentally magnificent survey of American political attitudes conducted by a team of researchers led by Theodor Adorno.[11] But for these writings, Hofstadter adamantly eschewed the archive, and he went still further: he called such research the purview of "archive rats."[12]

The source of this disdain is not entirely clear, but the effect is at best to have left the case for intellectualism incomplete and at worst methodologically ironic. Hofstadter, influenced by Adorno, concluded—rightly, I think—that what we call "McCarthyism" has been a cultural phenomenon. Yet the culture the historian had in mind was made and embodied in part by those who at the time remained unpublished or diverted into producing expressions not available (then or even now) on library or bookstore shelves. I do not claim that the materials rediscovered by archival work are "primary," but surely they can be just as suggestive and persuasive as materials that are readily available and require no such effort.

Almost two decades ago, I was in Austin to visit an uncle and decided to spend a few afternoons reading around in the unpublished papers of modern American poets at the Ransom Center of the University of Texas. To the archivist on duty at the reading room desk, I described my interest in modernists who had had actual affiliations with the political left—in particular, with American communism. We agreed that I should begin with Louis Zukofsky, an obvious starting point: I was as fascinated by the problem of reading Zukofsky politically as I was of doing the same with Wallace Stevens, whose political life, such as it could be construed, was my project at the time. Moreover, the Ransom Center has a treasure trove of Zukofsky's manuscripts. I read some edifying Zukofsky materials during that visit, but because my mind characteristically wandered "past Z," as it might be put, I began to move my research (and my archival methodology) in a new direction, putting together pieces of a puzzle that has occupied me on and off in all the years since. The method has taken me pretty much everywhere, and this book is the result.

What is literally past Z in the typical repository card catalog? *Miscellaneous, unidentified, anonymous, uncataloged, misindexed.* Even in the great archive, what is uncataloged is often merely that which has been quickly deemed "less important," not sufficiently a priority to merit the weeks and months—and real money—it takes to ascertain the identity of writers and recipients of personal correspondence, of pseudonymous authors of unpublished or unfinished manuscripts, of writers who neglected (or declined) to affix their names to or to date what they wrote. Now if you add communism to the mix of motives for anonymity, you get perhaps the ultimate reason why so much "ephemera" from the communist 1930s and the anticommunist 1950s awaits the scholar venturing past Z. Some communist and fellow-traveling writers used pseudonyms that, while not per se secret, are hard to identify now by anyone who has not developed a mental rolodex of the disappeared leftist network and its traditionalist antagonists or without careful cross-referencing to other correspondences in other uncataloged materials in other archives—or indeed without permitting the digressions from left to right and back again that are sometimes partially mapped in those unique materials. (Walter Lowenfels mentioned just once, in a personal letter to Granville Hicks, that he had published verse in the *Daily Worker* under the name "Arthur Coyle." Since Lowenfels never published a poem in the United States over his own name until his 1938 book, *Steel 1937*, the verse of Arthur Coyle is meaningful if one wants to learn about Lowenfels's transition from his expatriate, experimentalist 1920s to the "eleg[ies] for idealism" he wrote as a self-conscious communist.)[13] Of many twentieth-century American poets who wrote through a series of discrete aesthetic and ideological phases, who evolved through several literary identities, we often insistently but inaccurately describe a whole career, trace with critical hindsight a single creative and critical intelligence developing, without crediting or even realizing the degree to which such identification is a convenience enabled by the fact that they identified themselves consistently by name and were always thus bibliographically and archivally indexable.

Past Z that day in Texas I retrieved and examined with fascination a never-yet-read thick folder of unordered handwritten materials, mostly undated, that turned out to be a regular correspondence between a man named "Leippert" and another person then identified on the file only as "W.M." "Leippert" caught my eye because I had recently been visiting Chicago, where at the Regenstein Library of the University of Chicago I read letters the apparently conservative poet Wallace Stevens had written to "J. Ronald Lane Latimer." "Latimer" was the founder and publisher of Alcestis Press, which published two of Stevens's books of poems in the 1930s. I had learned there that the given name of this odd "Latimer" was George Leippert, born and raised in Albany, New York, and he had at least five other pseudonyms. I had already been to Albany to talk with contemporary residents named Leippert and had luckily found Melissa Leippert, sister of the pseudonymous publisher. I knew from the Latimer-Stevens connection that Willard Maas (my "W.M." at the Ransom Center) had been Latimer's associate editor and close friend, and I learned from Melissa that a half-century earlier, her brother had "run off with Maas," although until I read the unprocessed folder of letters in Austin I did not fully know what that meant.

It meant communism, among other things. The poet Maas had joined the Communist Party of the United States (CPUSA) and then had assiduously drawn Latimer in. And the letters I now studied, traded back and forth between the two excitable young red editors of modernist poets in the mid-1930s, taught me a good deal of the fecund modernist-communist relationship—and specifically the extent to which Stevens, a poet seemingly remote from politics, would have known about this context.

Latimer's semisecret modernist-communist nexus, almost entirely hidden outside the archive and mostly obscured even inside it, became a model for dozens of similar explorations I undertook in the years following. Typical of the exchanges I then sought and found in various archives, the "W.M."-"Leippert" letters also mentioned a myriad of other names, most of them indeed at first just names to me, "minor" literary characters—writers who, as I came to learn, were either part of a network that by the mid-1940s and 1950s was entirely scattered or, especially if by then they had renounced radicalism and had de-radicalized their version of modernism, were oddly now *in charge* of the reputations of their opposite numbers.

Bearing a list of everyone these two young radicals mentioned and accumulating longer lists as I went along, in Syracuse, Los Angeles, New Haven, Seattle, again Chicago, Durham, Boston, New York, Wilmington, Baltimore, Detroit, Truchas (in New Mexico—where I met Alvaro Cardona-Hine entirely by accident), Charlottesville, Palo Alto, La Jolla, St. Louis, Chapel Hill, Atlanta, Washington, and elsewhere, I followed leads and accrued a homemade cross-index. I wanted to write a book that described but also conveyed—and even embodied—the form of the scattering. I sought analysis of its effect on modern American poetry generally, and I began to identify the agents of an intra-American poetic diaspora—the agents themselves now shadowy figures no less, forgotten, discoverable mainly through the archive.

These radical and conservative networks largely did not overlap, especially as the 1930s gave way to years of anxious Cold War, yet the writings of and exchanges among members of each group plentifully referred to their detractors, and so, reading both, I began to shape this book's unusual dramatis personae. In the time it has taken to research and write the book, I have come to comprehend, through its materiality, the basis of what has been called a cycle of "repression and recovery."

Poetry is hardly immune to such political phasing. On the contrary, as I contend, poetry and poetics are especially sensitive indicators—not because the verse that ultimately interests me is particularly clear and indicative but because it is difficult, disrupted, open to counterargument. Through *Counter-revolution of the Word*, a detailed exploration of ideological antimodernism, I offer what I hope is a persuasive response to a fascinating and seemingly unanswerable question: Why has avant-garde writing been such a strong conductor of American conservatives' doubts and fears?

Acknowledgments

I wish first to thank my research assistants for sharing their enthusiasm for what can be found in the library and for their willingness to tolerate my mania for bibliographic detail: Kash Bahadur, Elissa Bassini, James Beaver, Robert Blum, Gordon Bond, Josh Boyette, Aichlee Bushnell, John Butler (at Brown University), Ross Chainin, Kerry Cooperman, Kalyani Fernando, Gabe Galson, Jill Ivey, Yumeko Kawano, Travis Koplow (at the Wisconsin Historical Society), Stephen Krewson, Matt Larsen, Elizabeth McDonnell, Suzanne Maynard Miller (at the University of Washington in Seattle and later at Brown University), Yaran Noti, Nitin Prakash, Zuri Rice, Lynn Roland, Eileen Romero, Matthew Rosenbaum, Avi Rubin, Sarah Ruhl (at Brown University), Danielle Siegel, Matthew Tanzer, Keicy Tolbert (at the University of Virginia), James Vergara, Kathryn Wege, and Elaine Woo. Arielle Brousse and Peter Schwarz ably helped me with permissions. Jamie-Lee Josselyn, Blake Martin, and Phil Sandick could not have been more supportive of my work generally; they are heaven's manna.

This book began and ended in the archives. Without the generosity, the timely response, and—quite often—the sheer enthusiasm of librarians of special collections and rare books and manuscript departments, this study would have lacked the depth, specificity, and newness I have tried to give it. I am grateful to John Lancaster (Amherst College: Bogan, Rolfe Humphries, Merrill Root); Fred Burwell (Beloit College Archive: Chad Walsh); Gordon Daines (University Archives, Brigham Young University: Cleon Skousen); Marianne LaBatto (Brooklyn College Archives: Kramer, Rosten); Frank Boles (Clarke Historical Library, Central Michigan University: Kirk-Eliot letters); Bernard Crystal, Jennifer B. Lee, and Patrick Lawlor (Rare Book and Manuscripts Library, Columbia University: Schneider, Joseph Barnes, Burke, radical oral histories); Jay Satterfield (Rauner Special Collections Library, Dartmouth College: Taggard); Noel VanGorden (Burton Historical Collection, Detroit Public Library: Dondero); Robert Byrd (William R. Perkins Library, Duke University: J. B. Matthews); James W. Greenleaf (Federal Bureau of Investigation: Freedom of Information Act materials on Cameron; Little, Brown; Rukeyser; Mike Gold; and others); Leslie A. Morris (Houghton Library, Harvard University: Hillyer); Patrice Donoghue (Harvard University Archive, Pusey Library: 1950 Conference on the Defense of Poetry); Sara Hodson and Rebecca Tuttle (Huntington Library: Stevens, Aiken, Florence

Keene); Cynthia Requardt and Margaret Burri (Manuscripts Department, Milton Eisenhower Library, Johns Hopkins University: Joseph M. Lalley); Nancy Birk (Special Collections, Kent State University: Cid Corman's copy of Matthiessen's *Achievement of T. S. Eliot*); Bob Schmidt (University Archives, Miami University of Ohio: Read Bain); Patricia Albright (Mount Holyoke College Archives: Viereck); Cynthia Wall and Diana Haskell (Newberry Library, Chicago: Cowley, Merriam, William McFee, Rolfe Humphries, Rexroth, Dillon, Floyd Dell, Jack Conroy); Peter Filardo (Tamiment Library, Elmer Holmes Bobst Library, New York University: *Daily Worker*, Counterattack, Taggard, Dahlberg, Lowenfels, Cowley, Bodenheim, Merriam–Cameron letters, Regnery, Jefferson School, Millen Brand); Marvin Taylor (Fales Library, New York University: for the M. L. Rosenthal Papers); Gretchen Feltes (Library of the New York University School of Law: Aesopian language in the Smith Act trials); Margaret Sherry (Princeton University Libraries: Neugass, *Story* Archives, Blackmur, Tate, Macleod); Leah Smith (Seeley Mudd Manuscript Library, Princeton University: Medina, Hillyer); Anne Englehart and Ellen Shea (Schlesinger Library, Radcliffe College: Eve Merriam); Abby Lester and Patricia Owen (Sarah Lawrence College Archives: Taggard, Gregory); Randy Bixby (Special Collections, Southern Illinois University: Bob Brown); Kay Bost and David Farmer (DeGolyer Library, Southern Methodist University: Smoot, *Facts Forum*); Ron Bulatoff, Pruda Lood, and Carol Leadenham (Hoover Institution, Stanford University: Hook, *National Republic*, Budenz, Dan Smoot, Freeman, Regnery, Buckley, Subversive Activities Control Board); Polly Armstrong (Stanford University Libraries: Creeley, Beach); Robert Berthoff and Michael Basinski (Poetry/Rare Book Collection, State University of New York at Buffalo: Merrill Moore, Williams); George T. Henke (Sunnyside Gardens [New York] Historical Society: Neugass); Kate Gorcyzynski (Thompson Public Library, Grosvenordale, Connecticut: Root); Leon Miller and Melissa Smith (Manuscripts Department, Howard-Tilton Memorial Library, Tulane University: Ben Lucien Burman); Steve Coy and Lynda Claassen (Mandeville Department of Special Collections, University of California at San Diego: Mac Low, Oppen); Ann Caiger (Manuscripts Division, University of California at Los Angeles: Rexroth, Babette Deutsch, Aiken, Kreymborg, Harriet Monroe); Carol A. Turley (University of California at Los Angeles Special Collections: Hughes, Lowenfels, Cameron, Rexroth); Dan Meyer and Jay Satterfield (Regenstein Library, University of Chicago: *Poetry*, University of Chicago Archives, Latimer, Weaver, Regnery, Amy Bonner, Dahlberg, Whitman centennial); L. Rebecca Johnson Melvin and Timothy Murray (Special Collections, University of Delaware: Kreymborg, Untermeyer, League to Support Poetry); Anne Turkos (University Archives, Hornbake Library, University of Maryland: Homer House, Susan E. Harman); John Beck (Albin Kuhn Library, University of Maryland at Baltimore: radical pamphlets); Linda Seidman and Peter Nelson (Special Collections, University of Massachusetts at Amherst: Bogan, Humphries, Viereck); Kathryn Beam and Kathleen Dow (Special Collections, University of Michigan: Rosten, Kramer); Karen Klinkenberg (University of Minnesota Archives: Joseph Warren Beach); Cathy Henderson (Harry Ransom Research Center, University of Texas: Zukofsky, Maas-Latimer, Merrill Moore, Lowell); John E. White (Wilson Library, University of North Carolina at Chapel Hill: Burke, Jackson Mathews Papers, *Contempo*); Nancy Shawcross and Daniel Traister (Van Pelt Library, University of Pennsylvania: Farrell, Mumford, Robert Spiller, *Alcestis*); Marie-Louis Kragh and John Plunkett (Albert and Shirley Small Special Collections Library, University of Virginia: Kreymborg, Leigh Hanes); Gary Lundell and Kerry Bartels (University of Washington at Seattle: Cowley, Malcolm Brown); Anne Posega (Washington University: George Marion O'Donnell, Rexroth, *Poetry*, Isabella Gardner, Robert Sward, Deutsch, Burke, Aiken, Lee Anderson); Nancy Baird (Kentucky State Archives, Western Kentucky University: Jessie Wilmore Murton); Harold L. Miller (Wisconsin Historical Society: Regnery, Eugene Dennis, Budenz, American Council of Christian Laymen); Patricia Willis (Beinecke Library, Yale University: Hughes, Lowenfels, McGrath, Cameron, Oscar Williams); and Diane E. Kaplan (Yale University Library's Manuscript and Archives Division: Norman Holmes Pearson, Williams, Hughes, Elizabeth Ames, Charles Humboldt–Alvaro Cardona Hines correspondence, Communist Party of New York State, V. J. Jerome). No archivist-librarian is better or more devoted to making rare materials available to scholars than the brilliant, meticulous, and bibliographically insatiable Kathleen Manwaring (Special Collections Research Center, Syracuse University: Sullivan, McGinley, Gregory, Hicks, Fulton Lewis, Roskolenko, O'Connor, Dahlberg, Leonard Brown, Brenda Putnam, Maas, the Huntingtons, Charles Wharton Stork, Earl Browder, Coblentz, Macleod, Kempton, Hillyer, Bob Brown, radical magazines), and I am endlessly thankful for her efforts. (In many instances, these individuals, representing the material rights held by their institutions, have given me permission to refer to and to quote from letters, manuscripts, and other unpublished materials.)

I am grateful to Josephine Hayes Dean for permitting me to quote from the poems of her father, Alfred Hayes. "Domes" is quoted by kind permission of Daniel Berrigan, S.J. Stephanie Viereck Kamath, Peter Viereck's granddaughter, authorized me to quote from his verse. For permission to quote from several poems by Muriel Rukeyser, I gratefully acknowledge the estate of the poet, represented by William L. Rukeyser. The verse of Genevieve Taggard is quoted with the kind permission of Judith Benét Richardson. I acknowledge the American Academy of Arts and Letters, New York City, for permission to quote J. Malcolm Brinnin. Joseph Warren Beach II has kindly permitted me to quote from a poem and from unpublished letters of his father, Joseph Warren Beach. Lines from the poem "Elegy" by Judson Crews are quoted with the permission of Mr. Crews, with gratitude to Carole Crews. Many thanks also to Marilyn Kane for permitting me to quote Carl Rakosi. Poems of Kenneth Fearing are quoted by permission of Russell and Volkening as agents for the estate. Martha Millet's poems are quoted with the approval of her heirs, Alexander and Emily Garlin. I am very grateful also to Patricia Rosten Filan, Norman Rosten's daughter. I quote from Walter Lowenfels's poetry by permission of Judy Jacobs. Alan Rosenthal has kindly extended me the right to quote from M. L. Rosenthal's unpublished papers and has made available—and given permission to use—a family photograph of his father. Howard Sparber's illustration for Stanton Coblentz's *New York Times Magazine* article is reproduced with his kind permission. Sidney Hook's letters are quoted with the permission of Ernest B. Hook. A letter from Murray Kempton to Granville Hicks is quoted by permission of Helen Epstein, acting for the estate of Murray Kempton. Georgiana Pine has granted me the right to quote the poetry and letters of E. Merrill Root. Peggy Fox at New Directions has been as helpful as always to me—and all of us who love to quote Williams and Pound. Acknowledgment of permission to reprint other copyrighted material appears in a section preceding the index.

Revised versions of nine scattered paragraphs in this book were published in an essay I wrote for *A Concise Companion to Twentieth-Century American Poetry* © 2005 by Blackwell; I gratefully acknowledge Stephen Fredman, the book's editor, and Blackwell for extending me the right to use this material. Several paragraphs that appear here in chapter 2 have been revised from a paper presented at a 2004 conference celebrating the fiftieth anniversary of Wallace Stevens's *Collected Poems* and then published in the *Wallace Stevens Journal*; acknowledgment is made to John Serio, Glen MacLeod, and the Wallace Stevens Society for permission to reuse this material. Several pages of analysis in chapters 2 and 13 derive from the preparation of my essay, "Tests of Poetry," for a symposium on history and u.s. poetics printed in the Spring 2003 issue of *American Literary History*; I am grateful to Robert von Hallberg for instigating these thoughts and to *ALH* editor Gordon Hutner for the invitation to participate.

Many people helped me by making themselves available for interviews, phone conversations, letters, and e-mail exchanges, providing contact information and historical and biographical background, vetting historical generalizations, verifying facts, and offering leads to new unpublished material and other people whom I should meet. I am especially grateful to Diana Anhalt, the late Herbert Aptheker (reading habits of CPUSA leaders), John Ashbery, Paul Barfoot (at Syracuse), Andrew Barnes (son of Joseph Barnes), Joe Beach, Walter Bernstein, Daniel Berrigan, Julia Budenz (a poet, daughter of Louis), the late Stanley Burnshaw, Louis Cabri (on Mac Low), the late Angus Cameron (whom I interviewed with Alan Wald), Alvaro Cardona-Hine, Don E. Carlton (at the Center for American History, University of Texas), the late Cid Corman, the late Robert Creeley, Tom Devaney (Rakosi), Rachel Blau DuPlessis, the late Howard Fast, Manny Filreis, Lawrence Fixel, Gene Frumkin, Estelle Fuchs, Marvin Gettleman (communist schools), the late Allen Ginsberg (on Ben Maddow), the late Irving Howe, Michal Kane (Lowenfels's daughter), Ann Kimmage, the late Aaron Kramer, Laura Kramer (Aaron's daughter), Sherman Labovitz (on Philadelphia communists), Matthew Lasar, the late James Laughlin, Sverre Lyngstad (Smith Act cases), the late Jackson Mac Low, the late Martha Millet, Myra and Deirdre Neugass, Bob Perelman, Jean-Michel Rabaté, the late Carl Rakosi, Naomi Replansky, Selden Rodman, Jerome Rothenberg, Ellen Schrecker (McCarthyism), Roger Seamon (Eda Lou Walton's nephew), Andrew Sillen, Tom Sillen, Ron Silliman (on Williams in the 1950s), Ted Smith (for help with Richard Weaver), the late Susan Sontag (aesthetics and anticommunism), Edith Stevens (for help with Alfred Levinson), Robert Sward, Harvey Teres (with whom I interviewed Stanley Burnshaw), the late Willard Thorp, Alan Trachtenberg (Lowenfels), Tom Travisano, Ted Watts (the one and only indexer of *New Masses*), the late Theodore Weiss, Fred Whitehead (whose *People's Culture* I found full of leads), and the late Ira Wolfert.

I am among those scholars and critics of modern poetry who can proudly say that Marjorie Perloff has been a crucial influence. No one in my field has been more consistently or energetically supportive of me, personally and professionally. (Many thanks also to Marjorie for putting me up in Palo Alto while I conducted research at the Hoover Institution and for hosting me in Los Angeles over lunch and dinner many times while I worked at UCLA and the Huntington Library.) In scholarly terms, one might say that Alan Wald is for me the literary left to Marjorie's modernism. Alan knows as much as anyone living about American literary radicalism; moreover, he has always been willing to share materials, cross-references, insight, and the stuff of his deep files—truly, the model citizen-scholar. Robert von Hallberg, aforementioned, invited me to present a version of the Cold War antimodernist story to his modern poetry group at the University of Chicago, an event that enabled us to continue a conversation about American poetry and politics that began with his generous support of my previous books; I have been guided and instructed here by the beautiful discernments of his long entry, "Poetry, Politics and Intellectuals" in the 1940–95 volume of *The Cambridge History of American Literature*, and I am grateful to know that we always converge on the importance of poetry as poetry. Charles Bernstein and Kenneth Goldsmith, through our work together on PENNsound, have, to say the least, enlivened my sense of contemporary poetics. Steve Evans, Ben Friedlander, and Burton Hatlen of the National Poetry Foundation (Orono, Maine) graciously invited me to present at length and enabled a critical environment in which I tested parts of this argument on a hundred poets, scholars, and critics in my field. Aldon Nielsen, hosting me at Pennsylvania State University, generously provided the same. Cary Nelson, like Wald an open book about literary radicalism, has been generous with his findings; his passion for lost or suppressed materials has positively affected me.

Sian Hunter has been an ideal editor, it seems to me: tolerant, responsive, and always ready to make a serious effort at understanding just how far I needed to go with this project. I am proud to publish this work with the University of North Carolina Press, well aware of the contributions the press has made over the years to scholarship on the American literary left, and to extend that special interest a bit by adding more poetics to the mix.

I express my deep appreciation for Rebecca Bushnell, who was instinctively supportive of my need to find time to finish this book despite the demands of many ongoing projects at Penn about which we both care; may she (and they) flourish. Peter Conn, no matter how busy, has always dropped everything he was doing when I called for help. From Bob Lucid, who died suddenly around the time this book went into production, I felt constant advocacy and the actual power of mentorship. Paul Kelly has been an unfailing supporter, friend, and real patron; he has made it possible for me to live intellectually in an environment (the Kelly Writers House and Center for Programs in Contemporary Writing, both entities I have founded and direct) in which the poetic experimentalism I study historically freely flows into the contemporary. John Richetti, whose own critical writing I deem lucidity itself, is a dear friend and the most collegial person I have ever met; when I write sentences, I think positively of John. Raymond Nelson and Art Casciato, an irascible pair, first got me interested in the literary left; Nelson's at-first inexplicable passion for Kenneth Patchen—and dislike of Wallace Stevens—caused me to ponder the radicalism-modernism problem for the first time in (as well as outside) the academic context. I still mourn Terrence Des Pres, who believed in my intellectual capacity before I did; I treasure the teachings of Margaret Maurer and the late Robert Blackmore, who opened the doors to crazy learning. Beyond academia, a mostly self-taught intellectual, my late great-uncle Carl Cherkis, lifelong public school teacher and rigorous urban liberal who lived for art and ideas, took the time to write long vibrant letters to a serious but yet-unskilled grand-nephew; it was Carl, now that I think on it, who set me first on the trail of this story. I am glad I have the energy of my mother, Lois, and the patience of my father, Sam, and wish to thank them once again for showing such faith in me.

This book is dedicated to Jane Treuhaft and to my children, Ben and Hannah. Ben and Hannah make my world go 'round (and 'round and 'round) and care about the best part of me. Among the myriad virtues of Jane's love are her deep sensitivities about art, drama, language, and, most of all, the way beautiful things are made and seen. Our time together has brought me to understand more than ever the merged concerns of this book, which are responsibility and beauty, with which she abounds.

Counter-revolution
of the Word

PART I

The Fifties' Thirties

The myth of the fifties may not be that the Communists dominated the thirties, but rather that there are no social passions.—Murray Kempton in a letter to Granville Hicks, 1955

The real question . . . was not so much a conflict between being both modern and communist, because we were all at that time modern in our writing.—Carl Rakosi, 2003

When I read *Proletarian Literature of the United States* [1935] (at about 14, halfway through school), I considered many of its poets to be modernists. —Aaron Kramer, 1994

Better Rethink Your Aesthetics

Near the end of World War II, a tough Brooklynite—she had grown up in a tenement and had worked many exhausting jobs—continued her work as an active member of the Communist Party of the United States (CPUSA). Martha Millet was also a poet. How unusual a party activist was she? She read and admired modernist verse and would then certainly have called herself a "modern" writer. The radical bibliography such as can be reconstructed—not easily—discloses Millet as the writer of occasional prose for tracts, pamphlets, and the like, edited, published and even printed by the party and by CPUSA-affiliated groups. Her poems, appearing in politically unaligned modernist journals such as the already venerable *Poetry* of Chicago and in communist-affiliated magazines such as *New World Review*, would have struck anyone aware of Millet's art as a whole to be a consistent verse project, undifferentiated with respect to poetics and partisanship. Or, on the contrary, was she leading two lives?

If as a writer Martha Millet was known at all by a literary readership beyond circles of political activists, it would have been as what was once called a "progressive journalist." Indeed, when she published her poems in the 1950s, magazines' "Notes on Contributors" sections would describe her as "*formerly* a *labor* journalist."[1] An odd tag, truly, for someone who had never really ceased her political writing. What did such a designation say? To call Millet a former journalist was to suggest—again, incorrectly—that by midcentury she should be or perhaps wanted to be known primarily as a poet. (In the late 1940s and 1950s, dubbing a poet "journalistic" could even, at times, be coded red-baiting.)[2]

Although Millet always had some doubts about "the 'cultural' wing" of Anglo-modernism,[3] the political poems she published during the Cold War were influenced formally and linguistically—at the level of the stanza and of the phrase (though less so at the line)—by specific modernist practice. There is little mistaking this. In "Mississippi," a poem about the horrific slaying of the young Chicagoan Emmett Till in 1955 for allegedly making a pass at a white woman in Mississippi, readers seeking or expecting a communist literalism or naive docu-mimeticism, an exposition in verse of the murder or the trial, might thus reasonably raise the same complaint that modernist poets had heard from their political detractors all along: the poem's language (multivocal, disrupted by ironized popular phraseology, idiomatic convention, and grammatical fragment) failed to record the history of an urgent, radicalizing moment (the Till case, a progressive cause célèbre) in a series of accessible word pictures, as verse in the communist *Masses & Mainstream* sometimes surely did. Indeed, one CPUSA official took exception to Millet's poem on such grounds, appreciating its apparent sentiment but raising serious "questions of content."[4] To be sure, more than a sufficient number of CPUSA poets always remained on hand to satirize comrades and fellow travelers who seemed paralyzed by mere aesthetic concerns, and the image of the ham-handed American communist poet has of course been derived from the former.[5] It must not go without saying that in the Soviet Union, experimentalists were suppressed, brutally and at times murderously, and after a brief postrevolutionary moment of tolerance, free verse was firmly condemned. It must also be remembered that several of the same complaints made by American conservatives against American modernists were those made by Communist Party leaders in the Soviet Union against Russian poets.[6]

Yet Martha Millet, in New York, an otherwise devout communist, in her language-conscious language "about" the Till case, gave us writing that draws readers' attention to the phrasal constructedness of what we are reading:

> crying out
> crying out
>
> "Do unto others . . ."
>
> yes[7]

The relationship between this affirmative "yes" and the fragment of the Golden Rule is open, unsettled. The overall point of the poem seems polemical (*we should never forget what racist hatred did to Emmett Till*), but its language was not that of leftist didacticism, in spite of official CPUSA policy at the time—weakly enforced then but unmistakable: writers should directly and realistically depict the Till murder.[8] For the reader willing to concede that Millet has a valid poetics, the loosened "yes" itself seems as much a chastened nod as a call to angry, certain defiance. Another of Millet's "radical" poems, "The Nearness," also published in the communist magazine *Masses & Mainstream*, might even cause a CPUSA traditionalist to complain of an abstract, fragmented, self-referential contentlessness. Doubters might worry that the poem's topic was the writing subject in search of proximity at a time of new cultural distance. The relatively difficult language—its effort, not entirely successful, at newness or freshness—could be said to bridge distances by a refusal to refer either narratively or depictively:

> Neither in mind
> nor in smile
> can any be
> remote enough—
>
> . . . .
>
> weather in New York affected.
> The desert
> still desert.[9]

Her "Orgy," published in *Meanjin* in 1954, reads similarly. As subject matter, it is not clear what the titular indulgence is except perhaps in the increasingly ecstatic singing of the poem itself, ending openly and paradoxically with an excess of similarity:

> What pulse is this
> That trips our blood
> Tilting the pavement, animating
> The profile on the war?
>
> The same
>   the same
> The same.[10]

When Millet's poetry students at the communist Jefferson School asked, "Do we mean that it is proper to make traditional, accustomed poetry techniques synonymous with progressive poetry?" her answer was *No*. Gertrude Stein and others, she told them, in their "breaking up of old forms, seizing upon and creating new ones," evinced a "radically different approach to the world . . . to ways of seeing and interacting with the world, people, what happens." But shouldn't radical writing be "*easy* to understand" and thus more "gripping?," the students asked. Their teacher replied, "What is less easy to grasp on the spot, in all its implications, may have an equal strength by gradual 'absorption' by the reader or hearer."[11] She was commending difficulty.

What was going on here? Is Martha Millet's communist poetry an instance of a strategic infiltration into modern poetic practice or perhaps conversely a modernist "boring from within" the heart of American communism, a double aesthetic counterspying—a sprung rhythm sprung on unsuspecting graceless cultural commissars?

Millet had had cordial relations with Harriet Monroe, the founding editor of *Poetry* magazine; Monroe was of course an avid proponent of poetic modernism and—this was well understood at the time, though forgotten today—an anticommunist.[12] But Monroe had gladly accepted verse by this young leftist in 1935, and Millet came to believe that poets in *Poetry* were "reacting sensitively to social evils (war, child labor, slums, lynching) *in their daring new forms*" and admired Monroe for publishing Lola Ridge, among others.[13] After the founding editor's death and the short conservative editorial term of Morton D. Zabel, George Dillon became editor in 1937—during a time of brief glasnost at the post-Monroe *Poetry*[14]—and he, too, eagerly published Millet (in 1938). But later, in the fifties, by which time the phrase "the thirties" spelled trouble, she, now "formerly" a labor journalist, returned to *Poetry* bearing poems that read like somewhat more venturesome versions of the "midcentury modernism" then regularly appearing in the magazine. Her poems varied: while some of her new pieces bore titles of perhaps too-obvious modernist vintage—such as the nonetheless lovely poem titled "Lines," after William Carlos Williams's imagist poem of the same title—others, such as her "Arts and Labor," proudly flew the red flag.

Scant extant evidence yields few interpretive options. One not unreasonable surmise is that by this point *Poetry*'s Cold War–era editors targeted Millet as a CPUSA hack trying to pass as a real lyric poet. Another guess is that the editors beheld the atomized language in poems such as "The Nearness" as intending antinuclear views and preferred to stay clear of such themes. Or perhaps the editors remained innocent of these latent ideological qualities and dismissed the work as aesthetically not up to their standards. By the end of this book, such assumptions of quietism or political circumlocution at *Poetry* magazine in the late 1940s and 1950s will not be surprising. In similar situations, the archival scholar can discern the editorial disposition at *Poetry* through extant interoffice notes, marginalia jotted on submitted manuscripts, and editorial correspondence. In Millet's case, we will never surely know, for each poem she sent to Karl Shapiro and Henry Rago—*Poetry*'s editors during this period—was returned to her without so much as a personally addressed rejection note. Nor was intramural editorial correspondence retained, if any was generated, about Millet's submissions. Although she had previously been published in *Poetry*, Martha Millet now received a standardized postcard rejection, unsigned.[15] In 1956 Millet tried once more, sending Rago the news that she was undertaking to edit "an anthology of the poetry of the [Ethel and Julius] Rosenberg case in the United States." She requested that *Poetry* run an announcement to help her gather material for the book, and she sought Rago's personal editorial "suggestions" for the project. Rago received dozens of such requests yearly. In all but two (of many) that I have found, he replied with at least a brief polite, personal letter, retained for the files and now available for readers of the *Poetry* archive in the Regenstein Library at the University of Chicago. In the top left corner of Millet's letter, Rago wrote merely, "No reply."[16] Rago was not normally a rude man. His time at *Poetry* is known as an era of good feeling.

What had happened between the 1930s and the 1950s to warrant this non-response by a normally cordial editor to a poet who had been a regular contributor previously and who had not had any particular falling out with the editors —a writer whom Monroe had felt went with rather than against the modernist grain? Millet was not alone. Norman Macleod, one of many modernists who had gone left—the well-known little magazine editor (*Front*, *Rebel Poet*, *Morada*, and later *Maryland Quarterly* and *Briarcliff Quarterly*) and staunch supporter of William Carlos Williams and Wallace Stevens who appears as a communist figure in Williams's verse—could not get a single poem published in *Poetry* between 1938 and 1957.[17] Walter Lowenfels published four poems in *Poetry* in the 1920s but just one poem between 1930 and 1960.[18]

Anticommunism helps to explain the situation, but not sufficiently. In general, what was happening in the 1950s was "an esthetic war between conservatives and radicals in poetry," as M. L. Rosenthal wrote during his stint as poetry editor of the anti-anticommunist *Nation*. But, crucially, Rosenthal added that critics and poets all "*played* with it"—this "war," he meant—"getting politics and technics and temperaments all blessedly confused with one another." Rosenthal did not mean that the work of formally and linguistically experimental poets (whom some on the political left typically and often inaccurately deemed "escapist" or "conservative" and whom the right typically and just as inaccurately deemed "deluded" or just plain "radical") could not be discussed in political terms.[19] He himself, here and there, did just this. He praised Williams's fourth book of *Paterson* in 1951 as a political poem and got slammed by six different angry conservatives, a telling episode in the deradicalization of modernism.[20]

When Rosenthal wrote that poets "played with" the "esthetic war between conservatives and radicals" during the Cold War period, he meant that communists and modernists (including some modernists who were communists) wrote poems, poem by poem, that were *sometimes* generalizable as "modernist" (by which most assumed anticommunist) but that no pattern imposed on "thirties poets" by midcentury poets and critics revealed the actual cut, style, and linguistic temper of the poetic line, let alone the content, political or otherwise. The communist editors of *The Left*, a magazine produced in Davenport, Iowa, in the early 1930s, deemed apolitical those who made the *distinction* between modernist and left-wing poetry, and their magazine's subtitle was "A Quarterly Review of Radical and Experimental Art." In the *Windsor Quarterly*, which under the editorship of F. B. Maxham in the early to mid-1930s published poets in the communist movement (Macleod, Don Gordon, Bob Brown, Solon Barber, Willard Maas, Harold Rosenberg, Carl Rakosi, Harry Roskolenko) as well as unaligned modernists (such as James Laughlin, Frances Frost, and José García Villa), the radicalism-modernism problem was circumvented by use of the term "vanguard." García Villa is introduced as a vanguard poet (a statement true only where "vanguard" equals "avant-garde"); Harry Roskolenko is said to be familiar to readers of vanguard magazines (true where "vanguard" equals "left-wing"); Carl Rakosi works "on the vanguard," and Macleod is known to readers of "vanguard poetry" (both assertions true in both senses). An ad for a new issue of the *Morada*, a Norman Macleod project, read,

poetry
prose
art
—e x p e r i m e n t a l
r e v o l u t i o n a r y[21]

Solon Barber's magazine, *Janus*, went both ways: despite its stated "policy of having no policy," its practice better followed the journal's name, featuring communist movement poets alongside Charles Henri Ford, Parker Tyler, Richard Johns, and others.[22]

"I suspect that 'esthetic' and 'Marxist,'" wrote Kenneth Burke in a 1936 letter to Isidor Schneider, "should not seem so different in emphasis as do 'esthetic' and 'sociological.'"[23] Burke, even then leaning more toward modernism than communism, was nonetheless a close adviser and theoretical mentor to a number of communist poets. This group included Schneider, who always agreed with his friend that the idea of radical writing composed "as though nothing but a shoddy sentence were really 'virtuous,'" was not just crude but politically ineffective.[24]

One communist poet, angry about a review by another leftist that had criticized the communist's indirectness, dismissed as "tripe" the "current theory on the New Masses" that "you've got to write exclusively of strikes. . . . I don't say JOIN THE COMMUNIST PARTY every second line. Poor fellow," he continued, imagining himself in the eyes of this critic, "we can't understand a word he's saying, because he's writing lyric poetry." He urged a comrade—another poet—to look for the "symphonic structure" of his poems.[25] Babette Deutsch, who published a perfect traditional sonnet bitterly lamenting the executions of Sacco and Vanzetti,[26] knew that the radical young poets succeeding the first modernist generation sought in reaction to their elders not extremity but "balance" (for instance, of song and speech), and she described many elements the two movements had in common, among them "sing[ing] of our urban and industrial environment, its paradoxes, its conflicts and its malaise."[27] Richard Wright published an article in the communist New Challenge in 1937 declaring that T. S. Eliot and Gertrude Stein represented a "gain in human thought" and needed to serve as materia poetica for the radical writer.[28] Although throughout Art and Society, Sidney Finkelstein held to the Democratic Front line emphasizing popular and folk art (and criticized "individual art" as having emerged in recent unimaginative centuries) and like most communist critics took Lukàcsian realism as the central aesthetic category, he nonetheless wrote sympathetically about Schoenberg, Joyce, Bartók, Picasso, Eliot, and Stein. The communist art theorist wrote that Stein "stimulat[ed] a sensitivity to the sound and rhythms of speech [and] a careful examination of each word." Finkelstein's interest in modernists extended in part from his critique of media monopolies that threatened to dissipate and distort their creative power. They were underdogs.[29]

Looking back seven decades later on the period 1935–40, what Carl Rakosi in 2002 remembered foremost of Walter Lowenfels was that "he was all over the place trying to be both a modern poet and a Communist poet." ("I remember, too, that I thought he was good enough that maybe he could be both.")[30] Even the lumberman Joe Kalar, while generally an advocate of communist poets who "disdain[ed] subtleties," agreed that "revolutionary poetry written in conventional rhythm and meter often enough seems naïve, sentimental and hackneyed."[31] "The newsstands abound with neat packages of grammatical offal," Kalar wrote, and so he sought in verse a disordered, ungrammatical alternative.[32] (Alvaro Cardona-Hine, taking Kalar to heart, later submitted poems without any punctuation to the National Guardian; when editorial associates questioned the practice, Cardona-Hine wrote to veteran communist editor Charles Humboldt, calling these editors "John Birchers" and arguing that "difficulty should be placed in the way of the reader in order to avoid careless reading." Humboldt, open to experiment, let the poems stand.)[33] A college freshman eagerly brought his rhymed stanzas to meetings of the communists who formed the staff of the Brooklyn College literary magazine, only to discover how deeply these young Reds were influenced by modernism; they pushed him toward experimentalism.[34] In 1937, as he grew disenchanted with erstwhile friends among literary communists, Merrill Root gave Rolfe Humphries one reason for his own rightward move: communists were taking on *too much* of modernism's modes. "They run to fads and fashions," Root wrote, "they tend to all technique and some of the moods of the artists of the dying world—from Joyce to Proust and Jeffers and Eliot. They are smart, sophisticated, decadent, etc.; they never go on . . . to say Holy Yea."[35]

Goddard Lieberson (later president of Columbia Records) zealously defended the craziest of party lines at a time when his main artistic project was setting music to passages from the "Anna Livia Plurabelle" fragment of *Finnegans Wake*.[36] Stanley Burnshaw's *New Masses* editorial colleagues dubbed him "the Aesthete with the Golden Scales of Judgment" because he reviewed poetry and modern dance; they were not joking, he remembered, because they wanted him in this role. "Was I pro-modern? Yes! I thought it was marvelous."[37] Even her conservative detractors described Genevieve Taggard as having taken "excursions among the experimental *and* proletarian sects of her time."[38] Eve Merriam deemed her most self-referential verse to be aligned with her commitment to communism, for instance in "Imagine Yourself":

> Name: Time: From Where: To Here: Date.
> Nib like a rider over the naked page[39]

George Henry Weiss, one of the ultraleft "Rebel Poets" who argued bluntly that "a poet to be of use to labor must win the broad mass of workers for an audience," just as adamantly insisted that "this doesn't mean that it necessarily has to be cast in old forms."[40] Bob Brown thought of his writing as "a moving type spectacle" of "eye-tickling interest" and said his readers needed to be "in a receptive progressive mood."[41] J. Malcolm Brinnin always maintained a passion for "poetry in the modern idiom" while publishing "Poem for the Birth of X" in *New Masses* (during the time of the Nazi-Soviet pact) and "The Fiery Exile" in one of James Laughlin's *New Directions* annuals.[42] (A Young Communist League veteran who was strongly encouraged in his poetry by *New Masses* editors, Brinnin enthusiastically organized readings by Eliot, Frost, and Edith Sitwell.)[43] A stalwart *New Masses* reviewer recommended one new anthology because it included John Donne's "The Ecstasy" and presented Algernon Swinburne, he of "unusually frail hands," so that "even the hard-boiled may be interested"—an attractive book, all told, bounded by a "voluptuous" cover.[44] Willard Maas, just when to one conservative observer he "seems to be veering toward the Left" (he was in fact already an active communist), was dubbed "another 'pure poet.' "[45] And what was the 1930s poetry of "objectivist" Rakosi, a CPUSA member, if not a project of making synoptic depictions of social relations in a modern idiom without a specific theoretical dependence on Marxism. As Rakosi wrote in "Surrealists" (1930),

I don't get you.
Why don't you talk in English?

You don't get me?
I have the blues, I have to tear.

But somebody has to drive the spikes,
pitch the gears, oil the cams. . . .

Say, could you stand an old man to a cup of coffee?

Listen, old man! I draw a sweet note out of myself
and have no time for other strangeness.[46]

"All of the objectivists were Marxists," Rakosi wrote, "[George] Oppen and I perhaps slightly more than [Charles] Reznikoff and [Louis] Zukofsky. Did that fact affect my literary form? Not at all." As a communist, Rakosi chose to write "in a free and open line" because it was "comfortable to use" and empowered his epigrammatic sensibility.[47]

Communists in the 1930s had often written "of strikes," of course, but they also had written love poetry, and lacy imagist ditties, and poems that were consciously "Parnassian."[48] They had conducted "elfin experiments" in verse[49] and had sometimes quoted "passages from revolutionary poems which are plainly precious,"[50] had loved and imitated "the orotund, rolling prose of Sir Thomas Browne"[51] and had praised "the little lyricists . . . who are finding a place in the memories of people who can and do, upon occasion, quote the great poets of the past."[52] And were praised as "brilliant revolutionaries" whose verse one cannot "fully appreciate . . . unless one knows . . . the poetry that belongs to the English tradition, with its classical background."[53] And were commended by poets on the *right* as "*not* attempt[ing] to reduce the question to an abstract argument,"[54] and counted among themselves one of the most stead-fast "disciples" of Robert Frost[55] despite Frost's reputation among communist poets as "giving us a feebler Vermont edition of MEIN KAMPF sweetened with a little maple-sap."[56] And wrote dissertations on Emily Dickinson.[57] Edward Dahlberg told Joseph Warren Beach in 1933 that his current writing project was a marriage of Karl Marx and Marcel Proust, and Beach knew enough of the literary left to take this news in stride.[58] Dahlberg introduced a new book of Kenneth Fearing's poems in 1935 with the judgment that Fearing's "fantastic patterns of slang and speech," his *symboliste* derangements, made him something of a Tristan Corbière "with Marxian insights."[59]

Indeed, if not for Fearing's association with communism as one of the original "Dynamo" poets, who would know (or rightly care) if his poem "Literary" did not merely give expression to modernists' keenest antibourgeois impulse, their repudiation of the means of mainstream literary publishing? Fearing's demotic, chatty, antic, digressive style made Allen Ginsberg's possible. "As for Allen Ginsberg," quipped Marya Zaturenska, "isn't ¾ of him straight out of Kenneth Fearing?"[60] The first stanza of "Literary" reads,

> I sing of simple people and the hardier virtues, by Associated Stuff Shirts
> & Company, Incorporated, 358 West 42d Street, New York, brochure
> enclosed;
> Of Christ on the Cross, by a visitor to Calvary, first class;
> Art deals with eternal, not current verities, revised from last week's Sunday
> supplement;
> Guess what we mean, in *The Literary System*; and a thousand noble answers
> to a thousand empty questions, by a patriot who needs the dough.[61]

In "What If Mr. Jesse James Should Some Day Die?," Fearing heaped scorn on capitalism's big shots:

> Where will we ever again find food to eat, clothes to wear, a roof and a bed,
> now that the Wall Street plunger has gone to his hushed, exclusive, paid-
> up tomb?
> How can we get downtown today, with the traction king stretched flat on
> his back in the sun at Miami Beach?[62]

M. L. Rosenthal called this work "the true poem of the early thirties," the kind of verse "that aroused the . . . ire of pure esthetes [and] Southern Agrarians." Its immediacy, clarity, and hyperbolic oratorial style, as much a mock of soapbox rhetoric as an instance of it, "was declared to be not poetry but propaganda." And yet in poems such as "Resurrection," Fearing's writing is "remarkable in its lyrical telescoping of personal emotion with sensuous imagery and critical thought," and like many poets involved with communism between the wars, Fearing "could hardly avoid the thousand experimental and symbolistic influences of the times." In the thirties, Fearing went through periods of Marxist "contempt and idealism" *and* of "Kafka-like obsession with fear, defeat, and confusion."[63]

Nor later, during the Cold War, was it honestly possible to predict what "communist poets" who had associated themselves with the 1930s milieu felt should be the *poetic* response to the anticommunist purge of poetry in the 1950s. Experimentalism was part of the heretical mix, as was honor owed to modernist experimenters. Lowenfels, an expatriate and High Modernist favorite in the 1920s shut out from *Poetry* in the 1950s, published a poem modeled on Ezra Pound's *Cantos* called "Masthead" in the *Sunday Worker* in 1954 to celebrate the thirtieth anniversary of that communist newspaper.[64] In a striking lyric published in *Mainstream*, Richard Davidson, the best of the communist confessional poets of the late 1950s, presented a portrait of the poet as a "young rebel": he mourns Joe Hill, adores Paul Robeson, supports Henry Wallace, and *reads Proust*.[65] Isidor Schneider deeply admired Henry James and was willing to say so in the communist papers.[66] Thomas Yoseloff prized Laurence Sterne as the "stylistic godfather" to Stein, Joyce, and Dos Passos.[67] Joe Freeman revered the work of Piet Mondrian.[68] Muriel Rukeyser, *because* she was driven by her "sense of righteous indignation," made her poems "an amalgam of modern styles."[69] Gene Frumkin, a protégé of the communist poet Tom McGrath and an avid leftist and probably a CPUSA member, published poems in the neoformalist *Beloit Poetry Journal* (with its bona fide New Conservative founder and faculty adviser, Chad Walsh), the middlebrow *Saturday Review*, and the hip *Evergreen Review* (which was making space for the avant-garde New American poets) as well as the communist magazines *California Quarterly* and *Mainstream*.[70] And as poetry editor of the communist *Coastlines*, Frumkin could hold to what he deemed a party line and at the same time request revisions in a poem that he felt was marred by "too much explanation": *Coastlines* just wanted good poems, and "we'll never turn a good poem . . . down."[71] As a poet, McGrath "simply disregarded the communist push without feeling guilty and also still remain[ed] pro-communist."[72] Isidor Schneider, writing for *Masses & Mainstream*, hoped readers would recall the *1920s* as a time when encroachments on writers' right to write whatever and however they wanted were "often met with picket lines," and Schneider—although by 1952 he was identified disparagingly as a "Marxian athlete" with "ideological . . . agility"[73]—submitted for serious consideration the idea that what made the 1930s so momentous was the great concern among the preceding decade's writers for "literary values" and that a major source of conformity in 1948 was "the *indifference* to literary values."[74] Kenneth Rexroth contended in 1952 that the communist *New Masses* had been the inheritor of the extraordinary modernist magazine *Transition*.[75] Edward Dahlberg urged the neophyte Robert Creeley to convene an avant-garde poetic company, a "vital little band of truthful people": without pausing, in a single paragraph, the elder writer recommended, for starters, the communist Lowenfels and also the heiress and former actress Isabella Gardner, a mainstream "modernist"[76] (and spouse of the reactionary Allen Tate, accursed on the left). Dahlberg, a ferocious maker of distinctions between and among poets and aesthetic camps—long after he split from the CPUSA—did not think twice about such a pairing. (More consequentially, neither did Creeley.)[77]

Babette Deutsch described the verse of Taggard, editor of the communist *May Days* anthology and a poet of overriding "concern with technique," as paying "tribute to that dedicated craftsman, Wallace Stevens."[78] Frank O'Hara learned to read Stevens seriously in the late 1940s from F. O. Matthiessen—not from Renato Poggioli or John Ciardi or from the young O'Hara's other teachers at Harvard. O'Hara wrote for Matthiessen a seminar paper on Stevens's "Chocorua to Its Neighbor." Under Matthiessen's influence, O'Hara voted for Henry Wallace, one of just 6 Progressive Party voters in Eliot House, out of 165, to indicate that choice.[79] Adrienne Rich also learned her Stevens from Matthiessen. She did not find it incongruent that at the same time he was the only one of her professors who alluded to events in Europe—indeed, to anything going on outside the classroom.[80]

Doris Grumbach, a college student in the 1930s surrounded by young communists, recalled in the 1950s that she had "confined" her radicalism "to books," working her way through *Anti-Dühring*, *Das Kapital*, and Lenin's *Imperialism* only to discover that engagement with these texts led her ("to a surprising extent") directly to the "literary, artistic and musical radicals of our time"— Kafka, Eliot, Picasso, Deran, and Matisse.[81] Malcolm Cowley always maintained that, as he wrote to Schneider, "All good writing is on the side of progress," and, even more important, that "I'm not sure that bad writing, whatever its merely explicit meaning, isn't on the side of reaction."[82] George Hitchcock, a regular contributor to the communist *Mainstream*, in a review of Edna St. Vincent Millay's *Collected Poems*, duly acknowledged Millay's elegies for Sacco and Vanzetti and for the "murdered" Spanish Republic but then berated her for insufficient formal independence from her literary forebears and *too much*—as opposed to not enough—"poetic attitudinizing."[83]

At the height of his affiliation with communism, Hitchcock (b. 1914) wrote a poem called "War" (1952) with lines designed to prove that in an age of nuclear annihilation one could engage surrealism as a form of radical realism:

The sky fills with teacups
and doorknobs,
the tibia of children . . .
What do you think, my brother?
Awaking at four sweating, the sudden erection?
The fat man at the hamburger stand?
The death of Mickey Mouse?[84]

Hitchcock grew up during the 1920s and 1930s in Oregon, where "the distant drums of surrealism, communism, and French decadence could be heard."[85] He became a longtime communist (still listing himself thus in the 1980s);[86] worked on the staff of the California Labor School for some years while holding jobs as a shipfitter, newspaperman, and seaman; and publishing poems in the communist *San Francisco Writers' Workshop Magazine* ("In This Third Year of a Useless War," an attack on the Korean War)[87] and *Masses & Mainstream* ("The Indestructible," to honor the communist-led Huk rebellion in the Philippines).[88] Here was a communist who venerated Hans Arp and Wallace Stevens,[89] whose editorial projects, including *Kayak* (founded in 1964) would always keep William Carlos Williams's aesthetic—a modernist sensibility "that operates on ordinary experience"—in the mix.[90] The first issue of *Kayak* plainly disdained the segregation of communists from experimentalists, including old-line communists H. R. Hays, Thomas McGrath, Gene Frumkin, and the Costa Rican–American poet-painter Alvaro Cardona-Hine, as well as John Tagliabue and the early work of avant-garde "talk poet" David Antin. To be sure, *Kayak* emerged late enough into the thaw that the convergence expressed through its table of contents was not especially remarkable. But *Kayak*'s open courtship of both leftists and avant-gardists was the key to its success among readers of contemporary poetry. "KAYAK," the first page of the first issue announced, "is particularly hospitable to surrealist, imagist and political poems" as well as "vehement or ribald articles on the subject of modern poetry."[91]

Judson Crews (b. 1917), editor and publisher of avant-garde magazines in the 1930s, 1940s, and 1950s (*Vers Libre, Motive, Flying Fish, Suck-Egg Mule, Deer and Dachshund, Naked Ear*, and others), was—and is—an anomalous poet with a mix of leftist and avant-garde passions, someone who "lived outside the common areas of recognition, surviving by his persistence," as Robert Creeley put it in 1961.[92] Crews was a surrealist who disavowed the surrealists' formalist tendency; he wrote politically radical poems; he ran a bookstore that became a focal point for advocacy of the avant-garde; in a profile, under the heading "politics," he puckishly checked "None," although he was involved with the War Resisters' League and the Society of Non-Violence against Nuclear Weapons. His poems at midcentury, such as "Elegy" in the mimeographed magazine *Iconograph* (ca. 1950), framed some sort of commentary on what he felt were the repressive conditions of the time:

> Now I have been
> plaguing the American embassy
> for days—to do something
> something drastic
> send me home in chains—anything.
>
> To get me out of this waste
> merely that I might be
> in New York—that I might say,
> "The hat's a crime, really,"
> "The chili's far too hot."

Yet Crews simply considered Wallace Stevens one of the "obvious influences" on his work. Crews's "Elegy" draws its surrealist politics from Stevens's "A Dish of Peaches in Russia" (1939), a poem that for many years seemed only to reinforce, by way of critics such as Randall Jarrell, Stevens's reputation as an apolitical modernist addicted to geo-aesthetic dislocations. Is it an act of American ignorance or of capricious globalism to place a dish of peaches in "Russia" —peaches that are "large and round, / Ah! and *red*"—and then to claim that "such ferocities could tear / One self from another"? That the speaker audaciously sees these peaches "as a lover sees" them and consumes them "with my whole body,"[93] seemed to indicate to Crews a way out of a political dilemma introduced by surrealist practice. He imagined an instruction to himself, a Cold War thought experiment: *Place a horse in Russia in a poem of 1950. See if he comprehends reality. Yearn simultaneously for the bohemian freedom of New York where one can say, in writing, that a hat is criminal.* But then, it seems, it *is* a crime, there, *here*, in the land of aesthetic liberty. Where in the world of Cold War are we? Or, as Stevens puts it, "Who speaks?" The subject enabled by political consciousness is unclearly delineated. Is it the "animal" that is for Stevens the Russian refugee? These are expressions of odd internal exile. The modernist's effect on the midcentury radical is not in the language per se but rather, surprisingly, in the way the younger writer felt free to harass the U.S. embassy, to repudiate Cold War binarisms, and to commit himself to the unremunerative life of avant-garde publishing and poetics. Stevens liberated Crews from his jar-in-Tennessee problem:

In Russia I saw a horse
walking on ice
as if he did not
understand himself
nor the world about him[94]

Horace Gregory, older than Crews by a half generation, had a personal history of association with aesthetic and political movements. Cranky by mid-century and no longer actively affiliated with communists, yet always an ardent defender of 1930s verse as having correctly interpreted 1920s modernism,[95] Gregory was reading several "bad, really bad books" by Richard Eberhart and Robert Penn Warren. He decried the stuffy poetic atmosphere that had been created by Yvor Winters and John Crowe Ransom and then wrote privately to M. L. Rosenthal that Eberhart's big reputation was merely an artifact of anti-communism. "Eberhart," Gregory wrote, "has been pumped up by [wartime anthologist] Oscar Williams in the 40s when the heroes of the 30s had to be eliminated." Notwithstanding Eberhart, the "best book of poems" that year was not that of some "social poet" in the sense Rosenthal might have expected but rather H.D.'s *Selected Poems*. Yes, Horace Gregory was commending Hilda Doo-little, a poet "whose exquisite gifts," Gregory felt, "have not been fully appreci-ated." It serves us well, I think, to ponder calls for greater appreciation of H.D. by a "thirties poet" as an alternative to the conformist aesthetic climate puffing Richard Eberhart—early modernism as one plausible, constructive response to the "eliminat[ion]" of *thirties* poets.[96]

We have no choice, I think, but to understand this gesture as a politically viable option for a former procommunist figure whose best verse was known to bespeak "the voice of the mass" in diction and meter that was straight out of early T. S. Eliot:

We are alive and do not die,
Not die, give us the power
Not to die but to return
At each imperishable hour.[97]

And yet on another day, without intending any contradiction, the same "thir-ties poet" might recommend the poems of communist Edwin Rolfe or the modernist *New Masses* editor Stanley Burnshaw. These are the actual details of individuals' poetic practice. No ideological prediction or generalization accounts for what version of the modernist aesthetic one would find in the work—in the writing itself—of a given left-wing poet at midcentury. Yet such generalizing about radicals became a staple of editors, reviewers, teachers, and critics.

The communist Martha Millet, our card-carrying CPUSA member, and anarchopacifist Jackson Mac Low (1922–2004), affiliated with the anti-Stalinist War Resister's League—otherwise two utterly different poets—were received with the same special indifference, or, depending on one's reading of the series of rejections, the same hostility, at *Poetry* in the late 1940s and 1950s. While Mac Low was in high school, George Dillon and Peter DeVries (editor and assistant editor, respectively) had encouraged him to revive the University of Chicago Poetry Club,[98] but he had been sending poems to Dillon at *Poetry* since he was fifteen years old in 1937—"and pretty often too," as he admitted to Rago in 1954.[99] No luck ever. Every poem rejected. Indeed, the more extensively Mac Low described in cover letters mailed with these submissions his emerging quasi-nonintentional writing practice—he submitted the now well regarded poem "Glass Buildings" ("WHEN FIERY WATER THIRDS FLAUNT SOLAR FUSION")[100] and wrote to Rago that it was "a calligramme & an attempt at expression by means of multiple ambiguity where all possible meanings are 'meant' by the poet"—the more grudging and laconic the editorial response. The top page of the sheaf of seven poems submitted with "Glass Buildings" (as well as "Winter Nausea," "Song of Homely Objects," and others) is marked by a single editorial word in red pencil: "Rejected." "Orasemosdp," a piece further venturing toward chance-operations writing, seems to have been rejected with no intramural editorial consultation or a rejection notice.[101] Mac Low's resistance to typographical convention was on record in *Poetry*'s already thick file on him. In 1951, the "penniless" Mac Low—he told Karl Shapiro pathetically that he was then holding down several jobs "to be able to eat & not fade out of the picture entirely"—was openly desperate to publish a review in *Poetry* if his poems were impossible. He submitted his review of Isaac Rosenberg's *Collected Poems*[102] but pleaded with Shapiro to permit some "deviations from the U[niversity] of C[hicago] Style Book"; Mac Low enthusiastically preferred the ampersand to the conventional "and." Prose should be no more "uniform" than poems. (When the review appeared in print, Mac Low's "deviations" had been silently "normalized.")[103] His poems continued to be rejected on the grounds that, for example, their experiments were marred by "over-cleverness." Shapiro leveled this criticism against Mac Low at the time he submitted what he called "the best poem I have ever written."[104] The final development of his nonintentional style

in 1954 and 1955 coincided with the height of Mac Low's participation in protests against the Cold War and his association with political heretics. (He published two poems in *Arena* while it was under attack as the "Communist inspired British 'magazine of modern literature.'"[105] One of them, "I Heard a
Voice," seems to have been read by the British communists who ran the magazine as part of the anti-anticommunist resistance: "I heard a voice that cried out
'Courage! Courage!' / The voice was mine;—it was not my own, / not *only* mine,
crying 'Courage! Courage!' / a very present help not *only* mine.")[106] In the early
summer of 1955, as the tenth anniversary of the dropping of atomic bombs on
two Japanese cities approached, Mac Low collaborated with a small group of
eminent protesters in refusing to participate in the mandatory nationwide air-
raid drill named Operation Alert, organized to prepare Americans to protect
themselves against a hydrogen bomb attack by the Soviet Union. A front-page
story in the June 15, 1955, *New York World-Telegram* prominently featured Mac
Low as among those arrested (along with Dorothy Day, the revered founder of
the Catholic Workers Movement) and included a photograph of Mac Low. A
policeman is leading away the poet, who holds a sign reading

Let's Face the Truth
There is NO REAL CIVIL DEFENSE
against H-Bomb[107]

Mac Low joined with the group of defendants to test the constitutionality of the
Civil Defense Act requiring participation in what they deemed useless dry runs
of nuclear attack; he prepared an eleven-page statement for Bayard Rustin,
explaining, in part, why he refused to plead guilty after the arrest (so that
"evidence as to the dangers from the test explosions . . . could be publicly given
during the trial").[108] The stationery of the Provisional Defense Committee,
which he used to raise funds from friends and colleagues, lists Mac Low along
with Rustin, A. J. Muste, and Michael Harrington. In early August, ten years and
a day after Hiroshima, Mac Low submitted his newest poems to Rago and urged
Poetry to publish a notice of the antinuclear protests sponsored by the War
Resisters' League, the *Catholic World*, and Julian Beck and Judith Malina's
experimental Living Theater. Mac Low sent Rago pamphlets (among them
"Operation Suicide—The HUSH-HUSH Story of the H-Bomb"), a copy of the
World-Telegram article bearing his photograph, a collage of other articles about
his arrest, a strident article from *Commonweal* titled "The Rights of Non-
Conformity,"[109] and an improvised press release (retyped personally for Rago)
in which Mac Low noted that he was fasting for five days during the period of
protest.

It is hard to imagine any other response from Rago—to the poems and to the request that *Poetry* print a notice of radical intellectuals' arrests for refusing to participate in H-bomb drills—than the one Mac Low indeed received, but what Rago wrote is nonetheless instructive in any attempt to discern the aesthetic scene: "I wish POETRY were the place to say something about your activities, but as you understand so well already, we aren't a political magazine." (Why Mac Low should already understand *Poetry*'s apoliticism "so well already" is not clear from any of the correspondence or from the poems Mac Low had submitted.) "If we opened our pages," the letter continued, "to the full discussion of these issues . . . there would be no drawing of the line against all others who would claim the right to speak their minds in our pages, and perhaps about other political matters besides this one. It is not a question of taboo; it is a question of what the job of this magazine is."[110]

It is my contention that to pursue Martha Millet's predicament as a poet during the Cold War, the literary historian who seeks to understand M. L. Rosenthal's sense of ideological "confusion" as part of modernism at midcentury or Horace Gregory's sense that H.D. was underappreciated as part of the ruthless campaign to deradicalize modernism and vilify the "Radical Decade" must first be prepared to view Jackson Mac Low's situation as similar to rather than dissimilar from Millet's, notwithstanding Mac Low's much deeper connection to modernist art and to an emergent postmodern disjunctive poetics and notwithstanding the fact that their similar views on the evils of Cold War culture led one to embrace the communist movement and the other, as an anarchopacifist, to distrust American Stalinists.[111] Henry Rago saw both Millet and Mac Low as aesthetically "wrong" for *Poetry* at a time when he saw it as his job to consolidate *Poetry*'s modernist legacy. A connection certainly exists between Rago's inability to appreciate the notion of "letting language speak for itself" and of "letting expression happen indirectly"—the original explicit basis of Mac Low's nonintentional writing—and his drawing a line "*against* [poets] who would claim the right to speak their minds" in *Poetry*, which since the days of Harriet Monroe had been committed to the modernist principle that anything can be the material of poetry, the great energizing letting of expression that had helped bring on modernism in the United States. The anarchist principle Mac Low discovered through his poetic procedure in the mid-1950s—what in 1997 he remembered as "a strain of so-called antinomianism" entailing an opposition to and breaking of rules and laws[112]—he was exploring by sending a modernist poetry magazine front-page newspaper photos of himself holding placards challenging inarguable, idiomatic, "natural" cultural logic (*we can defend against total annihilation by preparing for it*) as well as by asking for permission to bypass the *Chicago Manual of Style* in critical prose. Mac Low saw the two challenges as part of the same heretical impulse.

While the first half of this book describes what changed in the period from the 1930s to the 1950s, the initial consideration is something that did not change: in Millet's case, what had not changed was the poetry itself. The sort of poems that she submitted to *Poetry* and that were accepted in the late 1930s were the sort of poems rejected in the 1950s. Her consistency challenged what Mac Low perhaps unwittingly tested against *Poetry* as a modernist institution: the "limits of the modernist understanding of political action and of the political," as Louis Cabri has put it in an article about Mac Low's early radicalism. Such disruptive poets "want to extend and deepen representation—not abandon it." They wanted *in*, as hopefully and openhandedly as the sweetly ambitious young Jackson Mac Low. Despite what we might assume today about the communist and the anarchopacifist movement in the United States, neither Millet nor Mac Low was aware of the option of retreating to aesthetic categories outside of (or prior to or beyond) modernism; rather, in Cabri's words, they sought to stage "a confrontation with the limits of the modern."[113] Modernism was the mode, and surely the venue founded on modernism was a main site of acceptance.

Millet's aesthetic had not changed, but *Poetry* had. And as is often the case when we want to learn more about transitions at midcentury, we must back up a bit to the years of World War II, where this story of the anticommunist attack on modern poetry begins—back to 1943 and 1944, a turning point in the war, in the U.S.-Soviet alliance, and in the communist movement in the United States, as in (to continue our example) Martha Millet's productive although complex political identity as a modern poet.[114]

In 1943–44, working on behalf of the New York City Central Committee of the International Workers Order (a communist-dominated group), Millet was busily researching, writing, editing, and seeing through publication several persuasive tracts, including the sensational (yet sadly accurate) *Smash the Secret Weapon*, a pamphlet against anti-Semitism and genocide. Just then, political journalism seemed to her a full-time job, although unremunerative. But in 1944 also came a big literary break and with it the possibility of selling many books of her verse and of affiliating actively with modern poetry: Thomas Yoseloff, director of the University of Pennsylvania Press, recruited her to be part of an important "poetic symposium" to be published between hard covers and called *Seven Poets in Search of an Answer* (1944). Who were the seven? Aaron Kramer, a communist activist almost as busy as Millet, the young and talented poet, was brought into the project. Joining Kramer and Millet were five other poets, all either CPUSA members or actively affiliated with the communist movement: Joy

Davidman, Alfred Kreymborg, Maxwell Bodenheim, Norman Rosten, and Langston Hughes. Shaemas O'Sheel, a poet who had become so "wholly sympathetic with Soviet Russia" that he had turned (in his words) "practically vermillion!,"[115] was asked to write the preface.

Davidman (1915–60), forgotten today, was once a poet of real standing on the literary left; *Seven Poets* caught her at the height of her career. Dial Press had just published her *War Poems of the United Nations* (1943) under the sponsorship of the League of American Writers, a project that provided her the opportunity to bring CPUSA poets (Hughes, Kreymborg, Kramer, Rosten, Ruth Lechlitner, James Neugass, Eve Merriam, Naomi Replansky, and others) together with fellow travelers (Stephen Vincent Benét, Witter Bynner, J. Malcolm Brinnin) and sympathetic liberals (Oscar Williams, Mark Van Doren, and surrealist David Cornel De Jong). Davidman's "Poem for Liberation" (1944), about Spain, was widely circulated and reprinted.[116] By the time postwar anticommunism hit its stride, Davidman had left the party and moved far rightward. "Joy had found God and turned anti-left in 1949," Kramer remembered later. "Girl Communist" was Oliver Pilat's salacious twelve-part series in the *New York Post* about Davidman's life as a traitorous poet in the communist movement, written with Davidman's complete cooperation.[117]

After *The Weary Blues* (1926) and *Fine Clothes to the Jew* (1927) had established Langston Hughes as one of the stars of the Harlem Renaissance, he had turned sharply leftward in 1931 and then spent a year in the Soviet Union (1932–33), although he had earlier associated with Claude McKay and Max Eastman, from whom he had learned, as Arnold Rampersad has put it, a "model of the black writer committed at once to socialism, black progress, and literary excellence."[118] The bibliographical dossier on Hughes assembled by agents for the red-hunting files of the *National Republic*, now stored at the Hoover Institution, is one of the thickest in the archive.[119] In 1948 he was "exposed" as a communist ("a professed card-holding member of the Communist Party") by Howard Rushmore in the newspapers, by Henry Taylor on the Mutual Broadcast Network, and in the pages of *Reader's Digest*.[120] *Not without Laughter* and *Fields of Wonder* were later removed from the shelves of 150 State Department–sponsored libraries in sixty-three countries, and Hughes was compelled to appear before McCarthy's committee.[121] But even before *Seven Poets*, Hughes was a target of conservatives, including his own former Bible instructor at Lincoln University, Rev. Edwin J. Reinke, who, after seeing Hughes listed in *The Red Network*, collaborated with anticommunists in 1940 to expose Hughes as a subversive should Lincoln give the poet an honorary degree. ("His portrait has just appeared in the 'Lincoln University Bulletin,'" wrote Reinke, "and I expect that more is in the offing.")[122] By 1948, Hughes was writing to a public school superintendent in Michigan that "in light of what is happening in Washington I am rather flattered that they continue to keep me in print at all."[123]

Anticommunist critics attacked the poetry of Norman Rosten (1914–95) more viciously than perhaps any of the other writers represented in *Seven Poets*, including Hughes. One reviewer in 1953, using an anti-Marxist voice in which Rosten heard "overtones of hysteria,"[124] repeated these phrases in just three short paragraphs: "dialectical discords," "dialectical choruses," "dialectical miasma," and "dialectical situation."[125] (As we will see when we return to Rosten's career in chapter 6, the poetry in the book being so balefully reviewed, *The Big Road*, was not "dialectical" in the least.)

Since one aim of *Seven Poets* was to reach a noncommunist audience, the participation of Alfred Kreymborg (1883–1966) represented a strategic coup. Although it was inescapably true that his poems of the 1940s were impressed with the revolutionary stamp, bearing titles such as "Ballad of Art Young" and "Fellow Workers,"[126] Kreymborg was still associated in the minds of readers with New York Dada (he befriended Duchamp, and Man Ray collaborated with Kreymborg on the magazine *Glebe*); with the imagist *Others*, a project through which he gathered Stevens, H.D., John Gould Fletcher, and Mina Loy; and with early international modernism, through his superb work on *Broom* (1921–24). His modernist memoir, *Troubadour* (1925), a good seller among Americans wanting to know from an insider about the social life of the moderns, depicted "Krimmie" accommodatingly "Housing the Moderns" and sporting with "Old Forms and New"—mostly new.[127] Despite his ardent devotion to u.s. communism, he was invited to serve as president of the Poetry Society of America in 1943–44 (that group's last left-wing leader for several generations) and relished praise of his *Selected Poems* such as that it "escapes category."[128] Fletcher, by 1945 already an embittered ex-imagist and a political conservative, balked at what he called Kreymborg's limited "range of experience" (probably a euphemism for ideological narrowness) but nonetheless likened the *writing* itself to that of William Carlos Williams rather than any of the communist poets on behalf of whom Kreymborg expended his intellectual energies.[129] Certainly not Maxwell Bodenheim, who had blasted Fletcher's universalism in an ironic, perfectly regular sonnet, "To John Gould Fletcher," a devastating poem that *Poetry* had published. "The word eternity," it begins, "should not be carved / Upon the heights where poets stand."[130]

All expenses for Bodenheim's February 1954 funeral were paid by his friend and comrade, Kreymborg.[131] The murderer of the penniless Bodenheim (and the poet's obsessive wife, Ruth), when arraigned, had cried out, "I have killed two Communists. I should get a medal!"[132] Reporting these facts in the *Catholic Worker* in 1954, Dorothy Day was sure to refute such slander, for Bodenheim was another dead artifact of the Jazz Age, a victim of the still-cheap liquor of Greenwich Village and at the same time of its steepening rents, a writer to be remembered, as S. J. Perelman put it, as part of the "turbulent and frisky epoch" of the 1920s.[133] "Max was *only a poet*," Day wrote, "and his sympathies with communism were because they spoke in terms of bread and shelter, and he had lived long with hunger."[134] No one who had read the sensational *Replenishing Jessica* (1926) or any of his other antic Roaring Twenties novels could believe, for instance, that the sternly surreal "New Song"—Bodenheim's communist poem published in the *New Masses* in 1933[135]—was in earnest. But at least something was aesthetically new about "New Song," and indeed it lived up to the linguistic promise of the modern milieu in which Bodenheim had supposedly thrived more than did any of his flaperistic fictions, which were, aside from "liberated" subject matter, narratively conventional. For him, the innovative associations of the two decades swapped, but critical reception could never account for this resistance against expected politico-aesthetic pattern, and finally—sadly— Max Bodenheim was an easy target for the Cold War satires against bohemia. To some degree, Bodenheim merely traded one stylistic formula for another (even to the point where his new communist literary comrades had to ask, "Whither Bodenheim?");[136] and yes, many aesthetically newer songs were being written by radicalized modern poets than "New Song" or indeed any of the poems he now put into Yoseloff's anthology. Hart Crane had surely been right, moreover, when he wrote to Allen Tate in 1927 that modernism (both "our ideas and idiom") would only very slowly catch on, but whatever "we do win in the way of intellectual territory is *solid*": these gains, worth awaiting, stood firmly on a beachhead of innovative writing and "can't be knocked over by every wave that comes along—as could Masters, Bodenheim, Lindsay, etc."[137]

Such few serious readings as the communist Bodenheim would get suffered ipso facto from association with a narrow aesthetic identity. *Seven Poets* was hypothetically a chance for Bodenheim to break free of that. But Perelman's postwar perspective was typical, and not even the most energetic political writing in the thirties and early forties on the part of one so totally identified with the hopes and then the self-destructiveness of the century's adolescence in the teens and twenties could break the new antipolitical spell.

Aaron Kramer (1921–97), the last of the *Seven*, was too young to have had a High Modernist 1920s. He had come of age during the Depression.[138] Yet he spent much of the 1950s agonizing about the complex relationship between modernism as a social and aesthetic movement and leftist activism, often debating the topic with colleagues in the communist movement. The Cold War in poetry might be said to have begun for Kramer in 1945, the day he rode an elevator with *Masses & Mainstream* literary editor and poet-critic Samuel Sillen. They chatted about art. Kramer told Sillen about the poems he was then writing, work years later collected in *Roll the Forbidden Drums* (1954). "You know, Aaron," Sillen warned sagely, "some exciting young poets are coming home from the war; their art is denser, more sophisticated than yours, and theirs is the way of the future. If you don't want to be left behind, you'd better rethink your aesthetics now."[139]

In the 1950s, Jackson Mac Low and Martha Millet indeed did "rethink" their poetics but not in the dramatic (and, one might add, craven and paternalistic) sense Sillen meant in his confidential chat with his young comrade Kramer. Nor did Mac Low or Millet rethink their faith in modern poetry as a response to biases against people holding heretical views. The communist Millet, politically unwavering,[140] had to reevaluate not her poems but their relationship to acceptable poetic norms. Mac Low's move from subjective to aleatory writing in the mid-1950s resulted not so much from his inability to overcome (or to accommodate) Rago's double fears of *Poetry*'s being pushed toward extreme experimentalism and damnable association with anti–Cold War politics as from the theoretical failure of anarchopacificism in the realm of representation. This development led to Mac Low's formulation of a postmodern aesthetic that derived rather than broke from Steinian, Joycean, and Poundian modernism, making a lineage that bypassed the political torpidity into which modernism was falling in the late 1940s and 1950s, as witness Rago's impeccably cautious editorial regime. Although an utterly different poet, Millet also averted *Poetry*'s separation of modernism from radicalism and continued intrepidly to think of her poetry as partaking of both. But however successful these strategies were, they were largely invisible to the emergent formalistic critical generation, young writers and critics who would then and in subsequent years consolidate the modernist canon. Mac Low found a congenial political community—and an arts community *outside* the medium of poetry. Millet continued to print poems in the communist newspaper, the *Daily Worker*, and in the monthly *Masses & Mainstream*, offspring of the *New Masses*, itself the child of the original *Masses* (1911–18), where modernism and radicalism had been editorially accepted as one.[141]

Seven Poets in Search of an Answer was organized to imply a literary history through modern verse, but for the purposes of encouraging a positive reception for the book, this aim may have been its major failing. As the war drew to a close and as u.s. policy began to anticipate the bitter end of wartime alliance with the

Soviet Union, it was an inauspicious moment for communist poets to congregate in a single volume attempting such an undertaking. Hughes's "Good Morning, Stalingrad" ("Some folks try to tell me down this way / That you're our ally just for today")[142] was significantly tamer than "Good Morning, Revolution," "For Tom Mooney," "An Open Letter to the South," "Lenin," "Hero—International Brigade," and other poems he had published and would later publish in the communist press,[143] but the vernacular rendering of the pro-Soviet line in the poem about Stalingrad was transparent to readers looking beyond unified antifascism to inevitable conflict with the brutal regime of Joseph Stalin. Nothing about the language of Hughes's poems in *Seven Poets* seemed capable of accounting for its quickly passing historicity, notwithstanding the fact that resistance to such passing was generally the *theme* of "Good Morning, Stalingrad."

Conversely, Martha Millet's offerings in the book included a lyric called "Historians" that seemed to foretell anxieties of nascent cold warriors:

> They will say of this age:
> It set a blight
> On every living impulse. . . .
>
> They will say of this age,
> The chopping block. . . .
>
> But they will see
> Rising over these
> Whose beat was stilled that morning might be won.[144]

The "beat" here is not just that of hearts and drums of war but also the beat of the poem: its own cadences are at stake; history will determine how *they* are registered. Notwithstanding the diction of "might be won" (a dead giveaway, vintage idiomatic communism), the key lyric terms Millet chose have variable referents: "this" (as in "this age") and "they." The question implied by the poem—and by way of its title and indeed the whole of the 1944 anthology—is not *Who are they?* but *Who will they be?* Who will control what is said and seen of this age? The poem intends to participate in the making of a reasonable, historically generous "they" and does so in part by refusing to identify the pronoun.

Millet's critique of narrative functionalism is a more explicit version of the final lines of Gertrude Stein's "complete" verse portrait of Picasso (1924): "As or as presently. / Let me recite what history teaches. History teaches."[145] Millet's sense of the age in which she writes is contemporary and contingent. Her language, while not nearly as associatively open as Stein's, is organized to invite a politicized readership to review the problem of how history gets made—which is to say, by readers. "This age" is not merely the present—the time of worldwide war, its special destructiveness and political realignments that in any case *would* be written by historians of one ideological position or another. Millet's contribution to *Seven Poets in Search of an Answer* is also tonally elegiac or, more accurately, prenostalgic. "This age" seems already finished. Theology (for a communist poet) being no help, a poem is the only place where the strife between impulse and constraint, the impulse to make history checked by the constraint of poetry as a form, can enact the resulting despondency. Halfway between a free-verse lyricism (that of the modern Millet, well trained in the mode of the New Poetry), and an edgy, metrically regular didacticism (Millet the *New Masses* regular), she expresses a hyperawareness of a poem's transitional aesthetic situation. Is the communist poet's language moving in the same direction as her politics? Unfortunately, Shaemas O'Sheel's exhortative preface to *Seven Poets* gave no hint of this anxiety—"What more is needed?" he asked. "To postpone the threnody and sound the clarion-call . . . to stand less on the defensive, to attack more and on more fronts."[146] Nonetheless, that call can be heard in the language of many of the poems that take modernist modes as starting assumptions.

Millet certainly wrote a radical's modern poem prematurely on the defensive, attempting idiomatically to anticipate the literary-historical backlash. The attack that was coming very soon—within months of the war's end—was to be a repudiation of the left, but it was also an assault on versions of American modernism that had consorted with radicalism. The fifties' thirties was a period when it was widely believed that modernist techniques had simply not been available as a "resource" (to use M. L. Rosenthal's term) to the radical poets who had aesthetically come of age in the thirties and who now sought in the extreme pleasures of formal newness a devotion to ethical existence in the atomic age. Merely to suggest such continuity was to court disapproval. Merely to invite readers to see in the poetics of Gerard Manley Hopkins, for example, an influence on the lives of poets of Stalinist pedigree was in itself heretical. Yet the line running from prepolitical poetic forms of faithfulness through the development of a modernist language did pass through the thirties on its way to canonization in the fifties, and Rosenthal, among few others, dared to redraw this line. "The sufferings of the Jesuit poet Hopkins in the 1880s," Rosenthal wrote, "and his development of a metrical and imagistic method out of the conflict between sensuousness and devotion as it manifested itself in his own feelings, *created a resource for the secularistic revolutionary poetry of the 1930s.*" Modernist poetry fundamentally concerned "the strife between impulse and constraint in *any* context," including the context of what many poets felt had been a revolutionary moment.[147] (Hopkins's art might seem an unusual conduit between modernism and radicalism. But anticommunist antimodernists hated Hopkins as a "mumble[r]" of "incoherent theories" and purveyor of radical poetic practice that gave "latter-day rebels . . . unexpected precedent and reassurance." Hopkins, some conservatives complained, had the same radical impact on modern writing practice as Walt Whitman had.)[148]

Throughout his communist experience, Alfred Kreymborg wrote his poems out of just such aesthetic conflict. His poems were made of the tension between freewheeling social impulse and the tight formal circumscription he was proud to have learned during his days as editor of modernist ventures and early champion of H.D. and Marianne Moore, on the basis of which George Dillon's *Poetry* honored Kreymborg, even as late as 1938 (when he was known as a communist), as "an active force in the new poetry movement."[149] Yet Kreymborg's own standard for judgment consistently constrained him. He never believed in such a thing as a natural language. Nor did he relinquish the demands of form. His poems are "alternately pert and prolix," Louis Untermeyer noticed right after the war—"pert" being good, "prolix" a cause for concern.[150] The poem that perhaps most interestingly expresses Kreymborg's political radicalism, "One Face" (1937), is also his most "pert." If the impulse in this writing is to generalize widely and polymetrically about social and legal injustice, in the lines of the poem the poet recalls the focus necessary to make such charges precisely enough to ensure that the result (at least until the final line) remains similar to the social modernism of William Carlos Williams in his books of the 1930s, *An Early Martyr* (1935) and *Adam and Eve and the City* (1936). "Justice," Kreymborg wrote,

> has a
> single face
> composed
> of all
> the faces
> that brought
> a million
> actions in
> a million
> different cases[151]

The essence of M. L. Rosenthal's unique critical heterodoxy—he was writing his doctoral dissertation on Kenneth Fearing, Muriel Rukeyser, and Horace Greg-

M. L. Rosenthal in the 1950s. Courtesy Alan Rosenthal.

ory—was to assume just such a continuity, and the influence of Williams's social modernism was indeed its best indicator.

The poet A. M. Sullivan expressed a powerful opposing view when he confidently told a *New York Times* reporter in 1947 that good American poets are simply "not whimpering about social problems or ideologies which belong to the field of journalism."[152] Sullivan, the self-consciously Catholic poet and beloved president of the Poetry Society of America who in 1953 had to "admit" his opinion that Joseph McCarthy "was doing a good job and behaving himself,"[153] knowingly participated in a redefinition of contemporary writing that would pass the anticommunist test. But in practice it was not so much an empirical measure as a tautology one just abided (at risk of exile from the category of poetry): as a matter of course, real American poets remained strictly faithful to the poetic. This logic left poets to narrow the range of permissible poetic languages and genres that should be used to achieve a specific political effect; the remnant, like Millet, Mac Low, and many other heretics actively writing in several different arenas, felt forced to choose to be known on the one hand as "modern poets" or on the other as, for example, "formerly journalists."

A. M. Sullivan, a fascinating figure, was equal parts antimodernist and anticommunist, the hybrid of *antis* that is this book's topic. The two ideologies together made a potent combination, a doubling of socioaesthetic opposition. This convergence created an atmosphere in which poets' formal work meant once again counting syllables (to strive consciously for the effect of convention) while nonetheless trying to pass off subjective lyric poems as free and natural American self-expression—a special "bugaboo of young poets today," Jackson Mac Low observed bitterly as early as 1947, "beset as they are by such pseudo-'traditional' legislative critics as [Yvor] Winters and [John Crowe] Ransom."[154] Given Mac Low's and many other poets' association with organizations trying to legislate radical change, such a dismissive attitude toward mainstream mid-century verse struck some conservatives as the pot calling the kettle black. So the argument was on.

In the '30s, one's clinical vocabulary was limited to two words—escapism and subjectivism—and both of them applied only to other people's wrong political choices.—Diana Trilling, 1959

The Revolt against Revolt

The poems gathered in *Seven Poets in Search of an Answer* in 1944 show how these communist poets sought to shape the work of historians of modernism looking back on the period just ended. The most politically organized of the seven—Martha Millet and Norman Rosten followed closely by Alfred Kreymborg and Langston Hughes—by 1944 felt that they had been a part of a vital, historiographical colloquy in an era in which liberal and leftist poets allied and radical critical activity was generally tolerated, even accepted, as part of the American cultural conversation. "If the communists don't awaken the Negro of the South," Hughes had asked in 1932, "who will?"[1] Even the ultimate bohemian, Maxwell Bodenheim, had adamantly bespoken the liberal-left alliance of the 1930s: embraced by *New Masses* reviewers for writing (in *Run Sheep Run* and other books) "American revolutionary novels,"[2] Bodenheim had been permitted to publish in that magazine wild poems in Kenneth Fearing's comic political mode, such as "Tenderly" ("the dog / Ran amuck and bit a priest / Walking to the Armory / To bless the soldiers, bless the bayonets, / Bless the Springfield rifles . . . / Bless the Treaty of Versailles"),[3] and would be fondly eulogized by Catholic activist Dorothy Day as having been a communist because they campaigned on behalf of the hungry poor.[4]

Now the end of the war brought the demise, first partial and then almost total, of the alliance of cultural liberalisms and leftisms in the United States. This was the bitter conclusion to what one former communist, Robert Warshow,[5] called "the Communist-liberal–New Deal movement of the 30's."[6] Such a convergence —something of the same hyphenating of distinct political and cultural projects— would not form again until the mid-1960s or, arguably, not until the mid- and late 1970s. In the immediate postwar period, however, for nearly as many reasons as there were individuals, most liberals abandoned erstwhile leftist partners,[7] while autonomous, organized radical left activism stood alone, ever more discernible, exposed to the public eye.[8] That segment of the intelligentsia had defected, Warshow wrote in "The Legacy of the '30's" (1947), and "the *whole level of thought and discussion, the level of culture itself*, had been lowered."[9] "Because the victorious anticommunist liberals regarded Communists as illegitimate participants in liberal and labor institutions," John Earl Haynes has written in his summary of historians' postwar interpretations of u.s. communism, "they often saw such participation as 'infiltration' and refused to recognize Popular Front [1930s] liberals as fellow heirs of the New Deal."[10]

Now, in the postwar years, the term "Marxist criticism" was "rarely use[d]" without being harnessed to all manner of antipolitical adjectives—"mechanical," "banal," "platitudinous," and so on.[11] Now it was said to be axiomatic that the *writing* of Marxist criticism was robotic and that communist poets had not been so much "in search of an answer" as duped into believing they had not been given the answer by the Comintern and told to write their poems as if they were still searching—the process, in the modern poem, being as important as the outcome. Now, in the 1950s, the Filipino poet Carlos Bulosan was scheduled for deportation as a dangerous subversive—the same poet whom Franklin Roosevelt had commissioned to write an essay celebrating one of the Four Freedoms, "The Freedom from Want," for a 1943 exhibition in San Francisco. Just as significantly, however, Bulosan, a best-selling author during the 1940s (*The Laughter of My Father, American Is in the Heart*), was soon dismissed as a radical ethnic hack and then forgotten.[12]

Ten years after the end of the war, Murray Kempton could write that "the fifties are a graveyard for young writers whose art was molded by the myth of the thirties."[13] Conceived as a liberal-left anthology at the tail end of an era of united fronts, *Seven Poets in Search of an Answer* moved its difficult way through this ideological warp. By the time critics and editors received reviewer's copies of the book, a few pioneers in red-baiting excoriated a whole decade, such as Eugene Lyons—whose book *The Red Decade* (1941) Daniel Aaron later called "a melancholy record of self-delusion and even more reprehensible human failings"[14]—had already begun to change the way the cultural history of "the age" would be written. Anticommunists felt emboldened. In 1946, Lyons cheerfully accepted the label "red-baiter";[15] by 1953, he said he preferred hysteria to complacency.[16] "Over the next twenty years," Lisle Rose has observed of the period from 1941 to 1961, the Red Decade "ruined careers and lives."[17]

Ruined careers, yes, and livelihoods—but also many Americans' sense of political language. What shifted at the same time was the reputation of modern writing as befitting the historical sensibility, modernism as having something to say about political ideology. Speaking implicitly for the American Poetry Society over which he had presided—and purportedly as a postwar *defender* of the viability of contemporary poetry—A. M. Sullivan decried any connection between political utopianism or social change and verse in the United States. Answering a Soviet critic's charges against the superficiality of American poets,

Sullivan declared, "A poet without a purpose is a misnomer, but a poet with a cure is a bore and a charlatan." It was 1947, and the *New York Times*, which covered this "story," used Sullivan's anticommunist phraseology in forming its headline:

> Poets Here Scorn Soviet Attack on Work;
> Versifier With "Cure" Held "Bore, Charlatan"[18]

Communist poetry in the 1930s, apart from everything else, was a "bore." It had been nothing nearly as intrepid or extraordinary as earlier claims from both left and right had suggested. By 1950 a poem mocking the engagé artist could simply bear the title "Nineteen-thirty-seven" and readers would from that alone sufficiently comprehend the political satire: "Can there be worse / Than this extra-Auden-airy verse?"[19]

Lyons's *Red Decade* was among many anticommunist books that recorded not just personal acts of intellectual charlatanism, treacherous self-delusion, and stupid arrogance in the 1930s. Lyons argued explicitly for a change in Americans' innocent attitudes toward meaning making. That there had been a time, before the 1930s, "when words still had sensible meanings," as Lyons put it in "A Tour of the Leftist Press" (1946), was the new underlying assumption.[20] It made no difference that communist poets such as Martha Millet and Eda Lou Walton wrestled with the same issues as aesthetic problems. For conservative poet E. Merrill Root, it made no difference that in the late 1930s the *Harvard Communist* had "*combine[d] avant-garde experiments* with Communist ideology": notwithstanding these experiments, which imply a consciousness about poetry's formal concerns among the students who edited the magazine, the "style of the magazine is *pure* party jargon."[21] The poems Root quotes—and the rest of the verse published in the *Communist*—cannot be said to have succeeded in their linguistic ventures, and while thematically many followed a party line, as language they cannot rightly be called jargon. For conservatives such as Root, communist poets' stiff certainty—their sense of "cure," in Sullivan's pejorative sense—mooted a priori any relevance of aesthetic value. In the effort to refute the Soviet criticism of the superficiality of recent American poetry, T. O'Conor Sloane III, director of the Catholic Poetry Society of America, announced, "If a few . . . poets are moved to lyricize for political purposes," it "has [no] bearing on the quality or value inherent in their work."[22] The point was that the false connection of aesthetic value and "political purposes" was itself one form of communist charlatanism. In *The Vital Center*, Arthur Schlesinger Jr. observed that a "basic incompatibility" had existed between communism and "the creation of literature."[23] Ray B. West, editor of the *Western Review*, then published at the University of Iowa, already one of the creative writing capitals of the world, argued that revolutionary writers of the 1930s were "less interested in literature than they were in other matters . . . primarily social. On the whole such communities dislike, if they do not hate, genuine literary achievement." The now-defunct communist writers' "clubs of the 1930s," West noted, were "well-remembered, but little lamented."[24]

"The thirties" quickly became the term of choice for those who fingered the whole radical period (roughly 1927–46). For many, "the thirties" referred less to a decade than to vast and secret aims, to generational delusion, to collective bad style. In the literary world, the phrase "the thirties" became metonymic for communism's pernicious linguistic influence. "The thirties" encoded a horrible newfangled winning tactic. Sullivan of the Poetry Society of America felt this way, as did Sloane of the Catholic Poetry Society, two organizations whose boards were anxious to mount a "defense" of valued American poetry. More straightforwardly political people, ranging widely across the intellectual and literary-generic spectrum, shared the feeling. Lyons's book was followed closely by the reconsiderations of Freda Utley (*The Dream We Lost*), of the "sincere anti-totalitarian scholar"[25] William Henry Chamberlin (*The Confessions of an Individualist*), Robert Stripling (*The Red Plot against America*), and at least a dozen others. By the time the late forties and fifties arrived, "the thirties"— again, the phrase—tonally signified betrayal. Itself an epithet, it routinely implied scorn at "a sordid decade of liberal hypocrisy and self-deception."[26]

It is difficult to overstate the efficacy of the new rhetorical weapon. One scholar, defending himself in 1952 against an all-out barrage of red-baiting, understood that his accusers could "make [phrases] mean in the 1950s something quite different from their meaning in the 1930s";[27] the man's detractors were among those who felt that at best the decade was "a disaster that stimulate[d] enthusiastic intellectual activity" only possibly of value in support of that enthusiasm.[28] Leslie Fiedler argued that what he determined to be the deceptions of one man (Alger Hiss) actually indicated the guilt of an entire generation of liberals.[29] Peter Viereck, a much commended young poet (winner of the 1948 Pulitzer Prize for poetry) who doubled as a New Conservative cultural critic producing what M. L. Rosenthal called "endless slogans, precious credos, . . . saucy banalities about poetry and this harsh world,"[30] dared to use the phrase "the whole guilty 1930's" without blinking at such an unsupportably huge generalization.[31] In 1955, more flatly, Daniel Bell announced that "the generation failed."[32] The poet Louise Bogan, never so flat, nonetheless gave this pert history of modernism: a generation of writers entered their thirties in the 1930s and, instead of making a normal "transition from youth to middle age," embraced communism, "committed creative suicide," and forfeited the freedom they had brilliantly achieved in their teens and twenties, "thr[owing] over *every scrap of their former enthusiasms,* as though there were something sinful in them."[33] They were, for her, neither equivalent nor related enthusiasms. The first was commendable exploration of new ideas, but the second, communism, was simple delusion. For William Van O'Connor, the "upheavals of the thirties" drew experimental poets out of their usual isolated state, but "the pendulum swung too far the other way," verse went political and "became the poetry of a party," thus "forcing out aesthetic" concerns.[34] The liberal left, to Fiedler, was "stubbornly uncreative." If of a book of modern American verse that sold well F. O. Matthiessen had written that "such an audience is not to be scorned in a democracy," Fiedler replied, "Why *not*? The whole problem only arises if the critic abdicates his obligation to judge." The liberalism that had "emancipated" criticism in the 1920s had then become so "infected" with social faith that, far from being truly radical, "it had become in fact esthetic reaction."[35] Leo Gurko's history of poetry in *The Angry Decade* was similarly quick and dirty: "Why there should have been an outpouring of notable verse during the second decade of the century and not during the fourth, may be due at bottom to . . ."— whereupon readers of *The Angry Decade* are treated to Gurko's musings on the "accident" of history. It just happened that gifted people had come of age in the 1910s but not in the 1930s.[36]

Perhaps Viereck, although a truly extraordinary person, was only the most highly stylized of the many thirties-bashers. His anticommunism was more flamboyant and more for general public consumption than Bogan's or even Fiedler's, and Viereck was far less tentative than Gurko and O'Connor, both of whom sought in their work to recover a balance of views about the decade. Nevertheless, in many variations, quotings, and paraphrasings, gigantic assertions gained currency. *The whole guilty 1930s. Every scrap of their former enthusiasms. Stubbornly uncreative. Forcing out the aesthetic.* Whether such dismissive hyperbole was embodied in the phrase the "Red Decade" or in catchphrasing a bit more circumlocutious—such as the "angry decade," Gurko's choice, or the more ominous *twenty years of treason*—the words nevertheless disrupted and demonized.

"Twenty years of treason" was an especially effective formulation. It made one feel the imminent end of an era, that it was the eleventh hour—that one needed to look over one's shoulder or in the rearview mirror, keeping an eye on those sinners who had found their own aesthetic pre-Depression pasts "sinful." The term "communism" itself was "powerful enough," as Ben Hecht observed in 1954, "to flatten out all sanity,"[37] but "twenty years of treason" was terrifyingly ambiguous. The latter phrase at least subliminally referred to communism, yet when uttered by the Republican leadership it could be taken literally to refer to Democratic Party control of the White House, a connotation of the phrasing put into service by the victorious party in 1952 that significantly postdated Lyons's blunter epithet. By that year, a turning point, one could look back exactly two decades, to 1932, for conservatives an infamous revolutionary year in U.S. politics: the invention of the New Deal and what detractors saw as the aesthetic of absolutist accommodation. "Since 1933," wrote Dan Smoot, a Harvard teaching fellow in English and FBI agent, "we [have] place[d] our freedom and our lives in the hands of political servants in Washington, whose power to destroy us is unchecked."[38] In the pages of this man's remarkable newsletter, the *Dan Smoot Report*, New Deal liberalism was as treasonous as communism (1930s liberals were "Comsymps"),[39] just as for conservative theorist Frank Meyer the "Bolshevik revolution" and the "Roosevelt revolution" had "parallel" objectives.[40] The vocabulary of thirties-bashing was cast in the idiom of incurability; tropes of cancer and mass death abounded. Leftist writing of the 1930s was dismissed "in a phrase: it was an alien growth."[41] New Dealers' and procommunists' shared penchant for acronyms, according to the conservative rhetorical theory of Richard Weaver, expressed an "increasing tendency to employ in the place of the term itself an abbreviated or telescoped form—which form is nearly always used with even more reckless assumption of authority," thus violating Edmund Burke's main conservative dictum that "freedom inheres in something sensible." When "forces of government are referred to by these bloodless abstractions"—Weaver's examples include ERP, FDIC, WPA—an "abstract force" is unleashed whose "will is law" and whom "the individual citizen has no way to placate." Any new ethics of rhetoric would have to begin by unmaking all such acronyms, which lexically augured totalitarianism.[42] They denied individual responsibility. Another brilliant conservative, Ralph de Toledano, personally recalled the sanctification of the alphabet in the 1930s and realized only later that "repeated almost ritualistically," the way the acronyms sounded—the sound of the poetry, as it were, of the New Deal as a rhetorical world—seemed to "promise . . . the joyous destruction of the traditions."[43] Neither Weaver (ever) nor de Toledano (in the 1950s) would have much liked Edwin Rolfe's "Nuthin but Brass" (1932), a poem dedicated to Cab Calloway: "Let the old broken hag die on the street: / the DSC will haul the hulk away,"[44] or Langston Hughes's "Madam's Past History," despite its special bemusement about government-made jobs. Hughes's Madam (Alberta K. Johnson) has a "past history" of entrepreneurship, though she was barely profitable—in another poem she reports having ordered business cards chiefly because she wanted to see her name in print—and the New Deal job-creation program turns her down:

> Cause I had a insurance
> The WPA
> Said, We can't use you
> Wealthy that way.[45]

Radicalism for Weaver and de Toledano was at least as rhetorical as it was a matter of political activity. By taking "control of writing in the thirties," John Chamberlain wrote, "the Communists managed to poison the intellectual life of a whole nation—and the poison has lingered on." Now the "big job" was "to extract the poison."[46]

For the poisonous or cancerous ones, the treacherous betrayers of American culture, it was hard to know how to respond. In the end, surprisingly few took the very great trouble to defend "the thirties" against the barrage of underanalyzed, accusatory generalizations. One could extract the poison from Chamberlain's conceit of poison, but doing so did not begin to mend the underlying pain. Alfred Kazin, already famous for his precocious, comprehensive liberal-left survey of American writing, *On Native Grounds* (1942), wrote privately to Granville Hicks in 1953 that he had "begun to droop a little under the continuous impact of retrospective hysteria."[47] Not long before F. O. Matthiessen jumped from the twelfth floor of the Hotel Manger in Boston in 1950—an act many contended directly resulted from harassment by anticommunists[48] ("the cold war made its first martyr among scholars" at his demise;[49] it was a copycat defenestration honoring Jan Masaryk, a cherished acquaintance)[50]—he too had looked back on the thirties. Matthiessen wrestled with what he sensed was a false "retrospect" on the thirties as a time when "intellectuals commuted to radicalism and back." He had not "commuted"—he consistently called himself a "socialist" to the end; he proudly recounted his radical involvements from the day in 1923 when he joined the Labour Club while at Oxford to 1948 when he was Harvard's major campus supporter of Henry Wallace's presidential campaign, giving a speech at Harvard Hall in which he likened Wallace to Thomas Jefferson.[51] Yet even Matthiessen worried about the accuracy of the perception proffered by anticommunists in the late forties that smart people had in the thirties "bec[o]me Communists overnight."[52] The editors of the socialist *Monthly Review* knew that conservatives, "fear[ing] the danger of a radical coalition picking up where the New Deal had been broken off by the war," would feel the "necessity to split up and fragmentize all those remnants of the 1930s." To them the decade itself was being demonized, as was a certain language about the decade, despite the actual experience of many noncommunist radicals—among them the *Monthly Review*'s Paul Sweezy (1910–2004)—who in the thirties had found no radical mentors to teach them. Their radicalism was more stylistic and more solitudinous, less the result of mentorship, membership, or training, than detractors in later years claimed by means of conspiracy theories and tracings of secret networks and lineages of doctrinal influence. Many young radicals such as Sweezy had been forced to engage "in the process of teaching ourselves" Marxian theory, the Russian Revolution, and the culture of socialism in America. The teenaged Macha (later M. L.) Rosenthal was "entranced by the brilliance of Lenin's prose before I knew what he was talking about."[53] The poet Stanley Burnshaw (1906–2005), a literary editor of the communist weekly *New Masses* and infamous as Wallace Stevens's communist detractor, later admitted that he had been so busy doing basic literary work for the communist movement that he had never had a chance to read much Marx or Lenin and had never had a single theoretical conversation about communism in all his time in the movement. Yet he and his comrades talked a lot about *poetry*, and he felt himself a collaborative partner in radical activity as distinct from theory—activity that included editing leftist poets of aesthetic temperament. But in his development of a poetic language suitable for radicalism, Burnshaw had felt mostly alone.[54] In "What Happened in the 30's" (1962), William Phillips observed that for those wanting to understand why from 1940 to 1960 "everyone has been trying to forget what happened in the 30's," the main question was whether "the literary and intellectual side of the radical movement" was "so marginal, so parochial" or "so relevant and so central."[55] Nathan Glazer, who analyzed CPUSA demographics with greater precision than almost[56] anyone else at the time (including the FBI), evinced hardly less ambiguity than Phillips: while for twenty years (1930–50) "the extent and nature of Communist influence among writers" and other intellectuals "was great," it was also true that the "grouping" of intellectuals "surround[ing]" the party was "large" and "loose."[57] Notwithstanding his conviction that it presented an alluring "mirage of utopia," Daniel Bell knew that communism's influence "within American life" was "oblique,"[58] and only "for a small group" did the thirties, by the fifties, "have a special meaning."[59] Writing on the "social basis" of communism's appeal for Clinton Rossiter's liberal anticommunist series, *Communism in American Life*, Glazer mapped the American communist topography from ten thousand feet up. But every individual writer's "loose" connection to communism was *more or less* "loose" and was and is better understood through individual cases. Sweezy, the red-baited socialist editor and academic,[60] was not among Glazer's informants. In Sweezy's case, "the thirties" was actually a decade in which "Marxism . . . was very marginal in all of the centers of intellectual activity in the United States." He argued that instead of stealing or inventing the language of the American 1930s, as red-baiting antagonists later repeatedly claimed, radicals had been responding to the way the Depression was already being described by their detractors—responding, that is, defensively even then.[61]

In "How Red Was the Red Decade" (1953), Granville Hicks, although at that point himself a liberal anticommunist,[62] argued for the importance of "counteract[ing] the damage the myth of the Red Decade is doing to our national morale. Every time somebody says, 'Boy, the Reds nearly got us in the thirties,' his listeners shiver, thinking, 'It might happen again.'"[63] And what "it" was, in this particular argument, was influence on cultural language—on the way Americans talked and wrote about culture and language in the United States. The Red Decade thesis, Daniel Bell wrote in his contribution to *Socialism and American Life*, needed to be mindfully formulated despite the fact that "communism never won a mass following in the United States" but because "it did have a disproportionate influence in the cultural field."[64] The Reds had been routed in every common political sense, so the relevance of the "Red Decade" in the fifties was to the war against what remained: cultural power. Anticommunists owned electoral politics. Yes—but who owned the language? Who, in particular, owned the center of American language production, New York City? Kazin had recently published his celebration of New York's special liberal-ethnic style, *A Walker in the City* (1951), "a lyrical exploration of prose" and "a kind of 'documentary' poetry,"[65] a prose poem paean to the twenties turning linguistically into the thirties, lyric into document; the book was itself wonderfully an instance of such a style. Kazin was just then attempting to balance his image of Matthiessen's devotion to *The Waste Land* (the Wallaceite activist who loved Eliotic modernism) against the beloved "Matty," the dear friend who may have been killed by anticommunism[66] (the man on whom Counterattack kept a thick file, ready for sale to red-baiters)[67] and might easily have seen himself implicated in Chamberlain's description of communist "objective no. 1." That objective was "the capture of New York, the word capital of the United States." (And "there are more Communists in New York City," announced the leader of the reactionary Christian Crusade, "than in Moscow."[68] Until New York "lost its evil dominance," an ex-communist wrote, "the real voice of America" will never sing.)[69] The linguistic coup in New York meant that communists "have managed to put their coloration on the American Word." "This job was pulled off in the thirties."[70] And by no means had poetry been spared. Now it had to be liberated from this pernicious influence. After all, as the magazine *News from behind the Iron Curtain* reported in "Taming of the Muse," "poetry is an important aspect of the Soviet Union's ideological indoctrination program for the captive countries."[71] Was not New York City a captive country? Some anticommunists took this question very seriously; the answer could be sought, in part, through a survey of contemporary poetry, by tracking back along the traces of its radical origin.

One origin, much deplored by conservatives, was the New Deal's support of writers and painters. What was now, in the 1950s, "very reminiscent of the old WPA project stuff" was modern art that "is a lot of nonconformism for the sake of nonconformism." So the rabid anticommunist (and anti-Semite and racist) Fulton Lewis Jr. told listeners to his *Top of the News* radio program.[72] "The worst pressures toward conformity," wrote E. Merrill Root, "are not political . . . but cultural."[73] Thus anticommunists went in for aesthetic analysis. Lewis told his radio audience that modern artists' "extrovert complex" manifested itself in "moronic words" set to a "thyroidal conglomeration of noises in rhythm."[74] Gabriel Almond in *The Appeals of Communism* (1954) devoted a chapter to "Esoteric and Exoteric Styles" and spoke of "stylistic patterns," "differences in style and sentence structure," the "stylized motions" of writing, and enumerated "stylistic devices."[75] The "democratic egalitarian terminology" of the eighteenth-century Jacobins, "like that of the communists in the 1930s," had a "hypnotic attraction outweighing the despotic reality behind the terminology."[76] This radicalism had been linguistic.[77]

If Alfred Kazin really believed himself to be a target of thirties-bashers by 1953, it was tellingly ironic, at least from the point of view of writers and critics on the left who felt they had been misrepresented by Kazin's *On Native Grounds* when it was published in 1942. Despite apparently the best intentions to treat major communist literary figures such as Granville Hicks with equanimity, Kazin's comprehensive book, much praised in the reviews and critical press, fed rather than stemmed the flow of thirties-bashing.[78] This effect resulted largely from the language he used to describe the period. *On Native Grounds* characterized the thirties as "bent on liberation by conquest and extermination," "a subliterary calculus," "formula-mongering in conversation," "sad," "dull," "nothing but posturing bad taste," "rancor and prophecy trumpeting itself as disgust," "a bludgeon," "fratricidal," "exaggerati[on] with crude native force," "hoarse and coy emotionalism," and "a melancholy synthesis into which went the worst of Marxist tradition in polemic, the worst of the Russian example in criticism, the political influence of Stalinism, and a general mediocrity of local [American] talent."[79] Isidor Schneider considered Kazin a "hostile critic" for his view that the 1930s was a "period of the left-wing offensive as a domination which the Left lost through ineptitude."[80]

Critics in the late 1940s and 1950s significantly *less* sympathetic to the period than Kazin argued that writers of the 1930s had demolished the language—had poisoned it, had discolored words with radical subjectivities. These authors had sullied the lyric in particular. They had brought high art down to the level of the mass. One reason for our current crisis, postwar critics contended, was that the music of poetry had died. In an essay, "Why Modern Poets Have Failed," a Catholic critic, Mary Julian Baird—Sister Mary was both anticommunist and antimodernist—wrote that a dominating "socio-political group" of poets had "lowered the tone and content of poetry by thinning the music and levelling the intellectual content to suit the masses of people." She made a connection between communist betrayal and modernist subversion that many anticommunists took with deadly seriousness, as we will see in the second half of this book. Yet this anticommunist did not identify a single poem here, and she named only a few of the most obvious names. The alliance of traditionalist detractors of modernism and conservative/reactionary opponents of communism—an odd but powerful convergence—offers, to my mind, the most fascinating of the many tales to be told in the general narrative of the assiduous deradicalization of modern poetry at midcentury, the making of a "thirties" aesthetic apt for the fifties.

Finally, the sheer political fact of an alliance between anticommunists and antimodernists is less surprising than the unwillingness or inability of the most polemical advocates of this position, as a tactical matter, to name the names of those 1930s writers who really could be said, in critical terms, to have committed such errors. I became aware while prospecting the archives for a book titled *Modernism from Right to Left* (1994) that the degree to which poets of the left actually *accepted* modernist forms and linguistic concepts was quite great. It was not the case, as interpreters of the 1930s in the 1950s would assume, that "proletarian" writers hoped and expected their work to "outlive James and Joyce and Yeats and Eliot, because history was on the [leftists'] side."[81] Nor is it generally true that "in the 1930s the writings of the expatriates were filled with regret and remorse for past frivolities," despite Norman Cantor's generalization to this effect in *The Age of Protest* (1969).[82] Many poets affiliated with the CPUSA liked to assume, as Martha Millet and the other poets in *Seven Poets* did, that history was indeed with them, but that assumption did not necessarily extend to a counter-revolution undoing the Revolution of the Word (and indeed Cantor meant linguistic "frivolities" as well as drinking, dancing, and other social forms of Euro-flapperism). One *Daily Worker* critic in 1948 looked back at the "middle thirties" as a time of "collaboration" between poets and radical politics: in those days a left-wing poet "experimented with forms . . . *[b]ecause* of his discontent with what he saw and felt in that world," not in spite of it. Experimentalism "express[ed] his revolt."[83] "It would surely be unwise," a poet wrote in the New Masses, "to dispose of the vast contribution of James Joyce on the 'dung heap of decadence' to which some over-literal left-wing critics have consigned him." Perhaps this was a minority view, but it was offered to readers of the New Masses by the man who was then that magazine's literary editor.[84] In any case, another New Masses reviewer noted that "the prose throughout Ulysses has a remarkable suppleness of idiom which gives a constant sense of recognizable reality to the reader."[85] It was a myth invented in the late 1940s and 1950s (and surprisingly unquestioned by poets and modern poetry critics in the 1960s and 1970s) that all American communist poets in the 1930s had repudiated Eliot's verse—an error understandably compounded by true reports of attacks by official Communist Party critics in Eastern Europe on poets such as Tadeusz Rozewicz for their "imitations" of this "bard of rotting Western culture."[86] In fact, while some observers begrudged and dismissed Eliot's influence on modernism, a number of 1930s radicals in the United States took it seriously, and some responded positively. Solon Barber's "Nocturne in the Modern Manner" seems to parody the "g'night ladies" passage in The Waste Land yet expresses the desire to take the "modern manner" beyond the historical point (the end of the 1920s) when "the gin is gone / and the last broken-basked cigarettes / smoulder in the ashtray."[87] The same Rolfe Humphries who urged a straying comrade to return to the communist movement because "You have a world to gain!" observed at the same time that "Eliot's ear is good."[88] Although by 1936 Malcolm Cowley knew some of his comrades "jeer[ed] at such phrases as 'poetry renaissance,'" he felt strongly that "there really was something of the sort in 1912."[89] In 1938, reacting to some poets who were veering from surrealism's initial connection with parties of the left, Eda Lou Walton, a CPUSA member, wrote that "these writers forget that while they talk about the revolution of the word, the revolution of the world goes on under their noses." Walton simply assumed a natural relationship between modernism and radicalism;[90] while it was not an assumption shared by most party leaders, whom Herbert Aptheker later recalled had "very little knowledge and little interest" in modernism, this cannot be said of the literary regulars.[91] Walton was amazed that poets might not realize the radical potential in the modernist revolution.[92]

The interaction between and among upstart communists and by-then eminent modernist "elders" was more complex, freer, less predictable, than I would have guessed after coming of intellectual age hearing dismissive generalizations about "the thirties" as reported in the fifties and early to mid-sixties, a story that many intellectuals of the mid- and late sixties, obsessed with *new* lefts disconnected from old,[93] did surprisingly little to revise. One big myth about the thirties—perhaps the biggest, that communist poets hated the lyric—persisted into the late sixties, even in the work of a new generation of scholars who began to specialize in the thirties. Warren French's view in *The Thirties* (1967) that "the times conspired against the lyricist unless like [Wallace] Stevens he chose to sing largely unheard"[94] is wrong, I learned, on several counts, although it is one of those generalizations that seems to stick and has been unquestioningly repeated as fact.[95] For one thing, Stevens's *Ideas of Order* (1935), *Owl's Clover* (1936), and *The Man with the Blue Guitar* (1937) were loudly heard on the literary left.[96] When Stanley Burnshaw in 1961 tried to undo the confusions, he discovered that even otherwise perspicacious poetry critics had not even bothered to read —or literally could not find, since some libraries' shelves had been cleared of communist material—his *New Masses* essays, let alone taken time to relearn in any detail the socioliterary contexts of the thirties. Although he never claimed he was being red-baited by poetry critics who merely named his name (as if the name "Burnshaw" alone could stand in for all communist poetry critique in the decade), it pained him to have to start over in his explanation.[97]

Unlike Warren French, who offered no evidence for the alleged demise of the lyric in the 1930s, in "Why Modern Poets Have Failed" the anticommunist antimodernist Mary Julian Baird at least named a few names. But these hardly count. She tossed them off, just the obvious names—giveaways. Her gesture was akin to the cooperative witness giving the House Committee on Un-American Activities (HUAC) salacious generalizations along with a few pat, affirmative specifics they had heard a dozen times already but ceremoniously pretended to receive as revelations.[98] This always already ritualized smear tactic carried with it an eerie reluctance. Or perhaps more precisely, in Baird's case and others', hesitation was a version of aesthetic ignorance mitigated by little to nil political know-how. Introducing the reviled group of "political and social poets," Baird listed the three usual suspects—"W. H. Auden, C. Day Lewis, and Stephen Spender"—but mentioned not one American poet in this context; nor did she quote a line or even a title of a poem committing the political sins she assailed.[99]

Peter Viereck, although shrewder than Mary Baird, also did not name radical names or get down to cases when in 1954 he blamed the "whole" 1930s for assaults he claimed had been made against the "the dignity of lyricism." Young Americans learning the recent history of modern poetry would do well to forget or simply never learn about the 1930s. Indeed, Viereck claimed to know that "almost none" of the students and new poets whom he was meeting, teaching, and reading by the mid-1950s "would dream of returning to the . . . dry exaggeration of content and 'message,' which was popular in the proletarian verse of the 1930's." "God" himself was to be thanked for bringing on "Eliot and the Southern School formalists" to "rid us of that incubus!" Poetic form got neglected in the verse "of what the thirties called 'social responsibility.'" Such neglect was "deadlier to poetry" than the over-polished forms wrought by formalists in reaction. Here (and elsewhere) Viereck claimed to be no friend of "pure technical virtuosity." But if one had to choose—and in the 1950s, Viereck said again and again, one just had to choose—one took "unmoral *art-pour-l'art* formalism" over "soapbox poetry which prostitutes art to political propaganda, because at least unmoral virtuosity respects the dignity of its medium . . . which is more than Agitprop does."[100]

As poet and social critic, Viereck was an unusual conservative. He dubbed himself a "New Conservative" with a public-relations flair that itself alienated some bona fide conservatives[101] such as Russell Kirk,[102] Frank S. Meyer,[103] and Henry Regnery,[104] almost as much as he put off communist poets[105] and poets on the anti-Stalinist ultraleft. Among the latter was Kenneth Rexroth, who complained to Babette Deutsch that Viereck was "the loudest horn in the Stars & Stripes forever band of Political Sousaism so well represented by the recent parade in the Partisan Review."[106] The poet John Frederick Nims coined the verb "to Viereck" (as in "to Viereck [copies of his articles] all over Italy").[107] Yet the positions Viereck took earned the highest praise from E. Merrill Root, the ex-communist poet who was hard to please politically: in 1955, Root declared the New Conservatives "our only living radicals."[108]

One of Viereck's critical books received the title *Conservatism Revisited: The Revolt against Revolt* (1949), and in a later essay pairing a modern poet and a New Dealer who spied for Russia, he referred to "the philistine-baiting phi- listine, the avant-garde that has become a last rearguard resistance to the revolt against revolt."[109] Viereck appealed to some liberal anticommunist defenders of modern poetry, such as Selden Rodman and Karl Shapiro (the latter always loved a good revolt against revolt), as well as to conservative academics such as Harvard's ambitious and prolific Henry Kissinger who sought partners more rhetorically pugnacious than themselves in writing a workable cultural anti- communism. Pulling disparate anticommunist elements together, Viereck thus was for a few crucial years a major player in defining a new kind of modernism. This "new" "modernism"—a modernism of what Daniel Bell contentedly called *limits*, a "traditional modernism" befitting the age[110]—would, as Rodman put it (praising Viereck), make the "break with *the Eliot-dominated past*" while at the same time be so steeped in modernist modes of knowledge as to provide an intellectual "familiarity with cross-references almost Joycean in scope."[111]

Perhaps because Henry Kissinger's historical style was the dead opposite of

Joycean—*Bismarckean* might be the apt term[112]—he sought out poet Peter Viereck immediately after the young political scientist founded the international anticommunist magazine *Confluence* at Harvard in 1952. Kissinger, who was still then a graduate student, doubtless had seen Viereck's ode to the moderate undemocratic Metternich, the younger man's personal diplomatic model.[113] The piece Kissinger got from Viereck for the third issue of *Confluence*, thereby clinching the new enthusiasm for limits, was the remarkable short essay, " 'Bloody-Minded Professors': The Anti-Social Role of Some Intellectuals." " 'Bloody-Minded Professors' " was just about as vivacious a piece of thirties-bashing as any conservative in the political science arena could have hoped for. Although an inexactly reasoned essay, it nonetheless had a powerful, disproportionate effect. The case against communist polemic of the thirties seemed not to be marred by the poor quality of thought in this piece and, at certain points, of pure polemicism. In poured readers' mail, pro and con Viereck, addressed to Kissinger and often warning him about the direction of *Confluence*.[114]

This essay clearly showed that Viereck's version of blaming the thirties sharpened the anti-intellectualism already logically natural to many conservative anticommunists. Because so many progressive activists in the thirties had not been affiliated with the universities, the anticommunist project needed some handle on the aesthetic and theoretical "betrayal" of the academics. Viereck supplied a rationale partly through an analysis of left-dominated styles of interpretation, an approach that would soon have the effect, as we will see, of putting modernist poetry at risk of being red-baited. Leftist intellectuals had betrayed the West by an initial (in many cases, quite temporary) attraction to Marxism. Viereck cited a 1946 Gallup poll in which Americans were asked, "Do you believe Russia is trying to build herself up to a ruling power, or just building up protection against being attacked in another war?" The most educated gave optimistic replies—relatively uncritical of Soviet intentions. "From what Gallup called the uneducated 'manual workers,' " Viereck observed, came replies indicating grave doubts about the Soviets. Thus, intellectual status was "the main obstacle to understanding that communists are communists."[115] Education had taught Americans to misread truisms. Here, then, Viereck was a true anticommunist anti-intellectual; by means of such reasoning, the right—even Kissinger, among the most ambitiously academic of New Conservatives—could claim affinity with the working class at least as a matter of logic. Viereck noted that "these 'oppressed proletarians' " were the same folks who keenly predicted, in contrast to liberal-left pundits and professors, that "Russia aimed for world power."[116]

That this argument had much to do with modernist poetry was a point made clear by Richard Rovere. Rovere (1915–79) had been at the "center of the Communist group at college" in the 1930s[117] and served as associate editor of the *New Masses* from 1937 to 1939.[118] In the early 1950s he was fresh from two pointed expressions of postutopianism—liberalism without hope, as one might dub his credo of that moment. In the postwar period, Rovere was an ardent anti-Stalinist liberal with impeccable anti-McCarthy credentials.[119] Among those cultural anticommunists who nonetheless despised Viereck's " 'Bloody-Minded Professors,' " Rovere wrote lengthily to Kissinger[120] to explain the "dissenting" anticommunist view, a counterinterpretation of the relationship between modernism and radicalism in the 1930s. This was, it must be emphasized, an argument among anticommunists. While Kissinger wrote an editorial note to contend that publishing Rovere's dissent kept to his "policy of presenting as wide a range of opinion as possible," it was a limited claim, since one was hard-pressed to find an anti-anticommunist (let alone a communist) in the pages of *Confluence*. Rovere was there to say, in effect, that Viereck, of all people, had been too deferential to the aesthetic of 1930s radicals, and if anything he tended to red-bait an energetic, even reckless, but finally moderate red-baiter. To Rovere, Viereck's error was in assuming that 1930s radicals had cultivated some finely developed taste—that they were the least bit sensitive to modernism's project of challenging art's autonomous status and had applied to the praxis of movement politics the "literary (at first nonpolitical) anti-bourgeois crusade" of pre-Depression avant-gardism. Such a reading of modernism as having been at any point compatible with radicalism was to Rovere tantamount to being soft on communism.

Viereck's campaign generally sought to restore conservatives' place among nonconformists. But to Rovere and other more conventional (and more liberal) anticommunists, this was a mistaken tactic, for it conceded avant-gardism as a quality of the left. "Many liberals tend to assume," Viereck wrote, "that only the left in politics, only the avant-garde in literature are against conformity and philistia. Their bogeyman is a never-defined 'conservative.' "[121] For Rovere, conversely, Viereck erroneously assumed that communist intellectuals in the 1930s had gotten their critique of democratic capitalism from "their absorption in 'nineteenth-century French novels' "—a habit of reading that had put them in the mentality shared by noncommunists such as Ezra Pound and Henry Miller who had also gone in for the "familiar blend of an 'aristocratic' snob in art and a fellow-traveling 'progressive' in politics."[122]

Modernism and radicalism in the United States, in short, could seem to have shared original antibourgeois impulses. The extent to which the relation between political radicalism and modernism is an inherence or a case-by-case contingency became in fact the main problem that would have to be faced by theorists of the avant-garde who did their work during the height of the Cold War. For Hilton Kramer, the connection between avant-gardism and radicalism raised "one of the richest questions in modern intellectual history." But in his essay "To Hell with Culture," Kramer answered that question in the negative, giving a conspectus of the anticommunist view of the need to sever modernism from its radical connections: "The history of the avant-garde . . . cannot be made to conform to the history of radicalism." When "radical political interests and avant-garde artistic taste" converged between the late 1920s and the mid-1940s, the result was an era of convenient confusion during which political subversives, posing as avant-gardists, could irresponsibly criticize an age of sanity and affluent civility as "smothering orthodoxy and conformism." In Kramer's view, it was fortunate that at "the advent of the Cold War," the radicalism-modernism alliance was "finally shattered," those two movements sent once and for all in different directions.[123]

Somewhat less overtly than Kramer, Renato Poggioli similarly quarantined modernism from communism. This was ironic, for Poggioli wished in part to rescue the theoretical discussion of aesthetic experiment from politics. But in Poggioli's *The Theory of the Avant-Garde*, a study begun in the late 1940s[124] and finally published (in Italian) in 1962, the suppression of modernism in the Soviet Union casts on the book a shadow so long that it could barely be stated, even as a hypothesis then adamantly refuted, that there was a "tendency to equate aesthetic radicalism with political radicalism," an assertion no sooner made than dubbed "a tendency *already* questioned on theoretical grounds in this essay."[125] Poggioli's otherwise coherent study of avant-gardism goes fuzzily apolitical on the question of modernism's a posteriori close fit with political radicalism. Although his examples of antimodernism are all drawn from the experience of experimental artists facing their detractors in the West, Poggioli reminded readers that "the avant-garde, like any culture, can only flower in a climate where political liberty triumphs."[126] He could not seem to make straightforwardly the crucial point about form that Peter Bürger could make in *Theory of the Avant-Garde* when a decade later the younger theorist was in the revolutionary thrall of May 1968:[127] "When avant-gardistes demand that art become practical again once again, they do not [inevitably] mean that the contents of works of art should be socially significant."[128] But this was not news to modernist communists. In the 1930s, Stanley Burnshaw, Sol Funaroff, and Kenneth Fearing had known all along that insofar as they chose to relate to pre-Depression modernism, poetic form would be their connection to (respectively) Wallace Stevens, T. S. Eliot, and William Carlos Williams. Yet by the 1950s and early 1960s—Burnshaw, Funaroff, and Fearing all but forgotten as poets—with his nervousness about stating too openly the continuity from modernism to leftism, Poggioli on the key issue offers a theory of avant-gardism that Rovere as a liberal cold warrior had already more honestly articulated. To Rovere, the contention that modernism and radicalism shared the radical impulse was far from true a priori; indeed, it was fantasy. Sterner in this respect than Viereck's, Rovere's attack on 1930s aesthetics here formed an unholy alliance with the more conservative Mary Baird—as with the brilliant anti-Stalinist modernist[129] V. F. Calverton, the ex-Marxist critic of Marxist theory Stanley Edgar Hyman, the anti-Marxist formalist Eliseo Vivas, Diana Trilling, Stephen Spender, Leslie Fiedler, and the liberal, literary-minded journalist Murray Kempton, whose *Part of Our Time* (1955) presented "the social muse" as stupefied.

All of these complex, transitional figures contended that in one way or another political radicals had invariably brought poetry down low, had put verse in the hands of professional communists, "hard" people who "preferred the deed to the word,"[130] who had returned poetry to matters of mere content— a tendency that allegedly attracted mediocre people to writing as a career. This was indeed the subtext of theories of the avant-garde through the entire period. Calverton wrote privately to Max Eastman that literary Stalinism was a political tactic for explaining what is otherwise aesthetically unexplainable: writers without talent and lacking honesty sold copies and garnered reviews, while anti-Stalinists did not.[131] Attention paid to the second of these two qualities (Stalinists suppressing the literary careers of anti-Stalinists) begged aesthetic questions raised by the first (what literarily constitutes talent and honesty). "There was room within modernism," Spender wrote in 1954, "for an attack on our industrialized civilization by lesser writers."[132]

Eliseo Vivas also observed in 1954 that "the Marxists" constituted "the only body of men in our day who have had a consistently serious sense of the importance of literature" yet were "the very men who in their hearts least of all care for it." The assertion was made without example or footnote in an essay commending Allen Tate for his view that "the poet is not responsible to society for a version of what it thinks it is or what it wants" yet *is* responsible "for the mastery of a disciplined language."[133] Vivas had made the same generalization about Marxist writers (who believe simply that "all art is propaganda") in a 1935 paper on "Art, Morals, and Propaganda," but there and then, qualification was given in a thirteen-line footnote conceding that American literary communists held differing views and that individuals' opinions were changing over time.[134] Kempton in 1955 generalized that communist writers "were *all* very conventional" and "devoid of education"[135]—that the 1930s were not a time when "there was an 'idea' in life" but rather "a time of generally weak intellection," as Diana Trilling acidly put it on the evening she confronted the Beat poets in 1959.[136]

Kempton claimed to know that poet Edwin Rolfe had been in awe of James T. Farrell because Farrell had taken the time to read books by Alfred North Whitehead and was thus intellectually a cut above the comrades. He also claimed to know that Funaroff, one of the "Dynamo" poets (communists who satirized but also seriously engaged modernist forms),[137] preferred Mayakovsky to Pavlov because Mayakovsky wrote advertising slogans for the state and thus transcended Yeats.[138] That Willard Maas, as a bisexual communist poet who later consorted with "workers" at Andy Warhol's Factory, was elated that his poems, "whether . . . of love or revolution," were "suggestive of Wallace Stevens's serenity";[139] that the unswerving communist H. H. Lewis, author of *Thinking of Russia* (1932), had proudly won the Harriet Monroe Lyric Prize;[140] that at the height of Edna St. Vincent Millay's association with the Popular Front, Ruth Lechlitner criticized Millay's *Conversation at Midnight* (1937) as verse that was insufficiently poetic;[141] that Herman Spector interchangeably sent his Eliotic verses to *transition*, *New Masses*, *Contemporary Verse*, *Unrest*, and *Blues*;[142] that Walter Lowenfels, by calling Kenneth Fearing "one of the avant-garde poets," meant the highest sort of praise;[143] that Eda Lou Walton, a CPUSA member for decades, positively memorialized Yeats in verse[144] and had been so excited by Joyce that she risked arrest to smuggle into the United States a banned copy of *Ulysses*;[145] that Norman Macleod, a member of the National Executive Committee of the Rebel Poet group,[146] deemed himself a revolutionary imagist; that Frank Marshall Davis, the African American poet who later joined the CPUSA,[147] learned both modernism and communism at Kansas State College and did not until much later see them as exclusive in the least;[148] that Alfred Kreymborg, although a "red-hot"[149] communist, continued to depend on his "old friend Tom Eliot" for help getting published without feeling sly about it or ideologically contradictory;[150] that Walter Snow, coeditor of *Anvil*, regular contributor to *Rebel Poet*,[151] and union organizer for the Newspaper Guild, maintained a "passion" for "the early Pound";[152] that Isidor Schneider, editor of *Soviet Russia Today*, was pleased to publish there a poem by Amy Bonner, a *Poetry* editor and known anticommunist;[153] that Orrick Johns, an avid revolutionist by the mid-1930s, cherished the reputation he had gotten from being associated with the early modernist *Others*; that Burnshaw, while a *New Masses* editor, had closely followed *Poetry*, issue by issue[154]—these facts escaped Kempton's normally keen attention precisely because as he gathered material and testimonies for his book in the early 1950s his informed sources were *not* Lechlitner, still a radical and literarily underground; nor Spector, who from 1949 to 1959 drove a cab and did not publish;[155] nor Walton, who was almost hounded out of her teaching job by red-hunters cleansing New York University and whose husband was regularly stopped by FBI "as he drove to work just to let her know they were still attentive";[156] nor Maas, who now gathered semi-subterraneously with a proto-Fluxus crowd and experimented with limited-distribution film poems; nor even Lowenfels, who was in jail for conspiring to overthrow the U.S. government; nor Davis, who was selling paper and printer supplies and whose value as a poet would not be rediscovered until 1973. Rather, his source, his informant on these matters, was almost certainly the volubly, aggressively disillusioned James T. Farrell. As a matter of fact, Joseph North, notorious as the "political watchdog" at the *New Masses*, "knew more about poetry than anyone else in the editorial office."[157] Edwin Rolfe was almost as well read as Farrell, and Sol Funaroff steeped himself in the modernism satirized in his poems.

These facts had been generally stipulated in the late 1930s but were now unsaid, forgotten, or actively disbelieved. Tastelessness had become another communist polemical strategy in the arsenal, as Stanley Edgar Hyman observed in his 1947 critique of American communist literary theory. When communists such as Earl Browder claimed Marx and Engels to have been "the most cultured men of history,"[158] Hyman interpreted this as a shot fired by the blunt weapon of literary insensitivity. Communists were among those "haters of literature unprepared to appear under the true colors," wrote Leslie Fiedler. "Communists . . . fear and distrust art but like to boast that some of their best friends are poets."[159] Anticommunists started with the assumption that the Western communist movement had produced no "poet of stature" (or, as in Frank Meyer's begrudging reckoning, just one—Bertolt Brecht).[160]

Beware the communist with taste. But, more, beware the communist who claims Marxism offers an aesthetic theory that can accommodate modern writing. "The American intellectuals who fell hardest for Communism," Rovere chided, were hardly modernists but actually people "of tastes at once conventional and execrable." They had little interest in formal questions or in disruptions of social-aesthetic conventions. Some, as Kempton put it, "felt a kind of contempt for their craft."[161] For radical writers of the 1930s, Ray B. West wrote, "Art is the whipping boy, a scapegoat upon which to place the burden of their failure in other fields."[162] This was Rovere's point, and Viereck had erred when he "mingle[d] the jargon of the Communist fellow-traveller with that of the literary avant-garde." "Many of them, of course, had no literary tastes of any sort." Communists read journalism, not poetry. ("The poets were gone, and the journalists remained," wrote Kempton.)[163] "If they read poetry at all," Rovere concluded, it was likely to be that of Whittier and Carl Sandburg, not Rimbaud and Ezra Pound.[164]

This notion about what poetry communist poets admired and read—pure speculation that, as we see in *Modernism from Right to Left*, was in fact largely wrong, as was Bogan's notion that modernists in the 1930s "threw over every scrap of their former enthusiasms"—served conveniently as a rejoinder to anticommunist antimodernists. This more overtly conservative group contended that modernists had *engaged* in the radical excesses of the 1930s and remained in 1950 a serious general threat to American values and styles. But such a position at the same time fueled anticommunist defenses of modernism that projected onto the reemergence of experimental writing in the United States a total separation of modernism's antibourgeois aspects and the cultural critique of the radical left—what I call an *immaculate modernism*, conceived as a direct, unsullied continuity from the 1910s and 1920s. This belief is the basis of particular 1950s readings of the 1930s that enabled midcentury modernism to refute and even actively to suppress latter-day experimentalist challenges to its status as befitting politically sanctioned anticommunist culture. This "defense of poetry," specially styled for cold war, depended on the obliteration of any hint that the 1930s proffered contemporary cultural good sense. Here again, then, a strategic need existed for vast generalizations about the bad "taste" or "cultural tone" of an entire decade. These assumed, among other things, the successful power of u.s. communism as a cultural movement. Did communism in the United States actually establish the rhetorical register of that period? Would it definitively shape the cultural life and language to emerge after the world war? And what effect did it have on the legacy of modern experiment? Rovere, to the left of Viereck, felt that Viereck should have been "aware of the fact that the cultural tone [communist intellectuals] set in the thirties—and there can be little doubt that they did set the cultural tone of that period—was deplorable because it was metallic and strident. Communist culture was not aristocratic; it was cheap and vulgar and corny."[165]

Trying out his chapter-length survey of Marxist literary criticism on readers of the *Antioch Review* for later use[166] in a bombshell book, *The Armed Vision* (1948), Stanley Hyman rebuked literary Marxists of the 1930s. Hyman felt that V. F. Calverton had been "given to cheap tricks" by calling modernist writers nasty names. He said that communist novelist and critic Mike Gold had been "the most ignorant and provincial of all . . . a heroic warrior against Gilbert and Sullivan." He ridiculed Granville Hicks's *The Great Tradition* as "mechanical class-anglings based on the political criteria of the 1930's." (F. O. Matthiessen deemed the same book praiseworthy for having "compell[ed] the academic historian to remember that the bibliographical and aesthetic worlds are set in universes of economic and social discourse.")[167] Hyman saw Joseph Freeman and Joshua Kunitz, two communist literary commissars in the mid-1930s, as "log-rollers and strait-jacketers of literature." An entire section of Hyman's chapter-essay runs along in this vein. What made the diatribe rhetorically plausible was a previous section devoted to a skeptical examination of the evidence that had been presented by communists in support of Marx's (and Engels's) keen personal literary tastes.

The Armed Vision signaled that the battle for the modernist soul of Marx was on.[168] It was true, Hyman conceded, that Marx loved to read Paul de Koch and Cervantes, that he learned Spanish to read Calderón in the original, that as a young man he had steeped himself in the subjectivity of romantic lyricism. And he rightly despised the descriptive verse of Martin Tupper (the Edgar Guest of 1860s England).[169] But it is also true that as a disciple of Hegel, Marx trained himself to see the "inevitable decadence of art in modern times." Notwithstanding Georgi Plekhanov's complex intervention between Marx and post-1917 communist critics, we move with Hyman from such inevitability to "the straight political distortion" of the American Marxist critics of the 1930s, to all the "cheap cracks." The cheapest of the cheap cracks of the red literati was their crass claim that Walt Whitman "was our first poet."[170]

Purporting to scan the Marxist literary horizon of the era just ended, Hyman helped make possible a "corrective" modernism. As midcentury approached, he called for an "effective use of Marxism in moderation." One of the models for such a tempered literary Marxism, he claimed, was Matthiessen's approach to Eliotic modernism in The Achievement of T. S. Eliot. First published in 1935, Matthiessen's book was revised in 1947 for what was in effect a Cold War edition. The Eliot whom Hyman believed Matthiessen admired offered midcentury critics modern verse of the sort that was not "a wicked avoidance of contemporary social reality" but that would help refute "the narrowest [communist] concept of realism [that] hold[s] that an author necessarily acquires . . . virtue by recording the surface details of a middle western city instead of those [for instance] of eighteenth-century Peru." The charge of political escapism, made against modernists, generally "smuggles in [the] assumption . . . that it really is possible for [Eliot] to 'escape' the problems of his life and time in his work if he wants to." Thus Hyman's fully armed Armed Vision forged and tempered the Cold War weapon of "Marxism in moderation," in this instance by deradicalizing F. O. Matthiessen's reading of modernism. The modernist marched straightforwardly toward his problems "inevitably on another level, in another form."[171] Such judgment surely influenced Karl Shapiro's later in the 1950s: yes, Matthiessen's book on Eliot "was published during the height of the Depression and at a time when Marxism was strong," and "Matthiessen was perhaps the most intensely engaged political mind among the English professors of the day, and a leftist," but "he chose to cut himself off from the politics of Eliot's poetry . . . to talk about the 'forms.'"[172]

This is not, by any stretch, the critique of the politics of form Matthiessen had offered back in 1935, as William Cain and Giles Gunn have shown. Hyman apparently read the new preface Matthiessen supplied for the revised and enlarged 1947 edition of his book on Eliot and drew his conclusions from Matthiessen's quasi-confession that his *own* status as "a political radical" made him realize that the imperfectability of human society, the inevitable failure of utopian programs, "demands dynamic adherence from a Christian no less than from a democrat."[173] Hyman did not wonder (as Cain much later did) why Matthiessen's precarious predicament as a radical meant that he had to "underestimate [the] urgency" of the "political problem" entailed in his earlier views on Eliot. Among the questions Matthiessen did not or perhaps could not ask in the new preface was, "Are there not fertile opportunities and obligations for the radical, as Edmund Wilson has shown in *Axel's Castle*, when he engages and tests Eliot's and the modernist's ideas?"[174]

"One of the surest ways to fail to understand a poem," Matthiessen had written in 1935, "is to begin by trying to tear the thought from the context in order to approve or disapprove of what it seems to express. . . . [T]he only way of knowing what it does express is by a sustained awareness of all the formal elements of which it is composed."[175] Hyman assumed such statements to express Matthiessen's disenchantment with ethical or ideological criticism. That they represented a formalist critique of modern poetry, yet one suitable to a political radical, was not apparently among the theoretical options. Nonetheless, as Gunn has argued, *The Achievement of T. S. Eliot* had been a systematic effort to comprehend modernist verse as historically sensitive—following a kind of Baudelairean Marxism toward a politics of form that makes a radicalism of a "sustained awareness of . . . the formal elements."[176]

If Hyman missed or suppressed this crucial effort at synthesis, at least some of the new generation of avant-garde poets grappled with Matthiessen's Marxism as such. Cid Corman's personal copy of the 1947 edition of *The Achievement of T. S. Eliot* fortunately survives, along with his marginal comments, which he almost certainly made when he first read the book in 1950 or early 1951.[177] Corman (1924–2004), minimalist and objectivist-influenced poet and ambitious young editor of the Black Mountain School–affiliated magazine *Origin* (inaugurated in

1951), was tough on the book's Marxist excesses, catching Matthiessen's occasional binaristic crudities. Of Matthiessen's line, "Instead of being ornamental,
[an image containing divergent material] is wholly functional," Corman's marginal quip was "Ornament *is* a function." Where Matthiessen piously commended the poet's "mature realization of the existence between these forces,"
Corman noted that "these absolutes are phoney." Yet the young innovative poet
took seriously, as Hyman did not, Matthiessen's reading of Eliot as a modernist
who "must" (not just "should") write from social experience, pressing for a still
keener sense of this principle of historical "necessity." In Matthiessen's discussions of the free-verse movement, Corman marked passages in which modernism and radicalism converged to offer a cogent explanation for the angry reaction against the disturbance of convention. For instance, "He knows that the
main point about new poetry [of the 1910s and 1920s] is always 'how disturbing it
is to the conventional consciousness,' that the shock tends to be 'by its syntax
more than by its sentiments,' and that, speaking strictly, versification 'is essentially a disturbance of the conventional language.' "[178]

Readers both praised and criticized Hyman's *Armed Vision* for putting the
New Criticism at its silent center. The socialist literary critic Irving Howe was
among those who chided Hyman for masking his status as an "enthusiastic
defender" of antipolitical formalism and thus by implication Hyman's support
of Matthiessen's modernist Eliot as that of a "moderate" Marxist containable by
postwar academic quietism.[179] And it was surely convenient for Hyman to
misunderstand as formalist self-restraint Matthiessen's preface to the 1947 edition of his book. "I have not written about Eliot's politics or religion," Matthiessen wrote, "except as they are expressed through his poetry."[180] Supposedly
for Matthiessen, by 1947 modernism's political possibilities could be found in
the poems themselves. Yet was such a reading of the poetry in itself susceptible
to accusations of sedition from the vast extrapoetic forces aligned against the
Marxist proponent of modernism? Would, for instance, readers of an article in
the *Anti-Communist* headlined "u.s. Schools Graduating 6,000 Reds Annually,"
a piece that prominently featured the name of the dangerous red F. O. Matthiessen, really take the time to find out?[181] In such a sensationalist climate,
perhaps the leftist critic of modern poetry should have been grateful for the
moderating reading, for, as Matthiessen put it in the final words of his revised
book on Eliot, "reconciliation" is "the chief reality for which he strives in a
world that has seemed to him increasingly threatened with new dark ages."
Sensing an emotional ambiguity in the pronoun "he," Cid Corman jotted in his
copy of the book, "cf. M's own dilemma."[182]

What seems most important is to start afresh, and not to be paralyzed by memory. One of the virtues of American society in the thirties was that it appeared possible to do so. We did not have the apprehension that everything would be shadowed by the past and that we would have to spend the rest of our days defending or explaining or reciting plaintive recantations.—James Wechsler, 1953

I hide my fat urge
in the skinny land of the Thirties.
I am afraid of passion.
—Gene Frumkin, "This Great Burden of Loving"

Guilty Are Those Who Are Punished

The fifties' thirties was constructed of emotional penitence. At times the critic's job seemed to be to help extract shame. Even a sympathetic critical reader as late as 1957, beginning a review of a book that glancingly surveyed thirties writing, used a vocabulary of intensity: the book, the reviewer wrote, made him ponder "those whose lives were *drastically* affected by the emotional and intellectual *travail* of the thirties"; the book under review "will serve as a *sharp* reminder of the *anguished* doubts and *profound* self-examination which *beset* an *entire* generation."[1]

A number of poets who had been affiliated with radicalism but would not admit disillusionment were deemed self-obsessed, and such a seemingly personal judgment empowered critics to extend it to analyses of the poetic line. The man who would soon be elevated to the poetry editor's seat at the *New Republic*, Robert Richman, reviewed new poems by several former communists, noting that one of them "confused his disillusion [with] his former doctrine of revolution [and his] 1930's proletarianism . . . with 'a pity that borders on Narcissus.'" Apostatic drama in itself seemed to authorize condemnation on aesthetic grounds. Of another poet who openly repented his leftism, Richman's judgment was kinder: in general, without respect to the era, such a poet's ideology is "strong enough to bear the weight of major poetic responsibility."[2]

Malcolm Cowley broadly identified "something penitential in the behavior of liberals from 1948 . . . to the end of the McCarthy era."[3] The "retrospective hysteria" that Alfred Kazin privately admitted wilted him in the heat of the battle Cowley saw as calling for stiffer resistance. But Cowley dealt with the situation by producing his own version of the *twenties* for the fifties and got well around the problem of penitence (as we will see in chapter 4). His construction of a privileged High Modernism, his renewed attention to what British poet Kenneth Allott in 1960 called "the more private extravagances" of the pre-Depression years,[4] helped Cowley avoid feeling much guilt about what he wrote and did in the thirties. But it also meant that in calling for resistance to thirties-bashing, he completely missed the emergence of what became known as the New Poetry or, a little more specifically, the New American Poetry in the mid- and late fifties, which derived synthetically from various earlier poetics. Thus, to the young poet Donald Hall, commenting on the New Poetry for the paperback *New World Writing* in 1955, Cowley's focus on the discrete aesthetic radicalism of the twenties as a weapon against those antipolitical critics who would attack both modernism and communism prevented him from seeing how wrong he was by midcentury when he reported that "poetry seems to be retreating." Hall first observed that for Cowley the name "Lowell" inevitably meant *Amy*, the imagist matriarch, not *Robert*, the poetic enfant terrible then favored by those hoping for a restoration, after the war, of the knotty New England iamb as the metric of foundation-hard continuity—and, more relevantly, that in the highly touted "definitive" book, *The Literary Situation* (1954), it just happened that Cowley "mentions not a single new poet" while claiming generally that poetry was in retreat. A blindness to what would become the innovative New American Poetry—finally consolidated in Donald Allen's *The New American Poetry* (1960)—functioned from emotional projection of aesthetic innocence onto political guilt, a modernist prelapsarianism in its own right. "Today we worship the twenties," wrote Hall, barely suppressing his frustration at how the pre-Depression era was being politically exploited. Yet this led to Hall's and others' strong sense that "experimentalism has become a vested interest," a thing that critical and poetic schools thought they could own.[5]

So it was that the liberal ex-communist at midcentury, who had made his or her modernist mark in the 1920s and established his or her reputation as a radical in the 1930s, was in no position to observe how a resurgent poetic experimentalism could help the case against the red-baiters. For Cowley's part, the main concern was that 1930s radicals in the 1950s "were being punished for acting on what they had always regarded as the highest principles, and hence they came to feel that the actions were wrong."[6] Matthew Josephson, an avid defender of 1920s modernism as a social force, also called for resistance against liberal apologetics. "The trouble is that the repentant liberals overwhelmed with guilt at having sent $5 to Loyalist Spain prematurely, now try to hang on to the coat-tails of the McCarthys," Josephson privately wrote to Kenneth Burke in

1947. "Each outdoes the other in repenting, recanting, or whining."[7] Sorting out all aspects of the sorry political psychology that seemed to inhere in the situation would take some years—until the early 1970s—but by the end of the 1950s was barely beginning to be possible. After finally finishing his big literary-historical narrative, *Writers on the Left*, in 1960–61—a landmark scholarly undertaking at a time when little of the primary material of literary radicalism had been straightforwardly assessed and was mostly scattered in private collections, had been discarded out of fear, or had been impounded by the FBI—Daniel Aaron took advantage of an opportunity for retrospective. The impression that lasted, "all in all," was that in the 1940s and 1950s there had been so much "soul-searching, breast-beating, and mutual recrimination" that any narrative of the period had to depict the apparatus of filtering in the 1950s as well. Amplified by critics' and scholars' studied avoidance, forgetting, and denigrating, some writers who had flourished during the 1930s "flagellated themselves in print" while others "trivialized their radical enthusiasms as youthful aberrations or follies."[8] A special kind of blaming became an aspect of the new counterstyle.

Cowley eventually blamed anticommunist liberals for their "lack of resistance" and later remarked that "a few of the old-fashioned conservatives, easy in their consciences," were needed belatedly to make the effective stand. He was among the few who observed early into the anticommunist period that a close relation existed between, on the one hand, the ascendancy and indeed full-scale Americanization of psychoanalysis, with its therapeutic assumptions about political ritual and penitence, and, on the other, the making of a myth of the 1930s. " 'Father sent me upstairs without my supper,' the child says to himself. 'I *must* have done something wrong.' "[9]

Harold Rosenberg offered the clearest public articulation of this relation in an essay, "Couch Liberalism and the Guilty Past." Rosenberg had been a leftist poet, rebuking the poetics of individual feeling, as in "The End of the World":

And the archbishop
With enormous hands,
Kings, gypsies, generals, all
Thrown up by a dying age

Here at the bed
Of the Purely Personal[10]

Soon dissatisfied with Stalinism, Rosenberg briefly became a member an ultra-left group, what Kenneth Burke called "a splinter of a splinter of a splinter."[11] For a time in the late 1930s, Rosenberg had been among the most pugnacious

Marxist interpreters of contemporary poetry. He could force an essay into the pages of *Poetry* despite the editors' doubts about Marxist exegesis that was "not likely to be understood except by those who are already convinced of your point of view."[12] He had mocked Archibald MacLeish's soft, unrigorous association of modern poetry and the necessary steps writers must take to ease the crises of economic depression and fascism. ("Its absence *is* the crisis," MacLeish had said. Rosenberg satirized this by setting it against Herbert Hoover's statement in 1932: "What this country needs is a good poem.")[13]

Rosenberg's postwar anticommunism shaped "Couch Liberalism at the Guilty Past," although it offered a critique of political guilt. One of the essay's main aims was to disclose the creation of the myth of the 1930s. "What is remarkable about the manufacture of myths in the twentieth century is that it takes place under the noses of living witnesses of the actual events and, in fact, cannot dispense with their collaboration."[14]

The aforementioned Murray Kempton was even keener than Rosenberg— and far more earnest—in comprehending how the construction of a "twenties" to be admired in the fifties, as distinct from a "thirties" to be doubted, was closely connected to the personalization (and depoliticization) of what Kempton called "passions," a term that for him was a synonym for "ideas." It seemed suddenly possible to Kempton that the result of his work, just after its publication, was the opposite of what he had intended.[15] Even a noted anti-anticommunist must express feelings of guilt. The recipient of Kempton's rare raw moment of self-doubt was Granville Hicks. Kempton had not known Hicks personally before acclaim came to *Part of Our Time: Some Ruins and Monuments of the Thirties* (1955). Hicks had written to Kempton in praise of the book but pointed out, in Kempton's words, that *Part of Our Time* "constructed a counter-myth about the twenties." He told Hicks that he had also received a letter from James T. Farrell insisting that Kempton simply did not know what a "terrible decade the *twenties* was." Kempton wrote to Hicks, "I look back on [the twenties] and see [H. L.] Mencken laughing at everyone, and I look at the thirties and see [Heywood] Broun laughing at almost no one." He conceded that "in a sense I identify with Mencken and against Broun . . . and that is hardly a fair choice between decades." This judgment, essentially personal, made Kempton feel double political guilt. First there was the sin of leftism in the thirties. Then there was "the larger problem . . . that my unconscious . . . seems to have set me to swim against currents which are really not too important to books good or bad." Hicks had reminded Kempton that he had "made my own transient experience with the [communist] movement a universal one, and that, in deprecating myself, I deprecated persons who had lived more intensely than I."

Kempton had not intended to elevate the pre-Depression modernist period over the Red Decade as a means by which others could further deradicalize midcentury culture, yet in writing to Hicks, who despite a public rightward movement frequently remained a target of thirties-bashing, Kempton helped to create the thirties for the fifties. He described himself as thus capitulating to the present era even while as a journalist at the liberal anti-McCarthyite *New York Post* he seemed rather heretical, as in the column he wrote criticizing the government for denying Social Security payments to a jailed CPUSA official who had properly paid into the system for seventeen years.[16] (Kempton later remembered being among those who generally "found it useful to describe ourselves as anti-Communist.")[17] In the penultimate paragraph of his extraordinary letter to Hicks, Kempton wrote,

> I think the last and largest problem of all was that I surrendered to the time in which we were living. I wanted to do a book which was absolutely unique, and I wanted to make the reader say yes, that's how it really was; these were private quarrels; they were not universal; they happened to a very few people. I was, more than anything else, swimming upstream against [Whittaker] Chambers, who has, after all, had very little effect on our thinking in sum, and is himself a cardboard enemy. And so, I suppose, I tipped the balance another way; Marx is not all truth, nor is Henry James; the myth of the fifties may not be that the communists dominated the thirties, but rather that there are no social passions—there is only social observation—and that is the myth to which unconsciously I may have surrendered.[18]

Yet *Part of Our Time* did not convey such intense emotional ambivalence. There Kempton said that red writers of the thirties had been "graceless by choice"—styleless hatchet men "carry[ing] in their hands the ax and the spade to execute . . . the myth of the twenties." During the twenties, writers gloriously "search[ed] for individual expression, whether in beauty, laughter, or defiance of convention." Seen from the vantage of the fifties, the thirties' version of the twenties had brought out the disaster complex in these radicals; Kempton was hinting at the psychological concept of blaming the generational victim even as he expressly sympathized with those hurt by red-baiting in his own time. Because the "social revolutionary of the thirties" was "prepared to die by violence," his imagination imagined (and his writing, if he was a writer, conveyed) "almost every disaster except the one which has now overtaken him"—"now," that is, in the fifties. In a sense, then, the thirties radical helped bring on the anticommunist catastrophe by his earlier catastrophic imagination.[19]

In his analysis of the connection between the unmaking of the myth of the 1930s and the public psychology of liberal confession and self-criticism, Harold Rosenberg was silent on poetry. Similarly, the young film critic Pauline Kael, who edgily berated 1930s radicals for praising a work of art purely because it carried a socially redeeming message, told her KPFA-Berkeley/Pacifica Radio audiences that it was all a form of self-abuse. But although at KPFA Kael was surrounded by poets—Kenneth Rexroth, Lawrence Ferlinghetti, among others—by "art" she meant films only.[20] Of course, poetry was neither Kael's nor Rosenberg's intended subject, even though Rosenberg had been a member of the community of radical poets in the 1930s. When Kael mocked John Steinbeck's prose as a "blur of embarrassing sentimental pseudo-biblical pseudo-commentary," it was clear she would have said the same of radical verse, but it is nonetheless significant that poetry was never at issue for her.[21] The closest Rosenberg came to implicating modern poetics in his judgments on cultural anticommunism was his withering critique of Leslie Fiedler's "couch liberalism" in *An End to Innocence* (1955), a book that is now counted as among the classic works of anticommunism produced by a literary critic in the period.

Harold Rosenberg was a talented spotter of cultural trends but not when it came to understanding the lasting effect of Cold War degradation rituals. He roughly observed that "the Confession Era in the United States is about over."[22] This was 1958. The publication of Robert Lowell's *Life Studies* in the following year and the ascendancy of a fashion for Sylvia Plath's terse, impiously ribald voicing of taboo themes would be sufficient to disprove Rosenberg's prophecy. But there is even more to such prognostication than poor trend spotting, for the Lowell and Plath crazes and generally the triumph of therapeutic assumptions—the Americanization of Freudian experimentation-then-adjustment—developed in connection with a version of modernism befitting the fifties' thirties. In this respect, Rosenberg wrongly guessed that "couch liberalism" and its political influence would end when the language of red-baiting and ex-communist soul bearing lost its freshness. But the effect on poetry would last for many years—until, that is, counterideological studies of "repression and recovery," in Cary Nelson's phrase, or the rediscovered validity of "the revolutionary imagination," in Alan Wald's, forced at least some reexamination among poets as well as poetry critics of the history of interactions among modernisms and radicalisms that had not been carefully studied or seriously taught for two generations.

Rosenberg's main contribution to the discussion about 1930s culture in the 1950s was an analogy between the nuclear arms race and psychological warfare.

It was an outrageous comparison. Just as the Russians had stolen our atomic secrets, so, similarly, had we Americans "evened the score by mastering [Russia's] technique of psychological fission and fusion." This historical revisionist "technology" entailed "dissolv[ing]" segments of time so that we might forget and remake the recent past as part of the "modern politico-military struggle"— a psychic weapon as important "as the capacity to devastate areas of space." Fortunately for those who hoped for some enduring legacy of the 1930s, the "official investment in mythology" had thus far been part of the tactic of "limited" attack. Rosenberg's writing makes one ponder what an all-out war against the 1930s would have done. "A single full-scale blast" of this ultimate mental weapon aimed against bad decades, "and the years 1932–1952 could have been turned into a desert of 'twenty years of treason.'" He really did mean that the attack on the 1930s was limited warfare—that it might have been much worse.[23]

To be sure, Rosenberg's aim was to salvage something of the 1930s for the Cold War. Yet what he salvaged was unusable. Doubtless he saw himself as rectifying historiographical imbalances, "imped[ing] the process" of postwar readings of the Red Decade as describable by a "comic-strip encounter between a cock-eyed egghead and a right-thinking goon." But his tone and diction defied any persuasive conception of a workable centrism. Ex-poet, ex-radical, Harold Rosenberg was no Arthur Schlesinger or Daniel Bell, and of course his operating assumption was that American communist intellectuals had been unredeemably bad. This necessarily colored his view of liberal guilt: "Whatever its weakness in understanding communist power and techniques," he warned, "liberalism was in no sense responsible for Communist vileness." The problem was that in the late 1940s and early 1950s, notwithstanding HUAC's congressional masters and McCarthy, McCarran, and others in the U.S. Senate, there was "no one effectively to extract confessions"—not even Joseph McCarthy, Rosenberg noted from the relatively safe perspective of 1958, had ever created "the ultimate self-doubt" that was the "specialty of Russian interrogation."

Thus, to Rosenberg, the person who might have confessed political true crimes truly "had to supply *his own* heckling." Doubt ultimately came from within. And so "psychoanalysis assumes the function of the secret police."[24] "When the world we live in denounces us," Joseph Freeman wrote to Hicks, "we are likely to resent it—and to resent ourselves. There is self-hatred and hatred; many of the violent attacks by former radicals on their former friends [are] an expression not only of hatred but of self-hatred." Freeman asked Hicks to recall the suppressed chapter in *The Possessed* in which Stavrogin confesses his crime, to which Dostoyevsky's wiser confessor says, "He will forgive you if you will forgive yourself." Freeman knew by such psychological realism that "communists are human" even as he was reporting to Hicks his notion that the communist movement had earlier "attracted us by a sublime promise" and later "betrayed us not only politically" but as "human beings."[25] In Rosenberg's psychological reading of the ex-communist, the fifties' thirties was being invented by those who initially sought to salvage something from the period. While the conservative anticommunist would have annihilated it from cultural memory, the ex-radical "neo-liberal" actually damaged the story of the thirties as it got retold. Harold Rosenberg called this "guilt by rhetoric."[26]

Guilt by rhetoric led to some hilarious as well as pathetic results, as even the severest of ex-communists, such as James T. Farrell and Joseph Freeman, observed. "The final result," Rosenberg noted, "was that a neo-liberal became available to admit the justice of any accusation, no matter how ridiculous."[27] Even Farrell, usually sagacious in such matters, could barely fathom the quick rises and falls in the reputation of Hicks's important book, *The Great Tradition: An Interpretation of American Literature since the Civil War* (1933, 1935). Farrell observed rapidly shifting perceptions among anticommunists and communists as to how far Hicks had gone at any point to regret his own communist literary canonizing. Farrell sent Hicks a mock "Strike Bulletin," "URGENTLY CALL[ING] ON THE BOOK READING PUBLIC TO SUPPORT US IN OUR STRIKE. . . . LIQUIDATE THE GREAT TRADITION!" Among the demands were "WITHDRAWAL OF THE GREAT TRADITION FROM CIRCULATION," "BETTER GRADES AND MORE ENCOUR-AGEMENT FROM MR. HICKS IN OUR CLASSES," and the "PUBLIC PENNANCE [*sic*] FOR SINS OF LITERARY JUDGMENT." Farrell even included a mock "open letter" of counterprotest that contended that Hicks had earned his status as a great critic by hard, close study, by the application of good taste, and "by reading the works of Ralph Waldo Emerson."[28] Emerson! Just imagine! Farrell's move was characteristically sly; it was a doubly ironic nod at the constant Cold War countercanonizing in the great American tradition, a debate that *The Great Tradition* itself had reignited, with its 1933 edition ideologically outdoing Vernon Parrington's *Main Currents of American Thought* (1927), and a 1935 edition, with a new concluding chapter, the redder-than-red "Directions," meant to help the reader interpret the inevitable success of communist writers as they were projected back onto the Great Tradition and then brought forward from nineteenth-century vernacularist, realist forebears.

Now, at the height of the effort to dismantle not just the 1935 reading but also the 1933 reading and Parrington's still-earlier progressive reading, the ex-communist ironically slips Ralph Waldo Emerson through Granville Hicks's back door. Farrell knew perfectly well that the *later* Hicks, the Hicks now susceptible to regret, had come to valorize Emerson. (What he might not have known, so far from the Communist Party had he drifted, was that Marxist poets had also, by the 1950s, returned to Emerson, "who embodied, so wonderfully and richly, the tradition of the American revolution"[29] and whose writings were cherished by leftists for their aphoristic qualities. "If the 150th anniversary of Emerson's birth was [in 1953] ignored in Washington," they asserted, "it was celebrated by the Communists.")[30] In both 1930s editions of *The Great Tradition*, Hicks's initial goal was to revise, correct, and ideologically "update" not just Emerson but all of Parrington, whose book-length argument offered a usable U.S. literary tradition that began by in effect calling Emerson a failure. Emerson, the communist critic had then written, failed to discover a humanizing confidence in industrial society. In *On Native Grounds*, Alfred Kazin consciously stood alongside this "native" lineage; Kazin concluded as early as 1942 that rather than admiring the Great Tradition, Hicks, "lost in the tides of change," had been "vaguely hostile to traditional forms."[31] This was itself a version of the usual accusation against communists—that they tried to thwart the development of modern writing.

Later, in May 1958, Joseph Freeman struggled to prepare a talk on the thirties at Smith College for what would be his third visit there. Pondering this, Freeman recalled that the first had been in the thirties, when Hicks, then on the Smith faculty, had invited and hosted him. He thought back "fondly" on those days. The convergence of the memory of Hicks and Freeman together and the new evaluation of the period was fortuitous. To prepare for the new talk, Freeman reread *The Great Tradition* in the strident 1935 edition and then wrote to Hicks to say that despite his disillusionment about the communist movement in the intervening years, the "main theme continued to be valid." He intended obviously to make even the old book's revolutionary epilogue, "Directions," have some kind of current validity: at least a good measure of "the way we felt"—the emotional past—as a tool of study for those at Smith in the fifties who "really" wanted to understand the period immediately following High Modernism. Such teachers and students would first have to understand the basic radicalism of the twenties. As one of the American communist intellectuals whose radicalization formed a continuity from social experimentation (if not quite as much aesthetic experimentation) through the thirties—the "twenties" and "thirties" were not for him such discrete aesthetic categories—Freeman pointed out that *The Great Tradition* resisted the depiction of a sudden or *traumatic* quality about the thirties. (It was just this sort of actual experience in the period that, for Hicks, put the lie to Kempton's characterization of the outrageous, High Modern "twenties" that came crashing down in a decade that left us lots of "ruins" and a few "monuments.") "By the Thirties," Freeman wrote to Hicks, "the conflict of loyalties was more or less [already] resolved for most of us in the Left and that last chapter of yours is a true account of the certainty of our faith and its ethical character before historic events shattered it all into a mushroom cloud of dise[n]chantment."

Despite very different means of managing their disenchantment, by 1958 Freeman saw that he again shared common ground with Hicks: what they had once felt about the potential of the movement. Making the fifties' thirties was a blind revisionism disregarding feeling's connection to theoretical belief, all the more galling for its imposition of guilty awareness on the past. "The story now is that we knew all along the movement was a fraud and its members stupid, vicious and so on. Why we went in and why we sta[ye]d is never explained. . . . [T]here cannot possibly be disenchantment without there first being enchantment."[32]

Even the scant resistance that arose to the construction of a demonized 1930s in the 1950s was a changing, complex achievement, hard earned over time. Freeman, for one, had to move toward a relatively generous view of Hicks. Nineteen-fifty-eight was a better year for that than 1953 had been: it was the year in which Hicks seemed to Freeman to have been too cooperative with Joseph McCarthy's committee. Writing privately to ex-communist Floyd Dell, Freeman, despite his alienation from the CPUSA, sounded more like a party critic: "Adolph Hitler McCarthy . . . really infuriates me; the liberals make me sad. By approving McCarthy's alleged aim, the destruction of Communists, while deploring his methods, they played right into his hands. The great literary critic Granville Hicks has written a piece explaining why he gave HUAC the names of fellow-members of his Party unit at Harvard."[33]

At the time Hicks named names in 1953, a man named Philip Frankfeld was serving a five-year sentence in Atlanta, having been convicted under the Smith Act of conspiring to advocate the teaching of the need to overthrow the government of the United States at some (never specified) future point in time. A CPUSA hard-liner, Frankfeld was "shocked, morally revolted and physically sick" as a result of Hicks's testimony. When in 1954 Hicks published *Where We Came Out*, Frankfeld saw the book as "a miserable and shameless attempt to justify his cowardice." And yet when in an essay pseudotriumphantly titled "The Thirties! The Thirties!" Joseph North passingly offered a scathing retrospective assessment of Hicks,[34] Frankfeld responded by trying to save not just Hicks's work from the thirties but the very concept of "the thirties." *The Great Tradition* (of course he singled out the "2nd revised" 1935 edition) "was and remains an impressive work," "not dogmatic or sectarian by any standard." At the time that Frankfeld wrote "The Thunderous Thirties, and Granville Hicks," the main issue remained "deny[ing] ourselves." "Hicks, the Marxist," Frank-feld wrote, "is flesh and blood of our cultural heritage; he belongs to history and to us. By belittling or denying that fact of life, we belittle and deny ourselves."[35] By that point, it was the sixties; Frankfeld, an unrepentant heretic, was attempting to see the thirties through a lens *other* than the one ground in the fifties. It was like trying on new spectacles, disorienting at first no matter how right the focus.

Liberal critics of the 1930s in the 1950s relinquished the 1930s most easily when they could sever ideas from feelings. "The old passions are spent," declared Bell in *The End of Ideology*. "Temperamentally, the thing [the ideologist] wants is . . . devitalized"; a new generation sought objectives "within a framework of political society that has rejected . . . the old apocalyptic and chiliastic visions."[36] Poets particularly sensed this "chastened mood."[37] Robert Duncan sensed how "disruptive" were "passionate involvements, inspired necessities [and] visions."[38] The young Adrienne Rich—her father a liberal politically but a strict traditionalist aesthetically—was socialized to worry that, as she wrote in 1951, "a too-compassionate art is half an art."[39]

To be sure, "feelings" or "passions," it was repeatedly contended, could not and should not be negated outright. The best people could hope for in ideas was an "outlet for 'self-expression.' "[40] "Guilt is, after all, personal," wrote Kempton.[41] Freudianism suffused antiradicalism;[42] there was simply no denying inner, essential feelings, which were part of the inviolable human core, "beyond" culture's reach.[43] But certain "ideas," conversely—or "beliefs," the commonly used synonym—could be analyzed as illegitimate. The rhetoric of passion, though passé, might be salvaged as a critical object, a valid if curious or pathetic piece in the political history of modern poetics. After an agonizing correspondence with Hicks in the months right before *On Native Grounds* was published during the war, Alfred Kazin wrote to Hicks again a decade later, in 1953, to propose feelings cut off from ideas as a way of establishing a truce, an emotional stay against the confusion of conflicting theories, established between them for the purpose of determining a basis on which the two could discuss Kazin's *On Native Grounds* as some sort of successor to Hicks's *The Great Tradition*. "And perhaps, too," Kazin wrote, "there was nothing so very shameful—but on the contrary—in the idealism and sheer human hopefulness of many Communists in the thirties who, like yourself, knew what they believed in one year and in another year knew they no longer believed it, but can never, must never, go back on what they honestly felt."[44] The final phrase was something of an untruth. Close readers of *On Native Grounds*—in particular, the chapters "Into the Thirties: All the Lost Generation" and "Criticism at the Poles"[45]—can see that Kazin did not give credence to claims by Marxist writers and critics of the thirties that they had "*honestly* felt" that what they were doing and writing was not a sham. It was a key point.

If writers in the 1930s had made horrific aesthetic compromises—a premise for Kazin—the question became whether they did so deliberately. John Malcolm Brinnin, poet and editor of CPUSA-affiliated journals, called this problem "deliberate innocence" in a poem of politicoaesthetic retrospective on the 1930s, "Observatory Hill," published in Brinnin's book *No Arch, No Triumph* (1945).[46]

> Let Whitman go, and all the rest
> Who turned their broad glad faces on the West;
> Since all deliberate innocence must fail.

Brinnin's Whitman was the radical hero canonized during the Popular Front era, and Brinnin did not really mean that the left would—or could—"Let Whitman go" if and when deliberate innocence went out of fashion. Of course, the left itself did, and Brinnin found himself caught up in the recrimination, which for him characteristically became self-recrimination.

Brinnin's poetry, in *No Arch, No Triumph* and earlier in *The Garden Is Political* (1942), keenly records disillusionment with certain forms of radicalism yet always values deliberate innocence in the art of observing its intermittent failure in the practical sphere. *The Garden Is Political* infuriated conservatives who sought "dahlias, fuchsias, trees and lawns" in their poetic landscape, even at the time of the politicization of domestic horticulture as the home-front "Victory Garden." But Brinnin's book "has more to do with Republicans, Democrats and Communists than with dews and daisies." In this sense, its title was good, disclosing the poet's actual agenda: the connection between radical politicking and the modernist coterie. (To the antimodernist, he was "another of the graspers after that spurious originality which consists of contorting words . . . out of their natural orbits.")[47] In fact Brinnin struggled, in (as he put it) a "season of actual war," with his modernist training. He now saw how he had "walked blind with Joyce"; it was *not* as an apprentice to modern poetic practice but *now* that his "sight is fractured" (in the Joycean sense) "and set free" and, once liberated, presents "the stones of Stalingrad / And Wednesday's dead."[48]

Eda Lou Walton was another deliberate innocent. She had impeccable modernist-communist credentials. As a poet and teacher, she was devoted to modernist experiment; she was a mentor and friend—and lover for a decade—of novelist Henry Roth at the time he was writing *Call It Sleep* (1934); she drew Roth into the Communist Party in 1933.[49] She was formally a member of the

CPUSA for many years, longer than most others, probably from 1928 through the end of the McCarthy period. Walton had come of age aesthetically in the 1930s, but many of the poems she wrote in that period were not collected until *So Many Daughters* (1952), whereupon reviewers, such as the poet Leonie Adams, constructed a 1950s for Walton's 1930s. Adams felt that Walton's poems created the occasion for saying that "hers was a generation that saw the end of innocence, for its women especially, at a good deal of remove, and thereby the more unmanageably."[50] Many of the poems of *So Many Daughters* bear witness to the gloom that set in after a refusal to feel guilt, in a language edging toward unmanageability. The bitter sadness of Walton's writing sometimes takes aim at the poem's own forms. Yet even in her stoical, skeptical lyrics, through superficial political retrospect—an assumption about the entire decade and about the effect of Walton's radical activities on her verse—Leonie Adams found a way in 1954 to interpret "much conviction [that] was shaken, not so much by frontal assault, as by general consent."[51] Was Adams lamenting, on Walton's behalf, that poems had been cast adrift on the sea of 1930s leftist aesthetic and only now could be sorted out, like a few perfectly formed shells washed up with all the detritus? How did Adams miss Walton's frontal assaults? In her desire to affirm Walton's standing by the 1950s as a writer of "poems [that] are in the more tentative form,"[52] Adams repressed the quality in Eda Lou Walton's poetry that anticipated (and in my view, sometimes matches) Plath's anxious directness, poems in which the degree of formality in the constraint corresponded to the unmanageability of the female subject. Walton, as a lifelong radical, provides a sharp political edge to such confessions as Plath's poetry would lack. For Plath, the confessing subject was *analogous* to political hatreds, while for Walton, the personal deliberate innocence was *contiguous* with the political situation. It is hard to fathom how Adams neglected even to observe this "frontal assault," since the poem where it is most evident gave Walton's book its title. It is "Wreath for a Congressman (W.B.W.)," in which readers can comprehend a vital rebuke to the conservative political patriarchy as well as a daughter's dramatic counter to her father, William Bell Walton, who served in Congress as a representative from New Mexico:

I shut the door . . . I lock it.

For if he was my father, I am more
Than ever he bargained for,
As are so many daughters now
Pleading a calmed brow
Not rightly.[53]

That there are so many daughters constitutes a political threat of great psychic import—more reminiscent of a didactic final reprise of a play by Clifford Odets or the last mass scene of a proletarian strike novel than a predictor of Plath's or Robert Lowell's "confessional" poetry, in which the individual's struggle to be free of self-destruction might set the landscape of political repression, the Ike Age, "the tranquillized *Fifties*," in the phrasal, referential background, such as Lowell's mood-setting, easily scanned descriptions in *Life Studies* ("where even the man / scavenging filth in the back alley trash cans, / has two children, a beach wagon, a helpmate, / and is a 'young Republican' ").[54]

Walton's and Brinnin's poems evince "deliberate innocence" not as guilt about past radicalism but as a means of maintaining a heretical position with aesthetic integrity. For both, their sense of the depth of the heresy increased rather than diminished as the years passed. One always has a sense in reading Walton's poems that her commitments to extrapoetic life never left her enough time for poetic forms and so, when she produced them, they bore the full weight of her care. This *So Many Daughters* records. Like Brinnin in "For My Pupils in the War Years," which laments the wartime "narrowing plurality of choices,"[55] Walton took this complex regret to a poem addressing her students. In "Poet as Teacher," Walton sees the political irony:

My word is seasonal: I cannot say
"Believe me," for the contrary is true;
Fulness of time is being wrought and you
Are ample in your own day.[56]

They who were least engaged with the world had the most time to ponder forms of belief. Time outran consciousness.

In fact, this was Leo Gurko's phrase for the 1930s. In *The Angry Decade*, Gurko observed that "the decade of the '30s was uniquely one in which time outran consciousness, in which the sequential stages of depression and of reform appeared too rapidly to allow for accurate fathomings." To be sure, despite a generosity in guessing intentions, Gurko's study reproduces almost every anticommunist assumption about writing in the 1930s. Hicks, who had been to the communists "the St. Paul of literary criticism," applied Marxism to poetics, Gurko said, with "ruthless literalism." The antiradical analysis of the "dangers and sterilities of the literal application of Marxism to literature" comes off in *The Angry Decade* as shrewd and correct.[57] Leonie Adams noted that when many of Walton's poems were written (in the 1930s), "the poetic atmosphere was *less rigorous than at present* . . . and modes then flourished which young practitioners and readers, coming lately upon the scene, are accustomed to think of as belonging to the hinterland of the naïve and the second-rate"—a quiet but devastating critique of 1930s poetry nonetheless, again, founded on the assumption of naïveté.[58] Gurko pointed out that the left had roughly handled those who articulated this critique, consigning them to the margins. In the 1930s, he wrote, "literature seemed, on the whole, to be marking time," nostalgic for the 1920s and awaiting the 1950s. Still, in the pages of *The Angry Decade*, these were at least sins committed innocently,[59] and, again, Leonie Adams— herself a former communist supporter[60]—sympathetically mapped Eda Lou Walton's journey out of "the end of innocence," generously holding open for her, if she wanted to occupy it, a space between her poems and guilt for political misdeeds by assuming that as a woman Walton saw them "at a good deal of remove."[61]

Conversely, each of the many instances of the word "innocent" in Eugene Lyons's *The Red Decade* was simply ironic, flagged often as such by scare quotes. A list of communists, for example, was followed by more guilty parties, "a batch of liberal 'innocents.' "[62] Kazin, though far less adamantly, by 1942 also began with the premise that deliberate innocence entailed subterfuge, poetic skulking around, a dishonesty to be repudiated as a matter of style. To Kazin's mind, when Mike Gold "was only exaggerating with crude native force" in the 1930s, he knew better,[63] this being part of the inherent logic of force in literary hyperbole. When in Joseph Freeman's introduction to *Proletarian Literature of the United States* (1935), after "several perfectly valid propositions," he fell into a logical "trap," Freeman *knew then* that it was morally wrong to condemn every experience other than the proletarian.[64] Kazin condemned the "synthesis" of bad Marxist polemic, the worst of Russian criticism, political Stalinism, and "general mediocrity" of radicalized American writers that produced "nothing but posturing bad taste," and he meant that it was indeed a posture, a put-on, an evil mask for fronting intellectual violence.[65] Kazin wrote that Hicks too "often showed [right then in the 1930s] *that he knew what was wrong*."[66] Deliberate innocence in this context hardly differs from that proffered by professional anticommunist witness Louis Budenz, who in *Men without Faces* (1948) described the "Capture of the Innocents"—writers whose early naïveté gave way to a *stance* of innocence. Budenz's standard for discerning deliberateness was a good deal lower and cruder than Kazin's: writers whom one "discovered on three, four, ten or even a dozen" communist-front membership lists were writers about whom loyal Americans could ask, "Can he be so innocent?"[67] And Peter Viereck, while logically more refined than Budenz, was also rougher than Kazin by a good measure. Writing on "the anti-social role of some intellectuals," Viereck drew a line at the time of the 1939 Nazi-Soviet pact: anyone who "passed the test of left-wing decency" at that point (by abandoning communism, that is) was to be treated as an innocent; everyone else "should be . . . retroactively slandered as Reds today."[68] Kazin found no such clear boundary to mark the end of innocence. Nonetheless, the Granville Hicks who occupies several pages of On Native Grounds was a writer who produced "the work of an intelligent if not exceptional scholar on whom Marxism worked like strong drink."[69] And so Kazin condemned Hicks as conscious of Stalinist self-deception yet also demeaned that consciousness by characterizing it as not quite the result of will— more the result of a willful addiction, with the strong scent of pathology. So much for Kazin's private commitment in 1953 to respect what Hicks and others "honestly felt" as inviolable even while their ideas could be properly assailed.

At almost every point when Kazin discussed the 1930s in On Native Grounds, he implied that along with critical distance on the period came a more neutral, moderate tone—a mature analysis of excessive rhetoric committing no imitative fallacy, surveying an even plain from which to describe the erupted volcano. Insofar as the 1930s could be characterized as a kind of irresponsible adolescence, the maturity of the new era would be the implied main quality of the postradical critical subject position. Distance, knowingness, and acceptance naturally succeeded identification, deliberate innocence, and resistance. This was precisely Louise Bogan's take on her close personal friend (but political antagonist) Rolfe Humphries: reviewing Humphries's new book of poetry, Out of the Jewel, in 1942, poems telling of "his whole history as a fellow-traveller," Bogan marked out the range "from youthful rebellion against life to mature acceptance and praise." The natural valorization of lyricism made it perfectly clear where Bogan felt the radical poet—until 1940 Humphries was a leading activist in the League of American Writers, a procommunist, and coeditor of And Spain Sings (1937)[70]—should come out: "mature acceptance." As a poet, Humphries was finally "a lyricist, a man at ease with the humanities," and a man who in rebellion against "life" itself could be successfully "at ease"?[71] Insofar as such a thing as a conservative theory of the lyric existed during the immediate postwar years, Bogan's assessment of Humphries's poetic phases were widely shared on the middlebrow poetic right. Such a view was a staple of poems appearing in B. Y. Williams's Cincinnati-based traditionalist magazine, Talaria. Sophia Molk's "A Word in Your Hand" (1949), to take an almost random example from the pages of Talaria, held that words, standing alone, were "innocent," like "babes." But such innocence was not to be trusted, was not language's social state. Through sheer ingeniousness, words could be made into a "thunderous mob, / Inflamed by violence." At such times we must seek a "gentle master" in whose hands

Words
Are as sheep, browsing on a hillside
Permeating the air with deep
Peace.[72]

In staking out ground to be shared with conservative modern poets such as Bogan, with her severe doubts about relations to radicalism among avant-gardists, Alfred Kazin crucially shaped the way the political poetry of the 1930s would be understood during the Cold War, even though, of course, *On Native Grounds* was not except incidentally about poetry. He was saying something about, as one poet put it for Karl Shapiro, "the possibility of treatment as a lyrical exploration of prose." Kazin's underlying interest, in for instance *A Walker in the City*, was the convergence of prose, the lyric, and geopolitical fact—"prose as a kind of 'documentary poetry.' "[73] Indeed, his "postideological" observations about language, in relation to prose literature in *On Native Grounds*, actually had a *less* noticeable effect on postwar *fiction* than on poetry and poetics. This may be simply because "content" played so great a role in political readings of the many American novelists who repudiated the 1930s in the late 1940s and 1950s. But what was really at stake here was the idea that language and form, word-for-word literary style, could itself be a "crude native force" or "hoarse and coy," the dissonant sound of Sophia Molk's feared "thunderous mob," or could have an uneven "narrow tone," or be conversational or deliberately "formula-mongering."[74] That the survival of such a style was at issue was obvious to a generation of post-1930s poets who had to reckon with the conclusions of the young liberal-left Kazin: that the language communist writers had produced was merely "an eruption, a literary excitement" and that quality is what "is to be remembered."[75] This helped create a myth of the hackneyed 1930s vitally affecting the development of a "mature" postwar lyric, the lyric being the kind of writing that especially depends on perceptions of linguistic freshness.[76]

Thus, similar to anticommunist assumptions about rhetoric and word choice were those about genre or generic value. Doubtless not realizing that he was defining the genres of valid criticism so narrowly, Kazin described communist writers' collective failure to produce the big books, the major full-length critical statements—the work that earlier and later periods would deem central to any valid literary legacy. "Just as Marxism often became formula-mongering in conversation," Kazin wrote, "so conversation often became a form of criticism." The left's influence in the thirties was "almost exclusively in conversation and polemic, in casual book reviews, programs for action, and speeches at writers' congresses." As purely a rhetorical, low-generic, or linguistically ephemeral, demotic force—didactic subforms of journalism—its only "content" was in its general "influence."[77] The effect of this thirties-bashing line on anticommunist defenders of postwar poetry was incalculably strong. As we have seen, it became A. M. Sullivan's logic for distinguishing modern *American* poetry from modern *communist* poetry while giving Sullivan the opportunity to announce that American poets were aware of social content while knowing their proper generic place. Asked to counter a communist commentator who had asserted that u.s. verse was depthless, Sullivan replied that many American poets are responsive to life as it being really lived but are not ideological, for "social problems [and] ideologies" are alien to poetry and rather "belong to the field of journalism."[78]

It is obvious from Kazin's early thirties-bashing that if he was to carry it off, he would have to bleed out of his language all traces of "narrow tone," hyperbole, polemic, repetition for the sake of rhetoric, journalistic word choice, critical sloganeering—and would have to be neutral, nonideological. Calling the thirties a time of mere "literary excitement" in this way required a complete sobering up from the effects of Hicks's stiff drinks. When Harry Roskolenko accused Nelson Algren of suffering from "a political hangover of faith"—still buzzed from the thirties, Algren in 1942 had written for *Poetry* a devastating review of Roskolenko's book, *I Went into the Country*, showing that the poems linguistically indicated "a flight from industrialization into a sanctuary of disordered words"[79]—the angry ex-radical poet complained that the reviewer had tried to "avoid a political bias" but had failed.[80] Still dissipated from their Depression experiences, those attempting aesthetic judgment were obliged to write with rhetorical neutrality. Roskolenko's problem, as always, was that he was never sober in attacking what he deemed leftist literary excess. Nor was Kazin, normally an evenhanded writer, entirely successful at this. He did seek explicitly to counter communist linguistic violence with his own diction and tone and critical voice of equanimity, but at crucial moments even *On Native Grounds* participated in the rhetorical counterviolence in the name of getting beyond ideology that would in later years become the hallmark of the Cold War battle against linguistic disruption. Kazin's prose becomes worked up at the very end of the section on Marxist criticism in the thirties: there is a repeated coordinate sentence structure, and ironic hyperbole ("a literature of unparalleled human fellowship and dignity")—and the effect of the passage culminates in strong, biting sloganeering. Not at all beside the point is the fact that the coinage "a study of literature in its relation to society is not a feather bed for minds seeking cozy formulas" was itself the perfect formulaic set piece for the anticommunist stump circuit, a circuit Kazin's book rode a long way. This is much more like Peter Viereck's anti-thirties stylizings than unlike them:

It is thus precisely because the Marxist critic believes himself to be at once a historian, an expert analyst, and an agitator; precisely because he appears to be salvaging the best culture of the past and establishing the requisite foundations under Socialism for a literature of unparalleled human fellowship and dignity; precisely because he seeks what critics have always sought, yet seems to go beyond them in his understanding of the whole social context of culture, that his responsibility is so great. Criticism under Marxism usually becomes a form of *Kulturgeschichte*, but a study of literature in its relation to society is not a feather bed for minds seeking cozy formulas; it is, presumably, a rousing-up of the best intellectual energies and a stimulus to the richest structure imagination that criticism affords.[81]

Granville Hicks was surely right when he wrote to Kazin in the autumn of 1941, almost immediately after hearing parts of *On Native Grounds* (in at least one lecture) and after reading a draft of at least the chapter on criticism "at the poles." He pointed out that Kazin was emotionally and linguistically implicated in the rhetorical "violence" of the 1930s he purported to condemn and transcend. Hicks observed that this was not at all "simple anti-Stalinism" but that Kazin was nonetheless "influenced . . . by political considerations"—specifically, anticommunist "violence" posing as wisdom and analytical constancy. "I am not suggesting that you have been ruined by the Stalinist phobia," Hicks wrote, "as some of the Partisan Review crowd have been, but I felt in much of your talk an underlying pre-occupation that can only hurt your writing. It colors, I think your whole conception of the thirties, and involved you in an act of rejection as violent and as unjust as any of those earlier rejections you were speaking of. It enters into your passionate feeling for literature and perhaps corrupts it a little along the edges."[82]

Kazin protested. "I don't react against the thirties, now, in toto," he replied. "I don't bring violence to violence." But "I do ask . . . of all of us who are thinking and writing, who have remained alive and conscious in the face of so much abysmal stupidity and lying and violence and cheapness, an effort of imaginative vitality." And yet, in a closing paragraph in which Kazin worked hard to retain Hicks's friendship ("You're a wonderful guy, Granville, and I love you very much, even if you think me a stinker"), he conceded the close "relation of style to belief" even as he had resisted Hicks's suggestion—a correct one, I think—that Kazin himself at turns engaged in the stylistic "quality of brutality and shock and panic" he condemned along with communist theory. Kazin's letter to Hicks, which began with the younger man's contention that he felt "detached from the quarrel" about the legacy of the thirties, ended by revealing an almost complete absorption. He repeated his insistence that he was not "dismissing the thirties, as such" but rather was trying to understand what "seduced so many hundreds of writers into saying wild and foolish things." Kazin's answer? The literary tradition does not sufficiently explain it—the aesthetic line, say, that runs through Upton Sinclair and Jack London. Of course this was implicitly a comment on Hicks's *The Great Tradition*. What did explain the seduction was an allegedly common psychological flaw among those who went left, and such a kind of group psychology explained why "so many leftist writers petered out."[83]

In understanding Kazin's treatment of the literary left as "a crucial part of the book" not only because the book-length argument culminates in the 1930s but also "because of Kazin's personal ties with the Left," Alan Wald has refuted in some detail the contention at the end of *On Native Grounds* that literary radicalism was a "minor episode with no long-term future" and that radical writers on the whole stopped writing after the 1930s, "unable to follow up," as Kazin put it.[84] Where Kazin spoke of Edward Dahlberg, for instance, as "exhausted by his own sensibility," another radical dead end, Wald shows Dahlberg's dogged, energetic production of "original (and cranky) work"[85] through his dying day in 1975. Indeed, Dahlberg emerged as an idiosyncratic but effective critic of modern poetry at midcentury. Innovative poets were thrilled and irritated at turns but paid attention. Some knew that he had "very accurately located" the poetics and politics of Kenneth Fearing in various writings commending Fearing's poetics.[86] Paul Carroll of the hip magazine *Big Table* in the 1950s was happily "astounded" that a writer "so absolute and so odd"—"long one of the heroes of the literary Underground" because of his proletarian writing of the 1930s—could "despise . . . contemporary America" in the 1950s and still attract such a following.[87] Robert Duncan, disappointed generally that "passionate involvements, inspired necessities, visions, unpopular faiths" were conventionally deemed "disruptive to the requirements and dignities" of poetry fit for publication in the mid-1950s,[88] was pleased to turn, on assignment for *Poetry*, to Dahlberg's newest writing with an open mind, discovering that "his art is that of a collagist" and pleased (although also troubled) to see D. H. Lawrence's praise for Dahlberg thirty years earlier—Dahlberg's language "is a *willed* minimum, sustained from inside by resistance"—borne out in the new writing.[89] Dahlberg was urging young experimental poets to read Lorine Niedecker[90] and during a visit to Majorca told Robert Creeley that Zukofsky "needs the support of the young because he's a great teacher and great poet," whereupon Creeley contacted Zukofsky for the first time.[91] Dahlberg carefully read issues of the *Black Mountain Review* and corresponded with Charles Olson, attempting to "curb th[e] ferocious jackal" in Olson and serving for several crucial years in the 1950s as a mentor to Creeley and, after overcoming initial reservations, avidly promoted Creeley's poetry to others.[92] Dahlberg utterly belied expectations based on his having a regular column, "Second Harvest" (1950–53), in John Chamberlain's conservative magazine, *The Freeman*, for Dahlberg insisted that Creeley also get to know Walter Lowenfels, the modernist jailed under the Smith Act as a communist, "like some wild beast in an iron cage." While Dahlberg was by then no friend of the CPUSA, he admired Lowenfels and hoped Creeley would consider "why many [poets], utterly disgusted with cartels, cupidity, unlimited greed we miscall liberty, and the press which is eating up everybody's brain" would have turned to communism as he and Lowenfels had done.[93]

So Edward Dahlberg may have been, as Murray Kempton disparagingly called him in 1955, "a one-novel man,"[94] but there were of course genres other than fiction—poetry and poetic poetry criticism, to name two. Yet Kazin and especially Kempton did not look elsewhere. Why, after all, would a misanthropic, closed-minded old radical like Dahlberg—autocratic, insensitive, sexist—have any resonance for young writers in the 1950s? Yet Duncan, on record in *Poetry*, was not so very far away. Alan Wald is correct, then, in asserting that one can now see Kazin's hand in winding up the mainspring of collective critical forgetting of radical novelists—Dahlberg, Robert Cantwell, Edwin Seaver, William Rollins, Jack Conroy, Fielding Burke, Grace Lumpkin, Leane Zugsmith, and many others. Cantwell worked in film. Seaver, as an editor, sponsored many a young poet. Zugsmith, who in *The Angry Decade* is said to have "disappeared without a trace" and "with[drawn] into silence" after 1937, as a matter of fact published six stories, two nonfiction books, and a book of short fiction *after that date*, although even such facts do not tell the tale of the "falling off" of this radical writer. Her husband, a journalist, was blacklisted and hounded out of his job by red-baiters; needing an income and attracted by a new genre of writing, she joined him on the staff of the new liberal daily, *PM*; a few years later, fearful that her reputation as a subversive would prevent publication, she submitted new writing under at least one pseudonym.[95] This is hardly the "silence" of *The Angry Decade*. And certainly it was not "withdrawal."

To be sure, then, the burnout thesis was by no means Kazin's invention. Indeed, it was more frequently invoked to explain the alleged failure of radical poets than of novelists after the 1930s. Speaking about lyric poetry, Louise Bogan in the final weeks of the decade declared that "the day of chaste and noble proletarian myths should be about over. It has been recently proved that there is something hideously oversimplified in crude oppositions and blind idealism."[96] A few months earlier, in the *Partisan Review* symposium on "The Situation in American Writing," Bogan had argued that a generation of radicalized poets poorly made the personal transition to middle age in the 1930s, when *they* were in their thirties, took "refuge in closed systems of belief, and automatically (many of them) committed creative suicide."[97] Kempton in 1955 did not merely observe that "a former revolutionary poet [now] writes empty novels of derivative passion"; he went further, contending that no "literary generation can be said to equal [the 1930s radicals] for self-destruction." The question of political agency explodes on Kempton's normally lucent prose logic. While on one hand proletarian poets *"buried themselves* in Hollywood" after the 1930s, on the other they also were soon "to be *disinterred and cast to the winds by* the House Committee on Un-American Activities." Was the self-burial the cause of horrific disinterment? Did Kempton mean they should have stuck to their now-unfashionable craft? Was HUAC the radical's penitence for going Hollywood? It is hard to know how Kempton came up with the number, but he nonetheless asserted that "just one per cent" of 1930s writers on the left survived the twenty-year liberal-left era.[98]

Harry Roskolenko (1907–80), a poet who was briefly in the communist movement (his communist poems were written under the pseudonym Paul Goch)[99] but then in the late 1930s became a member of the ultraleft Socialist Workers Party[100] and the Trotskyite League for Cultural Freedom and Social-ism,[101] was for so long afterward an ardent anti-Stalinist that the transition to the Cold War politics and poetics of denigrating "the thirties" was relatively smooth (although in other ways the fifties were difficult years for Roskolenko). In a 1956 review for *Poetry*, he conjured "the angry Thirties" as a time when "Moscow . . . invit[ed] the hero of culture to make his pilgrimage," which left him "overtly stricken as a writer, shorn of his imagination." Roskolenko was reviewing Edwin Rolfe's *Permit Me Refuge* (1955), making a case that despite the book of poems in front of him, Rolfe had not survived poetically. Rolfe's "tender lyricism suffered," and "his growth as a poet" had been made "impossible" by his politics. Rolfe was in Kempton's 99 percent. The worst thing about Edwin Rolfe poetically was that his association with communism "persisted." That Rolfe *had* survived as a lyric poet despite unendurable tribulations otherwise— a person ill and impoverished, a victim of McCarthyism—awaited the evidence abounding in Cary Nelson's *Edwin Rolfe: Collected Poems* (1993) and *Revolutionary Memory* (2001), two studies that straightened out tangled lines of publication, ordered significantly delayed and never-published work, and clearly demonstrated late lyrics developed well beyond the early.

Roskolenko's was not the sort of judgment that required the historical or archival work that Nelson brought to bear on Rolfe's lyricism. It is not even clear from Roskolenko's review that he knew of Rolfe's premature death (1954). The uninformed assumption that Rolfe had *aesthetically* gone under after the 1930s was driven by an anti-Stalinism that was at this point contextless. In fact, *Permit Me Refuge* is almost entirely the kind of lyric Roskolenko claimed to have once liked in Rolfe.[102] Alvah Bessie, one of the Hollywood Ten and lifelong radical—and Rolfe's comrade from their days fighting with the Abraham Lincoln Battalion in Spain[103]—helped mark the obvious lines of battle, supporting the judgment of poet Thomas McGrath, also a communist, that Rolfe's last period was his best. Rolfe's poems of the late 1940s and 1950s were indeed "first poems," taking priority over work of the 1930s. Bessie thus provocatively reversed the usual denigration of the 1930s as the ur-period for radical art. He insisted that the posthumous book showed Rolfe's style furthering a "process of transformation," that his range was widening, his insight deepening. This was not just the opposite view from Roskolenko's; it was an effort to complicate a sense of the radical "period." Bessie read in Rolfe an understanding of collective political memory as a hedge against canonical forgetting: refuge was not just a political fact of the radical poet in cold war; it was also a "region of your brain"—*your* being the reader's.[104] Bessie saw Rolfe's verse epitaph as an essentially lyrical rejoinder to Bogan's attack on leftist poets as having taken "refuge in closed systems of belief."

Roskolenko, an uninventive anticommunist in this respect, abided a model for censuring the "angry Thirties" here and elsewhere that Kazin had helped to inaugurate. As a communist, Bessie did more than merely counter that model, pointing out as well that the communist artist in question made an art out of the repressive process itself. The deepening of Rolfe's lyricism included a consciousness of aesthetic aspects of repression. Here, on the aesthetics of political forms, Kazin offered scant insight. His role in creating the fifties' thirties finally had less to do with relations between language and style on one hand and, on the other, the actual experience of political idealism—Bogan's and Roskolenko's particular focus—than with the content of the "end of ideology" as later adumbrated and codified by Arthur Schlesinger Jr. in *The Vital Center* (1949) and throughout the fifties in essays Daniel Bell later collected in *The End of Ideology* (1960). This concept included, among other tenets, the notion that aesthetic ideology was always already an extremity—that political commitment was itself exhausted; that all -*isms*, including aesthetic movements, were similarly vulgar and conformist;[105] that ideological opposites are often of a piece and must be met by a kind of analysis that does not itself partake in the linguistic conduct of ideology; that good criticism opposes opposition; that "ideology" itself had become "an irretrievably fallen word."[106] One of the chapters Kazin chose to publish separately before the appearance of *On Native Grounds* was "Criticism at the Poles," eventually the book's fourteenth chapter. Published in the *New Republic* just a few weeks before the book was released, this essay summarized the two literary-critical extremes of the 1930s—communist cultural criticism and the New Criticism. The excerpt was intended to be evenhanded, and it implied, by the very balanced structure of its argument, that aesthetic ideology is flawed.

Here and especially in the full-length version of the chapter in the book, Kazin suggested that finally the communists and New Critics were the same. "Extremities always meet." While the "typical Marxist" who "subordinated esthetic values to a rigid social doctrine" and on the other side the New Critical formalist who "subordinated everything to his esthetic values" would seem to be "poles" apart, they are actually compatible.[107] Allen Tate's South was like Michael Gold's Russia![108] In literature and politics alike, extremity had itself become the "key symbol . . . of power and disaster."[109] And the solution to the disaster? Placing oneself "against" being so adamantly against—to find a non-opposition that effectively opposed ideology without being implicated in ideological terms. This would be well enough had Kazin created a real balance between his angry derision of the communist critical and literary legacy and his demulcent survey of the agrarians. On Kazin's particular native grounds, however, New Critical formalism was hardly the evil equal of radical poetics.

Although Kazin's summary implied that the New Critics' more recent position was a decline from the original agrarian "powerful moral critique of the superficiality and debasement of letters under capitalism," the "post-ethical" art for which John Crowe Ransom finally called was precisely the answer to the hyperethics of the communists, a shelter from the storm from which Kazin did indeed seek shelter. And while Kazin seemingly criticized Ransom's "proposal that 'the critic should regard the poem as nothing short of a desperate ontological or metaphysical manoeuvre,' "[110] and the poem was said to exist "as a technique of restraint," the urgent correspondence with Hicks makes clear that a functioning critical ratio became crucial to the operation of the fifties' thirties as a weapon against any furtherance of the relationship between poetic modernism and radicalism. The New Criticism was to the poem as Kazin was to Hicks; Kazin was to Hicks as the anodyne language of the "end of ideology" here was to the spiny radical critical style. Observed through this ratio, the New Criticism's poem was a desperate ontological strategy, a technique of restraint as itself a rejoinder to disruptive, excessive, unmannered socioromantic historicizing—in short, a fifties' thirties.

Kazin	Hicks
criticism at the end of ideology	the poem
1950s	1930s

It is all there in the fascinating Hicks-Kazin relationship from the dawn of the anticommunist era through Sputnik. Perhaps Kazin felt his language about formalism was barbed. Perhaps he wanted *On Native Grounds* over the years to be read as joining in a laugh at the expense of Ransom's unforgettably characteristic praise of Wallace Stevens's ostentatiously unhistorical poem "Sea Surface Full of Clouds" (1924): "The poem has a calculated complexity," Ransom had written, with an almost personal piquancy, "and its technical competence is so high that to study it, if you do that sort of thing, is to be happy." But the fact was that Kazin's "Criticism at the Poles" was itself a piece of calculated complexity, a kind of happiness after so much grimness: the end of the chapter, after the "opposites" of communism and New Criticism are described in turn, purports to create a continuity from communism, in the more moderate recent work of Edmund Wilson, Lionel Trilling, Harry Levin, Philip Rahv, and Delmore Schwartz. Yet the way these figures were described—Wilson in particular—provided evidence that the New Criticism colonized the critical dialectic here and that communism's influence on modernism had come to an end. Rather than befitting the thirties and then extending them, Wilson was better understood, Kazin concluded, as having endured and *survived* the thirties. (The same could be said of Trilling, Rahv, and Schwartz; all three did much to further a modernism swerving around the thirties.) Kazin's rendition of Edmund Wilson "gave meaning to the service of criticism and the honor of integrity and taste" and "excelled by *preserving an example in a bad time*, by illuminating the margin of greatness that keeps the spirit alive."[111]

For having created so soon after the 1930s a sense of that "bad time," Kazin's influence on anticommunist poetics was profound. One hardly thinks of Allen Tate and Alfred Kazin as belonging to the same camp. Yet Kazin's narrating what happened "after 1930," when American writing "became a search for fulfillment by the word, a messianic drive toward social action bent on liberation by conquest and extermination,"[112] caused Tate to recommend the *New Republic* excerpt to Wallace Stevens, John Peale Bishop, and other poets. Tate urged Bishop to read Kazin's piece for its description of "the way our totalitarianism will develop on the literary front."[113]

CHAPTER 4

I observe how my pen
gets embittered

and how the ink runs out
leaving the alloy dry.

—Alvaro Cardona-Hine, *Mainstream*

I was honest once.—Alfred Hayes, 1950

Repressive Rereadings

When he wrote *Writers on the Left* (1961), Daniel Aaron was not nearly as conscious of language as he might have been. To have read this big, groundbreaking book at the time of its publication was to experience twentieth-century radical writing as if it was nowhere self-referential, as if the writing of American communists and fellow travelers had rarely been about the writing, nor about how forms of writing *as* writing situate themselves politically—nor whether contemporary language was up to the task American radical ideologies set for it. The literary work featured in *Writers on the Left* was language conveying content, writing *about* heretical struggles real and realistically invented.

Of course, Aaron's main project was unearthing the names and biopolitical narratives of writers, many of whom had by then transmuted into midcentury centrists or had disappeared from view. The subtitle of his book was "Episodes in American Literary Communism," but a full sense of the literary—the politics of style—was lacking. Introducing "the Rebels" of 1900–1920 taxonomically, Aaron identified the "Literary Experimenters or the Priests of Art," lumping Eliot and Pound with Frost, Stein, and Bodenheim. He saved Vachel Lindsay for the "Unclassifiables," sequestering Waldo Frank in the "Apostolic 'Student Movement' "—and strongly implied, through the structure of his narrative, that in the story of "the impact of the idea of Communism on American writers . . . both on those who accepted it and on those who did not,"[1] the "literary experimenters" seemed little relevant, the category being—for the purposes of this story—a dead end. Aaron's long chapter on the movement "From Bohemia to Revolution" spoke not at all of language. Even "Literary Wars of the Early Thirties" came only a bit closer.

Yet when a few years later Aaron began more intently to study the question of memory, the aesthetics of political retrospect, he knew he had to face the problem of words as words, for repression, especially in the form of self-recrimination, entails denying language. When in the 1950s "former Leftists presid[ed] over the autopsy of the radical-liberal corpse," they found it to have been a death by language. Style, forms, syntax, phrases, idioms—these were the targets of assault. Anticommunists "took pains to announce in literary quarterlies, in class-rooms, in summer conferences for young writers, that the old formulas were hopelessly inadequate. Few had a good word to say for the popular Left-wing writers of the Thirties or for the literary forms and styles these writers had used."[2]

Aaron was now concerned with showing how liberal language had been caught in this dragnet. The anticommunist rebuke of engagé literature was really also a traditionalist attack on liberalism's aesthetic tolerance. The language of openness was interpreted as rigid, inhuman and—still worse—bad writing. "Vulgar" is the word Don Hager used in an essay of 1954. J. Donald Adams was willing to concede that "some valuable experimentation was done" in the 1920s and 1930s, but "too many poets had forgotten that poetry has its roots in emotion." The "word fabric" experimental poets had made was as "artificial" as the conventions against which this poetry had rebelled. What was needed (somehow) was an unartificial writing, for Adams disliked what he called the "telescoped and inverted English"—the "cablese"—of modern poets.[3] Hager's essay bore one of those Cold War–era titles, "The Rhetoric of Intergroup Liberalism," in which the mere appearance of the word "rhetoric" indicated the pejorative. In the book *Minorities and the American Promise* (1954), Hager had found the stunningly fractured anticliché "Social change is in the saddle riding mankind," and he assumed that the language—as sentences—grated on the American ear. He called it "curious syntax" and complained that it was "a tortured metaphor." The former charge was untrue as such, the latter contingent, of course, on one's view of history. The point of Hager's article was evidently to disavow a liberal language that used "the specious omnipotence of the winged word . . . and the merely hortatory approach." This sort of rhetorically inflamed antirhetorical attack on the vocabulary and figuration of liberalism worked simultaneously as an effort to redefine cultural pluralism so that it could be used to denigrate "mutual understanding" and to reinforce "the integrity of group *differences*."[4] Daniel Aaron, for his part, accurately realized that in such instances "not only Marxism was attacked. All the liberal clichés fell under the post-war ban."[5]

That liberal language was under fire had already been the communist position in the 1950s. This position was evident in articles on postwar illiberalism published in *Masses & Mainstream*. Milton Howard, a communist writer, critic, and *Daily Worker* editor whose main concern was the pragmatic politics of modern style (his essay describing cold warriors' praise for the language of Hemingway's *The Old Man and the Sea*[6] is a telling instance), struggled against thirties-bashing as a form of linguistic repression in "New Realities for the Intellectuals" (1955). The anticommunist narrative, for Howard, ran as follows: When the New Deal was infiltrated by communism, democratic liberalism was to be considered dead or dying—"and deservedly so." Thus, "any contemporary liberalism, or anti-McCarthyism must never again repeat the error of the 1930's of being in intellectual conversation, or practical collaboration, with Marxism in any manner, shape or form." This prohibition had dire consequences for liberal as well as radical forms. Howard understood the acceptance of formalist "literary withdrawal from history" as a result not so much of anti-Marxism per se but of antiliberalism.[7]

Aaron sensed a similarly close relation between the political reasons why scholars and writers in the 1950s "rather studiedly avoided the Thirties" and the critical "new line" dismissing liberal-left writers as "primitives, clumsy practitioners who simplified art."[8] Not everyone who regretted to some degree the political radicalism of the 1930s toed the new line by regretting also the linguistic forms associated with the period or by accepting the indictment of clumsiness. Thus, verse unsurprisingly has offered the toughest generic test, for in the world of poetry, there were significant points of continuity amid the flood of disruptions in the line running from the modernism of the 1910s and 1920s through the radicalized 1930s to the 1950s. Robert Warshow was among the few anticommunist critics of the 1930s who understood this. He knew that the main issue facing modern writers was how to find the language for experience in and with mass culture, a difficulty addressed most keenly by the poet. Warshow emphasized that this was a furtherance of early modernism through the 1930s. "The problem did not suddenly spring into being in the 30's; the poetry of T. S. Eliot is sufficient evidence to the contrary." It was just that "the center of the problem is in the political intellectual movement of the 30's. The problem developed over many years and through many historical factors, but it *happened* in the 30's." For that reason, according to Warshow, it was imperative by 1947 to create "some method of assimilating the experience of those years." (To be sure, he felt such a method would not only enlarge our "understanding of the cultural failure" of the period but again would also aid our sense of the unifying features of modernism and radicalism.)[9]

Even among poets who expressed real political regrets or disillusionment, it was quite another thing to accept the "new line" Aaron described—dismissing 1930s writing as crude—as a settled matter of poetic art. Alfred Hayes, born into poverty in 1911, once one of the most prominent as well as among the most dogmatic of the young revolutionary poets[10]—a typical contributor's note in 1935 observes that "he records himself a permanent communist"[11]—wrote in a 1950 poem of honesty about his communism as his most *aesthetically* heretical and dangerous quality. The memory that "I was honest once; or if not honest, / at least lack[ing] guile" was the single poetic virtue that "will serve me when nothing else will serve." "What would another age say?" Hayes wondered. "That we consumed ourselves, / and were self-deceived?"[12]

Horace Gregory later regretted having written—as he put it in a 1934 letter—"that the Communist Party is now the only valid third party movement in America, the only Party for all its blunders and mistakes that is gaining ground," but he never once felt he had been anything but truthful in his aesthetic evaluations, and in the late forties and fifties he was reviled by anticommunist poets.[13] But he had been no "mere time server." He had "proved my intellectual honesty many times" as a communist poet and critic. Although he had come to despise communism, he felt greater antipathy toward assumptions—a form of "inverted snobbery," he called it—that the poems he had written while in the communist milieu, especially love poems, were crude, "that if you've got a girl, she has to be a red hot revolutionary girl until you vulgarize every human emotion in your blood."[14]

J. Malcolm Brinnin, a poet much younger than Gregory, had been a member of the Young Communist League but was politically somewhat chastened already by 1945—and even more so by the time of *The Sorrows of Cold Stone* (1951)—yet continued all along to feel that a leftist's political survival inhered in the poetic line. In the ideation of disruptive language, even after social-political "failure," one may "move among your ruins conquering."[15] This brings us back to Brinnin's sense of "deliberate innocence" as a radical form of honesty, the ideological lie that Kazin and Leslie Fiedler decried ("the Popular Front mind at bay" by the late 1940s "was incapable of honesty"; "the avowals of innocence . . . were not affecting")[16] but that Brinnin in his verse quietly cherished. A poem Brinnin addresses to his university students imagines "the anger of your innocence" and teaches us how to view such a disposition as it enables modest restoration of the heretic, a tolerated (if not celebrated) homecoming—itself a note of dissonance in the 1950s. Here those who remained behind possess deliberate innocence. Neither Stalinist dupes nor ivory towerists, they make acceptance upon return possible:

When rebels ride to action, you remain.
For all the anger of your innocence,
Accomplished and free, they will ride back again.[17]

The one who remains behind in an age of radical activism was indeed a figure of the political modern poet common in 1930s poetry—for instance, much of the verse about the 1936–39 Spanish Civil War—although it became something of a convention in the "post-political" period, 1946 to 1960. Stephen Spender's most honest and most pointed poem about Spain might be "Thoughts during an Air Raid," a brilliant lyric about what is today called "hotel journalism."

> In the hotel bedroom with the wallpaper
> Blowing smoke through wreaths of roses, *one* can ignore
> The pressure of those names [of the dead] under the fingers
> Indented by lead type on newsprint.

The poet is "in country" yet composes in relative comfort and as a modern subjective lyricist includes in the language of the poem the pillow on the bed, the imagining of war's abruption onto the pacific, "impersonal" scene of writing.[18] Wallace Stevens's "The Men That Are Falling" (1936), an introverted "personal" lyric also about Spain that won the *Nation* prize, retreats even more honestly to the poet's intimate writing space.[19]

> What is it he desires?
> But this he cannot know, the man that thinks . . .
>
> staring steadily
>
> At a head upon the pillow in the dark,
> More than sudarium, speaking the speech
>
> Of absolutes, bodiless, a head
> Thick-lipped from riot and rebellious cries,
>
> The head of one of the men that are falling, placed
> Upon the pillow to repose and speak[20]

Brinnin's poetry fashions a postradical Everyman out of the one—the modern writer—who stays domestically behind the lines: "Their guilt is brave, and when you can believe it, / With a cold grace you will take their adult hands." This regretful post-1930s poetry was largely taken up with the retrospective view of radicalism, implicitly proposing a fifties' thirties that functions across space as well as time. Brinnin's "For My Pupils in the War Years" is a poem about staying behind spatially, across the widening distances separating forms of political activism—the angry innocence of getting formally educated in a time of others' engagement with antifascist war. Brinnin's collection, *The Sorrows of Cold Stone*, which Joseph Warren Beach in the 1950s observed was a book of "social faith grown thin or driven underground,"[21] collected lyrics contemplating the state of becoming an anachronism, every poem wrestling in some way with what William Phillips (dismissively) called the "combination of deception and self-deception" in the 1930s.[22] It is a book of self-consciously 1950s-style lyrics tracing the roots of content back to the 1930s, lyrics of guilt about innocence. Chronologically, Hayes similarly stayed behind—collecting poems into a striking but mostly ignored book, *Welcome to the Castle* (1950), a work also respected and featured by Beach. Hayes's verse ironizes the castle into a space for the poetics of political invisibility. He considers poetic gifts once generally cherished, but now "I think they're gone; and we've gone underground, / into our favorite darkness." The current "honest age" is one in which "our infamies [are] disclosed / all printed, up for self"—alphabetically outed, self-exposed.[23]

Beach's was the first substantive critical reading of Brinnin and Hayes of any sort, and one of the first of Gregory—let alone the first sympathetically political reading of them. If Gregory had written "precisely what I wanted to say in a manner that is now generally recognized as his own,"[24] Beach, among few others, now positively sought to describe this manner. Joseph Warren Beach (1880–1957) wrote and revised his masterwork, *Obsessive Images: Symbolism in Poetry of the 1930's and 1940's*, through the entire period covered by the present study. William Van O'Connor, also a member of the English faculty at the University of Minnesota—himself a shaper of a 1920s suitable for the 1950s[25]— watched his senior colleague and friend at work on this book from the time the older man retired in 1948 until his death on August 13, 1957.[26]

O'Connor was actively promoting the concept that poetry had reached the end of ideology at midcentury. He interpreted Stevens's "A Dish of Peaches in Russia" as contending "the unnaturalness of attempting to give one's allegiance to an abstract system"[27] and mistrusted all official versions of the real as "simple-minded," having seen, as he thought his mentor Lionel Trilling did, how liberals had become literal and unimaginative.[28] He argued that poets cannot be "civilizing forces" when their best poetry is written "outside the society," "divorced or exiled from the middle class culture."[29] "Those concerned with maintaining the freedom of the artist to create his vision of the work," wrote O'Connor in 1951, "have no inevitable allegiance either to the Right or to the Left," a remark that won the admiration of W. K. Wimsatt[30] and at the same time put O'Connor on the "excrement list" at *Partisan Review*, as he was delighted to learn from Karl Shapiro.[31] "With the political and economic upheavals of the thirties," O'Connor argued, poets had come out of their isolation with a vengeance: "The pendulum swung too far" toward engagement, "tend-[ing] to become the poetry of a party."[32] Even when O'Connor defended modernist obscurity, the assertion was so qualified that one extremist thirties-basher cited him as evidence to aid an attack on the experimental prosody of Archibald MacLeish's social poetry.[33] Beach's big book went against this grain, but it was not published until 1960, and it was O'Connor, fulfilling the duty of a departmental colleague, who edited the work posthumously.[34]

But if O'Connor was the consummate literary-critical midcentury centrist—mentored by liberal anticommunist Lionel Trilling and avidly promoted by conservative publisher Henry Regnery—Joseph Warren Beach was a leftist in his political views and a friend and supporter of left-wing writers (as well as a champion of modernist poets from 1915 on). Beach admired the radical novels of Edward Dahlberg (the antifascist *Those Who Perish* of 1934) and Waldo Frank (*The Death and Birth of David Markand*, a call for a workers' and farmers' government) and had corresponded enthusiastically with both in the early 1930s.[35] He passionately disagreed with Robert Penn Warren's neoconservative version of nineteenth-century southern white selfhood and, having read in manuscript Warren's book-length narrative poem about the 1811 murder of a slave by Thomas Jefferson's nephews, *Brother to Dragons* (1953), reminded Warren that Beach's "ethical 'ideology' . . . does not altogether jibe with what seems to be yours." He was "in much ideological disagreement" with Frost, Eliot, and Stevens.[36] He tried his hand at a poem unironically celebrating May Day in 1952, the coldest of Cold War years (a poem rejected by *Poetry* that year and not published until six years later).[37] He called John Foster Dulles a warmonger and felt that the Republicans might be willing to start a world war to win reelection in 1956.[38] Such dissident views encouraged Beach's already well-developed obsession with the then-dated political language of the liberal-left era, and he came to believe that by the 1950s a glossary might literally be needed for those who might want once again to take seriously the modernist poetry of that period.[39]

Beach knew he was working on the poetry of an era generalizations about which were typified by Leo Gurko's assessment in *The Angry Decade* that no poets from the 1930s would survive as an important part of our literature. ("Was fascism too immediate and ugly a matter to be suitable for poetry?" Gurko mused on possible causes; "Was the depression too smothering an experience?")[40] Giving no sense that the term "obsessive" in Beach's title meant to convey his passion for serious if overblown study of political poetics, O'Connor added a preface that, quite aside from expressing personal admiration for Beach, seems an attempt to restrict any critical foray Beach's book might be permitted to make into sincere consideration of "minor" poets of the 1930s. First O'Connor had somehow to account for Beach's unorthodox decision to write of two decades of modern poetry with little more than incidental reference to Pound, essentially no mention of Frost, and—utterly strikingly for a book on modern poetry of its time—a total of six words on imagism in 376 pages. This was the first study featuring poetry of the 1930s that did not sacrifice it at the altar of the 1920s. O'Connor's summary of Beach's approach to the younger poets of the 1930s and 1940s is far more patronizing than anything Beach wrote in the book O'Connor was introducing: Beach "sees the period as one of great earnestness, ingenuity, and sophistication," O'Connor observed, "but he does not see it as one that produced poets of the stature of . . ."—and then *he* names the big-name modernists of the 1920s.[41]

In fact, Beach's approach to modernists of the 1930s, with respect to the 1920s, was based on a heterodox distinction about formal experimentalism that he articulated to Robert Penn Warren in private correspondence: Beach "welcome[d] modernist innovations in poetry . . . but sheer clowning gives me the creeps, especially where it is the mask for solemn preaching."[42] And the main limitation of *Obsessive Images*, a quality implicit in the title, is not at all, as O'Connor for his own political purposes sought to imply, that from a Cold War perspective Beach derided radical poetry. Rather, it is that Beach took radical poetic content and put it through the structuralist symbol-hunting machinery du jour. This apparatus tended to obscure the fact that in certain readings of the development of modern poetry, such as those of Hayes and Brinnin, the issue was really the changing relationship between lyricism and communism. The 1950s-style schematization of this roomy, comprehensive book—chapters arranged by symbolic "order" and thematic development less important than typology—made it well-nigh impossible for readers to have a sense of the implicit narrative chronological shift away from radicalism toward the reaffirmation of the High Modern 1920s. This avowal O'Connor claimed was Beach's major point. It was not Beach's point, but to discern that, one needed to approach Beach's study as an active user of the book's index, for the index, rather than the table of contents, could serve as a guide to heretical figures otherwise not quite visible under the surface of commonplace literary-critical organization. We "may mistake for old-fashioned," a reviewer shrewdly observed, "what is essentially independent and refreshing."[43] The total space devoted to Alfred Hayes is nearly enough to have made for a discrete chapter on this poet about whom no one had yet written an article or book chapter. But readers must locate Hayes as *here* in a paragraph a user of the fearful tiger symbol, *there* in a sentence a user of the symbol of the assassin, *here* a poet writing on exile, *there* on "unfaith." In Beach's index, most poets of the 1930s receive a paginated entry under the depoliticized subheading "attitude toward present age." One might read against the methodological grain, rehistoricizing Beach's inclination toward the historical fact driving the story of radical poetry's demise by linking all the pages toward which indexed entries under "attitude toward present age" point.

That inclination did lead Beach to several key anti-anticommunist assumptions. These tend somewhat to resist the book's methodological deradicalization of the 1930s, and they become clear only when Beach considers the modern history of the symbology of exile. Although his book was all about poetry, when Beach sought a salient instance of Cold War literary politics at work in the shaping of perceptions about the 1930s, he came upon Malcolm Cowley—once himself a poet in the modernist orbit but best known in the 1950s for his lucid literary-historical prose. Reference to Cowley made good sense for a section on exile in a chapter on "Geography and Travel." In that chapter, Beach wanted eventually to get to Hayes's *Welcome to the Castle* and its antifascist charge of *la trahison des clercs* as an explanation for Jewish dislocation and extermination. While all

> over Europe the wheel of disaster turned in its grease[,]
> . . . they sat in the caves fierce about art
> The assassins were preparing masterpieces of their own.[44]

Malcolm Cowley offered Joseph Warren Beach a means of connecting the exilic mentalities of the modernist Joyce and the communist Auden to the modernist-communist poetry of Hayes. The making of this move provides a crucial moment in Beach's book, and it is the key, I think, to perceiving the deradicalization of poetic language generally: in Cowley's own revision of his sense of literary exile suitable for the 1950s, Beach interpreted a narrative structure of political regret.

When Viking brought out a new edition of *Exile's Return* in 1951, Cowley revised it. He altered some passages, deleted others, and added a new concluding chapter.[45] *Exile's Return* was already well known as a work that looked upon expatriation in the 1920s from the critical point of view of the radical 1930s. Its original final chapter, completed in 1934, read the end of the expatriate phase of American High Modernism as entailing what Beach called a "process of deracination." Writers, coming home from Europe, failed to reintegrate themselves "with the childhood culture-pattern from which they had cut themselves off," and so they remained exiles "in the sense that they had not found a completely satisfying homeland of the spirit." The final chapter originally proposed a High Modern 1920s for the book's own era, the communist 1930s; it suggested that the expatriates' class—the capitalist class—had little to offer them now that they had seen experimentalist Paris. The 1934 *Exile's Return* posited (in Beach's phrase) but "one available means of escaping the soulless isolation of the artist": class-conscious revolutionary politics, offered by the man whom conservatives dubbed "the Number One literary executioner of Stalin in America."[46] But in 1951 the anticommunist Jewish cultural magazine *Commentary*, anticipating the Viking Press publication of the book by a few weeks, published an excerpt from Cowley's new final chapter. For the magazine version only, it bore a subtitle that implied the Cold War rereading of the 1930s view of the 1920s: "1930: The Year That Was New Year's Eve: *The Great Binge and Its Leftist Aftermath*."[47] If to Murray Kempton the era was characterized by the movement from Cowley, who had been "a witness against the twenties to the thirties," to Whittaker Chambers, who was now "a witness against the thirties to the fifties,"[48] Cowley's appearance in *Commentary* hinted strongly that Cowley himself was being enlisted to make that move.

Cowley's moderate confession of deliberate innocence, in the context of satisfying "binge" and sterner, consequential "aftermath," was commended everywhere in 1951 in delighted reviews and appreciative ads, almost as if Cowley too had repented his former self, had turned state's evidence, had named names. The new *Exile's Return* "was as lyrically acclaimed as it had once been abusively condemned."[49] For Robert Spiller, who as general editor of the *Literary History of the United States* avidly recruited Cowley to write a coda on all modern writing, including poetry,[50] the author of *Exile's Return* was "*the* critic and chronicler of his generation" because he had settled into the second half of the century, had "bought a farm in Connecticut" rather than commit suicide like so many members of the generation he satisfyingly chronicles, now from a distance on the *thirties* as well as the twenties.[51] For Spiller and many other Americanists, Cowley's book provided the proper fifties reading of the thirties determinist reading of the twenties. This view joined the general rush toward a "twenties" liberated from thirties-style perspective—a twenties that outradicalized communists' insistence on literature's social role. Louise Bogan, a persistent defamer of thirties verse, confidently asserted in 1948 that "there is no doubt . . . that the postwar decade of the twenties opened more possibilities in the American arts and broke up more social and moral pressures than any comparable period of ten years."[52] And anticapitalism among twenties expatriates was blithely played down. For Princeton's Willard Thorp, American writers who fled to Europe "were not so much fleeing from an America in whose values, or lack of values, they could no longer believe, as searching for a new faith."[53] Edward Dahlberg mocked such views, which, he felt, seemed to imply that after the heyday of expatriation came a period of parallel linguistic and social retrenchment. "Originally [these alienated writers] had fled from trade and congealed academic stupidity to be free, deracinated writers in Paris," Dahlberg wrote in 1952, "Then they returned to America crying out, 'God is dead! Long live grammar!'"[54]

In reviews of and advertisements for the *Exile's Return* for the 1950s, one could almost hear the collective sigh—relief that even Cowley was repudiating the stringent view of the 1920s he had held in the 1930s. After "the bewildering ferment" of earlier decades and Cowley's friendships with the "truculently articulate" writers of the time, Lewis Leary observed,[55] here finally was a book of "fresh significance" because twenty years later it has been framed by a new "mellowed, reminiscent tone." Viking's ad in the *New York Times Book Review* cooed that Cowley had "rounded out" the story.[56] Arthur Mizener observed that the book had "improved with age"—by which he meant that our changed perspective had improved it. It was now possible to see Cowley's modernist exiles, once deemed heretical, as providing "our image of the good American."[57] Our literary exiles could *finally* truly come home. Home was the alternative to suicide—and also what Spiller, in an antimodernist moment, called "the meaningless ritual of their new religion of art"[58] (referring specifically to Dadaism). The once upstart experimentalists could now discover, instead of disaffection in 1934, acceptance in the 1951 remake of '34. By one of its chief original proponents, modernism had been rescued from the "grim realism of the 30's," in the phrase of *Commentary*'s anticommunist editors.[59]

Joseph Warren Beach's dissent from this totalizing view is not remarkable only for having been the first such to appear, the first to link the antipoliticism of the favorable critical response to the 1951 version to the general critical rehabilitation of the 1920s in the 1950s. It is also noteworthy because it brought the otherwise modest Beach closest to the point of demanding the anti-anticommunist interpretive assumption that operates eccentrically throughout his book. It was crucial, Beach noted first, to distinguish between the two editions of *Exile's Return*. While in 1951 Cowley did have the advantage of the longer view, nonetheless the "later version loses point in comparison with the earlier." The communist ending to the story of modernist expatriation just prior to the Depression was "historically and theoretically a matter of great significance" generally and to the study of poetic exilism, Beach felt. The communist had keenly understood a social aspect of modernism: why the "religion of art" had failed American modernists. "Like love-making and other forms of dissipation, [modern art alone] did not satisfy the craving for integration with something larger than the individual himself." The concept of collectivity functioned throughout *Exile's Return*, but the new Cold War ending concluded on a note

that while not quite *false* in 1951 nonetheless misread, for instance, the power of
the story of wild Harry Crosby, the intellectual lightweight, "symbolist epi-
gone," who, lacking the integrative social-aesthetic force Cowley could have
offered him in 1934, created in dissipation a fanciful personal mythology that
aesthetically justified useless suicide. "Crosby tried to live art," the ex-radical
Jack Wheelwright remembered, "rather than . . . to live for art."[60] In 1951 the
Crosby tragedy remained in Cowley's book. But now excised was the final word
given to the key idea of 1934: the capitalist class, despite having permitted the
rise of the modernist cult of art, as—in Wallace Stevens, Ezra Pound, and H.D.,
for example—a post-Christian successor to religion, had had no way of saving a
socially alienated fringe figure such as Crosby.[61] (And no mention was made of
Crosby's involvement, as a charter member, of the Rebel Poet Society, which
published one of the John Reed Club–affiliated magazines on the "proletarian-
didactic" side of the left literary spectrum, or of the fact that Crosby's poems
were included in the society's annuals, titled *Unrest*.)[62] The culturally "insoluble
self-contradictions" that lead to war, the communist Cowley had written, included the destruction of books, universities, museums, public intellectuals.
These conclusions "were in 1934 necessary to [Cowley's] solution of the problem of the exiles. . . . Their best hope then," Beach argued, "was to throw in their
lot with the workers." Beach's radical line on Cowley's revised reading of Crosby's alienation was precisely the approach taken by the communist poet Richard Davidson to comprehend the poetic fate of Hart Crane in "Death of a Poet,"
a poem Davidson published in *Mainstream*:

> Killed by indifferent firesides at home,
> Killed by empty mouths and roaring tongues.
> He came and went and there was no reply.[63]

Unlike Davidson, Beach was not endorsing "the Soviet type of socialism"
through this leftist reading of modernist expatriation, and Beach conceded that
some degree of anti-Stalinism was the reason why "in all sincerity" Cowley
made his revised version. But during the 1930s, these writers, among them
many of the poets whose work in *Obsessive Images* Beach reads seriously and
sympathetically, were not wrong or foolish then to seek their integration in
social-cultural collectivity.

Beach knew that his reading of Cowley went politically against the grain of
the 1950s. There had been silence on this matter, and he knew that to some
degree he was breaking it. After describing his preference for Cowley's 1934
version and quoting strong words about the inevitability of class conflict, Beach
wrote about the political process of canonical repression and recovery in the

1950s: "Well, whatever truth there may be in [Cowley's 1934 thesis], these are words that one no longer sets down in print in the United States; and they certainly do not represent the official point of view of our 'working class.' " And so as Beach turned back to poets nearly forgotten in the 1950s, he indicated even more strongly that in the radical version of the book, "Cowley was not suggesting that artists should turn to propaganda for their salvation." Cowley himself could not let such a view stand. His revisions were "*inevitable*," yet paradoxically, they "did *of necessity* weaken his book." The conclusion was that the fifties' thirties defied textual or internal literary logic by imposing contemporary "inevitabilities" from the temporal outside—a telling reversal of the usual charge against political poetry.[64]

Beach's dissent from Cowley's 1951 attempt to separate himself from 1934 makes it possible to see rare difference in the poetry of Alfred Hayes. In Hayes's 1950 book, a twitchy lyric in irregular trimeter, "After All These Years," refuses the midcentury construction of the Red Decade. Remembering when he "longed to hurl . . . the venomous on the smug" as the rich on the poor, the speaker feels his "acquired shrug" of the antipolitical present gives way to "the old familiar muscle" of the heretic, which "starts to twitch."[65] In "—As a Young Man," a wartime speaker recalls the image of himself in 1934, beginning,

> This portrait was taken when
> I was twenty-five
> Nineteen thirty-four
> A decade or so ago
> Before the present war. . . .
> The face that I was then
> Had a world of its own:
> The world of the private hurt
> And the disappointment known
> When one is twenty-five
> And imagines one is alone.
> But who remembers now
> The volunteer in Spain?
> Or how the minors stood
> Sullen and angry men
> In Lawrenceville in the rain?

In light of Cowley's construction of a fifties' thirties, this is temporally (although not otherwise) a complex poem. The current threat is actual and the thirties a time "Before the threat . . . / Was as real as it is now." The contemporary regret—that we will forget the "premature" antifascist who fought in the Spanish Civil War—does not mean that that period was a time of social consciousness while "now" is a time of political impoverishment. It was *then* that one romanticized—felt alone. This is a personal poem about the political period enduring its demise, cast in easy-seeming, freely flowing, enjambed, three-stressed lines (one hardly notices the rhymes). The perfect foil to Cowley, for Beach's purposes, Hayes's midcentury anti-anticommunism comes in verse that formally thematizes the rejection of the separation of modernism and leftism in the act of refusing the distinction between the "personal" and the "political"—between "the girls who knew Matisse" and "the girls who talked of Marx." Given the poem's geopolitical references to war, the idiomatic sense of the phrase "the talks" would seem to suggest political negotiation—the suing for peace—but again intellectual and personal (coming-of-age) excitements collide in recollection:

The talks that would begin
Under a hooded light
The curtains blowing in
The girls who knew Matisse
The girls who talked of Marx
And universal peace.[66]

Had Joseph Warren Beach not held onto his beloved book manuscript for so long past its due point[67]—had it appeared in the mid-1950s, when it was more or less complete—his relatively bold presentation of 1930s poetry might have had sufficient force or at least might have gotten some rejoinder from the thirties-bashers. Published finally in 1960, three years posthumously, it made little immediate impact.[68]

CHAPTER 5

The Proletarians & the Revolvers of the Word were right—
not the cottonbelt reactionaries.—Kenneth Rexroth

An Underground of the Unpublishable

Many cultural critics among anticommunist liberals theorized against the creation of oppositions, preferring consensus. Others who did make sharp distinctions (such as between and among choices of public policy) could be suspected of leading the camel's nose of treason under the tent of traditional American tolerance. The end of systemic disagreement betold the final repudiation not just of a certain political position but indeed of positionality.

This longed-for end of ideology meant the abatement of political difference and diminution of those who "took sides" in every conflict between aesthetic cultures. Most centrists were distinct from conservatives in this regard. If Americans were to focus on the culture against which the United States should clearly draw its own boundaries (the Soviet and Soviet satellite culture; the communist aesthetic in all its imagined and also its very real manifestations), then American culture makers would have to resist the temptation to create unnecessary oppositions *within* the West. T. R. Fyvel's essay, "Reflections on Manifest Destiny" (1952), gave readers the sense that it was as important not to exacerbate antitheses between the American and French ways of life as it was to keep up the contrariety between American and Soviet cultures. "While Coca-Cola is being advertised all over France," Fyvel wrote, "the French wine industry will naturally join the French anti-American chorus."

But here was the problem: the same argument held that imposing Coca-Cola on France—or exporting American anticommunist films even as "European film makers will regard [Hollywood] as the opposition"—was preconditioned by Americans' acceptance of their apparent postwar role as world arbiters of "modern" taste. "Such facts may be unpleasant," Fyvel noted, "but they are only aspects of the American imperial position, and as such not to be bemoaned, as some American observers tend to do, but to be studied, evaluated, and coped with—if possible."[1] Liberal anticommunists were also thus in the business of a celebratory cultural studies, interpreting pop along with high culture forms through the focus of U.S. imperialism.

Yet these liberal intellectuals were generally working out arguments *against* the growing influence of American popular culture, fearing that very influence, a power undermining the finest art a nation can offer others, as indeed a form of communist style, not its opposite. The cultural studies project proposed by some anticommunist advocates of the power of American popular culture as a stay against communist influence in Europe—a view embraced by the State Department and even the CIA[2]—was never generally accepted enough beyond its status as a hearts-and-minds-winning Cold War practical strategy as to receive theoretical standing. Thus, most promulgators of the strategy never got past this contradiction.

A month after Fyvel's piece appeared in the *New Republic*, the literary critic David Daiches published a commentary there on "American Culture in Britain." It is of a piece with Fyvel's. Daiches lamented not just that the term "chips" was giving way in London to "French fries." More distressingly, a "debased kind of American culture" was being "used so freely for export" and adopted by many British youth. The export was to be interpreted as a cultural debasement rather than, Daiches lamented, an American intellectual infiltration purer and more pleasurable and tolerable—something rather from "Jefferson's America or Lincoln's America or Whitman's America or even Carl Sandburg's America." But these latter forms of American "visions [are] wholly unknown" to the British kids lunching on French fries and taking the American aesthetic to entail "toughness, breeziness, cocksureness." To be certain, Daiches complained that "Europe is gradually being reduced to a low colonial status *vis-à-vis* America," but he did not say whether the complaint would remain valid if the American invasion were being backed by the cultural manifestations of Jefferson, Lincoln, Sandburg, or Whitman. Daiches worried that Americans might not be aware that they were being "misrepresented" and thus himself apparently did not worry whether a Jeffersonian or Whitmanian image would also constitute a misrepresentation and an imposition.[3]

After serving three years as second secretary at the tumultuous wartime and postwar British embassy in Washington, often interpreting British foreign policy for the Americans in Washington, David Daiches (1912–2005) was appointed professor of English at Cornell University, quickly becoming chair of the literature division. In 1948, as he became chair, Cornell's press brought out his *A Study of Literature for Readers and Critics*, a textbook widely adopted by instructors at America's burgeoning colleges and universities. He rapidly had become one of the era's sought-after cultural commentators, perhaps partly because of his ambassadorial savvy and surely also because he seemed unaligned with any of the various warring camps—although Peter Viereck was convinced that Daiches aligned with *him* (among the New Conservative "independent

Third Forcers" who were not "Eliotine adversaries" but opposed both modern-ism and communism).[4] In January 1955, Daiches traveled to Washington to help kick off the celebration of the hundredth anniversary of the publication of Whitman's *Leaves of Grass*, part of a yearlong series of events that the young Hugh Kenner deemed "oddly dispirited."[5] Why?

Three strong currents of Whitmanism flowed (roughly speaking) from left, center, and right. Left: on the day a century after Whitman published his unconventional book—July 4, 1955—the *Daily Worker* printed an anthology of his poems, including "Away with Themes of War!" and "For You O Democ-racy": "Come, I will make the continent indissoluble . . . / With the love of comrades."[6] Center: in the Coolidge Auditorium at the Library of Congress, where it was recorded for the "Archive of Recorded Poetry and Literature," Daiches gave a talk on Whitman's philosophy with the tempered ambition of correcting Americans' representations of Whitman.[7] Right: Conservatives in the poetry world (for example, the editor of *Wings* magazine) greeted books such as Leadie M. Clark's *Walt Whitman's Concept of the American Common Man* with expressions of disgust at "the deification of Whitman that has be-come more a matter of religious faith than of literary criticism" and with demands that Whitman "no longer be apotheosized as the poet of democracy [or] the poet of the common man."[8]

The official anniversary occasioned a display of Walt Whitman amenable to cold war—a nationalistic Whitman, a deradicalized Whitman, a Whitman whose language was not to be deemed revolutionary or whose language, as a poetics, was not really important at all. "I can imagine some of the [centennial celebrants] even thinking, 'It does not matter *how* he writes, but *what* he writes,' " one bemused poet wrote privately in his notebook.[9] Observers would hardly know, witnessing at least the public events, that Whitman in 1955 was the same poet who had said, "I sometimes think the 'Leaves' is only a language experiment."[10] A few dissenters grumbled, Hugh Kenner among them. If one got "to the very heart of the Whitman cult as it is at present administered," Kenner said as he prepared an essay after reading six centennial books, one saw that "its gambit is to restore the poet without attending to the verse."[11] Wit-tingly or not, Daiches joined the national administration of the 1950s Whitman, keeping in mind a sober concern for what the poet's writing, if properly under-stood, could productively add to the reputation of American culture in Europe.

As in his *New Republic* piece, Daiches in Washington did not mention that communism pervaded the critical background, yet it was his animus. If in one essay he worried that American culture failed to educate British youth—that it failed to do more for them than imbue cocksureness and a breezy tone—then in both pieces he was expressing the concern that other forces would prevail and that the postwar war for men's minds might after all be lost. The main failure was humanists' effort to prove to peoples of wavering democracies that art was ennobling. Implicitly, Daiches went to Washington to redress the image of Whitman as a radical socialist, an image that had flourished in the 1930s.[12] The deradicalization of Whitman befit Daiches's more general critical aspirations to "simplify" poetry through a responsible literary history of modern verse. In this reversal, Daiches could characterize the "histrionic doubling" of radical visionaries as overcomplicated while commending what happened to poetry in his own age, a time when "the hail" of bardic histrionics finally "became a whisper." This was, he felt, not such a bad thing. These phrases come from a poem Daiches published in *Poetry* at the end of this period, "Notes for a History of Poetry" (1961):

Absurdity was troubling:
See now the poet's task:
Leave histrionic doubling
To don a simpler mask.
Winds of the world were nipping;
The bardic robe was slipping.[13]

The centenarian Whitman in Washington donned just such a "simpler mask." Where Whitman had been accused of "putting the average man on a pedestal," in fact, claimed Daiches, he had actually "had no such idea in his head." Whitman had meant that "real human greatness" was independent of social position or formal education. Fair enough. The evil alternative Daiches cast was not (allegedly) leftist—not communist or even populist; it was rather the leveling and mediocrity of contemporary middle-class democracy. The bardic robe was slipping. The simpler mask was "normalcy," but actually it was not so simple despite the absence of histrionics. The equivalence of the error of seeing Whitman as having put "the average man on a pedestal" was not what Samuel Sillen and other communist interpreters of Whitman's radicalism claimed, but the mindless egalitarianism of "modern advertising which suggests that because more people are buying x or y then *you* will naturally want to buy it."[14] The Whitman Daiches alleged had been misconstrued as a radical in the 1930s was "the precursor of those opinion-seekers and pollsters who search after a statistical norm and then idolize it as the typical American." Whitman helped stem the tide of low-cultural American hegemony in Europe only if Americans understood their Whitman in the context of "political democracy" that could reverse the "greatness" of some and not all.

Walt Whitman in 1955 was certainly *not* the prophet of "the average" person. So it was declared that the centennial of *Leaves of Grass* marked the moment—celebrated it, really—when the political interpretation of Whitman was properly at a dead end.[15] This centrist view differed little from that promoted by intellectual conservatives of the time. *Lament for a Generation*, Ralph de Toledano's magnificently written memoir of his experience working his "way through the underbrush of the Right" in the 1940s and 1950s, summarized the conservative reading of Whitman: he was "a mediocre poet" proffering "an uncoordinated and double-jointed *mystique* of the common man, sexual in its palpitancy and Priapic in its celebration of democracy."[16] Richard Chase, in *Commentary*, went beyond disputing the radical reading of Whitman's poetry; he expressed amazement that such a reading had ever arisen. "The political radicalism of the 1930's enlisted Whitman in its cause," Chase wrote, but he wondered "how Whitman . . . could ever have been taken as a proletarian and revolutionary." The key to Chase's view was his conception of what it meant to be an "American spokesman": not to stand with definiteness but to evade any imposition. Whitman is a great poet, and typically American, because "he resists the identities he seems to invite."[17] This was not really so far from reactionary views of Whitman such as that of E. Merrill Root, for whom the poet "sought the inner kingdom" and had "nothing in common with institutions." As a poet and anticommunist, Root had learned from Whitman to discount the "fashionable virtue-word 'democracy,'" and to discredit those who "set the 'people's' outer good before man's intrinsic best."[18] In his book-length jeremiad against left-wing political correctness at the universities, *Collectivism on the Campus* (1955), Root invoked Whitman's great "cause" ("To thee, old Cause! / Thou peerless, passionate, good cause") in service of an urgent new conservative objective: the exposure of leftist brainwashers in the "war for the mind of the colleges." Root's Whitman stood for "the continuance of America's great tradition of liberty."[19]

Detractors of the radical Whitman realized the ascendancy of this view as clearly as his supporters. Samuel Sillen understood that at a time when the manuscripts of many heretical writers were "being rejected automatically by publishers and editors, not because of a deficiency of literary quality, but because they have dared being critical of prevailing political and cultural reaction," critics saw no connection to the Whitman who had to publish *Leaves of Grass* independently.[20] Some on the left went so far as to call this a "cold pogrom."[21] In the *Sunday Worker*, David Platt urged his readers to recognize the very few poets of the time—this was 1953—who followed in the tradition of poets such as Whitman who had joined "the fight against Negro slavery" and had "brav[ed] the McCarthyites of [his] day."[22] Leo Marx reported from the University of Minnesota that his students "like only exceptional Whitman poems, the more inward and strained lyrics." He could not "get them to see anything in writers who make strong statements. . . . Apparently it is Whitman's public commitments that seem embarrassingly naïve."[23] "The knowing quarterlies didn't have [Whitman] over socially," Ray Smith wrote in *Approach* in November 1955.[24] In 1954, the Library of Congress had recruited *Poetry* to run a special Whitman issue—and the editors planned to ask for statements from Robert Frost, Allen Tate, Wallace Stevens, Marianne Moore, Richard Wilbur, John Ciardi, Robert Lowell, Louise Bogan, Andre Breton, Paul Claudel, and Robert Graves, among others. This was to have been "a truly international" tribute, according to internal memos, but, interestingly, no Spaniard or Russian (or, for that matter, Italian) poet made the long list, even though Spanish antifascists, Soviets, and British communists,[25] for better or worse, were the world's most explicit Whitmanians of the moment (prior to the public emergence, a year or so later, of Allen Ginsberg). The plan for a Whitman centennial issue flopped because of a lack of interest inside *Poetry* and the tepid response the editors received from the few poets they contacted.[26]

At the University of Michigan, where he spent a year in graduate study and "draft evasion" (at the time of Korea), Jerome Rothenberg, later a Deep Image poet and advocate of a progressive international ethnopoetics, found himself "a lone defender of Walt Whitman." Rothenberg was seeking "the rebirth or reawakening of a radical modernism," as he put it, but he would not find it wherever the option of Whitman was refused, and Rothenberg founded his own heretical poetics on this conservative negative.[27] Harold Norse, the gay Beat poet who served as W. H. Auden's secretary in the late 1930s and who as a Brooklyn College student sporadically participated in radical activities, found midcentury verse "cold" and "bloodless" and craved an alternative, yet he knew the consequences of turning toward the Whitmanian mode. "In the forties and fifties," Norse later recalled, "mentioning Walt Whitman was heresy." (Norse finally chose to brave charges of heresy, and Whitman cleared for him a path straight to William Carlos Williams's door in Rutherford, New Jersey, a familiar destination for many radical poets who were attracted to experimental technique. Rothenberg too found Williams through Whitman.)[28]

Karl Shapiro, to his dismay, discovered Whitman's undying attractiveness to the left when he accepted the invitation by the State Department to teach in India. Shapiro was "in a fix," trying to find something about American poetry the discussion of which radical Indian students would tolerate, and "after fencing with Hindu leftists . . . for two months I gave up. Fortunately there was Walt

Whitman to fall back on." The Indian left loved Whitman.[29] E. Merrill Root, as we have seen, assailed liberal-left assumptions that Whitman wanted anything to do with organizations or with "the 'people's' outer good"; on the contrary, Whitman sought "absolutes of meaning" and should be invoked in the argument against "relativities, public utilities," and other "modern American delusions."[30] Kenneth Rexroth bitterly noted the absence at the Washington centennial not so much of poets but of *poetry* celebrating Whitman. The ideological dilution of Whitman was part of the McCarthyite reaction. Whitmanian poetry to honor Whitman? "No soap," Rexroth wrote Cowley. "They want to hear what Marse Allen [Tate] and Cunt Ransom say . . . —and no one else. These are the years of the Literary Black Hundreds."[31]

Leslie Fiedler's Whitman was an even stronger anticommunist than Daiches's and really just as extreme as anything Rexroth rudely predicted for Cowley. Fiedler, a former Young Communist League member who had repented in the early 1940s, accused the left of having turned Whitman "willy-nilly into a dangerous poet, a revolutionary." In "Images of Walt Whitman," Fiedler claimed to be surveying various of the poet's posthumous avatars, but he held his fire until he reached the story of Whitman's strong aesthetic and formal influence on American radicals of the 1930s. Such writers ignored the "facts" of Whitman's life (facts that were hardly—*are* hardly—confirmed). "Walt's Communist kidnappers"[32] foolishly ignored the "fact" that Whitman supported capitalism, that he hated unions, that he had little response to socialist advocates of his day. Never in the 1950s was Whitman quoted as having said, "Without yielding an inch the working-man and working-woman were to be in my pages from first to last"— but it was well known that he had said it[33] and that, as communist poet Samuel Sillen pointed out, he had warned writers "against the moral atrophy resulting from the 'depravity of the business classes.' "[34] As for capitalism, Fiedler had to admit that Whitman's support was qualified by "cagey reservations"[35] (just as Shapiro, stationed in India by the State Department, knew that you could offer the local Whitmanians "Whitman [a]s good American propaganda—unless you accidentally run into a Whitman expert").[36]

Despite the predilection against drawing lines, despite the "end of ideology," new lines were being clearly drawn. The argument about Whitman's socialism sometimes brazenly (but more often temperately) made by F. O. Matthiessen— or that implied by Stephen Vincent Benét's poem "Ode to Walt Whitman" set against the background of the Depression,[37] or in a beautiful, dispassionate assessment of Whitman's politics by Newton Arvin in 1938[38]—was losing the day. Whitman had really said to Horace Traubel, "I think of art as something to serve the people—the mass," Ray Smith noted in an essay that imagined a look back at the Whitman centennial from the year 2055. "The figures in the foreground of the American cultural picture in 1955," Smith continued, "never talked like that, but Whitman did." Smith predicted that "till the late 1960s" Whitman's influence would only be "latent." In the meantime, he saw in the Whitman centennial a clear "attempt to foreclose substantial meanings in American life [including] the stigmatizing of everything progressive as 'creeping socialism.' "[39] Matthiessen himself was of course gone—dead by suicide—by the time Fiedler finally buried the leftist Whitman; Matthiessen, anyway, had always skirted the possible connection between Whitman's homosexuality and his socialism, and this perhaps made it simpler for Fiedler to mock Whitman's encounter with a "beautiful young" socialist. (Fiedler aspired not at all to evidence here, depending—as elsewhere in his work of the early 1950s—on assumptions of homosexuality's antipolitical pathology. "After his one long interview with a Socialist proselytizer," Fiedler wrote, Whitman did not respond politically, rather murmuring, "What a beautiful young man!")[40]

In "The Education of a Socialist," which the radical *Monthly Review* published in 1950 in its Matthiessen memorial number, the doomed reading of Whitman's radical individualism got one last hearing: Whitman believed as Lenin did later in "the right of all to share in the common wealth." Whitman had begun to see that people in "a democracy should be both free *and* equal." Matthiessen wrote that Whitman "wanted nothing unless everyone else could have it on the same terms," and from the time of the great national strike of 1877 the poet moved "steadily, if by no straight course, towards socialism."[41] But the facts of Whitman's actual politics were finally of little consequence in the effort to deradicalize the powerful Whitmanian tradition in American poetry. With or without respect owed to the deceased author of *American Renaissance*, Leslie Fiedler was less interested in eliminating Matthiessen's political argument, revived through the radical left *Monthly Review*—whose editorial independence from American communists was largely assured[42]—than he was in making what amounts to a conservative aesthetic contention about poetics, a contention that was, I would aver, more devastating to the Whitmanian elements in the emergent disruptive American poetry than any political counterclaim ever was. R. W. B. Lewis's assessment of Whitman's language in the influential book *The American Adam* (published during the Whitman centennial) was that the poet is often "*telling* us too much": the more he tells us, the more we sense his anxiety, the "inflated utterance of a charlatan." The American response to such poetic explicitness is precisely the same as the response described (and mostly urged) by the end-of-ideologists: "We cling to our own integrity and we will not be thundered at."[43] Finding our inner American resources, we naturally resist Whitman's poetry in just the way we fend off ideology itself. Poets who do not work by implication deserve the same American response that we give anyone who presents us with "frontal assaults"—after which we, not he, retain integrity.

Fiedler's Cold War construction of the communists' Whitman is a poet who did not liberate the poetic line—did not break free of stultifying rhythmic and metrical Victorianism, did not really bring into poetic language the everyday and most certainly did not use the dogmatic, didactic, or propagandistic as a poetic element. (Yet in fact Whitman's ability to integrate dogmatism and experimental prosody would be his continuing attraction to the avant-garde in the last few decades of the twentieth century.) This particular charge against Whitman was almost certainly also a swipe at William Carlos Williams, whose praise for Whitman's innovative poetics (he "broke through the copied forms" of nineteenth-century poetry) coincided with his celebration of Whitman's affirmation of frank "propaganda" in verse. Later, in what I interpret as an almost desperate effort to revive the integrated left populism and modernism of Williams after these categories also had been separated by that poet's 1950s critics, M. L. Rosenthal quoted Williams on Whitman: "The structure of the old [traditional forms] is active, it says no! to everything in propaganda and poetry that wants to say yes. Whitman," Williams wrote, "broke through all that."[44]

Yet Fiedler saw no innovative aesthetic force arising out of Whitmanism. For him, the CPUSA's American bard should be likened to a bad translation: Whitman came to proletarian poets in the United States from *German* and other Middle European communist parties, like some thirdhand translation of Mayakovski. This trope aided Fiedler's characterization of the Whitman who influenced the poetic language of Ben Maddow (1909–92), for instance, by making the poetry seem like a false Americanism: a bad Soviet reproduction of an American original, secretly passed along by the Germans. This was the Whitman "practiced with fervor and *imprecision* in the darker 'thirties." Maddow's "Red Decision" was a poem, Fiedler alleged, modeled on this crude communist imitativeness: "Broad-hearted Whitman of the healthy beard / stiffen my infirm palate for this bread." But Maddow's poem is not formally Whitmanian in the least and was a poor instance of Fiedler's point. Using this poem as an example of Whitman-influenced communist poetry that "must stand for all the rest,"[45] Fiedler mistook the thematizing of Whitman in the poem for the actual influence Whitman's free verse exerted on modern poetry by leftists. It was an obvious aesthetic commie straw man. Had he cited Richard Wright's "I Have Seen Black Hands" (1933)—

I am black and I have seen black hands, millions and millions of them—
They were tired and awkward and calloused and grimy. . . .
And they piled higher and higher the steel, iron, the lumber, wheat, rye, the
    oats, corn, the cotton, the wool, the oil, the coal, the meat, the fruit, the
    glass, and the stone until there was too much to be used[46]

—he would have been offering his readers a more contentious example. Or
Leonard Spier's "Alien? Who Is Alien?" from Spier's book *You Own the Hills*
(1935), a poem of "satisfying breath" in the mode of a Whitman "chant."[47] Or Sol
Funaroff's "What the Thunder Said" (1938), which openly merged Eliotic modernism, Whitmanian ecstatic rhythm, and sectarian American communism. Or
Kenneth Patchen's "Joe Hill Listens to the Praying" (1934),[48] with its rough,
capacious Americanism ("From Kansas to the coast, wrapped / round brake
beams on a thousand / freights; / San Joaquin and Omaha / brush under the
wheels . . . / we've been / everywhere, seen everything")[49] disrupted by the
interlineation of bits of chanted conversation and slogans. And why not Lola
Ridge's "Stone Face" (1935), a Whitmanian direct address to a heretical hero
(Tom Mooney)?[50] Or Louise Jeffers's "My Thoughts Are Free" (1952), with its
repeated line beginnings?[51] Or Frank Marshall Davis's "War Quiz for America"
(1944), a poem in eight first-person voices exploring the generous racial and geo-
economic range of the American spirit.[52] Or known of Edwin Rolfe's new self-
critical "Catalogue of I" (1955), an exploration of the difficult political relationship between radical subjectivity and lists,[53] or of young Allen Ginsberg's visions
of a Whitman who "cried tears in Communist champagne glass."[54] If Leslie
Fiedler had really intended to survey the radical Whitman, he would have found
inscribed in that writing some basic lessons of American modernism. Concluding, rather, that "Whitman is an almost impossible muse,"[55] contrary to evidence
already available in the new ecstatic poets of San Francisco and New York writing
just when he was writing—including Ginsberg, who counted the fellow-traveling
Ben Maddow among his allies and mentors[56]—Fiedler went to great lengths to
show why the Marxists' "almost uncontested possession of the figure of Whitman" was unredeemably bad.[57]

Celebrating the triumphant American Whitman in Washington,[58] David
Daiches was claiming that the poet's political philosophy did not indicate democracy as an ideal collectivity. Rather, "political democracy makes it possible
for each individual to fulfill his own personality, to realize fully his free self."
Never mind the masses in Whitman's verse. This was a radicalism of the individual.[59] And in this sense Whitman's politics provided "a definition of his own kind
of poetry, *which is the new American poetry*."[60] So here, emphatically, in the

American capital, was announced a "new American poetry" that traced its lineage from a Walt Whitman who abhorred mass culture and had nothing to do with the attitude of cocksure certainty typifying the American Century. That's what the new American poetry was going to be. What it was *not*, Daiches had already described at some length during the war in his "comprehensive" history of modern verse, *Poetry and the Modern World*. But the conclusion was the same as stated in the positive. Whatever it was, the new poetry would not be like that of the 1930s. Two of this book's chapters on the poetry of the 1930s followed an uncritical chapter on imagism. Imagism had been naively erring in its tactics, charmingly and energetically wrongheaded for setting up unfollowable theories and ideals but good in its overall effect: "to keep English poetry from perishing from looseness and thin eclecticism"—a "tightening of the belt," in Daiches's economic trope of temperateness and sobriety. The first modernist movement in verse was admirably "narrow," understood the power of its "limitation,"[61] really knew the beauty of confinement. Did it have a strong connection to or parallel existence with the national disintegrations that led to World War I? Not in *Poetry and the Modern World*. One wonders where really was the modern world promised in Daiches's title. If anything, the origins of imagism in T. E. Hulme's cultural conservatism, the protest against romanticism, cosmic naturalism, bardic humanism, and utopianism are more important than the fragmenting social and political forces of emerging martial and technical modern life. As for imagism's mistaken attempts to rise again after its time, Richard Aldington's unfortunate nostalgia for the movement long after its moment had passed—for the *Imagist Anthology* of 1930—was to Daiches a quaint, understandable error in poetic judgment.[62] (Any such nostalgia for belated 1930s-style poetry that would animate art after 1945, Daiches more passionately repudiated.)

Daiches's two chapters on the 1930s dealt exclusively with British poets. And yet, whereas the chapter on imagism surveyed many poets (including some quite minor figures), in the 1930s section revolutionary poetry was represented exclusively by Auden, Stephen Spender, and Cecil Day Lewis. Wide-ranging references in the chapter on the 1910s and 1920s to John Freeman, Wilfred Wilson Gibson, Francis Ledwidge, T. E. Hulme himself, the American John Gould Fletcher, Richard Aldington, F. S. Flint, Amy Lowell, Nancy Cunard, Osbert Sitwell, and the 1920s satirist Humbert Wolfe created a sense of the texture and variety of the cult of the New—compared to a spareness in the two chapters on the left-wing poetry of the 1930s, which lacked any reference whatever to Geoffrey Grigson, Michael Roberts, Hugh MacDiarmid, Tom Wintringham, J. F. Horrabin, David Gascoyne, W. G. Golding, Winifred Holtby, Charles Madge, or William Plomer. Day Lewis's rapid disillusionment with radicalism must stand for half the revolutionary impulse among poets in the period when, while Eliot became crustily theological and Yeats patiently "waited for the phases of the moon to bring about the next phase in civilization," many, many poets—surely the majority of all those publishing verse—had turned significantly leftward.

By focusing on Day Lewis, Daiches managed to look back to 1936 as if it had been a time when already modern poetry was inscribed with "bitter foreboding" about what communism and fellow traveling might mean.[63] Such a move is made possible by the focus on a few prominent early adopters and quick disillusionists; this strategy situated Daiches's observations at the start of the postradical period. Of all versions of the erasure of the 1930s, this one was just about the soonest and neatest. Its sort of restrictive periodizing enabled the long, genial, ideologically omniscient view. Daiches could seem sympathetic, because at a little distance from a literary radicalism that he invented by marking an end of the radical poetry era at the mid-1930s, the whole problem faced by Day Lewis could be made to seem representative yet freakish, going along with "the naivete of the convert" and a "new-found attitude."[64] The latter phrase was a dull euphemism for radicalization. Daiches admitted that "to conceive of [the communist poets] as writing propaganda poetry to advocate remedies is grossly to simplify and to misunderstand their whole position," but he then did nothing to convey the setting or historical or political context that would make such counterunderstanding possible.[65] Neither Daiches nor Babette Deutsch in her later *Poetry in Our Time* (1952) gave credence to the mixture of radicalism and unconventional language in some communist poetry of the Auden group. Deutsch in fact went out of her way to find motives for line-by-line difficulty of some of Auden's poetry "*over and above* the abrupt syntax."

This represented a crucial antiexperimental and antiradical turn for Babette Deutsch,[66] who had briefly, years earlier, been aligned with American communist poets.[67] Kenneth Rexroth generally admired *Poetry in Our Time* but saw precisely how and why Deutsch was making her rightward move, and he wrote her a long personal letter about it soon after the book appeared. He scoffed at the notion of Auden as offering an instance of difficult language. To treat Auden mistakenly like "some wild incomprehensible 'modernist' like [Tristan] Tzara" Rexroth found part of the general pattern of midcentury efforts (he meant Deutsch's too, of course) to forget or conspire to repress both radical left poets of the 1930s *and* Revolutionists of the Word from the 1920s.

Rexroth found two kinds of "omissions." Because the book "purport[ed] to be historical," *Poetry in Our Time* showed political bias in leaving out completely the left poets of the 1930s. He mentioned Joy Davidman, Lola Ridge, Sol

Funaroff, Henry Potamkin, good poets among "hundreds" she might have mentioned. Most of what they produced the anti-Stalinist anarchist Rexroth found "no good. No *good at all*. But here and there is something. Don Gordon. Kenneth Patchen." Patchen was a special problem for contemporary poetry histories—always a radical but only briefly procommunist, a mystic, a maker of concrete and sound poems. Nonetheless, Deutsch was obliged at least to evaluate Patchen and the other hard-to-categorize heretics. The other category of omission was the avant-garde. "The Revolution of the Word was once a power in the land," wrote Rexroth. How could it be so completely ignored in a history of modern poetry? Where was mention, at least, of Charles Henri Ford, that adamant surrealist? In his published review of *Poetry in Our Time*, for the *New York Herald Tribune* Sunday Books section, Rexroth offered a milder version of this critique but chided Deutsch for knowing better about social poetry—she "never lets on that she knows that Sandburg's poetry lies in a region Back of the Yards where angels of the Higher Criticism could never dare to tread"—and added more names of leftists and modernists she should have included: Parker Tyler, Louis Zukofsky, Eugene Jolas, and Norman Macleod. This was a knowing selection: Tyler, Zukofsky, and Macleod, the first two certifiable Revolutionists of the Word and the third, a definite left-winger (editor of *Front*, signer of the original call for the American Writers Congress, contributor to *New Masses*, director of the progressive Bronx section of the Federal Writers Project *Guide* to New York City).[68] All three defied the notion of separate political and aesthetic spheres.[69]

Why the twinning of omissions—leftist and modernist? Rexroth does not quite say in his private correspondence with Deutsch. He is indeed certain that the "Proletarians & the Revolvers of the Word were right—not the cottonbelt reactionaries." Why the failure? "Was it market? The utter impossibility of anything but conformists to get a voice?" Even though the anarchistic Rexroth was a passionate anticommunist (he clearly told Deutsch so), he faced the emerging antipolitical canonical shifts, as evident in Deutsch's new book, with a joined defense of modernist and communist poetics as crucially relevant to the history of poetry in the United States.[70]

Here, then, lies an answer to the question about the connection between, on one hand, the apparent suppression in mainstream midcentury literary histories of the two poetic revolutions and, on the other, the emergence of a digressive, longer-lined, nonnarrative, frankly unadjusted verse. At least it is helpful to think of this aspect in the version of a new heretical poetics Rexroth would just at this time begin to encourage in San Francisco: the anarchopacificist poets associated with the rise of Pacifica Radio and other groups; the gang that gathered around George Leite's politically radical and proexperimentalist *Circle*; for a time, the Robert Duncan–Jack Spicer–Robin Blaser group; and, of course, the early Beats. In relation to the story of poetry's development, it was crucial first to concede, however reluctantly and riskily, that "the New Masses was [in the 1930s] the largest & best edited publication of its kind outside Russia." Rexroth noted that "this"—the relative success of the *New Masses* as a little magazine, the rightful inheritor of *transition*—"puzzles me—because I agree w/the revolutionists—and not with Elizabeth Bishop or Lloyd Frankenberg." At this juncture in his letter to Deutsch, it was no longer clear whether Rexroth meant left-wingers or modernists when he used the term "revolutionists." My point is that it did not matter. He was writing about the related misreadings and suppressions of each at midcentury. "I sometimes think American poetry," he concluded, "is a sort of conspiracy . . . that there exists a sort of poetic underground of the unpublishable."[71]

Unorthodox defenders of the modernist Revolution of the Word fairly easily saw that neither the specific social, extrapoetic sources of what experimentalism there was in the political positions of the Auden-Spender tribe nor the specific linguistically heretical company they kept among contemporary poets both American and British were described in supposedly "comprehensive" "histories" of modern poetry by critics such as Deutsch and Daiches. Yet the sort of analysis emerging from Rexroth—why modernists and communists were ignored in a single gesture of consolidation—got almost no press and appeared only in scattered reviews and notices. The realignment of modernism and communism had to entail some kind of forgetting or smoothing over of the political crises of the 1930s that so completely interested poets as scattered across the modernism-communism spectrum as Walter Lowenfels, the just-mentioned Norman Macleod, George Oppen, Norman Rosten, Alfred Kreymborg, Genevieve Taggard, the imagist-communist Whittaker Chambers, Kimon Friar, Naomi Replansky, William Carlos Williams, the lumberman Joe Kalar, Eda Lou Walton, the surrealist Charles Henri Ford, John Malcolm Brinnin, Claude McKay, the superexperimental "disturber of the peace"[72] Kenneth Patchen, Carlos Bulosan, Louis Zukofsky, Ben Maddow, Lola Ridge, George Bratt, Gene Frumkin, Isidor Schneider, Frank Marshall Davis, the communitarian and concrete poet Bob Brown, Dorothy Van Ghent, Stanley Burnshaw, Charles Reznikoff, Alvaro Cardona-Hine, Martha Millet, George Hitchcock, Maxwell Bodenheim, Carl Rakosi, Waldo Frank, Edna Millay, and so on. If readers were to trust Daiches, then the conclusion about C. Day Lewis's relatively rapid disillusionment, for instance, was that it arose from a condition no more specific than "*the delay in getting things done*"—an astonishing circumlocution for the democracies' sluggish response to fascism.[73] (The word "fascism" does not appear once in either of Daiches's chapters on the 1930s.)

Of Auden and Spender in relation to the larger modernist radical context, *Poetry and the Modern World* concedes, in the last paragraph of the section, only with a terse statement that "there were other poets in the 1930s." Some, like Louis MacNeice, were "good poets" as well as radicals for a time, but they would not add "any new insights into the nature of modern poetry." That Daiches does not mention any of these names or generally describe their engagement with the way in which "aesthetic and political problems became very closely related" in the period these chapters were supposed to address results from what he believed the reader in the 1940s would need: "The main types of situation existing between the poet and the modern world [in the 1940s] have been indicated, and further discussion, though welcome to the writer, would weary the reader, for it would involve much repetition."[74]

Although Louise Bogan was never shy about lambasting radical poetry, she wrote of the 1930s with the same sense of impatience as Daiches in *Poetry and the Modern World* and from the same assumption about the American radical poets' destruction of the necessary "lively interest in their craft"[75] as Deutsch in *Poetry in Our Time*. Bogan's summing up of the place of modern poetry at midcentury was *Achievement in American Poetry, 1900–1950* (1951). Of the book's 111 pages of text, 10 were devoted to the entire period from 1930 to 1941. And of those 10 pages, 4 were devoted to Eliot (*Ash Wednesday* was published in 1930, thus barely making it into the period), Yeats (not American, of course), Pound, Joyce (well, the ban on *Ulysses* of 1922 was lifted in 1933), Tzara, Eluard, and a few others—to the "non-Marxian elements released into the creative stream of the times." But the tributary here rushed more vitally than the river. The justification for the imbalance—and, really, the eschewing of organizational logic—was that these merging elements "endured after Marxian piety had faded," thus implying from the start that the digression was going to be the main topic, that radical poetry was the subtext, an underlying pressure against the movement flowing from the real "postwar achievement" (which was the title of the previous chapter on the 1920s). Of the remaining 6 pages on the 1930s, a 3.5-page section stipulated that the period was *not* the Red Decade after all but rather a time "in which a variety of influences" operated and then offered the finally failed career of Hart Crane as a misguided acceptance of Eliot's "penetrating analysis of modern" ills. Had he lived a little longer, one vague implication was, Crane might have been influenced by "the decade's more rigorous formulations of Marxian theory and practice." And so it was possible for Bogan as a conservative modernist to interpret Crane's "efforts to absorb and acclimatize the machine into poetry" and to extract symbols from urban, mechanized culture—*and* his unhealthy assumption of Whitmanian optimism—as tainted, in effect, by the communism that *might* have affected him for the worse. That left 4 pages to explore the political poets of the left. But here Bogan treats Auden, Spender, and even MacNeice at length in a book whose author profiles are otherwise exclusively reserved for American poets. It seems that the titular purpose of exploring the *American* achievement in poetry, when it came to the 1930s, could be abandoned (without explanation). Only the transition back from MacNeice to American radical poets hints at the digression: "While" these fleetingly radical British poets, "in neat and telling stanzas, invented effective symbols" for the political problems of the day, "American poets settled down to an almost unbroken level of gloomy conviction and gloomier hope." This left exactly one paragraph, in which only Muriel Rukeyser and Kenneth Fearing were identified and succinctly (and negatively) assessed. Closing out the discussion of the 1930s, Archibald MacLeish receives more than a full page, he who embodied "the most dramatic and unexpected conversion to a political point of view." Yet the discussion is almost entirely about how MacLeish's writing was really not of the thirties: his first books belonged properly "to the aesthetic of the twenties"; his influences were among the French experimentalists (with no bearing on radicalism); he integrated Pound's method, Eliot's tone, and Hopkins's compression; he took a "firm stand" *against* poetry as propaganda. In a few sentences, we see MacLeish announcing political convictions, no sooner described than condemned. The final sentence of a chapter called "Ideology and Irrationalism, 1930–1941" runs, "For a short period, middle-class hostilities to art became open and general, but, happily, this hostility lessened, or at least became less vocal, as the war ended."[76]

Bogan's *Achievement* was an impressive piece of literary denial. In a sense it was a culmination of her effort to situate herself at the center of a certain "reasonable" or genteel anticommunist modernist taste making. The book several times made explicit through its pedagogical tone and its format that it was designed to serve as a primer for poetry of the era. This aim certainly was furthered by the short anthology published to accompany *Achievement*, which included poems discussed in the book (although none of those mentioned in the chapter on the thirties). Yet when in the book itself Bogan finally arrives at the contemporary period, she declines to engage in "a naming of young names"— although she does finally mention Viereck, Shapiro, Bishop, Lowell, Randall Jarrell, and Richard Wilbur, with a moment's glance toward Richard Eberhart and Theodore Roethke—and she notes that "the student of the subject" can make his way through the contemporary midcentury scene by following the "broad outlines" of the overall achievement.[77] Those contours carefully circumnavigated a path around the 1930s, a longer but safer route. One could study the poetry of the American 1930s through Eliot's influence, by way of Crane's incipient and Mac-Leish's overt political failures, steering among British poets. *Achievement* was pedagogically the natural next step in Bogan's career as poetic arbiter —as poetry reviewer for the *New Yorker*, where she had consistently and sometimes brutally attacked communist and other political poetry since the late 1930s.

As early as 1939, Bogan had identified American writing in the 1930s as "more symptomatic of a spiritual *malaise* than is generally supposed."[78] She despised "the sentimental come-ons and [the] exhortations of demagogues" in radical poetry.[79] She praised the "conservative tendency" in the poetry of Yvor Winters because it had by 1944 "become so rare . . . that it is again almost *avant garde*"—and she generally enjoyed brandishing the term avant-garde as a form of heroic illiberalism.[80] She stood firmly on the right although she fully engaged in dialogue with the left—far more willing to deal with opponents than would be apparent in *Achievement*. She argued with Fred Dupee of *Partisan Review* about whether Marx had been a prude (Bogan said yes).[81] She bemoaned the journalistic "fact fiction" modes encouraged by New Deal federal patronage and promoted by communist poets who admired constructivism; and she mocked the public's new perception of "series writing" as "thinly documentary."[82] While most noncommunist poets in the 1930s were timid about drawing clear distinctions between modern American poetic ancestral lines, Bogan did so boldly, courting argument. In the widely read *Partisan Review* symposium on the "Situation in American Writing" (1939), she wrote that her usable past lay in Henry James and not Whitman. Whitman she "do[es] not return to, and I never draw refreshment from his 'thought' "[83]—a criticism of the Whitmanian leftist strain that helps to explain her otherwise vague connection between Crane and communism in *Achievement*. She was ready to contend with communist poet Ruth Lechlitner about whether D. H. Lawrence's poems were both "lovely" and at the same time "definitely Marxian in outlook, in symbol."[84]

She corresponded with Lechlitner on the communist interpretation of Bogan's disappointment about Millay in the 1930s, with Bogan arguing publicly in her review of *Conversation at Midnight* (and privately in letters to her leftist colleagues, who were delighted by Millay's moves leftward) that the beauty of the poetic line, the forms of "inarticulate tears and joys," inhere in the art itself, bearing no relation to external circumstances. (Bogan was at that moment in a position to review Ruth Lechlitner's book, *Tomorrow's Phoenix* [1937], published in a tiny run by a fly-by-night communist-affiliated modernist press.)[85] It was a point to which Lechlitner passionately asked, "But *are* these joys and tears in existence apart from, and in spite of, the 'beliefs, dilemmas and despairs' current . . . and continually articulate elsewhere?" In the epistolary dialectic, Bogan caused the communist Lechlitner to concede, "This does not mean, to me, that a poet must become a 'pupil of his age' if he does write of current dilemmas and despairs. It all depends upon how he writes of them."[86]

How he (or she) writes of them. This was the key for Bogan, always. When MacLeish wrote "official" verse in *America Was Promises*, it mattered not that he had in fact rejected the "sentimental come-ons" of communist poets; the "difficulty of writing political poetry, even a kind of official poetry," was that the "strict checks and disciplines" entailed in writing poetry "for itself" do not hold. Bogan's anticommunism for poetry was always strictly a formal affair. She claimed, in a sense, to behold as a function of the lyric ear what was dissonant and disgraceful about leftist poetry. The phrase "America Was Promises" even an "untrained ear instinctively rejects": "it sounds ugly." No political reason need be brought to bear on it. It is "impressive" but "ugly"—inherently.[87]

Louise Bogan's anticommunist modernism was as purely about language as anticommunism could get. After all, the same poet who became irate about the roaringly approving reception given by members of the League of American Writers to a speech by MacLeish, "In Challenge Not Defense"—containing language that was "the most awful tripe," the worst "tub-thumping . . . I ever read," "the kind of sophomoric oration that brings the house down at college reunions"—was in fact briefly at the same time a supporter of League efforts to raise money for relief to the Spanish republic.[88] When a figure such as Eugene Lyons, hit hard by communists, felt ready to do battle against them, it was obviously because of Stalinist politics American style but not really because of *style*; what infuriated Bogan was primarily style in the serious sense of the term—that "the poetasters have got us"; that MacLeish could dare to "tell of the 'pure poets,' and the leaners toward posterity." "From now on," Bogan angrily wrote to Rolfe Humphries, himself then a procommunist poet,[89] "I'm not going to pull my punches about that bird." She was "terribly mad" at "the C.P., and all its works" because when she was greeted by some radical "girls at the subway entrance," they bespoke ruleless, unlyric, feelingless words, did more damage to beauty than their opponents did in the political sphere. Even their "soft tones" infuriated Bogan: "Stop the mad dogs of Fascism," these young communists mildly offered, "help our boys dodging Franco's bombs." "Frankly," these words "make me sick," Bogan wrote. "If the C.P. doesn't stop all this 'mad-dogs' 'depraved' stuff it will lose" the respect of cultured prospective supporters; this was a matter less of political action than of words. At stake was the fact "THAT POETRY HAS SOMETHING TO DO WITH THE IMAGINATION." And: "I STILL THINK IT OUGHT TO BE WELL-WRITTEN."[90]

"Discipline" cut just one way. Poetry that checked itself against external discipline, that followed a nonpoetic "line," as it were, changed for the bad, going in for terms suited to policy. This did not count as imaginative writing. Yet writing that submitted to the "strict checks and disciplines" of poetics— verse written "for itself"—was disciplined in the positive sense, in the sense of a writer whose poetic development emerges naturally, continuously, following an aesthetic direction traceable through the verse itself. Praise for poets who had carefully "stayed the modernist course" "despite" the sudden allure of communism was founded on the valorization of "natural" poetic growth. Quick aesthetic shifts were bad. Bogan's reviews and her *Achievement* strongly reinforced such terms. The young poet Frederick Morgan followed suit when in an omnibus review for the *Hudson Review* (his own magazine) he compared MacLeish and Winters, both of whom had published *Collected Poems*. Morgan praised Winters's poetry for giving "evidence of a sturdy talent that has grown— slowly and organically—into major proportions." MacLeish, conversely, was "the perpetrator"—carefully chosen word—of "hortatory effusions," sudden bursts of aesthetically changing winds.[91]

Bogan, Morgan, Peter Viereck, James Burnham, the ex-radical Harry Roskolenko, and Conrad Aiken all accepted the contingency of aesthetic value and more or less supported the continuation of modernism; the question was *how* contingent.[92] Too much stylistic contingency and there was the risk of—indeed, a sign of—communism. In one of the earliest pieces of anticommunist poetry criticism about "the thirties," Aiken urged poets to quit politics altogether and get "Back to Poetry" (1940). Poets should resist the high-speed changes forced on them by the "shadow of social pressure" (in "the form of war, revolution, change," and so forth) and summon the will to develop "calmly and steadily" "that they may know and *separate* themselves."[93] Burnham, one of the most prolific anticommunist intellectuals of the fifties, wrote an essay on anticommunist uses of the contingency of value, "The Calculus of Diffusion" (1953), published in Kissinger's magazine, *Confluence*. This denunciation of the method by which communists spread their ideas—by forcing apparently natural but fast-changing "elements of aesthetic style"—began with an anecdote about art and design in the thirties. Burnham remembered visiting the Paris Salon des Arts Decoratifs in June 1932, surprised to find that in just one year, the straight lines, parallels, and right angles of the prevailing doctrine of rectangularity had suddenly given way to new curves. Simple curves were then suddenly the rage. "How could this be?" Burnham asked. He associated the shift with the bottoming of the economic depression. Between curves and depression Burnham evidently made no connection, though a pall is cast over the essay by the intimation in the story of the demise of straightness and the apparently sinister emergence of indirectness.[94] By telling a tale of changing "style," Burnham was tapping into a common understanding about the consciousness of datedness. Yet the awareness moved in only one direction. Frederick Morgan had no intention of scrutinizing the social force driving his own changing preference for the "unswervingly true," "austere," "rightness, . . . modesty, dignity and perfection," the "mature, hard-earned awareness" of Yvor Winters's verse as against Archibald MacLeish's fulminations and "liberal-pamphleteering poems." Morgan could say, without pressure to provide evidence, that poems as "pamphlets"—the very *idea*, in other words, quite aside from the diction such a formal choice conveys—are "very dated" and thus are "probably the worst" of MacLeish's poems.[95] "Dated" is ipso facto bad. Yet a young poet imitating John Donne or indeed T. S. Eliot just then, Morgan would not have been called "dated." In "Beyond Revolt," Viereck argued that poetry in the late forties and fifties postdated linguistic disruption or experimentalism and the rapidly shifting poetic values associated with obeisance to political pressure. He claimed that thirties poets had a phobia for "alliteration, rhetoric and strong musical rhythms"[96]—a baseless charge. Viereck comes the closest of these anticommunist poet-critics to making the connection between the hatred of linguistic experiment and the obligation of critics to warn of the sinister "calculus of diffusion" by which communists spread their rhetorical poison. Not an active anticommunist, bearing the hope that his *Hudson Review* could shore up modernist conventions through a respectable reaction against the extremity of styles of the previous era, Morgan discerned the same connection. His uncharacteristically furious dismissal of MacLeish's communist-influenced social poetry must be closely associated with his assumption that "readers of poetry today are accustomed to highly-charged systems of imagery, and to poetic statement that is violent, dramatic and disjunctive" and thus that "there *was* a balance to be righted." Poetic centrism entailed not a little of this and a little of that but actually "a job of house-cleaning." Modesty was a mask here for a sweeping away of the disjunctive and bringing on the "rightness" of a poet such as Winters—hardly a balance.[97]

Burnham, for his part, understood the diffusion of aesthetic value as inevitable in all social systems. Several aspects of dissemination informed the basic tenets of modern advertising and public relations, yet totalitarian movements add to this phenomenon "the cadre structure of organization," first, and methods of concealment, second. These make all the difference, he contended; the communist plot is the ultimate underlying force behind value change. "The Calculus of Diffusion" is really an essay on the theory supporting already then well developed anticommunist practices aimed at disclosing behind the Marxist cultural-critical rhetoric of impersonal historical "forces" its real operation: the willful, planned spread of ideology. The enemy spoke in the language of "natural" or "spontaneous" meaning. The relevance of this to poetry was immediate: any claim to spontaneous style was assimilable in the theory of the communist calculus of diffusion—a linguistic communist front. The "natural" could be part of the plot.[98]

Burnham's theory against theory was relatively unusual among published considerations of the ill effect of the 1930s on midcentury aesthetics. Much anticommunist commentary on poetry opposed theory as a mode that brought on the trouble. Aiken's "Back to Poetry" called for clarity in response to "the shadow of theory." Poets should be skeptical of too much conceptual apparatus. "Where there is so much supporting theory, so conspicuous and intricate an apparatus for care and repair . . . one . . . begins to suspect there may be something wrong with the poetry." Poems are not made by theories. Moreover, "the theorist isn't a poet" because what he wants is "poetry without nonsense." It is here that Aiken associated left-wing "social theorists" among poets with writing that bears an "emphasis all on *technique*." The return to poetry is the return to humanity after a period—"the past decade," Aiken notes—of dogma. Theory is inhuman.[99]

Burnham and Aiken reached conceptual extremes, and Bogan was never quite of that camp. But the anticommunism of her reviews could be just as strong. She felt that poets who strictly followed (leftist) theory lacked humanity. (Poets who were ultimately human were those who resisted communist "come-ons" and hewed to "strict checks and disciplines" of autotelism.) Although Bogan did not once mention the word "communism" in her negative review of Muriel Rukeyser's *A Turning Wind*—in 1939, when the younger poet was just twenty-five—the claim there that Rukeyser lacked humanity was about as aggressive an anticommunist poetry aesthetic as the postwar period would ever produce. To Bogan, Rukeyser was interested in "the state of society to the almost complete exclusion of any conscious 'personal expression.' " This was of course a criticism of a stylistic approach—Rukeyser's repudiation of the by-then conventional modernist subjective lyric—but the *feel* of the review was that of a personal attack. For M. L. Rosenthal, whose New York University dissertation included a long chapter on Rukeyser's poetry, Rukeyser was a significant part of modernism's continuity, and he thus put her with Eliot, Pound, and Crane in a sweeping conclusion to his argument that all modern poetry embodies a valuable "unconsenting spirit": "From *The Waste Land* to Muriel Rukeyser's *Elegies*, from Pound's *The Return* to Crane's self-analyses, the . . . struggle for such continuity . . . [has] made for a richly varied *yet unified* literature."[100] But to Bogan, "The suspicion arises that Miss Rukeyser is deficient in a sense of human life." She had become a poetic automaton, an ugly emissary in the sinister calculus of worldwide diffusion—moral values washing up, like pods, on American shores by way of "social" (as "opposed" to "personal") poetry. Young Rukeyser had become one of *them*—an ideologist, one of the "terrible simplifiers," for whom, as Daniel Bell wrote, "it was unnecessary . . . to confront individual issues on their individual merits."[101] Bogan's review has the force of painful-but-good-for-you deprogramming, an offer of rescue from cultist thinking. Rukeyser lacked the "rough joy and silly pleasure" or "horseplay." She needed to get a life. Her world was "static" and "literary." To Bogan, thus, something must be eerily wrong with this picture. The literary had become a false mask—the near-miss attempt of a catechized involuntarist trying to seem "natural." For the purposes of such a critique, it made little difference that Rukeyser was more of a voluntarist than any other communist-affiliated poet of this time; that her one true belief was a belief in poetry; that she in fact did "not belong to any party" (and "that is why I say I am vulnerable to both sides").[102] Vulnerable indeed—since there was hardly a more effective anticommunist countercharge than the one Bogan leveled at Rukeyser, the hegemonic move made by those favoring "humanity" over "theory" for rescuing the "literary" from those whose inability to fake true "personal expression" must be revealed. This piece ended the decade for Bogan (it was dated December 16, 1939) with a condemnation of the 1930s and the sort of "oversimplified . . . crude opposition" she found in Rukeyser: "The decade which outlawed from poetry personal emotion, individual insight, and straight looks into the flawed human heart now closes." And, to anticipate Aiken by a few months and Morgan by more than a decade, Bogan concluded that true art always develops in a poet slowly and surely, resisting even drastic pressures to change. That progress is quiet and certain, while conversely, "There's nothing brisker and more vocal than politics."[103]

It is true that once the poetic revolts had been firmly put down, Bogan's appreciation of the slow and sure continued—for instance, in the influential essay "Modernism in American Literature" (1950), where she argued that poets at midcentury would give up avant-gardism quietly and voluntarily since there was "no real need for a further restless forward movement any longer."[104] But the counterreformation Bogan had been among the first to call for spawned a new brisk and vocal politics—this time, of course, an avid politics against the 1930s. When in "Poets versus Readers" (1947) the brash Viereck announced that "the spirit of revolt is over, the revolt against poetic forms and disciplines," there was more than a little gloating at the triumph; a new energetic poetic conservatism—a distinct politics of anticommunism that sometimes rebuked modernism and more often proclaimed it as befitting the anticommunist midcentury—was being born. Viereck knew that the "uprising was less against form than against formalism." He deliberately did not distinguish between the aesthetic radicals of early modernism and political radicals of the 1930s, and for the moment here (but not elsewhere), this conflation of modernism and radicalism nicely served the purpose of his declaration that an age of conservatism had been ironically enabled by the rebellion. Poets calling for radical disjunction "served a conservative and traditionalist function: sweeping away—by a temporary esthetic crisis—the misuses of form." They "paved the way for the present return to more rigorous and exacting forms."[105]

By the time of Bogan's *Achievement*, the enemy having been vanquished, the radical could be almost entirely ignored. There were even slight concessions. In the two lines Rukeyser got in the book, Bogan conceded that she composed with "an amalgam of *modern* styles,"[106] it being harmless at that point to bring at least this radical poet toward the triumphant modernist camp. All was well. "Foundations devoted to the subsidy of creative talent generously function." The poet now "deals with incidents of everyday life." Only in this sense is poetry assumed to have any importance. Perhaps the only completely ambiguous sentence in *Achievement in American Poetry* speaks to this matter: "The poet of the future need waste little time and energy in establishing the fact that his art has importance."[107] John Ciardi, whose critical style was doubtless too satiric for Bogan, took this to heart, acting on an energized sense that the opposite of being a political poet in the 1930s was to go before an audience at a College English Association annual conference during the 1950s to bespeak the potential "importance" of modern poetry to businessmen in an only somewhat facetious talk called "An Ulcer, Gentlemen, Is an Unwritten Poem" later published in *Canadian Business* magazine (1955). Ciardi quoted Spender looking back on the "thirties from the vantage point of 1950, summariz[ing] the poet's then-sense of himself as very much a warrior of the practical world." "It was still possible then," Ciardi quoted Spender, "to think of a poem as a palpable, overt, and effective anti-fascist action." A poetic assertion in the 1930s seemed then "to be a bullet fired in the war against human repression." But now? "I know of no sane poet today," Ciardi observed, "who persuades himself that the action of his art and imagination has any significant consequence in the practical reality of Dow-Jones averages, election returns, and state of the nation."[108]

Ciardi was not altogether "sane" per his own definition. He was out there as ever on the stump, defending modern poetry against charges that it was "ugly, coarse, immoral, and debased,"[109] persuading audiences that no poet should believe in the public significance of poetry. But this was a pose—an effective one. Ciardi was among those building careers on the "crisis" of poetry's settled affairs. Spender, on the other hand, was by this time the epitome of the sane ex-radical anticommunist poet who knew enough to lament previous excesses in assumptions about poetry's capacity to support or induce political change. Spender's "Can't We Do without the Poets?" (1951) made two points—the same two points Bogan had felt in 1939 that the young Rukeyser had wholly missed. First, it was fine for poets to become politicized, but it should be understood that "they are bad party men": "It is always a bad time for poets when the social or religious cause they have inspired and propagated comes into power." (This was a version of the anticommunist cry against theory that Aiken and Bogan had first formulated: "Poetry . . . cannot be responsible to the logic of theories and events, and attempts to make it so are fatal to the poetry. Poetry is responsible to the logic of poetry." This was just as well, Spender suggested, since "the Government probably does know best.") The second point, closely related to the first, maintained the essential serious unseriousness of poetry, content being roughly the serious part, poetic form being roughly the unserious part. This observation associated the failures of the social and aesthetic experimentalists; both groups needed to recognize that Shelley, had he lived long enough to see his utopian legislation enacted, would have felt among the first to be condemned by means of it. Poets at midcentury had to know that since they "write in meter and perhaps also in rhyme," they illustrate the inherent divided loyalty of poetry—radical content, conservative form. This created an inevitable political ambivalence not well resolved by emphasizing radical content or by rejecting the inherent traditionalism of poetic form. Adherence to the little rules of poetry distinguished the good poetry of a poet who understood form as enabling what Bogan deemed Rukeyser to be lacking: "rough joy and silly pleasure." The error of modern poets had been that they thought their deadly serious revolt against convention meant serious content as well as serious form.[110] "The old Irish freedom-fighter O'Leary," Viereck liked to say, "once remarked to Yeats that you may be permitted almost any crime for the sake of your country except bad verse."[111]

What really angered Louise Bogan about the poetry of the 1930s was not its serious content. It was the (alleged) effort to "sweep away all standards." For her red friend Rolfe Humphries, she mocked the experimentalism of the communist: "Where are your little rules as applied to the works of Shakespeare? Where are your little rules as applied to the works of Dante? How small your little rules look." This was what led Bogan, at least privately, to reveal that she was ready "to put up a lot more fight" and to sign off her letter with a joking yet pointed, "Your Fascist friend, / Louise."[112]

Here was the heart of the fascinating relationship between American anti-communism and modern poetry in the postwar years. In an unquiet yet quietistic time, it was a desperate fight about the "little rules." Ironically, the modernist at midcentury sought to defend and maintain them. If modern poets still wanted to sweep away form's rules, it might be appropriate to ask: Were they, or might they have ever been, communists? Were they perhaps anti-anticommunists? Would it do to bait them with the sharpened new weapons of anticommunism? Ciardi was at least right in implying that the outcome of this struggle would determine whether the modern poet would be invited to bespeak any kind of relation to the Dow Jones average, the election results, the state of the nation.

CHAPTER 6

Poetry is not about crisis, it is the resistance to and escape from crisis.
—Henry Rago, editor of *Poetry*

History sounding on the gong of glacier!—Norman Rosten, *The Big Road*

Anti-Anticommunist Poetics

Is there a useful category, *anti-anticommunist poetics*? Were those who resisted anticommunism themselves deemed to constitute a threat like that posed by American communists?

The latter question, at least, is valid and has been posed—far more often by diplomatic historians than by literary historians—but it has not been and perhaps will never be definitively answered. Most of those known as "anti-anticommunists" were not communists; nor were they necessarily defenders of U.S. communism per se. Nonetheless, the gesture of accusing someone opposed to anticommunism of being part of the communist conspiracy became a well-established tactic. To have stood against anticommunism—indeed, against anticommunism's effects on American verse—became, if only in context, some form of radicalism. My aim has been to show that among such radicals were modernists who sought an alternative to the anticommunist version of modernism.

Possibly it is unhelpful to use so subtle a term in connection with postwar poetry and poetics, for "communist" or even "procommunist" would seem sufficient for denoting the bearer of heretical ideas troublingly sustained during cold war, at least with respect to verse, which is always at most an indirect form of political activity. That is certainly how most anticommunists felt, judging anti-anticommunism to be an irresponsible evasion.[1] How precise after all, how logically necessary, could the relation between modernism and communism be? Again these are apt questions and, leaving aside for a moment the problem of modernism's reputation among the relatively few poets and poetry critics on the noncommunist left who declined to join anticommunist ranks, there is indeed the crucial matter of terminology.

No one knows if the anticommunists or their detractors first used the term "anti-anticommunist."[2] The distinction became, regardless, an anticommunist construction, useful when an anticommunist purported to have discovered the term being employed deceptively by a communist who posed as a nonpartisan. The problem was that the writer who insisted that he was quoting a communist in anti-anticommunist disguise was in fact quoting a fellow *anticommunist*—to wit, Arthur Koestler.

Koestler did as much for the intellectual anticommunist cause as anyone. He was the author of *Arrival and Departure* (1952), *Arrow in the Blue* (1952), and *Darkness at Noon* (1941) and was the target of Merleau-Ponty's series of counterinterpretations of the Moscow Trials in *Les Temps Modernes* (1946–47). In the 1950s, the stable presence of *Darkness at Noon* on college syllabi was one key indicator for conservative observers of the strength of anticommunism (or, when the book was absent, of communism) among the faculty. An assistant professor of English who complained of Koestler's removal from an introductory course was said by poet Merrill Root to have "tripped over the Party line, stretched in the dark for unwary feet."[3]

In the *New Leader* of June 17, 1950, in one of his "Where the News Ends" columns, the conservative critic William Henry Chamberlin, a member of George Sokolsky's "Ancient Order of Red-Baiters,"[4] doubted the idea that a noncommunist might defend the civil rights—the right to due process—of communists living within a polity guaranteeing these things or might utter an indicative cautionary "but" after the phrase "I'm not a communist." Chamberlin argued that there was no such thing as a defender of communists who was not thus himself or herself a communist. In provocatively collapsing a basic distinction, he assumed a position of preeminence among the many conservatives seeking to mitigate the political language of the 1930s. Again the issue was interpretation: freedom-loving defenders against communist transgression had also to be well-trained readers of the increasingly complex nature of the conspiratorial identity. No problem was now to be solved straightforwardly; everything was elaborate, especially the subject position of those whose writings treacherously argued for straightforwardness. According to Chamberlin,

> As the fellow-traveler [of the Popular Front era, 1935–39] fades in political and intellectual influence, a new and more complex type has been filling the vacuum left by his departure. This is the anti-anti-Communist, to borrow an apt phrase from Arthur Koestler—the man who prefaces his remarks with: "I'm not a Communist, but . . ."
>
> The AAC . . . [s]ometimes is simply an individual who is cheating the Communist party of its dues, whose professions of antipathy to communism are only a camouflage for views which are in line with Kremlin goals. More often he is . . . afflicted with a bad case of political astigmatism.

The "AAC communist"—the anti-anticommunist who was actually a communist—was so well camouflaged that the only way he or she could be outed was through written signs of aversion to "doing anything about" communism. Yet linguistic evidence of the difference between the communist and the "AAC communist" was hard to decipher. If such a radical wrote the sentence, "You can't stop an idea by force," the distinction was practically moot. Similarly, the AAC communist wrote that there was nothing illegal about the *theory* of communism—and did not grasp the nondistinction between a theory of acts and the actual activities of a conspiracy to act.[5]

That the anticommunist liberal had similar problems dealing with Koestler's anticommunism indicates the ideological range and reach of the construction of the 1930s in the 1950s. To Alfred Kazin, for instance, the formulation was "Ideology versus the Novel"; the two terms belonged to exclusive categories. The phrase was the title of Kazin's brief but devastating piece, published not quite a year after Chamberlin's article on anti-anticommunism, about *The Age of Longing* (1951), Koestler's novel of Arabs and Jews in Palestine. Koestler, Kazin conceded, wrote despondently about "the impotence of all present classes, ideas, and intellectuals before the Communist threat to the West" and reminded his readers that, at bottom, Koestler "hates Bolshevism." Nonetheless, if in its Soviet Diplomat the novel acidulously presents a fictional character whose talk "reads like an anthology" of political clichés, thus murdering language, the reviewer in making such a judgment should perhaps have noted that this was an *anticommunist* aesthetic standard: the cardboard communist.

Not so. For Kazin this was a sign of a writer's clinging secretly to communist literary fantasies, his lingering distrust of individualism, his continuing commitment to the discredited aesthetic of unindividualized types. After all, good novels skillfully representing nuanced or "unique" political contexts could always be said finally to be about the "healing love of individual existence"—in other words, writing that is in some sense *about* its opposition to ideology. Fiction that failed to rise above one's socialization to type (except if that education happened to have inculcated the desire to see in all politics "the sacredness of each individual") increased the danger of cultural annihilation. "No matter how full of sociological cant your education may have been, the whole point of writing fiction in our day, it would seem to me, is that you begin by accepting in your characters that simple, healing love of individual existence which so much else today constantly threatens to destroy." This passage turns on the phrase "writing fiction in our day." In contemporary writing, the point was that writers accept as a premise one kind of characterization because the alternative is an ultimate destructive force, the enemy's aesthetic. True enough, but does not historicizing characterization qualify the assertion of the timeless beauty of the individual? Indeed, if just fifteen years earlier, in the mid-1930s, a novelist had done what

Kazin blamed Koestler for doing in 1951—if he "represent[ed] individuals as types because the original models weary and disgust him"—he might have been lauded as a writer with something new to say about relations between the novel as a genre and the social conditions giving rise to its contemporary generic formulation. Yet now when the idea of the individual left Koestler cold, he was to be criticized for not recognizing the "simple, healing love" of selfhood.

So Kazin found Koestler not just guilty of being "a political novelist who conceives of his characters as types"; he is not simply "less of a novelist"[6] than Ignazio Silone or George Orwell, who offered popular allegories of antipolitics in *Bread and Wine* (1937; in its first major American translation, 1946—essentially a Cold War book)[7] and *Animal Farm* (1945; first American edition, 1946), where characters are by design no more than types. Murray Kempton did not understand this intention when he similarly castigated Edwin Seaver's antifascist novel *Between the Hammer and the Anvil* (1937) for offering "characters so deliberately faceless that they were even named Mr. and Mrs. John Doe."[8] Kempton meant that Seaver's communist novel was not a bad novel—indeed, that it was not really a novel at all, as novels should be. Kazin was more explicit in his functionalist logic about how decent critics and readers were to respond when writers violated basic rules of the genre. Kazin's version of Arthur Koestler "is against the novel itself."[9] Given the wide range of experimental novels written before and since, characterless novels, novels in which the politics of individualism are played out through experiments with character—let us say, Samuel Beckett's *Watt* (written anxiously in Vichy France), a nonnarrative fiction that can be interpreted as enacting a form of antifascist resistance through an extreme language-ing, as we might say, of the self—such a statement must be understood in the broad context of anticommunist culture, just as William Henry Chamberlin described it. Indeed, Chamberlin and Kazin, although not normally deemed to have shared any political ground, a conservative and a liberal, made precisely the same point about subversion: the literary AAC communist poses the same threat as the communist. Here, then, is why to Kazin Arthur Koestler was so incondite, why his novel was "against the novel itself": "For though he hated Bolshevism, he had accepted the fatal Bolshevik premise that individuals are not interesting in themselves."[10] Anticommunism again took aesthetic measure. In an era typified (in Daniel Bell's formulation) by an exhausted repudiation of exhortatory language and of didactic rhetorical passion, the end of rhetoric, and at the same time a valorization of caution, sobriety, limitation, and individuation,[11] even anticommunist writers could be accused of aesthetic anti-anticommunism—of "betray[ing] a distaste for human passion" that evinced the communist threat.[12]

In the second half of this book, we will explore how political poetry could be deemed by anticommunists as *against the poem itself*. Verse very often was judged thus, in terms nearly identical to those Kazin used for Koestler and Kempton for Seaver. We have already seen Louise Bogan on Muriel Rukeyser: the radical's verse expresses distaste for the delights of human passion, creating a "seriousness . . . unrelieved by . . . moments of lightness."[13] Poetry had to be about individual passion, the emotional source work of a deep, variable yet finally constant self. The refusal to explore or disclose that depth was a subversive sign—was another quality shared by the stubborn remnant of the 1930s left and by advocates of experimental writing as it emerged out of modernism in the late 1950s. Most suspicious to anticommunists was the "progressive depreciation of the value of personality," as Frank Meyer put it in *The Moulding of Communists*. In remarks made upon sentencing Ethel and Julius Rosenberg to death, Judge Irving Kaufman listed their "crime[s] *worse* than murder," among them chiefly the "denial of the sanctity of the individual."[14] A subversive was unable to form an "attachment to another person," Meyer observed, "—filial devotion, love, or friendship—deep enough to create values independent" of abstract political belief.[15]

Instances of the kind of critique Bogan aimed at Rukeyser abound. Henry Rago, reviewing Genevieve Taggard's book of poems, *Slow Music* (1947), saw in the writing only "her humorless faith," no humanity. Rago "wear[ied of] following Miss Taggard around," mindlessly historical and mechanically incurious about form. Taggard's poetry did not count as poetic. Poetry was not "poetic comment on the news." And "poetry is not about crisis, it is the resistance to and escape from crisis, but of course only those people sensitive enough to know what crisis is will take the trouble to resist it!" Taggard—she had served as an executive officer of the League of American Writers, the communist writers' front, and Rago knew it[16]—was not, to him, among those poets "sensitive enough" to present human depth. "He comes out for art," Taggard wrote in notes toward a never-published rejoinder, "at my expense. How brave of him." The logic of Rago's critique is circular; as Taggard put it, "Where is all this talk about paying strict attention to the poem, regardless of political color?"[17] He did not credit as poetry her line, "Let it [poetry] have heart-beat," because he was not convinced the poet had a heartbeat.[18] Taggard was heartless. Her linguistic surfaces were like those of the newspaper headline, of the clipped, subjectless language used by reporters and political commentators.

But what if that kind of language was itself the poem's concern? In agonizing over the declined or constrained role of the poet, it might have plenty of heart. Taggard's poem, "Poet," published in the *New Masses*, begins straightforwardly enough, the speaker a poet (indeed) who has worked in the fancy, high-minded mode:

> Tragic meaning was my altitude.
> Took it for mine, felt it lift
> Very high, learned to live holding it behind diamond eyes

But that is the last we see of the subject in a poem of five six-line stanzas. The poem is increasingly about the poet's new linguistic options—about lines that are end-stopped or not, about poetic units of measure that can be slowed or sped up. Yes, the poem's "line" is the "party line" of the time: poets have a responsibility to widen the scope and role of poetry to include "the crisis hurrying." But because the metrical heart of this poem about poetry beats with that urgency, the party line must be in the poetic line. Prosody and grammar have ethical aspects. The commentator's stinting language (lacking subject, missing articles, and so on), of which Rago complains, is actually the basis of the communist poet's claim to aesthetic relevance. "Poet" concludes:

> Toiled in unit of slow going; in the line as it stops;
> With stop after stop, the signal awaited. One
> In the lock with all, chained but never slave.
> Here sweat out struggle nothing-sweeter than history.
> Web of feet, working over dark bloody ground.
> Heart plunging neatly, spasm on spasm.

The poet once of rhetorical and stylistic "altitude" comes finally to be associated with a disturbance of the lyric line. The poet willing to write "Here sweat out struggle nothing-sweeter than history" brings the disengaged conventional tragic mode, with its obvious subjects and objects (poets and historical matters), down to the level of the line. The poem has heart, all right; its humanity, though, is in the meter of "spasm." Party line; disruption of lyric convention; anxiety about verse as ultimately a thing made out of words: all converge. "Does it follow that Poetry is solely an affair of words?," Taggard would ask her students at Sarah Lawrence College. "Yes," was the correct answer.[19]

In a critique similar to Rago's of Taggard, Theodore Weiss (1916–2003), editor of the modernist *Quarterly Review of Literature*, looked back at the 1930s verse of Edwin Rolfe, compared it with that which Rolfe published in the 1950s, and concluded that Rolfe's poetry "successfully resisted poetry." It was, Weiss felt, a conscious effort to realize Rolfe's "singular faith," an antipoetic "utopian dream of a simpler, purer world" in which the poet can eschew poetry itself "as one of the main accesses to and of truth." To Weiss, Rolfe's 1930s-style radicalism put him outside the tradition of Milton and Marvell.[20]

And the poet Winfield Townley Scott (1910–68) was more than a little appalled when he saw in the verse of the young, suddenly popular Australian poet John Manifold an urge to "make frequent identifications for the individual with general society." Scott wondered if such poetry was going to make a resurgence among modern poets returning from the war. What horrified him was the bitter implication of a review that might otherwise have been read as a polite, even cautiously encouraging comment by the colleague of a young, heroic "war poet," each of them trying to comprehend a changed relation between modern poetry and the social crisis from which they now emerged. Modernism itself was at stake. At the very beginning of the Cold War, in 1946, Scott examined Manifold's *Selected Poems*, recognized Manifold's talent for making of poems out of "Guerrilla words" "declamation[s] in the crowded square,"[21] and did what just then, in the first months after the war, might have seemed an odd thing: he mounted an extraordinarily disproportionate effort to characterize Manifold's work as outmoded, immature, and foreign to what American poets do. "In his Marxist politics he relates directly to the poetry of the 1930s," Scott wrote; Manifold thus was at best quaintly vivacious "in favor of the underdog." Manifold's political ballads "have the virtue of being indigenously Australian" and indeed curious and primitive—apt for condescension: "There is always in the deliberate primitive an antipathetic sophistication, and such artless art commits suicide."[22] Manifold's poems can be enjoyed in postwar days because, with his "drive" and "gusto" to make clear his poetry ideal, he can be thought of as very unlike us.[23]

As we have seen, the making of a conception of the 1930s well suited for the 1950s was getting well under way in 1946. Reviewing five new poetry anthologies for *Poetry* that May, M. L. Rosenthal, writing as "Macha," his given name, was shocked to see how rapidly the deradicalization was occurring. He learned that Conrad Aiken had helped produce a book called *An Anthology of Famous English and American Poetry* that featured Maria White Lowell, Richard Realf, and Cale Young Rice, while "Horace Gregory, William Carlos Williams, Kenneth Fearing, and practically the entire American literary left are nowhere to be found." The omission and the political reasons for it were obvious to Rosenthal; after all, it was perfectly in line with what Aiken had been writing since 1940. Yet in the preface to this 1946 collection, Aiken no longer mentioned politics, depending, rather, on the vocabulary of aesthetic value. Aiken gave the "vague assurance that 'the esthetic judgment . . . is the only sound basis of procedure,' " an outright lie, Rosenthal felt, that expressed "once again the arbitrary, irresponsible nature of so much publishing today . . . patriotic businessmen responsible for the decision to censor American critical intelligence."[24] Aiken, Rago, and Winfield Townley Scott were hardly alone among poets and poetry critics in rigidifying definitions of what was to be disliked about poetry of the 1930s. And in the same year—again, 1946—in which Scott categorized Manifold as a primitivist antifascist poet born too late, another young poet, William Meredith, attacked Norman Rosten's political poetry as reductive "posterwriting" that merely "evoked a primary response."[25]

At twenty-nine, Meredith was a heralded new postwar poet—he was in Princeton's war-bound class of '40; he was a navy pilot; he had had been named the Yale Younger Poet for 1944—whose assessment profiled radical writers of the 1930s "as primitives, clumsy practitioners who simplified art,"[26] notwithstanding the fact that one of his strongest supporters in the early 1940s had been Muriel Rukeyser,[27] chief among the accused simplifiers. Why the radicals' use of "blank and free verse [that] read like a shopping list" (by which Meredith meant something poetically quite deficient) "evoked a primary response," while what Meredith and his postwar colleagues were now doing presumably "evoked" something more sophisticated—less animal and more human—was left unsaid. Then there was in Rosten's writing "the omission of articles and an excessive use of participles" and, worse, "words and phrases connected by commas where conjunctions are wanted," and "clauses and sentences joined by conjunctions where periods and a breath of air are needed."[28]

Narrowing the Scope of Poetry

In criticizing Norman Rosten's ambitious book-length poem about the building of the Alcan Highway, *The Big Road* (1946), William Meredith made a connection between, on the one hand, these particular syntactical failures and, on the other, radical poetry written before the war "in which political ideas were presented in a simplified form" and "advanced causes important to poets and free men."[29] Small effort was made here to countertheorize the politics of poetic form. Even in poetry written explicitly as tracts, such as Eve Merriam's "Pamphlet in Poetry" issued later by a blacklisted publisher to mark the third anniversary of *Brown v. Board of Education*,[30] the communist poets these critics attacked often inscribed into their writing their own aesthetic struggles, as we have seen in the writerly anxieties of Taggard's "Poet." Merriam's wartime poem, "A.W.O.L.," comes to an intentionally abrupt end in such self-awareness: "Conscience reminds me / back to black and white, to billboard-crude."

"A.W.O.L." is a political poem risking accusations of didacticism that is *about* conditions in which "I can leave off writing poster-crude," the moment when the poem's own style becomes unnecessary.[31] Meredith's assessment of Rosten's verse in *The Big Road* as "poster-writing" contained no admission that modern poets who were communists agonized in this formal way. Nor was there acknowledgment that *The Big Road* was working in a mode of which Hart Crane's *The Bridge* (1930), Charles Reznikoff's *Testimony* (1938), Muriel Rukeyser's "The Book of the Dead" (1938), and some of the earlier work of the Dynamo poets were examples. It seems that Rosten's writing was to be disconnected from that part of the modernist legacy of the 1930s in which, as Michael Davidson has put it in *Ghostlier Demarcations* (1997), "narrative becomes a vehicle for a critical reappraisal of nationhood."[32] Instead there was only the assumption that when on the pages of *The Big Road* Rosten transcribed army radio transmissions or inserted a bulletin or document with its language intact, when in such passages articles were omitted and conjunctions appeared in lieu of full stops, these represented poetic "shortcomings," "a real carelessness with regard to the sound of the verse." If postwar readers were to agree that "Mr. Rosten's book would be more readable if it were better poetry," Meredith nonetheless left it to them to assume what that more "readable" poetry would be, except to say self-fulfillingly that it would have "the form, the precision and the scope of art."[33]

Once poets who were or had been "ideologists" could be said thus, ipso facto, to be "terrible simplifiers"—to use Daniel Bell's term in *The End of Ideology*—only a short next step led to the conclusion that such a poet's writing bore no concern for intrinsic merit. "One simply turns to the ideological vending machine," Bell wrote, "and out comes the prepared formulae." Yet if anything, the "prepared formulae," formally speaking, of *The Big Road* had been set by the various modernist documentary-allusive styles of Pound, Rukeyser, Dos Passos, and Reznikoff. Instead of merely representing the world in which the big road is constructed, *The Big Road* incorporates linguistic pieces of that reality, occasionally—at its best—presenting contingent stories (in the mode of Dos Passos), "discursive 'excrescences'" (in the mode of Rukeyser), and multiple yet contradictory witnesses (in the mode of Reznikoff).[34] The charge made against the literary left by theorists of the end of ideology could be turned around and made against Meredith exactly as he assailed Rosten, although Meredith surely thought of himself as a poet whose concern for individual aesthetic value remedied communist reductiveness—or, in other words, "ideology makes it unnecessary for people to confront individual issues on their individual merits."[35]

At around the time of Meredith's criticism of Rosten, an aesthetic for the postwar period was emerging in reaction against something the hatred of which could now be culturally sanctioned yet left unmentioned as such. Even the subtlest poetry critics fell into the anti-ideological pattern. This is surely the case with Richard Blackmur's 1945 rebuke of Rukeyser, whose "amorphous" meters in *The Beast in View* (1944) supposedly failed. Blackmur's judgment was actually harsher: her meter was not even "representative of the tradition of craft in English poetry"! This prosody, claimed Blackmur, had "nothing to do with the speed and little to do with the shape of the poetry." Without overtly conceding that his bias against Rukeyser's use of "direct perception, reportage, and *the forces to which she gives in*"—a transparent circumlocution for communism—was a repudiation of political poetry and its modes, Blackmur spoke of the poet's poor metrical control as a drag on otherwise strong generic and even topical aspects of the blank verse.[36]

What book was Blackmur reading? Meter was hardly the thing that could truly have irked him when he read the lines

> The *girl* whose *father raped* her *first*
> *Should* have *used* a *little knife*[37]

That passage of Rukeyser's "Gift-Poem," emphatically (and aptly) iambic, was almost but not quite in a ballad stanza—a ballad wrenched just slightly, aided by the thematic violence: "Failing that, her touch is cursed / By the omissive sin for life," as rhymed follow-on, is somewhat disappointing, but not because of its meter.

In the end, Blackmur's readers learned summarily that Rukeyser was "confused about sex" (this noted in an essay otherwise avoiding thematics) and were instructed to imagine "what she ought to have done and could do" in her poetry, "at some future stage of itself": instead of the "rough blank verse," "rough rhyme," "half rhyme," reportage, the immediacy of direct perception which "usually takes over the verse," there would be more formal lyrics such as those—here Blackmur reached for a certifiably canonical counterexample—of John Fletcher:

> Lay a garland on my horse
>   Of the dismal yew;
> Maidens, willow branches bear;
>   Say, I died true.

Blackmur promised here that he meant Rukeyser should follow "the *form*" (Blackmur's emphasis) although not the sentiment of these lines.[38] It is difficult to imagine that the connection between Rukeyser's rough meters and her "confus[ion] about sex" was not wholly relevant to this judgment. Rukeyser was beginning to be aware that the criticisms of poetic form by otherwise perspicacious critics sometimes now masked homophobic and antiradical reactions. She overheard publishers talk of Robert Duncan's poetry—that it "lacked what [Yvor] Winters calls 'moral fibre' "—which was the very same "strength of [Fletcher's] sort of form" that Blackmur was calling for. Duncan had come out in *Politics* in 1944,[39] and, Rukeyser observed, "the echoes have not faded." She heard a poet say of Duncan, "Intellectual torment. Sexual confusion." "Now the two touchstones of American sentimental reactions," she wrote, "are . . . the names of communism and homosexuality[,] signals to the unsure for fear-trigger response that will be identical."[40]

In strong form ("the metre, the musical phrase, the attitude, the whole weight of previous use"—by which, thus, he meant traditional form), Blackmur discerned a force that "pulls the poem into . . . a state of autonomous being," a poem so formally right and good that it can live without reference to its social thematics.[41] This is the same R. P. Blackmur who in 1934 had written to Allen Tate in overtly conservative language ("There is no . . . party dogma which does not sicken me. . . . The general problem of politics is the problem of securing balance between forces from the outside and responsibility within")[42] and who had neglected Matthiessen and Perry Miller out of discomfort, as Edward Said later observed, with a whole "generation of tendentious Americanists."[43] But now, during the Cold War, Blackmur's distaste for political poetry could finally be stated in terms of the failure or success of autonomy or could be hidden in praise for the most formally conservative aspect of a radical's poetics. The latter impulse drove him to look in *The Beast in View* for lines that might bring Rukeyser up "to the strength of th[e] sort of form" he found in traditional poetry as a model—and he found them:

> The world is full of loss; bring, wind, my love,
> My home is where we make our meeting-place,
> And love whatever I shall touch and read
> Within that face.[44]

Yet this poem, Rukeyser's sweet-sad lyric "Song," is not at all typical of the political and sexual radicalism of *The Beast in View*, which Blackmur politically eviscerated without feeling the logical need to refer to politics at all—only to the failures of form, and to a (vague, unnamed) "force" to which Rukeyser as poet submitted herself.[45]

This sort of averting to form was much more effective than if Richard Blackmur or William Meredith had felt any obligation to spell out the emergent antipolitical counteraesthetic that would rebuke the work of Rukeyser and obliterate Rosten from the poetic landscape. The praise of Rukeyser's "Song," a completely integrated lyric effort, implicitly cast doubts on the disruptions of poems such as "Who in One Lifetime," where the linguistic difficulty of the first lines becomes a medium for the convergence of domestic/sexual and wartime/international radicalisms. The poem reads, in its entirety,

June 1941

Who in one lifetime sees all causes lost,
Herself dismayed and helpless, cities down,
Love made monotonous fear and the sad-faced
Inexorable armies and the falling plane,
Has sickness, sickness. Introspective and whole,
She knows how several madnesses are born.
Seeing the integrated never fighting well.
The flesh too vulnerable, the eyes near-torn.

She finds a pre-surrender on all sides:
Treaty before the war, ritual impatience turn
The camps of ambush to chambers of imagery.
She holds belief in the world, she stays and hides
Life in her own defeat, stands, though her whole world burn,
A childless goddess of fertility.

One begins this poem trying to decipher the grammar of the first line. Is it an interrogatory without a question mark, asking who sees lost causes? Rather, "who in one lifetime" is the grammatical subject of a fragment—*it is she who* has witnessed the war-torn world and "has" or feels or, more properly, comprehends sickness. So much has happened by June 1941. Vocabularies collide somewhat ungrammatically. "Love" could also be the subject and "made" thus a transitive verb, making a noun have a quality (love has been made monotonous). But the noun follows the modifier (monotonous fear), so that it might refer to the *kind* of fright love makes. Or monotony may be made into fear by love. Domestic and geopolitical qualities are confused, as then, after love, there are armies: an "and" ("and then the sad-faced . . .") seems colloquial, a parataxis, creating a connection between unconnectable parts. This is not the way history is usually told: *and* then this happened, *and* then this, and so on. Or perhaps the connection makes sense and love is meant to be making other objects into other qualities, "sickness, sickness" being the quality love bestows on the armies no one can stop, as on the ground falling out from under their feet. The cause that is lost is the sure, level ground: connection between sentences and phrases; the normal, logical way in which history, in language, proceeds. And yet, of course, the poem is grounded and assured by the blessings of literary history: it is a Petrarchan sonnet, with an octet and sestet, a lyric diction, and a rhyme scheme sufficient to remind us of its formal pedigree.

In the text, "Who in One Lifetime" is dated "June 1941," the great turning point in World War II, when the Soviet Union joined the Allies and a second front opened. The poem is about a woman, not herself a warrior, who upon finding "pre-surrender on all sides" discovers the abandonment of prewar treaties, the rhetoric of peace betrayed—"turn[s] / The camps of ambush to chambers of imagery." She presents a poem as a form of infuriated feminized helplessness, which, she implies, serves us as a model not for just one lost cause but for all. Is "Who in One Lifetime" a "communist" poem? Does it follow the platform of a revolutionary party? These are not simple questions. Nonetheless, the skeptical or antipolitical critic, assuming the answers to these questions are inherently yes, might well assail the poem on aesthetic grounds. The poem itself allows for this. What enables the poet to "turn / The camps of ambush to chambers of imagery"? Is it verily the sonnet, the classic "chamber of imagery," a result of "ritual impatience"? The speaker maintains "belief in the world" by epitomizing the ultimate paradoxical form for a political woman poet, "a child-less goddess of fertility." The c-rhyme in the sestet, which is supposed to rhyme *abcabc* (one of several conventional options for a Petrarchan sonnet), should be *imagery/fertility*. But after *sides/hides* and *turn/burn*, that final rhyme is odd and disappointing, and metrically the line falls a beat short. Poets have long derived a sense of clarity and unity from the sonnet. This is a sonnet made both in and about June 1941—a time of extraordinary unity among allies, when antifascism finally seemed ubiquitous and the war seemed possible to win—that undermines its expression of "belief in the world" by enacting, through its form, the same "ritual impatience" that normally renders the agony into the solaces of poetry in time of war. The antifascist poet, rather than feeling clarification at the reentry into the war of the world's one communist government, is confused by what it means. The work of reconstructing the political context—a context of which the poem is evidence and to which it contributed—is difficult.[46]

Regarding the communist Rosten, Meredith claimed that "the issue here is not intelligibility *vs.* obscurity, or popular as against private poetry," but he was protesting too much. These were exactly the issues. The political poetry that had come before had deliberately engaged popular forms, low-cultural diction, frankly integrated slogans into the writing, and incorporated documents—and would now be made to pay for that descent below the proper station of poetry. That is why, we may suppose, Meredith used the loaded phrase "the scope of art."[47]

He and others, in the name of modern poetry, were engaged in the work of renar-rowing that scope that had been widened first by modernists in the 1910s and 1920s and then by radicals in the 1930s; both movements had urged that nothing be considered in itself not the material of poetry (to state the point the way Wallace Stevens put it in the 1920s and William Carlos Williams did in the 1930s).

Others feared this freedom more than William Meredith, to be sure. In an antimodernist anticommunist essay, "Poem vs. Slogan," published in the liberal Jewish magazine, *The Reconstructionist*, Norman Friedman argued that it was "time that the issues were plainly stated: (1) the basic question is the use of language in poetry, (2) an artist who allows the language of prejudice to write his poems for him is selling himself out." Slogans were the formal instantiation of prejudice, and since prejudice led to the loss of agency, poets that used slogans were tools of an alien force. Thus "any poet who [uses] sloganisms in his verse for the purpose of furthering their *sloganistic* effects can be said to be truly vicious, both as a poet and as a man."[48] The landscape of Norman Rosten's poetic language in *The Big Road* was marked and variegated by all the "sloganis-tic effects" of public language. Yet by Friedman's rationale, applied with a finer, more ambiguous touch by Meredith, Rosten's verse, and that of many others, would have to fall outside the proper "scope" of poetry. Why? For one thing, according to Meredith, "it has . . . [a] catchy design [and] the crude color of a poster," qualities that have all to do with the key questions of intelligibility and obscurity.

Meredith's logic in 1946 was indeed exactly that of much poetry criticism in the anticommunist period through the early 1960s: claimed to dislike what the poster or the slogan said and how it said it, but really the crudity lay in the use of poetry as a poster or sloganism. The most effective way of repressing the prewar period was to impugn the forms (aesthetic judgment); then one could not be accused of mere disagreement with the content (just politics).[49]

Red Cauldrons of the New

For his own part, Norman Rosten felt that he must continue to champion politically and formally "alternative" poetries, something other than what Wil-liam Meredith and Winfield Townley Scott and others sought from a "mature" subjective-lyric verse for the postwar period. My sense is that Rosten's aesthetic choices in this period were often framed by a defensiveness that had its source in feelings about attacks against his verse such as Meredith's on *The Big Road*. For example, when James Decker, whose ambitious small press ran out of Prairie City, Illinois, asked Rosten to write a preface to the first book of poems,

Cauldron (1948), by a talented young poet, the unknown Alfred Levinson, Rosten went unstrategically to the barricades. So far as we can tell, neither Levinson nor Rosten benefited from Rosten's intervention.

Alfred Levinson's poems in *Cauldron* were actually in no need of Rosten's denunciation of the contemporary stupefied trend, "a period when so much of modern poetry suffers from a kind of intellectual trauma, enmeshed in complexities and guilt."[50] Slipping into leftist orthodoxy, Rosten seemed to forget how far radical poets had come toward modernism in the 1920s and 1930s; indeed, Levinson chose as the title for his first book the name of one of the revolutionary magazines inspired by the communist-led John Reed Clubs, a site for the gathering together of experimenters and leftists. It was not just generally a poor literary-politicking on Rosten's part but also specifically an inapt characterization of Levinson's work to speak of it as if Walt Whitman's rough, innocent yokel-prole had to be reinvented for an anti-ideological age of irony, subtlety, anxiety, and complexity. The anti-anticommunist lyricism of Levinson's first book of poems is not particularly that "of a poet with unbuttoned collar, strolling at ease among people, as if to say: Here is where I was born and grew up, here is what I know, remember, feel."

Rosten seems to have used Alfred Levinson's debut as an opportunity to deride the "school" of poetry of which Meredith was a student and the young Levinson was most certainly not, "doing brisk business" and dedicated to "the proposition that poetry is mainly a linguistic exercise," that was producing "the sickliness of all technical thought or refinement in itself." Rosten advocated "our greater tradition, stemming from Whitman"—a "social poetry." But he mapped this social poetry along uninventive lines, even conceding that Levinson's topic "covers well-worn ground."[51]

Alfred Levinson was hardly either a yokel or a prole, but he was, then and later, a political radical. His parents were Russian; he had been born in Southampton, England, and had come to New York by way of Buenos Aires, a typical exilic path for Jewish families in the late 1930s and early 1940s. He was an aesthetic internationalist, well versed in the multiple languages of modernism. The book of poems Decker published for Levinson has in it some trite work of the neophyte, but in any event it is hardly the kind of radical poetry Rosten had to defend—perhaps not so much a communist resistance to modernism as an attempt at experimentation *within* the communist aesthetic. Poems such as "Aura in War-Time" ("Today, with wisps of love my thoughts are plumed" is the quite regular opening line of what is essentially a traditional war poem) and the book's first work, a set-piece invocation titled "Me and the Sun," have little unusual about them; they are not even in the left-Whitmanian vein, despite

Rosten's implication. The proletarian road poem "Hitch" is vaguely imagistic, even, in the final stanza, down to the image-focused, nominative tagline in the haiku mode (it is reminiscent of Ezra Pound's precise early efforts, such as "The Encounter"):

warm Packard people, ghost
faces in paling light.

Drenched white line bending
through the mist . . .
miserable finger curved.[52]

But Levinson's most politically radical poems are in fact also his most linguistically inventive. It is precisely what this study has been written to discern, exactly what Rosten missed in his effort to counter the anticommunism of the end-of-ideology modernists. Levinson's poem denouncing American education as rote transfer of authority passing itself off as knowledge forms a thin vertical line of words. The poem's overall effect is to offer its words visually as words. Perhaps Levinson meant the look on *his* page as presenting an alternative to the lined paper framing the "ink-stained" hours of Americans' useless formal instruction. The poem is called "Education, with Seal of Approval":

Nerves
In meat of fingers
Speak:

a hard-point ball

caress
a fleshy sandwich.[53]

The longest poem in *Cauldron* is in some ways a by-then generic communist strike poem, "A Storm Grows in the Wind." It features at least two destitute factory workers at the onset of a cold evening, the (presumably shut) factory part of a boxy background horizon. Some stanzas are little more than vertically lineated versions of strike writing of the 1930s:

Tomorrow
We
Strike
Tomorrow
We
Move in Picket Lines.

But there is also a different language: "light flickers from his fingers / they swirl in cash—."[54] Levinson attempts to diffuse the strike poem subject and to alter the linguistic common sense of the sentence as the poem moves toward the disintegration of its radicalized speakers. It is not entirely successful, but the effort at disfigurement is marked. It is finally a communist poem yet not categorically a "thirties" poem. The inexorable movement toward the Big Strike, toward the realization in the disorganized speakers that organization among them is necessary, is not accompanied by an increasingly linguistic organization and integration. On the page, the poem looks rather as if the situation trails off, open-ended, so that lines such as, "This is it, yes this is it" and "At least one smile at coffee"[55]—optimism of a sort allegedly required in this radical genre—become ironic within the larger context created by the poem's refusal to conclude successfully.

The political reading patterns established in the 1910s and clinched in the 1930s tell one that *Cauldron* is a revolutionist's book. In the late 1930s, Decker had run a quarterly poetry magazine (and had solicited poems from many of the "social poets");[56] now, directing his press, among the modernist works he published were a share of those by communist fellow travelers and pinks— including two of Ruth Lechlitner's books, *Only the Years* (1944) and *The Shadow on the Hour* (1956); Zukofsky's *Anew* (1946); Frank Marshall Davis's most radical book, *47th Street* (1948); as well as Norman Macleod's *Calendar* anthologies. Decker presumably knew why to put on bright red covers when it befit the poems. The contents of the Decker Press *Cauldron* mark out a section for poems "of war," including those titled "Song for a Fascist," "Song for Partisans," and, in a section for poems "of oppression," a lyric implying a better future, "From our Ashes" (the poem is actually about the affiliations, through radical history, of blacks and Jews).

It was 1948, and while there was some continuity from the radical poetry of the 1930s, here there is a distinct difference. The historian of this political poetics has little choice but to make a case on insufficient evidence for a poet's talent, just then, for integrating radicalism and experimental writing. How can one securely comprehend a poet such as Alfred Levinson? There is little or no additional internal or external evidence to support this first book as auguring a new direction for a young post-Holocaust communist modernist or in collaboration with others of like mind. For after *Cauldron*, a modest but promising poetic beginning, the trail goes cold, despite every effort to follow it. Given what I know from researching dozens of other little-known leftist modernists of the postwar period—many people like Levinson—it has seemed possible that for several decades this writer simply disappeared from the poetry world.

Much later, Levinson taught in the theater program at New York University's School of the Arts, and he was for a time dramaturge at the New York Shakespeare Festival Public Theater.[57] In 1968 we can find him writing as he travels and resides among new revolutionists in Paris and elsewhere (publishing at least one poem about the cycle of New Left rebellion and repression that spring);[58] he made stops that year as well in Leningrad and Moscow. *Paris, Lost and Found*, a slight book of verse, with another foreword by Rosten, was produced by the mostly francophone pan-Africanist publishing project, Poésie Vivante. Another book of Levinson poems is called *Travelogs*, published in London in 1981. In 1982 Levinson was advocating the Palestinian cause.[59] Two further books, *Shipping Out* and *Millwork*, appeared from Oracle Press in 1987, perhaps published posthumously. What we can surmise from *Cauldron* is that the young poet meant the title not to suggest the volatile stirrings of revolutionaries (although that is certainly a viable reading) but rather the merging of poetic traditions, canonical or traditional on the one hand and radical and experimental on the other. The final poem of this little red book is not a glance forward toward social utopia but is actually a poem about poetry—more specifically, a declamation against the do-nothingism of traditional form ("Your well-formed phrase / Your past technique / Are shadows written of the sand"), the slender expression of hope in "poets of a new time," "inheritors of past" making way for "red cauldrons of the new." Open and self-referential, the verse calls for integration of poetic and political forces. The book's final line, "Your blood is one with ours," is not addressed from a poet to the people, to radicalizable readers, but from a communist poet to antipolitical experimenters. So much for Meredith's and Scott's implicit claim that the time had come to retake the language about the postwar politics of form from the "social poets." Norman Rosten, Levinson's advocate and Communist Party sponsor, for one, actively criticized what Scott, Meredith, and others saw as politically inspired revisionism—but Rosten's poetic career, too, was subject to deformation in the process.

The Rise and Fall of Norman Rosten

Rosten's book-length poem, *Return Again, Traveler*, had been published in 1940 as part of the Yale Series of Younger Poets, with an introduction by Stephen Vincent Benét, Rosten's mentor. Three years later, he published a book about the 1930s, *The Fourth Decade*, put out by a respected publisher, Farrar and Rinehart. *The Big Road*, the target of Meredith's disparagement, was another book-length poem (Rinehart, 1946). Three books of poetry in six years; at least one play, *Concerning the Red Army*, which was published among *The Best*

One-Act Plays of 1944 by Dodd, Mead in 1945; and scores of reviews and notices in the communist press. Typifying the latter was his celebratory review for the glossy *Soviet Russia Today* of Boris Skomorovsky's account of the siege of Leningrad, which Rosten called "a record of heroism [in] which the Soviet man takes his honored place in history."[60] It would have been difficult then for Rosten to imagine that just a few years later he would anxiously await even mere "hints" from publishers that they might publish his poems or that he would term such faint signals "food for a long winter."[61] In 1946, Rosten was a prolific, widely admired, eminently publishable poet, just thirty-two years old, with the Yale Younger Poets honor on his résumé and continuous access to a reliable press.

Stephen Vincent Benét (1898–1943) had gladly supported his radical protégé, but he died suddenly in March 1943. Rosten had become Benét's dear friend, had deeply admired the hundred-thousand-word poem *John Brown's Body* (1928)—the most widely read long poem of its era[62]—and felt at the time of Benét's death that his elder represented the best potential for radicalizing eminent noncommunist writers. Under the auspices of the Council for Democracy, a Popular Front group, independent but supported amply by wartime government funding—with some monies and lots of airtime provided by NBC's "Inter-American University of the Air"—Rosten took the one completed section of Benét's in-progress *Western Star*, a national epic, and prepared it as a radio dramatization in verse.[63] It was broadcast on March 19, 1944, under the banner of the Benét-Rosten/liberal-left "collaboration," with Raymond Massey's rock-solid, confidence-inspiring voice and an announcer auspiciously chanting that Rosten's completion of Benét's work posthumously enabled the "final great legacy of an artist to his people" to be a "soaring hymn to the spirit and beginnings of America."[64] Such praise by communists—and complaints from conservatives[65]—earned the deceased Benét a few years later a place on Joseph McCarthy's list of "communist authors" whose books Roy Cohn and David Schine had unhappily found on the shelves of American libraries overseas. The Steinbeckian language of Benét's *Western Star*—muscular, idealizing simple physical feeling, of the body needing and working—certainly records Rosten's aesthetic influence on his eminent friend, although it was, to be sure, like no other language Benét had produced. Benét linguistically morphed Daniel Webster into a kind of Tom Joad: "He began with the simple things that everybody's known and felt—the freshness of a fine morning when you're young, and the taste of food when you're hungry, and the new day when you're a child. He took them up and he turned them in his hands. They were good things for any man. But without freedom, they sickened. And when he talked of those enslaved, and the sorrows of slavery, his voice got like a big bell. He talked of the early days of America and . . . he made you see it."[66] Louis Untermeyer, former *Masses* editor and fellow traveler in the 1930s,[67] was so taken by this particular language that he decided that "no poet has ever written a better epitaph for himself." The proletarianized writing in Benét's remarkable deconstruction of the simple sentence "I am a citizen of the United States" for the *Yale Review* in 1941 restyled patriotism with a radical American idiom, under the rubric "The Power of the Written Word."[68] Soviet critics were persuaded, too; Benét was hailed in *Literaturnaya Gazeta* as one of just a few American poets who dared to "go against the stream of reactionary and 'apolitical' works."[69]

This was a specific victory for Norman Rosten and for the Popular Front. To follow the wartime movement toward the center by this young communist poet and the leftward pulling of fellow-traveling liberal eminences such as Benét is to learn a good deal about the radical poet's moment of prominence. The wartime work of the Council of Democracy, an uncontested site where communist or fellow-traveling poets' radicalization of literary Big Names could take place in the early 1940s, ranged across art and ideology more variously and unpredictably than later detractors of government "support" of communists would discern or concede. The Council for Democracy published Carl Sandburg's antifascist commentary for the defense film *Bomber*;[70] issued its dialectical *Advance through Crisis* (1941) as part of a Democracy in Action pamphlet series; corresponded engagingly with fellow-traveling intellectuals;[71] published the extraordinary *Write Now* magazine in May 1942; and freely took on leftist issues, as in its twenty-one-page pamphlet, *The Negro in America: How We Treat Him and How We Should* (1945).

No one at the Council for Democracy in the early 1940s would have doubted —or much worried—that Rosten was a communist; he simply was and apparently had been. It was generally known in poetry circles, for instance, that he had been helping to select poetry for publication in the *New Masses*.[72] Although he was relatively young at the onset of the war, the radical connections in his writing had already been established, and his reputation as a procommunist playwright preceded him from the University of Michigan. *Labor for the Wind* seems to have been his first produced play there. By the late 1930s, Rosten had written full-length plays (such as *Wait for No Morning*, 1936) as well as verse dramas (*The Proud Pilgrimage: A Poetic Drama of America*, 1937). *The Proud Pilgrimage* was also first produced by Michigan's University Theatre in 1938 and won Rosten the university's prestigious Hopwood Award.[73]

It is difficult to know what happened to Rosten's attitudes toward his writing and to the usual mainstream outlets for his poetry between 1946 and 1953. In any case, the period between 1946 and 1951 is an almost total blank, with the exception of his ideologically ill-conceived preface to Levinson's modernist-communist poems in 1948, two unpublished drafts of poems he mailed to Aaron Kramer in 1947, and a few more in perhaps 1950. Almost immediately after *The Big Road*, Rosten's new poetry mostly disappeared from view. Letters he wrote to Kramer, who had become a close political ally and personal friend, indicate that Rosten had all but abandoned poetry before he began drafting verse that would eventually be collected in a book called *The Plane and the Shadow*. A few typescripts came to Kramer with a note lamenting, "all I've done since 'The Big Road.'" Rosten remained optimistic about his verse, hoping Kramer agreed that "I've learned a lot since [*The Big Road*]."[74] Kramer's reply apparently does not survive; in any case, what Rosten seems to have "learned" was about what kind of lyricism was now publishable. During this period, he did not publish poems in the little magazines or quarterlies. But neither did he go back to playwriting, although he made at least one false start in that direction.[75] The critical attack on *The Big Road*, its failure to find any sort of ideological or generic fit with the times, helped bring on this silence after so much vehemence and activity.

"These Poems Need an Extremely Large Context"

As with many other radical poets in the decade beginning in 1946, the beleaguered poet seems, at least briefly, to have decided to attempt a change in genres—twice, in fact. Through Alan Wald's comprehensive studies of radical writers, we have learned that an extraordinarily large contingent of communist novelists and poets moved into popular genres such as mystery and detective fiction, children's books, softback thrillers, cookbooks, popular psychology books, radio and television screenwriting, sci-fi, dime-store romances, and the like.[76] There are as many reasons for these shifts as there were individual writers facing the new difficult period, and not all, obviously, have to do with the anticommunist movement's successes in pushing radical writers out of the main literary arenas. In Rosten's case, we can track the swerving course less accurately than in others'. Yet such situations as his are perhaps more instructive than the more easily documented ones, precisely because of the way in which extant records of this period are limited.

The reason for the dearth of records is in itself worth studying and is a central part of the story of the communist-modernist relationship. Dozens of leftist poets who had thrived as writers in the 1930s and early 1940s were in some fashion exiling themselves—were (or felt) forced into exile—during the early years of the postwar period. Some, like George Oppen, left the United States for Mexico, literally avoiding or escaping red-baiters, professional anticommunists, FBI men seeking "interviews," deliverers of subpoenas. Before Rachel Blau DuPlessis set out to edit Oppen's letters for publication, so little was known about Oppen's twenty-five-year "period of poetic silence" (1934–58) that she came to depend on the FBI's file on the poet, which she obtained through the Freedom of Information Act, as the only source for many of his activities, especially between 1936 and 1941.[77]

Margaret Larkin, the poet married to Albert Maltz, also spent the blacklisting period in Mexico.[78] Robert Friend (b. 1913) left for Israel in 1951, when HUAC threatened to rescind his passport.[79] On December 7, 1948, Frank Marshall Davis left for Hawaii and did not return until 1973, a retreat that initially signified his "capitulation" to the FBI and other anticommunists who were hounding him. He had taught what was probably the nation's first history of jazz course at a school that was listed by HUAC as a communist front; he was a member of the CPUSA (although he never admitted this); he had been under intense scrutiny by the FBI since 1945. The sudden big move, the fear under which Davis lived at a crucial time in his poetic development, and his complete departure from the world of poetry for a quarter century, has made the work of gathering Davis's materials an enormous undertaking for his editor and biographer, John Edgar Tidwell.[80] Davis's verse disappeared until in the early 1970s Dudley Randall campaigned to revive the reputation. Only then did Randall learn that it was not only Davis himself who had been removed from the scene; his books, too, had been pulled from library shelves "and stored . . . in the basement along with other controversial literature," as Davis put it, "until the nation began returning to sanity."[81]

Norman Macleod, the "revolutionary imagist" who had been closely associated with *The Left*, the *New Masses*, and the Federal Writers Project, founded and directed the New York Poetry Center from 1939 to 1942 and was appointed chair of the Briarcliff Junior College English department in 1944. He left Briarcliff in 1947 (reasons unknown) and taught at a prep school in New York (1948–49), served as administrative assistant in the public relations section of the New Mexico Department of Public Welfare (1951–53), spent one academic year (1954–55) as assistant director of the poetry center at San Francisco State University, and then taught high school in Gardnersville, Nevada (1958–59). In what he later called "the difficult summer of 1950," with plenty of relevant experience—he had been a tenurable assistant professor of English at the University of Maryland in the early 1940s—Macleod received an appointment to become an English instructor with the U.S. Air Force in Okinawa. He visited the

Pentagon for inoculations and to view training films on Korea but then received a letter from a Colonel Lindsay of the Armed Forces Information and Education Division advising him that he "did not have the 'necessary' qualifications for the job." Later, when composing his autobiography, the still unpublished 750-page "Generation of Anger," Macleod chose to begin with this 1950 scene at the Pentagon: what amounts to the blacklisting of a poet, a man whose unemployment insurance was running out and who was caring for a two-year-old son while his wife battled cancer, was his main motive for memoir, a work he called a review of "the dissident heredity."[82] A few young poets at *Golden Goose* in the Bay Area eventually somehow made the connection and did an all-Macleod issue; by 1962 Macleod, still insolvent, generously donated money to restart *Measure* under John Wieners's editorship, thus having a hand in publishing verse by Robin Blaser, Ed Dorn, Larry Eigner, Barbara Guest, and Wieners. But between 1949 and 1960, Macleod moved at least seven times, and notwithstanding revived associations with the new poetry, the archival record of his writing of this period—letters and poems—is limited.

Other poets, even when not moving from city to city or enduring the decline from house to apartment or from larger to smaller flats—such moves, of course, often meant discarding letters and manuscripts—stopped saving personal correspondence; thus the archives, normally sites for recovering something of the shape of the distorted literary career, with its gaps, transitions, breaks, and silences, are a limited resource as well. Given that Genevieve Taggard was temperamentally a keeper of letters and manuscripts, there is a relative paucity of extant materials about her personal life, notwithstanding good collections (which helpfully include her teaching notes) at Dartmouth and at the New York Public Library.[83] Taggard died young in 1949; as she began to suffer her final illness, she told a Sarah Lawrence College colleague that "*they* destroyed me," and stories circulated that a red-baiter—another poet—had been undermining her standing at the college; in any case, she was forced to resign after a nervous breakdown.[84] Was it during this period that she discarded letters or asked her correspondents to do the same?

Materials pertaining to Millen Brand's popular books and mainstream activities are relatively plentiful and available, but little survives of his years of involvement with CPUSA protests and projects *or* of his poetry. The twenty-three-page typewritten report on Brand's communist doings, prepared in December 1949 for the red-baiting enterprise, Counterattack—and now filed in the 178th folder in the twenty-eighth box of the Counterattack Papers at New York University's Tamiment Library—remains the fullest extant account, errors and all, of Brand's radical career.[85] Ronald Lane Latimer, an ambitious although unremarkable poet yet a brilliant editor and publisher of important books of poetry in limited editions, joined the Communist Party but then, at the end of the 1930s, fled from a convergence of nightmarish sexual and political discomposure; Latimer disappeared into New Mexico and surfaced later in Japan; when he returned to the United States, first to Santa Fe and finally to Florida, he had given up the literary life. During his strangely hasty retreat from New York, most of the editorial materials and correspondence—much of it directly connecting modernist and communist poets (he published Willard Maas, Ruth Lechlitner, Williams, and Stevens, among others)—was lost or scattered. Only recently has some of this been discovered, as I suggested in this book's preface, in archives here and there—typically uncataloged or misfiled, almost unretrievably, under Latimer's five or six known pseudonyms.[86] I am certain that if Latimer had remained in the picture, the poetry of Maas and Lechlitner would be better known and in the case of Maas might have encouraged third and fourth books of verse at a time when his passion for vanguardism was directed toward other art media. Other poets, by the late 1940s and 1950s, had to spend so much time defending themselves legally and otherwise as "premature" antifascists or anti-anticommunists that they literally ran out of the time they felt they needed to devote to especially unremunerative writing—particularly the experimental.

Some poets who had depended on sympathetic editors watched in horror as they were removed. Angus Cameron, a prominent book editor with a legendary talent for spotting good writers for Boston's Little, Brown,[87] was fired from that firm after being named by Joseph McCarthy. Cameron formed several new presses, including Cameron and Kahn, and did what he could to publish blacklisted and other unpublishable writers; among them was the feminist Eve Merriam, the communist poet who had introduced modernist women to WQXR's listeners to her show, *Out of the Ivory Tower*, but who now had few outlets. Facing major shifts in taste by magazine editors and book publishers, some poets just stopped trying to publish their work. Merriam was lucky to relocate Cameron, an old friend loyal to her from the 1948 Henry Wallace campaign. John Beecher (1904–80) had become a poet during the years when he worked twelve-hour shifts in front of an open steelmaking furnace in Alabama; he was active poetically and much in demand in the 1930s, but in the 1950s he and his wife resorted to publishing his poems themselves.[88] Edwin Rolfe published *First Love* (1951) himself; the book came out under the name of the Larry Edmunds Book Shop, but Rolfe worked with (and paid) the printer and personally sold the books.[89]

Eda Lou Walton was red-baited as often as any poet. In *Conquest of the*

American Mind (1956), Felix Wittmer identified her as among New York University's "faculty stalwarts on the pinko fringe."[90] In *American Legion Magazine*, Louis Budenz named her a subversive educator in "Do Colleges *Have* to Hire Red Professors?"[91] And as a (paid) cooperative "witness" before a 1953 hearing of the Subversive Activities Control Board (SACB), Budenz defamed her by association because she taught evening writing courses at the Jefferson School of Social Science. Budenz told the SACB that he knew her and then admitted that his witnessing of her subversive acts amounted to having overheard others mention her radical connections. Nothing about her poetry or teaching was ever introduced as evidence:

> CHAIRMAN HERBERT: Did you know Eda, E-d-a, Lou, that is L-o-u, Walton, W-a-l-t-o-n, and if so, when?
> BUDENZ: Yes, I knew her . . . particularly in connection with her activities with the Communist Party in the educational field and her association with a number of organizations connected with the Community Party.
>   The reason I hesitated there for a moment about whether I knew her personally was that I am not certain whether I met her during the campaign for [poet and critic] Morris U. Schappes's release. But at any rate I have constantly been informed officially of her connection with the Communist Party and her connection with these various organizations created by the Party in the educational field and in some other fields.[92]

The SACB never could decide if poets who taught poetry writing at a school sponsored by communists were ipso facto treasonous in doing so. Others were surer: Jefferson was dubbed a "center of Communist indoctrination" in *The Conquest of the American Mind*,[93] and Fulton Lewis Jr. in his radio program, *Top of the News*, referred to Jefferson as an "espionage school" and told his audience that in "these refresher courses . . . word filters down to [students] from the Kremlin."[94] When Frank Meyer testified, he led the SACB in a discussion of "a whole set of courses on literature, art, and so on" in the Jefferson School catalog (where the board had gotten Walton's name in the first place). But even when pressed, Meyer could say only that such courses as Walton's "look to me primarily to be attractive courses [that is, window dressing], but certainly some of them and in some way—depending on the teacher—may have been of some use in developing Marxist-Leninist ideas. But," Meyer, an economist and political scientist, working in a distant academic field, added, "I don't know who the people were."[95] No testimony was introduced about what poetry Walton taught in her courses or about how they were taught; nor was Walton able to appear to describe her art or pedagogy, since SACB hearings were held in secret.[96]

Eda Lou Walton's job at New York University apparently was saved only by the intervention of her department chair.[97] Red-baiters in San Antonio nonetheless got her name through the various red channels—reports spread around after Budenz "named" her by saying he had heard from others of her subversive books—and civic-minded Texans in turn listed her as a dangerous communist in a report made available at all public libraries in that region.[98] The campaign against her depressed sales of her works to libraries. To this day, it seems likely that no public library in the state of Texas owns a copy of *So Many Daughters*, a book that was available to acquisitions librarians just at the time of the smear campaign.[99] Walton did publish *So Many Daughters* during this difficult moment, and this in itself would seem to suggest poetic activity, but in fact the book gathered several decades' poems.[100] Later, doing a rough stint[101] at Howard University and taking teaching appointments at, for instance, a small black women's college in North Carolina, Walton found the "hours . . . long and I did not manage my writing."[102] "Our Daily Death" is written out of the dissonant response Walton received:

> Ear could not catch the song
> And the rhythm was wrong
> And the smell of the earth was fear.[103]

Alfred Kreymborg, survivor of decades of literary wars, from the 1910s through the time of *Seven Poets in Search of an Answer*, told one editor (who had rejected all the poems Kreymborg had just sent) that he knew his political views and reputation were making it difficult to find a publisher for his manuscript, then called "The Heavenly Blues." Kreymborg's "old friend Tom Eliot" was reading the work for Faber in London, but because of its "embattled pacifism"—which is to say, its advocacy of "peaceful coexistence," its anti–Cold War stance—"it won't be easy to place in the current marketplace."[104] Kreymborg, who endured sectarian wars and line changes within the communist movement[105] with a "temporarily exhausted and depleted heart" (as he put it in 1946 during the worst of such times),[106] was finally "bludgeoned into silence by the McCarthy period," according to Kramer, who knew Kreymborg well through this era.[107]

The poet and anthologist Louis Untermeyer, his radical past at the *Masses* having been disclosed and his dissident view of World War I (that it was strictly a creature of imperialism) now repeated back to him, was named before HUAC and was sacked from television's *What's My Line* in 1951. Arthur Miller recalled that Untermeyer was so shocked by his blacklisting that, struck down by an "overwhelming and paralyzing fear," he did not leave his apartment for eighteen months[108]—an exaggeration, apparently, but one that helps us understand Untermeyer's meager production as poet and editor in those years.

Carlos Bulosan died penniless and in literary obscurity—blacklisted, scheduled for deportation, and depressed.[109] "But we are not really free," he had written in "Freedom from Want" for the *Saturday Evening Post* in his heyday, "unless we use what we produce"—and he meant his own writing as much as anything else.[110] Alvaro Cardona-Hine, a "non-Party Bolshevik" poet, shared Bulosan's sense of the importance of the CPUSA's stated commitment to " 'anti-colonialism' and 'anti-racism.' "[111] Cardona-Hine's "Bulosan Now" responded to this wasteful death synesthetically, just as the poem, in the mode of elegy, turns from lament to encouragement: "I can raise the thankful inwells of my voice."[112]

Ben Maddow, who had taken the name David Wolff to keep his identity secret from employers, launched a career in Hollywood after the war, only to be blacklisted for eight years beginning in 1952. His experimental documentary "cine-poem" for the Nykino project—innovative writing in which diction and word choice are used to accentuate or conceal a visual detail, retard or increase the tempo of images—has gone largely unnoticed in part because "David Wolff" (his communist handle) was credited for the project.[113]

Isidor Schneider left his editorial post at the *New Masses* in 1946 not so much because of ideological conflicts there, although he was embroiled in the controversy stirred by Albert Maltz's article calling for greater aesthetic latitude among CPUSA-affiliated writers, and he admitted that he had lost the capacity to "take the political mind." Mostly, Schneider wanted time to work on two books and hoped for a salary sufficient to give his daughter, Emily, an education. First he sought part-time jobs in the book business, but because of his "identification with the Party press," there was little work for him. Months after leaving *New Masses*, he had no "feeling of security for more than two weeks ahead."[114] Malcolm Cowley privately warned Schneider that it would be at least a year before he would get decent work or sell his writing. When a new job at *Soviet Russia Today* opened up for Schneider, Cowley warned that "a job at SRT would be a greater bar to your getting strictly literary employment than even a job at NM. . . . You'd better make the break now, and get started."[115] This was in August 1946. In January 1947, Schneider was ghostwriting for a dermatologist.[116]

At the time of Herman Spector's death (at the age of fifty-four) in 1959, after a decade of driving a taxi and selling photo coupons for a commercial photographer, he had become, in George Oppen's words, "perhaps the loneliest of the impoverished men of his time." "1929 and a decade [were] audible" in his experimental verse, which in the 1930s Alfred Hayes deemed Zukofskyian[117] and which Oppen and Carl Rakosi always greatly admired. But Spector had been "haunted and jostled" by conflicting audiences through the decades. Before he died, "fear had abolished the poetry." Oppen wrote to Spector's daughter after the poet's death, "I think your father stopped short, or was stopped."[118] Forty percent of the posthumous collection of his writing is taken up by work he was unable to publish in his lifetime.

It is not clear why the poet James Neugass did not actively pursue his various verse projects. He certainly never regretted signing the original call for the formation of the procommunist League of American Writers in 1935[119] or fighting against Franco as a member of the Abraham Lincoln Battalion in the late 1930s, although all Lincolns, as "premature antifascists," faced red-baiting beginning in the 1940s. To countersubversive investigators, Neugass was an unreconstructed red into the 1950s, living, they thought they had discovered, in Long Island City and still reading the *Daily Worker* daily. The *Worker* subscription, as usual, tipped off Counterattack, the for-profit anticommunist "research" group, that Neugass was still a traitor; they had pilfered from the New York office of the Communist Party a run of addressograph mailing labels for metropolitan *Worker* subscribers. But the poet had died in 1949, and it was actually James Neugass's wife, Myra, who had kept up the subscription.[120] Neugass had published poems pseudonymously, but by the early 1990s his widow had long forgotten these names, so this verse presumably is lost.[121]

Rukeyser was followed by an FBI agent pretty much full time during the height of the Cold War. The 118-page portion of Rukeyser's FBI file I have read lists ten different informants who presented investigators with "evidence" of her communism. "Confidential Informant T-5" learned that another government agency doing a security check on the poet said that Rukeyser was known "to have been active in Communist literary circles and as a writer," supporting evidence coming from the *Oxford Book of American Literature*, where she was listed "as a 'left-wing poet.'" As T-5 did his or her groundbreaking lit crit, informant T-4 had already advised the FBI in 1951 that she knew the poet to be a communist "as a result of conversations she had with the subject" even though "this informant advised that no specific instances or statements could be recalled" ("but further advised that the subject had also visited with Mr. and Mrs. HAN[N]S EISLER on one occasion").[122] When Sarah Lawrence College hired Rukeyser, the American Legion convened a meeting at which 150 legion delegates applauded a report condemning the college's president for "the recent hiring of 'a celebrated Leftist,' identified as Miss Muriel Rukeyser," as a *New York Times* article put it. Merrill Folsom's story listed no fewer than seven of the subversive organizations to which the legion report said she belonged, including the National Dance Congress. The copy of the *Times* story I consulted for this book was a photostat the FBI made for its file, all Folsom's references to her radical associations marked up for cross-indexing in related agency files. Here the FBI got its intelligence on Rukeyser from the Legion report through the *New York Times* report on the latter.[123]

Kramer was one poet who continued to publish after his publisher turned against him, but from the mid-1940s through the early 1960s, doing so was sometimes not easy. As early as the winter of 1942–43, soon after he joined the Astoria Club of the CPUSA, he went to the Fifth Avenue branch of the New York Public Library and surreptitiously pulled all catalog cards indicating communist subvention of his first book, *Another Fountain*.[124] In 1954, the William-Frederick Press editor who had published *Thru Every Window!*, the second of Kramer's four anti-McCarthy collections (1950), got scared weeks before the scheduled release of *Roll the Forbidden Drums!* William-Frederick returned the galleys with apologies and a frank admission that Kramer's name at that point would make it suicidal for them to give the book their imprint.[125] Angus Cameron not only took up and published *Roll the Forbidden Drums!*; he and his associate, Albert Kahn, himself a blacklisted writer, proposed to back Kramer in a series of volumes that would be designed to turn American history into modern verse.[126] Even the energetic Kramer had his low moments—such as in mid-1950, when his embattled work as bookkeeper and office manager at Local 16, United Office and Professional Workers of America in New York, which was fighting against the widespread removal of communists from union leadership, caused him severe bleeding ulcers.[127]

Millen Brand had regularly published poems in *Poetry* before the war. Although his lyrics were typically too political for Harriet Monroe, she sometimes accepted them.[128] But while Brand's career as a novelist and screenwriter showed surprising continuity, notwithstanding his radical politics and the red-baiting he had to endure (his name appeared, for instance, in the sensational "Hooray for Murder!" chapter of *The Red Decade*),[129] the poetry went out of view. Brand, when he is remembered, is known as the writer whose career took off with the novel *The Outward Room* (1937), continued with *Albert Sears* (1947) and his screenplay for the film *The Snake Pit* (1948), and fully emerged with the remarkable success of *Savage Sleep* (1968). Brand became a successful editor at Crown, managing to keep his job while being listed in every manner of red-baiters' scandal sheets (typical was *REaD-READING: A Report on Our San Antonio Public Libraries: Communist Front Authors and Their Books Therein*, which urged citizens to remove Brand's books from library shelves everywhere).[130] Wald's sense of popular genres as safe havens for radical writers is apt in Brand's case, but with a further complication pertaining to the political nonviability of Brand's commitment to modern poetry *as* poetry. Cut off from forums for modern verse in the late 1940s and 1950s, he concentrated on the generic options open to him; thus his success there does not mean that aesthetic-political repression did not operate on his writing project or specifically on his use of language. For an analysis of that operation, the extant archive is insufficient. We do know that members of the generation of young writers who were not as swayed by the 1950s construction of the 1930s as their elders cherished the bits of Brand's new verse they could find. Indeed, as a poet Brand had a samizdat reputation. He, in turn, wrote letters to some of the young idiosyncratic poets whose work he followed.[131] To find the oddly dislocated or unlocal lyrics of his "Local Lives" series, the new poets had to go back to the Popular Front anthology edited by communist Edwin Seaver, the 1945 *Cross Section* annual,[132] and the June 1949 issue of *Masses & Mainstream*,[133] where one read, here and there, a conscious modernist reckoning of language mixed thematically with political radicalism. For the political sensibility of the new poems— independent of communist calls for direct political writing—one could go back, during the heyday of left sectarianism, to Brand's off-key response to the question "For Whom Do You Write?" (Whereas the typical communist writer's response was "I write to make such contribution as I can to the dissemination of the most important truth of our times. Capitalism today is monstrous. . . . Communism alone is the way out," Brand remarked that he wrote foremost for his wife and for "those who are interested in work that does not deal directly with social protest or struggle, but has serious or tragic significance.")[134] "The Factory," which had appeared first in *Cross Section*, is typical of the emergent "Local Lives" series. The shrill sound of a machine saw occasions a renunciation of simile, beyond the simple "circle" (the shape of the blade?) which is barely visual; it is less an image than an aspect of the continuous sound. The observation of the way the people of the night shift live their lives, inscribed by that sound, refuses to take its eye, as it were, off the sound. The poem's refusal to refer to language outside itself is modeled on William Carlos Williams's experiments in antimetaphor—for instance, in "Flowers by the Sea" (1935), where the sea is "likened" to the plantlike stem of the flower rocking within it, a likening that gives way to the observation that the flower's stem is in turn like the rocking sea. In Brand, for example,

> The whine, like a circle,
> is the sound by which men live—

yes, and the living goes
even beyond
the sound[135]

Again because *Poetry* retained its editorial files, we gain at least a partial view of Brand's poetic silence. Having had nothing but rejections during the previous eight and a half years[136] and no ongoing relationship with the magazine in fourteen, since *Poetry*'s December 1941 issue,[137] he tried again in late 1955, writing to Henry Rago that "for quite a while I sent my best work to Poetry." With this letter he included "An Old Man toward the End." The poem had been rejected at *Poetry* but eventually found a place with *Accent* of Urbana in 1953, and it was in *Accent* where some of the younger poets had picked up traces of Brand's poetic survival.[138] "I ask myself," Brand wrote, "why the continuity of the relationship with *Poetry* broke down. . . . The fact remains that I feel *Poetry* as a kind of lost home."

Brand also sent Rago a group of poems from his new poetry manuscript, then titled *Local Lives* (it was not social published until 1975).[139] The *Local Lives* project operated from the assumption that portraiture had lost almost all of the aesthetic valuation it once had, had fallen into total utilitarianism; Brand sought, passionately but *uncreatively* (through what might be called nonimaginative writing), to do in his poems what portrait painters traveling back roads across America did with their rolls of cheap canvas—"painted the people who otherwise would have died without record," a census-taking gesture initiated without any concept of its value as social archive or as art. Brand would do a six-month stint in Hollywood, making enough money to live on for another six, and then spend that time in small eastern Pennsylvania hill towns, an itinerant maker of these portrait poems. Brand told Karl Shapiro in 1952 that the project, already then 350 pages of poems about the people of a single community, was "something in the nature of a life work" and "a work of love."[140]

A few weeks after Brand submitted these poems, Rago wrote to explain why all the poems were being rejected. "I think I agree," Rago wrote, "that these poems need an extremely large context before their true 'poetry' reveals itself."[141] Such language was typical of Rago's rejection-letter style. It was effective—much more effective in calming angry, rejected poets, especially those who felt an antileft and/or antiexperimental bias, than almost any of the rejections sent out by Rago's predecessor, Shapiro. Nonetheless, the letter is revealing. The "extremely large context" Brand's poems required was, for one thing, page space in a fiscally tight little magazine; it also referred to the need of socially allusive or referentially complex work for expanded historical setting, prefatory materials, notes, or prose annotations. The note accompanying Brand's "The Lute" in *Masses & Mainstream* took up six lines of type, explaining the setting of the series in a "plain sect" Mennonite community. (Actually, *Poetry* sometimes ran longer context-setting notes.)

Poetry in the Rago years could not make room for the "large context" Brand's poetry augured, and its editors could honestly report back that this was a managerial and financial problem—almost a layout and design problem as a function of budgetary constraints—rather than an aesthetic and political matter. Of course it was also very much the latter, and Brand knew it when he wrote that he had lately been finding *Poetry* "somewhat hard to read." (He meant this literally.) It seemed to him "to be much more limited than it had been" in earlier years, when the look of the short lyrics on the page was not so strictly determinative of what verse was acceptable in the first place.[142]

Millen Brand, creating a modern documentary in verse, was urging *Poetry* to value a valueless poetics, writing that "is different from the current definitions." He hated to think that such a poetics of "clear perception" lacking any rhetorical claims would "cut me off either from poetry or POETRY," but that is what happened.[143] What had originally driven the larger context for allusive verse was the modernist revolution of the word, not the social and political revolution Brand in the 1930s (and later) bespoke. Indeed, one of the reasons George Dillon in the late 1930s opened up *Poetry* to some "social poetry" was that the "context" for unannotated short lyrics was easier for readers to follow than for the various modernist epic fragments the magazine was also publishing by then.[144] But by the 1950s, the two revolutions were being quietly undone by Rago's competent rejection notes—neither admittedly. Had Rago recognized the antipolitical bias of this "inherent" editorial limitation, he would, I think, have accepted it; had he understood ways in which this transformed *Poetry*'s relation to the modern, he would have been appalled.

The End of the Line

Millen Brand never overcame the aesthetic sense of this rejection, but fortunately his commitment to fiction and nonfiction were sufficiently urgent, and the political situation of the American novel was more transparent than that of modern poetry, so Brand went on in fiction. Norman Rosten, on the contrary, more or less failing in his other generic commitments, turned longingly and somewhat desperately back to poetry, capitulating to the new editorial regime. This is why it is useful to attend to Rosten, for his case thus provides one way of narrating the fifties' thirties in poetry.

He seems first to have attempted a new career as a songwriter and composer of vocal scores and more or less simultaneously as a screenwriter for television; he also tried his hand at short fiction.[145] The TV work he did, "not the best or the most," provided no pleasure, but it was "enough to keep ahead of the rent."[146] It seems likely that his good friend Arthur Miller helped him make some Hollywood connections, although there is only indirect evidence of this. For a short time in 1951, Rosten worked on a film script for a Joan Crawford vehicle, but the project was never completed.[147] He had tried his hand at song-writing in earlier years; he now considered this activity akin to his work as a successful lyric poet, and he seems to have put everything into the attempt. At the height of the Popular Front, when communist writers could be found among teams of artists creating patriotic, antifascist short films, features, public performances, traveling exhibits, and the like, Rosten had worked with Leo Sowerby (1895–1968) on the elaborate orchestral *Song for America: Chorus for Mixed Voices*. By the end of the 1940s, desperate for work and money, Rosten very nearly accepted a project writing musical "historical spots" for a program being produced for the u.s. National Guard. In the end, he could not go through with this project—no matter if it put some money in his pocket, and no matter if it might mean liberalizing the product a bit. Still a supporter of the communist movement at the time, though disaffected by some communists' literary policies, he felt "political responsibility" that transcended the tactical advantage of cultural boring from within and noted that such a potential subversive engagement, even for a starving leftist poet, was more complicated— more closely bound up in the dire need for cash and work and thus at least superficially not really a political decision—and "far less diabolical" than critics on the right, and even those on the noncommunist left, would perceive it to be: a communist poet writing for the National Guard.[148] Turning to music more seriously around the same time, Rosten completed work on libretti for the song cycle published by Simon and Schuster as *Songs for Patricia* (with decorative illustrations by Alexander Dobkin). The next year, 1952, he created the musical settings for another personal song cycle, *For My Daughters*. Whatever the re-sponse to this new work, if any (records apparently do not survive), it seems not to have been enough for Rosten. And he was finally accumulating a small sheaf of unpublished poems. He sought a big return to poetry and to active participa-tion in the poetry scene.

The result was a book, *The Plane and the Shadow* (1953). It was finally published by Bookman Associates of New York after a bitterly disappointing rejection by Twayne of Boston that proved to Rosten that the antipolitical backlash against his mode of constructivist multivocality had stuck. From that experience emerged a distortion of Rosten's earlier approach to poetic language as a means of conveying the wide social landscape: a retreat from the boldness of the modern documentary epic to the quietude of the meditative, "tight" personal lyric that was now characteristic of the modernist inheritance in u.s. poetry, a trend at least editorially endorsed during this period by Rago and other editors. Yet this was not a poetic mode in which Rosten thrived, the social form well captured in Rukeyser's dictum, "Not Sappho, Sacco." Rosten's experimental use of language is to be found in the audacious Popular Front leftist epic derided by William Meredith in 1946; once he conformed aesthetically in the 1953 book, his poetry lost rather than gained in its engagement with the linear and stanzaic disruptions that centrist critics alleged had been opposed by radicals. Insofar as *The Plane and the Shadow* discloses the internalization (although perhaps not quite acceptance) of Meredith's anti-ideological condemnation of communist-modernist writing, the new book was a disaster for Rosten's poetics. Indeed, for all intents and purposes, 1953, intended as a comeback year, marked the end of Rosten's career as a poet of significance. In *The Plane and the Shadow*, Rosten inscribed his own fifties' thirties.

Rosten's 1953 book presents us with the slightly modified political ballad in "Prelude," giving us something of a Kenneth Fearing of the 1930s absent the wit:

> Today you will sell out
> Today you will take the bribe
> It's the way of the world
> And you'll stay alive[149]

There was also unproductive tension (or obvious contradiction) working clumsily inside a formal generic invocation, a genre that communist poet Ruth Lechlitner in the 1930s had mastered with sharp feminist irony, in, for instance, "Lines for an Abortionist's Office" (1936):

> Close here thine eyes, O State:
> These are thy guests who bring
> To gods with appetites grown great
> A votive offering.
>
> Know that they dare defy
> The words of law and priest—[150]

Here, in Rosten's hands, the genre falls metrically (and otherwise) flat: "Help us, Father. / (For we still must have Authority.)"[151]

The Plane and the Shadow even offers a summoning of the premodern. It is as if Rosten wrestled with his uncomfortable status as a midcentury poet by, here and there, seeking tonal affinities with his modernist precursors. An example is "Gloucester Port"—a "Gloucester Moors" for the 1950s that seemed to trace a threadbare lineage back through modernism to William Vaughn Moody, back to Moody's sullen American Victorianism at twilight. Moody's heavy-toned scene setting in the widely anthologized "Gloucester Moors" is rightly said to be among the late-century models against which Williams, Moore, Pound, Stevens, and even Frost reacted. Rosten's version goes as follows:

> By dawn the ghostly tide is in.
> The harbor, enmeshed with sails, soon dancing
> With daylight and buoys; to the rotting docks
> Fish-smell and motors heavily cling.

The poem nonetheless conveys unhappiness with the status of (mere) observer, the tourist-poet who comes to such a scene "with verb and camera, to survey and leave," who "must simulate" and "never be." In an earlier draft of "Gloucester Port," which Rosten mailed to Aaron Kramer in 1950, the opening stanza used Moody's line more straightforwardly to match the end-of-an-era mood:

> From morning's tide, ghostly with gongs,
> The jungular day with its buoys drifts;
> Fish smell and motors, the rotting docks
> Where the water sinuous and heavily lifts.

One would not find two inversions forced to favor meter and rhyme ("drifts"/ "lifts"; "water sinuous and heavily lifts") in all of *The Big Road*, 233 pages long. Nor did Rosten's readers find words like "jungular" in the earlier book, certainly not in descriptions of the sea. The draft Rosten sent Kramer ended with an effort to undo the poem's own studied innocence—the premodern archaism of its own lines—with a bit of didacticism projecting fear of political knowledge outward, to "the seekers, the workers, the oblivious poor." This line was gone from the published book.[152]

The problem was that by this point Norman Rosten was far too self-conscious of the radical poetic legacy as it had to operate in the 1950s to manage a leftist's homage to William Vaughn Moody's downbeat protomodernism. The distinction between linguistic seeming and embodied being, between scene setting and action, is lost in the obvious tonal effectiveness. That such a poet really "grapple[s] with a literary idea of fate" (the awkward phrase in the final version of "Gloucester Port") is just not believable. The poem does not so much long for "Gloucester Moors" as for the preexperimentalist era in which Moody might operate, innocent of such self-reference and formal inwardness, relieved of the imaginative burden of the documentary modernist mode the communist poet had mastered in *The Big Road*, not in spite of but because of his political commitments.[153]

To be sure, the 1953 book bore a few extant signs of Rosten's radical energies. "The Portable Electric Chair," a poem about the denied civil rights of Willie McGee, takes that narrative of communist martyrology forward with some of the linguistic force reminiscent of *The Big Road*. One section of the book is taken up by the long titular series, "The Plane and the Shadow." In a sequence of cantos, each in a different stanza form, picking up snatches of airline commonplaces and smartly ironizing the peculiar modern solitude of commercial flight, this long poem charts the adventure of a plane that makes a forced landing. But for each poem like the titular poem or the homage to McGee there are five like "Song for the Make-Up Man," a work based on a theatrical cliché (that under the made-up face of a performer lies blank terror) set in a clichéd stanzaic form:

> Did you ever see
> Such a hiding of possessions
> Did you ever see
> Such a washing of sins[154]

In just a few years, then, Rosten had set aside the mode of *The Big Road* and with it a critical reappraisal of nationhood generated in the documentary epic that engages, like Crane's bridge and Williams's city, an overarching symbol of human aspiration. It refused to tell its story from a single point of view but instead used myriad other voices and testimonies to bespeak contingent and partial stories. By collecting individual elements of the colossal objective of building an interconnected postwar world yet rejecting the urge toward world-historical synthesis that had in the first place created nationhood, *The Big Road* argues that indeed "poetry can extend the document" (in Rukeyser's phrase)— that such writing can be deemed, as Rosten puts it in a prefatory note, "a poem as well as history." The endpapers glued to the bright red cloth cover of Rinehart's edition of the book bear stylized world maps drawn by George Annand, indicating the continents connected by one big worldwide road. The maps might seem at first to gesture toward a simple unified postwar utopianism, a One Worldism in which a triumphant national narrative delivers its message unimpeded across cultural multiplicities, having used world war as an aesthetic-strategic bulldozer. In this light, *The Big Road* seems the work of one of Chamberlin's unremarkable (although geographically minded) AAC communists. But readers of *The Big Road*

George Annand's drawing for the endpapers of Norman Rosten's
The Big Road. © 1946 by George Annand.

quickly realize that the world of this written road is constructed of parts; that the road enacts a multilateralism; that history's temporality cannot be contained in a lyric of a single subject's epiphanic moment; and that the part is to the whole as what is deemed nonliterary materials is to the literary.

In the material text of *The Big Road*, readers find verbatim ancient instructions for engineering, marginal documentary cues (dates marking diary entries; further instructions such as "Gremium / the subsoil base"), phrases from Tokyo Rose's radio shows, announcement notices ("Notice is given / that a company will meet at the Block House / on Sunday"), diary entries, songs of westering ("I shall soon be in Frisco / And then I'll look around / And when I see the lumps of gold / I'll pick 'em off the ground"), glossaries of construction standards ("Clearing, 32 feet wide minimum"), rosters of the multicultural highway crew ("Homer Childs, Hercules Stamps, Al Antonini, / . . . Rodolfo Reveulta, Alvarez Sanchez . . . / Eddy English, George Kotrodimos"), inventories of heavy equipment, passages from letters written home from the site ("Dear Wilma, they made me a tractor driver which is the nearest thing to tanks in this man's army"), road signs ("YOU ARE LEAVING VALDEZ / RICHARDSON HIGHWAY"), newspaper headlines, personal testimonies of Pacific Front trauma ("*Piling the dead and wounded in our tunnel / The jig is up / Corregidor used to be a nice place / But it's haunted now My name is Irving Stobing*"), an extract from the diary entry of a Russian soldier whose wife was killed in a German siege, the complete lyrics of spirituals sung by African Americans among the Army Corps of Engineers, the allegorical tavern limerick sung by those on a day off ("There was a young lady named Banker / Who slept while her ship was at anchor . . ."), the transcript of one side of a telephone conversation ("It's me, honey, callin' from up Alaska way / just to hear your voice"), the ecstatic call-and-response of an evangelist and his audience, transcriptions of Ezra Pound's wartime radio talks, the play-by-play sportscast of a baseball game (and the exclamations of men listening), the anthem sung by the Abe Lincoln Battalion in Spain after the battle at Jarama, boring transmissions overheard on the army's radio ("18 calling 97 over / 97 go ahead 18 / At Donjek equipment icebound"), expressions of exasperation among enlisted men ("I'd go AWOL / If there was some place to go"), and a collage made of all the announcements on a bulletin board that served as much as a site of communal expression as a means of passing messages, read from top to bottom:

Will the man with those French postcards
    kindly post same on bulletin board?
Dottie Duzzit, BR. 9-8280

(by one who has been there before)

WANTED: A FEMALE TO DISCUSS BOOKS

Joe Blaine, Minneapolis.

Marty the Goon, Cincinnati.

    Don't waste gas, boys,

    think of the folks back home

Anyone passing through Cleveland

  phone 2-34160 and mention Joe.

       Cpl. J. L.

    Hang out the gold star, mother,

    your boys in the QMC.

WILL SWAP BRAND NEW PURPLE HEART FOR

  CHEVVY COUPE AFTER WAR UNDER 50000 MILES

      Mack, Co. B.[155]

The Big Road is something of the "palimtext" Michael Davidson identifies in the work of other documentary modernists (and Michael Thurston sees in Rukeyser particularly).[156] But what might have kept us from seeing this complication? Perhaps the book's simple internationalist epigraph from a speech by Henry Wallace? The political correctness drawn into George Annand's maps for Rosten's book, a top view depicting Africa above and North America below? The unavoidable fact that the author was a known member of the Communist Party even as late into the bloody century as the time of publication—1946? A critic's complaint that the poem used "blank and free verse [that] read like a shopping list"—although it was by then a standard criticism of, say, a William Carlos Williams poem, normally the sort of traditionalist complaint that proponents of modernist poetry ignored—won the day because what was in essence a critique of modernism's difference was carried aloft on the strong anticommunist current.

Modern American poetry had come to the point where the poem that "read like a shopping list" could be red-baited on formalist grounds and then soon forgotten. But if, as one detractor put it, "the 'minute particulars' carry Mr. Rosten far afield," perhaps the way the field was bounded was what needed reconsideration.[157] If of writing that sought to serve "a pragmatic function" it could be said that "that function is extra-aesthetic"—and if "to make a good poem" even the poem that was "a cry for social justice" must "come in the individual voice of the poet"—then perhaps the "extra-aesthetic" could be shifted to the realm of the aesthetic and a "good poem" could be made of other voices.

Mona Van Duyn, the poet who aimed these objections at Rosten, who found Rosten's writing "singularly annoying," at least made no effort to hide her dislike of "second-hand and very diverse forms" in modern political poetry. In Rosten's verse she found the influence of Kenneth Fearing and disliked that too. Van Duyn was writing in April 1946 about Rosten's book *The Fourth Decade*; the title refers to the fourth decade of the twentieth century—the 1930s. This topical fact seems to have led Van Duyn to assert that the book's political themes "need not be assessed in a consideration of the poems as poems,"[158] but that is precisely what was (and is) necessary.

PART II

Anticommunist Antimodernism

CHAPTER 7

Free verse was not born in freedom, suckled in freedom, or matured in freedom; nor have any of the various [t]ypes of modernism or surrealism tolerated freedom. All that they have done is to substitute one form of repression for another.—Stanton Coblentz, *The Anti-Poets* (1955)

In the long view a due respect for the canons of grammar seems a part of one's citizenship. One does not remain uncritical; but one does "go along."—Richard Weaver, *The Ethics of Rhetoric* (1953)

What is the lesson when progressivism, after sincerely setting out to liberate literature and politics, ends by flirting with treason? Avant garde and liberalism [are] the two halves of Babbitt Junior, in culture and politics. —Peter Viereck, "Symbols: Hiss and Pound" (1952)

Poetry in the Hour of Need

We have seen that as the anticommunist intellectual movement grew rapidly in the late 1940s and early 1950s, one of its fundamental assumptions was that in the Red Decade—the years of "deception," "treason" and "betrayal"—communists in the United States exerted an "oblique control of writing."[1] For conservative anticommunists in particular, this assumption extended to poetry. And if communists and fellow travelers, or "dupes of Stalinism," could be said by conservatives to have "controlled" writing just as they had controlled (for example) the executive branch of government during the New Deal years, it was hardly surprising that in the late 1940s and throughout the 1950s, when anticommunists sought to invite authorities to speak on the matter of poetry, they turned to a world of people *outside* poetry. Persuasive indictments of New Deal experimentalism had to come from people beyond the field in question or—using a strategy that had already been perfected in twentieth-century electoral politics—from insiders who could suddenly reinforce their outsider status. In any event, insiders were suspect.

Indeed, in many local precincts, poetic expertise was in receivership. A soldier and prep school headmaster who frequently decried modernist effeminacy, Colonel Cullen Jones, was chosen to give the keynote address at the Twenty-fourth Annual Poets' Dinner in Berkeley in 1950.[2] An academic sociologist became the poetry editor of *The Humanist*, thereupon from this platform pronouncing his hope that "the ultramodern poet," having wandered into the "dangerous wilderness" of too much freedom, would be "wiped out on the bloody slope of verbal anarchy."[3] A supertraditionalist who had edited a little-known magazine called *Wings* for years out of his Mill Valley, California, cottage and who believed that "the sharpest revolution in the history of literature has overtaken poetry," "the revolt of a small discontented avant garde," received large space in the *New York Times Magazine* to vent his extreme views.[4] A man who taught in the engineering school at the University of Michigan founded and led the Poetry Society of Michigan.[5] A Dutchman of letters who did not at all circulate among contemporary poets, Jan-Albert Goris (1899–1984), was summoned to speak about the state of the art. Goris had published under the pen name of Marnix Gijsen and was known in New York for *Belgium in Bondage* (1943), which had been urgently published in English by Louis Fischer during the darkest days of Nazi occupation of the Lowlands. He served during the Cold War as Belgium's commissioner of information—in effect, that nation's propaganda minister.[6] He was invited to speak by officials of St. Bonaventure University in New York at a program on the topic "Tradition and the Controversy in Poetry."

Since Goris's knowledge of poetics was limited (and his understanding of American culture outside New York admittedly nil), he naturally confessed surprise at having been asked to speak on such a topic. Yet he certainly seemed game. He began his speech by wondering aloud why the Japanese did not like to break with poetic tradition, since surely this was a good thing. Perhaps there was a model here for postwar Americans. When the Japanese had recently held a poetry contest, eighteen thousand poems were submitted, and the winner was . . . *Emperor Hirohito himself.* While not entirely discounting "servile flattery" as a factor in the judges' decision, Goris observed that Hirohito's poem did after all scrupulously respond to the contest requirement for a specific "mathematical effect . . . of verse." The emperor had produced a perfect *waka*, the ancient form of five- and seven-syllable lines precisely alternated. It was a form that his grandfather, the unshakably formalistic Emperor Meiji, had made central to the patrilineage. (Meiji wrote one hundred thousand such poems. One of the most often cited has been translated as follows: "In a world of storms / Let there be no wavering / Of our human hearts; / Remain as the pine tree / With root sunk deep in stone.") For Goris, the poetic performance of the current emperor, fallen from Meiji's godly station in a time of American domination and yet *aesthetically* stalwart, a former enemy of unbowed tastes, was evidence that our new allies would do well to hold onto traditional poetic artifacts while being inundated with just about every other cultural form from the West (including political poetry such as that published in a bold new Japanese magazine, *The Waste Land*).[7] Goris saw that the few Japanese poets who wrote "unconventional verse," following the Anglo-American trend, were meeting with "little or no success." Without citing evidence he proffered the statistic that "90% of [Japanese] readers do not care" for poetry other than strictly traditional.

Rhetoric about poetic form was often unacknowledged Cold War politics. The Belgian minister did not ascribe to subject matter the poor reception of experimental verse or to the very favorable response to Hirohito's traditional verse. He might have. A modern poem Goris quoted was *about* the devastation of Hiroshima, while the emperor's *waka* was about a cloud drifting over a mountain (translated in part, "A white cloud like a sash moves over / Nasu peak, soaring beyond the plateau"). Commissioner Goris conceded that "in our estimation," Hirohito's poem was no major contribution, while the modern poem about the atomic bombing was "powerful" and "of significance."

Still, two lessons could be learned about the consequences of poetic tradition: first, control of the means of expression; second, self-determination in free societies. "Each reader deserves the poetry he reads—like every people has the government it deserves." And "poetry, however cryptic, is a means of communication." In contending that in this obviously political context "eloquence" is always better than cubistic "stammerings," however charming or skillful such stammerings may be, here was a prominent cold warrior pressing a social interpretation of modern art: "Recently a cartoon in the *New Yorker* showed two puzzled men in front of an abstract painting, one addressing the other and saying: 'Maybe he doesn't want to communicate anything at all.' Many poems of that kind are written now, but it is not probable that this extremely narrow conception of poetry will triumph. If we may compare poetry to painting, I would dare to say that, after all, the language spoken by Velasquez, Rembrandt, Van Eyck or Rubens will always be more moving than that used by Mondrian or Pollack."

The Belgian concluded for his collegiate audience that the term "pure poetry" does not describe an extreme state, a stance in opposition to political poetry. It suggests, rather, the moderate center in a balance of qualities that *include* "politics" as just one of them. It is only when one quality dominates others that "poetry becomes impure." That is why "the world over now, pure poetry is praised and considered above controversy."[8]

We do well to pause on this ratio: "Each reader deserves the poetry he reads—like every people has the government it deserves." Such a statement was enough to make one think that linguistic disintegrations and discontinuities entailed dangerously toying with a free way of life. Thus many conservatives believed. In *Faith and Force: An Inquiry into the Nature of Authority* (1946), Joseph M. Lalley, the *Washington Post*'s conservative literary critic, wrote that

"Maybe he's trying <u>not</u> to tell us something."

"the decline of authority in the state is very closely analogous to the decline of authority in language," and his argument in this influential treatise[9] that traditional forms of authority must be reasserted was founded on his sense of what happens when the modern imagination "has grown enervated": "opportunity lies open to the revolutionist."[10] "A sound national life and a sound literature are almost synonymous," wrote the author of "Literary Decadence and World Decay" (1947), a piece that assigned part of the blame to the verse of Marianne Moore.[11] The founder and director of World Poetry Day spent her time supporting poets who fought modernism, "urg[ing] people to show their allegiance" by pointing out its nonsense "whenever they see it instead of being afraid of it." She lauded an Irish antimodernist crusader as a hero of the Cold War, *commending* him for telling her that the best way for Americans to win the love of the world—"poetry, alas, will not do it"—was to use "a plentiful supply of what you are now manufacturing in Nevada" (strontium, for atomic weapons).[12] One skeptical critic described the logical leaps taken by "conservative art judgment": "The weird cacophonies and twisted watches of the modern era harbor God knows what threat to law and order, probably communism itself—almost certainly communism."[13] Jacob Hauser, the poet and editor of *Solo* who was a master of this special political logic, called the world imposed by modern verse an "anti-democracy." Modernism "tolerates no departure from its inflexible requirement of distorted, pathological incoherence."[14] The "leading warriors and agents of the Revolution . . . founded the court wherein all literary aspirants and offenders are tried and sentenced according to a code in whose making they had no share. . . . The verdict of 'Literary decapitation!' will issue inexorably."[15] Robert Hillyer assailed modernism in the *Saturday Review* as "an illusion of independent thought"—a "propaganda" machine sponsored by "a group which has a genuine power complex."[16] He referred to the enemies of traditional poetry as "the powers of darkness"[17] and induced in other antimodernists the feeling that they had "company and moral backing."[18] In the *Bulletin of the Poetry Society of America*, Hillyer went further: there he announced that modern verse had introduced "cold conformity of intellectualism," had eliminated "diversity," and had instituted "a critical censorship, in its effects like that of the Kremlin."[19]

The penchant among avant-garde poets for "expressing rather than describing life" had "gone too far," Gilbert Malcolm Fess wrote in a 1952 issue of *Books Abroad*, a magazine that had for years published news and analysis of world literature from the American perspective and by 1950 featured an anticommunist editorial policy. "Intellectual intolerance, striking at all simplicity of form . . . now rides the world," Fess continued. Some American publications, he noticed, "especially among the 'little magazines,' would today unhesitatingly reject any contribution if it made complete sense, irrespective of its aesthetic value.... Poetry must be 'hard' (to grasp), relatively unintelligible." Modernism "has lasted much too long" and behaved "like a totalitarian dictator gone to seed."[20] Modernists were said to have "stood on the rostrum and shouted themselves hoarse," like any political zealots.[21] They used precisely the Big Lie tactics perfected by absolutist governments: "If we tell the people often enough it is poetry; if we keep on saying it is poetry, and get critics to tell them it is poetry, in the end they'll disregard the testimony of their own sense, and believe it is poetry."[22] "Under the false flag of friendship," modernists had captured poetry's "citadel—a little as if the totalitarians, beneath the banner of democracy, had taken the capitals of the free world, and enforced freedom by means of secret police, concentration camps, and execution squads."[23] Modernists operate "with an intolerance which denies others the right to exist."[24] The editors of *Pinnacle*, the magazine of the League for Sanity in Poetry, described modernism as genocide: poets were being exterminated. ("The actual mandate, to be precise, prescribes not that all poets be exterminated, but only those who respect the literary traditions of three thousand years.")[25] To this murderous "revolution," wrote another antimodernist, "there must be a counterrevolution.... The world has no ... use for any kind of bigotry and regimentation."[26] It was "futile ... to seek the cause of the rise of our poetic dictators in any agency or factor outside their own little, warped minds and hearts," a conservative editor wrote; so, he continued, "the only way to eliminate the trouble is to eliminate *them*."[27] By imposing a "tabu against beauty, modern poets ... have unwittingly signed their own death sentence."[28]

After World War I had laid the land to waste, "with the general let-down and loss of human integrity," poetry had not made a great advance but had in fact "suffered its greatest degradation," wrote Mabel Gregory Wuesthoff, a metrical poet from Berkeley, author of three books of verse. Alice Hunt Bartlett, the antimodernist American editor of London's *Poetry Review*, quoted Wuesthoff approvingly, added a call for poets of "balanced judicial mind" to "storm the gates of stress," and then bespoke her hope that after World War II, modernism's ugliness, chaos, and incomprehensibility would finally be thwarted—that "good" poets *this* time "will sing themselves into each nation's development."[29] But Bartlett's close friend,[30] Stanton Coblentz, did not share her optimism: as of 1950 "a small discontented avant garde" still cowed young poets by "bullying" them, "converted publishers," and "stifled ... much that is best and most authentic in our verse" by enforcing a "type of freedom enjoyed by the citizen of a totalitarian state, who is unrestrained in expression so long as he follows the

Party line."[31] Just as for some anticommunists the source of Marxism's appeal in the United States was in the way proponents of the socioeconomic theory "twist the meaning of words from their common usage,"[32] for Robert Hillyer the language of modern poetry was "voodoo jargon to overawe the young." And for Hillyer, like Coblentz, modernism was inscribed by "the party line."[33]

"Party line" was of course a phrase borrowed from the communism/anticommunism debate. It referred to the iniquity of (leftist) ideology. Yet this was modern *poetry*. There had indeed been both critical and popular outcry against the new poetry in the 1910s and 1920s: complaints against urban, mechanistic, or "obscene" subject matter;[34] against the modern preference for manner over matter[35] and the abandonment of poetry's duty to give readers a sense of what Conrad Aiken (when attacking the imagists) had called "organic movement";[36] against the repudiation of pleasant, natural settings and of uplifting tones; against the demise of both hard work and elegance ("What is dashed off *reads dashed off*");[37] and against the uselessness of experiment, as in the "art as madness" debate stirred by Elsa von Freytag-Loringhoven's poem, "The Cast-Iron Lover," in 1919.[38] But the postwar case against experimentalism was different—shriller and apparently more desperate and borrowing heavily from the new national political rhetoric. Amy Lowell's *Tendencies in Modern American Poetry* (1917) had once "sounded the battle cry of the rebels," but now, wrote one anticommunist in 1947, " 'modern' methods have become more vociferous, and their departures from earlier practice more radical."[39] Why "*more* radical" now? The perceived urgent threat of domestic communist subversion provided special rationale for those who deputized themselves as social authorities in order to roll back modernism's claims of immediacy and its attack on art's autonomous status—an attack that had radicalized some modernists in the 1930s and induced them to join the communists' view "demand[ing the poet's] conscious participation in the whole nation's life."[40] Poetry in the 1930s had emphatically rejected the notion of poetry's separate sphere, in this sense continuing rather than reversing modernism's reversal of late-nineteenth-century aestheticism.[41] Modernism had always meant the "erasing of all distinctions," the replacement of truth with fact and prose with verse, the merging of the discrete social and aesthetic fields, and the destruction of "the metaphysical community of language," according to Richard Weaver, but it also, Weaver lamented, "result[ed] in an inability to interpret current happenings." This last malady made for a dire situation in 1948 (the time of Weaver's writing).[42] Whereas John Livingston Lowes had teased the avant-garde poet for his "mad metaphor" in 1916, not intending the complaint to produce any particular political consequence, by the late 1940s the League for Sanity in Poetry argued that the modern poet's madness led directly to disloyalty and subversion,[43] and the league's remarkable bulletin, the *Pinnacle*, by spreading widely the charge that experiment destroyed poetic form, elicited letters of praise from conservative groups that were taking the lead in the fight against domestic communism and had had nothing to say theretofore about poetry. The managing editor of the magazine published by a large fraternal organization praised the league for cleaning up "the nauseous messes" made by modern poems, while in nearly every issue of this man's magazine, such a phrase described the confusions caused by Reds. One cannot say the message about poetry was merely subliminal.[44] The league's magazine issued a warning in an editorial coinciding with the end of World War II, signaling the tougher battle ahead: "The modernists are of a different type than . . . any previous innovators: they are not only more radical, they are revolutionary."[45] Again, this political inflection was new to the postwar period. Take, for example, the charge of objectification. Whereas Padraic Colum in 1915 criticized Richard Aldington because the girl in Aldington's poem "Daisy" "becomes, not a living creature, but a shell,"[46] accusations that modern writing dehumanized its subjects now had the strong rhetorical backing of those expressing fears that certain political systems robotized its artists, who then transformed the people about whom they wrote into machines. The "conflict" between "the aims of art" on one hand and "the heart of man" on the other now had deepened. "The cult" that favored aesthetic technique over human emotion was "strong and sinister, . . . taking us away from life in the name of art." In 1950, it could be said, as it could not have been said in 1915 or 1920 or even in 1925, that "existence as we know it on this planet" was threatened because modernism had set poets' "hearts on ice."[47]

Such charges of dehumanization, long the stock in trade of antimodernism, now struck a loud note in the chorus of national anxieties, while Colum's old critique had once been dismissed as meaningless art-world infighting motivated perhaps by the jealousy of a poet suddenly going out of fashion. Colum's "Egoism in Poetry" might well be explained as revealing his own bruised ego as he came to resent acclaim accorded the "clean-cut and virile" work of "Some Imagist Poets."[48] Conrad Aiken's "The Place of Imagism" (also 1915) was not just a little envious of the fame quickly coming to "a very loud-voiced little mutual admiration society."[49] Aiken saw no danger that anyone would really believe claims that, for instance, "Miss Amy Lowell's work is as important an event in the world of poetry as the European war is in the world of politics." If "Amygism," easily demeaned, survived the poetry wars, so be it, but this was not itself—and not even really *like*—the world of politics.[50]

Thus, whereas in the 1910s and 1920s the modernist challenge to convention "had withstood charges that it is distorted, unintelligible, unreal, specious, ugly, et cetera," a 1949 article in the *New York Times*, "Modernism under Fire," summarized the postwar situation in this way: when American culture seemed most in need of protecting and defending, "subtly, through its opposition to the time-worn traditional," modernism was "somehow possessed of the devil and, through the extensions of aesthetic frontiers," was deemed "dangerous to American culture and realism."[51] The "cubist witch," observed R. B. Beaman, also in 1949, feeds on the fear of "unseen dangers," and modernism, which "arouse[s] hostility of things new and strange," is deemed "by now a 'hostile act.'"[52] Abstractionists who eschew imitation and mimetic composition were said to be part of "an organized heresy."[53] Harry Truman, whose cracked anti-modernist aphorisms were a regular feature of newspaper columns, turned serious for once on the subject of modern aesthetics, opining for White House reporters that "the ability to make things look as they are is the first requisite of the artist."[54] Was it not true that the United States needed to be well depicted if it was to be well defended? Welford Inge, offering his version of anticommunist antimodernism in an essay, "The Poetry of Fear" (1956), stressed the timing of this necessary defense of cultural freedom. It was no longer the freewheeling 1920s, when experimentalist antics were disagreeable but finally tolerable in a world uncertain of value:

> For a long while the modern poet, deviously exploiting snob appeal, man-aged to convince some readers that because his poetry was difficult to read and understand it must therefore necessarily possess some great "literary treasure." But the public is no longer hoodwinked by snob appeal. The strange and the baffling, through familiarity, have become commonplace and shopworn. And the long-suffering public, taking another long clear look at modern poetry, begins at last to distinguish the evidence of death and decay it bears within it, to hear the thin piping of self-pity and irrespon-sibility, to sense, intuitively, the message of despair. The public is no longer interested in a small tombstone, firmly bedded in matter, and bearing on its face the forlorn legend, "All is misery, all is woe." The public once again is beginning to demand life, to search for courage . . . to seek out heroes.[55]

"Heroes" now were needed who could stare down the menace or at least recruit an opposition. The lyric poet Joseph Auslander, poetry editor of the *North American Review* and compiler of the best-known classroom anthology of American verse, paid courtly visits to the immensely wealthy reactionary poet Archer Milton Huntington (1870–1955) during Huntington's final years, hoping that the tycoon would assert his might (and money) against modernist barbarism. When Huntington published his *Collected Poems* (it was a privately produced edition, as were all but three of Huntington's twenty-four books of poetry), Auslander's elaborate praise was uttered "in the fear of God": "You are a troubadour from the Golden Age when song was sovereign, in this confused and sordid hour of barbarous dissonance."[56] Maxwell Anderson, famous for his plays but less well known as a poetry editor (of *The Measure*, 1921–26), joined Auslander in urging Huntington to take his place as a natural leader in the fight for traditional poetics. Of the poems in *Recuerdos* (1949), Anderson wrote, Huntington had "turned back the clock and written some real and moving lyrics" at

> a time in the age of our planet
> When the old faiths fail,
> And nobody's running it if anybody ran it
> And there aren't any rules at all.[57]

Archer Milton Huntington, as we will see, did rise to the occasion, using his wealth and encouraged by his knack for being "imperious . . . impatient . . . and biased"[58] to keep the modernist revolution from spreading further. In the meantime, he replied that "the poet's ship has barnacles over and under it, and the pumps are out of order"; "even Picasso is trying to get aboard."[59]

Huntington, son of railroad emperor Collis P. Huntington, was in demand mostly, to be sure, because of his great capacity as a patron but also because he was one of the few active poets of true American aristocratic mien, had impeccable right-wing credentials, was by marriage an insider (his wife, Anna Hyatt Huntington, was a sculptor, art-world politico, and board member of nearly every traditionalist society for the plastic and visual arts). Huntington could even be said to be in conversation with the community of those editing and curating the moderns, as he was the favorite uncle and regular correspondent of A. Hyatt Mayor (1901–80), the legendary prints curator, avatar of photographic history with a genius for "editing by juxtaposition," and coeditor with Lincoln Kirstein of *Hound and Horn* (where Mayor edited R. P. Blackmur's first full treatment of Wallace Stevens's rhetoric).[60] The letter Huntington wrote to Nicholas Murray Butler, then the president of the American Academy of Arts and Letters, which Huntington had supported for many years through large endowments and the donation of its building, is a model of antimodernist gentility. He led the reaction against the admission to his beloved academy of poets whose modern ideas he felt would weaken the club's strict standards. "I am not depressed or in mourning," he wrote after years of hard work backing the academy. "These things must happen, but the pleasure I had in taking the thing through is in the ground. . . . This is the letter of a man who has had an almost lifelong sense of the obligation due you in so many ways by the people of this nation." Yet Huntington made the antimodernist case with a prejudice that took its cues from a favorite figuration of nativists and anti-immigration conservatives, warning Butler that "inferiority breeds like the herring and it is conceivable that one day an inferior person may slip into the Institute—and spawn."[61]

Archer Huntington could be counted on to enter the art-politics fray with all his political might and a tone of brave condescension, expressing his hatred of modernism in a style that itself maintained a heroic dignity the loss of which all reactionary antimodernists lamented. They craved such heroism. One antimodernist dubbed another "fearless" simply because the second man had coined the "word" [sic] "the slovenly school" to describe modern verse when he stood up for metrically regular poetry "in the very face of the modern writers."[62] Cullen Jones, the soldier-headmaster-poet who railed against modernist abnormalities and mocked Gertrude Stein as "that mental genius-giant of the short—but oh, so poetic!—vocabulary,"[63] saw the "poetic wisdom of the masters," including a very few twentieth-century American maestros such as Robert Frost, as providing a model of male boldness. They courageously offered "humanistic clarity," revealing "the potential greatness of man," pushing back against the "chrome-plated death-a-second annihilation of man-measured time" and the "synthetic, paper-thin passion and smirking satire" of the "so-called poetic leaders" of the modernist era. Such "leaders" in fact abandoned America, adducing a false aesthetic freedom from the "vastly more efficient, cruel and confused [place] of their own minds."[64] In a private letter to Karl Shapiro, the poet Donald Jenks accused experimental writers of "a particularly obnoxious sort of smug self-righteousness" that undermined their claims of liberating readers from stultifying tradition: "You self-conscious modernists are just as firmly stuck in the goo of your own set of conventions as the traditionalists are in theirs."[65]

For antimodernists such as Jenks, Jones, and the poet Alfred Ralph Korn, the modernist case for freedom meant the opposite of freedom, just as "progress" really meant retardation—and the issue was rhetorically if not always substantively political, for in modern writing one reads what Jones called the "dextrous shifts of responsibility for impending disaster" brought off by "lost men, the uprooted, the physically and psychically expatriated," poets who "rush about wildly under the grinning mask of emancipation."[66] Shapiro, although he never quite accused High Modernism of communist subversion and could not be counted on as a reliable ally of conservative antimodernists, nonetheless rarely tired of making the analogy on the basis of aesthetic dictatorship: "The condition of poetry in America today is similar to that in Russia; the creative spirit is not free; it is dictated to from above."[67] In an editorial for the *Christian Poet*, Korn insisted that a "poet should enjoy the utmost freedom in employing those forms of poetry for which he has a natural inclination. . . . But there are fundamental principles which cannot be ignored." He went on to ridicule those "who would . . . substitute license for freedom."[68] The last of the ten official principles guiding members of the League for Sanity in Poetry reads, " 'Freakishness' is not a synonym for 'Freedom.' "[69] From this it followed for Stanton Coblentz that modernism was to be deemed a wing of the Progressive movement. It seemed to him "that we have made a fetich [*sic*] of the idea of progress —and that this fetich has hampered true attainment in literature, and particularly in poetry."[70]

Coblentz (1896–1982), critic, anthologist, science fiction writer, poet— author of twenty-one books of poems—and for many years (1933–60) editor of *Wings: A Quarterly of Verse*, was a leader among those who contended that the cold war against modernism was a fight for political as well as poetic liberty. Coblentz always saw antimodernism as a "cause": he sought to locate the traditionalists who had been "crying in our poetic wilderness" and to persuade them that he and they were "working for the same cause, and against the same forces."[71] In an essay/editorial called "The Walls of Freedom," Coblentz summarized the successes of the "insurgents" who had begun by exclaiming, " 'Free! Free! We want to be free!' "[72] and who then proceeded to "substitute one form of repression for another" and finally instituted "their particular form of control." That control was "harsher, narrower, and far more restricting than" the traditionalism it replaced.[73]

Coblentz saw this as part of the political history of radicalism. Breakers of chains are bringers of chains. The French people of the 1790s were released, only to be plunged into bloody despotism. Revolutionists later threw off the shackles of the Russian czars, and now communism is "still more ruthless." The analogy to "unrelated field[s] such as poetry" might not seem to follow. But indeed it does: "Similar psychological forces have been at work" in and among modernists. "Having assaulted the ancient strongholds," the modernist radicals issued "their declaration of independence": "anyone may write in any manner, any mood, and from any point of view." Under the new regime, a poet's "model may be Spenser, Herrick, or last week's newspaper columnist." This is liberty? No. Secretly, "free verse was not born in freedom, suckled in freedom, matured in freedom; nor have any of the various [t]ypes of modernism or surrealism [*sic*] tolerated freedom."[74] Modernism was an instance of pure dogma; it was as vicious and tenacious as the Russian Revolution because "one of the most insistent of modern dogmas is that which [pretends to] oppose the dogmatic."[75] Modernists clandestinely impose rules "of an ironclad dogmatic quality." They are, in short, keen political ideologues, brandishing a ruthless hegemony of cultural freedom, "demand[ing] everyone be free in their way"; thus, like the communists, modernists "clamp . . . down an intolerable tyranny." They put their opponents in "six-by-eight" isolation cells of "unbounded liberty."[76] The revolt that got under way in the 1910s and 1920s was consolidated during the Depression, the 1930s having been a time when many let "our crumbling economic foundations undermine their poetic foundations."[77] When for the purposes of an editorial Coblentz invented a typical unrelenting modernist Poet (with two figures operating behind the scenes—one named the Politician and the other the Press Agent), he noted that after four or five years of appearing in avant-garde magazines, the Poet's work was now picked up by "the editors of *left-wing* publications," who began to speak of him as "one of the most promising of the younger coterie."[78] In a series of editorials, books, anthologies, and memoirs, Coblentz repeatedly offered a political history of modernism as follows: World War I led to "a mood of creative nihilism" that had aesthetically led to "the feeling of 'Oh well, what does it all matter anyhow?'" and then to the "abandon[ment of] standards in poetry" and "literature of high aspiration," which in turn was "powerfully accentuated by the wars and revolutions that made a shambles of a great part of civilization while slaying uncounted millions."[79] Coblentz was applying specifically to poetry an assumption generally shared among anticommunists who studied the "psychology" of the ideologist. Eric Hoffer's book, *The True Believer* (1951), through its taxonomic approach to various categories of radicals and fanatics, began with the assumption that revolutionaries feared liberty more than they feared persecution. The "experience of vast change" offers a "sense of freedom," but changes are "executed in a frame of strict discipline."[80] For Coblentz, this explained the despotic cult of newness in the New Poetry.

A poet-critic somewhat more of the mainstream who partly shared a sense of this conspiracy was Robert Silliman Hillyer (1895–1961). Hillyer had won a Pulitzer Prize in 1934 for his *Collected Verse* and by the 1950s had become a regular reviewer of poetry for the *New York Times Book Review* and *Atlantic Monthly*, a cultural commentator for *Saturday Review of Literature*, and president of the Poetry Society of America. He was a religious man (a practicing Episcopalian) and believed that most modernist poets were nihilists who felt that "life is evil in itself."[81] He thought that "royalism is politically reasonable."[82] His new poems in the 1950s regularly appeared in the *New Yorker*. He was a

Republican and a traditionalist, a proud literalist[83] who had a large middle- and upper-class readership. He was an unironic advocate of suburbanism at a time when literature everywhere, even middlebrow novels, satirized the boredom of posturban uniformity; recommending his book *The Suburb by the Sea* to the antimodernist poet Phyllis McGinley, author of "Suburbia, of Thee I Sing," he wrote, "I think that the civilized suburb is America's great contribution—look at us!"[84] As a critic, Hillyer sought, in Karl Shapiro's words, "to make a facile marriage between avant-gardism and political wickedness."[85] He was certain that the assault on traditional poetry was being launched by radicals. In 1948 he pondered one "sudden and unaccountable onslaught" against his own poems and confided to Leigh Hanes, editor of the *Lyric*, that "the impulse is probably left-wing, that is where most of the attacks have come from."[86]

Hillyer had a special tutor in bearing the burden of the postwar heretics' ire, for his brother-in-law was Judge Harold R. Medina, a devout anticommunist who wrote a jacket blurb for Hillyer's *In Pursuit of Poetry*[87] and recruited Hillyer to select all two thousand books of literature for the library in Medina's Manhattan apartment.[88] He was the Circuit Court of Appeals judge who sternly presided over the infamous first "Foley Square" Smith Act trial of CPUSA leaders just at the time (1949–50) when Hillyer was most deeply embroiled in literary politicking: lauded by nearly every newspaper editorialist for summoning the stoicism needed to resist attempts by communist attorneys to "taunt the judge . . . with foul abuse, provocatory taunts, and cynical jibes . . . into losing his temper sufficiently to make an error and in that way be able to declare a mistrial,"[89] Medina, by his own account—a narrative perfectly befitting the new genre of anticommunist spiritual autobiography—remembered the precise moment he "realize[d] what they were trying to do to me." He added, "But as I got weaker and weaker, and found the burden difficult to bear, I sought strength from one source that never fails" (the account is called "The Judge and His God").[90] Any real difference between Hillyer and Coblentz depended indeed on the former's relative dispassion and facility in the public forum. On at least one occasion, however, Hillyer, contravening the model of Medina's saintly calm, really let loose, identifying "The Crisis in American Poetry" as caused by the communist-style strategies of penetration used by modernists, who "through logrolling, discreet acquaintanceship, academic positions, and brow-beating the public, . . . acquired power" to control all discussion of modern poetry.[91]

Coblentz at *Wings* and other conservative antimodernist editors such as Robert Greenwood of *Talisman* and Leigh Hanes of the *Lyric* searched for signs of such power-mongering and responded aggressively to any article that smacked of the modernism-radicalism conspiracy to erode tradition. When

Robert Hillyer. Courtesy Special Collections Research Center, Syracuse University.

Lawrence Lipton began in a series of articles to promote the development of "a poetry of the spoken word" as a possibility reopened by modernism, he knew that his calls for a return to a "poetry of passion" might be misread by those of the Pound-Olson-objectivist cluster as allied with conservatives who had been criticizing modern verse for its alleged impersonality. To ward off this assumption, he made a point of reinforcing his abhorrence of *Wings*, which he said fomented a "rear-guard action against all 'radical' poetry."[92] Coblentz wrote immediately to the *Nation* to complain.

Lawrence Lipton's characteristic mix of modernism and radicalism in fact made him the Cold War antimodernist's perfect target. He was exploring the implications of modern poetry that such conservatives most feared: the poet who, as Lipton put it, was marked by a convergence of "such qualities as the rhapsodic, the lyrical, the vatic, the direct, topical, nonconformist, democratic and libertarian." In his *Nation* article, Lipton named some poets who would form the basis of a new modern poetry movement built on interest in the jazz idiom as a model for experimental linguistic structures and in the performed (and recorded) word. Among his models for spoken-word poetry were three well-known communists, William Pillin, Hugh MacDiarmid, and Thomas McGrath.[93] Lipton dubbed the New Criticism as no less "class-angled" than the *Daily Worker*. He criticized Cleanth Brooks and Robert Penn Warren's *Understanding Poetry* for omitting Rexroth, Zukofsky, Dahlberg, Rukeyser, Gregory, and especially Kenneth Patchen, implicitly accusing the formalist editors of blacklisting leftists. Eventually, through *The Holy Barbarians* (1959) and through his beachfront Beat salon in Venice, California, Lipton became known as an explainer of hipster alienation and a supporter of vatic verse performance. But in the mid-1950s, he was the consummate mix of modernist and political radical— once a friend of Harriet Monroe from the 1920s Chicago circle,[94] the supporter of poetry as a force for a more "truly functional society" as a community,[95] the multiculturalist who believed that the further development of modern American poetry depended on "Jewish, Polish, German and now Welsh elements . . . as well as Italian, and of course the always leavening Negro element, which is no longer confined to music."[96]

No record survives to show Coblentz's private response to Lipton's claim, but Leigh Hanes of the *Lyric*, in a file he labeled "Poetry Society of Virginia: Efforts to Have School Children Read Poetry Orally," kept a copy of Lipton's essay as well as a letter he wrote to a friend expressing his disgust. Hanes found himself "in open rebellion." He in effect called Lipton a Jewish carpetbagger who sought to impose communist modernism on southern populations. Hanes was not "awed by any of the high priests [of modern verse] coming South to tell us what poetry is or how to read it." Lipton, he wrote, was part of "this stinking clique" that should be "eliminate[d]"; we must not be "encouraging them by having them come South." In such language one can sense not just southern recalcitrance but racism in this version of anticommunist antimodernism. Hanes was not impressed "by [Lipton's] appearanc[e] in the *Nation*," he continued, "nor in any other publications north of the Potomac. Some of their stews have pretty bad meat in them."[97]

In the exchange between Coblentz and Lipton, Coblentz was not drawn into a discussion of the multiculturalist's assertion that the participation of Jews and African Americans would save modern verse. Focusing instead on the assertion that *Wings* "oppose[d] 'all radical poetry,'" Coblentz replied first by claiming he sought modernism's defeat yet supported "poets of social criticism" and then insisted he was beyond ideology, for the kind of poetry promoted by Lipton was vilified in *Wings* "in a rear-guard action and in a left-guard action and a frontal attack and every other form of assault." Lipton replied by reminding the *Nation*'s readers that the social poets Coblentz commended ranged unventuresomely "from Shelley to Masefield," a conveniently narrow and obsolete selection, to which Lipton responded by asking how Coblentz stood "on Fifty-four forty or fight! or the Greenback issue," while in *Wings* he still excoriated William Carlos Williams, Kenneth Patchen, José García Villa, and e. e. cummings, whose character, Olaf, was a conscientious objector. "I can only say with Cummings' Olaf . . . 'There is some s**t I will not eat.'"[98] Lipton could safely abstain. Coblentz's anticommunism was unequivocal: "I too abominate," he wrote a fellow antimodernist about another poet, "these persons who, in the name of social progress, actually are espousing the cause and methods of communistic Russia against our own standards and ideals."[99]

Coblentz's editorials in *Wings* were read by a small devoted readership, yet they were quoted and recommended and remailed and footnoted by many cultural conservatives. He also published several widely circulated articles, including the sensational "What Are They—Poems or Puzzles?" (subtitled "Modern poetry has been overrun by pseudo-poetic usurpers, says a critic. The result is chaos."), which the conservative Sunday editor Lester Markel—probably with the support of J. Donald Adams of the *Book Review* department—published in the *New York Times Sunday Magazine* at the outset of the Cold War. In all, Coblentz made ample use of anticommunist vocabulary, diction, and tropes. The Churchillian diction of "Poetry in the Hour of Need"[100] is also notable (only) in this respect. The conclusion of "The Walls of Freedom," describing the Iron Curtain descending down across the terrain of poetry, reads like the speech of the most strident jeremiad in the mode of Joseph McCarthy. One need only substitute "our nation" for the word "poetry": "A form of servitude, beyond anything known in all the past ages of poetry, has fallen upon us; we are in bondage to rules, and to the promulgators of rules. And it does not help that we dignify our slavery by the name of liberation, and crow from behind bars about our glorious independence. Only when poetry is truly free again—in other words, when all men are free to choose their own rules, rather than the pre-scriptions of a group or faction—will poetry once more be able to expand and blossom as during the splendid unmanacled centuries that gave us the timeless body of our traditional work."[101]

In 1949, conservatives were offered the sale of a book in which the central chapter was titled "Freedom—What Price?" Was this another Cold War analysis of the failure of democratic liberalism to thwart world communism? No, the book was Coblentz's *An Editor Looks at Poetry*. The argument runs along these lines: a poet must accept his lack of freedom; if he does, he will no longer seek freedom and thus has a chance to become a great poet. "That which we know as freedom," wrote Coblentz, "when it does not descend toward disintegration and chaos, is not really freedom at all. . . . The fact is that the restraints of technique, while they lie like iron about the wrists of the tyro, are the merest tissues of gossamer to the accomplished hand. The . . . poet who has mastered [the traditional rules of poetry] will no longer think of freedom or ask for it, since to all practical intents and purposes he *is* free."[102]

If Terence once said, "Nothing human is alien to me," the Modernist could say with equal fervor, "Nothing inhuman is alien to me."—Daniel Bell, "Modernism and Capitalism"

Attack Is the Best Defense—title of an editorial in *Pinnacle*, the newsletter of the League for Sanity in Poetry

Invasion of the Modernists

The poets and critics who defended modern poetry keenly felt the assault launched by the traditionalists introduced in the previous chapter, whom collectively the defenders began to call "the enemies of poetry." Cranky as Cullen Jones, Alice Bartlett, Stanton Coblentz, Leigh Hanes, Welford Inge, Robert Hillyer, and their ilk were, their views gained credence; so it seems from personal correspondence, editorials, newspaper stories, readers' responses to magazines, summaries of conversations one finds in letters exchanged among poets on both sides of the issue. The antimodernists' charges seemed to stick in the minds of readers who had heard about or been taught cubism, surrealism, and imagism and who, trying to make sense of these within the broader modernist revolution, began to understand *-isms* generally as system-asserting fixations, similar sorts of (false) belief systems that compelled one to be part of an oppressive "movement." After all, had not imagism demanded "*absolute* freedom in the choice of subject?" And was it not, as one conservative poetry reader worried, "a doctrine of revolt?" This reader understood Conrad Aiken's article of backlash against the 1930s, "Back to Poetry," to have called for a "return to sunsets and passion" as a response both to early modernism's antiromantic "hard and clear" language and "the present wave" of passionless zealots whose "verse incited for the glory of society's 'underprivileged classes.'"[1]

The *New York Times* speculated that the anticommunist detractors of modernism successfully shifted the conversation about art back "to the old talk about 'isms' (which were operating before communism became an issue), identifying facets of the modern movement as destructive weapons of Communist propaganda." When Robert Hillyer spoke of Eliot and Pound having a "single point of reference," he knew that phrase connoted political intolerance as well as aesthetic didacticism at a time when ideology itself was suspect.[2] Many who had spent the 1930s asserting that the separation of art and politics was false were now hard-pressed to give a persuasive rejoinder. The *Times* observed that those who offered answers to the denunciation of experiment—for instance, to the demonization of cubism as communist[3]—found themselves facing the task of "bombarding a fog."[4]

Modernism's supporters were indeed on the defensive. When Lawrence Lipton began to promote spoken-word poetry arising out of the radical poetic tradition—an argument that, as we have seen, necessitated condemnation of conservative antimodernists—he was nonetheless careful to suggest that his call for a social revolution led by advocates of a new poetics was noncommunist. "A truly functional poetry in the old bardic sense," Lipton wrote, "is not to be expected, of course, until we once more have a truly functional society, a community, *not a collective*, in which a population area is called a 'market.'" (He went on in this piece to urge a new market and new media, including LP records, for the new poetics.)[5] And when William Rose Benét wrote to a *Poetry* editor who had attacked Hillyer's attack on modernism, Benét prominently displayed his own anticommunist credentials. "We have attacked Communism, and thereby, I supposed [*sic*] 'aroused base emotions and played upon people's fear,'" he wrote. "I have said what I think of Communism as a philosophy, and I know what *Masses & Mainstream* thinks of me."[6] What was Benét implying? That the enemy of the enemy of modernism was aiding the communist cause and that, on the contrary, he, an enemy of the enemy of the enemy of modernism, was not? Yet at *Poetry* and elsewhere, many of the people who were appalled by Hillyer were themselves sincere anticommunists; as we have seen, they typically responded to the criticisms of anticommunist critics of modern poetry by disconnecting the 1930s from the literary history of modernism. They tended to deradicalize modernism's experimental project and sought to gain and share the high ground held by proponents of the agreeable political culture "beyond controversy" of whom the Belgian propaganda minister spoke and from there beheld what seemed a purer poetry. "It now looks as though," William Phillips summarized in "What Happened in the 30's," "a radical literature and a radical politics must be kept apart."[7] A new defense of poetry was thus logically weakened, and the defenders' antimodernist antagonists took full advantage, noting the "astonishing paucity of arguments this clique is able to summon against a reasoned attack." The vulnerability further emboldened conservatives: "Organization and repeated counter-attack by the defenders of sane, orderly, lucid, singing and readable poetry are necessary if the betrayers are to be sent reeling back in defeat."[8]

This statement was published in the spring of 1950, and a few months later, from August 14 to 17, the Harvard Summer School sponsored a Conference on the Defense of Poetry, which turned out to be, indeed, a celebration of "sane, orderly, lucid, singing and readable poetry." Participants included John Ciardi, John Crowe Ransom, Randall Jarrell, Marianne Moore, Peter Viereck, Stephen Spender, Donald Davidson, Theodore Roethke, and Robert Lowell. No one who was then writing formally experimental poetry was present, save perhaps Marianne Moore; nor was anyone there to speak for or from the left—or even formerly of the left—save perhaps Kenneth Burke (but all his remarks were on other topics). Three of the speakers (Davidson, Ransom, and Viereck) were themselves outright antimodernists, and their arguments would be embraced, whether aptly or not, by the same "enemies of poetry" whom everyone assumed constituted the reason for holding the conference. Even Ransom, who came to Harvard to "deplore . . . the 'nausea' of modern poets and urge that their vision be directed away from the negative,"[9] expected "that we were going to discuss poetry and defense against its enemies" and was surprised, when he received the tentative program a few days before traveling east, to find "no mention of the enemies of poetry" and thus could "forg[e]t that poetry had so many enemies."[10] Ransom then proceeded to mention the effect on poetry of "urbanization"—was this term a euphemism for the post–World War I migration of African Americans from the South to northern cities, or was it shorthand for the major demographic circumstance of the Depression? "Urbanization" had caused poets to replace "the love of nature" with "a social feeling." Then there was the adoption by many of an "almost incredible ideal of a society without the arrogance of classes"—and this, a little more explicit, must have been a reference to communism. Poets "in the twenties and thirties" wrote in "that vein," and the result was verse "perhaps less lyric, contain[ing] less of the essence of poetry."[11] Peter Viereck then announced that "truly modern poetry is no longer modernistic." Modernism mistakenly "continu[ed] the . . . easy, glib, smug, outworn conditioned-reflexes of revolt," but now, when "modern" poetry has been stripped of its "modernist" qualities, poems will become "conservative . . . and conventional"—and *this* was "the mid-century revolution in poetry." The enemy of poetry, "straggling" and "sniping," was not the rear guard but the avant-garde. The "pantingly progressive generation" had become old-fashioned. Creative members of the democratic polity had a responsibility to reject extreme experiment, which subordinated ethics to innovation—the reverse being the main tenet of conservatism. "The artist, being a citizen, should be critical of innovations that are uncreative, the craving for radical novelty in art and politics."[12] Ransom and Viereck gave their talks on the first evening of the conference, and while several participants referred to these points in subsequent discussion, they were not doubted or questioned, except indirectly by Pierre Emmanuel, who was introduced as a writer who been denied a passport the previous year by the u.s.

State Department and then spoke about the sense of political urgency achieved by writing in Occupied France. Hillyer was incidentally mentioned once, on a matter of style. Pound was mentioned once, when Lowell spoke about the modern epic, but no reference to the 1948 Bollingen Prize for *The Pisan Cantos* awarded him in 1949. In a sense, this "defense of poetry" proceeded from the assumption that the (unmentioned) enemies of poetry were generally right about the modernist avant-garde and were generally, though perhaps irrelevantly, right about the poetic legacy of the literary left.

Modernism's defenders at midcentury may even have *wanted* to respond as they did to the apparent paranoia of Cullen Jones and Stanton Coblentz. They may even have felt poets would fare better if a deradicalization of modernism and a dissociation from 1930s poetry could be managed in the name of fending off unreasonable people by making reasonable distinctions between and among versions of modernism. This was indeed the accusation made especially in the mid- and late 1950s by a new generation of poets for whom their elders' implicit and explicit claims of victory against conservatives seemed empty. The creators of *Golden Goose* in Sausalito—it thrived in the independent radical poetic nexus of which *Circle*, the Rexroth salon, Madeline Gleason's Lucien Labaudt Gallery, and the Spicer-Duncan-Blaser group were elements—quoted a private letter they had received from an editor at *Poetry*: "The battle for modern poetry is won—in spite of Hillyer. It is obviously won because there isn't any other kind of poetry being written." But the young editors noticed that, to their view at least, the pages of *Poetry* had already been purged, so "a good percentage of the poetry in his own magazine reflects something hardly modern." And if only *this* "kind of poetry [is] being written," then "something new is needed"—whereupon *Golden Goose* published a mix of radical and avant-garde verse by Robert Creeley, the old communist-modernist Norman Macleod, Lorine Niedecker, William Pillin, the twenty-year-old Theodore Enslin, Robert McAlmon, and so on. In the young experimentalists' lamentation that the "Revolution, the men who made the Revolution, and the good accomplished by the Revolution has been betrayed," the revolution was modernism and the betrayers were its midcentury *defenders*, including the people mounting "The Defense of Poetry" at Harvard.[13] In every manner of investigation one can conduct of the defensive advocates of modernists in this transitional period, it will be clear, I think, that by holding their ground, they largely lost or abandoned it. As we see in *Golden Goose*, they were completely disconnected from a new generation. And while they sometimes used the rhetoric of the anti-anticommunist left (the mode of beleaguered leftists defending themselves against HUAC, Senators McCarran and McCarthy, and the like) they also mishandled the claim that such abrogation of the civil liberties of poets could be likened to violations perpetrated by international communists against free peoples. Thus, anticommunist modernists—modern poetry's defenders who were not willing to disavow the anticommunist aspect of attacks on modernism—sometimes even stooped to red-baiting the red-baiters. They surrendered to an urgency driven by the failure of some of those responsible for the reputation of modern poetry at this time to acknowledge the risks inherent in making a poetics palatable to political moderates as well as conservatives.

Hayden Carruth, briefly in a lead role for the defense, responded with a tone edging momentarily toward panic against the "slanderous methods of political attack" used by ruthless antimodernists.[14] These mean-spirited people, Carruth argued, threatened the civil liberties of contemporary poets, going "even to the extent to invading literary debate." As a result of this invasion, "the free right to thought will become quite as meaningless in America as it has in the totalitarian nations overseas." Carruth was certain that the enemies of poetry were prepared to engage "in public, if not directly political, action against most working critics and poets today."[15] The rest of his essay on this occasion was a good deal less fearful, but for a signal moment, this editor of *Poetry* sounded ever so much like callers to arms in popular anticommunist movies of the day—for instance, in the classic anticommunist speech performed by Mary McCarthy's brother, Kevin, as he played that reasonable extremist, Dr. Miles Bennell, in the penultimate shot of Don Siegel's *Invasion of the Body Snatchers* (1956). The enemies of poetry are . . . *everywhere*; they're out to get *you*.

There can be little question that a cold war was being waged for or about poetry—with the crucial qualification that opposite sides in the cold war in poetry were on the same side in the cold war against communism. Carruth contended that if the antagonists would just calm down for a moment, they would see that the case against Ezra Pound—the controversy stirred by Pound's winning the 1948 Bollingen Prize for *The Pisan Cantos*—had very little to do with the political attack on modernism. This was a smart observation and seems to me borne out generally in the writings of the anticommunist antimodernists. Yet the Pound crisis "merely provided an opportunity" for these cultural conservatives. They "imput[ed] as many as possible of Pound's defections to 'modern poetry' and the 'new criticism' generally," and their intention was actually to "discredit all of us."[16]

Some expressions of this opportunism were subtle, some not, but they almost always tended to disclose the anticommunist basis of the attack. One reactionary poet-editor, joyous about Hillyer's assault on Pound, mentioned it only as a case "against experimentalism"—and then went on herself to smear William Carlos Williams as a communist.[17] In a tirade against the Bollingen committee, another poet, an ex-radical, argued that Robert Lowell's well-deserved credentials as an anticommunist were destroyed by his vote for Pound; in that gesture were also "destroy[ed] the Waldorf questions" about art and ideology that Lowell raised along with other anti-Stalinist writers who crashed the communist-dominated writers' and artists' peace conference at the Waldorf Hotel in 1949.[18]

After many letters from defenders of modernism made rejoinders to Hillyer's initial June 1949 statement in the *Saturday Review of Literature*, where he condemned the choice of Pound for the Bollingen, conservative antimodernists began to protect Hillyer against further counterattacks.[19] They wielded the rhetorical broad brush of red-baiting. Offering his opinion just when T. S. Eliot appeared on the cover of *Time*, Hilton Kramer wearily noted that Pound had provided foes of writing that they did not understand "with the opportunity to launch the argument in the name of patriotism."[20] In the *Catholic World*, conservative culture-warrior James B. Sheerin was the sort of strange anticommunist bedfellow that kept Kramer awake at night. Sheerin's logic began with a refutation of the elitism in Eliot's notion of what Sheerin called the "caste system of experts in literature" for the American intellectuals' failure of nerve in the Pound affair. This was a standard approach: a traditionalist decries the errors of other, *different* conservatives—in this case, what we would now call the New Critical right. The best and brightest found themselves creating art that had turned inward: the "hodge-podge of private symbols, weary epigrams . . . and polyglot malapropisms" that Hillyer denounced in the *Pisan Cantos*. Yet for Sheerin, it was but a quick logical move toward anticommunism in the attack on modernism's violation of language. (Sheerin not only praised McCarthyism and Joseph McCarthy himself. He seems also to have derived his move against modernism from several preferred McCarthyite tactics by way of reactionary Catholicism.)[21] The "growing movement among college professors," Sheerin noted, who "set themselves up as a caste" had joined the elite that had then awarded Pound the Bollingen. These are the sort of people who "resent any attempt to examine their attitude toward Communism."[22]

In lining up behind Robert Hillyer against the language of modernism—the linguistically heretical mode that seemed to cold warriors "to destroy the designed order"[23]—the cultural right claimed affinity with "the people." The people would rise up against this experimentalist cadre. "Some day," Hillyer wrote threateningly, "someone is going to adopt a rather cross attitude towards the editor of *Poetry*. Maybe America."[24] An antimodernist compared the Bollingen affair with the Judith Coplon spy trial. Members of the jury in the Coplon proceedings were regular folks, and they convicted her as a Soviet espionage agent. The Pound jury, consisting of an intellectual caste, instead of condemning Pound for treason, prized him for the "highest achievement of American poetry."[25] Harry Roskolenko also likened the Bollingen judges to "a trial-jury" in which the verdict was fixed, itself constituting a crime.[26] The Pound case, which ostensibly had little to do with communism—and which *should* have enabled the left to distinguish itself from the right—became another weapon in anticommunists' arsenal against modernists. A crime had been committed by one; then others, asked to judge, pronounced him innocent. Many on the antimodernist right assumed (though not as openly as Sheerin) that proponents of Pound and the Bollingen were typically liberals and leftists who had come to hate mixing poetry and politics—an assumption with many ironies, since numerous leftist intellectuals joined the campaign against Pound, although it cannot be said, as I will show, that they endorsed the attack on modernism. Those on the Bollingen jury who could not even be dubbed fellow travelers were logically dismissed as "extras fitting into a mob scene."[27]

The writing of these subversives was said to be in "strangely muddled English" —odd, stilted, foreign, cursed. In a rebuke of modernism and Pound and a defense of Hillyer, Philadelphia poet-critic-novelist and travel writer Struthers Burt[28] accused Carruth of chanting "well-worn incantatory phrases." To Burt, Carruth belonged to a "cult" whose members employed the language of "witchcraft" and at the same time used freedom-denying methods. Carruth's language was said to be the same as that "being used by the authoritarian-minded as a rebuke for the honest expression of opinion." Carruth's allegiant rhetoric, which had been summoned in defense of the modern, actually reminded Burt of the inhuman syllogism of domestic communists: "Mr. Carruth's reliance on this non sequitur reminds one of Miss Lillian Hellman's equal lack of logic when, last winter, she reprimanded Norman Cousins [then editor of the *Saturday Review of Literature*] for his bad manners because he told a largely pro-Communist gathering, imported and domestic, what Americans really thought."[29] Carruth was being *found out*. In defending a fascist modernist, he was really fooling no one, and actually he was hiding behind modernism a habit of mind that enabled rude, red Hellman to judge modest, liberal Cousins ill-mannered for saying something to an audience of communists that was disagreeable to communists.[30]

The "disclosure" of communist casuistry was a trait of the special illogic of cultural anticommunism. The very trope of disclosure, of locating dangerous people having something to hide, of stripping them naked, was of course a staple of red-hunting rhetoric. The danger lay in -isms inside which communists were able to hide. They lurked in the Americanism of organizations such as Labor's Non-Partisan League, even in the patriotic language such organizations used. Yet if conservative activists could "bring these groups into the open [and] drive from behind the folds of the Flag those who would tear it down," such language could be shown for what it was: deceptive, connotatively tactical, difficult to interpret but in any case dangerous. So argued John D. Home, chair of the American Legion's Americanism Committee.[31] In the Subversive Activities Control Board (SACB) hearing against a Marxist school, the government based its case on the ex-communist witness who acted as a close reader of communist language: the government's attorney put into the record the "fact" that the witness had been "likened" by the judge in a previous trial to "a conspirator who understood the language used by members of the conspiracy."[32] W. Cleon Skousen, former FBI agent and director of the alumni relations office at Brigham Young University, sought to strip communists of their obfuscatory language by providing models of interpretation. His book, *The Naked Communist*, taught teachers and students how to read writing that was aslant and to discover its "true native elements."[33]

Hillyer associated the "sterile pedantry" of the amoral aestheticism exhibited by the Bollingen jurors—some of whom he claimed to know had not understood or even read the poems they were judging—with "what happens when a dictatorial will moves through a group wherein right and wrong are no longer clearly distinguishable," the result being not as much fear of fascism as tolerance of the "enforced conformity" of the left. The most dangerous aspect of this conformity was linguistic "difficulty." Difficulty was a divisive ploy. It muted or stunned rational centrism, just "when," Hillyer argued, "quietists must be heard loudest of all"—a standard conservative contention of the time. Since "history shows us that a civilization is always destroyed on the cultural level before the politicians and military take over," and since subversives' grand design was to "reduce all . . . divisions of the American people to a mental state where they do not have the slightest idea of . . . what to believe *about anything*" (fear of this outcome was a founding motive of the John Birch Society in the late 1950s),[34] conservatives would do well to analyze why the Quiet Center had been so duped by the tactical "blurring of judgment" inherent in the language of modernism.[35] Welford Inge contended that "the modern poet . . . is compelled to be obscure" because "he has something to hide." That he has dared to reject romanticism he keeps from his readers; by this, Inge meant the mythic and figurative but also the metaphysical quality of "real" traditional lyric. The modernist believes only in "assiduously observing the material phenomena of life in a vacuum"—in sum, materialism. Like the communist, "that is the modern poet's first fear, that he be found out, and it is always with him. And so he must be obscure in order to hide this *guilty evidence*."[36] In his satirical yet finally embittered antimodernist epic, *Peter's Progress* (1953), Geoffrey Parsons describes a young writer's attraction to "contemporary poets": although "the phrasing may be quite vernacular," Peter soon discovered that

> This use of words to hide what you are thinking
> Has always been a *diplomatic* ruse;
> Why poets now into the vice of sinking,
> Employing verse to camouflage their views.[37]

The zigzagging, disarrangement, tortuousness, and circumlocution of modernist writing, the "vice" of using language as "camouflage," ridiculed by conservatives before the 1930s as adolescent game playing, was now viewed with a seriousness that one was duty-bound as a loyal citizen to trace as communists avoided detection. After all, the tactic of camouflage Peter the Modernist learned was borrowed from the world of diplomacy. For the "modern cultists," wrote sociologist-poet Read Bain, "indirection had become no-direction or all-directions." Bain was less concerned about "no-direction." "The ultramodern poet" who sent his "verbal and ideational anarchy" in "all directions" did the greater damage.[38] In *An Editor Looks at Poetry* (1947), Coblentz explained his view that modern "uncommunicativeness, vagueness, obscurity" were the true sins.[39] The main quality of this "newer poetry"—its "opacity"—was tightly linked with the style of political zealotry these writers allegedly used: poets of opacity were the same "spokesmen of the new school" who emphasized clarion oratory and "shouted themselves hoarse." Yet conservatives in the poetry world had "been unorganized and leaderless."[40]

If a linguistic conspiracy was afoot, a counterconspiracy was warranted. The modern revolt against poetic cliché endorsed an antirhetorical dogma that let in a flood of oppressive clichés, but now, instead of being permitted to write that the "sky is blue" (its "normal color"), the poet must make his sky a "rarer color," nondenotative but a dumb substitute for the word "blue." It was a code cracked by poetic restorationists who understood the "modern dogma . . . that . . . opposes the dogmatic."[41] Modern poets were a "literary army" formed of "psychological misfits . . . fanatically upholding illogical and inartistic precepts." We might "let this poetic army bivouac," but we must not commit "our reserves until we have a clear picture of the 'situation,'" lest it "result in annihilation."[42] The communists sought to take over American English; thus it could be said that others who did damage to normative syntax aided the communist movement. That, in short, was the point of Harry Hodgkinson's *Doubletalk* (1955) and R. N. Carew Hunt's *A Guide to Communist Jargon* (1957).

Repeatedly after 1946, both popular and scholarly interpreters of American communists denounced obscurity and implication as sinister deception, like deliberately leading readers down a blind alley to "lose" or "shake" them. International communists were experts at separately deploying languages of theory and of action.[43] Gerhart Neimeyer contended in 1956 that communists must "argue their goal according to one set of terms and . . . pursue it according to a different set of terms."[44] Summarizing a decade of abstract art as having been part of an "organized heresy" and indicting modern poets along with painters as purveyors of rootless antiart, a writer in the conservative *Modern Age* mockingly advised young painters curious about the fashion: "To be intelligible today, Wilde said, is to be found out."[45] Readers of Russell Kirk's columns heard much about "confusion" as itself a deadly communist tactic.[46] For Cullen Jones, "our modern geniuses-of-confusion" murderously lured talented young American boys (like Hart Crane) into expatriation and insane associative and surrealistic writing as an ideology rather than a social outlet for personal inadequacy, teaching them that "the Philistine of Capitalism" is "to blame for my weaknesses, my bad habits, . . . and my obviously self-procured insanity."[47] Subscribers to the American Legion's *Firing Line*, a biweekly newsletter published by the legion's National Americanism Commission in Indianapolis, learned that the major problem was anticommunists' "inability to understand" communist indirection. Subversives were "confusionists" and "diversionaries."[48] A new education in interpretation was needed. In Louis Budenz's *Men without Faces* (1948), Robert Stripling's *The Red Plot against America* (1949), Carew Hunt's *The Theory and Practice of Communism* (1951), E. Merrill Root's *Collectivism on the Campus* (1955), J. Edgar Hoover's *Masters of Deceit* (1958), Skousen's *The Naked Communist* (also 1958), Stefan Possony's "Language as a Communist Weapon" (1959 testimony before HUAC),[49] and Fred Schwarz's *You Can Trust the Communists (to Be Communists)* (1962) many pages were devoted to the tactics of self-concealment. Literal strategies of avoidance (in cars and on foot)[50] are linked to the linguistic encoding of party statements and classic Marxist texts in contemporary political context. This lay at the heart of Louis Budenz's paid hermeneutical service to the prosecution in conspiracy trials against communist leaders under the Smith Act, the foundation of the "Aeso-pian Language Thesis" as itself "evidence" for the state. Since communist writ-ers did not mean what they wrote—when what they wrote did not incriminate them—they were enacting an official strategy of literary evasion.[51] As the pref-ace to Hodgkinson's *Doubletalk* states, "Language was to Marx the 'direct real-ity' of thought. . . . The meaning of a Communist word is not what you think it says, but what effect it is intended to produce."[52]

Several of the most reactionary antimodernists took the anticommunist language thesis a step further, assuming that a "beautifully" written poem might be just as seditious as a ham-handed poem. One such person was Jessie Wilmore Murton, a sanatorium medical secretary who edited *Peninsula Poets* and was named the first poet laureate of the Michigan Federation of Women's Clubs. She was the author of, among many other books of verse, *Whatsoever Things Are Lovely* (1948). Murton prepared a report for the head of the Kellogg Company that sought to persuade Kellogg to pressure the superintendent of the Battle Creek public schools to campaign against communism by way of teach-ing children how to read good poetry. This remarkable "report" reads, in part,

> The forces antagonistic to the American way of life have not overlooked this most powerful weapon. Their ideas are thrust at us through every form of the written word—prose, verse, radio. . . . We must learn to recognize the poison quite often wrapped in an attractive package of words. This "camou-flaging" can be done much more easily in verse than in prose, because of the symbolism or imagery that is part of poetic technique. Poetry is a brief, highly concentrated for[m] of expression, its real meaning—whether good or bad—often clothed in beautiful similes and metaphors of imagery; and, therefore, frequently lost to those readers who are not familiar with, or interested in, this form of writing. . . . It is this characteristic of verse, or poetry, which makes it such an effective weapon in whatever cause it may espouse. A poor grade of verse, where the meaning was completely obvious —if subversive—would be recognized as such at once. But a finely written poem, carrying an evil intent beautifully camouflaged in lovely imagery, would be infinitely more dangerous.

With her report, Murton enclosed a sampling of "communistic poems."[53] The Kellogg CEO received an anthology of Langston Hughes. Those at whom Mur-ton directed her campaign received a mimeograph titled "Horrible Examples," which included William Carlos Williams's "Folded Skyscraper," Lorine Niedec-ker's "Canvass," and Louis Zukofsky's "Song 27—¾ Time":

```
Right out
        of
                Das Kapital
Vol. 1
        Chap. 3
            2
                    A
"who has
        a
                taste
for something
            that will
                    warm
                        up"⁵⁴
```

Whereas for conservatives prior to the Cold War, the evasive tactics of leftist writers seemed (literally as well as strategically) meaningless, now the discernment of meaning necessitated outing the heretical poet with his or her secret—materialism, the fetish of the document (such as derived from *Capital*), the rejection of poetry's idealist lyric origins. This is what Welford Inge meant by the ominous phrase "something to hide." Experimentalist writing that was unintelligible was far worse than meaningless; it was dishonest. In 1951 the editors of the *Lyric*, a magazine published for many years by the Poets Club of Norfolk and by the more aggressive Lyric Foundation for Traditional Poetry of Christiansburg, Virginia, and New York City, praised the "beautiful and gracious" writings of a poet who had criticized modernist despoliation of tradition while editorially "pray[ing] that American publishers may soon demand the highest standards of intellectual honesty" that comes only with intelligibility. The "honesty" of poets was directly connected here to the fate of a world ripe for overthrow: "As we pray for sanity in the arts," cried the *Lyric*, "let us pray that the world may not be plunged into the darkness of political and economic barbarism."⁵⁵ For reactionary antimodernists such as the editors of the *Lyric*, members of the League for Sanity in Poetry, Inge, Murton, Skousen, Archer Huntington, Cullen Jones, and Coblentz, modern poets were linguistic skulkers along meaning's back alleys, trench-coated, bearing illegible sectarian messages, picking among the litter, and avoiding the light of clarity. Jones contended in 1951 that "the calm of the inevitable that one finds in things universal," traditionalist poetic essentialism and masculine wisdom, could "draw . . . aside the veil from confusion" and would "light with regenerative . . . clarity" the way toward lyric freedom.[56] The critical commentaries appearing in the *Lyric*, *Pinnacle*, and *Different* had more linguistically in common with such articles as "Turn the Light on Communism" appearing in *Collier's* ("there must be . . . constant exposure"; "the spotlight of an aroused public opinion must be focused")[57] than the staid editors would have wanted to admit. Seeking methods of counterattack, Coblentz and the *Lyric* editors took their cues from the "real life" of fighting communism: "In literature as in life," wrote Coblentz, "there is only one way of overcoming the interloper, the trespasser, and the fraud: to fight actively against them, to expose them, to unearth them."[58] The preferred tactic of the League for Sanity in Poetry was to "flood editorial offices with letters of protest against insane poetry."[59] League leaders found modern poets "hiding under the cloak of the American government in order to flout American principles" and called for an "investigation."[60] In what he too thought of as "investigations" of modernism in the late 1940s, Robert Hillyer claimed to have uncovered a conspiracy, the modernist "power complex," and so his articles for the *Saturday Review* went well beyond the Pound controversy, extending the notion of "what happens when a dictatorial will moves through a group wherein right and wrong are no longer clearly distinguishable." Hillyer's rhetoric was that of the counterspy. "When I began the research for these articles," he wrote, "I was quite unaware how deviously the trails would lead me toward one concept: totalitarianism."[61] Although in his *American Mercury* "J'accuse," "The Crisis in American Poetry," Hillyer wrote that he "need not" name the names of those modernists who had learned their style of attack from the communists, he characterized them as loutish types who were "always clamoring to be named" and whose *writing* in any case would out them: "They can readily be identified by their references and by their style."[62]

A self-described extremist, Coblentz on principle opposed accommodation. After quoting e. e. cummings's phrase "*&(all during the*," Coblentz wrote, "There can be no compromise, any more than we can compromise clean water by mixing it with mud and expect a pure drink."[63] Should readers tolerate Walt Whitman and Gerard Manley Hopkins, although these writers led to "free versifiers" and H.D. and the imagists? No. "What is commonly regarded as tolerance . . . might more properly be labeled lack of foresight."[64] Irish playwright and poet-aristocrat Edward John Dunsany shared this view. In an essay complaining about orthographical "radicalism," he noted that an anthologist who had given over fifty pages to poems that looked strange on the printed page "subsequently committed suicide rather than face an American court enquiring into Communistic activities." Dunsany was implying, first, that the anthologist summoned to name names before an antisubversive investigation had been caught red-handed; second, that his suicide resulted from guilt at having been caught rather than from depression over this sorry state of affairs; and third, that a connection existed between his giving ample space to incomprehensible modern poetry and his treasonous association. Communists took political advantage of experimental verse. Dunsany would be rid not just of the modern poet but of the anthologist who made room for such poetry. No accommodation should be made for those who accommodate modernism, since communism accommodates modernism.[65]

Lilith Lorraine (1894–1967), an ex-communist, similarly established the connection between avant-garde poetry and political subversion: modernists write recondite verse, deliberately alienating American readers, so that "the people will repudiate . . . ALL poetry," which is precisely what "some one at the back of the whole movement has in mind, because once poetry is discredited, one of the most effective weapons again[st] evil and oppression is destroyed."[66] To counter this conspiracy, Lorraine founded the Avalon National Poetry Shrine, at which poets were welcome as long as they were traditionalists who deemed poetry to embody the "pursuit of eternal values" and they "believe[d] in the democratic way of life."[67] The ideas and rhetoric of Coblentz, Dunsany, and Lorraine befit antimodernist antipathy toward the liberal-conservative (or centrist) consensus of the period, an alliance founded, of course, on agreement about anticommunism. The consensus they denounced was based on the assumption that common ground was itself good and that politics was finally, at long last, to be characterized by ideological reconciliation.[68]

The significant and perhaps surprising aspect of the story of the anticommunist antimodernists is that the reactionaries one meets in these pages, such as Coblentz, Hillyer, Inge, Dunsany, Joseph Lalley—and, among others, Gerald Kennedy, the Catholic historian of American preaching; Henry Regnery, founder of the most important conservative publishing company of the era, who "went into book publishing . . . to break the almost complete control of American intellectual life by the left";[69] popular regionalist writer Ben Lucien Burman; Homer House, the chair of the English department at the University of Maryland for sixteen years who upon retirement had declared he was a visceral poet and opposed the "labored intellectual effort of the modernists";[70] Jacob Hauser, whose poems were published in *Future Harvest* (1943) and *Man and Nature* (1946) and who hated modernism's alleged repudiation of naturalistic description; the abovementioned Lilith Lorraine, whose magazines the *Raven*, *Different*, and *Flame* provided safe havens for antimodernist members of the League for Sanity in Poetry and whose battle cries in the mid- and late 1940s were "Sing loud for loveliness" and "Character against chaos";[71] Skousen, who for years edited the magazine *Law and Order* and became Salt Lake City's chief of police; Albert Ralph Korn, sponsor and underwriter of a series of aggressive "Clarity in Poetry" campaigns[72] and cofounder of the "This Is Poetry and This is NOT Poetry" department in *Wings*; and the brother-in-law of *Poetry*'s Peter DeVries, Carl Edwin Burklund, with his dystopic vision of "the treason of modern poetry"—were not finally the people who inflicted the greatest damage. Poets and critics whose antimodernism was less extreme in fact put the anti-communist argument forward more effectively than did the extremists in the effort to purge modern poetry of its radical character. This latter group is typified by J. Donald Adams, a man of impeccably acceptable right-of-center credentials, who in 1953 was moved by the apparent diminution of a "true Right" among literary people to declare the "Right to Be Conservative." Adams called for the cultural radical and cultural conservative to get along; the two, he said, are like the string and the bow.[73] To Adams, truly patriotic writers, who "strove to retain a vision of American purpose," could steer a middle course between modernism and communism. They had "held their *balance* during the Twenties and Thirties," neither getting lost contemplating their navels nor conforming to narrow social mimeticism.[74] When Adams referred to "the confusion and stupidity in modern verse,"[75] the editors of *Poetry* felt the need to give his "arraignment" space in their magazine and introduced Adams generously as a decent person who "*does* read poetry, would like more people to read it, and has made some genuine efforts in its behalf."[76]

Among such doubters of modern poetry who thus might be called *moderate* anticommunist antimodernists, in addition to Adams, were the poet turned novelist Gilbert Neiman; Catholic poet and cultural critic Joseph P. Clancy; Douglas Bush of Harvard's English faculty; sociologist Daniel Bell; poet and Romance languages professor Robert Avrett; the exceptionally talented poet and attorney Melville Cane; Adams's younger colleague, Russell Baker of the *New York Times* Washington bureau; the New Conservative poet-critic Viereck; and several literary eminences, including Robert Graves, Upton Sinclair, and ex-imagist John Gould Fletcher. For them, some kind of coexistence with modernism was not just possible but perhaps desirable. Most of these people understood how traditional forms were contingent. They were "modern" enough to know that one could not tenably argue that the sonnet was always already the form of poetic greatness or that Wordsworth's choice of the ballad was a choice for universality. They reckoned that experimental writing was sometimes not so radical after all. If modern poetry was at its worst "a method sterile at the core" (in J. Donald Adams's phrase),[77] it could also be put in context through the application of conventional, commonsense criticism. This did not make avant-garde poetry good, in Adams's opinion, but did make it a reasonable response to the cultural situation, and thus a reasoned counterresponse was in order. Poetry criticism, in short, should never itself engage modernism's obsession with new forms. Daniel Bell—famously an anticommunist but by no means a conservative—hoped for "limits." "Limits" was the "keyword" as "we grop[e] for a new vocabulary" now that ideology has been exhausted. Since "we now seek to return economics to moral norms," Bell added with a post-Marxist logic, "is there not a similar warranty for culture?" Because "modernism was the major effort to break away from th[e] restrictions [imposed by moral systems] in the name of . . . the aesthetic and the experimental and, in the end, broke all boundaries," the best way to end the "tedium of the unrestrained self" was to apply such "limits" to modernism—to discourage experimentalism.[78]

Robert Avrett's position was similarly centrist and even ambivalent. On one hand he felt that the modernist-traditionalist binarism had been overstated and was pleased to report to readers of *Writer's Digest* that "Modernists and Traditionalists reluctantly have been drawn somewhat closer together"—that modernists were "trying to make sense, to use somewhat more restraint," while traditionalists, responding to the shrinking of venues for metrically conventional verse, strove for "fresher imagery and more precise expression" and had "partially repaired" the damage done by the poetry wars.[79] On the other hand, Avrett was an active member of the League for Sanity in Poetry, served on the editorial board of its newsletter, was for a time the editor of the *Lyric*, never once himself published an unrhymed verse, lamented the demise of nature poems ("What poet dares to speak today of Spring?"),[80] and classified contemporary American poetry into one enemy camp and another enemy camp, "escapists" in one and "defeatists" in the other. Modernists were the defeatists, seeking "ephemeral satisfactions" and expressing vaguely heretical notions (for example, "The times are out of joint, nothing is right").[81] Avrett warned fellow traditionalists to avoid *Poetry* magazine, where "the slant is increasing to the left" and where "meaningful poems appear [along] with relatively incomprehensible verse." *Poetry* remained the "ultimate in publication goals for the modernists," and traditionalists were urged to "save time and postage" by staying away.[82] (In such a view, Avrett stood with Coblentz to the right. Coblentz observed bitterly that the *Nation* and *New Republic*, "being liberal if not radical in their political doctrines," adhered to the "principle that acceptable poems must be radical *in form*.")[83]

The key for these antiradicals was who would get to tell the literary history of modernism, especially how the Red Decade episode would be narrated. Some constructive engagement with the chief ideas of the 1930s would be required.

And some adjustment to the "permissiveness" of modernism, its "anything goes" quality and its "ephemeral satisfactions," in Avrett's terms, was inevitable if reconciliation was to be made and if *Poetry* were to be brought back rightward from the "left" and if the *Nation* and *New Republic* could be persuaded to publish poetry that was formally conservative even if its content expressed radical views. For the reactionary, *no* communication with the enemy was good or even in fact possible, since communication itself was the matter at stake. Conservatives such as Frank Meyer (he criticized Viereck as "passing off . . . liberal sentiments as conservatism") argued that the moderate antimodernist was right to celebrate the sturdy, recalcitrant "unadjusted man" but, alas, could not stand him to be "too unadjusted, mind you, [only] just enough to get him in on the ground floor when the bull market in 'adjustment' levels off."[84] On the question of modernism as a movement, conservatives accused centrists of enabling betrayal; it was an aesthetic failure of nerve every bit the equal of the liberal democracies' Munich giveaway of 1938. Those who doubted modernism but nonetheless had permitted it to survive had betrayed poetry itself. As we have seen, the prewar period had been the fateful era when territorial concessions had been made with avant-gardists whose derangements had ruined language at the level of the line, phrase, and (worst of all) the word, subversives whom Coblentz scorned for their illegibility—"the authors of aberrations of the *rr y on* and *Oattumbll* types (to quote lines from an applauded recent volume)."[85]

Coblentz was here again referring to e. e. cummings. An immediate result of any compromise made with such all-out assaults on coherence was that coherence then fell on a spectrum of meaning. It became merely one of many possible coordinates on the axis from sense (truth and civility) to nonsense (deceit and social subversion). This marked the beginning of the end. When the Academy of American Poets gave cummings its annual prize, Jacob Hauser complained that even those who peopled the academies, once traditionalist enclaves, in an attempt to get along, had gone over to the other side in the Cold War. Now that an award went to a poet whose reputation was wholly based on his linguistic disruptions, "it must be conceded that the academician of today is synonymous with *radicalism* and verbal *anarchy*." The academy was as much the betrayer of American values and truths as the modernist.[86] For Carl Edwin Burklund, who had once consorted with radicals,[87] the "treason of modern poetry" was aided by supposed "friends of 'advanced' verse" who no longer bothered to defend the tradition against the new poetry, which they did not admit confused them.[88] The academy prize given to cummings was another form of treachery that reinforced for traditionalists the general inadequacy of liberalism: the betrayal of poetry meant the compromise of *all* values, not just the poetic. "The issue reaches beyond poetry," as Coblentz warned traditionalists who pondered which strategy to accept. "It extends into all departments of life, into one's treatment of personal and political problems."[89] It was best, this argument went, to recognize the general problem first as a political one, and so one would do well to fight modernism just as one must fight communism—as a totality.

Neither Stanton Coblentz nor Jacob Hauser—nor, for that matter, the super-prolific Texan, Lilith Lorraine; nor Alice Hunt Bartlett, the influential columnist on American poetry for the *Poetry Review* of London; nor Mabel Gregory Wuesthoff, who had contended that 1919–25 was the epoch of poetry's "greatest degradation"; nor Florence Keene, editor of the aggressively conservative *Westward* (calling itself the "entirely independent" poetry magazine "for the articulate minority"); nor B. Y. Williams of *Talaria*; nor LeGarde S. Doughty, traditionalist poetry editor of the *Augusta Chronicle*; nor editor from 1949 to 1952 of the *Lyric* and creator of the Lyric Foundation for Traditional Poetry, Virginia Kent Cummins—none of these productive poets ever once graced the pages of *Poetry*, even though at the Chicago offices of that magazine the editors considered long and hard how open they should be to attacks on modernism to maintain their standing as defenders of "freedom" in verse. Hillyer, whose writings the *Lyric* featured regularly, especially after he became a martyr of the anti-avant-gardists during the Bollingen affair, always smarted from having been told by Harriet Monroe in 1916 never again to use "thee" and "thou" in verse. ("Naturally," Hillyer told readers of the *Lyric*, "I determined at that to use nothing else . . . in protest to the rising tide of revolt.")[90] By the end of the 1950s, editorial insiders at *Poetry* seemed to agree privately with one editor who argued that "I don't think POETRY ought to review Hillyer at all" because "the magazine is for people who know something about the art, as opposed to the craft."[91]

Despite a bias born of anger, surfacing here and there, against antimodernist sinners such as Hillyer, *Poetry* variously published moderate antimodernists. Gilbert Neiman (1912–77) was one. *Poetry*'s editors had begun to reject the poems Neiman sent them when he claimed to have had a revelation about politics, modern verse, and *Poetry*. He was encouraged to write this up as a prose piece, and produced an essay that helpfully connects (1) the general perception that *Poetry* had lost its innovative edge, (2) the commuting of writers from verse to prose as a means of social and emotional adjustment; and (3) the idea that poetry was "making a last ditch stand against politics," as Neiman put it to *Poetry* editor Karl Shapiro in a 1951 letter.[92]

Having previously published poems in "the avant-garde back alleys," including *Pagany* and *Accent*,[93] Neiman had then become a respectable mainstream fiction writer. He contributed short stories here and there to the little magazines through the 1940s. Now he was the author of a novel, *There Is a Tyrant in Every Country* (1947). Unlike Coblentz and the people who published the *Lyric*, Neiman now thought of himself as an outsider—typical, he contended, of many who had once loved modern poetry. In the late 1930s, he had translated Lorca for one of James Laughlin's *New Directions* annuals. Three of his poems had appeared in *Poetry* in 1942.

Neiman's contribution to the antimodernist campaign, the self-effacing complaint commissioned by *Poetry*'s editors, received the title "To Write Poetry Nowadays You Have to Have One Foot in the Grave" (1949). Neiman's tone was not that of the extremist's fury but a moderate's disappointment. Antimodernists should take solace in the fact that critical history will look back on "poetry from the twenties to the fifties" and "classify [it] as anything but experimental." It was rather "a shading-off of the Victorian." Here even Joyce was not avant-garde; he stood, rather, at the "dead-end . . . of prose (under the guise of innovator, of course)."[94] The best way to counter modernism was to refuse to recognize its radical or originary qualities. What was the proof that modernism at midcentury was derivative? Criticism. The ascendancy of criticism as a favored expressive medium among poets, a preference that coincided with the demise of the primacy of verse. This was of course the sweetest sounding of antimodernist refrains. Poet-critics were what reactionaries such as Coblentz and "moderate, temperate conservatives"[95] such as Viereck called the "anti-poets" (against which Carruth and Shapiro answered with the epithet "anti-critics"). Their simultaneous recognition that a critical coup had taken place— that the "infiltration" (Hillyer's preferred conspiratorial term) of the modernist poet-critics was the key event in the institutionalization of modernism—paired the moderate with the reactionary, for both centrist and rightist antimodernists saw modernist strategy as a sign of cultural totalitarianism.

In the new regime, wrote Neiman in *Poetry*, "criticism, instead of being complementary to the creation, is needed to supply what the poem lacks"—that is, coherence, clarity, and common sense. "We *have to be told* what to read into the creation" sounds much like Coblentz's freedom-fighting counterdicta in "The Walls of Freedom." More theoretically, Neiman felt this was an issue about what constituted the object and what the subject—and who could claim to control what words were "about." "Our avant-garde has become less and less creative and more and more critical," he observed. "No longer is the poem *a thing*, an object, and the criticism *about it*."[96] The real poet writes poems, publishes them in *Poetry*, and then in due course brings out book-length collections. The world of prose—of society, of politicians, of compromise—is a world *from* which one comes, escaping the world, like coming home, when one wants to leave the ideologues to their unclean business. The moderate especially lamented the literary-political dynamic of attack and counterattack that seemed endemic to the modernism wars. In this, the reactionary antimodernist had more in common with the anticommunist modernist than with Neiman; *they*, like Coblentz, felt criticism as counterattack to be an obligation, something very much like rather than different from the obligation to write poetry itself. One of the reasons for Hillyer's special hatred of the modernists was that "they are a disputatious lot."[97] It was a staple of the conservative case against communist writers that they, captives in the "Iron Tower" of aesthetic party discipline, quickly tired of writing in the imaginative genres and took "the path of least resistance," turning to articles and literary criticism.[98] In the 1950 editorial launching the *Beloit Poetry Journal*, Chad Walsh, to whom we will return in chapter 12, noted sadly that *Poetry* had in recent years "given so much space to . . . analysis of the political implications of poetry that its subtitle is in danger of becoming a magazine *about* verse."[99]

The "poet" in a *Saturday Review* cartoon that had originally appeared during the war but was reprinted during the Pound controversy in August 1949 looks like the intellectual as veteran rejoinder maker, the rumpled middle-class post-war culture warrior. Stacks of paper lie on the floor; false starts fill the waste-basket. The man types with a scowl. "No, he's not writing a book," says a woman, presumably his wife, standing with a well-dressed visitor in the study of what seems to be her and the writer's home. "He's holding up his end of a literary feud that began in 1903." The choice of year seems intended to suggest both that the "feud" has something to do with the first shocks of the modern era—incited among critics by, for instance, Kandinsky's first exhibitions—and that the message seems to be, in part, *c'est la guerre*. The scene at first seems settled, well-off, bourgeois and perhaps suburban, the home of the culturally mature. But the writer's wife hints at the domestic dystopia of nonlyricism.[100] More explicitly than Gilbert Neiman, Peter Viereck associated prose with liberalism, poetry with conservatism, and hardly anything could irk an antimodernist more than the brazen way in which the communist poet ignored the distinction between the proper stations and functions of the two—Eve Merriam, for instance, in "Said Prose to Verse":

Listen, my insinuating poem,
stop poking your grinning face into every anywhere.
I have trouble enough keeping my house in order

without a free-loading moon-swigging boarder around
making like of solid ground.[101]

For Viereck, conservatism "embodies" rather than "argues," and whereas poetry in the 1930s argued exactly as if it were prose, conservatism could claim a
closer connection to poetry than did the liberal left. The liberals of Viereck's
time could have prose; poetry—real poetry that did not poke its face into every
empirical anywhere—would best be realized by conservatives. Following Yeats's
distinction between embodying truth and knowing it, Viereck wrote, "Poetry
tends to embody truth, prose to know it. Conservatism tends to embody truth,
liberalism to know it."[102]

In the days when Gilbert Neiman was an experimental writer and a friend of
Bern Porter—when he lived in Los Angeles in the early 1940s—he had felt the
heady bohemian absolutism of the pure poet, indifferent to publication, unwill-
ing to "compromise" with social standards. From this aesthetic ideology he
moved toward its putative opposite, toward "reality": having chosen a form in
which "prose meets society on its own terms," he wrote two of his novels.
(Neiman's "realistic" literary politics later became fairly well known, especially
among poets—including Robert Creeley[103] and Harold Norse—who visited or
corresponded with North American writers in Central and Latin America.
Neiman founded and edited the important magazine *Between Worlds*—and
thus published Porter, Larry Eigner, Mina Loy, Anselm Hollo, William Carlos
Williams, and Creeley—in association with the well-financed InterAmerican
University of Puerto Rico, a project subsidized [as Norse mused to Williams] by
the Ford Foundation.)[104] A friend had recently lent Neiman a copy of *Poetry*.
He had opened the issue, anticipating a pleasurable return to the intrinsic place
of verse beyond ordinary society.

But what Neiman found, after just a few years away from verse, gave him
a "terrific . . . shock." The experience of reading *Poetry* he had craved produced
the feeling of a homecoming—a return to privacy, a peaceful withdrawal, to a
form of writing that "creates its own terms." To understand the political rhetoric
here, again we need go no further for the moment than *Invasion of the Body
Snatchers*, that unlikely model for understanding the poetry wars. The withdrawal Neiman covets when returning home from prose to verse, from social
meaning to autoteleology, should be a repossession or restoration, comforting
like the image of a familiar village. But as in the paranoid *Invasion*, nothing is as
American as it seems. Rereading *Poetry* in 1949 was for Neiman "like returning
to the Old Home Town again, the same Main Street, only everything smaller. My
life no longer depended on poetry. Just having finished my second novel, it was

like descending from Mars. Only in reverse: it seemed to me that the poets were the supermen, and that I had been one of them once."[105] Neiman could not tell who was Other, the modernist or himself. Likewise, it was hard to know who, upon his own return home to poetry, had changed and who remained the same. Who disturbed the peace? Perhaps by now *they* had established the domestic tranquillity, the sense of familiarity, and *you* were the one who seemed alien, awkward, not right. Which—you or the alien—was from Mars? As in liberal anticommunist science fiction,[106] the aliens were far more terrifying and disconcerting than those in reactionary films, where the unknown intruder was unmistakably Other (thus easily targeted and destroyed) and *we* were unambiguously our loyal selves. Although increasingly isolated in our discernment of the awful problem of inauthenticity, we can tell, as the few patriots in *Invasion*'s quiet town of Santa Mira can detect in others who had already been botanically overtaken, that "there's something missing. Always when he talked to me there was a certain look in his eyes. Now it's gone. . . . The words are the same, but there's no feeling."[107] Not to belong to the town meant extreme alienation. The distinctions were stark. In the eyes of those who enforced "adjustment," Joseph Freeman lamented, people politically tainted as radicals did "not belong to the human race."[108] The writing Neiman now found in modern verse implied to him the constructedness of the person. Here again, anticommunist rhetoric was having its effect on varieties of antimodernism. If, in Williams's oft-repeated dictum, "There's nothing sentimental about a machine, and: A poem is a small (or large) machine made out of words," and if, as conservatives assumed, "The Communist is made, not born," then unnaturalness could itself be a sign of subversion. Readers of *Wings* knew the ten modernist commandments, horrid *Thou shalt nots*, including the sixth: "Thou shalt not express personal emotion."[109] Douglas V. Kane in a bitter (though perfectly regular) sonnet tells the nightmarish tale of the inhuman modernist teacher etherizing a poem upon a table, passing across her once "smooth antique body" "the prodding scalpel of our modern views"; he urges his modernist acolytes to "*Experiment* upon her," and this seditious surgical pedagogy leads to the dehumanization of poetry as she "turns cold, with love and logic fled." " 'Surreal,' we call her, without form or face!" Kane's poem is called "Poetry Seminar."[110] The subversive person is grimly clinical in just such a way, wrote Frank Meyer in *The Moulding of Communists*, participating in a "narrowing of the area of awareness of men as men," in a project aimed at the "shifting of affect from real people and real situations to" abstract tenets. "All affect drains out of situations" not relevant to the mechanistic goals of these inhuman people.[111] This critique of the critique of capitalism led Daniel Bell to see the dangers in modernism's "rage against order, and in particular, [against] bourgeois orderliness." Here precisely is where Bell pointed out that "if Terence once said, 'Nothing human is alien to me,' the Modernist could say with equal fervor, 'Nothing inhuman is alien to me.'"[112]

J. Donald Adams, never as uncertain as the residents of Santa Mira in discerning a real, spiritually whole poetry criticism from materialist analyses (those who made poetry "a training-ground for science"), referred to "these strangely hybrid critics" who "dominated the field" and "retarded" the "revival of poetry" in our time. The weird hybrids were "bleeding it to death," he warned readers of the *New York Times Book Review*.[113] Modern writers and critics, Ben Lucien Burman wrote in 1948, "avoid any appearance of humanity" and thus "outlaw the objective author who lets mankind reveal itself."[114] William Phillips, influential coeditor of the *Partisan Review*, spoke of communist writers of the 1930s as embodying "something alien, something inauthentic." Phillips blamed crude sectarianism, which had "squeezed" iconoclastic writers into the two-dimensional shape of the zealot; one could always tell the dishonest imposters, for, try as hard as they might, the alien force (Euro-Russian Marxism) never could teach its American followers "to take on a native accent and thus [they] seemed all the more alien."[115]

Which is to say—in the case of writers—you could tell their Redness, thus their inauthenticity, by their mutant wording. By 1955, E. Merrill Root had completed his study of every issue of a collegiate communist magazine published in the late 1930s and discovered, to his consternation, that the young editors chose to print poems that "combined," within the poem, avant-garde experiment and "Communist ideology." Thus Root worried that readers of a later time would miss the communism for the modernist linguistic surface. Perhaps such naive people would "smile and say, 'It was long ago—and far away.'" Root wanted readers of this verse to be alert to the dreadful consequences of such tolerance of the 1930s in the 1950s: Yes, "it *was* 'long ago.' [But] insect eggs are laid long before they waken to devour the living host." Unless they are vigilant, at any rate, *his* readers might not realize that the deadly parasite here was political subversion expressing itself as modernism.[116]

Phillips had engaged the trope of the alien as an anticommunist strategy to make a point about the failure of communist aesthetics. On the question of modernism, he was hoping for a middle way, convinced that the main lesson was that "the radical movement of the 30's *broke* the radical spirit of literature" and hoping for a return to modern writing that had nothing to do with the Red Decade.[117] Coblentz saw modernists and communists as aliens invading in the same forms, and he, moreover, was not just a poet and antimodernist editor and publisher, for if he had any popular renown in his day it was as a science fiction and fantasy writer, author of *After 12,000 Years* (1950), *The Planet of Youth* (1952), and other sci-fi classics and a winner of many prizes in these genres.[118] In *The Blue Barbarians* (1958), he depicted a people for whom the world revolved around a green glass pointedly called "gulag." *After 12,000 Years* featured gigantic insects as soldiers in the war to control the weather. Yet it was in a book about modern verse that Coblentz wrote, "There may be mutants; let us fervidly hope and pray that they will be favorable mutants; but when they appear, they will be found to bear family resemblance to all the poets that have ever glorified the language of civilized man." Until such resemblance grows from these synthetic seeds (at which point we will be blind to all difference), we must be on guard to protect "the natural world" in which "no plant is disconnected from its past."[119] To Gilbert Neiman, modernists' "gestures were alien, diminished in magnitude, false." He finally knew *they* were the invaders, numbly imitating humanity. But how would *he* be perceived by others? Modernism was being accepted. The pod people had taken over the town—or had always been there. Would others believe him? The sci-fi-like confusion in this scene of prodigal return is even more pointed in Neiman's private correspondence with *Poetry*'s editors: perhaps he had become the imperceptive one, he conceded. The opposites were dullness on one hand and the capacity for love on the other (precisely the extremes plaguing Santa Mira). It was "a great defeat to me," he wrote to George Dillon, "that I become dull to the loves I had once, Eliot, Tate, Auden, and naturally Stevens, Mina Loy . . . and Marianne Moore."[120]

The antimodernist founder and executive secretary of Poets of the Pacific, poet Jan Kujawa, wondered "*what could* have happened" to poetry that two Americans calling themselves poets—cummings and Kujawa himself—could be "as strange to each other as beings out of two different worlds." As with Neiman, Kujawa's first response to the modernist as hideous Other is to think, "I want to know how he got that way." But then Kujawa realized that the hard battle against modernist incursion faced by these Pacific Rim traditionalists— poets in the association, "valuing poetry for its cultural influence" and ranging from Dorine Goertzen of Idaho to Jock MacDonald of western Canada to Gertrude Wellington from Hawaii to Pearl Wimberly in South America to Ling-Fu Yang of China—was the work of an overwhelmed but dauntless minority against a powerful alien American force, a force so great and strange that even a poet as sure of his antimodernism as Kujawa must wonder for a moment if he is the one of whom it should be asked, "What could have happened?" "I want to know how [the modernist] got that way. Or how *I* got that way, if *we* of the traditional school are off key. . . . I think that each of us feels the other is simply 'touched,' that is all. . . . Is he?, or is there something I do not understand?"[121]

Colonel Cullen Jones knew for a fact, he said, that Hart Crane had been driven to homosexuality and "insanity" after being infected by the "ratty-minded sophistication and psychosis" of modernism. He was certain that the fellow-traveling Louis Untermeyer, just for handling Crane's poems so kindly and gently in his anthologies, should be dubbed "an alienist." And although "normal men walk away" from modern poetry "with a feeling of acute nausea," perhaps finally it was he, Jones, who should be fitted for a "padded cell in some institution." Perhaps it was he, the normal poet, who did not belong in the awful dystopia he described, in which "long-haired, lisping sweet boys rushed to the arts for haven, even as Crane's gentry still haunt and engrave public toilets."[122]

Once the modern mode became an operative force in public discourse, it could be depicted by its detractors as a hegemony featuring malformation of natural difference. Modernists, "motivated by a frantic desire to be different," wrote Jacob Hauser, produced "something weird, fantastic, out of this world,"[123] yet at the same time "theirs is never the modesty of a faction content to acknowledge itself as a faction."[124] Once again, the confusion concerned which segment of the poetic population was ideologically (not just aesthetically) Other, and Neiman, in part because he was more temperate than Hauser and Kujawa, knew that confusion was his sharpest weapon as a skeptic. We have seen that he suggested that Joyce was not actually an innovator, and he anticipated revising the whole history of modern writing from the 1920s to the 1950s so that formal experimentation ("innovations of punctuation, spacing, and idiom")[125] could be ignored and a label of "Victorianism" applied. Still, for Neiman as for the leadership of Poets of the Pacific, this sci-fi-like bewilderment was also horribly shocking. Modernism had become an enemy within. You could not go home to get away from them: they're *there*.

Despite the use of the conceits of anticommunist science fiction, this solution to the problem of the enemy within was not violent. Neiman's response, typical of the moderate antimodernist, was, like Bell in *The End of Ideology*, to use the weapon of historiography—to doubt their literary history of radicalism and their claims for the newness of experimentalism; to deradicalize the avant-garde by rewriting the narrative so that modernism marks an end of something old, not the beginning of something new. The reactionary antimodernist, on the contrary, called for total annihilation and used the anticommunist trope—one of J. Edgar Hoover's favorites and that of Edward Hunter, the authority on communist psychological warfare, and again, of course, a standard screenplay analogy in Cold War sci-fi—of the foreign invasion as an infectious disease, or mutation, or weedlike destroyer of the natural. On the floor of Congress,

George Dondero referred to modernists as "the human art termites, disciples of multiple 'isms.' "[126] Hunter called communism "the insectization of human beings," leading the author of an article, "Termite-ism Compared to Communism," to remind readers that as the "termite bores into the fibre of a structure, causing serious damage," so the communists "bore into the fibre of American character through certain tricks of psychology."[127] A little more precise in his troping about the demise of the natural than Hunter and other psychoterrorism experts, Edward Dunsany likened the actual *lines* of the modern poem to weeds, "hiding for a little while" along the "bases of the pillars of the temples" of godly canonical versifiers (for him: Homer, Milton, Shelley).[128] "The only way in which falsity and affectation" in modern poetry "can be uprooted," wrote Coblentz, "is by exposure to the light of day."[129] E. Merrill Root published a poem, "Consider the Lilies," satirically proposing "a new and needed Commissar" whose "duty was to stain red each yellow rose," "to suppress all wildflowers that grow / At beauty's whim" and to "destroy / Brown ox-eyed daisies," and so forth—and what was implicit here (although explicit elsewhere in Root's writings) was that the strict traditional form and meter of the poem, a perfectly regular sonnet, was itself a weapon against the "resolute arch-enemy of joy." The nightmare in Root's sonnet took place in the United States after the communist takeover, in "these new People's States." The flowers bore the first sign of political doom.[130] For Coblentz, the verse of the antipoet was also a tenacious weed, a false flower, marauding in meadows of beautiful delicate poems. The false must be uprooted entirely now, or it will take over. That outcome was frightful not only because foreign weeds inevitably crowd out native flowers and the few good poems that survive will have to struggle toward sunlight. Worse still, admirers standing at the edge of the field, fooled by the inhuman invaders, will actually begin to esteem the weeds with exclamations of "Flowers!" It was "a species that may have originated on the planet Mars, since nothing just like this was ever known on earth before."[131] Elsewhere, Coblentz likened the modernist to a gardener who sets out to uproot the weeds and "ends by tearing up the pansies, sweet-peas and petunias."[132]

When the regionalist[133] southern writer Ben Lucien Burman (1895–1984), a Harvard alumnus and wounded World War I veteran famous for his *Catfish Bend* books, assailed the poetry of Gertrude Stein in 1952 with charges of unintelligibility familiar from earlier decades, the new metaphorical twist was the use of the anticommunist rhetoric then being perfected by Hoover in his speeches and in the pages of the biweekly *Firing Line* of the American Legion and by Burman himself: the analogy to immunology. In a *Firing Line* issue of May 1952, readers learned that communism in the United States was "the Red plague"; fellow travelers were "the Typhoid Mary's" [sic] who spread it; and, most important, learning to understand communist language entailed "be[ing] able to spot Stalin's viruses and bacteria."[134] Burman wrote that leftist absolutism was a "disease" so pernicious that "we may contract the malady and become totalitarian ourselves."[135] For Burman—a much-practiced anticommunist who believed that plainness and clarity would keep "Ivan" from "pulling the trigger"[136]—difficulty, artificiality, and especially the abhorrence of regional writing sapped American cultural strength.

Burman's criticism of modern writers—they "have sinned too often against art and objectivity, . . . they have destroyed poetry"—was always linked to his belief in the power of "homespun" locality.[137] In every book set in Burman's fictional Catfish Bend, a conservative's paradise of simplicity based on Louisiana river life and the author's hometown of Covington, Kentucky, "the antisocial are simply put to rout" and "World Government" is unlikely ever to have effect;[138] the denotative, concrete sense of the local was the best bet against globalist totalitarianism.[139] (Burman was a local hero of antimodernists. Robert Hillyer lavished praise on Catfish Bend as "the product of a mind at peace,"[140] and J. Donald Adams urged his readers to heed Burman's warnings against "the contemporary literary scene" that show how dangerously "our standards are blurred, our perceptions blunted.")[141] "Because all culture is local" and because the clearest truth derives from specific knowledge of and devotion to a place, international modernism brought on rootlessness, incoherence, and lies. The falsehood of foreign abstraction spread because no root held it firmly to veracity. "*There are no international roots*," wrote the brilliant reactionary rhetorical theorist Richard Weaver in "Reflections of Modernity." "All of the world's cultures have been *regional*. . . . Loyalty begins with what is near."[142] What was culturally foreign tempted disloyalty. So Ben Burman read the poetry of Stein, the quintessential twentieth-century American internationalist, and from the very fact of her success concluded that allegiant Americans were fighting back against foreign entanglements with the wrong weapons. You do not combat a disease with the tools of conventional battle; this was not hot but cold war. Midcentury Americans, Burman argued, were bold when it came to overt political opinion. But they were sickeningly timid when it came to literary opinions. Thus whereas in politics we were safe from destruction by communists because we were tough and certain, when facing modernism we were damnably soft and, thanks to the treason of liberal critics, susceptible to invasion. The influence of Gertrude Stein is "still to be found in many strategic strongholds, like the lurking germs of a yellow fever, they must be constantly fought and sprayed with violent chemicals lest the microbes develop again and start a new infection."[143] "Who has let into our homeland," George Dondero asked in Congress, "this horde of germ-carrying art vermin?" Dadaism, cubism, surrealism, abstractionism—"all these isms are of foreign origin, and truly should have no place in American art."[144] In a widely circulated article appearing in the national *American Legion Magazine*, a woman named Esther Julia Pels described the "Modern Art Swindle": modernism sponsored a political revolution. She noted that "books written by or about leaders of 'social protest' . . . were [being] published or sold by the Museum of Modern Art." "The way was open," wrote Pels, "for the virus of foreign-spawned 'Isms' to be injected into the bloodstream of American culture, and it was."[145] (Esther Julia Pels was also known as Mrs. Karl Baarslag, wife of the man who was head of investigations for HUAC.)[146] Modern poetry created intellectual stagnation, wrote Hillyer; poetry now "serve[d] as a breeding place for influences so unwholesome."[147]

Making his case against relativism, Weaver turned to a "biologist friend of mine [who] caustically expresse[d] the modern attitude thus: 'Why face facts: they may turn out to be no facts at all.'" Such pernicious ideas about meaning—that it floats freely—were for Weaver a ghastly political epidemic: since modernist ideas about language are espoused by liberal members of "our once respected Supreme Court," "it is little wonder . . . that our young people have succumbed to this when it infects the highest echelons of our social and political organization." Weaver quoted Oliver Wendell Holmes's language theory, loathed by conservatives: "A word . . . is the skin of a living thought and may vary greatly in color and content according to the circumstances and time in which it is used"—and even Chief Justice Fred Vinson, whose statement that "nothing is more certain in modern society than the principle that all concepts are relative: a name, a phrase" made him disloyal to the new right.[148] Tolerance of variations in meaning furthered the spread of the linguistic idea that "all things flow," to Weaver a disgraceful attitude that thwarted "the preservation of freedom."[149]

A medical doctor from Philadelphia wrote to the editors of the *Saturday Review* in 1954 to praise Dunsany's attack on modernism, which had introduced the trope of the leaden bell. For Dr. Frederick Fraley, this rang true to his experience in immunology: "Many years ago, as medical students learning the art of Physical Diagnosis, among the adventitious sounds we were supposed to recognize was one by the name of the 'cracked-pot' sound, which precisely described it. This note appears to be a frequent sign in the pathology of Modern Poetry, and points toward a correct diagnosis in that variety of virus infection."[150] Once modernism, like communism, can be said to be like a virus, openness is no longer appropriate; extremism is affirmed, tolerance ridiculed as abetting, not reducing, the illness. "You do not willingly allow half a bite to the mosquito that sucks your blood," wrote Coblentz of modernism, "or inaugurate a policy of 'Live and let live!,' whereby half or one quarter of the tuberculosis or typhus germs are tolerated and protected."[151] "We cannot come to terms with . . . the parasite in the grain . . . ; our only recourse is to suppress the menace."[152] The horror of relativism, wrote Weaver, is that it has encouraged moderation and tolerance as weapons in the fight against wrong. "Between contradictories there is no middle ground." The disease is a philosophy of meaning that holds A to be implicated in not-A. But "it is a law of logic that where A and not-A exist as alternatives, you cannot have both of them nor can you squeeze in between them."[153]

Edward John Moreton Drax Plunkett, eighteenth Baron Dunsany, undertook to read "a good many lines of modern verse" and did not like what he saw. His special tactic for expressing this animosity—he yanked passages from difficult, satirical, or densely contextual modern poems to display them as nonsense —was enormously influential among traditionalists. One was Mary O'Connor, an antimodernist poet and founder of World Poetry Day (notwithstanding the word "World," the day was limited to writers in the United States). Through O'Connor's advocacy of this celebration, she urged "all who care for poetry . . . to show up 'modern verse' for the nonsense that it is and for metre to be written again," and she revered Dunsany for supporting conservatives who continued to write no matter what, "in these days of 'modern verse.' "[154]

What little Dunsany actually knew about experimental poetry in the United States he gleaned during several lecture tours in the early 1950s, where huge audiences heard him say that publishing a modernist poem was like bringing a dirty roll of paper to the bank and passing it off as a hundred-dollar bill.[155] He also learned about the situation in American poetry from the negative examples —typically lexicographical and typographical verse experiments—that Stanton Coblentz quoted in the book-length diatribe against experimentalist subversion, *New Poetic Lamps and Old* (1950).[156] Dunsany wondered how it was possible that "the United States that had, amongst others, Edgar Allan Poe, and has Stanton Coblentz to-day," tolerated such lines and even "rewarded the men who wrote them." In claiming to have found the sentiments of political radicalism hiding behind enigmatic language, he made the connection between the left and the avant-garde that thenceforth required no external evidence. That is to say, the presence of difficult language itself provided evidence of cloaked heresy. Dunsany made this point in "The Fall of the Muses" (1952) in the *Poetry Review*, by wholly inventing his horrifying examples—standard revolutionary fare, a parody of 1930s poetry as imagined by the midcentury antimodernist:

They all die, die, die,
The tram-conductors, the cops, and the players of baseball,
The keepers of confectioners' shops and the owners of motors,
The presidents of railways and building contractors,
They all die.

Here, then, was precisely where experimental writing was concocted—at the point when the "thirties" "radical," author of such subversive lines, realized that his radicalism might be discovered or outed by his writing. "But if it all went like this," Dunsany observed of his own fantasized "radical" verse, "they might be found out; so they write passages which you, my reader, will not be able to understand, such as this"—at which point Dunsany, still making it all up, presented a "sampling" of communist modernism. This modern verse is a nightmarish linguistic world in which nothing is what it seems, in which words are the opposite of denotative, and—like the use of the "Aesopian Language thesis" in the Smith Act trials, already under way—in which the writing of communists is discernible precisely because it refuses to mean anything revolutionary at all:

The moon is not the moon
Nor the sea the sea.
And yet the sea draws the moon as much as the moon draws the sea
And drowns the moon in unplumbable ages of filth
For ever and ever and ever.

Dunsany's gloss on this "sample" of modern verse is a classic instance of anti-communist interpretive logic in the world of poetry: "Only nonsense can never be plumbed."[157]

CHAPTER 9

Deep Pinks, Medium Pinks, Door Openers

Not long after his muses fell, Lord Dunsany was elected president of the Authors' Club in London. His acceptance speech was another jeremiad against modern poetry. News of the pronouncement was cabled far and wide. In Boston, the editors of the *Saturday Review of Literature*, doubtless still stung by the counterattack against Robert Hillyer a few years earlier, discussed Dunsany's speech among themselves as if it were a message from an emergent new front in a secret war. To them he was not the consummate insider, the president of a staid academy, but a proud aesthetic exile, leading a noble resistance, saying the unsayable.

Edward John Dunsany had again associated the rise of modernism with revolutionary politics. But unlike most of the American reactionary antimodernists, his position was frankly aristocratic. Following Stanton Coblentz, Dunsany dubbed his enemies "anti-poets," adding an urgent political twist: "They are to Milton and to the Muses what Robespierre was to the Court of France." He warned fellow members of the Authors' Club to watch their necks: "The *sans-culottes* did not call their leaders aristocrats. They chopped off the heads of men and women because they thought them out-of-date, as these [modernists] speak of the great poets. They thought them mere traditionalists, and they were sick of tradition." Dunsany contended that the problem was not itself the experimentalist argument against tradition but the fact that modern poems celebrated ugliness and formally attempted to replicate political chaos, marring "our glorious language."[1]

William McFee, a conservative poet, wondered if indeed modernist ugliness was a hoax. "There [is] an awful lot of hoky-poky in our trade," he wrote, asking his friend Malcolm Cowley to "suppose a poet were to offer such a line as 'The scent of these armpits is an aroma finer than prayer.' Would the publisher accept it? Maybe. . . . I grew up on Kipling," he continued, "and shall never regret it and [he] will outlast your enthusiasms."[2] McFee was irked by the linguistic quality of the straw-man modernist line (which he, too, invented). The same approach drove his attack on William Carlos Williams.[3] For McFee, as for Dunsany, that poets were permitted to write so freely was not freedom but force. "The imposition of style on a disparate and chaotic reality," a conservative art critic wrote, "seems to force the impression of negation on the aesthetician."[4] That assessment appeared in the upscale conservative venue *Modern Age*. Dunsany, an after-dinner speaker on the stump, agreed but was blunter: "If this is poetry," he cried, then "there is plenty of it on the walls of lavatories."[5]

Poetry's capacity to convey the beauty of the English language, carried rhetorically aloft by "high" poetic diction as well as by the use of "positive" or uplifting subject matter (not "the sordid things of everyday"),[6] was now deemed a fundamental form of patriotism. B. Y. Williams, the editor of *Talaria*, praised a new book of poems by Michigan's "beloved" poet Jessie Wilmore Murton because she "avoid[ed] being didactic," presented "the precious eternal verities," and grouped her poems under six essential headings: Things That Are Lovely, Things That Are True, Things That Are Praiseworthy, Things That Are Virtuous, Things That Are Pure, and Things That Are of Good Report.[7] Ben Lucien Burman warned against modernists who "hunt in packs . . . baying Joyce and Stein" and "see no beauty in the world."[8] Nor did Charles Wharton Stork (1881–1971) find much uplifting in the writings of his modernist colleagues. Poet, friend of literary figures in the 1920s, former editor of *Contemporary Verse*, and president of the Poetry Society of America, Stork bitterly satirized modernism in a pamphlet titled *A Vision of Misjudgment: An Adventure among the Latest Poets* (1958). Stork had previously had no trouble publishing his verse, but by the late 1940s he was being ignored by the major periodicals. Stanton Coblentz's Wings Press came to the rescue in 1948, publishing Stork's *On Board Old Ironsides*,[9] which Coblentz promoted across conservative America. (He shipped complimentary copies to Admirals Chester Nimitz and J. H. Hawley and to Republican perennial Harold Stassen.)[10] By the time of *Misjudgment*, Stork had completely soured on modernism and had come around to Coblentz's view of the new poets.

Stork's Virgil, guiding him through the avant-garde nightmare, is motivated by an evening listening to Aaron Copland under a painting by Salvador Dalí: he is a figure named Usurpy, the Tenth Muse (the other nine having been executed). Usurpy will help the dreamer "understand the New Poetry." They meet the modern poets Mr. Scummings and Mr. Teazy Sellalot, but Stork notices the absence of Starchbold MacYeast, whose long poem "Contwistedbores" should have made him eligible for modernist canonization. "While his case was being discussed," replies Usurpy, "he unaccountably lapsed into a sanity and patriotism and that put him quite out of the running." But surely a

"New Poetry séance [should] include Mr. Carl Sandburg and Mr. Robert Frost," Stork wonders. They give "a pleasant impression of human nature," Usurpy patiently explains, and, committing the greatest sin, "they wrote favorably about America."[11]

Notwithstanding the simplicity of Stork's vision of the modern poetry world, detractors of modern writing found it easier to assert the claim against disloyal or un-American subject matter in fiction than in verse. Poetic form presented the special difficulty. Even Stork's satire had to grapple with the problem of poetic form in *The Vision of Misjudgment*. Journalists covering the modernism wars assumed that it was easier for readers of antimodernist screeds published in mass-circulation magazines to comprehend doubts about American *novels*—to discern as a matter of content which writer "wrote favorably about America," as Stork's Usurpy put it, as part of the anticommunist movement as a whole. When in 1952 John Lydenberg, a leftist critic and something of a literary historian of American radicalism, anxiously surveyed assaults on modern American fiction, he discovered diatribes in "magazines as diverse as *Fortune, Life*, the *Saturday Review of Literature*, and the *New York Times Book Review*." This was "certainly not planned to be part of a coordinated campaign,"[12] but overall the attacks aimed at what an article in *Life* called a misanthropy that was "not representative of the country." "We need a novelist," the August 16, 1948, piece in *Life* opined, "to re-create American values instead of wallowing in the literary slums."

It is fair to say that when anticommunists referred to "modernism" in American fiction, they did not really mean the mode ascending from Stein's *Three Lives* (1905–6), John Dos Passos's *Manhattan Transfer* (1925), Ernest Hemingway's *In Our Time* (1924), Henry Roth's *Call It Sleep* (1934), the early Nathanael West, or the Djuna Barnes of *Nightwood* (1937) but were thinking more of the literary naturalism of the modern period: Stephen Crane, Theodore Dreiser, Sherwood Anderson, the Hemingway of *For Whom the Bell Tolls* (1940), Richard Wright, even Michael Gold and (to the extent that anticommunists knew of these works) other communist naturalists of the 1930s such as Grace Lumpkin and William Rollins. The *Life* editorial decried the "modernism" of Mailer's *The Naked and the Dead* (1948) because, in its likening of wartime behavior to qualities in American domestic life, that novel was too negative. Mailer ought to have seen the value in "marrying and procreating and raising a family or master[ing] an art or a profession or building a business or beating the Japs."

Here and throughout this period, *Life* expressed a yearning for the particular modernism of the 1920s, for the purer, originary modernity imagined with the help of political hindsight that we have seen at work in other contexts. Readers and critics in the 1950s longed for the writing of the 1920s because "the Hemingway generation" had then exhibited "animal vitality," a quality lacking in nihilistic leftist GI writers such as Mailer.[13] Since varieties of antimodernism depended on the aesthetic medium and—within the broad field of writing—on the genre, a comparative look at poetry, painting, and fiction is instructive.

The anticommunist assault on modernism waged against postwar fiction was almost purely a matter of thematics. "Our novels are 'unhealthy'" because of what they are *about*.[14] This simple conservative view gave expression to the shame traditionalists felt when they reckoned that the postwar leaders of modern fiction "wouldn't dream of writing a novel about a Republican any more."[15] But in poetry, antimodernists really did mean to stand against formal and linguistic resistance to convention. They really were concerned about the social consequences of the dissolution of the work's customary unity. In that distinctive sense, they feared a dangerous "new freedom" that along with disintegration, "negativism," loss of control, and subversion had infected the language word by word.

So while on subject matter, antimodernists in fiction, poetry, and painting had a great deal politically in common, in poetry and painting, form had to be dealt with if the conservative case was to be persuasive. One local activist who complained about red influence in modern painting, Charles Plant, argued plainly that "art is supposed to be pleasing and uplifting to the people who view it." Writing to the commissioner of public buildings to denounce the Rincon Annex Murals in San Francisco's post office, this man noted that the murals, which he called "Frankenstein monsters," were the work of anticapitalists.[16] Although not a professional art critic, Plant assumed he had an obligation to speak about the work's aesthetic in some sort of detail. So, too, with most anticommunist critics of modern poetry. They now took for granted the need for some sort of close reading. And just when the anticommunist's attention focuses on the manner and form of the work itself, getting beyond subject matter, the great fear of disjunctive language becomes manifest. When Burton Frye wrote to Hillyer to complain about Hayden Carruth's rejoinder to the antimodernists, his real worry—the concern that takes up most of the letter— was whether Hillyer would also hold to a hard line against ballads in which the quatrain leaves the first and third lines unrhymed.[17]

When Coblentz and Dunsany took the time to examine modern poetry line by line, the lines became the source of their keenest rage. Dunsany offered three examples of verse of the sort he consigned to the bathroom wall:

Brown grass, gray rocks, rust forest beds, no heartbeat is now
At kick.   (William Gibson)

That every damned American
Eats crow   (Reuel Denney)

1-2-3 was the number he played but today the number came up
    3-2-1   (Kenneth Fearing)[18]

This was quintessential antimodernist manner, a quick and dirty anthology of
hateful experimental verse, "a few don'ts for the anticommunist poet" implied
and only somewhat explained. The technique of associating such poets is a
scattershot attack. Kenneth Fearing, closely identified with the Marxist movement between the wars and a favorite target of antimodernists,[19] whose great
subject was the predicament of the modern individual and who went through a
Kafkaesque phase obsessed with fear and confusion; William Gibson (b. 1914),
author of *The Miracle Worker: A Play for Television* (1957), a one-book poet
(*Winter Crook* [1948]) who almost always wrote in elevated diction ("What
gnarl of idiom roots my tongue awry / So all my limbs, deformed / Hang out of
hand my gifts, to dry"),[20] dubbed a "modernist" in error and then reviled by
conservatives through a chain of unquestioned guilty association;[21] and Reuel
Denney, a modest University of Chicago critic-sociologist (coauthor with
David Riesman of *The Lonely Crowd*) whose main topics were mass communi-
cations and Great Ideas, and whose poems—"The Honest Retired Lodger on
the Porch" (1955)[22] is typical—rarely venture toward the open form. Dunsany
clearly conducted no background checks before naming modernist names, but
neither did he sense any diversity in his victims' writing. Everything ranging
across modernism, from left to right, fell into the same trouble. What tended to
enrage anticommunist antimodernists, when they observed modernity at work
on the poem's page, was the combination of common idiom, the discoloration
of natural subjects, insults hurled at a great nation—executed or actualized by
some at least superficial deformation of the line.[23] When Dunsany quoted an
abhorrent line, presumably for its violation of the poet's idealist promise—for
instance, "The 9:25 train may be rather later / this morning, but not very"—he
did not set to wondering about the dull, common subject matter but dolefully
asked, "Have the poets of the world labored in vain for three thousand years if
their *meter* was quite unnecessary?"[24] (His choice of Gibson was a special error
in this regard, for that poet rarely strayed from the regular metrical foot.)

In an essay for the *Atlantic* called "Prose or Poetry" (1945), Dunsany had
made the point still more forcefully:

How often does something like this get into print nowadays, to be accepted as poetry:—

The charge for announcements in the
    Personal Column is 6s. per line
(Minimum 2 lines)
Trade announcements 25s. for 2 lines
(Minimum)
A box number forms part of
The advertisement
And counts as six words.

How does this come about?[25]

Here Dunsany caught himself in one of the paradoxes that often marred the antimodernist case. He claimed to want simplicity. "What authority have [the modernists] to give you their message in other than plain English?" Yet chief among his own heroes was John Milton, whom he put on the wrong ideological side of the analogy in his quick Tory history of poets and revolutions. Moreover, the modern line Dunsany quoted (the one about the belated 9:25 commuter train) could hardly have been plainer.[26] And the "found poem" in arrhythmic vers libre suggested distinctions between newspaper ads that otherwise read similarly, presenting a complex conception of art in utterly simple terms. One cannot read these lines of "prose" as lineated thus—

A box number forms part of
The advertisement
And counts as six words

—without indeed thinking about the sort of spare yet constrained language that can derive its value only literally by the word, here in a five-word line about an advertising figure valued as if it were six words. It might not have been art to Dunsany, its formal irony entirely accidental, but its ambiguous status as an object in the realm of poetry distinct from prose did after all force him to ponder self-consciously what art is. For Dunsany, such linguistic forms did *not* "come about" because "the public scorned all the arts . . . abusing Keats."[27] It might have been "accepted as poetry," but it was not thusly intended, for the idea that this *was* a poem was entirely Dunsany's. The antimodernist himself had committed the constructivist sin of "anything goes" and then conveniently caught himself in the act.

Indeed, this trick at least partly backfired every time an offended antimodernist used it. The British poet Alfred Noyes (1880–1958), one of the earliest avid detractors of modernist writing, delighted in the hoax—which he called "an experiment"—perpetrated by one of his students on "a well-known journal." The student "deliberately wrote down the most complete bosh he could think of" and submitted it. The poem was printed, and there ensued a series of letters from readers, some defending modernism but not the poem, others defending modernism and the poem (one called it "beautiful"); still others took Noyes's position in rejecting the assertion that " 'fine' modern poems are a meaningless 'jumble of words.' " All this affirmed Noyes's view that "the confusion of standards at the present moment is appalling," but nowhere did he consider even passingly that when the student "deliberately wrote down the most complete bosh he could think of" he had discovered a way to liberate himself from Noyes's own traditionalist pedagogy *and* win Noyes's affections at the same time—and that the deliberateness of the act, rather than the poetic tradition from which it broke, was its source of creativity.[28]

When antimodernists contended that the main issue for them was restoration of truth and beauty, they spoke of these qualities as aspects of cultural fealty, civic instruction, and the revival of historical standards. Carl Edwin Burklund, in his raging essay "The Treason of 'Modern' Poetry" (1949), argued that modernists betrayed poets' "obligation to the public," rejecting a role inherent in "three thousand years [of] our Western tradition" that ought to culminate in efforts to "clarify our understanding of the world."[29] For Dunsany, in part, such duty originated in the impulse of an "author, soldier and squire"[30] to protect the English verse legacy of Keats from the prosemongers. For Hillyer, patriotism and anticommunism were always available as analogies; the operation of one subversive force was like the other. When Hillyer exposed the power-hungry modernists in 1950, he took full measure of their "trickiness." It was "scarcely exceeded by that of the Communists, whose tactics of infiltration into our colleges [the poet-critics] have imitated."[31] He meant that modernists had learned subversive strategies from communists and thus were *like* communists. He fell short of saying they *were* communists. In the case of Coblentz and the *Lyric* editors, modernism and u.s. communism functioned not just similarly but actually conspired together. Yet, again, the goal of both groups of antimodernists—moderates and reactionaries—was to persuade the reading public of a seemingly counterintuitive claim: what really threatened postwar u.s. culture was the subversive linguistic strategies modernists and communists had commonly developed. Modernism in this sense, as a development of cultural un-Americanism, was actually more threatening than communism in the active, political sphere because of its formal disjunction. The proper response by those at the center and on the right was "anti-ism-ism": for the centrist, such a position was not itself an *-ism*; for the conservative, it unproblematically was.[32] What seemed to be at stake, even for readers of the blundering American Legion magazine *Firing Line*, was control over the ability to interpret, to discern or "spot" subversion in texts. It was hard interpretive work, but it had to be done. Citizens were rallied to the hermeneutical cause. While Willard Thorp of Princeton, a moderate, had no intention of winning adherents to one struggle or another, his entry, "American Writers on the Left," in *Socialism and American Life* (1952) nonetheless lent credence to the idea that reading red in texts required superacuity. "To ascertain precisely how the party line for America was determined, . . . whether in the Kremlin or by the Comintern or by party headquarters in New York, would be beyond the detective prowess of any scholar. *But . . .*," added Thorp, undaunted—whereupon he pressed further to locate the aforementioned "party line" in the verse of several communist-affiliated poets.[33]

So anticommunist antimodernism was founded on a series of related fears— a fear of the godlessness entailed in "obscurity"; of the abandonment not just of "positive" subject matter but, far worse, of content altogether; of the disruption of the lyric line (for instance, of overused enjambment); of the rejection not just of natural description but of imagery itself (somehow, modernists "scoff at imagery");[34] of the combination of difficulty and " 'intellectual' poetry" producing "simply bad craftsmanship";[35] of the "*rhetorical* smoke screen created around abstract art";[36] and of the communist-modernist prohibition against any free and open "discussion of [bad] tendencies in modern American poetry."[37] "Because conservatism stresses concrete emotional loyalties more than allegiance to abstract syllogisms," wrote Peter Viereck, "it overlaps more frequently with poetry (that crystallization of the emotional and the concrete) than do any other political isms."[38]

Anticommunists attacking experimentalism and abstraction in modern poetics took cues from the well-organized campaign against modern painting, and the archives of conservatives in both media are full of letters exchanged between them. Alice Garrett, who fought modern painting, wrote Hillyer to praise his strategy of commandeering a popular magazine for his cause and now gained some hope that an "opposite number" of the *Saturday Review* could take up the conservative countermovement in painting.[39] And, vice versa, antimodernist poets took courage from statements of government policy against modernism such as A. H. Berding's pronouncement in 1953 that "we are not interested in purely experimental art."[40] Doubters such as Garrett asked, Was it not true that Stuart Davis, a modernist and a communist at once (and at turns), had stressed abstraction's left-wing heritage throughout the Red Decade? Had not Ad Reinhardt been a favored illustrator for the communist *New Masses*, a protégé of perhaps the most talented and attractive member of the *New Masses* staff, David Leisk (a.k.a. "Crockett Johnson")?[41] Did not abstraction in itself undermine the American literary traditions of regionalism, fidelity to the local landscape? Was it not the case that the radical, fellow-traveling art critic Herbert Read, a British eminence with a large public following in the United States, had argued in 1935 that abstract artists were "the true revolutionary artists, whom every Communist should learn to respect and encourage?"[42] Abstract art wrought destruction "by the creation of brainstorms," announced a congressman on the floor of the U.S. House of Representatives.[43]

The partnership between radicalism and modern painting became an electoral campaign issue for this intrepid member of Congress, Republican George A. Dondero of Detroit. It was also a means by which artists who felt neglected could once again grab the limelight. Wheeler Williams, president of the American Artists Professional League (AAPL), whom Dondero mistakenly called "our foremost American sculptor," was one antimodernist, very much like Coblentz in the poetry world, who went completely for McCarthyite rhetoric, claiming at one point to have documentary "proof" that modern art was a communist plot: "*I have before me* the complete notes sent me by a secretary of a communist art cell in the U.S. who left the party in disgust. They confirm in detail Dondero's findings: 'Our plan: to encourage, to promote, ugliness, repulsive, meaningless art. People are more influenced by their art than they realize—subtle, unconscious but effective means to depress spirit . . . speed internal disintegration, destroy faith in our culture by removing all inspirational ideals of beauty—substitute insane, ugly, revolting art.' "[44]

Dondero's career as an anticommunist antimodernist culminated in 1957 when the International Fine Arts Council (IFAC) presented him with its gold medal of honor, issuing statements of praise (each reiterating the dire threat posed by modernism) that were read into the *Congressional Record*. His career as a foe of the left had commenced suddenly in 1947 with a speech urging a Roanoke, Virginia, Rotary Club Ladies Night audience to stop all foreign ideologies, every day and everywhere, including schools and colleges,[45] but he received scant national press until he trained his gaze on modernism. Unlike several other legislators—such as Fred Busby of Illinois, for whom modernist human forms were unnatural, and Edward Cox (Democrat of Georgia), who deemed modern art an adumbration of insanity—Dondero specifically and personally appealed to traditionalists in all the arts, including poetry. Many of his correspondents among artists were susceptible to this appeal because they had begun to feel neglected by the museums, magazines, and the market. Working directly with Dondero, they pulled antimodernists from a variety of traditionalist academies into the anticommunist political world, where they made the case—fronting for him—in an aesthetic language in which Dondero himself was unfluent. These antimodernist organizations included the National Sculpture Society, the AAPL, the National Academy of Design, the Salmagundi Club, the IFAC, Education Information, and the Allied Artists, among other groups.

Dondero's activities and speeches, such as "The Communist Infiltration in American Art," delivered March 17, 1952, created a boom in antimodernist research. Such investigations had implications for writers. "In 1935," Dondero announced in Congress, "Earl Browder, General Secretary of the Communist Party, and Lewis Mumford, John Reed Club organizer . . . took part in [a] sinister act to gain control of art and literature in the United States." Mumford fired back, not against the notion of a conspiracy to control modern "art and literature" but against Dondero's faulty fact-finding. In a letter demanding retraction, Mumford challenged Dondero's "tainted sources," denying that he had ever been a member of the John Reed Clubs.[46] However many errors Dondero made in naming names—and he made many—the generalizations stuck: American visual and literary art should be gladdening not depressing, orderly not chaotic, whole not disintegrated, native not foreign-influenced. At this point, Dondero's attacks never penetrated much past content.

Until, that is, a traditionalist poet intervened. Among conservative poets such as Archer Milton Huntington, who by the late 1940s felt that he did not belong in magazines and journals that had once published him—excluded by the now-dominant world of modern verse—what must have made particular sense was Dondero's claim that modernism's mode of difficulty was itself a form of radicalism.

Huntington was becoming a mordant traditionalist in his own poetry. *Lace Maker of Segovia* (1928) had received some favorable critical attention, as did *The Ladies of Valbona* (1931). But then, although Huntington published book after book of accomplished, well-wrought poems, his work was neglected: *A Flight of Birds* (1938) was ignored; *Spain and Africa* (1943) caught only a bit of war-related notice; *Recuardos* (1949), *Turning Pages* (1950), and *Tapestry* (1951) came out in quick succession—three years, three volumes of poems—but generated no response from critics and little from readers. How vexing it must have been, too, to produce a 424-page *Collected Verse* (1953) and be entirely ignored except by a few politically sympathetic friends. Huntington certainly knew that going against the "modernistic" mode was tantamount to self-destruction, and one could only facetiously "revel in the modernistic," for "at any rate" it is a "relief from the portraiture of magnates and the war memorial" (both traditional art forms he had commissioned and written). So he could sometimes laugh at the poets' nonsense: "Laughter . . . is one of the few things left in our lunatic asylum!"[47] But he was also troubled by what the nonresponse to his postwar poetry signified politically. That his "poems have had no response in America"[48] at many points infuriated him about the many terrible influences in his family's native land, as it was to be associated with the fact that any "criticism [of modern writing] melts as before a new atomic bomb." Huntington knew that the avant-garde had learned how to construct "a modern poetic literary reputation" and had taken over the means of poetic production.[49] Thus, he declined to participate in the bastardized poetic economy. He refused to send out his books of poems for review. He declined the use of book jacket blurbs, which he despised as anathema to true poetry. A loyal conservative, Huntington began to feel that American verse had reached the nightmarish end of ideology, and the result was a dangerously wide acceptance of "moderation"—that the whole life of poetry had fallen into the state of the Academy of Arts and Letters, following the admission of several free-verse big shots. He detested the indulgent centrist conclusion that these problems "cannot be redressed in political terms," as Daniel Bell later put it in *The End of Ideology*. Huntington reluctantly understood, as Bell wrote of the 1950s, that "American culture has almost completely accepted the avant-garde, particularly in art, and the older academic styles have been driven out completely."[50]

Then came Dondero. Archer Huntington was also already a supporter of conservative cultural causes. He had famously resigned from the Academy because modern artists—men of mere "moderate" talent—were coming in through the modernism-friendly parent organization, the National Institute of Arts and Letters. Through his books on traditional Spain, he had become a devotee of Francisco Franco, with whom he exchanged lavishly friendly letters. (In one personal note to Franco written in the mid-1950s, just after the time of the worst Francoist repression, Huntington described himself as "an admirer who believes in the splendid work you have done.")[51] He frequently spoke out against "the hauteur of the modern poets I know—(Lord! I know a number!)."[52] When his nephew, A. Hyatt Mayor, sent him a book of modern poems in 1945, he described it as "the portal of a new garden of Alice in Wonderland. . . . And one feels the vanishing grin of the Cheshire was not less modern than even Dalí on a nature raid."[53] "As to poets, God made 'em no doubt, but I'll bet He's forgotten why. And now as He looks at the damn things I can see Him scratch His head (if that is not impious) in grave doubt."[54]

Archer Milton Huntington.

Dondero had begun corresponding with Huntington's wife, the sculptor Anna Hyatt Huntington. Soon after the congressman began making his widely publicized speeches about the red modernists, he secretly[55] recruited the painter Dorothy Drew, a close friend of the Huntingtons, to help him fight the subversion. As membership chair of the AAPL and prominent painter with many close connections throughout the traditionalist museum, gallery, and studio worlds, Drew began feeding Dondero tips about agitators using insider information. She passed red-baiting confidences to him by letter and by telephone messages left with his staff. A note on House Committee on Public Works stationery, a message taken by a Dondero staffer for the congressman, survives in the Dondero Papers in the Archives of American Art in Washington, D.C. It reads: "Dorothy H. Drew telephoned. . . . Beware of following: Eleanor Gay Lee, Appolonia Cassidy, Albert Gunn Assoc., Burr Gallery, Whistler Society."[56]

Anna Huntington soon became a member of the AAPL advisory board. At an AAPL annual dinner, the dais included Dondero and Drew and one unusual speaker: Frank B. Bielaski, former chief investigator during World War II of the Office of Strategic Services, forerunner of the CIA. Bielaski had burglarized the offices of the leftist scholarly journal *Amerasia*, had broken that case for anti-communist senators in 1946, and subsequently played a major role in launching Joseph McCarthy.[57] Bielaski had headed a "dirty tricks" investigatory team for the Republican National Finance Committee in 1936, making illegal audio recordings of Pennsylvania Democrats as a political operative for reactionary industrialist Joseph N. Pew in a drive to "crush" the New Deal in Philadelphia.[58] Bielaski's brother, A. Bruce Bielaski, had served as FBI chief until 1919, preceding J. Edgar Hoover in that post. Their sister was the infamous application-denying chief of the State Department's passport division, Ruth B. Shipley, who always seemed to have more information about writers wanting passports than she should have had.[59] Bielaski obviously was not at the AAPL dinner to talk about the aesthetics of modernism, but he did introduce Dondero. And odd partner for a poet? Not in those days.

In 1949, Bielaski had set up shop as the Research and Security Corporation. While Dorothy Drew was writing to Anna Huntington, enclosing lists "of the very deep pinks"[60] among artists, Bielaski began writing directly to Archer Huntington, describing the "funding" he needed to "further . . . our campaign against the influences of Marxism in art."[61] Drew's deep pinks included "several well-known 'door-openers' ": among the deepest of the pinks were Peter Blume, Stuart Davis, Ben Shahn, and Max Weber. This was referred to as "*your* list"— names on a page typewritten by Anna Hyatt Huntington and mailed to Drew for annotation, who went to Bielaski for help. The letter from Drew notes that

"Mr. Bielaski checked on his list, too" and that Bielaski asked to have Anna Huntington reminded that even if names were not crossed off—a group that included Andrew Wyeth and William Zorach—"this does not mean that [they] may not be at least—'medium pinks.'"[62] At the same time, Bielaski was writing to Archer Huntington that "the only way to restore American Art to the high level that it should enjoy is to continue an unremitting attack against the debasing influences in Art today"; this letter acknowledged "receipt of your contribution made to Miss Drew."[63]

The result of this campaign: Archer Huntington sent Dondero a check for two thousand dollars through Bielaski as conveyed to Bielaski by Dorothy Drew. An extraordinary invoice[64] from the Research and Security Corporation, headed "Communism in Art," indicates the cost of printing and distributing twenty thousand copies of Dondero's August 16, 1949, congressional speech (an effort intended to "rouse further the conservative element of American art")[65] as well as the expense of conducting research and of hiring agents to investigate red writers and artists, the latter aspect of the job costing Archer Huntington nearly a thousand dollars for two weeks' work by Bielaski's antimodernist field agents. The money with which Archer Huntington supported Dondero was the first of many installments over the years.[66]

Despite her claim that those who fought for conservative poetic values were like the early Christian martyrs in suffering the ridicule of the vast majority, Lilith Lorraine knew what Dondero knew—and she was willing to admit, at least to fellow antimodernist Joseph Lalley, that there was good money in this martyrdom and that the social conservative network was organizationally available to the savvy activist in the poetry world. "We have secured ample funds," she wrote to Lalley, "to carry this fight to its victorious finish." By 1946, the mailing list Lorraine had assembled had already grown to seventy-five thousand. Since Lorraine was the founder and director of a traditionalist poetry center and was also a key officer on the board of the League for Sanity in Poetry, she freely used the rolodex of one to attract adherents to the cause of the other. Moreover, she knew that it was an advantage to goad her promodernist antagonists into "their rantings, and deliberate misrepresentations of us as fascists," since that political positioning greatly improved her groups' access to conservative donors. Lorraine's poetry projects were set up in the South because "a lot of us down here love sincerity" at a time when "poetic values" were lacking elsewhere, but their main means of gathering money and supporters was through an angry reaction against leftist cries of fascism—in other words, a poetic anti-antifascism—that readily brought rightists into the aesthetic fold.[67]

One way or another, anticommunist antimodernists were tied into the whole red-baiting apparatus. Although I have found no hard evidence that A. M. Sullivan officially named names of radical poets, he wrote privately to Phyllis McGinley, saying, "I know of at least five or six people in the Poetry Society [of America] who were reds or pinkos," and he worried that his once close friendships with "many extreme leftists" including "the tragic Max Bodenheim" and Kenneth Leslie, a "dear friend for many years," who "went berserk politically and edited a Communist Front paper," might make Sullivan vulnerable to a " 'guilt by association' assault of the subpoena-swinging legislator." What would he do then? He did not blame Senator McCarthy, whom he "admit[ted]" was "doing a good job." Rather, he tended to blame writers on the left who used the word "McCarthyism" as an epithet. "The term McCarthyism," wrote this poet, "may be a boomerang on some of those who are turning it into a term of opprobrium."[68]

It is not clear how much of an anticommunist network singled out poets in particular. Extant letters exchanged between Frank Bielaski and the maniacally systematic (but often imprecise) J. B. Matthews—Joe McCarthy's chief of staff, whom William F. Buckley admired as "veteran anti-Communist researcher, sleuth, and theorist"[69] and Murray Kempton dubbed "a Pied Piper entombing his children"[70]—specifically show that Bielaski's research at least in part entailed going to the usual professional anticommunist sources to check names of Reds and gather evidence of subversive membership, activities, and associations—lists that included many of the communist and anti-anticommunist poets discussed in this book.[71]

Bielaski dared not go very far into aesthetic questions. The closest he came, typically, in his letters to Archer Huntington was to suggest that it was "pitiful" that there did not exist "a Right-Wing, conservative art magazine which could carry on the struggle . . . and challenge and refute the statements made constantly in the Left-Wing art publications that seem to have gone all out for Marxism in art."[72] (Bielaski seems not to have been aware of Lilith Lorraine's *Different* or Stanton Coblentz's *Wings*. Or perhaps when making his pitch to Huntington, Bielaski knew it was advantageous not to let on that such efforts already existed.) Huntington would not have taken this comment seriously as part of an aesthetically coherent countermovement; he knew full well what Bielaski was after—practical means of counterattack and (always) funding. But some antimodernist operatives actually spoke the language of aesthetics.

One was Lorraine. In fund-raising and efforts to enlarge the mailing list for the Avalon Poetry Shrine, she knew with the certainty of a zealot that she had found an ally when she discovered a poet or editor publishing "poetry that is technically sound and idealistic in content"—the two qualities, for her, being logically mutual necessities.[73] Another was C. O. Garshwiler, editor and general manager of Education Information, a tax-exempt nonprofit outfit "dedicated to sound American philosophy" in education, writing, and the arts.[74] In the late 1950s and early 1960s, Garshwiler's group reprinted Wheeler Williams's *Minutes of a Communist Cell on Art*[75] (an effort made possible by a thousand dollars from Archer Huntington),[76] bitterly fought communist-dominated "monopolies of the perverters of beauty on boards and in art juries,"[77] and carried on energetic, detailed correspondence on aesthetic matters with various antimodernist writers.

Notwithstanding the seemingly clear statements of their leaders, these red-baiting projects created a great confusion of terms, a jumble typically no worse in anticommunist attacks on modern painting and sculpture than those on modern poetry, because, fundamentally, the relationship between radicalism and modernism in the 1930s was as tangled and interanimated in poetry as in other arts. It was everything defenders of modernism could do to reassert plausible definitions of aesthetic movements, such as "social realism," while making rejoinders to individuals' red-baiting them—all while remaining committed to a form of anticommunism that necessitated some kind of reconstruction of the 1930s for the present day. Antimodernists' confusions in painting are especially instructive. At the very end of the 1950s, the liberal National Council of Churches—called communist-affiliated by red-baiters[78]—held its triennial conference and hosted an exhibit at the San Francisco Civic Auditorium. First prize went to Bruce Conner, a devotee of Duchamp and bohemian confrere of Rexroth and Michael McClure who had run Ezra Pound for U.S. president in the 1956 elections.[79] The prizewinning piece was Conner's *Box*, a mixed-media sculpture consisting of an old carton wrapped in cellophane arranged with miscellaneous items including a torn nylon stocking. The people at Education Information were incensed, seeing this "grotesque 'sculpture'" as a "link in a long line of subversion" that ran from "the left-wing dominated" National Council of Churches through Conner himself and exhibit judge Peter Selz to Selz's home museum, the Museum of Modern Art (MoMA), and from there back to the National Council, with its conference theme of "clarify[ing] and visualiz[ing] concern for human suffering," and thus into the White House, where Jacqueline Kennedy's then-new White House Conference on Children and Youth was aiding the "social welfare" program in the communist conspiracy. The link that logically breaks the chain, however, is Garshwiler's notion, borrowed from William Wheeler, that Conner's *Box* was an "excellent example" of "*social realism.*"[80]

Antimodernists sometimes sought to resist an assumption, ascribed to the communist left, that depictive or narrative artists were better suited to radicalism than those whose work was abstract, undepictive, surreal, and/or nonnarrative. Anticommunists in fact became furious when both leftists and modernists used the terms "traditionalist" and "conservative" to describe nonmodernist left-wing art. Ben Shahn and William Gropper, both well-known supporters of radical programs in the 1930s and somewhat later, were caught in the categorical bewilderment. When editors of the newsletter of the Westchester County Committee on Un-American Activities, the *Spotlight*, saw in the *Scarsdale Inquirer* an article called "Art Week to Be Celebrated in Local Scarsdale Schools," they went looking for communist modernists and found Gropper. This educational exhibit was organized by a promodernist art outreach group called Art on Tour. Understanding the Edgewood School to be "conservative," the Art on Tour curators felt it was appropriate to be "showing such *traditionalists* as Gropper." The *Spotlight* spelled out the radical pasts of both Gropper and the Edgewood School. The school was guilty of having celebrated Lincoln's birthday in the past by staging the "communist cantata, 'The Lonesome Train.' " As for Gropper, a key force in the movement from bohemianism to radicalism in the *Liberator* of the 1920s, he was no "traditionalist"—and as proof the *Spotlight* quoted George Dondero's March 1952 speech in Congress, where Dondero had named Gropper as one of the "modernists" who betrayed the United States by painting a mural for MoMA "which thousands of people visit weekly and . . . shall . . . expos[e] the war plot against the Soviet Union."[81] The Gropper work in question was on loan from the Whitney; that museum came under attack for its part in the conspiracy.

Brenda Putnam, an antimodernist sculptor who in the early 1950s was a fellow of the National Sculpture Society (NSS), led a protest against the Metropolitan Museum, which in 1952 announced that it would spend one hundred thousand dollars to bring the sculpture collection "into balance with the painting," which had been more energetically modernized. The NSS antimodernists saw this sum as red-stained dollars, part of the communist takeover: "Having complete possession of the Whitney Museum for their experimental work, having taken over MoMA, which was planned for contemporary, not predominantly modernistic art, a very active group of artists is now in the process of establishing its control of the Metropolitan." This was a "serious cancer" spread by "extreme modernistic and negative tendencies [and] mediocre left-wing work at that" and had to be treated with doses of "constructed forms of art."[82]

The protest against the Met noted that every country that had fallen victim to totalitarianism had also fallen "victim to this insidious idealogy [*sic*]. Modernistic art proved a most effective vanguard." The war was being waged against Americans by "victims of psychiatric delusions, who torment themselves with visions of an agonizing, sordid, or abstract character."[83] Wheeler Williams and other NSS officers wrote to all members urging them to see that "the Modernistic Movement threatens not only art, but the fundamental freedoms of our American way of life" and to resist "the increasing power exerted by a left-wing art group" that would undermine "the whole philosophy of national normalcy."[84]

Striking back at the NSS conspiracy theory was James Thrall Soby, one of the most energetic and eminent anticommunist defenders of modernism. Soby was a friend and Hartford neighbor of Wallace Stevens, the person within the curatorial establishment whom Stevens trusted most to lead him toward relationships with cubism, surrealism, and the work of the exiled antifascist neoromantics.[85] Soby's article on this issue quoted Williams's and Putnam's complaint to the Met and showed the link between this sort of antimodernism and Dondero's broad-brush red-baiting. Then Soby offered the obvious refutation of the NSS version of recent political history: European totalitarianism has not in fact been kind, to say the least, to modernism. By using the example of the Soviets' demonization of modernists—the Communist Party in the USSR felt that modernism evinced the "evils of disorientation"[86] and so promoted "anti-experimentalist poets" who boasted of "being too wholesome to look at modern art," as Viereck later observed firsthand[87]—Soby was also submitting evidence of his own Americanism, threading his way between cultural anticommunisms. Although using the tone and rhetoric of someone boldly taking sides on the question of modernism, Soby tried to clear up confusions about representation and radicalism. The real issue, he urged, was how to understand that fine art is "more than an expression of commemorative verisimilitude." Here Soby waved the victory flag in the face of traditionalists. Because modernism had so effectively "left the reputations of most academic artists hopelessly in arrears," traditionalists now ruthlessly fought "a bitter rear-guard action." At least in the old days, when conservatives got some share of critical attention, they took behavioral cues from their own staid art, acting with "a certain dignity, . . . solemn and calm." But now *they*, not the rude red modernists, were "fight[ing] like Bowery thugs."[88]

Roles were reversing. Modernists seized the moment to stand for apolitical art, while in the fight against political art, antimodernists took up the political role. By the mid-1950s, this was a key shift in the antimodernist/modernist balance. It furthered the deradicalization of modernism as a strategy available to its defenders. And it would have a real effect on the way the battle was waged between and among poets and in poems.

The thuggish approach worried a number of the anticommunist opponents of modern art, even the most energetic of them. Harry Cohen, president of the

IFAC and strongest champion of the idea of awarding the organization's highest honor to Dondero, was one antimodernist who felt anxious. Cohen wrote a confidential letter to the congressman expressing concern over what was becoming of the once-apolitical IFAC now that its artist-officers—struggling, elderly traditionalists, most of whom had never been political—found themselves in the business of gathering information on the questionable political opinions and associations of artists whom they wanted to recruit as members of a group that existed to sustain art that was not about political opinions. This contradiction had never before been an issue, certainly not in the 1930s, when the lines had been clearly drawn: art having nothing to do with politics stood against art dirtily engaged with it. It had been easier to take sides. But, Cohen lamented, "we have this year been very careful about the selection of artists for nomination and for [our] final award [the IFAC Gold Medal]," so it was with some hesitation that Cohen now asked Dondero if he could use his contacts with the congressional anticommunist network to arrange for IFAC officers to get access to the records of the HUAC—"if," for instance, "we had a person [suspected of left associations] recommended for active participation."[89]

Raised in such a way, this problem was similar to the one Soby outlined for conservatives generally. Believing art to be nonideological, traditionalists had become politicians. They had become all too "conscious" of the relation between art and ideology. They longed, in a way, to return to their preferred roles as what Cohen called "purely art minded." And to some degree they, now politicized, were accusing modern abstractionists in particular of going too far into the art of pure forms, of forgetting the patriotic responsibilities of representation.[90] "Extreme abstraction" was so obstinately formalist, wrote one conservative, that it constituted an actual "organized heresy" and had to be stopped if the imitative tradition, the "graphic patrimony, a signal of civilization," was to be saved.[91] To be purely art minded on either side of the battle lines was now not enough.[92]

So one solution was to seek red-baiting information from HUAC rather than retreat to the high ground: focus on form, "quality" and "craftsmanship." This strategy was overall the cause of greatest confusion among the anticommunist antimodernists in poetry as well as the visual arts. The traditionalist argued practically for the necessary abandonment of art for art's sake as an operating principle resistant to leftists, while other anticommunists, following the lead of J. Edgar Hoover, the American Legion's Un-American Activities Committee, and federal Smith Act prosecutors, were just then identifying "Art doesn't exist for art's sake" as a basic Leninist principle that modernists had adopted for the purpose of effecting cultural revolution.[93] Ben Lucien Burman, in his 1952 attack on Stein, Joyce, and others in the "Cult of Unintelligibility"; Gerald Kennedy, in a piece called "Poets, Politicians, and Preachers" published the same year; and Hillyer in his clearest antimodernist statement prior to the political confusions caused by the *Pisan Cantos* crisis, "Modern Poetry versus the Common Reader" (1945), were all conservative antimodernists who enacted this ideological reversal. For Hillyer, the switch depended on the developing Cold War–era construction of the Depression, to be deemed a period of "the violent swing to materialism" in poetry, a time in which the high modernism of the 1920s had gone awry and given rise to rather than resisted the "new esthetes" of the present.

The postwar reaction against modernism's audience-denying excesses marks the moment when modernist "insistence on the sensuous image as opposed to the abstract idea" met the "tradition of catalogue"—paratactic lists of things— "as exemplified in the work of Walt Whitman." What was emerging was a modernism of all style, little or no sense—"the fallacious separation of *being* from *meaning*."[94] In the postwar poems of Wallace Stevens, a headliner modern who was reviled as "the arch-abstractionist" in *Wings*, "the voids grow voider and voider . . . in every line." Following this course of conservative thinking, Stevens's "The Ultimate Poem is Abstract," published in *Poetry* in 1947, "openly professed" a "credo": "Modernity, *per se*, could guarantee poetic values." In truth, the argument ran, Stevens's poems "had about as much intrinsic coherence as the contents of a shopping bag," and this was inimical both to good sense and to goodness. Stevens was the "minister" of a "creed," and his abstract verse was "the augur of an inscrutable heritage."[95]

In these examples, the conservative calls for social content while accusing the modernist of pure art. For Gerald Kennedy, the problem was that the "new poetry" had dangerously influenced the language of "modernist" *politicians*: it was all poetry—all sound, pure music—evading the responsibilities of meaning, thus threatening the nation's ethical structure. The pure music of the new language was a cause of the current political crisis.[96] Richard Weaver sadly realized that function had become more important than status. When the relationship between permanence and nature on one hand and form, process, and identity formation on the other became skewed, dire consequences arose "both in intellectual outlook and in social regime." Here is where Weaver observed that "modernism is everywhere stressing function at the expense of status." He continued, "It is repugnant to mind as well as to feeling to think of the world as pure becoming or as something which never is because it is forever in process."[97]

Burman noticed in his own argument—that "words must communicate or they are worthless" and that modernism "enthrone[s] incomprehensibility"—a similar tendency to associate modern poetry with pure art. Whereas arguments against the radicalism of 1930s writing, usually made by liberal anticommunists who favored modernism over "social art," associated pure art with anticommunism, Burman and other conservative antimodernists associated *their* position with "content," "realism," "communication," art that responsibly says what it means. Burman took this point to a revealing extreme. After identifying modernist language with the nonsense or unmediated words of lunatics, he created an image of pure sound jangling the nerves of the poetic fundamentalist by comparing it to the fears of the colonizer who is threatened by countercolonization—an image of African "natives" about to cannibalize visiting Westerners—in a passage doubtless meant to be as horrifying as any anticommunist space-invasion conceit. "We can listen for a while to the pure music of language, flowing like water over a falls," Burman wrote. "But soon we must have something other than mere murmur and rhythm. A telegraphic ticker sends out a varying pattern of sounds, but it is the message they form that is important. Sound by itself may create a totally false impression. In the African jungles I often heard the telegraphic drums rolling in irregular thunder, their tones so sinister it seemed the natives were surely preparing our massacre."[98]

Coblentz's response to this situation was a sort of aesthetic isolationism. It was not only safer not to go exploring into alien (and "irregular") rhythms. It was more responsible to remain within the hearing of familiar aural and metrical traditions. "While it may be legitimate for a poet to set out for virgin territory and untraveled paths," Coblentz wrote, "his attempt would be presumptuous not to say preposterous were he unacquainted with the territory. . . . The poet who rides into the *terra incognita* of rebellion [is] on the ticket to failure."[99] Richard Ashman, the geneticist and physiologist who edited the *New Orleans Poetry Journal*, feared the demise of pleasurable meter, noting bitterly that "every savage tribe has its drums" and that "modern poetry has few or no readers because it ignores . . . inherent qualities" of "an advanced civilization."[100] Burman certainly agreed with Coblentz that American writers should stay home—as we have seen, he was a staunch regionalist—but in conjuring his misadventure into African arrhythmia, he meant to imply that when one reads Gertrude Stein's *How to Write* and so must cope with sentences forcing one to understand, from scratch, what a sentence is, one should think not of the madness of the quaint childlike idiot variety but of the truly strange, cultural heart of darkness, a racist's linguistic demilitarized zone. The ultimate form of cultural subversion is not the forward march toward radical content—*that* Americans could defend themselves against—but a primitivizing backward step into the most blindingly elemental questions about how we mean, every bit as basic and underived as a cannibal met off the beaten path. So Burman quotes from Stein's *How to Write*, wanting his readers to hear a sinister irregular thunder:

> A sentence is proper if they have more than they could. They could. Without leaving it. A sentence makes not it told but it held. A hold is where they put things. How what is a sentence. A sentence hopes that you are very well and happy. It is very selfish. They hate to be taken away. The minute you disperse a crowd you have a sentence. There were witnesses to it even if you did not stop. There there is no paragraph. If it had a different father it would have.[101]

[Modern verse is] as unreadable as the page of history in which
it is written.—Robert Hillyer

Hard Times in Xanadu

Since, as we have just seen, their antagonists now claimed that
modernists subversively produced pure poetry while traditionalists, pulled into
activism by their enmity, seemed to have little choice but to be concerned with
political realities as well as imitative styles, it is little wonder that conservatives
were upset when some of their own political leaders began to sound as if they
were falling under the influence. The accused within the traditionalist ranks
seemed now sometimes even to borrow from modern art the "art" of not
meaning what one says. This particular moment of rhetorical interanimation
was a turning point in the new conservative epoch. It attended a special paranoia of the successful group, and such apparent capitulation conjured the
ultimate nightmare for the anticommunist antimodernist: the realization,
stranger still, that absolutely everyone, even those one needed to trust, could be
infected, that a reckoning of the real (but also, crucially, of *realism*) was being
squandered.

The anticommunist attack on incomprehensibility extended to the right-
wing distrust of Congress and of Washington politics generally. Gerald Kennedy wrote his essay "Poets, Politicians, and Preachers" mainly to address this
problem, profiling politicians of the suspiciously irresolute New Conservative
variety—which is to say, right-leaning moderates who claimed to mistrust ideology, along with their more conservative allies. They, Kennedy felt, had lost the
passion for arguing from stable, principled positions against modern poets
whose language lacked clear force.

A scholar and something of a historian of American preaching who also
published widely on the sermonic literary mode as a form of teaching,[1] Kennedy sought to integrate new forms of American religious practice with the
writing of Auden, Eliot, and others. To this end, he immersed himself in Amos
N. Wilder's *The Spiritual Aspects of the New Poetry* (1940), a book serving as a
guide to Christian defenses against Christian antimodernists. Wilder was a
leftist, a feature of his advocacy of modern poetry that is mostly well hidden in
Spiritual Aspects; his political view is clearer from his appreciation of Kenneth

Patchen's "revolutionary and proletarian poetry"—in Patchen "we have the Marxian version of [the] Early Christian apocalyptic with its imminent and predestined triumph"[2]—and is still more evident in *Voices of Our Day: Social Issues in Contemporary Poetry*, a 1941 monograph that was issued by the Council for Social Action of the Congregational Christian Churches. Kennedy found Wilder on balance unconvincing and came away from *The Spiritual Aspects of the New Poetry* persuaded that Wilder was "just not sure what the boys mean." Wilder's defense of the purity of modern verse merely reinforced Kennedy's clarion call for transparency: "Is it really impossible to write poetry that is plain? Must a reader spend a lifetime in special preparation before he can be expected to understand poetry?"

Wilder also put Kennedy in mind of the general analogy between poets and statesmen and of the special hateful politics of modern language. So while Kennedy claimed to be "on the side of the poets," chastising others who caricatured the poet "as a long-haired, slightly effeminate fool," he excoriated modernists for their failure to be comprehensible and thus for "find[ing] it easy to capture a very large audience," discerning in this misadventure political treachery. Like many of the antimodernists already discussed in this book, Kennedy feared that the postwar period had become the "Age of Obscurity," but for him it was very specifically a problem of politics, of American political life, and the "heavy and obscure verbiage" was a political form of modernism.[3]

If Gerald Kennedy saw an aspect of modernism in the politician's vile technique of using opaque "poetic" language to flip-flop on policy positions, Stanton Coblentz, too, not surprisingly, saw the American political linguistic habit of "adapt[ing] . . . to the proposition that *x is y* at the same time as . . . s[eeking] to prove that *x is not y*" as, armed with this Aesopian weapon, "invad[ing] the arts" and thus "pernicious."[4] Poetry, like politics, should be a form of "public service." Through modernism we enter "the sphere of the seeker who lets himself be diverted from a goal of public service to one of self-service"—of the guilty bystander, "the onlooker who merely winks an eye and passes on at the sight of misrepresentation and chicanery." As Coblentz put it, there were modern "poets who changed their allegiance" and "straddled all issues in a manner hardly to be surpassed by the experts on Capitol Hill."[5] For Kennedy, modernists had joined the ranks of political operatives, having entered "the realm in which politicians . . . may let their early shining aims be corroded with the acid of opportunism."[6]

At the end of the 1950s, Russell Baker, then a staffer at the *New York Times* Washington bureau, undertook to survey poems American politicians had recited on the floor of the House or Senate and had entered into the *Congressional Record* from the 1930s onward. Fresh from this research, Baker observed that an anthology of such verse would chart what he only half-jokingly called "the depth and quality of Congress' poetic instinct." He noted two trends. First, the poems members of Congress read into the record between 1936 and 1959 moved discernibly away from political and nationalistic themes toward nature lyrics. The trend tellingly coincided with the reemergence of what the young critic Robert Langbaum was just then calling "the new nature poetry."[7] Noticing that poems read into the record became less political over time, Baker also saw that they became *more modern in form*. As the 1930s gave way to the 1950s, these poems became less metrically conventional and more often than before were written in blank or even free verse. Lacking a complete reading of the *Congressional Record* during these years (where the index does not specify poetry as a category), one can only guess at how accurately representative Baker's compendium is. It does at least indicate his (and possibly his notion of his readers') assumptions about the way in which the relationship between poetry and electoral politics had changed from the mid-1930s to the end of the 1950s, from New Deal to Cold War.

The poem "Probe into a Sit-Down Strike" was both written and read into the record in 1937 by a Republican congressman from Michigan, Clare Hoffman. Baker aptly identified this strike poem as "typif[ying] the poem with a social theme that characterized the New Deal era." Yet this was thematically as well as formally conservative verse; it conveyed bitter anti–New Deal sentiments, and it was strictly rhymed and metrical—but also, of course, strictly "social" in content. Baker was also right to point out that "Golden Fingers," read in Congress by Melvin Price of Illinois in the first 1959 session, a poem in free verse apparently singing the glories of midwestern corn, indicates "the complete absence of the eloquent social outcries which distinguished so much of the poetry of earlier Congresses":

> Under the sun's torrid rays
> It thrives,
> And from the rain's glistening fountain
> Does it drink . . .
>
> No beauty here?

More significant, as Baker also pointed out, was the "distinct trend away from the orderly classic forms." Congress, he noted, was "finally opening its mind to modern rhythms." Baker's article was illustrated with a sketch showing a jaunty, self-satisfied, business-as-usual congressman entering a door once marked "Congressional Record," now bearing a sign reading, "Poetry Corner."[8]

To be sure, in this period there was no Poetry Corner in the White House. Perhaps the modern aesthetic had slowly infiltrated the lower house of Congress, but it hit a glass political ceiling nearer the highest levels. Harry Truman once compared modern art to scrambled eggs[9] and at another time called it "merely the vaporings of half-baked lazy people."[10] Truman's view here fell right in line with antimodernists who were arguing that unrhymed verse was unfinished poetry drafted by slothful albeit sometimes talented writers: "Blank verse . . . comes from . . . lazy drowsiness . . . and . . . should be . . . accepted as poetic exercise."[11] So, too, traditionalists alleged that a "modern precept" was this: "The easiest way to do a thing is necessarily the best."[12] The poem Truman always carried around in his pocket was a martial cadenza from Tennyson's "Locksley Hall," unlazy lines one could almost say clinched the connection between traditional high verse-rhetoric and the dropping of atomic bombs: "Heard the heavens fill with shouting, and there rain'd a ghastly dew / From the nations' airy navies grappling in the central blue."[13] Nonetheless, Baker's satire on modern poetry in the nation's capital—based on the consequential idea that verse sometimes served as a rhetorical substitute for political positions—would have been meaningless without this basic cultural assumption: modern poetry was becoming acceptable to the American public. But if acceptance came just as overt political language was much diminished, why is it that every anticommunist antimodernist whom I have found in doing research for this book complained bitterly of modern poetry's dissociation from its democratic audience? Even seemingly apolitical calls for a solution to the poetry-public split went in for counter-revolutionary messianism. Observing that "anthologies of Significant Modern Poetry" excluded poets of light verse—that "our serious poets" wrote only for an elite and "despis[ed] the average reader" and had "ruined poetry in the minds of the general intelligent public"—Morris Bishop reasoned that the Light Versifiers should take over, at least until a new generation of "serious poets," unrelated to the modernists, could come of age. In the meantime, poets of light verse—he suggested Phyllis McGinley, author of "Manners Are Morals" and "Party Line," the latter a piece about giving a good party[14]— could hold "poetry's little forts amid the desert sands . . . awaiting the relief that shall come when the Poet arises, to fill our world with his overwhelming music."[15] (Bishop, a professor of Romance languages at Cornell University and a light-verse poet himself, made "The Case for Light Verse" in *Harper's Magazine*, and it was well received.) Other antimodernists, such as Coblentz and Kennedy, less hopeful that "mid-form" poets could hold the fort while modernists ruined audiences, blamed the alienation of American poetry readership at least partly on the language and tone set by American politicians. On the promodernist side of the question, Lloyd Frankenberg was typical in blaming not the American people but the American postwar habit of impatience, a matter that also, during the Cold War especially, presented a political problem. Frankenberg published a book-length general introduction to modern poetry, *Pleasure Dome* (1950), with a main aim of inviting common readers in.

M. L. Rosenthal was more skeptical about the prospects of healing the poet-public split. Rosenthal boldly used an analogy to Cold War reconstruction of former enemies to explain why Americans' apparent surface ability to read and admire modern verse will not be sufficient when antagonisms, cultural and political, reside deeper down. He proposed this daring ratio: Americans of the late 1940s were to German citizens receiving Marshall Plan dollars as modern poets were to a public readership facing "difficult" verse. Reviewing Frankenberg's *Pleasure Dome* for the *Nation*, where Rosenthal was soon to become poetry editor, he agreed that the optimistic advocacy of modernism "may work with the already half-converted." But these were "hard times in Xanadu." Persuading Americans to admire modern verse "does seem a little like selling democracy to the Germans. The resistance goes deep; many people, tragically insecure, simply do not trust their own resources."[16]

Despite Rosenthal's and Frankenberg's differences, both men were among modernism's defenders. Neither would stoop to blame the poets themselves for the dysfunctional relationship between American readers and modern poetry, while anticommunists once again were quick to make the modernist their target. Harvard's Douglas Bush was one temperate antimodernist who contended that poets themselves were responsible for the gap between modern poetry and a potentially vast readership in the United States. In a paper Bush gave before the sixth annual Conference on Science, Philosophy, and Religion, he argued that modern poets' "concern with the world's ills" should make them move linguistically and formally toward the American mass audience and strive for comprehension rather than retreat and thus become "difficult." On the contrary, ran this line, "the modern poet is not altogether fulfilling his traditional function."[17] The speech Bush delivered before members of the Catholic Poetry Society, who were celebrating the twenty-fifth anniversary of the founding of the society's magazine, *Spirit*, became a rallying cry for the moderates.

So inspired by this centrist rebuke of experimentalism was J. Donald Adams, a witness to Bush's Catholic Poetry Society speech, that Adams devoted his next "Speaking of Books" column in the *Times* to Bush's view that "while holding to what has been gained for poetry through years of experiment and revolt[, we should also] recogniz[e] what was worth preserving in the poetry of tradition: [the] freedom from fear at finding something beautiful." Its patriotic and internationalist rhetoric, its vague Four Freedoms–style emphasis on basic human rights ("freedom from fear"), made what was essentially a cranky assertion of traditional aestheticism sound downright contemporary, globalist, and liberal. When all humanity is at stake, better beauty than experiment. Modernism had lost poetry its audience; innovative writing is inevitably tempered when "the human need for an audience," which "can never be too long denied," comes back, like part of nature.[18]

Douglas Bush's opinion carried great weight beyond academia; for one thing, Adams, with his own huge American readership, followed every word— and passed it along. Bush's critical judgment of modern poetry was all the more significant because of his general standing, the hard work he had done to produce accessible academic prose for nonspecialized literate readership. In scholarly journals, Bush continued during the early Cold War years to publish on Milton and on seventeenth-century British literature generally, and among scholarly circles outside his field he was fairly widely known as among those openly doubting the New Criticism. Peter Viereck, presenting the New Conservative platform for a general audience in *The Unadjusted Man: A New Hero for Americans*, praised Bush for expressing concern that the "rising flood" of GI Bill–funded postwar students, which bolstered the pedagogy of close reading, would in fact lead to barbarism.[19] "Education for All," Bush proclaimed in the *New York Times Magazine*, "Is Education for None."[20]

Bush was also one of the few traditionally trained literary scholars who published in the critical quarterlies and a few mass-circulation weeklies and monthlies; he tackled "Sex in the Modern Novel" for the *Atlantic*, examined the whole question of humanities education for *Daedalus*, and gave subscribers to the *Virginia Quarterly Review* a clear description of the intramural fight being waged between "scholars" and "critics" and its deleterious effect on readers. He argued that the scholars were "closer to the reading public" than the poet-critics, who, following Eliot, were said (mistakenly) to have won the non-academic ground. Here Bush clearly voiced the antimodernist argument, and in making this point he connected his goal of reversing the critics' defeat of the scholars with his tendency to blame modern poetry for abandoning the affirmative literary heritage in being "content" to "start from scratch." (He identified Karl Shapiro as "one welcome exception.") "The layman," Bush wrote, "may at least wonder if the poets who have kept on playing the fashionable pipes of panic have not been a little too easily overwhelmed by the modern world, which is what it always has been, a bad world."[21]

Bush came no closer to contemporary poetry than in the *Virginia Quarterly Review* piece and in "The New Use of the Word" (1957), written for the inaugural issue of the *Centennial Review*.[22] Had he admitted relative ignorance about what modern poetry actually was, these bits of irresponsible antimodernism might have provided useful perspective. The battle waged between scholars and critics really had less to do with harm wrought by modern poets than Bush alleged. As for his ignorance about the new poetry, Bush privately (in letters to his friend Rosenthal) admitted that aside from having attended a reading by W. B. Yeats in 1919 or 1920, he was unmoved by modern verse. He doubted the fitness of Rosenthal's taste for Williams and Stevens and implied polite disdain for Rosenthal's "imperfect sympathy" for Robert Frost, whom Bush felt was a better model for the modern poet. Notwithstanding what Rosenthal would aver was a basic misunderstanding of what in practice constituted poetic modernism—Rosenthal felt Williams was truly a poet of the people, a better instance of "start from scratch" modernism than the "critics" (for Williams, too, opposed the "critics")—Bush's word on contemporary verse was efficacious.[23] His regretful feeling that the poet was no longer "regarded as a teacher and leader of his age" and his nostalgia for a time when "nearly all the greatest poets have been more or less popular"[24] were widely shared.

The Canadian poet Ralph Gustafson, another moderate, saw poetry "in such a sorry state of neglect" as to compromise the value of any claim that verse "is written to better the world." Here again, antimodernism embodied what might be called the "political" position in the debate with defenders—who were, in Gustafson's critique, "critics of the new school" (that is, the New Critics) who defend modern poetry by arguing that "poems are not written to effect any of these tangibles and to define their function in terms of science, politics, theology." Defending modern verse in this way "misjudg[es] the nature of poetry." This withdrawal from the public sphere had worsened "the despised state of poetry," which was becoming "isolated." Gustafson's skepticism about modernism, like Bush's, was founded on the assumption that "the widest possible communication" of the claims for poetry must "be accepted and found"—that this public positioning of poetry's defense is not only "the best hope for removing the misapprehensions which have socially beggared poetry" but also the best way of curing verse of radical modernism, where national "responsibility has largely been walking around . . . inside the limits of esthetics."[25]

The idea that critical "authority is urgently needed outside"[26] poetry was the basis of Gustafson's and Bush's complaints. For such critics, the "difficulty" of modernist form was reactive rather than original in its impulse, arising from the unfortunate need modern poets felt—allegedly in response to the radical externalizations of the 1930s—to find authority within rather than beyond poetry. "Does it seem reasonable to you," the poet Donald Jenks wrote privately to the editors of *Poetry*, "to identify this art, in which fewer than 10,000 people find any value, with contemporary life itself?"[27] Publicly noted awards to poets were one potential way of closing this gap between modern poets and the democratic culture, at least ceremonially. But a 1951 symposium on "What's Wrong with the Nobel Prize?" cast serious doubts on the validity of that major award.[28] And of course the value of the Bollingen Prize had been compromised by the crisis of 1948–49. When in 1957 the Pulitzer Prizes were announced on radio and television, the winners for biography, history, and journalism were named (no prize was awarded that year for fiction), but there was no mention that Richard Wilbur (for *Things of This World*) had won the prize for poetry, causing traditionalist poet-professor[29] Joseph P. Clancy, editor of the magazine *A.D.*, to observe once again "the split between the poet and the general public." Clancy's "Lament for the Readers" (1958) focused even more narrowly on a specialized "public" readership for modern poetry one would think perceived no such split: "readers who are college graduates." But in fact, Clancy noticed, it was difficult for anyone who "is not in graduate school, is not a poet, a critic, an English teacher, and is not married to one or all three" to find and comfortably exist as a reader in the world of contemporary verse.[30]

There is little doubt that when Robert Hillyer took up the question of American readers' alienation from experimental poetry, he believed he too was taking a moderate position on the matter. He never conceived of his antimodernism as fixed or absolute. Yet his *Saturday Review of Literature* essay on the "common reader," subtitled "Too Many Poets Are Living in a Metaphorical Age," set off an avalanche of anticommunist antimodernism. Hillyer began by *lamenting* that modernism's "new esthetes" gave the movement a bad name, leading to "the common reader's opinion [that] all modern poetry is obscure." When he defended his verse against this charge, it might have seemed that he would conclude that what was needed was a proper return to modernism's primary impulses, a course correction. In one of his poems, Hillyer had written the line, "Arcadia means the land of bears," which had provoked "many requests for explanation." But, he protested in exasperation, "Arcadia *does* mean the land of bears, and that is all there is to it." He might have assumed this to be an anecdote aiding a defense of modern poetry as sometimes innocently misunderstood. He read it, rather, as a tale about betrayed trust. In Hillyer's mind, his perfectly clear language necessitated requests for explanation by readers who would have had no trouble understanding him literally were it not for poetry's contemporary bad reputation—were it not for the widespread addiction to language that is the opposite of transparent, to "figurative language as a source of obscurity," in which "*meaning* (which is, in critical fact, the true *being* of a poem) is so laboriously evaded."

From this point in his argument against contemporary poetry, Hillyer lost all temperance, quitting any defense of modernism by name for the larger project of tracing the invidious politics of the new language-centered poets. The final paragraphs of "Modern Poetry versus the Common Reader" treated his large readership to a quick and dirty literary history in which modernism is associated with godlessness, confusion, chaos, egotism, effeminacy, and anti-heroism. In the "violent swing to materialism" of the interwar years, poets had taken the idea of free verse to extremes and at the same time had "reacted *against* the looseness of free verse," so that "poets writing today," bearing the burden of the double negative legacy of the 1920s and the 1930s, are "hair-splittingly conscious of the subtleties of language, of the single word." A too-intense focus on the language, this revolution of the word, brought on "stylistic chaos" as the swing to materialism "crashed into the stone wall" of World War II. The pendulum, supposed to move back to formalism, was then "self-shattered and unbalanced" and instead carried a superconsciousness about language into the political disruption of the times. Poetry needed rational (and political) postwar planning. "The mind of the present is like a beleaguered city, milling with misdirected traffic and thick with refugees." Any continued Revolution of the Word carried with it the risk of sedition, extremists taking advantage of the chaos. Beware "much modern poetry" because indeed it tends to be "as unreadable as the page of history in which it is written." What the "Dadaists triflingly sought in the languor of a doubtful peace, the modernists accomplish in the frenzy of war." Modernism must be succeeded in the postwar period by a tough, American-style rejection of unmanly selfishness—a new "age for heroes in the arts as elsewhere."

Here again, a conservative antimodernist was attempting to take the social-political ground from what he roughly dubbed the modernist left. The counter-revolution against the New Poetry revolution would usher in the language of the truly democratic poet-heroes, "simple and melodious in the ears of the common reader, the common man, for [the hero-poet] is one of them."[31] To bring modern "poetry back to the really heroic" is mainly also what John Gould Fletcher (1886–1950) sought in the postwar period.

Both Hillyer and the conservative ex-Fugitive poet Donald Davidson revered

Fletcher as one of the founders of modernism in the United States through the imagist revolution[32] and as an antimodernist defector.[33] Fletcher, whose Pulitzer Prize for *Selected Poems* in 1939 was generally understood to have been a popular nod toward imagism's original importance,[34] complained to Winfield Townley Scott, worried that nothing could "be done to take poetry . . . out of the hands of the slick, opportunist-minded brittle intellectuals." Fletcher saw this as a "struggle for some sort of decency" in the context of the day's "obscene chaos." He saw Eliot's essentially positive influence wholly degenerated into the political verse of the British politicians—Auden, Day Lewis, et alia. He saw William Carlos Williams, among poets of the "prevailing fashionable school" of which Stevens (whom he preferred) was a part, as "stuck fast" in the political precincts—"at best half-a-poet" in the "industrial slums of Paterson, New Jersey," and from this context comes the damning observation that "his prose is often better than his poetry." The counter-revolution, which Fletcher knew would attract Scott, should restore something like imagism, and it had to stop the further development of an ugly mongrel modernism made of indecency, opportunistic Eliotic radicalism, slums and slumming as *materia poetica*, prose, rigid intellectualism—and also, by the way, Jewishness.[35]

So when experimentalists—including the young Jackson Mac Low, who was then earnestly searching for models of sustainable and ethical avant-gardism— read John Gould Fletcher, they tended to find not just that he was "still an imagist" but that he "*still* writes symphonies." Diction once consciously wrought now seemed "careless, often banal." A poetics implicitly of urgent ideas compressed into hard forms now actually seemed anti-intellectual.[36] There was a little in Fletcher for a young language-centered poet such as Mac Low—but only a little. The heroism Fletcher wanted restored to American modernism entailed both a masculinist rejoinder to the fragility of the "brittle intellectuals" and an antipolitical rejection of the dogmatic obduracy of the political poets—the style he saw operating in Williams. Mac Low, who happened to be reviewing books by Williams and Fletcher together, was the sort of languagy avant-gardist who fueled Fletcher's antipolitical fire: Fletcher was indeed "still an imagist," whereas Williams, who retained a "knowledge and feel of the verse line, especially 'free verse,' the line augmenting and diminishing with the thought," had in the documentary modernist epic *Paterson* moved beyond, providing an "extraordinary complex formal organization of the work, binding the most disparate elements into an aesthetic unity," which was in sum the modernist project that Mac Low here strongly commended—all of it founded on the collective and the social.[37] Fletcher's attack on the politico-aesthetic dogmatism and antiheroism of the Williams style was more a contradiction—a problem, a fallacy about political poetry—than a paradox. Fletcher was typical of moderate antimodernists, like Ralph Gustafson, in looking for ways in which to pair the two antagonisms. In his letter to Winfield Townley Scott, Fletcher found this in a phrase Kenneth Patchen had used to describe Karl Shapiro's verse: "iron turds in lavender water."[38] The epithet drew Shapiro to heights of uncharacteristic redbaiting: "*Kenneth Patchen*: Rabid anti-American poet," Shapiro wrote, "sometime social revolutionary, visionary of destruction of industrial world and its standardized population."[39]

In many respects, neither Robert Hillyer nor John Gould Fletcher properly belonged with the most conservative among the anticommunist antimodernists. Hillyer's anticommunism, while unmistakable, was neither as dogmatic nor as well formulated as that of Coblentz. And Fletcher, suffering from acute depression—he took his own life before the workshop-style short lyric of midcentury modernism really began to dominate journals and magazines—spent his final few years clinging to the memory, now misty, of original imagism, because of which, among poetry circles, his was something of a household name. Hillyer's antimodernism seems in part personally motivated: he felt rudely "cut out" of the anthologies edited by Shapiro and Richard Wilbur, "the younger poets [who] took over," and as Hillyer prepared to publish his "final Collected Poems," he fully expected it to become "the victim of that Ciardiism that seems to have enveloped Parnassus." He liked sweeping statements such as "Modern literature [is] mostly junk," yet his place in literary politics cut across several positions in the poetry wars: Theodore Roethke referred to Hillyer in front of younger poets as "my old mentor"—also telling them, to the same mentor's dismay, that Hillyer's poetry was being "neglected." At the same time, Hillyer had been Peter Viereck's teacher and was described by Hillyer's antimodernist colleagues as having "a vigorous pipeline into the new generation—Viereck."

Hillyer admired Viereck and largely agreed with him, although Hillyer was proud of his moderating influence on the younger man's extremist impulses. ("You may think him wild," Hillyer wrote to Howard Nemerov, "but you should have read him before I got hold of him.")[40] Moreover, Hillyer's pining for a "heroic" poetry is modestly traditional—not violently so, as in the poetry of Viereck or Roy Campbell or ex-communist (and pro-McCarthyite)[41] Max Eastman—and for the most part kept him out of literary politics. Few combatants in the poetry wars referred to Robert Hillyer's *poetry*. Even in a poem such as "Elizabethan Pastoral Landscape," longing socially and linguistically for the imperial age in which poets and "Tall captains" alike

fold[ed] their fiery wings at Court,
To claim the smile of their mysterious Queen
Too dazzling to be more than briefly seen.[42]

The heroism—or, in the case of poems such as "A Voice in the Night" (1947), the craving for heroism—came in the mildest of premodern romantic forms:

That echo melting away in its own wistfulness!
A woman's voice? A child hurt in a play?
The voice retreating from the stage of starlight
Into the wings of night, finale of hush
As the heart dies? Dies in the play? Or dies
In the breast following the echo beyond life?
What charm, what sweetness, what divine despair,
Has for an instant made me feel again,
Who have lain so long alone in the grave of the world?[43]

Yet on the matter of modernism's alleged abandonment of its American readership, the antimodernisms of Hillyer, Fletcher, and Coblentz were essentially one. For Coblentz, readership was the issue that brought him indirectly to his own workable definition of ideology, although he offered it without mentioning the term. Modernists radically resisted normative communication. They evinced "the unconscious dogmatism of one who assumes that every wise man will share his own point of view: he who thinks otherwise automatically proves himself unwise,"[44] and so once again if modernism was not itself a far left political doctrine, it operated like one. Precisely this analogue informed the anti-ideological meaning of Hillyer's invective against modernists as unheroic opportunists in times of war and doubtful peace both: didacticists, "materialists," mere describers of what they deemed reality—and makers of poems consisting of images as "objects" and, somehow at the same time, cultist evaders of meaning.

There is no use lamenting over the end of this movement. The reasons for the decline, partly political and social, also lie partly within literature itself. . . . Several works have been written during the first half of this century which should terminate not with FINIS or THE END but with the warning DEAD END.—Stephen Spender, 1954

Lyricism, Freedom, and Art Education

Robert Graves, Melville Cane, Peter Viereck, and to a lesser extent Stephen Spender—four very different poets, of distinct generations—turned separately against modernism during the Cold War. They concurred, though, on one matter: the necessary relation between lyricism and cultural freedom.

Graves criticized "a-metrical practices" and worried about good poets becoming aesthetically "em-Pounded."[1] For Graves, there "are only poems" (very few in any era) and "periodic verse-fashions." Modernism begot the latter.[2] He groaned that "modern poetical experiment" was being modeled on nonrepresentational painting.[3] He lamented the "abandonment of metre," a retreat that had been made, he felt, under the command of modernist abstraction. Such abandonment meant inevitable failure in free verse. The disappointment, Graves observed, coincided chronologically with the bitter end of Lost Generation expatriation and the coming of radicalizing depression, and thus with the emergence of "new *isms* and new stylistic excesses." Stylistic excess added to other causes of Depression-era ideologies a still stronger will to sacrifice individual freedom. And yet, Graves argued, individual freedom had always been the precondition for lyricism.[4] Promoters of modernism were unusually strategic; Graves noticed that young poets "have been acquiescing" to this "organized attempt . . . to curtail their liberty of judgement." This was not so much the "Age of Consolidation" as the "Age of Acquiescence"—which "of course, in the Welfare State, covers a wider range of subjects than poetry and literature in general." The acceptance of modernism—not its rise in the first years of the century but its ascendancy as the dominant mode of the 1950s—was a socialist, paternalistic phenomenon. In a capsule history of the twentieth century, Graves could thus describe "the Modernist Movements of the 'twenties[,] which merged into the Left Wing Movement of the 'thirties," its decline from freedom to "idolatry" following inexorably thereafter.[5]

In his own vexed poetry of the 1950s and early 1960s, Graves sometimes employed metrical convention with what seemed to many an angry vengeance. At least one leftist-modernist veteran found the result "very silly."[6] Once, in the first years of the Red Decade, Graves had been grouped together with those modern "extremists" attacked by Max Eastman in *The Literary Mind* (1931) for praising poems so linguistically self-referential, so conscious of constructed-ness, that they were verily "made out of communication,"[7] a critique deepened by the feeling on the left that, as one *New Masses* critic put it, "Graves seldom lets social questions intrude."[8] But by the latter part of the 1950s, Malcolm Brown of the University of Washington, asked to say what lately impressed undergraduate English majors, noted that for them "the intellectual event of the past year was Robert Graves's common-grave interment of Eliot, Yeats, Pound, Auden, Spender and [Dylan] Thomas."[9] Brown was referring to the last of the 1954–55 Clark Lectures—later published in *The Crowning Privilege* (1956) —and to a feisty essay Graves had published in the *New Republic*; both gave big boosts to conservative antimodernists.[10] Stanton Coblentz and Charles Wharton Stork reinstated their correspondence in response to this essay, roused by the news of "Graves's strictures against" modern poets, although Coblentz was "at a loss to understand" why Graves still chose to keep cummings, "one of the worst offenders of all," off the enemies list.[11] Nevertheless, Coblentz gladly added Graves to his growing roster of defectors from modernism. By 1958, Robert Creeley was politely telling the editor of *Poetry* that Graves was "the most accomplished '*traditionalist*' now writing,"[12] and by the 1960s, Horace Gregory, sensing Graves's antiradicalism and antimodernism more keenly than Creeley (who always maintained an ecumenical approach to Graves), observed that the old poet's new poems "might as well be written by slick paper women's magazines." Fervent adherence to meter shifted the sound of Graves's verse toward "unseriousness,"[13] not typically a successful tenor for him in what Creeley evenly called "the content of [Graves's] obligation to [poetry's] pattern."[14]

That so major—and, especially to the young undergraduate male of the 1950s, so influential—a figure as Robert Graves had turned against the poetic modernists bucked up second-thoughters of lesser standing such as Winfield Townley Scott. It was one thing to see Yeats and Eliot "attack[ed] out of the exacerbated disappointments of Robert Hillyer," Scott wrote. "But Robert Graves!" Graves's move against modernists "could be the beginning of the end of their reign."[15] To this sense of denouement, Melville Cane, the brilliant lawyer-poet and author of the influential *Making a Poem* (1953), added his forceful essay, "Are Poets Returning to Lyricism?"

Cane identified lyricism with antimodernism, just as the anticommunist editors of the *Lyric* repeatedly did. In declaring that "we believe in lyric poetry as the only true type of poetry," Leigh Hanes, the Roanoke, Virginia, lawyer who was Virginia Kent Cummins's predecessor at the magazine, rejected poems that responded to the "human woe that fills that world." Hanes noted that the decline in the quality of poetry coincided with poets' interest in political "strain and stress," and he reasserted the equation of lyricism, individuality, "quiet and reflection," and apoliticism.[16] Wondering a bit more optimistically than Hanes whether American poets were turning to lyricism, Cane worked against a basic Popular Front belief about Whitman's positive impact on modern verse. He suggested that that influence, while superficially "liberat[ing] our poetry from the shackles of convention," connected two conditions. First, liberation from convention meant tolerating poetic ideals that are "essentially those of a religious or humanitarian crusader"; second, freedom was the result of "sacrific[ing] and scrap[ping] the basic distinction between verse and prose," which Cane argued had inflicted "an injury to poetry," causing the demise of the lyric.[17]

The precondition for a return to lyricism in the 1950s was the unlinking of the role of the poet as ideologist from the acceptance of prose as available to the vocabulary and diction of lyric poets. The first counterrevolt would follow from the second. For Cane, the restoration of the lyric would cause the demise of ideology. The counterrevolt would be a bloodless coup, no actual political battle being necessary. The alternative to the coup was a shying away, the sad retreat, made by those disappointed with the failed direction of modernism by the late 1940s. As we have seen, Gilbert Neiman's experience rereading *Poetry* again after a few years away "made [him] glad that I got housebroken into prose" because poetry had failed to remain sufficiently distinct in its versification. "The great unnaturalness has crept in," Neiman complained, and we no longer "know how to treat our consonants any more. We can't rival the vowels any more." Poetry was "home" to Neiman, we saw, but his homecoming was marred by finding prose there. "Housebroken into prose" *elsewhere*, now exiled from verse, he remembered that "I once lived with this."[18]

A far more avid anticommunist than Graves, Neiman, or Cane, Peter Viereck more explicitly conveyed the political import of the lyric at midcentury. In "The Dignity of Lyricism," Viereck charted a middle course "between" the Marxism of the 1930s and its alleged destruction of lyricism on the one hand and the "dry formalism of the 1940s" (the New Criticism) on the other. The result would be, indeed, lyricism—"the one great function left to the poet."[19]

Thus did the lyric come most clearly to be identified with the postideological moment—as a beleaguered but tough center that would poetically hold. Pressed properly into service, lyricism became a form of freedom fighting, a mounting of resistance against left and right "totalitarian twins." Real aesthetic individualism was nonconformity, set against the invading armies of avant-gardists. Cullen Jones challenged modernist effeminacy and its "sexual abnormality," called for natural, nonpolitical, individualistic "strong male exhibitionism" as a weapon against the "high-pitched agonized mousy squeaks of the psycho-terrified middlesex pseudo-artists as they beat their self-constructed padded cells."[20] "Poetry," Jones wrote elsewhere, "is the virile after-life of a civilisation."[21] The "unrecognized turning-point" leading to the ultimate degeneration of the lyric impulse, according to Viereck in *The Unadjusted Man* (1956), occurred when "a popular-level weekly . . . suddenly put T. S. Eliot on its cover instead of Marilyn Monroe." This signaled the triumph of "banality's New Look of introverted sensitivity," an "abstract, explicit, formulated code" that needed refreshing by the true lyric, which is concrete and passionate.[22] To illustrate an article called "How to Dislike Poetry," *Time* magazine featured a photo portrait of the strong-chinned, dauntless-looking prep-school poet and teacher Leonard A. G. Strong, bearing the caption, "No thanks to Oscar Wilde."[23] Strong was trying mightily to get teachers to learn to like the poetry they taught.

The image of this Mr. Strong appeared in a back-to-school issue of *Time* (September 15, 1947). Its "Education" section featured two items of news. One, simply called "Back to School," rounded up new and perhaps frightening trends for the anxious time. Young children who were the leading edge of a generation to become known as baby boomers already taxed the capacities of existing schools, while for older students, "study abroad" was all the rage. Readers of *Time* now had to contemplate potential troubles associated with hordes of cocky American undergraduates cruising the *Queen Mary*, bound for fragile democracies in Italy and France with thriving communist parties. Here was an at least subliminal reminder of the radicalization of college students in an earlier decade, for this was "the largest such group [of students abroad] since the 1930s."[24] *Time* misread or ignored what Leonard Strong was actually trying to achieve; for one thing, he felt that his goal of engaging his fellow teachers would be better realized if he could persuade them to introduce *more* modern poetry. In summarizing the new troubles, the magazine noted only that "hostility to poetry dates from the careers of Byron and Shelley, reinforced by that of Oscar Wilde, which have connected it with effeminacy, goings-on, incapacity for sport." Strong was quoted out of context on this point: the teacher who tries to hide *this* bias by "conceal[ing] his feelings . . . can be far more dangerous."[25] The obvious implication in *Time* was that stalwart dons such as Strong were being undermined by unknowing academic dupes of poetic perversity.

Jacob Hauser, the descriptive poet from Brooklyn, saw how hyperintellectual modernists stormed the walls of a new kind of academy, the "Academies of the

Perverse," pushing so hard at originality that they created "a bizarre or insane regimentation of *un*intelligibility."[26] "What confronts us," Viereck warned in "The Dignity of Lyricism" (later collected in *The Unadjusted Man*), "is whole robot-armies of regimented 'poets,' critics, professors, and [as *Time* implied in its back-to-school warning] secondary-school teachers with *The Waste Land* tucked under an arm and stiff ruler in hand. Each *robot* intones dutifully, 'I'm a real human being, an independent, nonconforming, avant-garde aesthete, just like everybody else.' "[27] The modernist barbarians, posing as "progressive" educators, were at the gates. (And, in postwar Europe, they awaited America's children.)

Lyricism in the postideological world meant individualism, to be sure, but certainly not individuation, an aid in the coming to consciousness. The properly restored modern poet was free but not merely self-expressive. "Free association" for Viereck had little or nothing to do with psychology. It was a matter of poetry's widest range of effects, and it resulted from more rather than less use of traditional form. "The stricter (more 'enslaving') the form," Viereck wrote, "the freer is this free association."[28]

The greatest threat to the application of this fundamental antimodernist tenet came from the Education through Art movement. Led by poet and political heretic Herbert Read—a man who "tried to bestride the Marxist, Freudian, and Surrealist steeds all at once"[29] and who felt that "a belief in Marx should be accompanied by a belief in, say, Cezanne"[30]—the movement was founded on the progressive conviction that modern education and the modernist aesthetic were well paired in the effort to support the growth of the individual. Contrary to Read, antimodernists of Cane's, Viereck's, and Graves's variety by no means sought lyricism as a form of cultural freedom to entail either a hermeneutic principle of "anything goes" or poetry for everyone. Lyricism did not mean to them that every American undertaking the effort of lyrical self-expression, no matter how formally, could count as having joined in the advance toward Viereck's postideological Third Way. That was a place reserved for true poets. The random "poetic" products of the liberal cult of personal expression did not produce true poets. One of the criticisms of Anglo-modernism here was that it tended to suggest to the public that art is easy and that personal writing, no matter how uncommunicative, is a priori good. And Herbert Read's ideas about education seemed to confirm this view.

The key to poetry, argued Read, was "sincerity of expression"—the "fundamental and revolutionary" innovation inaugurated by Wordsworth and carried "a step further" by modern poetry.[31] "The whole question of talent is immaterial," Read wrote provocatively in the preface to Richard Ott's *The Art of*

Children (1952). "Every individual has certain sensations, emotions, intuitions, and certain impulses to express" himself or herself aesthetically.[32] This was the heart of the modernist-liberalism alliance that Viereck and Cane—and Russell Kirk and Richard Weaver, far to their right—denounced: it made for "unintelligible incompetence" that passed for poetry, and if anyone, such as Max Eastman, exposed it as such and called for a "return to communication," he would be "slandered by the would-be avant-garde as . . . attack[ing] serious, difficult, or experimental writing" and permitting "demogogic surrender" to middlebrow convention and commercialism.[33] Similarly, Cane's strong preference for a poetry that did not accommodate itself to prose implied strict lyrical standards for inclusion in spite of his ideological affiliation with liberals heralding "the individual" as the answer to communist groupthink.

This was going to be the tricky thing about such a version of moderate antimodernism, for it seemed to bring on as allies the facile midcentury "modernist" liberal, with his adaptive ideas about individual expression as a result and indeed an aim of living the modern life. Viereck resisted this idea repetitively in *The Unadjusted Man*, where he argued that the self-satisfied, talkative "well-adjusted" person was a weak social attribute of modernism's easy aesthetic of fragment, skill-less implication, and undemanding dissociation. And in "Gnostics of Education," Weaver attacked the idea that "the child should be encouraged to follow his own desires" by summarizing modernist education: "The general aim is to train the student so that he will adjust himself . . . to society conceived as social democracy." This was for Weaver "a virtual educational *coup d'état* carried out by a specially inclined minority . . . in essence a cabal."[34] What was wrong with teaching a changeable art? "We are told by [progressives] that we are 'living in a world of change'; but the 'catch' is that they are in charge of the change." Weaver distrusted the modern penchant for argument from circumstance. The liberal shibboleth "We must adapt ourselves to a fast-changing world" was not really an instance of rhetorical cause and effect but a brutal dictum. The left would have been better off frankly revealing its rhetorical mode and shouting instead, "Step lively."[35] In an essay for *Pinnacle*, the magazine of the League for Sanity in Poetry, Robert Avrett observed that the new young poet either "buckles down" to do the hard work of writing within the grammatical tradition or takes the "easier course" of "adopt[ing] a distorted stream-of-consciousness technique that critics hail as the epitome of Modernism," thus joining "the motley gang of poetic renegades who similarly have taken the easy way."[36]

Such views on the technique-centered easiness of modern verse befit Coblentz's hatred of "expressiveness," although in his exhortation, "Freedom—

What Price?," we have an extreme version of the position: Young poets are permitted to dream and imagine, yet poetry will "rise or fall by the principles of artistic expression," and "such delineation cannot be accomplished willy-nilly, as the wind blows; it is possible only by means of skill." And Coblentz defined skill as total acceptance of "the restraints of technique."[37] Similarly, E. Merrill Root loathed pragmatism's emphasis on the basis of art as experience, the idea that the "temporary lack of adjustment with surroundings" resulted in artistic divulgence—poetry as "a brute formless contact with events" rather than what it should be, "expression-for-itself" (as distinct from expression in response to stimuli), "a selection and patterning of events into meaning."[38] In *The Conservative Mind* (1953), a book many consider the Bible of the modern right, Russell Kirk took the Eliot of *The Idea of a Christian Society* (1939) and *Notes toward the Definition of Culture* (1948) and formulated "the most influential poet and critic of his age," "a principal conservative thinker in the twentieth century," the one living poet to whom "many conservatives turn for insight." Eliot's key insight for midcentury conservatives: "Liberalism [is] a relaxation of discipline."[39] Weaver's *Ideas Have Consequences* (1948), a book "from which the postwar conservative movement took its start,"[40] condemned "an infinite-valued orientation" that made "certitude and the idea of the good impossible" and encouraged writers not to engage the real "Power of the Word" through use of words' strict, clear definitions but "to choose words and illustrations which will arouse the proper mental associations with his readers" (and "if he doesn't succeed with [those words], he should try others"). For Weaver, modern liberal ideas about language permitted "the easy divorce between words and conceptual realities." He longed for a return to the model of "the poet's unique command of language" and called for an end to asyntactic "looseness and exaggeration," the latter especially being "a form of ignorance."[41]

In locating the root of the problem in the modernist preference for "art *expressing* rather than describing life," Gilbert Malcolm Fess blamed the "pouring-out-of-oneself" aesthetic, a radical neoromanticism that produced "a large star of ink on a painter's canvas, entitled *Crossing the Bridge* . . . express[ing], darkly, the artist's emotions while performing the action." Orientation to process, the hallmark of modern theories of progressive education, manifested itself in the transformation of the Freudian unconscious into "*conscious* social living." Modernism's social theory, implicit in the generatively expressive inkblot, led to intellectual isomorphism and intolerance, diminishing "intellectual freedom and variety."[42] When from the 1950s through the 1970s Daniel Bell stressed the simultaneity of "the exhaustion of Modernism" and "the aridity of Communist life," he equated "the tedium of the unrestrained self" in modernist art and the "meaninglessness of the monolithic political [system]" inherent in communism.[43]

E. Merrill Root's enmity toward communism was linked to his growing disgust with modern poetry through the idea in both movements of "life as a flux of quantity," the Deweyite notion of what Root assailed as "an indiscriminate *flux quo*." In many articles and reviews and in his book, *Collectivism on the Campus* (1955), Root argued that pragmatic poetics entered all areas of human knowledge through "free expression" curricula in the schools—or, in short, that when John Dewey's "object[ion] to reverence for great works of art" was accepted in u.s. education under the guise of respecting individuals' "experience," modernism led directly to general subversion.[44]

Geoffrey Wagner, who blamed many social ills on abstract art, hated the notion that "the most important new concept in American art is that 'everything' can be art and that art can be 'everything,'" the radical opening of the field heralded in American Dada by Marcel Duchamp, as part of the organized progressive heresy.[45] In 1952, Viereck used the *Political Science Quarterly* to make this case emphatically. There, in an influential essay, "The Revolution in Values," he argued that the modern "anything goes" aesthetic led to communist (and fascist) mass murder, a claim even Root and Coblentz for the most part shied away from making openly. Genocide apparently had *not* as a matter of fact been the result of the systematic imposition *of stricter and narrower* rules on citizens, limiting their employment, then their legal identity, and then their permitted residence based on a state-driven idea of absolute truth; no, the origins of totalitarian mass murder drifted in the refrain of what Viereck calls "an unconscious Broadway jazz echo of the [medieval Syrian] Assassins: 'Anything goes.'" (The supersubversive secret Order of Assassins had uttered, "There is no truth; everything is permitted.")[46] In this context we see how Bell's postideological reading of modernism in relation to capitalism depended on the assumption, taught him by the poets, that the (to him) dangerous legacy of the political period in which modernism and communism simultaneously thrived was "the impulse of Modernism . . . to leap beyond" and specifically the way in which the modernist move "beyond nature," the cult of the "aesthetic and the experimental," was "driven by the self-infinitizing spirit of the radical self." Bell's social narrative telling of the convergence of communism and modernism led him to propose a "vital center"—in Arthur Schlesinger Jr.'s celebrated term—where "limits" could be placed on the urge toward "anything goes," an attitude symptomatic of both communists and modernists, movements that had "exhausted" American readers after the 1930s.[47]

Working hard to overcome the criticism that modern poetry had become disconnected from any audience, those who sought to defend poetry in general took as much advantage as they could of moderate antimodernists' calls for "individuality" over the supposed tyranny of avant-garde groupthink (cliques, movements, manifesto-animated cadres). Claiming to stand with the antimodernists after ideology's death, such defenders also heralded the individual's special potential relationship to modern as opposed to traditional poetry. One master of this strategy was A. M. Sullivan—poet, Poetry Society of America leader, member of "the realistic school,"[48] enemy of "the obscurantists, the Freudians [and] the exhibitionists" among poets,[49] host of the *Radio Forum for Poetry*, business counselor ("The alert manager is often autocratic—with good reason"; "he knows that the democratic . . . decision is usually late, second-best, mediocre")[50] and, in his day job, director of public relations at *Dun's Review* (later *Dun and Bradstreet*).[51] He was a devout Catholic who believed that modernists were "the poets of little faith."[52] He claimed to be bringing the issue of audience to "all the discussions of poetry by the various schools, coteries, or fronts." He could make a reasonable "defense" of modern verse without having to disagree with anyone about the pernicious influence of the left.

Thus, one solution to the problem of its alienated audience was to recognize that modern poetry in particular—free verse and other open forms, Sullivan meant—was in effect the expressive birthright of all Americans. In "The Poet in Search of His Audience" (1951), he urged fellow poets and readers to consider that they actually "live in the most poetic epoch in world history," in spite of the fact that "the stature of the poet as a public being is smaller" than traditional "competitors" for that low status—the lawyer and the politician. The paradox presented by these contradictory facts could be resolved if poets and teachers realized that American children and modern poetry had much in common. "What can we do to restore the poet to his audience?" Sullivan asked, answering that the poet should "become as a child again." Sullivan's "evidence" was not Wordsworthian romanticism but modern developmental psychosemanticism: "Children speak poetry before they learn prose." When faced with an assignment to write a poem, one little boy asked, "What shall I write about?" Understanding the "educational" virtues of the modernist dictum that anything can be the material of poetry, the modern teacher replied to the child that "Anything, your house, your wagon, your dog" would do. Sullivan's readers were treated to lines quoted from children's "modernist" poems, which he affirmed with superficially legitimizing tags such as "imagistic and dramatic." The psychosocial rule was that in general, "children are imagists."

But children were imagists only if they were permitted to be, only if teachers truly conveyed the idea that students could write about "anything." Sullivan noticed that for one teacher—she had a "dominant" personality and held rigid, traditional beliefs about poetry—children produced bad verse: for instance, "carefully rhymed, obvious, . . . dull quatrains." This, argued Sullivan, was the best response to the usual centrist claim that *they* had the postideological answer to what Sullivan also called "the debate among the critics of the carping, intellectual Left or the smug traditional Right on [the issue of] clarity in poetry."[53]

Conservatives were horrified enough by the liberal fallacy evident in such self-help books as *Art for All* (1942), an upbeat you-can-do-it volume that undertook to refute the notion that "art . . . is for the few [or] that it is for those who have special creative talent." (Rather, art "is all around you. . . . It is important in everything we do. . . . Make whatever you have as good to live as possible.")[54] Still more appalling was the liberal-modernist idea that *imagism* in particular, arguably the foundational movement of Anglo-American modernism, had by the late 1940s and 1950s become the formal and pedagogical means by which modern art was truly democratized. If this was one result of New Deal/Popular Front–era cultural liberalism—that *imagism* by 1950 could seem a force for general popular improvement—it only added greater urgency and even panic to anticommunists' sense that the 1930s and the High Modern period needed to be kept far apart in the emergent literary history that would underwrite the new curriculum. In response to Horace Gregory's likening of British Marxist critic Christopher Caudwell to the imagist philosopher-poet T. E. Hulme, Stanley Edgar Hyman in his mostly calm negative assessment of u.s. literary Marxism became irate, calling the comparison of Hulme to Caudwell "absurd and insulting."[55] For although, indeed, most advocates of the applicability through education of modernist *-isms* such as imagism were themselves anticommunists, nonetheless these ideas again raised the specter of a tyranny of a modernist cultural left: aesthetic regimentation and mass education through the back door of otherwise healthy American institutions. The traditionalist teacher with her "dominant personality" and rigid commitments to rhyme and meter, doubted by A. M. Sullivan, in fact embodied Viereck's ideal Unadjusted Hero. She stood as an educational bulwark against cultural communism. If postideological imagism for every American, starting with grade school, was loathsome enough to antimodernists, still worse was the way in which the radical ideas in the mass "Education through Art" movement as founded and led by Read—a sometime fellow traveler, a sometime anarchist, "an early disciple of T. E. Hulme" and "prophet of the modern movement in art and literature"[56]—were now infiltrating the moderate modernist defense.

The wartime first edition of Herbert Read's *Education through Art* (1943) seems to have stirred little antagonism among conservatives. The 1950 edition generated greater concern. While Read avoided the relativist-populist claim that " 'free' expression is necessarily 'artistic' expression,"[57] the book nonetheless clearly showed that modernism made progressive mass education viable. Such democratic modernism favored, at turns, expression over selection, process over content, "making" over meaning, "spontaneity" over restraint, a plurality of values over antirelativism,[58] aesthetic "integration" (Read's favorite term) over elitism. Education through art assured the final ascendancy of modernism: the rough equation of "child-art" (illustrations of which filled Read's book) with bona fide modernist movements and categories, of a piece with Sullivan's identification of individual grade-schoolers' poems with one modernist -ism or another. Read spelled it out more systematically than Sullivan, to be sure, endorsing the physio-aesthetic connection between surrealism and "feeling" as it might be found in a child's art, expressionism and "sensation," constructivism and "intuition," and so forth.[59]

At midcentury, a number of conservatives worried about the strong influence Read exerted on their potential allies among antimodernist moderates such as Sullivan. Read's ideas were taken quite seriously in the United States. His merging of pragmatism, modernism, and radicalism made modernism seem strikingly coherent and relevant. He spent an academic year (1953–54) at Harvard, occupying the Charles Eliot Norton Chair for poetry. He was a guest lecturer favored by civic organizations whose members were trying to grapple with modernism's social implications. His engaging talk swept freely across aesthetic and political categories and respected no boundary that separated sister arts.

Education through Art represented an enormous sociopolitical synthesis of modernism in Euro-American culture. Its pages provide an encyclopedic range of progressive-modernist reference: Croce, Dilthey, Dos Passos, Dvořák, Forster, Fromm, Gropius, Hulme, Shelley, Tagore, Van Gogh, Poincaré. Constructivism, cubism, expressionism, imagism, futurism, and surrealism stand alongside annotated summaries of the classroom system, the so-called Project Method, Franz Cizek's Juvenile Art Class in Vienna, Georges-Henri Luquet's studies of children's drawings, and the liberal-left Spens Report on secondary education (1939).[60] While Luquet was no modernist per se, he showed generally that young people can recognize and accommodate stylistic differences, and in *Le Dessin Enfantin* (*Children's Drawings*), he specifically contended that children enter a potentially productive stage of "failed realism" in which "the limited and *discontinuous* character of the child's attention" finds aesthetic embodiment in forms requiring evaluative criteria other than representational.[61]

Read's interpretation of the influential Spens Report held that *Spens* "finally" had contended that teaching children "through the application of drawing to . . . branches of the work of a Modern School" should "be recognized as of greater importance than . . . imitative accuracy" in fostering "the spontaneity, the freshness and vigor which are characteristic of the free expression of young children's drawings."[62] Read frankly advocated modernism as liberal-left education theory by bringing together John Dewey's pragmatist *Art as Experience* (1934); the report of the U.S. Commission on Secondary School Curriculum, *The Visual Arts in General Education* (1940); and avatars of modernist education such E. A. Kirkpatrick, whose *Imagination and Its Place in Education* Read admired. This convergence of progressive ideas about aesthetic expression befit a world of new teachers who would know something of Kurt Koffka's work on gestalt in the mid-1930s—ideas that criticized the old-school system in which facts and factuality are overestimated at the expense of meaning.[63]

Proponents of the child-art movement, otherwise easily belittled as irrelevant even to the most serious modernist social practice, gained status through Read's synthetic writing. Seemingly silly, reductive ratios between modernist movements, such as those Sullivan breezily advocated without any scholarly apparatus in the pages of the *Saturday Review of Literature*, gained intellectual legitimacy in Read's work. Partisans of child art such as Reginald R. Tomlinson (*Children as Artists*) and Wilhelm Viola (*Child Art*), when such liberalism was aggressively put in context with the modern work of scholars of Henri Rousseau, such as Ernest Hunter Wright, seemed to make the psychology of modernist primitivism tenable. H. Teasdale's innovative effort to scientize what avant-gardists knew as the early Poundian project of a modernism of images, now seen as reviving optical impression with hallucinatory clarity, might never have been taken seriously by the literary left or its detractors had not Read juxtaposed Teasdale's otherwise forgotten "Quantitative Study of Eidetic Imagery" (1934)[64] with the general movement toward the new leftist social-political forms of intercultural cooperation and popular self-government.[65]

Commentators on the 1950 edition of *Education through Art* perceived, as the wartime reviewers had not, the specific political import of Read's advocacy of "integration." Arthur Lismer, of Montreal's Museum of Fine Arts, thought that only someone who is "a poet, a critic, an educator, and a psychologist who understands the relationship of art, childhood, and of education to human aspirations, growth, and world problems" could make such a case for modernism on behalf of the "society" side of the individual-versus-society debate, now with its Cold War overtones. Lismer saw this as a book about the "unity of consciousness which is the only source of social harmony."[66] Writing in the journal *Psychiatry* to express doubts greater than Lismer's, C. Hans Syz, an art collector and expert on the social interpretation of neurosis,[67] nonetheless acknowledged the social force derived from the relationship between leftism and modernism. When art becomes the basis of education, "individuation" becomes a matter of "integration," which answers conservative objections to modernism by proposing "the reconciliation of individual uniqueness with social unity," the "primary unity of social interrelations, an organic confluence of the mind within and world without." That confluence had been prevented by an educational system that failed to comprehend modern art—that permitted disruption by "secondarily developed moral impositions and alterations," as Syz put it,[68] including, Read argued, adult socio-aesthetic standards for legibility, readability, sense making, beginning-to-middle-to-end narration, mimeticism, tonal restraint, and a check on intuition in the area of "the written word" as well as "in the language of drawing."[69] Such critics had no illusions about the liberal-left origin of all this: they knew that Read advocated the "creation of a sense of mutuality," a system of teaching in which "feelings of separateness and oppositeness must not be allowed to intrude," and he understood that the one process is "group-education."[70]

In *Art and Society* (1937), Read had noted with approval the surrealist's "claim that he is a more consistent Communist than many who submit to all manner of compromise with the aesthetic culture and moral conventions of this last phase of capitalist civilization."[71] Once the goal is the "cultivation of the capacities of expression," then education can entail "the creation of artists"— but, indeed (as Hans Syz saw), it is an art particularly modern in its breakdown of the apparatuses that used to form a wholeness difficult for anyone to attain in reaching toward the status of artist. Art "consists of nothing other than the good making of sounds, images, movements, tools and utensils."[72]

Supporters of modernism who were also anticommunists, such as Robert Richman, literary editor of the *New Republic*, were nervous about the social implications of such a "theory of everyday art." Richman's general concerns about political criticism[73] emerged most tellingly in his commentary on Ott's *The Art of Children*, a work implying a modernist pedagogy[74] that owed a good deal to Read, who wrote the preface. Here Richman worried about "mass imagination" and its effects on the development of aesthetic sensibility in American children; he was referring to a danger created by the advance of technology. Yet the vocabulary of threat Richman used was the language of anticommunism. (In this period, of course, communism was represented as forcing on its subjects, especially children, a standardization of expression.) Richman's criticism of the "uniform mental images spewed out of the television sets" and retinally burned-in images of Walt Disney's cartoon Johnny Appleseed implied that cultural collapse might well come not from the outside but from within the very heart of the American cultural rejoinder to communism—through the patriotic "standardization of all our public arts forms" that developed as a response to communist "mass imagination," allegedly the main aesthetic legacy of the 1930s. The way out of this nightmare of internal subversion, Richman suggested by way of praising *The Art of Children*, was through a counterstandardization. Liberal self-expression thus provided a bulwark against more radical forms of "social mutuality," to use Read's phrase, which was here being turned against the child-art movement. Richman felt that the American parent "should take a vow . . . to honor the pictures his child makes." If "conventionalization is hard upon them," children should be encouraged to create art, and we should say it is all good. That American homes were going without such "honor" owed to self-expression constituted a threat; Ott's book is "forceful testimony of these dangers."[75]

A more successful strategy for co-opting or deradicalizing the advocacy of democratic "free expression" as attainable through pushing universal "artistic expression" in American homes and schools via modernism was to depict the modern movement as having come home—normalized, domesticated, stripped of its shocking qualities. By the time Richman wrote about Read, such deradicalization was well under way. "The adventurous young modern" whom we meet in *Art for All* "wants his furniture as up-to-date as his automobile or refrigerator."[76] The eight-year-old child, left to "appreciat[e] real poetry" on his own, will inevitably choose verse over other genres because the "lines of type [a]re short," and the child is, after all, "his own best anthologist."[77]

In 1955, Robert Richman brought the "theory of everyday art" to the pages of the *Kenyon Review*, where he praised Read as at "the center of the modern movement," then quickly deemphasized all the radical qualities of Read's ideas. The real Herbert Read was never actually "restrictive or prescriptive." Rather, he was committed to the moderate principle that the "choice of form had to be determined by [the artist's] circumstances." The fellow-traveling Read of *Art and Industry* (1934) and his long reformist service as chair of the Committee for Industrial Design were reduced to tiny domestic triumphs: was it not Read who had helped replace outmoded horse-and-buggy design, ridding us of the nostalgic miniature metal horse from the hoods of the first automobiles, whose makers had failed to match modern engineering with modern design concepts? Richman contended that it was *not* as if "the fine dinnerware of Arzburg ha[d] been designed by the German designer Platz with Herbert Read standing at his shoulder giving a gentle suggestion *here* for that [modern] proportion, or even a gentler chiding *there* on the relation of the handle to the teacup," but nonetheless one finishes this tractable version of Read with the distinct feeling that such containable formalities were actually the essence of his role as change maker. Never mind that this was the same Read who lavishly praised George Lukács and spoke of the Hungarian theorist's "twelve *fruitful* years" in Stalin's Moscow.[78] Better to redesign teacups than the state.[79]

Further undertaking the project of deradicalizing modernism, Richman put together a handsome volume, *The Arts at Mid-Century* (1954). The large-format book was aimed at the general reader, the new art-minded American middle class. Here the domestication of modernism's dissident qualities was fairly well complete. Richman's preface celebrated the fact that in the 1950s, "the arts of the twentieth century were being accepted in the home, in the museums, and in the universities," for what had been "shocking and modern in the arts at 1913 was respectable and curricular at the midcentury." Richman and most of those whose short essays were included in the volume saw this not as a dull time, as one might conclude from the narrative and imagery of gray-brown domestication, the "smell of autumn and maturity . . . in the air," but rather as an "exciting stage of civilization."[80] One read the contributors' essays, including writers who elsewhere were energetic commentators on the crisis caused by communism in the arts, with a distinct impression that politics was a sideshow.

The Arts at Mid-Century contained an important essay on "The New Orthodoxies" by Stephen Spender, who was something of an exception in the collection. This piece spoke forthrightly about an aesthetic "answer to Marxism," giving the sense that we ought to accept and quietly rejoice in an age of criticism in which "the shock of art is lost when it is absorbed into a complicated machinery of exegesis." By recalling that "twenty years ago T. S. Eliot was being denounced by dons for a drunken Bolshevik," Spender was less interested in distinguishing modernism from radicalism—in taking any time to prove these dons wrong—than in showing how "today [Eliot] is accepted, partly because we have become familiar with his kind of sensibility (and this is a distinct gain) but partly because no one who can be the object of so many university theses could possibly be regarded as a drunken Bolshevik." Spender's sense of writing was less relevant to Eliot than to the horrid specter of the smashed red running amok in the ivory tower. The impact of *The Waste Land* surely had over time been softened by this trend; in this passage, Spender expressed hope for a less "intellectual" analysis, one more focused on poetry's rhetorical qualities. Overall, Spender defined an orthodoxy of choice: Would it be the communist and communist-influenced orthodoxy, or the "new orthodoxy" of the West manifested occasionally in art overseen by "Committee taste"? This was supposedly a tough choice. Whereas "Committee taste is a nice compromise between what is conservative and what is advanced," such "acceptance" is far preferable to the orthodoxy of communist art through which the state seeks control of the telling of history. As with many of Spender's anticommunist essays of this period, the one he contributed to *The Arts at Midcentury* made a tricky argument. He never came out in favor of "Committee taste," yet the reading of the history of modernism here does imply such a view.

Spender's essay perfectly befitted Richman's liberal anticommunist objective of producing a "respectable" book about how the arts are "accepted in the home" of the 1950s. Modernism in its original iconoclastic form was by 1950 insufficiently responsive to "contemporary reality." Joyce's originary modernism assumed the subversive task "of re-experiencing everything as though it had never been experienced before, and then expressing it not in terms with which traditions and education have made us familiar but in new ones." But "values have to be created *by the total submission of poetic sensibilities to contemporary reality*," and "in the end," this kind of revolutionary modernism would be just too hard for readers in a "contemporary reality," making full reexperiencing untenable and thus *unrealistic*. Better, then, to call Joyce "a fanatical traditionalist" without a tradition who thus wholly invented one of his own.[81]

This was the literary centrist's circumvention. Retrofitted as a benevolent new orthodoxy, modernism could accommodate much, even radical denunciations by writers, as long as these writers remained minor. Indeed, "there was room within modernism," wrote Spender, "for an attack on our industrialized civilization by lesser writers who simply had the sense of belonging to such a general movement." Modernism was less an ideology in itself than an accommodator of notions with a bona fide distant ideological past, based on the mature ("realistic") aesthetic assumption that accommodation grants the status of "lesser" to the accommodated.[82]

Spender was arguing the same point about aesthetic value made by Eric Hoffer in his "psychological" taxonomic profile of the radical ideologue. In *The True Believer: Thoughts on the Nature of Mass Movements* (1951), one finds the category of "The Creative Poor" among the listed types of radicals. The "fading of the individual's creative powers" reveals a "pronounced inclination" to join a radical movement. The camps of extremists are filled with lessers, among them "the slipping author" whose "creative flow within" has dried up.[83] This was typically how Maxwell Bodenheim's modernism was explained to postwar readers: it was not so much modernism in any true sense as a noxious combination of communism and personal degeneracy. Bodenheim's poem "To a Revolutionary Girl" was surely a joke; such a man had to be using the communist movement merely as a way of updating *Replenishing Jessica* and other sexy narratives for the postflapper epoch of substance and seriousness. Greenwich Village sincerity was to be generally mocked on similar grounds—in a 1948 *Commentary* "profile" of the urban bohemia, for instance: real freedom-loving innovators after World War I had given way, alas, to "the bastard Stalinist type . . . with his slogans, his cast-iron frame of mind, his dog faith, and his carefully cultivated mediocrity."[84] Crude bio-interpretations of "bad" poets abounded in spite of the strictures of the New Critical age. We have seen what formalists did to the work of Norman Rosten, a far more consistent figure than that cut by Bodenheim. Richard Rovere, replying to Peter Viereck's claim that communist intellectuals had truly "damaged their country," came to agree with Hoffer on this point (and indeed to quote him): Communist writers should be disliked not so much for their political ideas but because their art is so bad. Red poets were hacks—lessers, poetasters, pseudoartists with a hidden agenda, writers who at first opportunity went west to hack for Hollywood, press agents, ad men, and so forth.[85]

In this situation, it was just as "difficult" to "accept ethical and social responsibilities" as it was for readers of modernism, toward the middle of the century, to comprehend and accept the radicalized rhetoric of modernists' expectation —such as Williams's in *Spring and All* (1923) and Bob Brown's in *Toward a Bloodless Revolution* (1934)—for the energetic reinvention from scratch of the world through language. "Because meanings have been lost through laziness or changes in the form of existence which have let words empty," Williams wrote, "the man of imagination [must break] through layers of demoded words. . . . Then at last will the world be made anew."[86] Such revolutionary rhetoric was especially difficult for those advocating the new language who were incapable of significant aesthetic achievement. Literary critics would almost inevitably point out that efforts by leftist reformers to improve social conditions had led to centralization. Spender contended that Herbert Read had himself helped to prove that centralization was anathema to art. He quoted Read at length in contending that when authoritarian regimes seek to find a place for the artist in industry, they tend to "keep his mind off disturbing problems" by, for instance, having him, as it were, "decorate the canteen." Spender's version of Read spoke compellingly for the writer living under Soviet-style communism who would "look for *something* to the West" more integral than gussying up the service facilities. "All attempts of the State to find a place for the artist," wrote Read as quoted by Spender, "have merely created a type of lifeless academicism which has no relevance to the desires and aspirations of the people at large." As a matter of fact, in *Art and Industry*, Read was just as worried about the state centralization entailed in programs by which *American* artists painting murals in post offices—the very domestication of art Spender and Richman *accepted* for the midcentury—and about American academicism as about Soviet regimentation.

Efforts at midcentury such as Spender's and Richman's to deradicalize Read neglected the fact that he was still calling mass education through modernism a "revolution"—indeed, the "Necessary Revolution." That incendiary phrase was the title of the epilogue in *Education through Art*. The call to aesthetic-educational arms originated in Tolstoy's socialist tenet that "all the great revolutions in men's lives are made in thought" and rang out in every chapter of *Education through Art* and in almost every other work by Read as a function of language, which was to him a larger and more basic category of signification than was drawing or painting. This enlargement was the gist not only of Read's *Poetry and Anarchism* but also of *The Education of Free Men*, both works published by the anarchist Freedom Press.[87] The basis of this kind of modernism was language not as a form of depth in itself but as sensation or surface indication of identity and "true" thought below.

In Read's poetry of the 1950s, this concept of the connection between language and liberal-left mass education led him to recognize a "true" poetic modernism founded on the linguistic root of cubist, surrealist, or constructivist sensationalism: the reinvention of reality through the disruption of the normative line and the word. In *Poetry and Anarchism*, "the cause of the arts is the cause of revolution."[88] In *Education through Art*, "the necessary revolution" of modernism was no less political, derived from the thus-far implicit radical ethical system in modernism's project to Make It New. Using a phrase pointing toward political hypocrisy and warmongering, even E. M. Forster saw in Virginia Woolf's modernist language a political lesson about how disrupted surfaces of meaning—consciously juxtaposed words—carry "the importance of sensation in an age which practises brutalities and recommends ideals."[89] This is the aspect of modernist liberal education that would be most bitterly fought by conservatives in the American populace—in the parent-teacher associations, school boards, and public library committees—and most aggressively exploited by those anticommunists who equated abstraction with subversion (as did Max Eastman), modernist primitivism with false revolutionary ideas (as did Wyndham Lewis and Roy Campbell), and the "relaxed, 'democratic,' shoulder-rubbing camaraderie" of modernist pedagogy with "a concept of education treacherous to our regime" (Richard Weaver).[90] Read pointed out with some dismay that even when the authors of the reformist Spens Report advocated modernism in art instruction, they took pains to remind teachers that the "normal child" needed to "make progress toward adult standards in the language of drawing as in the written word"—in other words, that once children have discovered "free" self-expression, they should be encouraged to unlearn the illegibility of the sensational, nonnarrative, nonrepresentational, abstract forms produced in that exercise and then (but only then) to learn to make the move toward maturity that the century itself had made,[91] the move, as Spender imagined it, from drunken Bolshevik to domestic acceptability.

Antimodernist anticommunists were far less equitable than the Spens authors about legibility and its relation to intuition, feeling, and spontaneity. The committee that produced the Spens Report contended that "the value of information has been grossly exaggerated" and urged a principle of students' self-discovery, which was "worth more than all the riches handed out to us by our teachers." Language, they suggested, was not a series of formulas "but a living function of the mind whereby it expresses living ideas." They argued that awakening a child's aesthetic sensibility generally was "as important as the training of the intellect through grammar, science and math." They divided "activities" of a learning community into "conservative" and "creative," heavily stressing the latter. They doubted the term "subjects" (preferring "activities" and "projects") as running the risk of emphasizing "bodies of facts to be stored rather than as modes of activity to be experienced." But overall, the Spens Report advocated careful balance between free expression and the ethical responsibility of consciousness and comprehensibility as derived from traditional descriptive, imitative, and narrative skills, often stressing the "influence of a concrete tradition" and national culture.[92]

Read's advocacy of modernism in the schools came at a time when, as one defender of modernism put it in an essay on "Poetry for Children,"

> the imaginative imagery of the contemporary poet is rejected as meaningless. Children are to be protected from this because it is obscene, modernistic, or futuristic! . . . Rhyme is [thought to be] an essential, [experts on schooling] are convinced; and that a proper poem would never mention breakfast dishes or anything so personal as a detail from a dream. . . . A writer like Joyce is dubbed indecent and dangerous, but no objection is taken to literature of extremist political parties. . . . It is as if there were some general fear abroad of what might happen if words and phrases charged with emotional content were released and approved of in children.[93]

What Read made clear, for instance in the Norton lectures at Harvard, was that the postwar period in art criticism would be characterized not only by the celebration of the "pure intuitional basis" of Picasso and Braque in their cubist periods but by the extension of this as a mass-educational principle through which the benumbed "introverted" type of modern child-citizen, frightened by global brinkmanship, will be taught to create meaning in feelingful "*nonfunctional* abstract[ions] . . . where the artist's intuition is *not directed to any external purpose beyond the expression*, in the concrete elements of mass, outline, colour, and tone."[94]

Deeming Read a pernicious influence, antimodernists warily tracked his reputation in the United States. When a young abstract painter "yipped" that "feeling and thinking are one," Geoffrey Wagner immediately assumed that the artist rode in the "frothing wake . . . of Sir Herbert Read's *Icon and Idea*, his Charles Eliot Norton lectures at Harvard."[95] Eliseo Vivas in *The Moral Life and the Ethical Life* (1950) called the Deweyite school traitorous.[96] In "Gnostics of Education," Richard Weaver, specifically following Vivas, disclosed the movement as "actually a group of fanatical partisans who are determined to spread their special theory of human nature in opposition to all that history and the humanities have taught us."[97]

Read's celebration of "the spontaneous product" of a five-year-old girl, a schoolchild "of working-class origin," innocent and unsophisticated yet able to produce a pencil-and-ink drawing—an abstraction of a snake and a boat that Read called "a symbol for which the unconscious mind of the child had already found a verbal equivalent"—was to the antimodernist just the sort of basic evidence of the atheistic and subversive intentions of the advocates of formlessness. The girl's drawing was reproduced in Read's book exactly in the way an esteemed artwork would be presented in conventional art criticism, illustrative of a critical point and a made object to be viewed with pleasure in itself. By saying the girl had found the "verbal equivalent" of the drawing—"a snake going around the world and a boat"—Read was again insisting on a modern linguistic intelligence.[98] The *Catholic World* ran an article, "Why Modern Poets Have Failed," making in effect the opposite point. It was problematic enough that "the socio-political group" of poets in the 1930s had "lowered the tone and content" of verse by "leveling the intellectual content to suit the masses," but what was far more destructive was the recent addition to this—the conspiracy to promote intuition and childlike or "free-form" abstraction in modernism generally. The radicalism of the former and the anything-goesism of the latter were together more subversive than either separately.

Testifying before HUAC, Wheeler Williams called Jackson Pollack's *Cathedral* a "childish doodle," seeking to tell HUAC not that it was not art but that it was communist art.[99] Although otherwise perfectly willing to attack nonnarrative, disjunctive poetry as the fruit of mindless leftism, Harry Roskolenko found that the "literary crime"[100] committed by Kenneth Koch in these lines—

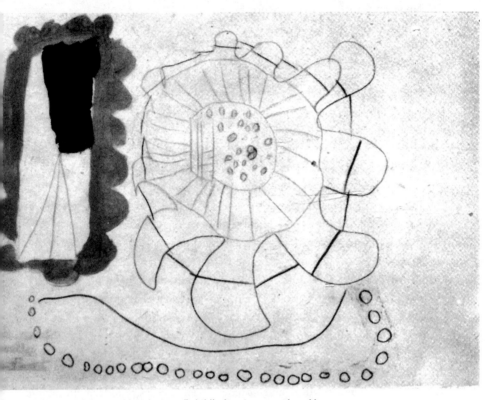

"Snake round the World and a Boat," child's drawing reproduced by
Herbert Read in *Education through Art*.

Beyond the costly mountains
Some pills are going to sleep
Frank will cover them with blinding bloomers
Janice appears from multiple nowhere
The sun was a hot disk
How do you spell "dish"?

—was what Roskolenko termed "infantilism." He quoted ex-communist Max Eastman: it was also "lazy verse." "Children," Roskolenko observed, "often work up verbal nonsense, but it's still infantilism, no matter whether you call it avant-garde or rearguard."[101] In a published riposte to Roskolenko, Frank O'Hara—the very same "Frank" who makes a cameo appearance in the poem—had urged readers to consider Koch in the modernist tradition ("Mr. Koch intends to 'make it new' "), but that only made the conflagration worse.[102]

In a paper on "The Future of Freedom"—that future was bleak—presented at the anticommunist (and CIA-funded) Congress for Cultural Freedom in 1955, Daniel Bell quoted Ortega y Gasset to the effect that modern culture, by seeking a "free expression," becomes "an unrestrained 'spoiled child' with no controlling standards."[103] In his scathing attack on abstraction in painting and poetry, "Non-Communicative Art" (1954), Eastman again clinched the connection between the crisis of the Cold War and the "functional insanity" of modernism. Citing Plato, he conceded that "the poets" "have to be a little crazy"—"have to be child-like" and "have to play seriously." Very well, but that does not mean that critics, curators, reviewers, and poetry editors have to accept unquestioningly "all sorts of ideas and nonideas." The child-art movement should remain an instructional tool, teaching self-expression, but when the craziness is coming from Gertrude Stein and is widely accepted as great art, attaining the power of a movement, the result is akin to "what is happening in the political world": the acceptance of "a return to mumbo-jumbo," "put . . . over" on the public "in the name of intellectual culture," which leads to the "surrender of mental and moral integrity" and "threatens our whole . . . civilization with ruin." To assert his point, Eastman repeated his old trick of twenty years earlier, but now, placed in the Cold War context, it gained new political meaning. Just as he had in "The Cult of Unintelligibility" (in *The Literary Mind* [1935])—one of the earliest political attacks on modernism—he again quoted Gertrude Stein, "high priestess" of the cult:

> I was looking at you, the sweet boy that does not want sweet soap. Neatness of feet do not win feet, but feet win the neatness of men. Run does not run west but west runs east. I like west strawberries best.

Then, in 1954 as he had in 1935, Eastman "revealed" that the passage is not from Stein but from the stenographic report of "the ravings of a maniac" quoted by Emil Kraepelin in *Clinical Psychiatry*. Stein's modernist language thus can be said to be acute linguistic prematurity, or an autism, "an extreme withdrawal into a world of private values and meanings." Eastman next offered an actual passage from the real Gertrude Stein and judged it, although without explanation, "perpetrated . . . not so well" as the linguistic performance of the maniac. There was of course a contraction here: Stein's writing, not automatic but constructed, not unconscious but crafted (Eastman would say too crafted), is by definition *not* the "literary and artistic talking-to-oneself" Eastman deems moronic. The presence of an aesthetic movement against which politically incorrect people must do conscious political work implies no such pure interiority.[104] When the "metaphoric topsy-turvydom" of poetry is put into the hands of people offered "too many degrees of freedom," the result is "verbal and ideational anarchy" as well as "word-hash, gibberish." So wrote Read Bain, the poetry editor and sociologist. Modern poetry was "a cult," he continued, "because devotees have to learn the 'personal language' of the genius they admire, much as the psychiatrist has to learn the personal language of a schizophrenic."[105] After reading Richard Weaver's *Ideas Have Consequences*, Joseph Lalley bitterly argued that modernism put us at the "brink of cosmic nothingness"—that modernism's ethical correlative in physics was atomization; in medicine it was cancer (another perfidious parts over wholes, "the development of certain cell tissues without relation to the whole bodily organism"); and in psychology, "the dominant mental disorder of our times is schizophrenia."[106] Coblentz characterized intentionally undecipherable poems "the sputterings of a madman" with "no observable relationship to the waking content of a healthy mind," but what really frustrated him was that traditionalist readers, in whom "the remedy rests," did not cry out "Insanity!" By our willingness to accept such language, "our peril" was the toleration of "departures from 'rhyme and reason,'" for the "battle is one between reason and unreason, between solid values and chaos."[107]

In Max Eastman's terms, the political demise of the West ("our whole Graeco-Christian civilization" was his phrase) that results from child art, especially from the left's brand of modernist primitivism, had nothing to do with witting subversion. It is hard not to imagine that as he dredged up his old gambit, his crazy faux Stein, Eastman smiled at the suddenly allegiant Cold War–era relevance of the phrase "I like *west* strawberries best." It reads like a mild parody of a title of a Stephen Spender essay or of a Congress for Cultural Freedom conference paper from this hyperpartisan period. Yet made by Eastman's own sleight of hand, it is *not* Stein's line but part of the lunatic "innocent" unconscious, to which civilization should in fact not listen. That it rhymes, too, becomes a political irony.[108]

No antimodernist writing in the 1950s drew the connection between modernist art and leftism more vehemently than Wyndham Lewis in *The Demon of Progress in the Arts* (1954). Eastman on Stein and Lewis on Stein, by 1954, are hardly distinguishable. But of course Eastman was a liberal (or anyway libertarian) ex-communist,[109] and Lewis was a reactionary ex-modernist (or, rather, a consistent exponent of modernist illiberalism), the pair showing again the ways in which anticommunism grew "Up from Modernism" as well as out of the usual disillusionment with communism. (It also shows the complexity of being an ex-communist at a time when some conservatives felt that once a literary communist, always a literary communist: reactionary red-baiters *still* published Eastman's name on lists of writers whose evil "crusade for world government" entailed "abolish[ing] the United States.")[110]

In Stein one could see the political effects of Herbert Read's ideas about the democratic "tendency" in the "impressionistic" forms of modernism Wyndham Lewis generally despised. Stein is Lewis's exhibit A: "Miss Stein gives proof of all the false 'revolutionary,' propagandist plainmanism of her time." It is no wonder that by the 1950s, conservatives such as the publisher Henry Regnery, William J. Casey, billionaire conservative H. L. Hunt, and such otherwise nonpolitical traditionalists like the poet Winfield Townley Scott were taking up Wyndham Lewis and Roy Campbell as anticommunist hero-poets and indeed martyrs in the modernist-communist war who nobly "persisted" in the face of "the Eliot tone" on one side and "the new Auden verse and politics" on the other.[111] Russell Kirk admired Lewis because he "refused to sing Hallelujah to the river-god" as we were all carried along by the "flood of modernity."[112] The Catholic press praised Campbell not just because he fought for Francisco Franco (although he did that) but because his poetry "is born of neither *Angst* nor social realism."[113] It was Casey—formerly an OSS spy and now an attorney in private practice representing Spain's Franco, among others—who urged Henry Regnery to publish Campbell's *Light on a Dark Horse*, "sure of [his] consistent . . . stand against communism,"[114] and direct though unpublicized funding to Regnery from H. L. Hunt was used to purchase fifteen hundred copies each of Lewis's and Campbell's books to donate to university and college libraries. ("Hunt must be given credit," Regnery wrote to William F. Buckley, "for understanding, as few businessmen do . . . that it is ideas that shape history.")[115]

The anticommunism of the *Catholic World* article, "Why Modern Poets Have Failed," took the argument against subversive abstraction even further

than did Eastman. "Ultramoderns" are "extremists" when they commend poetry as a "waking dream state," "a pure psychic automatism." This dangerously
"substitut[es] for intellect an emotional privacy" such that poetry's meaning is
a secret "known only to the poet's psychiatrist." To close "the gap that lies
between poetry" and normal, conscious Americans, poems needed stable,
sanely conscious, wrought forms. Free verse was "the absence of all control
exercised by the reason and outside the aesthetic or moral preoccupation." Here
the *Catholic World* critic, Mary Julian Baird, quoted the surrealists—as devils
who, once exorcized, made way for advocacy, through the writings of the
monk-poet Thomas Merton, of a self in poetry that "is *not* 'a subjective, psychological thing' " but an object of true faith.[116]

CHAPTER 12

For what, and to whom, the modernists pray, no one knows—unless it be for universal destruction and Beelzebub.—Jacob Hauser

Poetry is vision, . . . not the stringing together of words.—Stanton Coblentz

Formlessness Is Godlessness

To Mary Julian Baird's "Why Modern Poets Have Failed," with its equation of free verse, communism, and atheism, another Catholic critic replied with a negative defense of poetry. The latter, Mary Faith Schuster (b. 1914), was a Benedictine nun with a 1953 literature Ph.D. from St. Louis University. She taught college-level poetics. Her essay, "Poets Have Always Failed," presented a typical promodernist rejoinder to the anticommunist. What is notable, though, is its praise of a few faithful modern poets whose experiments with dislocated language can be said otherwise to meet Christian pedagogical goals.

Antimodernists, Sister Mary Faith contended, were missing the point when they submitted modern poetry to a litmus test for religious consciousness, "check[ing] too soon [the poet's] IQ for the infinite." She continued, "The poet, Herbert Read has said, is the most unpoetic thing on earth. He has no self. He just goes through life trying to be faithful to reality." A modernist paradox—that poetry must flirt with the unpoetic if it is to signify with sufficient acuity—enabled an argument defending formal inventiveness yet upholding religious practice. Modern poets are "so used to failure that they keep on believing in ultimate victory." And "Father Berrigan," Sister Mary Faith added, getting down to cases, "will have to say his message again a thousand times before he dies" and will still "probably think he has 'failed.'" This poet-priest could bear repetition not for reasons the antimodernists were claiming—not because his poetry is formless and incomprehensible—but because his language productively troubles the faithful reader.

Schuster had been teaching a poem by this "Father Berrigan" to a class of ninety students, on the semester's first day, in a temporary college classroom set up to accommodate the great influx of students, an uncongenial deskless auditorium. It was a difficult poem, the problem of teaching it made surely worse by the makeshift setting, so typical of Cold War teaching. The poem somehow featured the Kremlin's lovely domes and seemed to touch on themes of victory and defeat and the repression of free writing. It shored up the Catholic pedagogue's use of modernism in the initiates' classroom. "A boy of nineteen came up [to me the next morning] to say, 'I couldn't sleep for a while last night, Sister, thinking of that poem.'"[1]

The poem that kept the boy awake was Father Berrigan's "Domes," and he, of course, was Daniel Berrigan (b. 1921): son of a railroad unionist; a Jesuit priest ordained in 1952; a teacher of French, English, and Latin at St. Peter's Prep in Jersey City until 1949 and at Brooklyn Prep from 1954 to 1957, with a frightful stint in war-tense Europe in between. Berrigan's radicalization, begun when in France he fell under the sway of the worker-priest movement and culminating in his partnership with David Dellinger, a four-month sprint evading capture by the FBI, and imprisonment from 1970 to 1972 for the destruction of draft files, developed much more slowly than did his progression from rhymed traditional stanzas betelling pious thoughts in received forms (and weighted by religious allusion) to an intense political ethics running in free-verse lines that digress to the point of referring to themselves as a main means of human liberation. The freest and most inventive of Berrigan's poems in the late 1950s were indeed metapoems—poems about the art of poetry. The Catholic teacher assumed that Berrigan's "Domes" was a piece of self-conscious writing that young students would find "relevant" to their lives in the 1950s; and she knew it was a persuasive answer to traditionalists who worried overmuch about the end of the union between the firm structures of belief on one hand and poetic form on the other. She understood that the connection had to be severed. The conventional Catholic/aesthetic uplift, apparently mindful of George Santayana, in Berrigan's opening lines—"Domes / that raise the improbable to an art"—eventually suggests that *these* lines, the poem itself, can raise such faithful capitols. In the phrase "I had rather written such a line," the poem refers to its own opening language as an antityrannical alternative.

"Domes" had not been included in Berrigan's first volume of poetry, *Time without Number*, which had won the annual prize awarded by the Academy of American Poets; the Catholic magazine *America* asked Berrigan for new unpublished work, and he sent them this piece. The poem reads in part,

> Someone must be born to say:
> I had written such a line and
> died without signing it, than borne home to my
>
> empress, encircling Moscow's sword.
> Who says it?
> no reward is commensurate[2]

The poem figures itself as a "wing studied for the space of its alighting shadow." Its inscription of faith is as a belief in the power of the modern mind. In this sense, it valorizes the modernist cult of the imagination. Berrigan recently recalled for me that in the shadow of the poem was also the influence of Marianne Moore's modernist writing practice: first a given exemplary instance, then an oxymoron, followed by judgment, "esthetic to be sure, [yet] all but ethical."[3] The message of the poem's formal challenge is that true human resistance is in the words. From "*such a line*," not *that* line but *this*, the one here in front of you, the improbable becomes art. The "someone" who "must be born to say: / I had rather written such a line" is not Christ but the poet himself, here in the writing, where there is no such perfection but where one can find "reasons for living [that] remain / supreme." Berrigan never makes it clear why writing a line but remaining anonymous is a preferable alternative to "encircl[ing] Moscow's sword." And the poem only roughly suggests that the achievement of art as a form of belief (a *modern* savior, like "*Rouault's* Christ" in the poem) can be likened to the acceptance of defeat as a key element in the making of these domes.

Yet, writing that she felt "wistful tonight for the poets" of free forms to defend themselves against traditionalist doubters, Sister Mary Faith read right past Daniel Berrigan's self-referential humility—and his apparent longing through the poem to be an antipoet—and rather went straight to her own point, her rejoinder to Catholic antimodernist critics: here is a Jesuit modernist who after all *does* salute the flag. "Domes" put her in mind not of the Kremlin (despite the clear reference to Moscow's built symbol of authority) but to an American occasion: "On this Lincoln's Birthday," she pondered the u.s. Capitol, "which," she noted, "also raises the improbable to an art." Perhaps then, she wondered, modern poetry could after all serve a Christian anticommunist pedagogy. "How many of these students," she rhetorically asked, "will one day teach children to love their country more earnestly, because we read that poem" in class? Here, then, in an effort to save modern art from the antimodernists, a faithful defender provided a close reading of a poem as allegiant in its particulars.[4] It was not merely, I think, a politically strategic misreading of the poem's themes; it only vaguely admired—and did not much account for—the poem's efforts at verbal disjuncture.

Mary Faith Schuster's appreciation of Daniel Berrigan is but one of a myriad instances one can find. Patriotic readings of promodernist liberals abound in the period 1945–60. Yet Christian antimodernists—in the United States they were among the fiercest of all anticommunists—were not shaken from their view that true freedom implies decorum, not disjunction. In a poem such as

"Domes," again, it was difficult to ignore the analogue between acceptance of defeat and improbable art. Postwar chaos should be met, they argued, by a poetics of clarity, sanity, narrative and thematic order, moral temperance, and unambiguous victory of the good. Thus Alice Hunt Bartlett, who in her regular "Dynamics of American Poetry" column chastised "the young poets of the present time" for their "vague, non-understandable" verse and hoped that "out of things that are chaotic" they will "produce something sane,"[5] observed that she "has *invariably* found poetry of the Catholic Sisters of significant worth." Bartlett gave so much space in *Poetry Review* to the American nuns whose verse British readers did not otherwise see that the British might well wonder about the narrowing range of writing in the United States. One featured formalist, a Sister M. Maura, then a graduate student at Johns Hopkins, was said to write so beautifully in "cloistered loneliness" that those of us "who live in the hurly burly of life" might be made to wonder if more new poetry should be attempted there at all:

My words might bruise your whitest thought,
    might break some waxen leaf,
    might bring your templed loveliness
    to sudden human grief.[6]

For the sake of preserving such conventional verse, the poetry editor of *Poetry Review* recommended to people living in the chaotic postwar world that they "storm the gates of stress" and restore "something sane and something immortal" to the nation's poetry.[7] "God gird our walls," wrote Sister Maura in a poem "Against Post War Platitudes," "God make us strong. / Against the slow, deliberate deceit."[8]

J. Donald Adams of the *New York Times* held similar views. His main criticism of modern poetry was that its obsession with method and form implied a "spiritual poverty." Modernism was the "literature of disillusionment and despair," and this quality drew young poets toward subversion, to the rejection of "honor, loyalty, patriotism" and, most disturbingly, of every "manifestation of the spirit."[9] Its spiritual emptiness left modern poetry criticism open to Marxists and materialists. Liberal intellectuals, weakened by their "ingrained love of novelty"[10] and their attraction to avant-gardists, have done little to prevent the "domination of the field of poetry criticism"[11] by materialist critics who supported—as Adams wrote in "The Right to Be Conservative" (1953)—"some of the most pretentious nonsense and some of the most blatant stupidity that has found its way between book covers."[12] When he wrote in *Literary Frontiers* (1951) that "literature is not a branch of sociology or economics" and that contemporary writing suffered from the "tense battle between conflicting ide-ologies," Adams was referring to the cultural damage done by the literary left before the war.[13] He evidently felt Kenneth Burke was one such ruinous critic. Burke's criticism, only vaguely or viscerally Marxist by this point—with his talk of dynamos and magnetic fields, "repulsive forces" and "arrest[ed] problems," its "science" of aesthetics, and its ugly phraseology about a poem as "a wholly dynamized dialectic,"[14] his admiration for what was later despised as "the new metallic music of machinery"[15] and verse that ran like an automatic dish-washer[16]—contributed further to the already demonstrable "stupidity" of mod-ern poetry. Adams felt that Burke's analysis in *A Grammar of Motives* (1945) of John Keats "bears about as much relation to the essence of poetry as surgical technique to the nature of religious ecstasy."[17]

Lilith Lorraine founded her Avalon National Poetry Shrine, which she claimed was "the world's largest school for poetry,"[18] to "take a firm and de-cided stand" against "the obscene, incoherent ramblings" of modernists "who, when their work is stripped of its obscurity, and [the poet's] libido of its defense mechanisms against inferiority," can be understood as little more than "the sort of thing that little Johnny wrote on the seats of vanishing American institu-tions." Her zealous efforts on behalf of this nondegree residential program for conservative poetics—and for the magazine *Different* and the League for Sanity in Poetry—constituted an all-out culture war. The struggles of "pioneers in this field," the few intrepid traditionalists who knew that "sincere poetic values" would eventually triumph, betold a story that, for Lorraine, "reads somewhat like the story of the early Christian martyrs."[19] (Lorraine, a pseudonym for Mary Maud Dunn Wright, presents another complex, shifting figure: she pub-lished in the *New Masses* in the 1920s, earned the Old South Award from the Poetry Society of Texas, and much later won a cult following for her quasi-feminist fantasy writing; the FBI gathered a file on her, apparently because of the startling savagery of her vision of Armageddon.)

Michael Francis Moloney, a Jesuit who taught at Marquette University in Milwaukee, hated cultural disunity and all forms of disintegration, sought in religion a means of achieving intellectual responsibility, and deemed modern-ism a "darkness at dawn." In a diatribe against all modern literature, published in 1951 in the Catholic magazine *America*, he wrote that "the majority of con-temporary literary men have . . . wandered dazedly amid the rubble, fixing upon a beam here, or a concatenation of mortar there as still possessing value."[20] Moloney's life's work, which finally resulted in *John Donne: His Flight from Medievalism* (1965), argued that Donne, at heart a medievalist who had to face "the rising tide of modernism," is said to have finally identified with the latter and to have enabled a poetics of juxtaposition and disjunction. But in Moloney's view, this was an error generated by a historical misreading of the poetry promulgated in the twentieth century. And so he argued for the continued relevance and value of the medieval tradition (in particular, Catholic mysticism and the theological power of aesthetic wholeness) with which Donne, unfortunately, had been "forced to break when he cast his lot with modernism."[21] The implication: the Eliotic poetics Donne inspired was bad history.

Chad Walsh was a little known poet-professor (and English department chair) at Beloit College in Wisconsin. In 1950 he had cofounded the *Beloit Poetry Journal* and was its guiding spirit, but its success among mainstream poets was not associated with his name. Walsh's efforts were relatively obscure— that is, until Peter Viereck identified him as a member of a small team of terrific "young scholars known as new conservatives." Viereck named Walsh and Hyatt Waggoner "in literature," Clinton Rossiter in history, Will Herberg in social theology, and a few others.[22] Walsh was an ordained Episcopal priest and author of several books of poems, including *The Factual Dark* (1950). He was working on a study of students' attitudes (indeed, he thought, very poor) toward religion, published in 1953 as *Campus Gods on Trial*, and, with Moloney at Marquette, stood nearly alone in this period as a promoter of religious art as having a vital role to play in contemporary culture.[23] Walsh admired and taught his students some modern poetry (Eliot in particular) but bemoaned modernism's easy connection with kitsch. "Avant-garde art," he wrote in *From Utopia to Nightmare*, "teaches its technical tricks to those artists who prepare advertisements in the glossier magazines; eventually the lowly cereal package shows the trace of modernity."[24]

Chad Walsh believed that non-Christian critics and teachers were simply not as competent as Christians to teach T. S. Eliot's poetry and poetics. "The little boy who maneuvers his tin soldiers may talk glibly about strategy and logistics," he wrote by way of explaining this controversial position, "but when he is drafted and sent to a battle front he begins to understand war for the first time." What about the converse? "Cannot the agnostic turn the tables and challenge the Christian to show how he would teach . . . one of Zola's annals of the slums . . . ? Can the Christian imaginatively enter the one-story house of naturalism and guide his students through it as understandingly?" Walsh's answer: "*He can.*" Moreover, "in any work of literature where Christian insight is needed, the Christian has the obvious advantage."[25] Although Walsh's tone was casual and his occasional accommodations to popular taste were knowing,[26] this New Conservative was quietly advocating a hermeneutic crusade.

The extremist's version of this Christian argument—somewhat to the right of Adams and Lorraine and well to the right of Walsh and Alice Hunt Bartlett—held that modernism was satanic and that vigilant believers were required to keep up with modernist trends. In a 1951 editorial for the *Lyric*, Jacob Hauser declared that modernists pray "for universal destruction and Beelzebub."[27] "May it not be," Edward John Dunsany asked in an article criticizing a poet who experimented with alternative orthographies, "that Communists are attacking whatever is spiritual and good . . . ? We know that the Communists are against religion. If they succeed in overthrowing it, and sanity, decency and poetry too, what will be left?"[28] Modernism, Stanton Coblentz felt, empowered any "obscure bard in an avant-garde magazine [to] hurl the beauties of religion into the mire with the swine by referring to 'The snout of God.'"[29]

Coblentz frequently attacked for its impiety the disjunctive verse of the New American Poets—those gathered by Donald Allen in *The New American Poetry, 1945–1960* (1960). The godlessness of experimental poetics inevitably gave way to what Coblentz deemed radical political themes. While for instance the New American Paul Blackburn was no radical pacifist in the ordinary sense, his lines came in for special excoriation: "Emasculate his god and general manager in charge of / blow his earth up." Coblentz despised such discontinuity (the logically dangling preposition, the asyntactical enjambment, and so on) in the service of atheist themes. He attacked Jack Spicer, too, for writing about ugliness in a form that was itself ugly:

God feeds on God. God's goodness is
A black and blinding cannibal with sunny teeth
That only eats itself.

Godlessness and formlessness—for Coblentz, Spicer's verse could as easily be prose, thus lacked authentic poetic form—were qualities closely connected in this repugnant New American poetics.[30]

Peter Viereck was hardly an ally of Christian anticommunists of the sort who joined the powerful American Council of Christian Laymen (ACCL) or the Christian Crusade led by Billy James Hargis, and who supported the campaign launched with *Jesus, a Capitalist* or *Satan Goes to School* or ACCL founder Verne Paul Kaub's *Collectivism Challenges Christianity* (1946). Viereck called himself "a moderate, temperate conservative, in the tradition of [Edmund] Burke, plus the peaceful cosmopolitanism of Metternich."[31] Yet he founded his poetic career on the idea that the opposite of decorum was terror, a binarism particularly attractive to ACCL anticommunists and Christian Crusaders who associated linguistic disruption with atheism.[32] Not even much of a religionist, Viereck nonetheless intended for the connotations of the word "terror," as an antonym of "decorum," to conjure the political histories of revolutions that toppled forms of belief. Yet many of his poems were about contemporary American banalities. Terror/decorum was the insistent binary, notwithstanding Viereck's constant claims to be standing in a new ideological place.

Setting terror against decorum by switching terror's place was perhaps the shrewdest answer ever given to the anti-anticommunist rebuke of McCarthy-ism.[33] William F. Buckley surely learned the technique from Viereck, whose New Conservatism Buckley otherwise distrusted. In *Up from Liberalism*, Buckley merely turned the phrase "Reign of Terror" around, ridiculing liberals who regarded McCarthy as a terrorist simply by ironizing anticommunist First and Fifth Amendment rights violations through facetious overstatement: "We should not forget the bloodchilling descriptions of the dissolution of our free-doms at the hands of . . ." and so on—and by proposing order, faith, and anticommunism as the triad of Christian values in response to the "terror" of liberal-left dogmatism.[34] The dust jacket blurb for Viereck's *Terror and Decorum: Poems, 1940–1948* (1948), made up of saucy sentences and phrases cooked together from his various articles, claimed that the neoconservative formalism of these poems "reject[s] alike the one-sidedness of modern neo-classicism, with its crossword-puzzle pedantries, and the one-sidedness of ro-manticism, with its gush and formlessness."[35]

This rhetoric better befit Viereck's many prose dicta on the matter of mod-ernism and ideology than the poems, which only occasionally espouse decorum and mostly otherwise satirize terror. One such poem, "Don't Look Now but Mary Is Everybody," condemned the high jinks of the free-form secretarial class of postwar America. Mary is bored by her boss's kisses, ready to "quit desk," to flee the job she is in fact lucky to hold, to run off and "eat new freedom up." The poem cannot bring itself to use as part of its satire the free form tried on by the likes of Mary; the stanza conveying her escapade (she steals her employer's yacht for a joyride that ends in "tragedy") concludes with four perfectly orga-nized, proficient end-stopped lines: she knew "by four signs," correctly dis-played, that the "jig was up":

> [She] buoyed the life-preserver down, not up;
> True was the pistol's aim, but in reverse;
> The compass steered, but only toward abysses;
> The little lamb nipped Mary's thighs and roared.[36]

The final words pick up rhymes not only according to a strict stanza form but also by thematic match, so that *reverse* extends the rhyme from the poem's line 4:

"Compass and pistol took she in her *purse*." (We have evidence, thus, that this was a premeditated unrestrained reign of terror!) How can the tragedy of Mary be other than the "terror" of the "new freedom" of her class (and gender)— employable, although she is stupid and trivial, because of the war and various large cultural trends pushing liberation, including High Modern flapperism. The old form had properly restrained her rebellion. Yet it conveyed a violent, sordid conclusion to her tale: Mary had shot herself in the loins. It seems that everyone, even our American Marys, can get into the modern act. As J. Anthony Marcus of the Institute of Foreign Trade put it in a 1949 letter to Hillyer, "Any neurotic, idle woman who does not know what to do with herself goes into the 'business' of writing poetry." And, Marcus urged, "A housecleaning is in order."[37]

The idea that terror was the implication of modern formlessness attracted an antimodernist following far rightward of Viereck, typically, though, with little of the witty magnificence of his satires. *Challenge*, the newsletter of the ACCL, made the point often, as did editorialists at the Catholic *Brooklyn Tablet* and the Paulist *Catholic World*, reports emerging from the News Service of the National Catholic Welfare Conference, and the Catholic bishops who coauthored the "Crusade for Christian Democracy."[38] Such views were also shared by the Christian Freedom Foundation and its president, Howard E. Kershner. And they were available regularly to readers of the reactionary conspiracy sheet *Dr. Berry's One-World Church Report* and to parishioners within earshot of the sermons and speeches of Francis Cardinal Spellman of New York, for whom youths attracted to chaos were vulnerable to "Satan-inspired Communist . . . anti-Christian minds drenched and drugged in the devil's cauldron of hatreds and iniquities."[39] More cerebral traditionalists such as Richard Weaver and Russell Kirk supported Christian rhetorical order against what Weaver called "the New Deal or totalitarian liberal point of view"[40] as well. Kirk later remembered Weaver as having "reminded the academy that the Word still may be either holy or diabolic."[41] In Weaver's *Ideas Have Consequences*, the act of defending property rights against invasion by the socialist state entailed the same rhetorical activity as recovering respect for the symbolic value of words— for instance, by rejecting jazz, which Weaver called "a music to go with empiricism." Too, such antistatist resistance and antimodernism involved the same act of "recapturing *pietas* toward nature."[42] *Ideas Have Consequences* is a full argument against "modernism"—Weaver frequently used the term—as the direct expression of nominalism, which in turn had arisen after the abandonment of belief.[43] Cold War antinominalism—opposition to the idea that nothing has a definite nature other than that which we ascribe to it through our invention of words—became, after Weaver, a main way in which conservative anticommunists expressed their enmity with almost greater theoretical coherence against modernist verse than against communist theory. (After all, some communists, when initially reading objectivist poems in the early 1930s, had launched charges of nominalism against the poets, preferring what was in essence a brand of idealist historicism.[44] Language-centered nominalism often better characterized modern writing than did American communism, especially when objectivists, Reznikoff and Zukofsky in particular, ventured toward postmodernism.)

Viereck returned to the topic of form, belief, and language as a technique of indefiniteness in *The Unadjusted Man*, and here he sounded a good deal like Weaver as the reactionary theorist of rhetoric. In a "note on values" titled "The Inarticulate Roots of Free Values" and again in a mini-chapter on "Drive-in Churches: The So-Called Return to Values," Viereck, it seems, intentionally rambled. At such moments, in his poetry and his critical prose, he wanted readers to believe he blurred, even confused and confounded, lefts and rights; in doing so, he managed, as skillfully as anyone of the era, an anticommunism founded on antimodernism. By the end of "Drive-in Churches," decorum signifies a willingness to come out honestly in favor of "debat[ing] ideas . . . with gusto," while terror is "a bland savoring of technique." Of course, the distinction was connected to the "external threat to academic freedom"—McCarthyism—denounced by the academic and literary liberal-left. But as Viereck insisted, what "that mood fears is not merely the anti-intellectual demagogue"—McCarthy, Hoover, Dondero—"but the ridicule of fellow pro-intellectuals." The intellectuals write poems in which anything goes, yet actually they have made such a "free form" wholly the "bland savoring of technique." To the charge made a few years later by Susan Sontag that this sort of critique (and its attendant "return" to religious faith) is "piety without content," many antimodernists would have said that, sadly, modernism's aesthetic terror followed from Nietzsche's dysangel, heralding God's death. Sontag, writing in 1961, noticed that intellectuals' renewed interest in religion in the 1950s *coincided with the attack on leftist politics*. The seriousness with which 1950s intellectuals took religious decorum came "in the backwash of broken radical political enthusiasm." "Religious fellow-traveling" in the 1950s was the Cold War version of intellectual affiliation with revolutionary politics in the 1930s, one main difference being that indecorousness now suggested a gendered radicalism: in this climate, Sontag wrote, "to be anti-religious (like being a feminist) was old hat."[45]

How terrifying, then, Viereck was implying, that Mary is Everywoman. "Anything goes" is not creative freedom but terror. Such false liberalism emboldened the secretary to steal her employer's yacht, an act that the public might even hail as liberated. Freedom, defined as a style of terror, became not spontaneity but a deceptively "elegant knowingness": "The preference is for ideas, poems, creeds made impregnable against ridicule" by such freewheeling smugness. Typical of his antiradical sleight of hand, Viereck managed to equate modernist formlessness with the facile "return to . . . spiritual values" in the 1950s—with the easy, "modern," anything-goes approach of Norman Vincent Peale's *Power of Positive Thinking* (1952). "Normally, one would expect the universities to be a gadfly-corrective against this folksy-wholesome spirit." In part, campus apathy, a lack of resistance against Peale's easiness or against the fad of drive-in churches, resulted from the dominance within the academy itself of the preference for poems of mere elegant knowingness.[46]

Viereck's *Strike through the Mask!*, subtitled "New Lyrical Poems" (1950), was meant to provide example after decorous example of verse resisting such elegant knowingness. Several depend on a complicated, negative relationship with modernism. The "Love Song of J. Smith," a domestic poem about the second coming, absolutely orders itself—one almost wants to say, *tidies* itself— in preparation: it consists of two quatrains (rhymed abab) alternating an ostentatiously "simple" five-line stanza rhymed abaab, where b is the single monosyllable "comes."

> Not you will recognize
> Him when again he comes.
> Only our loveless eyes
> Will love without surprise
> Him when he comes.[47]

By its first line, directing the children to "wait" in orderly fashion, the poem presupposes the "love" of Mr. Smith to be apparently that of sweet Christian decorum—and of a kind of accepting maturity. No passion attending *this* mid-century second coming. The voice of the "Love Song of J. Smith," such as it is, bespeaks the Prufrockian burgher of the 1950s. Weakly he gathers the children to wait for a "great hour" of a day, where Eliot's anxious modern sense of waiting (wandering, aimless and anxious, anticipating failure or nothing, "Till human voices wake us") is finally "resolved."

It is as if the proper answer to T. S. Eliot by 1950 was, *It would have been worth it, after all.* Form finally locates belief. The poem is a restoration of Eliotic modernism of sorts. Rhymes, for one, are no longer ironic. In *Strike through the Mask!*, "The Dignity of Lyricism," and elsewhere, Viereck's project sought to restore the relationship between belief and form by way of decorum's fight against terror. The terrorists described in "The Dignity of Lyricism" were the liberal-left "nonconforming avant-garde aesthetes": modernists as "machine-armies" who "have made compulsory official uniforms for poetry of even the most threadbare and discarded garments of Eliot and his generation."[48]

So despite every denial, Viereck's "defense" of modernism is essentially anti-modernist because it is founded on anticommunism: in poems and prose, Viereck urged on "the great conservative rebellion" against innovative form as part of the terroristic tactics of avant-gardists. "A Masque of Tears" (collected in *Strike through the Mask!*) tells of the ghostly return of the beheaded. They have been asked to howl their old outmoded art, and do so—and Viereck almost *likes* the result because it is *not* the formalism of the terror that decapitated such art. In "The Dignity of Lyricism," Viereck dares to steal Make It New for the conservative resistance to totalitarian experimentalism: "The great conservative rebellion against the formless, radical, materialist thirties will not be complete if it has nothing more profound to conserve than—the rhyme scheme of *terza rima*. What a mockery! As if Dante's *terza rima* pattern were something in a vacuum! —instead of the mere shadow thrown by a vaster spiritual pattern for man."[49]

Of course, conservatism against formlessness must itself seek new forms. At times Viereck was among the very few anticommunist opponents of formally innovative poetry who hinted at alternative stanzaic and metrical forms of belief. "Prospero Boasts Too Soon of His New Freedom" shows such an effort. Here Prospero, a member of the modernist cult of the imagination somewhat in the manner of Wallace Stevens, comes back to the language of earth, as it were: "Now clouds are merely clouds and eyeless; / All winds are prose and unaware." He had claimed his "new freedom" too soon.[50] The poem in its way poses the question asked in "The Dignity of Lyricism": How can the lyric make its rejoinder to godless formlessness? Beware the new freedom, for the very survival of Shakespearean lyricism is at stake. When the claimant for its proper inheritance contends, what is at stake is political. The conservative must not vie with terza rima. So he asks, "What song is worth my safe new peace?" "Prospero Boasts Too Soon of His New Freedom" offers *itself*, reasonably, as the apt New Conservative song. Its long lines, slant rhymes, the laxness of the diction (one line is "Too long I've tracked each tune down that brushed me with light wing"—rough and almost interminable iambics, rare for Viereck), suggest that the poet knows what the song of the new peace should be: conservative, formally (as well as thematically) standing against the avant-garde, yet hardly a throwback to old conventions.

"A Masque of Tears," however, is quite something else—and more typical of Viereck's lyric counterattacks against modernist terror. The old czar's lyric, although pounded out on an "old wild yataghan," is supposedly so sorrowful that readers might await the Russian counter-revolution on aesthetic grounds alone. The little tale—replete with toasts "To Terrible Ivan!"—imagines the return of the decapitated czarist bards once "every hundred years," when "a yawning earthquake re-appears / Across the land of Rus": an aesthetic natural disaster sweeping away the Soviets. This event, a formalist counterreformation, with its refreshing "pompous airs," "Gangle[s] the shaggy ghosts of tsars / Like bears from lairs." The poem is anticommunist through its satire, and so perhaps does not warrant a strong political reading. Yet taken together with Viereck's call for conservative forms more inventive than terza rima in a vacuum, the poem can hardly be said in this respect to advance the New Conservative cause. While four straight rhymes of the *eers* sound would seem not to beggar belief in structure's decorum, the disproportionate effort to find three subsequent rhymes for the word *Turkoman*—a real challenge to the non-Russian sonorist—does make "A Masque of Tears" an anticommunist project rather of the sort of conservative retaliation against formlessness Viereck deemed a "mockery" of the cause:

> At midnight every hundred years
> A yawning earthquake re-appears
> Across the land of Rus and leers
>   With grin so fierce. . . .
>
> "Hurrah," they cry, "a Turkoman:
> A khan, a khan from Astrakhan!
> Pull out your old wild yataghan,
>   Pound us a Tartar tune."[51]

The wild song within the poem, not by any means the poem itself, is of course barbaric—not the conservative's sort of aesthetic—but when *contained* thus it satisfies a need for a New Conservative revolt.

Singing praise for rude lyric essentialism, contained by strict meter and rhyme, was in fact a staple of the antiexperimentalist activists. It is not that the New American Poet would write about the Soviet Union (that enemy state receives no mention in the early writing of John Ashbery, for instance). But if one did, as Frank O'Hara did in "A Poem about Russia" (1951), the attractive masculine roughness of "Rus" is not to be satirized within a controlled stanza but is enabled by an exciting, impetuous loosening of syntax:

> the beating
> dance and all music's
> most passionate blood

the wind of your steppes
swept my cluttered heart . . .
And my hatreds were your
rich fire of longing.

If O'Hara's poem can be said to resist the logic of anticommunism, it is because it derives from the image of "the last mystic land" the sort of sexy, fierce breathlessness that in itself was the hallmark of O'Hara's and his New York School colleagues' nose-thumbing at Cold War conformity.

Among anticommunist poets, Viereck was merely the best at containing atavism by formal strictness, but many others tried their hand at it. The Anglo–South African poet Roy Campbell and the ex-communist E. Merrill Root were two who occasionally mastered a similar strategy. Root dubbed communist poets "damned thin cerebralists" who produced a cultural "barrenness, a vacuum that should be a living soul," and decided that the "simple strong Mud Folk are far, far better"[52]—and somehow he managed to drag said Mud Folk into some of his traditional sonnets. While Campbell's "jokes are sledge-hammer, his rhythms rocking-horse," and while he tended in poems to eliminate his enemies by "tell[ing] them . . . they are stupid and homosexual and smell bad," he was at least successful in producing precisely the kind of writing that "was very popular from 1820 to 1840." (This was Randall Jarrell's sour view of Campbell, and it earned him the wrath of editor-publisher Henry Regnery.)[53] But for every Campbell or Root there were a dozen plain failures. In "Rhythm Is in Disgrace" (1949), one such anticommunist antimodernist mockingly imagined a dystopia: the poetic scene after meter and rhyme had been drummed out by the modernist enemy. "Chanting leaves [would] be still," spring would no longer come, and so forth:

The winter blast must end her cycled blowing,
Rocking the Andes and the Arctic shore;
And stop, you ancient dancing in my mind—
Barbaric cadence for the deaf and blind![54]

What a difference between this quatrain and the final lines of O'Hara's "A Poem about Russia," where unconcern for Cold War topicality leads to hurried strings of nouns and exclamations:

Oh now I cry you black
jellied rivers heaps of
startling lovers tundras
of quick wolves! oh tears[55]

The author of "Rhythm Is in Disgrace" was Cullen Jones, our Nevadan and former U.S. Army colonel. Jones settled down after the war as a boys' school headmaster, but soon he was out stumping against " 'modern' theories" that had made a "nuttery for nuts."[56] The poem is typical of those published in the *Lyric*, cautiously rhymed and rhythmic yet conveying apocalyptic scenes of modernist formal destruction. The antimodernist culture war compelled Jones into poems about poetry—modeling the traditional while keenly conscious of its repudiation of modern self-consciousness.[57] In one sense, Viereck's poems—from this special vantage, not much different from those of Jones and any number of other beset lyricists forced into metapoetry—offer a glimpse of the conservative-reactionary alliance as an aesthetic matter: in the decorous New Right lay the wilder aspects of the Old. "With a whoop and a roar," Arthur Schlesinger Jr. observed, Viereck had "materialized out of the wilderness . . . rearing high on a charger while he fires his six-shooter vigorously in all directions."[58]

Viereck admired regional writers from the West and the Southwest, such as Thomas Hornsby Ferril (1896–1988), the publicity director for the Great Western Sugar Company whose prolific Rocky Mountain verse Viereck hailed as inspiring a bold "new creativity" in music, art, and letters. Viereck appreciated conventional tough-guy poets such as Ferril because they cockily favored poetic manifest destiny and repudiated the dandified, "overadjusted spirit irreconcilably inimical to the creative imagination."[59] He hated the "artiness" of "introverted professional wincers" and argued that "there are worse cultural alternatives than back-slapping philistinism; better a real huckster than a fake sensitive-plant."[60] The New Conservative understood the value of the West's predilection for the aspect of lyricism Viereck praised in *The Unadjusted Man*: "the unformulated."[61] This particular antimodernist spirit was well captured in issues of the magazine *Westward*, which was edited by Stanton Coblentz's friend and League for Sanity in Poetry activist[62] Florence Keene, whose remarkable unpublished papers have found their way to the Huntington Library. The strictly traditional poems of conventional sentiment that Keene and her guest editors published ("If the Dawn gives no promise / Of loveliness to see, / Be patient, heart, / Speed not the day toward eternity") were meant to befit this "entirely independent" poetry journal flying on its masthead a brash Americanist motto: "Westward the course of empire takes its way."[63]

But Viereck's "Big Crash Out West" stands apart from Ferril and Keene's *Westward* in this respect, a consciously *formulated* response to the New Conservative urge to join the ranks of the roughly passionate:

They call streets "boulevards" and build them huge
Where grandpa's oxcart could not budge;

Here's room for elbows, land of the brave fourth gears.
Speed is the bridge for spanning loneliness.
Until.
    This is the western way to die.
And when the car stops burning, thar he'll lie,
Surrounded by the brothers of his lodge.
O Crash for whom their boredoms cry,
Is there—in your sensuous instant—time to guess
At what's unspent, unsensuous years
Never hot with doubt nor faith nor reverence for tears?[64]

In fact, the prospective alliance of new (East Coast) conservative and reaction-ary Old Westerner—keeping these two together was the single major concern of the Republican Party in the 1950s and early 1960s—was spoiled here. The con-servative discovers that even "out west" modern forms have taken over. The roads are not big in the traditional sense but merely instances of modern excess—four-lane highways. It is not the land of big hearts and boldness but of fast new cars, not of tough patriotism but of outsized adjustment: in one of Viereck's smartest poetic phrases, the "land of the brave fourth gears." The American West has lost the tradition of being "hot with doubt," of "faith" and "reverence for tears." "Big Crash Out West" is newspaper diction. Lodge broth-ers' response to the death of a compadre by car wreck is sensationalistic in that dull, salacious sense, "a crash for whom their boredoms cry." What disappoints the speaker of this poem is the failure of Wild West nerve, just what made the speaker of "A Masque of Tears" yearn for the Russian czars.[65] Elsewhere, Viereck lamented the end of westering as a male coming-of-age tradition that validates a real cultural alternative for American intellectuals. "The motto of the urbaner graduates from the English departments of Harvard, Yale, Princeton," he wrote, "is no longer 'go west, young man' but 'go to the Little Magazines.' "[66] In the poem, this abdication becomes nothing less than a defeat of faith, induced by the facile attractions of modernism. The speaker wants his American to strike through the modern mask. In the epigraph to "Big Crash," he stresses his disappointment with the demise of Old West visionary passion. It consists of a banal quotation taken from an ophthalmologist's handbook: "Consult your physician at once if you see haloes."[67]

Viereck's New Conservatism obsessed over the alleged loss of vision evident in the twin ascendancies of liberalism and modernism. On this point, the otherwise different celebrations of unadjustedness by Viereck and Weaver and other conservatives coincided. "Middle-of-the-roadism is not perspicacious,"

Weaver wrote in his pamphlet against linguistic relativism. "It doesn't see with its own eyes. It tries to get along by borrowing a little from those who have done the hard work of seeing the principles through."[68] For Viereck, adjustment was a form of blindness. Imagination was the "bringing together of vision and beauty."[69] For Coblentz, the opposite of vision was cult and ideology. The poet was "the man of universal vision," prophetic and Arthurian in mode, who "restores us to fundamental emotions." "Poetry is vision, . . . not the stringing together of words."[70] In expressing alarm at a modern poet who is "the perpetrator of this horrible conglomeration," a *Wings* editorial called for verse that conveyed "a vision for the totality of things."[71] The Catholic philosopher Frederick Wilhelmsen, favoring a prerationalist traditional society on the model of medievalism prior to the day when "poetry . . . went its [own] way and sought a lonely destiny," argued in 1955 that "modernity is man's disenchantment of the real" while conservatives, conversely, "have nothing to offer the world but our vision." Wilhelmsen hated Mallarmé's construction of a poetics seeking to "divorce itself . . . from natural being." Modernism was that which sought to supplant the world of created things; vision, modernism's antithesis, was natural.[72] E. Merrill Root arrived at his rightward tipping point when he discovered that "a fundamental thing in poetry is vision (not of the eyes alone)."[73]

A section of Viereck's poems under the heading "Americana" begins with several epigraphs. The last of the three, again suggesting a new conservative's admiration of the passions of the extremist figure, quotes Melville's Ahab: "Strike through the mask!" Viereck means this to be about vision, seeing deeply. The second epigraph quotes a book by ophthalmologist Dr. Sidney A. Fox, *Your Eyes* (1944), and suggests what is wrong with the modern rejection of vision, another call for the "Unadjusted Man" as a hero in an age of compromise and accommodation. It conveys, from the other side of the argument about liberalism in the Cold War, just the sort of quietism or somnambulism Peter Biskind meant to convey in the subtitle of his book-length survey of Cold War ideology in film, "How Hollywood Taught Us to Stop Worrying and Love the Fifties." The following is the opthalmopathogenic warning Viereck satirizes from the right: "Glaucoma is more likely to occur in the excitable, highstrung individual than in the calm, non-worrying type. Avoid worry or disappointment. At the movies, choose subjects that are not depressing."[74]

Here Viereck skillfully confuses (1) the rise of anything-goes incomprehensibility, (2) liberal uplift and the failure of faith as a informing structure, (3) modernism's dissociation of static image from bardic or Christian *vision*—the wrong legacy (Viereck would contend) of Ezra Pound and T. S. Eliot, and, now, (4) the medicalization or bourgeois literalization of the culture of adjustment.

"Well, offhand, I'd say it was something by Ezra Pound." Cartoon appearing in the *Saturday Review of Literature*, August 6, 1949. © 1949 by Lloyd.

In conflating these tendencies for the purposes of promoting a neoclassical formalist strain in modern poetics, Viereck befits the larger pattern of anticommunist antimodernism. The campaign against experimentalist illegibility used satire most effectively not when depicting the familiar befuddled museumgoer standing before a modernist abstraction. Ben Lucien Burman's diatribe against Gertrude Stein reached its peak not when he quoted "difficult" lines from her poetry but when he likened Steinian poetics to disease, infection—something *really* dangerously wrong. The twentieth-century metaphorization of cancer as the dreadful work of agents of impersonality, coming from the "non-self," enabled right-wing fantasies of a society ridded of cancer to stand in the stead of the usual diatribe against the cultural invasions of communism. The same John Birch Society that produced a forty-five-minute film, *World without Cancer*,[75] strenuously contended against liberalism as a failure of vision. The right was not alone in metaphorizing vision, which is the way in which, as Susan Sontag has shown, the center figured cancer. The *Saturday Review of Literature* cartoon mocking the *Pisan Cantos* depicted a middle-aged man in a suit, sitting in the patient's chair at his ophthalmologist's office, trying in vain to read the random letters on the eye chart. The humor plays off the simple observation that eye charts, requiring an unpredictable, nonalphabetical array if vision can be objectively measured, resemble radically lineated modernist verse—to be sure, something more like cummings or Duchamp or Stein in the popular imagination than Pound. And that is the point of referring to Pound. The issue of vision was a vital matter of contemporary cultural politics. When the patient, realizing the fact of his worsening vision, tells the doctor, "Well, offhand, I'd say it was something by Ezra Pound," the alleged "anything goes" cult of modern art—in which *anyone* can be an artist, in which the patient is in *any* case seeing the eye chart correctly—becomes a matter for the "actual" health of the body politic.[76] For anticommunist proponents of "vision," such misreading produced greater terror than analogies to invading aliens. This was about who would see nonsense for what it actually—objectively—was.

Hillyer says [the iamb] can't be varied; but that's because *he* can't think of any way to vary it.—William Carlos Williams

Save man's capacity to *be* when words are stale . . . not done.
—Kenneth Patchen, "We Hold These Truths to Be Self-Evident," 1936

The Good Grammar of Citizenship

Peter Viereck's approach to the Ezra Pound controversy, we have seen, further politicized an already overwrought situation. And yet Viereck really did claim to see in those taking sides on Poundian poetics an ideological swap and merge of positions, literary lefts become indistinguishable from rights. This, he implied, nullified the old partisan approaches to the matter of a poem's content, and thus he could claim to focus on what he took to be the politically *neutral* question of form.

With such a postpolitical approach in mind, Viereck returned to the Pound problem in 1953, after the commotion of 1949–50 had abated. In this supposedly calmer climate, he observed that "the 'proletarian verse' Marxists of the 1930's were right about Pound for the wrong reasons" (overly narrow politics, indifference to the dignity of lyricism as a self-justified genre). Conversely, "the New Critic formalists are wrong about Pound for the right reasons (at least they are concerned with the dignity of poetry, not with degrading it to soap-box propaganda)." Viereck now contended that readers and critics were supposed to argue about Pound on the "level of poetry," not on the "political economic level" of the "coercive statist[s] of the far left," who are "unimpressive as friends of liberty," and the "free, ethical, nonstatist" formalists. These political positions—the leftists who were wrongly right and the formalists who were rightly wrong—canceled each other, "each group point[ing] out unerringly the fatal one-sidedness of the other." Viereck stood somewhere else altogether. Where? With lyricism, the formalistic defense of which was not political yet was politically efficacious.[1]

In the end, conservatives' problem with the Poundians could be summed in a phrase: "the canto-technique." This term stood in variously for collage-based poetics, the aesthetic of discontinuity, and modernist verse historicizing, but at base it meant repudiation of the iamb as fundamental expressive element. Once again, something in modernism had gone terribly wrong at the level of the line. The New Conservative could correctly admire Pound's "exhilarating lyrical middle period," that enabling moment after vorticism and before the *Cantos*. But the canto technique was being justified by the "superficially plausible" yet finally fallacious assumption that iambic pentameter, "the traditional norm of our poetry," was outmoded, inappropriate to modern times, thus disabling the poet trying for new effects. The "canto-technique" was a "non-Euclidian" geometry being applied to poetics. "The anti-traditional assumption ends by justifying as 'modern'" the ultimate form of disruption: the "free-wheeling 'anything goes' chaos in poetry."[2] What could be done?

Willing at the end of the day to negotiate on the question, Viereck finally felt that something indeed could be done. The major midcentury poets to whom he looked—let us say, to take one representative example, Theodore Roethke (as opposed to, for instance, Charles Olson)—could be counted on to lead the way out. *They*, the moderately modern Roethkes, neither wrongly right nor rightly wrong, were the best refutation not just of the extremist canto technique as a matter of poetics but the cult of antilyrical liberalism brought on by the 1930s liberal left. Charles Olson might well have been among those to chafe under Viereck's contention that "Whitman, Williams, Pound, and Ginsberg" measure themselves only against the pure positive nature—a physical essence[3]—of iambic pentameter when trying alternative rhythmic effects. In later years, hearing the avant-garde opposition contend that "the iamb's not a normal measure of speech," Viereck wittily invited his antagonist to submit that retort to scansion.[4] Or, as Robert Hillyer put it, "Let our iambs be of granite, and we need not heed the pulpwood words of our bedevilers." Here Hillyer was advising Leigh Hanes of the *Lyric* on how best to stave off the vers librists: traditional form was the best defense against modernist enemies. The best antimodernist offense was a strong iambic defense. So get on with your traditional poem, Hillyer urged Hanes, "and forget the foes of poetry. It is better to make our turrets impregnable than to make sorties on unprofitably territory."[5]

Viereck's interesting case demands that attention finally be paid to the specific Cold War politics of poetic form, which is the emphasis I bring to this concluding chapter, and such emphasis makes possible a few final distinctions between and among antimodernists. While for absolute traditionalists such as Hillyer, Merrill Root, Richard Weaver, and S. B. Lush—it was Lush who deemed modern poetry "prose tortured into clever stops," a quality that led to "blank verse that leads us to blank walls"[6]—an ethics of rhetoric might only be restored through the iambs of order, for Viereck as well as Louise Bogan, though the latter two poets angrily disputed indictments against traditional meter and other lyric norms, there was, through moderation, a poetic way out, a midcentury middle ground, indeed a responsive New Conservatism that would become the rightful inheritor of modernism.

Bogan really did assume that after "more than quarter century of 'experiment'"—she put the word in scare quotes—formal innovation was dead or at least dying. The formalists who superseded experimentalism (she praised them) were criticized by Marxists for dwelling in the "ivory tower," hiding behind "their limited and old-fashioned reproach." Yet in these formalists, she felt, such as Robert Penn Warren and Robert Fitzgerald, was the last hope of modern poetry. They knew to avoid both the "confusions" of surrealism and "the bigotries" of 1930s-style leftist polemic, yet in reaction they never engaged in "slick rhythm" and were really quite thoroughly *modern*. In Warren's case, we get a "clever approximation of 'folk,'" a refreshingly real topic for the modern American poem, combined with the critical method of the "late Eliot."[7] Such was Bogan's view of the situation.

To the extremist, as we have seen, no prosodic, grammatical, or linguistic compromise with modernity would do, and this prohibition extended to poetic genre. Stanton Coblentz, we know, tirelessly patrolled the borders separating poetry from "non-poetry." The separation was simple and absolutely enforceable. "No one will contend that if a stranger is found at midnight stuffing his pockets from a bank vault, the charge of burglary will not apply," so why would readers of poetry ever say, "Poetry is what I see as poetry!" Why would they espouse that "rabid creed?" Writing that is "non-poetry" is as identifiable as the thief caught red-handed. "A house . . . is not a poem, nor is a palm-tree." Nor is . . . any of the verse displayed in the popular "This Is NOT Poetry" section in *Wings*, which included passages from William Carlos Williams's *The Desert Music*, from e. e. cummings, Kenneth Fearing, Kenneth Patchen, and from poems published in George Leite's anarchist little Berkeley magazine, *Circle*.[8]

As for rhyme, Hillyer announced to members of the Poetry Society of America that the modernist imposition of conformity—that crude force with effects like that of the Kremlin—had led to "bullying" young poets into "cultivat[ing] the slightly off rhyme." Hillyer's statement was meant as a warning for decent poets, loyal to the language, to keep ears peeled for the suspicious slantings of sedition.[9]

And as for meter, Richard Weaver hated jazz because syncopation enacted a radical "restlessness," an attempt at realization that dangerously bypassed the "going through the aesthetic ritual" from a proper start proportionately through to a full finish. It was the most basic dissolution of form. "By dissolving forms, [modern life] has left man free to move without reference, expressing dithyrambically whatever surges up from below."[10] The social consequences of "the modern style," with its refusal to "mark . . . beginnings and endings," were significant: "In place of a meaningless continuum, rhythm provides intelligibility. . . . Rhythm is thus a way of breaking up nihilistic monotony and of proclaiming that there is a world of value."[11] From *Ideas Have Consequences* (1948) to *The Ethics of Rhetoric* (1953) to "Reflections of Modernity" (1961) and ultimately in *Visions of Order* (1964), Weaver far more comprehensively than Hillyer contended that rhetorical modernity had encouraged the acceptance of any "expression"—that uses of language were being shaped by "the whole trend of our commercial, political, and social world" that commits "the fallacy of presentism" and assumes out of a pious modern love of newness the primacy of young people. Functionalism, activism, the bending of grammatical rules, the whole rhetoric of advertising, "the cult of political liberalism" (or "liberal-collectivist theory"), and "the impulse to standardize everything in the present" —all follow from the one ur-error of rhetorical compromise.[12] Fragmentation, the main quality of modern life, along with "obsession," was a "flight toward periphery," to dangerous extremes where general knowledge was *not* power and where "the modern knower . . . fixed tenaciously upon certain details."[13] Conversely, canons of grammar were the fundamental laws of good citizenship.

Facing the challenge of the canto technique, Viereck—a compromiser, compared with Weaver—was prepared to find in new kinds of contemporary poetry an adjusted lineage for the modern poetic line. In typically overstated terms, he approached the whole problem of the Bollingen controversy as a matter of survival: "For it happens to be a fact," he wrote, "that the day can still be saved for the still untapped resources of iambic pentameter; new magical effects can still be achieved by alternating the alleged monotony of iambics with the kind of conversational *spondee* measures found in Roethke and Hart Crane. . . . The quick, flexible nervous rhythms . . . of Yeats[ian] . . . iambic tetrameter . . . proves [also] that variations with the iambic tradition can still achieve more excitement and originality than Pound's ingenious search for originality outside that tradition. In short, literary evolution and not revolution is the way out of the present impasse."[14]

Such tempered passages present Viereck more as a conservative ally of the liberal proponents of a modernism made tenable for the 1950s than a friend of the extremist detractors Huntington, Hanes, Murton, Burman, Hillyer, Weaver, Welford Inge, and others. Yet, as Viereck shrewdly recognized, "such is the company one inevitably gets oneself into." So Viereck conceded when asked to speak about the consequences of resisting modernism—in spite of his "aggressive . . . determin[ation] to safeguard my complete independence and integrity from all schools."[15] (If this was bait, then Hillyer took it, believing from 1949 on, as he wrote to Hanes, that "it was wonderful luck to have Peter Viereck—so admired by the young—come out on our side.")[16] Viereck did ponder what would happen when his argument about the canto technique was taken up by the antimodernist far right. He claimed to be unbothered by the prospect of being misunderstood as an ally of old conservatives—a danger, but not, he felt, an "ineluctable danger." "Anti-Communism can or cannot play into reactionary hands," he added. Viereck meant moderate anticommunism as an example, but as we have seen, "the reactionary fate" (his phrase) of antimodernism was the same. In "Pure Poetry and Impure Politics," he took pains finally to point out that he was not regretting modernists' doubts about traditional poetics to praise the poetics of Edgar Guest or Austin Dobson as an alternative. He did so to commend "the most sensuous lyricism" of "Yeats, Hart Crane, Theodore Roethke, Richard Wilbur, and Louis Simpson."[17]

But unlike Weaver, whose reactionary views were authentic, the figure of the antimodernist calling for the poetics of Eddie Guest was a straw man. For not even Welford Inge in "Poetry of Fear"—nor Henry Regnery, who published editions of Guest—wrote or said anything like that.[18] And anyway, as Viereck wrote in The Unadjusted Man, "those who begin by being ashamed to like the literature of Edgar Guest will end up by being ashamed to like the Republican politics of the old inelegant hucksterism." It was not that Viereck admired popular middlebrow poets but that he distrusted more acutely those "Protestant bourgeois self-haters" who dreamed of dying young "with open collars in Rome" or "at least sip[ping] an aperitif there." He knew that by "criticizing the stereotyping of liberalism and avant-garde," he would seem "guilty of that ultimate crime: playing into Wrong Hands."[19]

Peter Viereck's impatience with ideological challenges to poetic syntax and linguistic convention did for a fact fall into reactionary hands. His analyses of the faithlessness of modern formal disorder and of the "'anything goes' chaos in poetry" were exactly those that irked and stirred Weaver and Hanes as well as other conservatives, such as Michael Moloney, Joseph M. Lalley, and Donald Davidson.

Leigh Hanes, for one, expended great energy denouncing non- and antinarrative poems, writing that seeks to "get rid . . . of the time chronology that [as modernists alleged] falsifies the experience of seeing several things at once." Narrative cause and effect was natural. "Nature," Hanes wrote in "Poetic Doodles" (1946), "has never required [poets] to destroy the continuity of time and see all, be all, and write all, all at the same moment."[20]

And Donald Davidson (1893–1968), Richard Weaver's teacher at Vanderbilt, observed in the modernist use of the "conjunction *and*" a "latent" rhetorical betrayal that had dire political consequences. It was but one step from the expression of a pet peeve against parataxis to the conservative's domino theory of communist succession. When Hemingway's writing connected an A to a B— "I told it to a doctor *and* he said I was lying";[21] "He was an old man who fished alone *and* he had gone eighty-four days now without taking a fish";[22] and (in a passage about wailing victims of genocide) "We'd run the searchlight up and down over them two or three times *and* they stopped it"[23]—the modern writer was failing to create a meaningful relationship between the conjoined elements "other than a simple coupling." Davidson continued,

> "A" and "B" are there. The inescapable act of vision tells him so. But Hemingway rarely ventures, through grammar and rhetoric, to go beyond saying that "A" and "B" are just there, together. Similarly, our diplomats and Far Eastern Experts long had a habit of declaring that there was a Red Russia *and* a Red China, with the tender implication that such a conjunction was entirely innocent. [Liberal] [p]olitical theorists for nearly two centuries have coordinated liberty *and* equality, but have too often failed to tell us, as history clearly shows, that liberty and equality are much more hostile than they are mutually friendly.

Rejecting historical sequence and the grammatical hierarchical imperative, parataxis was bad. The paratactic, ironic "and" was just as bad—perhaps worse, for it pretended narrative order.

Davidson saw a treacherous political irresponsibility in the act of eschewing relations of cause and effect while the related elements were left to stand in unordered, unsubordinated lists.[24] Although cause and effect is a "less exalted" rhetorical mode, added Weaver, "we all have to use it because we are historical men."[25] Coblentz was similarly incensed when he ran across verse hailed as "advanced" where the syntactical connections had been removed (even the emptied-out "and"), such as these lines, which Coblentz loved to hate, from Kenneth Patchen, "the well-known modernist" who had once also dared to publish a Leninist poem called "Lenin" (1932) in the *Rebel Poet*:[26]

Behind this familiar scenery of words
The fear-stained placenta
The mulchronated cowlknife
The enchorial puddercap
The dissentient conglutination
The dagglesome crassitude
The spool-mouthed gaddement
The ruck-souled concinnity

Never mind that the passage can be said to cohere through the variation of otherwise closely matched grammatical pairs (*article/{compound-}adjective/noun*) and that it is more strictly "grammatical," despite its neologisms, than some of the vers libre nature lyrics Coblentz lavishly praised in his anthologies. Patchen's poem "And a Man Went Out Alone" (1949)[27] seems to me just successful enough to obviate any need to spell out what is fairly obvious to the reader—that in writing this verse the poet was collecting fragments to strive for a sense of sanity and to form, against the backdrop of insanity, a patterned "scenery of words." Yet for Coblentz, this Patchen was of the same disruptive ilk as the author of the "These fragments I have shored against my ruins" passage from *The Waste Land*, where the modernist evinced a culture-denying "crassitude" no less assailable under the conservative's strictures ("Why then Ile fit you. Hieronymo's mad againe / Datta. Dayadhvam. Damyata").[28] Responding angrily to a mode in which José García Villa (whose verse an editor of *Poetry* called the work of "a pure lunatic")[29] would insert a comma after every word, Donald Jenks published "Tell Me No More" in the *Humanist*, bearing the opening line, "Tell me no more the covert significance of this man's commas." Jenks's poem is about the connection between the fragmentation of poetic language, the development in poetics of a focus on "parts," and the modernist attack on humanism. Jenks's speaker realizes here that his own "divergence" from the new poetics

> has now reached such a pitch
> that I have dared to peep at the humanist heresy
> that life has scope for many arts and skills,
> the sum of which is greater than any part.[30]

For Davidson, Coblentz, and Weaver alike, tradition blessed grammar with the means by which all elements in a piece of writing were not created equal. "The forces of modernism conspire to extinguish" the faithful idealism expressed through tradition and eloquent wisdom that characterized the American South prior to 1861—so Weaver contended in 1948—bringing on "fragmentation" that "leads directly to an obsession with isolated parts."[31] The appeal of antebellum rhetoric for southern apologists Weaver and Davidson was its rejection of the illegible list and the modern nonconjunctive "and." Rather than accepting as true the A and B conjoined, the open-form "and" favored by Hemingway and Stein merely confirmed the stark choices *between* the two, which reminded Davidson of the conservative's noble preference for liberty over equality. This radical-democratic parataxis eventually must give way to civilized subordination, the ranked and ordered list, the proper hierarchical place of rhetoric as a decent public force. Modernist grammar, "the mark of timid evasiveness" that led to the acceptance of successive communist regimes— *first* Russia, *then* China, *then* . . . ?—must finally cause "the prevalence of liberty" and "may very well require some subordination of equality." Once modernist parataxis staved off subordination, anything and everything could be thrown together, and that was the beginning of the end.[32] Here avant-garde writing was such a strong conductor for the doubts and fears of the American conservative because it represented a style that refused to subordinate what the conservative felt were inherently unequal elements.

An editorial in *Pinnacle*, the magazine of the League for Sanity in Poetry, listed "the ordinances of the new authoritarianism": "Discard clarity! Discard music! *Discard consecutiveness of thought* . . . *!* As a reward [for following these rules] we will acclaim you as a modernist!"[33] "A poem written merely to prove that the contents of an ashcan may provide material for a poem," J. Donald Adams wrote, "belongs in the place of its origin."[34] "So much anguish" had been caused by modernists' "practice of stuffing their text[s] with oddments," wrote Hillyer.[35] This was "a crisis in language," wrote Joseph M. Lalley, brought on by "the reckless and mendacious inflation of words."

In his conservative theoretical inquiry into authority, *Faith and Force*, Lalley argued for a kind of immigration quota on words: the "number of English words in circulation" had increased (it was one result of rising literacy in the United States) to the point where language was in a "state of chaotic inflation." Linguistic latitudinarianism had led to the liberal state in which an American could "make words mean what he chooses them to mean, or, if he chooses, to make them mean nothing."[36] Thus, the ultimate nativist nightmare had come true: words' referential force and precision (and thus reason in language) had eroded as "the ratio of words to facts and ideas" had grown larger and larger. This is why Lalley admired the reactionary, antimodernist alternative put across in the writing of Roy Campbell, whose *Selected Poetry* Lalley edited and intro-duced for Henry Regnery's publishing company,[37] and why he had no use for modern poets who were "elliptical, allusive, ambiguous" and who "abandoned the traditional verse patterns." Lalley preferred Campbell's "master[y of] the familiar prosodic patterns" and sought out the power in Campbell's use of a language that tends to reduce the word-to-thing ratio back toward one. But, Lalley lamented, Campbell's poetry "ran counter to the tendencies of the times,"[38] in which "each man finds himself suddenly free"—"*free*," Lalley ob-served, "like Humpty Dumpty."[39] "Fragments connote disorder," concluded Welford Inge. Poetry had had a great fall. The "stubborn rock of density and confusion" that characterizes human activity in this life must in poetry find the "language and syntax and diction" of order and integration "to hew clarity and simplicity" from modern existence.[40]

Sidney Cooley, an antimodernist poet in Los Angeles who urged that we "choose up sides now and pick our philosophy," warned of a "lax syntax that has invaded verse."[41] Under "Suggestions for Parents," W. Cleon Skousen in *The Naked Communist* contended that only the restoration of form and order, the total rejection of aesthetic permissiveness, would prevent our children from becoming the sort of "hoodlums with maladjusted personalities who are likely to fall for every 'ism' that comes along."[42] J. Anthony Marcus of the Institute of Foreign Trade, who wrote and lectured on the communist menace,[43] was ready "to assist in getting some Congressional action" going against modernism, not because he wanted to follow the money to subversive sources and duped foundations but because he was horrified that modern poems "were just words, words, words, without any connecting sense of them."[44]

It was on the basis of this special political viewpoint, in part, that even the most progressive literary education began to edge young poets toward the short and coherent "precise" lyric, thwarting forays into the Poundian mode of cyclonic history, the conversational poem that resembled the prosody of casual human interaction, the incoherent epic-lyric sectional collage on the *Paterson* model that freely integrated stretches of document and narrative—all courting *genre* confusion. Genre confusion was bad enough for American adults but was specially inimical to the development of children living in a democracy, for the greatest long-term danger of modernism was its "rebellion against distinctions."[45] The young David Antin, who was learning in English classes at the City College of New York that "the literary world was in a conservative mode"—and knew already in 1949–50 that the ensuing decade would be a time when "poets were supposed to be picking up the meters again"—came across a sound recording of Gertrude Stein's *Three Lives* and "was blown away by the flattened blues music of 'Melanctha' " and then reveled in the realization that it had not "occurred [to him] that these were not poetry."[46] In 1952, when Yoko Ono, at nineteen years old, was a student at Sarah Lawrence College, she tried her hand at poems that would satisfy a desperate need for happiness after her harrowing experience as a child fleeing ruins left by incendiary bombs rained on her family's neighborhood in Tokyo. "Whenever I wrote a poem, [her teachers at Sarah Lawrence] said it was too long, it was like a short story." (She also wrote a short story that was said to be "like a poem.") The talented sophomore, already trained in the classical forms, was made to feel "like a misfit in every medium" because she sought happiness from her art rather than instructive adherence to generic rules or conventional distinctions between poetry and prose that she in any case knew well.[47] Moloney, in "Modern Literature: Darkness at Dawn" (1951), explained his conviction that the primary contemporary evil was free forms generated by "the doctrine of human self-sufficiency"—not communism as much as the larger (or rather perhaps synonymous) category of collectivist materialism.[48] In this view, poets of the canto technique were to be seen as less interested in poetics than in "self-display."[49] Daniel Bell concluded that "one cost" of modernism's critique of capitalism "has been the loss of coherence in culture," and he associated this with "the preoccupation with the medium": an example was the choice of "the aspirate rather than the syllable as a measure of line" in the poems of Robert Creeley. These were, for Bell, "all . . . expressions of the self, *rather than formal explorations of the limits . . . of the medium.*"[50]

The focus on the bodily human self—following the admonition of "the inevitable T. S. Eliot" to write poetry not out of the heart but from "the digestive tract"—had led, after the ruinations of a second world war, to a self-satisfied aestheticizing of disintegration, a sin the young Ono, seeking radical forms of personal pleasure through aesthetic rule breaking, was in fact learning to commit. Ono, Antin, and many other nascent artists were preparing themselves to push still further what Herbert Read concluded about modern poetry's revolutionary quality: insofar as poetry is sincerity, Read wrote, it "has no essential alliance with regular schemes of any sort," and thus "the modern poet has no uncompromising theory of metrical composition."[51] But "poetry of the modern kind suffers from the anthropocentric delusion," Weaver wrote in "Etiology of the Image" (1948), and whereas poets were once "concerned with truth," now, having "lost belief in the existence of that order," the poet has come to believe that "a poem today is the communication of a quality of experience rather than a meaning."[52] (It should be noted, especially because Weaver had had little contact with contemporary poets, that the typescript of *Ideas Have Consequences* submitted to the University of Chicago Press apparently had less to say about poetics than the final version. Cleanth Brooks was one of the anonymous readers for the press: he had a "definitely favorable" response to the book manuscript yet suggested that Weaver clarify how his indictment of "the fragmentation and general break-down of our civilization" pertained to "the irrational, obscurantist art of the lunatic fringe.")[53]

Thus had conservative detractors of avant-garde art come to dislike the modernist "preoccupation with disintegration" in language.[54] "Cubism," said one congressional aide in 1949, was part of the communist conspiracy because it too "aims to destroy by designed disorder."[55] Whereas the red-baiter in politics learned the phrase "known Communist" in the rhetoric of naming names,

Merrill Root, a prolific namer of poets' names, used the phrase "known *disintegrator*": for instance, "The Indiana Association of College Teachers of English," he reported in 1952, "selected as their annual speaker a known disintegrator of art and life, with a long record of fronts, Dr. William Carlos Williams."[56] Ben Ray Redman in the *Saturday Review* condemned modern poems that "largely disintegrate into quotations."[57] Hillyer, referring to Redman's analysis of the "errors produced by this mosaic style," called that style a "pathetic" attempt to make modernism a "substitute for aristocracy," an effort to "fabricate a language" without context, constructed of passages from older and nobler writers.[58] Weaver's *Ideas Have Consequences* argues that the "erasing of all distinctions" in modern life poorly passes for a commitment to equality, the imputed equal value of ideas and writing. But for Weaver, equality is a disorganizing concept,[59] and his one great subject was "the restoration of language."[60] The League for Sanity in Poetry (headquartered in Lilith Lorraine's Texas home and in the village of Rogers in southwestern Arkansas) fought the Bollingen Award "to preserve our poetic heritage and against such disruptive forces," these forces being the lines of offending poems.[61] Welford Inge wrote that the modern poet's " 'fragments' consist inevitably of either a disgusting querulous self-pity or a kind of crude and pathetic bravado that seems to whisper, 'Not daring to live bravely and gloriously, I shall examine my insignificance and woe.' "[62] In the pamphlet issued by the league, no attempt was made to find fascist content in *The Pisan Cantos*. A passage was quoted from canto 74 ("The enormous tragedy of the dream in the peasant's bent / shoulders") to demonstrate that *literary judgment* could be brought to bear on the radical demoticism and parataxis in these lines:

> Pisa in the 23rd year of the effort in sight of the Tower
> and Till was hung yesterday
> for murder and rape with trimmings   plus Cholkis
>   plus mythology, thought he was Zeus ram or another one
>   Hey Snag, who's in the bibl'?

The connections had been severed. Aesthetically, "this so-called poetry" could "confirm the findings of the psychiatrists" that Pound was insane. Yes, sane poetry was politically responsible—did not "flout American principles"—but first and foremost this complaint was issued by real Americans "concerned solely with literary qualities." Sanity was continuity; "plus Cholkis / plus mythology" was not. Similarly treacherous was the use of a conjunction that refused to conjoin.[63] And prosody too was a measure of sanity. "Regular meter

. . . is psychologically necessary," wrote Coblentz. The supposed "abandonment of meter" in modern verse had led to "insanities" like comparing "a flower garden with a thistle."[64]

So although it was far more elegant to speak in Viereck's plausible and winsome manner of the annihilation of iambs as a non-Euclidian approach—revolutionary and counterintuitive, but at least with a tried and tested intellectual heritage—at heart Viereck's stand against fragmentation particularly was akin to Moloney's and Davidson's and not so very far from that of the aesthetic Texans and Arkansans who manned the regional outposts of the League for Sanity in Poetry and managed the Avalon National Poetry Shrine: distrust of discontinuity. One of the reasons why anticommunist sci-fi could serve Gilbert Neiman and Ben Burman and others as a metaphor for articulating their hatred of Steinian and Poundian and Patchenesque aesthetics was that sci-fi in the 1950s, fueled by its enemy-within paranoia, succeeded in expressing American concern over what Susan Sontag in "The Imagination of Disaster" a few years later called "the aesthetics of destruction." Anticommunism was the means by which this loathing—this obsession with "wreaking havoc, making a mess"[65]—could be effectively expressed. Conservatives, influenced by Viereck's approach, began to regret the initial right-wing strategy of praising traditional poets "for reasons which were *outside* the realms of poetry." Such campaigning was "as detrimental to the cause of criticism as was the irresponsible adulation which was given by the other side" to left-wing poets.[66] "It is futile . . . to seek the cause of the rise of our poetic dictators in any agency or factor outside" poetics. The modernist dictatorship "has come about by reasons of influences that may be found *inside* our language."[67] The long poetic tradition had given contemporary poets great tools for techniques, but the modernist "disdains all connection with the past." Yet would a physician, while "naturally striv[ing] for new methods and techniques, . . . throw away his microscope [and] discard his medical library?"[68] They—the *conservatives*—sometimes complained that the *modernists* did not in their essays and speeches "venture . . . to any appreciable extent if at all into the exacting lanes of technique."[69]

Again this makes the gathering conservative backlash against modernism significantly different from that faced by avant-gardists in the 1910s and 1920s. When in 1915 the poet William Ellery Leonard, who in American modernism's *annus mirabilis* published a magnificent traditional sonnet sequence, *Two Lives* (1922),[70] issued in an newspaper satire what Renato Poggioli called "the quadruple *bon mot*" against the imagists—"1. The Imagists can't see straight. 2. The Imagists can't feel straight. 3. The Imagists can't think straight. 4. The Imagists can't talk straight"—his countermanifesto made its charges of dehumanization and disfigurement out of an unwillingness to take seriously the language the imagists actually used.[71] Poggioli later was probably right to group Leonard with the majority of modernism's early detractors, who "attack it from the viewpoint of its extra-aesthetic peccadillos, the avant-gardists' violations of the book of social etiquette or the moral code."[72] That is to say, he was right that this characterizes the denunciations of modernism at that time, but Poggioli in the 1950s and early 1960s was offering a general theory of the avant-garde, by no means its specific literary history. The attack on modernism in the period from 1945 to 1960, even that waged by many conservatives beyond the academy and outside the usual circles of intelligentsia, focused extraordinarily on the aesthetic challenge the avant-garde represented; the social implications of that challenge followed from the formal aspect of "wreaking havoc."

Anticommunism provided the rhetoric and the political agency that could be used effectively against antipoetic language and the threat that artists would abandon art's autonomous status represented by modernism's continuity out of radicalism.[73] Some anticommunists logically backed into a focus on poetics, to be sure: if to the form-hating communists, for whom "formalist" was an epithet akin to "cosmopolitan," "formalism does not refer to style but to 'treatment of an untrue, adulterated subject,'" then an anticommunist language theory had to attend to form as a style.[74] And it is true that some angry, inelegant critics such as Virginia Kent Cummins also often reminded readers of the personal sins and errors, the "extra-aesthetic peccadillos," of radical modernists in the late 1940s and 1950s, a rhetorical staple of red-baiting from the moment HUAC and smear-mongering columnists began naming names. But in the end, Archer Huntington was most disturbed by the demise of rhyme and meter; J. Donald Adams at the New York Times felt greater anxiety about modernism's "poverty of method" and the "strangely hybrid critics" that grew up around radicalism and modernism than about the Marxist background of Kenneth Burke's view of a poem as a "dynamized dialectic";[75] Belgium's commissioner of information, Jan-Albert Goris, finally did prefer the waka of Hirohito; Merrill Root was most upset by the way young poets "combin[ed] avant garde experiments with Communist ideology" to produce "a stiff, synthetic pastiche," "stiff" and "synthetic" being for him the worst possible qualities of a poem;[76] Coblentz hated Ray Bremser's poem in Donald Allen's The New American Poetry more because the New American had the gall to use the word "transvestite" as a transitive verb ("transvestite my human animal until I walk / with knuckles on the ground. . . . / call me a communist, or this and that / I am a traitor traitor traitor") than because the poem's sentiment was obscene or because Coblentz believed this Beat was a treasonous red (he was not);[77] and Cullen Jones sought most of all to restore poetry's natural irrelevance to political life when he insisted that "the truly poetic mind is out of balance with . . . 'practical' affairs."[78]

There were of course the Edgar Guests of modern verse—market-minded folks who sought an audience among members of a new suburban middle class decorating their mod split-levels with biomorphic furniture and knew the phrase "April is the cruelest month" from ad campaigns for household wares.[79] But these Americans were, of course, anathema to the true antimodernist conservative. Members of the League for Sanity in Poetry were calling for strict stanzaic convention and high poetic language, such as in Hillyer's poems— anything that would stand against Pound's adamantly demotic, unpoetic, post-iambic speech ("Zeus ram or another one / Hey Snag") in the *Pisan Cantos*. Yet, frighteningly, the Eddie Guest of the Cold War adapted with great facility to the new modernistic modes, caved in and found a market for fragmented syntax in a lax, liberal world of postwar consumerism. Some antimodernists simply accepted this as a function of the free market without overtly endorsing free verse. Lee Richard Hayman, a poet-columnist for *Writer*, a trade magazine for freelancers, was one of these people: modernism, he mildly argued, was to be accepted as a fact of marketability. Not surprisingly, Coblentz rejected the position, seeing here a furtherance of the sinister plot among radical modernists to penetrate the literary marketplace with linguistic disruption. Nor would poet Donald Davidson, "the most unreconstructed of the Vanderbilt Agrarians,"[80] who in a 1957 speech about the situation of the southern writer in the academy condemned anyone who "traffics with . . . modern collectivism in terms of the market that it controls," thus surrendering his independence and permitting his language to be "processed (heavily edited)" to conform to "stock patterns, which are aimed at the mass mind."[81]

In his "From Our Rostrum" column in the September 1949 issue of *Writer*, Hayman, a contributor of light verse to the *American Mercury* and other such venues, urged his readers to recognize that the "market for free verse is constantly widening" and that both magazines and poets were "dipping into the pool of unrhymed poetry," including even *Good Housekeeping* and *Harper's Bazaar*.[82] Two years earlier, William Meredith had already noticed that "the new idiom—the manner taken for the substance—has now reached the lyrics of the family magazines."[83] Hayman found some poetry journals that actually *required* submissions to be "unrhymed and experimental." Others, such as *Experiment* of St. Paul, paid up to fifty cents per line, no matter how short the line. *Experiment* thus enabled freelancing William Carlos Williams look-alikes to maximize poetry's slim profits.

Hayman was merely reporting the news that modernism was entering the "pay-market field." He then outlined simple steps poets could take to write and to sell such verse. He instructed readers in the verse of "E. E. Cummings (the lower-case poet)" who "places part of single words on separate lines." (This too went opportunistically with tidings that modern verse now paid relatively well by the line.) Hayman noted that some crusty opponents resisted this trend, such as indeed Stanton Coblentz himself (whose "What Are They—Poems or Puzzles?" had by then received mass circulation). But Hayman was willing to conclude that "even the most rabid antagonists of free verse are beginning to realize that it is 'here to stay.'" Hayman's article nonetheless reproduced a basic premise of the traditionalist right in the new context of analyses of the modernist market-takeover: "among the widest markets for free verse" were the *New Republic*, the *Nation*, the *Partisan Review*, and the communist *Masses & Mainstream*, which "readily accept *unrhymed poetry which stresses social themes*."[84] True conservatives wanted nothing to do with facile skeptics of Hayman's kind, those who would permit the modernist wave to wash over them. Although he was himself known as a conservative poet, Hayman was accused of being soft on modernism.

Notwithstanding his traditionalist inklings, Hayman, in Coblentz's view, was the typical contemporary American poet—the type Coblentz dubbed "Author A" in his jeremiad, *The Anti-Poets*. Author A's sin was in looking to economic trends for guidance and thus, for the sake of getting published, tolerating the verbal discontinuity du jour. The "driving force" behind A's grammatical base was just as weak as that of the copywriter for a Madison Avenue ad agency who followed the rules being set out by David Ogilvy, the father of modern advertising, who discovered in the 1940s and 1950s that the key to print selling was in knowing how to arrange the words on a page.[85] To the indecisive A, linguistic convention can be sacrificed in favor of "cater[ing] to popular taste," making money, achieving marketability. Worst of all, to such a modernist poetic advertiser, ideology is merely a means to a slick end, thus hiding the political implications of the disparate modern idiom. "Author A aims his work [equally] at [the communist] *People's Weekly* or *Housewife's World*." In this particular version, antimodernism deemed the marketplace itself insufficiently strong to withstand subversion and unable to enforce ideological boundaries. That modernism pays was another traditionalist's nightmare, a conquest of cool.

Bad as Author A was, Author B was even more frightful. B was a modernist because he came of age as a writer in the modern era. His "earliest efforts are rhymed and conventional in form . . . due merely to the accident that his friends and teachers favored rhymed, conventional work." Although Coblentz did not mention him by name here, B was this conservative's take on the life and career of William Carlos Williams. The young Keatsian poet, hinting at genuine retrograde talent, had then met and consorted with Pound, "an apostle of the 'newer freedom,'" and eventually "entrust[ed] his lower-case contributions to various frenzied-looking sheets, from which . . . he [drew] not only recognition but prizes." Why? "They pay, do they not?" Success encourages B, and he in turn becomes an apostle of the newer freedom, recruiting successors, filling new bottles with old snake oil. Coblentz's antimodernism matched his concern about what cultural capitalism had become. If the modernist revolution had brought about the "transformation in . . . the physical structure of our poetry," it coupled with radical changes in the "physical structure" of the economic marketplace for culture; they "converted publishers, magazine editors and anthologists, enlisted critics and critical organs," and thus "captured most of the leading prizes," attached academic salaries through "the cold conformity of intellectualism," and cornered the market on whatever money there was in poetry. The antimodernism of poetic form in this sense led to (rather than followed from) the anticommunist protection of free markets.[86] One could see in many of the traditionalist send-ups of Williams's prosody and lineation in the 1950s a criticism directed at "the value" of the equivalent in modern verse of a Marcel Duchamp readymade, something bought cheaply from the local hardware store and then made into much-discussed experimental art. For instance, Ralph Gustafson, the skeptic we met in a previous chapter, published a poem, "For William Carlos Williams," in *Poetry New York* in 1950 :

> It was one of those immortal wounds
> Mister Frost talks about
>
> a poem
> sixteen words
> it was made of
>
> concerning the value
> of a 1923 wheel
> barrow
>
> I was struck dumb
> anything modern
> could last
> so long[87]

The paradoxically immortal (not mortal) wound is the poem itself—or, rather, is inflicted by the weapon that is the poem: writing that had already generated such canonical value. And the poem, this conservative metapoem expressing shock at such a modernist economy, manages minimally to say what can be said by the traditionalist at this point, his voice having been otherwise disabled ("struck dumb"). The fact of a modernist market had become the issue. As we have seen, Richard Weaver no more trusted the marketplace (now that it was "controlled"[88] by revolutionists) to underwrite the ethics of rhetoric than did Coblentz. Weaver saw the canons of grammar, traditions of good sense making, sacrificed not only by the language of modernity but by the rhetoric of advertising, all fitting into the larger category of the "cult" of political liberalism. The subversive Poet B—William Carlos Williams or another of his adaptable ilk—by selling modernism like a sideshow charlatan, had created a rationale for the final defense of capitalism as a form of traditionalism against the twin encroachments of advertising and modern writing.

When Coblentz's bombshell article, "What Are They—Poems or Puzzles?," was to run in the *New York Times Magazine*, editor Lester Markel hired Howard Sparber to create a wild illustration spread across the top half of the first page. Sparber read the essay and decided to depict two poets, one traditionalist and the other modernist, each entrancing a segment of the audience. The traditionalist, dressed as an Elizabethan, sells "English Sonnets written TO ORDER." But he seems hardly different from the beret-clad modernist, whose placard reads, "get your modern poetry here," in lowercase letters. The curtain pull to the modernist's left is an eye of Picasso's *Guernica*; we also see the folded, weeping pocket watch of Dalí and other surrealist/cubist memento mori. The point of Sparber's drawing was not that modernism was bankrupt or that traditional verse was a healthy alternative, but that even the Shakespearean sonnet had been penetrated by dislocated language—such that even rhyme is no defense against it. (And Picasso's eye was surely a semisubliminal red herring. By the time the U.S. Information Agency canceled an exhibit put on by the College Art Association because it included a Picasso, certain "trademark" Picasso designs had become associated in the public mind with both radicalism and modernism.)[89] Sparber's caricatured modernist hawks his lines predictably:

> but my eye was a sot
> in a bowl of acids, must lidlift to know

The disturbing thing about the drawing, however, as about Coblentz's article, was that the rhymer presented no constructive alternative. The audience seems to be duped by him just as by his opposite number. This was no choice between sides but an illustration of the collapse of choice and of the idea that there are sides, the ultimate tyranny of nonsense. The sonneteer was meant to be no

Drawing by Howard Sparber to illustrate Stanton Coblentz's "What Are They?—Poems or Puzzles?," *New York Times Magazine*, October 13, 1946. Courtesy Howard Sparber.

better—perhaps indeed another modern poet in traditionalist disguise. He rhymes but makes little sense beyond metrical regularity and seems logically to have borrowed from Steinian tautology (a primrose is a primrose is . . .): "A primrose by a river's brim / A yellow primrose was to him."[90]

Even antimodernists who had higher hopes for rhyme's future than was implied by Sparber's drawing for Coblentz's dystopian essay—such inveterate rhymers as Paul Scott Mowrer—now evinced at line's end a desperation that barely hid the new conservative politics of poetic form. The derogation of rhyme contravened human nature, but the response to that unnatural threat almost had to force itself, had to overprotest. In a poem called "In Praise of Rhyme," Mowrer wants to help keep William Carlos Williams from becoming a rhyme-hating "bigot"—wants to save him not for his political views but in response to his statement (in a *New York Times* interview) that "it is impossible for an alert man to rhyme, and say what he wants to say," a tricky reversal of the natural:

Though bigot carpers frown askance,
Come, poet, seize the rhymer's chance
And bring the bonnie words to prance
　And play together
Like frolic lambs that frisk and dance
　Through highland heather.

A rhymer is a rhymer born.
The gift of rhyme, that some may scorn,
To him is like an angel's horn.
　He did not learn it.[91]

Attacking the market from the inside, posing as a natural talent, the subversive who peddled lines of disintegration and associated rhyming with dullness and free forms with acuity and taunted the sane with insane juxtapositions did greater damage to the cultural field than "open" communists whose rejection of capitalism actually came in readable, legibly oppositional cultural modes of the sort one could reject, sense for sense. The modernist line the eye could not so easily reject, what with its implicit formal claim of freedom. Posing a threat worse than the outed communist, the modernist radical manufactured verse:

MONEY　:　JOKE (ie., crime
　　under the circumstances　:　value
　　chipped away at accelerated pace.)
—do you joke when a man is dying
　　　of a brain tumor?

Money: Uranium (bound to be lead)
throws out the fire   .
—the radium's the credit—the wind in
the trees. . . .

Money sequestered enriches avarice, makes
poverty.[92]

The passage is an example of what anticommunist antimodernists meant by warning against the poet who resembled Coblentz's Poet B. When disorderly language seems a resistance against money because capitalism is disintegrative —impoverishing and murderous—it presents an unanswerable style.

This passage comes from Williams's fourth book of *Paterson* (1951). Antimodernists criticized the entire range of forms and practices enacted in *Paterson*, as by the idea of the project as a whole, which daringly engaged a modern aesthetic with the intention of claiming for the exclusive purposes of that style the depiction of the American community as tragic. The tragedy entailed the failure of official descriptive languages to find "a firm grasp on the American idiom," as one favorable reviewer put it.[93] This particular passage was especially provocative, since it seemed to be offered as text to accompany—as a kind of caption for—a full-page advertisement that appears as part of the poem's text on the previous page. Apparently introduced by the phrase "as you may see" in Williams's verse on the page just before that, this was a reproduction of the paid advertisement of an extremist, a man named August Walters of Newark, New Jersey. Walters, Williams had noticed, took out newspaper ads urging Americans not to borrow money from private, profit-making banks but to borrow on the credit of the United States for the purpose of funding the manufacture of airplanes with which to bomb the Russians. "To win the cold war we must reform our finance system."

Williams's response to this tragicomic confusion of credit theory right *and* left with Cold War right—arguably the most politically radical moment in all *Paterson*—also enables a passage linguistically and idiomatically among its most experimental. The self-referential and self-critical refusal to deliver a verbally complete depiction of a person in "Portrait of a Lady"—

the tall grass of your ankles
flickers upon the shore—
Which shore?—
the sand clings to my lips—
Which shore?

Agh, petals maybe. How
should I know?[94]

—is here brought forward into the world of Cold War economic theory and
instigated by the presence in the poetic text of the unironic political document:

                    an advance over the
        market price for
                        "hospital income"
        Who gets that?   The poor?
                        What poor?[95]

Responding to Walters's contention that "the Russians understand only
force" and that reforms of the financial system would produce that force,
Williams comes as close as he would in this period to thoughtful anti-anticommunism, implicitly calling for American defeat in the Cold War as a means of
finally disclosing the inequalities in the u.s. economy, a set of structures in
which patients die because they are "penalize[d] . . . with surgeon's fees" indexed to the "market price for / 'hospital income'" and where the value of
radium, the enabler of atomic weaponry and itself an element of the credit
system, ends up in the economic as well as literal air we breathe. "Trade winds
that broached a continent" is a remarkable phrase that summons among other
things the image of a Cold War version of the first capitalized invasions of the
American continent by Europeans. Thus,

        Defeat may steel us
    in knowledge : money : joke
    to be wiped out sooner or later at stroke
    of pen   .[96]

Which stroke of pen? *This* one? The "defeatism" here, which might finally be
good for Americans, in the context of cold war certainly risked accusations of
sedition. But equally risky is the obvious engagement of Ezra Pound throughout this section of *Paterson*, not just thematically (his theory of American credit
as "cancer" and as a form of usury—both images making their way into *Paterson 4* here)[97] but also the Poundian poetic mode.

For several pages in *Paterson*, Williams at this point tries on the canto
technique loathed by Viereck, with stanzas organized around merged ideas, the
question-and-answer mode, the use of bits of untranslated foreign language as
epigraph-like provocations set off by colloquial local responses, where the basic
poetic measure or "foot" is not the "goddam iamb" Pound hated[98] but the

Full-page political advertisement by August Walters, reproduced in William Carlos Williams, *Paterson 4* (New York: New Directions, 1958), p. 181. Courtesy New Directions Publishing Corporation.

social-economic unit of thought rendered as cultural phrasing—all with explicit nods toward Pound. Williams was positively stimulated by the several qualities antimodernists feared: the social import of an anything-goes form ("'poems' that look like the nightmare of a delirious printer")[99] and the market rhetoric of advertising. All with a Poundian emphasis on making it—*it* being society—new:

IN

    venshun

O.KAY

     In venshun[100]

One of Williams's signal inventions for American modernism developed from his fascination with forms of advertising. For conservatives urging a return to nature poetry, the sort of analogical inversion Williams had been practicing from the time of *Spring and All* (1923), with its jarring aestheticism of metal roses ("The rose is obsolete"), was worse than just ugly—far worse, for it undermined the way language is supposed to work in relation to the world. J. Donald Adams believed that modernist claims for the beauty of the metal rose emerged from the fact that "all experiments necessarily have a measure of recklessness." Reckless and irresponsible was the destruction of nature poetry in the modernist movement, but now that "inevitable reaction has set in"—a good thing for the "constitutionally middle-of-the-road" Adams—and now that new "young poets are coming up," "nature is no longer abhorrent."[101] Galway Kinnell, just the sort of young poet Adams meant, made this point in a special 1953 issue of the *Beloit Poetry Journal* featuring three "technically conservative" poets (Anthony Ostroff and Winfield Townley Scott as well as Kinnell): "Only meaning is truly interesting," and "this explains why the so-called experimentalist schools are the most boring and imitative of all." By "occupying themselves with their discrete effects," by being "more *an imitation of language* than of nature," modernist writing "lose[s] real connection with nature itself."[102]

For years, the *Lyric* had been animated by opposition to the subversive substitution of language for nature. And in the extremist interlude when Virginia Kent Cummins replaced Leigh Hanes as editor of that magazine, the anticommunist implications of this particular position erupted, focusing on William Carlos Williams. In the end it led to bizarre drama, just as Cold War blacklisting often did: at one point, Williams, too ill (from a stroke) to respond with characteristic pugnacity, asked his wife, Flossie, to call a Mr. Clapp in Washington after a special delivery letter had informed the poet that he would not be permitted to assume any of the activities of the poetry consultant at the Library of Congress until the matter of his communist affiliations was "cleared up." Flossie described her phone conversation with Clapp in a letter she wrote to Conrad Aiken: "*He said*—Dr. Williams has been around a lot.—When I asked what did he mean by that—he replied he was in Germany and Austria. Yes—I said—he was—what about it? Well—just that he said."[103] A poet friend who was also a psychiatrist suggested that it would be helpful to get a letter of support from a local veterans organization.[104] "The dark ages," Flossie wrote to an academic supporter of her husband's verse, "surely are looming up again and the generous spirits are being stifled."[105]

The red-baiting of William Carlos Williams is either a story of an absurd, aberrant American political moment that has little finally to do with the language/nature problem modernism posed for traditionalists or indeed lies at the heart of the problem. The narrative of Cummins's relentless campaign in 1951 and 1952 to prevent Williams from taking up his appointment as consultant in poetry at the Library of Congress was first told in detail by the Cambridge University scholar Mike Weaver, who for his book *William Carlos Williams: The American Background* (1971) dug into old issues of the *Lyric* and corresponded with Sidney Hook, one of the most brilliant and persistent of the anticommunists who had come to ridicule Williams for his "political naivete" in the 1930s.[106] In issues of the *Lyric* Weaver consulted, he discovered a separately printed insert that laid out the case for Williams's communism. It was an open letter red-baiting Williams on seven counts, including his official opposition to HUAC in 1940 and his involvement with a League of American Writers project in 1937.[107] Mike Weaver's correspondence with Hook survives in the Hook Papers at the Hoover Institution. "We were annoyed with [Williams]," Hook told Weaver, "for his silly fellow-travelling in the '30s[,] particularly a letter he signed August 14, 1939 in the *Daily Worker* . . . denouncing our [Committee for Cultural Freedom] as 'Fascist and allies of Fascists.'"[108] Weaver conceded that he thought Williams "boobed over this and many other things," and added, "As a good Social Crediter he should have stuck to his 'normal' principles of individualism. . . . I think he simply let his good socialist heart—his belief in socialized medicine touches a chord in the Britisher [Weaver]—overflow into channels dug [by communists] specially to exploit him."[109] Hook mentioned that one of his former students, the poet Vivienne Koch, as she prepared to write her book *William Carlos Williams* (1950), had (allegedly) learned from Williams that he "had second thoughts about his Stalinist associations."[110] Weaver apparently did not pursue this lead with Koch.

Actually it was not Virginia Kent Cummins who inaugurated the anticommunist antimodernist offense against Williams in 1951–52. Stanton Coblentz did so in 1949. He wrote to Luther Evans, the librarian of Congress, on July 7 of that year to complain of Williams's "stand against the ideals for which America has fought and bled" and urged that Williams's appointment, an "insult to the American people," be withdrawn. Coblentz then sent a carbon copy of this letter to Robert Hillyer.[111] Coblentz had already written to Hillyer to suggest that Williams's political views "may have some 'implications' . . . in regard to the poetry set-up of the Library of Congress." Hillyer passed along this letter to an editor at the *Saturday Review*, asking if the evidence against Williams was "of interest."[112] Coblentz used Williams's radicalism as a means of bringing Hillyer —at that moment the most powerful of the conservative antimodernists—fully into line with the extremist faction: "I am writing you," Coblentz remarked in yet another letter, "in the belief that those of us who are working for the same cause, and against the same forces of corruption, do like to hear from one another and to know that we have company and moral backing."[113]

Missing the *Wings* network made for no great flaw in Mike Weaver's study. But had he followed the trail from Cummins to Hook to Vivienne Koch, he might by that means too have discovered the broader aesthetic context for the anticommunist thrust against Williams. It was not the aberration merely of a bad political season. Koch, Hook's student, had been trained well in the post-ideological strategies of anticommunist poetics. Reviewing Alfred Hayes's *Welcome to the Castle* in 1951, she described the poet as "tired, bitter, and essentially a journalist." Having experienced "the revolutionary commitments of the Thirties and the disillusion of the Forties," Hayes "never rises above a pleasantly 'poetic' liberal-magazine rhetoric of the social Thirties." And then the key indictment: "He speaks, as Wallace Stevens says of someone in a poem, 'below the tension of the lyric.' " Hayes's "hate and self-hate" derive from his inability to rise to a new— but unexplained—lyric standard of "tension" (a New Critical use of the term Stevens had not meant at all).[114] For Koch, poems should not offer "diagnosis of our present economic ills." But that is precisely what she found in the fourth book of *Paterson*. Such ideological force was a "serious weakness" of the poem and was connected to another—the disconcerting formal practice Williams attempted here, more than in previous installments of the epic, to pull into the poem whole documents, such as August Walters's political ad, which, Koch irritably noted, took up "a whole page." It made *Paterson* "terrifyingly simple." To be sure, a poem of *Paterson*'s length necessarily accommodated " 'let-down' passages" that relieve the reader from "the more intense, pure poetry in it." The collage—the "intense, pure" lyricism set aside a full-page political advertise-ment—created for Koch "a re-iterative stridency."[115]

The red-baiting of William Carlos Williams—whether of Cummins's and

Coblentz's thuggish sort in the mode of Joe McCarthy or of Koch's sort in the keen critical mode of her mentor, Sidney Hook—tended to mask the degree to which Williams's work with the communist poets of the 1930s led him toward what is arguably his furthest extension of the modernist project, in poems of *The Wedge* (1944) and in *Paterson* (beginning in 1946). Deep inside the file Cummins gathered on Williams's un-American activities was a significant item: at the time of the Third Writers' Congress hosted by the communist League of American Writers, on June 26, 1939, Williams went to the George Washington Hotel to join a symposium featuring himself and Taggard, Fearing, Maas, Freeman, Schneider, Funaroff, and Countee Cullen. The topic was "New Mediums in Verse," and Mike Weaver was exactly right to conclude later that the session was "to provide an influential background for Williams's use of documentary in *Paterson*."[116] By then, the communist poet's interest in a lyric of document, as we have seen in the case of Norman Rosten's *The Big Road*, depended on the modernist advance forward from a supposedly natural language to an accommodation of the word as such. Fearing, for instance, was more interested in posters, ads, and signs that pointed to social reality than in any purported transparent realism. The poem's medium could be thematized, and this was centrally part of the modernist-communist conversation. Thus, we return to a radicalism in the substitution of language for nature. In *The Wedge* and *Paterson*, sensing already that he, among others, was the target of condemnations by such young "technically conservative" nature poets as those who would gather in Chad Walsh's New Conservative *Beloit Poetry Journal*, Williams showed insistently once again that beauty for him—for instance, in an image of pink roses awash in springtime rain—could be *like* a store's sidewalk advertisement, rather than the other way around, or like nothing but naturally itself. In a lyric passage from "To All Gentleness" (published in *The Wedge*), Williams wrote,

> Like a cylindrical tank fresh silvered
> upended on the sidewalk to advertise
> some plumber's shop, a profusion
> of pink roses bending ragged in the rain—
> speaks to me of all gentleness and its
> enduring.[117]

M. L. Rosenthal published a strong defense of Williams's postwar poetics, and for it he too suffered assaults from antimodernists. Rosenthal observed that "Williams is always a committed poet," and meant it politically. Into the Cold War era, Williams continued "taking his chances," pushing "In venshun," without ever retreating from the earlier aesthetic movements that had enabled his progress. Rosenthal was one of the very few defenders of modernism against its detractors in this period who did not submit to the temptation to scissor out the poet of the 1930s from the literary history of modernism. He was the first in fact to see a modernist continuity through the radical poets of the Depression. Many pages of his first book-length critical work—his never-published dissertation—were taken up by praise of the radical modernist poetics of Gregory, Fearing, and Rukeyser.[118]

Rosenthal's stepfather "would explain" his ardent socialism to the young Macha, and even as a child Macha held the conviction that "Communism was the way of peace and fraternity," as he later wrote in an unpublished memoir titled "Confessions," "and that in a wilfully [*sic*] barbarous world, revolutionary force was necessary." As a teenager he was "entranced" by the "brilliance of Lenin's mind." He was frequently beset by the feeling of being "a Communist of inadequate sincerity," although a stint working on the staff of the Illinois unit of the Federal Writers Project (in 1938–39) gave him the sense that he was doing something politically efficacious with his skills as a writer.[119] In 1944, Rosenthal dared to praise a poem that ended with "a barrage of slogans" although he knew that doing so would "arouse . . . the united ire" of anticommunists in the world of poetry criticism. "But the perspective of a decade must teach us that this poetry was not written simply to win people over to unorthodox ideas," he noted. "For it sprang from the conviction that programmatic struggle is as much a part of experience as a subject-matter for art as are passively observed facts or the emotions of love and sorrow or the dissolution of the inhabitants of the Waste Land. It must not be thought that this view is unphilosophical or merely topical."[120]

As early as 1946, Rosenthal was willing to refute Stanton Coblentz's equation of "clarity" and antimodernist verse—his dictum that it "must be lucid"— noting that if Coblentz truly admired clarity, he would not reject "Fearing, Gregory, [Marya] Zaturenska," choosing those three for their leftist reputations.[121] During his years as poetry editor of the *Nation*, he insisted in various ways that poets of the 1930s be taken seriously as part of the tradition of American poetic innovation.[122] Rukeyser appeared on a list including Williams, Hart Crane, and Charles Olson as American poets for whom the "struggle" of using an American language is "hardly to blot out the past; rather, it is to make it heard in a new *contemporary* way."[123]

Rukeyser helped Rosenthal create a counterdefinition of aesthetic innovation. "Experimentation in verse is largely a matter of adjustment [of] available traditions, language and all the other elements of the art being by definition a matter of social heritage."[124] He argued for a sense of modern poetry as "varied yet unified." He was one of a very few critics of modern poetry in the 1950s—perhaps there were just two in the United States, Joseph Warren Beach being the other—who consistently refused to disconnect the 1930s from the 1920s; this critical move was itself, for some, tantamount to radicalism. "Our poetry of the twenties and the thirties might almost be described as a concerted effort to re-establish the vital continuities with the past . . . and to achieve a cultural breakthrough . . . in search of fresher meanings."[125] Rosenthal rejected the view that poetry of the 1930s uniformly advocated collectivity; it was often, he said, "anarcho-individualistic, Freudian," and written as much "in the image of D. H. Lawrence" as of Lenin.[126] He intrepidly connected the New American Poetry with the 1930s. His open view of Paul Blackburn (who had been his student) was that he wrote in the tradition of Fearing.[127] As a serious poet himself, Rosenthal was pleased to join the company of Joy Davidman, one of the com-munist *Seven Poets* poets, in her anthology, *War Poems of the United Nations*.[128]

So when in the *New Republic* Rosenthal emphatically praised Williams for attempting "to see what meaning, if any, can be read into a given cultural unit, . . . symbolic of life in America," he did so on the assumption that *Paterson* owed its status as cultural commentary to the continued validity of the modern-ist revolution of the twenties and the political revolution of the thirties. In short, *Paterson* resists the fifties' thirties. Williams "is one of the few writers who have gone on from the twenties and thirties without rejecting what once was valid for them but always ready to find new meanings and better ways to state them." Rosenthal was frankly affirming Williams's version of the canto tech-nique as the only way in which the poet can ask if "the violent gestures of graceless lust and hatred and self-destruction define irrefutably a 'world of corrupt cities' lacking continuity with past tradition or future perspectives."[129]

Swiftly came the antimodernist counterattack—against both Williams and Rosenthal. The elderly novelist Upton Sinclair started it, and subsequent re-sponses from Stanton Coblentz, William McFee, S. Beryl Lush appeared in the *New Republic* itself, as other rejoinders avalanched[130] across weeklies and monthlies. Sinclair disarmingly asked Rosenthal, then a young New York Uni-versity professor, "to take pity" on him, an old writer out of his element, yet the criticism here was unremitting. Sinclair could not fathom Rosenthal's praise of the passage from *The Wedge* that began with a single unlineated line of proselike verse: "Like a cylindrical tank fresh silvered upended on the sidewalk to adver-tise some plumber's shop, a profusion." Sinclair claimed to be less concerned about the disruptive sense of the words—the juxtapositional loveliness of sign advertisement, the sort of thing that attracted Williams's attention on the streets of Paterson and Manhattan—than about "why a line of poetry should start a new clause or a new statement, beginning with an indefinite article and a noun, and then leave the rest of the clause to be carried over as another line of poetry." Sinclair recalled forty years of trying to "make anything out of what is called modern poetry": first he had given up "looking for rhyme," then he "gave up looking for any rhythm," then "any melody . . . any beauty, any wisdom, and even any sense." The not-so-hidden subtext of Sinclair's complaint about Williams's seemingly random lineation was a new dramatization of his old concerns about the proper relationship between political radicalism and aesthetic experiment, a topic inelegantly introduced in the final didactic chapters of *The Jungle*, in which a long lesson in socialism is taught through the extended quotation of a dinnertime diatribe. After that performance, Sinclair had almost instantly become "a one-man press agent for the workers," as Leo Gurko put it critically in 1947.[131] Then when Village radicals and anarchist bohemians became passionate about modernism, Sinclair had complained to the editors of the *Masses*, as that magazine had undertaken its own feisty synthesis of modernism and radicalism; the socialist committed to the style of imitative description, Sinclair found a threat in this synthesis. Modernism's forays into radicalism might even be said to have caused the final decline in the influence of Sinclair's novels after *The Jungle*. The anger directed at Williams's lineations and at Rosenthal's daring praise of them as both lovely and socially conscious is discernible even when the grounds of the complaint are "merely" formal.[132]

That Upton Sinclair's censure of modernism indicated his rightward movement at this late and bitter moment in his career was a point hardly needing reinforcement,[133] but Coblentz supplied it. Writing the *New Republic* to defend Sinclair's traditionalism, Coblentz restated the dire need to "put a finger on an index to the whole malodorous infection of modernism." He "outed" Sinclair as a conservative antimodernist per se, observing—accurately—that Sinclair's rebuke of Williams assumed the basic equivalence of modernists' claims as "apostles of 'progress' " and their violation of "elemental rules of sentence structure."[134] "The old poetry," Coblentz wrote in "Freedom—What Price?," "is not the imprisoning and constricting thing that so many rebels suppose; even though it never renounces the control of law, it does allow the writer . . . to be . . . free. . . . But in order to express himself successfully, every writer *must follow the laws*."[135]

The un-Americanism of disjuncture in modern language was at every point the issue, the greatest threat to freedom, whether the notion was asserted clumsily by proud anticommunists such as Coblentz through tactics resembling McCarthyite guilt by association, or half-consciously by the rueful ex-socialist Sinclair, or with the self-conscious theoretical acuity of Richard Weaver, or through the prosecutorial rhetorical strategy employed by Justice Department attorneys in a series of Smith Act trials during which the "Aesopian Language Thesis" was put in evidence for the purpose of sustaining Louis Budenz's testimony that whenever an American communist wrote something innocent or gradualistic, it probably meant its opposite.[136] Disjunctive poetics violates the rules of "language citizenship" and gives readers uncomfortable with experimental writing reason to suspect a "latent ideology" hidden under the linguistic surface, which it is the job of anticommunist critics to bring up through and beyond the language. This was the theory of language behind the Smith Act prosecutions that had begun in 1949 and subsequent anticommunist notions of leftist language for the next forty years. "It is . . . the latent ideology that needs to be studied," a Reagan-era anticommunist critic wrote in *Encounter* to summarize the case against "esoteric elements" in communist language (and to add new support to Budenz's old accusations). "This is not easy," continued this critic. "How do we know what a man believes in the absence of his own testimony?"— that "testimony" being what readers *cannot* discern from a subversive writer's "esoteric" phrasing. "In general we must judge his actions more than his words. But his words too can be revealing of thoughts he may wish to hide. This is particularly so when these words seem odd, incongruous, and inconsistent." How then in this period would readers know if there is a latent radicalism that needs to be interpreted in a piece of writing? Answer: when the writing is "odd, incongruous and inconsistent." One need not normally suspect conventional language of subversion. But "odd" writing, while not itself the carrier of communist content, is the indication that subversion is afoot. Guilt is not in the linguistic difference but is the sign of that treason otherwise hidden from view, a method of detecting communism that obviates the legal requirement to prove illegal action rather than prosecuting free speech.[137]

The standard for linguistic citizenship as Richard Weaver conceived it required no such trick of asserting latency. Weaver despised trickery and directly went after disjuncture. In the fervent conclusion to "Aspects of Grammatical Categories" in *The Ethics of Rhetoric* (1953), Weaver argued that "like the political citizenship defined by Aristotle, language citizenship makes one a potential magistrate, or one empowered to decide." Here the absolutist advocates a writer's adjustment or acceptance, for it is a gesture of accommodation to an a priori truth about grammar's rightness. One should not—one cannot—unthinkingly adopt the conventions of one's language or approach them with "the attitude of personal defiance" but should in the end consciously accept them and thus accept the notion that to renounce them is to give up voluntarily one's social belonging. While it cannot be proved that "grammar is determined by the 'best people,'" it was true, Weaver insisted, that strict adherence to canons of grammar "incorporates the people as a whole." Weaver strove for the most capacious historical perspective: "In the long view a due respect for the canons of grammar seems a part of one's citizenship. One does not remain uncritical; but one does 'go along.'"[138]

In the poetry wars of the late 1940s and 1950s, the very definition of citizenship was at stake. Writers who now sought social belonging, such as the aging Joseph Freeman, feared the flattening of language. In a long letter about the effect of McCarthyism on writers who refused linguistically to go along, Freeman wrote, "The serious writer today writes in an atmosphere of fanatical persecution. . . . THE WAR IS AGAINST WORD MAGIC."[139] For Viereck, the experimentalist was guilty until proven innocent, and he knew well that this reversal of American democratic convention constituted a great revolt against revolt: in an essay on social change in the mid-1950s, he suggested that whereas liberalism forced the anti-innovative to reckon, conservatism put the burden of proof on the innovator.[140] In the wide world of arguments about modernism, Weaver's insistence that one should show fealty to the rules of grammar or figuratively risk the denaturalization of citizenship was the theoretically sophisticated equivalent of telling the practitioners of disjunctive poetics that if they don't love it, they can leave it—or, in the still cruder red-baiting parlance of the day, to go back to Russia.[141]

Of course neither Weaver nor Viereck nor Robert Graves literally meant that modernists would actually feel at home in the Soviet Union. But as I have shown in this book, a few nativists actually came to believe this. It is true that conservatives who disdained Whitman's influence on modern poetry or appreciated it only after it had been deradicalized had made the connection between the poet who thought of the "arts as something to serve the people—the mass" and the poet whose verse was open, unfinished, "on the way," "not the *object* but the *process*" of communicating. This is precisely why Whitman's reputation suffered by the accident of having fallen at a time that "breathed reaction," for Whitman actually "taught us to see language as mediate," as Ray Smith put it in 1955. More relevantly (because of his importance to young avant-gardists who would emerge later), it is also indisputably one reason why William Carlos Williams had to endure similar anticommunist assaults: he sought in Whitman an affirmation of "a relative measure"—for Weaver and Leigh Hanes this was the dreaded aesthetic thing—and Williams then boldly claimed that such an open form was the "order . . . essential to the new world, not only of the poem" but of all cultural aspects of democratic life in the United States.[142] Something of what the poet Ron Silliman today calls the "Desert Modernism"—he is playing on Williams's *The Desert Music* (1954), a book expressing isolation and the emptiness of a poetic generational interregnum crucial to the earliest developments of Silliman's own poetics[143]—reached its crescendo not during the red-baiting of Williams but in the years just afterward, for the period roughly from 1957 through 1962 was a time when Williams's official critical reputation had been both fully deradicalized and demodernized. In the summer of 1959, in the "contemporary poetry issue" of the *American Scholar*, Karl Shapiro announced that Williams was simply "not modern,"[144] and in October 1962, in a speech delivered at the National Poetry Festival sponsored by the White House (during the Cuban Missile Crisis), Randall Jarrell observed that Williams's verse had none of the "mooing awe for . . . the Common Man . . . that disfigures so much contemporary poetry."[145]

It is probably more accurate to say that the final phase in the deradicalization of modernism commenced with Robert Graves's coming out against modernists in the mid-1950s, a move clinched a little later in his much-discussed essay, "Wordsworth by Cable," the embittered commentary published in the *New Republic* in 1957. There he drew the connection between the emergence of "new *isms* and new stylistic excess." While Graves knew well that Gertrude Stein would not bring down freedom in the West the way Earl Browder might have—Graves was no Ben Lucien Burman, anxious about the spread of viral modernist germs—nonetheless it struck him that "stylistic excess," when mixed with other great causes of Depression-era ideologies, induced a still stronger will to sacrifice the individual's freedom. And political freedom was the precondition for lyricism.[146]

Faced with this logic, what ardent, open defenders of modernism there were did not typically feel, for the moment at least, that they had in their arsenal of rejoinders any sort of defense of communism or even of anti-anticommunism. It did little good to point out, as James Thrall Soby, Thomas Hess, and R. B. Beaman did, that foreign totalitarian regimes of the left had in fact done their best to *suppress* most forms of modernism and that when conservatives allied with groups funded by poet Archer Milton Huntington shrieked "Communist!" to protest a Los Angeles exhibit of modern art, "Stalin was also there agreeing."[147] A very basic logical—as well as, of course, political—aspect of the refutation of the antimodernists was systematically removed from among the choices. Had anti-anticommunism really been an option among strategies, the conservative antimodernist argument might have disappeared soon after it was first offered. But absent that option, it was difficult to side against the anticommunist basis of attacks on experimentalism. This situation substantially helped to give rise to the bland topical subjective lyricists—the "midcentury modernists"—who have sometimes been called (although not quite accurately) the New Formalists. As Ray Smith succinctly stated, "Conservative fears . . . compelled a false armistice of the forms."[148]

Two poets, each important in a different way—one an eminent reactionary who entered the 1950s with a reputation as a mainstream figure, the other a young New Formalist—made replies to Graves's "Wordsworth by Cable," with its sublimation of radicalism within the history of modernism combined with a definition of poetry as inherently "linked with metrical forms" (which is to say, *traditional* meters). The two replies came from John Crowe Ransom and William Jay Smith. Neither poet bothered to defend experimentalism, even hypothetically. Smith respectfully chided Graves for being outmoded. There was no sense in condemning contemporary poetry because of its use of free verse. Charges against modernists as careerist "great new experimenters in the line of Eliot and Pound" were irrelevant. Why? Well, "for the past ten years," Smith observed, "there has been on both sides of the Atlantic a conscious swing away from *vers libre* and a return to the metrical norm."[149] For Smith, Graves's point was not wrong; it was moot.

And John Crowe Ransom? With deference to Graves, Ransom stressed the domestic ending to the long story of William Wordsworth's protomodernist phrase-based construction of poetry—extracts from scrapbooks consisting of random observations made during "walk[s] around the world." In the end, the superannuated radical wrote out poems from these scrapbooks "when he had to sit at home," settled, domesticated, unworldly, far in time and location from revolution. For Ransom, this process, composition as a poetic practice of homecoming—in "the humorless complacency of his old age," as Mark Van Doren had put it in 1950[150]—is a productive and admirably "tidy sense of the uses of poetry."[151]

So much, then, for a response to attacks on free verse or a defense of constructivist writing. These were evidently yesterday's problems. From Ransom and Smith's statements, one would have thought Graves's essay had given a judicious summary of the situation. Yet to Graves's wildly overstated charge that modernist "experimentation . . . is already dated as a streamlined pogo-stick with decorative motifs from Tutankhamen's tomb" and the absurd and perhaps merely provocative claim that "the true American masters of experiment were such poets as John Crowe Ransom and Robert Frost,"[152] Smith and Ransom remained silent. What was really being fought here was the assumption that only the left in politics and only the avant-garde in literature were against conformity. And aside from the glad embarrassment of having been himself so pointedly complimented, John Crowe Ransom nodded at Robert Graves in the direction of Williams Wordsworth's domestic happy ending. Experimentalism likewise had come home. It was a time for tidying up.

The traditionalist Anna T. Harding announced in the newsletter of the League for Sanity in Poetry, "When experimentalism has exhausted its energy, the poet, weary of the 'uncharted freedom' of which Wordsworth admittedly 'tired,' may yearn for convention's very aid."[153] Just as it had become difficult to challenge Peter Viereck's assertion in 1956 that the "social poets of the 1930s . . . sloppily ignored the need for form" (and yet they had not), so similarly was it a special *political* challenge for formally and linguistically innovative writers to counter the observation that "among the younger contemporary poets, free verse is dead and forgotten."[154]

What had been and what would later again become the alternative to such a tidied-up poetics? This book has looked back, but another study could extend the story forward.

As a starting point, we might take Kenneth Patchen's apparently meager connection to contemporary poetics as an almost random example from among many possible. In a sensitive study of Patchen's work, Raymond Nelson notes that Patchen's distinction as a heretic was not in "what he says" when condemning conservative poets (for instance, "the [Allen] Tates throb . . . on the bosom of Jeff Davis")[155] but in "the way he goes about saying . . . such things," reminding us yet again that poetry—even or perhaps especially radical poetry—succeeds or fails because of its form. Nelson, personally familiar with the "downright hostile" response to Patchen, for various reasons delayed his book for nearly two decades. He well understood that Patchen's bad reputation came in large part because he had once been the darling of the communist left ("a young Shelley, who might discover a truly eloquent literature in the proletarian movement"), had moved away from organized socialism, was a pacifist when the CPUSA advocated the two-front war, later attacked liberalism from its left, created ideological antagonisms nonstop, and could by 1961 be lamented as almost entirely "Out of Sight, Out of Conscience" by poet Jonathan Williams.[156] Nelson deplores the long "adverse" view but is still more rueful that such judgment has been rendered about the poetry without any rigorous study, and so it is rigorous study that he calls for at the end of his book. Finally, Nelson hopes that Patchen will eventually achieve a living reputation *because* his strange writing is understood to be that of someone "who is always suspect."[157]

Patchen's first volume of poems, *Before the Brave* (1936), has been in my view correctly described as "combin[ing] a strong sense of design and formal shape with a lyricism that took Popular Front organizing verse in a strikingly new direction." It is also accurate to say, as the editor of a new newsletter devoted to this poet asserted in 2006, that Patchen, alas, "had no distinct social formation with which to be identified from 1940 until his death." The line that might have discernibly run from the merge of radical decentralism, alphabetic freehand drawing, performance, docuidiomatic aggregation, and vocalism in Patchen's writing to the work of recent experimental writers such as the Canadian poet Barry Phillip Nichol (bpNichol) or on the documentary side to Jena Osman—and to some recent visual, sound, and concrete poets more generally—was made well nigh impossible to follow by the direction in which the ridicule and vilification of Patchen during the Cold War pushed the writing and its core of devoted readers. Quite aside from their political strategies, it was not factually wrong of his traditionalist detractors to associate Patchen with radicalism. Indeed, he thought of himself as writing out "the story of the working-class artist."[158] Yet pinning him down ideologically tended to suppress otherwise direct connections not so much to the Beat poets as to a larger category of more linguistically innovative New American poets and to those of subsequent language-oriented and concrete poetry movements that in the late 1970s and 1980s would claim and commend the antiliterary impulses of writers such as Patchen and the fascinating Bob Brown, the communitarian (and commune resident) who alternately wrote utopian political tracts and books of participatory, typographically weird, and conceptual poetry. In the late 1940s and 1950s, attacks on Patchen and the complex of forces contributing to the almost total disappearance of Bob Brown's uncreative writing[159] seemed to be using excessive literary-historical force, far more than was necessary to put down the former and forget the latter. Why the excess?

In these and the cases of so many other beset writers mentioned in this book, there was always more linguistically to the story. The editor of *Celery Flute*, the intrepid Patchen newsletter, is not wrong to lament that in general "we [do not] have a[n] articulate program for finding continuity of purpose among innovative American poets from 1935–1950,"[160] a statement, I have found, that can be applied to a good many interesting poets, particularly if the latter date is extended to 1960 or so. *Counter-revolution of the Word* is in part a history of a disruption that sought to prevent a special lineage, the finding of that continuity of unorthodox literary purpose.[161] Even now, a relationship between Patchen, Brown, Norman Macleod, the Dynamo poets, or Eve Merriam, and bpNichol, Kathy Lou Schultz, Rodrigo Toscano, Jena Osman, or Lyn Hejinian (to take only a few suggestive possibilities) seems very odd and untenable. So do the relationships that are ascertainable between, on the one hand, contemporary makers of leftist documentary word collages, such as those of Osman,[162] and even Nichol's influential anarchic practice of "ideopomes" and "border-blur," and, on the other, their unknown radical predecessors. The political ground having now been mapped, these sort of connections can be made.

Then there is the work, difficult but pleasurable, of reading the poem *as poetry* while maintaining an awareness of a deep history of ideological readings that have already deformed the poem's career among the reading public. In historical terms, these poets believe such deformation to be the "social fraud," to use Hejinian's phrase, perpetrated by official American language about radicalism—the language against which many young political poets in the 1970s and 1980s, such as Hejinian, sought redress in organizing or constructing the process (in other words, the *writing*) of their own writing. Hejinian's seemingly nonpolitical *My Life*, written in the 1980s[163] and augmented through the 1990s in 2003,[164] presents a political portrait of a young artist as a languaged self passing through periods—especially the late 1940s and 1950s—in which language seemed to her the expression of that social fraud. "Deceptive metaphors," such as the trope that nations were dominos falling in set-piece order to communism, "establish[ed] the pretense that language is 'natural'—that we speak [in a Cold War sort of] way because there is no other way to speak."[165] Many American poets, after the demise of communism and the diminished relevance of anticommunism, continue to seek in poetry today an alternative to that naturalness.

Notes

Abbreviations Used in the Notes

b	box
f	folder
s	series

HI	Archives of the Hoover Institution, Stanford University, Stanford, California
KSA/WKU	Kentucky State Archives, Western Kentucky University, Bowling Green
MLR/F	M. L. Rosenthal Papers, Fales Library, New York University
PMP	*Poetry* Magazine Papers, Regenstein Library, University of Chicago
SUSCRC	Syracuse University Special Collections Research Center, Syracuse, New York
TL	Tamiment Library, Elmer Holmes Bobst Library, New York University
WU	Special Collections Department, Washington University Libraries, St. Louis

Preface

1. Renato Poggioli, *The Theory of the Avant-Garde*, trans. Gerald Fitzgerald (1962; Cambridge: Harvard University Press, 1968), p. 12.

2. See, e.g., Read Bain, "Poetry, Prose, and Criticism," *Humanist* 16, 3 (May–June 1956): pp. 148–49.

3. A. M. Sullivan to Phyllis McGinley, February 12, 1954, Phyllis McGinley Papers, SUSCRC.

4. Archer Milton Huntington to Nicholas Murray Butler, March 8, 1941, Archer M. Huntington Papers, SUSCRC.

5. Virginia Kent Cummins, "What Is Traditional Poetry?," *Lyric* 29, 2–3 (1949): pp. 195–96.

6. Jessie Wilmore Murton to Stanton Coblentz, February 22, 1949, Jessie Wilmore Murton to George S. Schuyler, February 3, 1949, Jessie Wilmore Murton Papers, b1, f14, KSA/WKU.

7. Stanton Coblentz, *New Poetic Lamps and Old* (Mill Valley, Calif.: Wings, 1950), p. 130; emphasis added.

8. Ibid., p. 129.

9. Peter Viereck, *The Unadjusted Man: A New Hero for Americans* (Boston: Beacon, 1956), p. 11.

10. Richard Hofstadter, *Anti-Intellectualism in American Life* (New York: Knopf, 1962).

Although written after the decade had ended, Hofstadter's book "was conceived in response to the political and intellectual conditions of the 1950's. During that decade the term *anti-intellectualism*, only rarely heard before, became a familiar part of our national vocabulary of self-recrimination and intramural abuse" (p. 3).

11. T. W. Adorno, Else Frenkel-Brunswik, Daniel J. Levinson, R. Nevitt Sanford, *The Authoritarian Personality* (1950; New York: Norton, 1982); Richard Hofstadter, "The Pseudo-Conservative Revolt—1954," in *The Paranoid Style in American Politics, and Other Essays* (New York: Vintage, 1967), pp. 41–65. The term "pseudo-conservative" was itself borrowed openly from Adorno ("Pseudo-Conservative Revolt," p. 43).

12. Qtd. in David S. Brown, *Richard Hofstadter: An Intellectual Biography* (Chicago: University of Chicago Press), p. 143.

13. Walter Lowenfels to Granville Hicks, January 5, 1938, Granville Hicks Papers, b35, SUSCRC.

Chapter 1

1. E.g., *Antioch Review*, September 1953, p. 313; emphasis added.

2. See Vivienne Koch, "The Necessary Angels of Earth," *Sewanee Review* 59 (1951): pp. 9–10; see also chapter 13. Koch was thus denigrating the poet Alfred Hayes.

3. "The leaders of the 'cultural' wing of today's capitalist-approved culture (and it is important to make the distinction as to leaders and more-or-less led), as Rossell H. Robbins has made it so surgically clear (in *The T. S. Eliot Myth*), are by and large the reactionary Southern Agrarians, Tate, Ransom, Warren, and their *Partisan Review* allies who have eased into control of criticism, the most important literary reviews, [and] college instruction" (Martha Millet, "Modern Poetry: For or Against?," *Masses & Mainstream*, March 1955, p. 41).

4. Herbert Aptheker, "Letter," *Masses & Mainstream*, December 1955, pp. 58–59.

5. See, e.g., Al Goeddel's "Art for Art's Sake," a satirical sequence of three sonnets (*New Masses* 52, 2 [July 11, 1944]: p. 11).

6. See Deming Brown, *Soviet Attitudes toward American Writing* (1962), esp. pp. 13–14. "In Soviet Russia," Herbert Read wrote, "any work of art that is not simple, conventional, and conformist is denounced as 'leftist distortion.' Any originality is described as 'petty bourgeois individualism'" (*Poetry and Anarchism* [London: Freedom, 1941], p. 27). My view coincides with that of Richard Hofstadter, "The Pseudo-Conservative Revolt," in his discussion of "fear[ing] the power of international communism": "Why do some Americans try to face this threat for what it is, a problem that exists in a world-wide theater of action, while others try to reduce it largely to a matter of domestic conformity?" (*American Politics, and Other Essays* [New York: Vintage, 1967], p. 50).

7. Martha Millet, "Mississippi," *Masses & Mainstream*, October 1955, p. 44.

8. See Christopher Metress, ed., *The Lynching of Emmett Till: A Documentary Narrative* (Charlottesville: University of Virginia Press, 2002).

9. Martha Millet, "The Nearness," *Masses & Mainstream*, November 1954, p. 23.

10. Martha Millet, "Orgy," *Meanjin* 13, 2 (Winter 1954): p. 202. To be sure, Millet

published her share of radical poems in traditional forms, such as the anti-McCarthyite "Many Are Called," a tritely rhymed, sing-songy piece that begins

One day—one not too far-off day,
A son of your own will say:
"When you were called upon the stand,
Did you take Honor by the hand?
When you were threatened with the ban,
Were you a creature—or a Man?"
(*Daily Worker*, June 2, 1953, p. 7)

11. Millet, "Modern Poetry," pp. 36, 44; emphasis added.

12. Alan Filreis, *Modernism from Right to Left* (New York: Cambridge University Press, 1994), pp. 187–88. See Daniel Cahill, *Harriet Monroe* (New York: Twayne, 1973), pp. 80, 86, 124.

13. Millet, "Modern Poetry," p. 40; emphasis added.

14. See Filreis, *Modernism from Right to Left*, pp. 186–94. Dillon's left-leaning editorship was cheered by the literary left: "Now that the chariot has swung low for sweet Harriet," Merrill Root wrote to Rolfe Humphries, "maybe there's a little more guts and zip. Must be, if George [Dillon] opens the pages to you. Hurrah!" (November 4, 1937, Rolfe Humphries Papers, b1, f6, Amherst College, Amherst, Massachusetts). Dillon read the *New Masses* and participated in Humphries's antifascist poetry project, . . . *And Spain Sings: Fifty Loyalist Ballads Adapted by American Poets* (New York: Vanguard, 1937) (Dillon to Humphries, April 27, May 18, 1937, Humphries Papers). Dillon made sure *Poetry* sent a delegate to "the poetry craft session" at the Congress of the League of American Writers in 1939 ("Poetry at the Writers' Congress," *Poetry* 54, 4 [July 1939]: p. 229). Dillon was never scared off by radicals' Marxist readings of their own submitted poems, though he might not ideologically agree. When Ruth Lechlitner sent "At the Road's Turn," she wrote forthrightly, "In the poem I've used as symbols the two most potent escape elements in bourgeois society: sex and religion, and showing how these stand against the realization, till too late, of the swift advance of Fascism and its attendant ills." Dillon accepted the poem and it ran in the March 1942 issue (59, 6: pp. 322–23). In 1948, Lechlitner wrote to Marion Strobel, one of *Poetry*'s conservative postwar editors, to submit "Lines for the Year's End," which she frankly called "a political poem" while expressing the hope that "we [would] swing back . . . to the idea that poets are 'legislators, logicians, or critics of life' "; the poem was rejected (Lechlitner to Dillon, June 27, 1941, Lechlitner to Strobel, June 6, 1948, PMP 1936–53, s1, b15, f2).

15. The typical practice at *Poetry* in the late 1940s and 1950s was to send at least a brief personal note explaining the rejection.

16. Martha Millet to Henry Rago, April 8, 1956, PMP 1954–61, b23, f15.

17. Norman Macleod to Henry Rago, July 22, 1957, August 14, 1957, PMP 1954–61, b22, f3.

18. The prose poem "Homer" appeared in 1938 (*Poetry* 52, 5 [August 1938]: p. 255).

19. M. L. Rosenthal, "A Note on Tradition in Poetry," *Nation*, May 11, 1957, p. 419.

20. See chapter 13.

21. A copy of the ad (n.d. [1931?]) is in the radical periodicals collection at SUSCRC.

22. *Janus* 1, 1 (Autumn 1929): p. [1]. These magazines were following in a tradition established by the old *Masses* and especially the *Liberator* in the second decade of the century. New York–based modernists in particular deemed the work of Max Eastman, Floyd Dell, and others "indispensable," according to Margaret Anderson, editor of the supermodernist *Little Review* (qtd. in Adam McKible, *The Space and Place of Modernism: The Russian Revolution, Little Magazines, and New York* [New York: Routledge, 2002], p. 24).

23. Kenneth Burke to Isidor Schneider, January 12, 1936, correspondence b "A–L," Isidor Schneider Papers, Rare Books and Manuscript Library, Columbia University, New York.

24. Ibid., October 3, 1932.

25. Horace Gregory to Selden Rodman, n.d. [1934], Horace Gregory Papers, SUSCRC.

26. Babette Deutsch, "August 23, 1927," *Modern Quarterly* 4, 3 (Winter 1927–28): p. 247.

27. Babette Deutsch, "Understanding Poetry," *American Scholar* 10, 1 (Winter 1940–41): p. 68.

28. Richard Wright, "Blueprint for Negro Writing," *New Challenge* 2 (Fall 1937): 53–65.

29. Sidney Finkelstein, *Art and Society* (New York: International, 1947), pp. 23, 28, 114 (on Schoenberg), 157–64 (Eliot), 202, 203, 233 (Bartok), 236–40 (Picasso), 194–98 (Stein); for "stimulated" etc., see p. 196. See also Andrew Hemingway, *Arts on the Left: American Artists and the Communist Movement 1926–1956* (New Haven: Yale University Press, 2002), pp. 219–220. *Art and Society* was written in the 1930s but was published by the communist press, International Publishers, in 1947. It should be noted, however, that beginning in 1950, the *Daily Worker* and *Political Affairs* attacked Finkelstein's work as ruined by "gross theoretical error."

30. Carl Rakosi to the author, December 8, 2002.

31. Joseph Kalar, "Pamphlet Poetry," *New Masses* 16, 6 (August 6, 1935): p. 24.

32. Joseph Kalar, "He Wants to Know," *New Masses* 5, 4 (September 1929): p. 22.

33. Alvaro Cardona-Hine to Charles Humboldt, November 8, 1962, Charles Humboldt Papers, b2, f38, Manuscripts and Archives, Yale University Library, New Haven, Connecticut.

34. Aaron Kramer, *Wicked Times: Selected Poems*, ed. Cary Nelson and Donald Gilzinger Jr. (Urbana: University of Illinois Press, 2004), p. xxxiv.

35. E. Merrill Root to Rolfe Humphries, January 30, 1937, Humphries Papers, b1, f6. This was of course the time of the Popular Front, when CPUSA policies sought inclusion of political liberals and literary diversity.

36. Richard Rovere, *Final Reports: Reflections on Politics and History in Our Time* (Garden City, N.Y.: Doubleday, 1984), p. 64.

37. Alan Filreis and Harvey Teres, "An Interview with Stanley Burnshaw," *Wallace Stevens Journal* 13, 2 (Fall 1989): pp. 110, 113.

38. Morton Dauwen Zabel, "Two Years of Poetry, 1937–1939," *Southern Review* 5, 3 (1939): p. 585.

39. Eve Merriam, "Imagine Yourself," *Poetry* 58, 6 (September 1941): p. 314.

40. Henry George Weiss [*sic*], "Poetry and Revolution," *New Masses* 5, 5 (October 1929): p. 9. See also Cary Nelson, *Repression and Recovery: Modern American Poetry and the Politics of Cultural Memory, 1910–1945* (Madison: University of Wisconsin Press, 1989), pp. 154, 302 n. 194.

41. Bob Brown, *The Readies* (Paris: Roving Eye, 1930), p. iv; Bob Brown, "Writing Readies," *Morada* 5 ([1930?]): p. 16.

42. J. Malcolm Brinnin, "Poem for the Birth of X," *New Masses* 35, 6 (April 16, 1940): p. 16; J. Malcolm Brinnin, "The Fiery Exile," *New Directions in Poetry and Prose* 8 (1944): pp. 183–92; J. Malcolm Brinnin and Kimon Friar, "Poetry in the Modern Idiom," in *Modern Poetry: American and British*, ed. Brinnin and Friar (New York: Appleton-Century-Crofts, 1951), p. ix.

43. See Alan Wald, *Exiles from a Future Time: The Forging of the Mid-Twentieth-Century Literary Left* (Chapel Hill: University of North Carolina Press, 2002), pp. 306–7.

44. E. A., "Poems for Enjoyment," *Sunday Worker*, February 14, 1943, p. 13. This was a review of Louis Untermeyer's *A Treasury of Great Poems, English and American* (New York: Simon and Schuster, 1942).

45. Harry Brown to George Marion O'Donnell, September 11, 1938, George Marion O'Donnell Papers, letters to Brown 1936–38, WU. As for Brown's conservatism: "I am so damned tired of having these violent fools whining about the workers of the world that I could almost welcome Fascism" (Brown to O'Donnell, September 11, 1938, O'Donnell Papers). Maas was among the signers of the original 1935 call for the formation of the League of American Writers ("Between Ourselves," *New Masses* 14, 10a [March 12, 1935]: p. 30).

46. Carl Rakosi, *Selected Poems* (Norfolk, Conn.: New Directions, 1941), p. [4]; Carl Rakosi, *Poems, 1923–1941*, ed. Andrew Crozier (Los Angeles: Sun and Moon, 1995), pp. 166–67.

47. Carl Rakosi to the author, July 2, 2003, February 23, 2003.

48. Isidor Schneider's poem "Dawn" consists of these two lines: "O auroral obfuscation! — / lace sleeves over the hard grasp of day" (typescript in PMP 1912–35, b21, f29). See also Harriet Monroe's response to Stanley Burnshaw's "Eartha" sequence (Filreis, *Modernism from Right to Left*, pp. 198, 346 n. 94). "Parnassian" was Burnshaw's term for the poem he submitted to the *New Caravan*, which was being edited by a communist (Filreis and Teres, "Interview with Stanley Burnshaw," p. 112).

49. Louis Untermeyer, "War Poets and Others," *Yale Review*, n.s. 35, 2 (December 1945): p. 336.

50. Stanley Burnshaw, "Notes on Revolutionary Poetry," *New Masses* 10, 8 (February 20, 1934): pp. 20–21.

51. This was the "worker-writer" Jack Conroy, describing the writing of *The Disinherited* (1933) in his essay, "Home to Moberly" (*Missouri Library Association Quarterly* 29, 1 [March 1968]: p. 49), qtd. in Lewis Fried, "The Disinherited: The Worker as Writer," *New Letters* 39, 1 (Fall 1972): p. 33.

52. Isidor Schneider, "Hard Luck of Poets," *New York Times*, April 9, 1932, sec. 1, p. 16.

53. Babette Deutsch, "Poetry for the People," *English Journal* 26, 4 (April 1937): p. 274.

54. Robert Penn Warren in a review of Isidor Schneider's *From the Kingdom of Necessity* (*Southern Review* 1, 3 [1935]: p. 647).

55. This was E. Merrill Root, a poet and political extremist who was briefly, in the early 1930s, associated with the communist movement. In 1932, after some time as a contributor, he became contributing editor to the *New Masses*. Root's continuous devotion to Frost's aesthetic and person dated from his years at Amherst as a student (see Rolfe Humphries, "The Other Side of Sound," *Poetry* 54, 5 [July 1939]: p. 225). Root described his involvement with the *New Masses* in Root to Humphries, January 30, 1937, Humphries Papers, subseries A, b1, f6.

56. E. Merrill Root to Rolfe Humphries, March 7, 1942, Humphries Papers, subseries A, b1, f6.

57. Morris U. Schappes began his Columbia University dissertation on the poems of Emily Dickinson after he received a master's degree in 1930, at the same time he joined a Marxist study group. He formally became a member of CPUSA in 1934 (Alan Wald, *Trinity of Passion: The Literary Left and the Antifascist Crusade* [Chapel Hill: University of North Carolina Press, 2007], pp. 201–2).

58. Edward Dahlberg to Joseph Warren Beach, January 3, 1933, Joseph Warren Beach Papers, University Archives, University of Minnesota, Minneapolis. In this period, Dahlberg was still affiliated with the CPUSA. He reported the Washington hunger march in 1932, warned of Hitler's power in 1933, covered fascist movements for the *New Masses* in 1934, and in 1935 helped organize the first American Writers' Congress, where he delivered a provocative paper, "Fascism and Writers."

59. Edward Dahlberg, introduction to Kenneth Fearing, *Poems* (New York: Dynamo, 1935), p. 11. See also Edward Dahlberg, "Kenneth Fearing: A Poet for Workers," *New Masses* 15, 8 (May 21, 1935): p. 24.

60. Marya Zaturenska to M. L. Rosenthal, January 27, 1958, MLR/F, b1, f41.

61. Kenneth Fearing, *Collected Poems of Kenneth Fearing* (New York: Random House, 1940), p. 79.

62. Ibid., p. 47.

63. M. L. Rosenthal, "The Meaning of Kenneth Fearing's Poetry," *Poetry* 66, 4 (July 1944): pp. 215, 217, 208.

64. Walter Lowenfels, "Masthead," *Sunday Worker*, January 31, 1954, p. 10. One passage reads,

> (You will demand
> full payment for the centuries
>   killed by sleep.)
> From my mouth you have taken away the food . . .
> Every beast that preys on man is a wolf.
> It need not have hooked nails or bloody teeth.
> Just the same it devours human flesh
>   (Po Chu-Lee said it in China 800 A.D.)

And Diogenes Laertius 2,000 years ago—
    The most beautiful thing in the world
        Is freedom of speech . . .
All that poets have sun
    moonlit seas

65. Richard Davidson, "A Garden of Chicago," *Mainstream* 13, 4 (April 1960): pp. 34–38.

66. As literary editor of *New Masses*, Schneider decried communists' "misevaluation of Henry James" ("Probing Writers' Problems," *New Masses*, 57, 4 [October 23, 1945]: p. 23); see also Isidor Schneider to "Joe" [North], June 15, 1946, Schneider Papers.

67. Thomas Yoseloff, *A Fellow of Infinite Jest* (New York: Prentice-Hall, 1945), p. xi.

68. Joseph Freeman to Floyd Dell, April 14, 1953, Floyd Dell Papers, "De Reserve Box," Newberry Library, Chicago. Freeman's relationship with CPUSA was dynamic and vexed, one of the fastest of moving targets. In this case particularly, one must attempt to track the extent to which a communist-affiliated poet's taste for modernism was tolerated by others in or near the party. The finest account of Freeman's connection to radicalism appears in Wald's *Exiles from a Future Time*; see esp. pp. 9–12, 178–91. For more on Freeman's shifting connection to communism in a contemporary literary account, see Willard Thorp, "American Writers on the Left," in *Socialism and American Life*, ed. Donald Drew Egbert and Stow Persons (Princeton: Princeton University Press, 1952), vol. 1, pp. 611–13.

69. Louise Bogan, *Achievement in American Poetry, 1900–1950* (Chicago: Regnery, 1951), p. 92.

70. These poems and others were collected in Gene Frumkin, *The Hawk and the Lizard* (Denver: Swallow, 1963).

71. Gene Frumkin to Robert Sward, February 15, 1959, Robert Sward Papers, sI.1, b12, f19, WU.

72. This was the recollection of Carl Rakosi (letter to the author, January 11, 2003).

73. Thorp, "American Writers on the Left," vol. 1, p. 607.

74. Isidor Schneider, "Writers after Two Wars," *Masses & Mainstream*, November 1948, p. 36.

75. Kenneth Rexroth to Babette Deutsch, June 16, 1952, Babette Deutsch Papers, WU.

76. Donald Hall deemed Gardner's poems relatively "original . . . in a time of conservatism" (*New England Quarterly* 29, 2 [June 1956]: p. 249). In reply to a tirade against modernist incomprehensibility and excess, Karl Shapiro noted in 1952 that "the extreme period of a difficult kind of poetry has now passed and . . . nearly all poets are writing in a manner that is acceptable to most literate readers." Shapiro's example of such "acceptable" verse is Gardner's (Karl Shapiro to Sidney A. Cooley, June 4, 1952, PMP 1936–53, s2, b2, f14).

77. Edward Dahlberg to Robert Creeley, March 14, 1958, Robert Creeley Papers, b31, f16, Manuscripts Division, Stanford University Library, Stanford, California.

78. Babette Deutsch, "Lyrics from Ecuador and New England," *New York Times Book Review*, February 16, 1947, p. 4.

79. Brad Gooch, *City Poet: The Life and Times of Frank O'Hara* (New York: Knopf, 1993), pp. 137, 129.

80. Adrienne Rich, *Arts of the Possible: Essay and Conversations* (New York: Norton, 2001), p. 46.

81. Doris Grumbach, "The Lost Liberals," *Commonweal* 55, 25 (March 28, 1952): pp. 609–10.

82. Malcolm Cowley to Isidor Schneider, August 30, 1946, Schneider Papers.

83. George Hitchcock, "Intact Vision," *Mainstream* 10, 3 (March 1957): p. 55.

84. George Hitchcock, "War," in *The Wounded Alphabet: Poems Collected and New, 1953–1983* (Santa Cruz, Calif.: Jazz, 1984), p. 4.

85. George Hitchcock, "On *Kayak*," *TriQuarterly* 43 (Fall 1978): p. 439.

86. *Contemporary Authors*, New Revision Series, vol. 13 (Detroit: Gale Research, 1984), p. 255.

87. George Hitchcock, "In This Third Year of a Useless War," *San Francisco Writers' Workshop Magazine*, Spring 1953, pp. 30–32; see also "Among Our Contributors," p. 47.

88. George Hitchcock, "The Indestructible (for Mariano P. Balgos of the Hukbala-hap)," *Masses & Mainstream*, September 1953, pp. 40–45.

89. Hitchcock, "On *Kayak*," p. 439.

90. Edgar Robinson, "Nine Kayak Books," *Chicago Review* 20, 1 (1968): p. 156.

91. *Kayak* 1 (Autumn 1964): p. [1].

92. Robert Creeley, untitled review, *Poetry* 98, 3 (June 1961): p. 198.

93. Wallace Stevens, *Collected Poems* (New York: Knopf, 1954), p. 224.

94. Judson Crews, "Elegy," *Iconograph* 4 (n.d.): n.p. (edited by Kenneth Lawrence Beaudoin); Judson Crews, personal statement, in *Contemporary Authors*, New Revision Series, vol. 24 (Detroit: Gale Research, 1988), pp. 136–38. See Wendell Anderson, *The Heart's Precision: Judson Crews and His Poetry* (Carson, Calif.: Dumont, 1994).

95. During a period (the early and mid-1930s) when Gregory held a reputation as one of the most successful communist poets, his poetry was nonetheless accepted as derived from Eliot and Crane and even, in its specific style of allusiveness, Pound. For more on Gregory's communist modernism, see, e.g., R. P. Blackmur, "The Ribbon of Craft," *Poetry* 42, 4 (July 1933): p. 219. Joseph Warren Beach later referred to "the Horace Gregory imitations of Eliot and Crane" (Beach to Robert Penn Warren, July 29, [1956], Beach Papers). Gregory was a signer of the "Call" to the first League of American Writers Congress in 1935 ("Call," in *New Masses: An Anthology of the Rebel Thirties*, ed. Joseph North [New York: International, 1969], p. 349). A 1955 editorial in *Wings* quoted lines from Gregory as the writing of a "run-of-the-mill 'modernist' poet" ("Beauty Is Truth, Truth Is Beauty," *Wings* 12, 1 [Spring 1955]: pp. 4–5).

96. Horace Gregory to M. L. Rosenthal, January 27, 1958, MLR/F, b1, f41.

97. Qtd. in Leo Gurko, *The Angry Decade* (New York: Dodd, Mead, 1947), p. 254.

98. Jackson Mac Low to the author (e-mail), March 14, 1999.

99. Jackson Mac Low to Henry Rago, October 19, 1954, PMP 1954–61, b22, f4.

100. Jackson Mac Low, *Representative Works, 1938–1985* (New York: Roof, 1986), p. 15.

101. Jackson Mac Low to Henry Rago, October 19, 1954, PMP 1954–61, b22, f4.

102. Jackson Mac Low, "A Poet of Movement," *Poetry* 80, 2 (May 1952): pp. 101–4.

103. Jackson Mac Low to Karl Shapiro, March 13, 1951, PMP 1936–53, b15, f10.

104. Ibid., April 22, 1951.

105. "News Notes," *Books Abroad* 26, 1 (Winter 1952): p. 117.

106. Jackson Mac Low, "The Ice-Furnace" and "I Heard a Voice," *Arena* 2, 6 (February–March 1951): pp. 26–27.

107. "31 Pacifists Defying Drill Arrested in City Hall Park," *New York World-Telegram*, June 15, 1955, p. 1; a copy of this story, in a collage of related news items apparently constructed by Mac Low, is in Jackson Mac Low Papers, b32, f4, Mandeville Collection, University of California at San Diego, La Jolla, California. For more on the Operation Alert protests, see John D'Emilio, *Lost Prophet: The Life and Times of Bayard Rustin* (New York: Free Press, 2003), pp. 213–14.

108. Jackson Mac Low to Bayard Rustin, n.d. [July 1955], Mac Low Papers, s9b, b79, f3; "Pacifists Plan Test of State Defense Act; Seized in Raid, May Go to High Court," *New York Times*, June 18, 1955, p. 8.

109. A reprint of this article is in Mac Low Papers, b32, f4.

110. Henry Rago to Jackson Mac Low, August 17, 1955, PMP 1953–61, b22, f4.

111. In later years, Mac Low characterized his early political views in starkest contrast to communist political theory. Documents in the Mac Low Papers amply bear out his anti-Stalinism, but he described his views on the debate between utopians (a term aligned with anarchists and pacifists) and "scientific-socialists" (a term associated with theoretical communism) as "neutral." "I certainly lean toward the utopians; but most precisely: I am neutral." He added that he was "a presentist (or, as the French like to say now: an 'existentialist')" as well ("Utopian Dreams and Libertarian Ethics," typescript, September 17–18, 1946, Mac Low Papers, b68, f21).

112. Jackson Mac Low, "Intention/Nonintention/Chance/Choice/Other," lecture, University of Buffalo, October 9, 1997. The late Jackson Mac Low generously provided me a typescript copy of this paper.

113. Louis Cabri, " 'Rebus Effort Remove Government': Jackson Mac Low, *Why?/Resistance*, Anarcho-Pacifism," *Crayon* 1 (1997): p. 68.

114. For more on Millet's life and work in the 1950s, see Walter Lowenfels, "A Visit with the Author of 'Alabaster Cities,' " *Sunday Worker Magazine* (New York–Harlem Edition), October 19, 1952, sec. 2, p. 7.

115. Shaemas O'Sheel to Horace Gregory, September 10, 1937, September 18, 1937, Gregory Papers. For "practically vermillion," see Shaemas O'Sheel to Rolfe Humphries, September 6, 1937, Humphries Papers.

116. Joy Davidman, "Poem for Liberation," *New Masses* 52, 11 (September 12, 1944): p. 8.

117. Oliver Pilat, "Girl Communist," *New York Post*, October 31–November 13, 1949. Davidman's turn away from atheism is recorded in a series of 1948 letters to V. J. Jerome (V. J. Jerome Papers, Yale University Library, New Haven, Connecticut) and in Kramer's notes provided for his archivist at the University of Michigan, interleaved in files containing correspondence from Norman Rosten (Aaron Kramer Papers, University of Michigan Special Collections, Ann Arbor).

118. Arnold Rampersad, "Langston Hughes," in *Encyclopedia of the American Left*, 2d ed., ed. Mari Jo Buhle, Paul Buhle, and Dan Georgakas (New York: Oxford University Press, 1998), p. 340.

119. *National Republic* Papers, b240, HI.

120. "Communism in Education," *Reader's Digest*, July 1948, p. 124.

121. "Banned, Branded, Burned," *Masses & Mainstream*, August 1953, p. 8; Arnold Rampersad, *The Life of Langston Hughes* (New York: Oxford University Press, 1988), vol. 2, p. 211.

122. Edwin J. Reinke to Elizabeth Dilling, December 10, 1940, *National Republic* Papers, b240. On others' neglect of and Hughes's later ambivalence toward his radical poetry, see Anthony Dawahare, *Nationalism, Marxism, and African American Literature between the Wars: A New Pandora's Box* (Jackson: University Press of Mississippi, 2003), pp. 92–110.

123. Langston Hughes to Virgil M. Rogers, October 5, 1948, Jessie Wilmore Murton Papers, b1, f14, KSA/WKU.

124. Norman Rosten to the "editor" of *Poetry*, February 15, 1954, PMP 1936–53, s1, b22, f5. Nicholas Joost, an associate editor, in an intramural note to editor Karl Shapiro, conceded that *Poetry*'s reviewer had given Rosten "a hard time" (PMP 1954–61, b29, f21).

125. Harry Roskolenko, "The Shadow Is Not the Rose," *Poetry* 83, 3 (December 1953): pp. 176–77.

126. Alfred Kreymborg, "Ballad of Art Young," *New Masses* 50, 5 (February 1, 1944): p. 24; Alfred Kreymborg, "Fellow Workers," *New Masses* 58, 3 (January 15, 1946): p. 4.

127. Alfred Kreymborg, *Troubadour: An Autobiography* (New York: Boni and Liveright, 1925).

128. Untermeyer, "War Poets and Others," p. 336.

129. John Gould Fletcher, "A Gentle Satirist," *Poetry* 66, 4 (July 1945): pp. 218–19.

130. Maxwell Bodenheim, "To John Gould Fletcher," *Poetry* 54, 5 (August 1939): p. 249.

131. Dorothy Day, "Max Bodenheim," *Catholic Worker*, March 1954, p. 8.

132. Dorothy Day, *Loaves and Fishes* (New York: Harper and Row, 1963), p. 155.

133. S. J. Perelman, "Cloudland Revisited: Great Aches from Little Boudoirs Grow," *New Yorker*, July 9, 1949, p. 16.

134. Day, "Max Bodenheim," p. 8.

135. Maxwell Bodenheim, "New Song," *New Masses* 9, 1 (September 1933): p. 30.

136. John Herrman, "Whither Bodenheim?," *New Masses* 7, 10 (April 1932): p. 26. This is a review of *Run Sheep Run* (1932).

137. Hart Crane to Allen Tate, March 30, [1927], Allen Tate Collection, Princeton University Library, Princeton, New Jersey.

138. For a biographical profile of Kramer, see Wald, *Trinity of Passion*, pp. 176–80.

139. Sillen as quoted from memory by Aaron Kramer (Kramer to the author, July 23, 1994).

140. Unlike other poets who were members of CPUSA or were closely affiliated with the party, most of whom typically broke away at some point (and left more or less decipherable traces of the break), Millet seems to have remained with the party even past

the fateful 1956 public revelations about Stalinism. Indeed, in 1965, Kramer, writing about the idea of a reunion edition of *Seven Poets*, noted that six had either died or moved away from the party: "Only Martha Millet remained as ever" (Kramer's annotation on a postcard from Rosten to Kramer, n.d. [1965], Norman Rosten Papers, Harlan Hatcher Graduate Library, University of Michigan, Ann Arbor).

141. See, e.g., Allan Antliff, *Anarchist Modernism: Art, Politics, and the First American Avant-Garde* (Chicago: University of Chicago Press, 2001). Antliff seeks to "recover the creative agency of those who invented, shaped, and implemented modernism for radical ends" (p. 3).

142. Thomas Yoseloff, ed., *Seven Poets in Search of an Answer: Maxwell Bodenheim, Joy Davidman, Langston Hughes, Aaron Kramer, Alfred Kreymborg, Martha Millet, Norman Rosten: A Poetic Symposium* (New York: Ackerman, 1944), p. 44.

143. Langston Hughes, "Lenin," *New Masses* 58, 4 (January 22, 1946): p. 5; Langston Hughes, "An Open Letter to the South," *New Masses* 7, 12 (June 1932): p. 10; Langston Hughes, "Good Morning, Revolution" and "For Tom Mooney," *New Masses* 8, 3 (September 1932): pp. 5, 16; Langston Hughes, "Hero—International Brigade," *Daily Worker*, July 22, 1952, p. 7.

144. Yoseloff, *Seven Poets in Search of an Answer*, pp. 87–88.

145. "If I Told Him: A Completed Portrait of Picasso," *Vanity Fair*, April 1924; reprinted in Gertrude Stein, *A Stein Reader*, ed. Ulla Dydo (Evanston, Ill.: Northwestern University Press, 1993), pp. 464–66.

146. Yoseloff, *Seven Poets in Search of an Answer*, p. [9].

147. M. L. Rosenthal, "A Note on Tradition in Poetry," *Nation*, May 1, 1957, p. 421; emphasis added.

148. Stanton Coblentz, *New Poetic Lamps and Old* (Mill Valley, Calif.: Wings, 1950), p. 26. Coblentz pairs Whitman and Hopkins in chapter 1, "Forbears of the New Movement" (pp. 13–26).

149. "Notes on Contributors," *Poetry* 51, 5 (February 1938): p. 292.

150. Untermeyer, "War Poets and Others," 336.

151. Alfred Kreymborg, "One Face," *Poetry* 51, 5 (February 1938): p. 243. The poem was accepted for publication in December 1937 (PMP 1936–53, s1, b14, f10).

152. "Poets Here Scorn Soviet Attack on Work; Versifier with 'Cure' Held 'Bore, Charlatan,'" *New York Times*, January 7, 1947, p. 25.

153. A. M. Sullivan to Phyllis McGinley, October 7, 1953, Phyllis McGinley Papers, SUSCRC.

154. Jackson Mac Low, "John Nerber's *The Spectre Image*," *Contemporary Poetry* 6, 4 (Winter 1947): p. 15.

Chapter 2

1. Qtd. in Anthony Dawahare, *Nationalism, Marxism, and African American Literature between the Wars: A New Pandora's Box* (Jackson: University Press of Mississippi, 2003), p. 94.

2. John Herrman, "Whither Bodenheim?," *New Masses* 7, 10 (April 1932): p. 26.

3. Maxwell Bodenheim, "Tenderly," *New Masses* 10, 7 (February 13, 1934): p. 21.

4. Dorothy Day, *Loaves and Fishes* (New York: Harper and Row, 1963), p. 155.

5. For a sense of Warshow's postcommunist views, see Alan Wald, *The New York Intellectuals* (Chapel Hill: University of North Carolina Press, 1987), p. 324.

6. Robert Warshow, "The Legacy of the '30's," *Commentary* 4, 6 (December 1947): p. 539.

7. See David Caute, *The Great Fear: The Anti-Communist Purge under Truman and Eisenhower* (New York: Simon and Schuster, 1978), pp. 161–263.

8. See Maurice Isserman, *If I Had a Hammer: The Death of the Old Left and the Birth of the New* (New York: Basic Books, 1987); Robbie Lieberman, *The Strangest Dream: Communism, Anticommunism, and the U.S. Peace Movement, 1945–1963* (Syracuse, N.Y.: Syracuse University Press, 2000).

9. Warshow, "Legacy of the '30's," p. 538; emphasis added.

10. John Earl Haynes, "The Cold War Debate Continues: A Traditionalist View of Historical Writing on Domestic Communism and Anti-Communism," *Cold War Studies* 2, 1 (Winter 2000): p. 78. Haynes is a persuasive "traditionalist" in the traditionalist-versus-revisionist battle among historians of American communism. In the passage quoted, though, he begins his survey by necessarily acknowledging that many "First Wave" chroniclers of communism, bearing "intensely emotional" views of the 1930s experience, tended not to give sufficient due to the liberal-radical alliance that enabled the New Deal they so admired. They "interpreted the New Deal in their own [liberal anticommunist] image" (p. 78). Haynes's summary in "Cold War Debate" and in *Communism and Anti-Communism in the United States: An Annotated Guide to Historical Writings* (New York: Garland, 1987) are indispensable guides to successive interpretations of communism in the 1930s and their Cold War legacies. Among the "revisionists," whose influence on the present study is greater, are Mark Naison (*Communists in Harlem during the Depression* [Urbana: University of Illinois Press, 1983]), Ellen Schrecker (*Many Are the Crimes: McCarthyism in America* [Princeton: Princeton University Press, 1998]), Alan Wald (*Writing from the Left: New Essays on Radical Culture and Politics* [New York: Verso, 1994]; *Exiles from a Future Time*; "Communist Writers Fight Back in Cold War Amerika," in *Styles of Cultural Activism: From Theory and Pedagogy to Women, Indians, and Communism* [Newark: University of Delaware Press, 1994], pp. 216–32), and Maurice Isserman (*Which Side Were You On?: The American Communist Party during the Second World War* [Middletown, Conn.: Wesleyan University Press, 1982]), among others.

11. Isidor Schneider, "Sectarianism on the Right," in *Years of Protest: A Collection of American Writings of the 1930s*, ed. Jack Salzman (New York: Pegasus, 1967), p. 283.

12. E. San Juan Jr., "Carlos Bulosan," in *The American Radical*, ed. Mari Jo Buhle, Paul Buhle, and Harvey J. Kaye (New York: Routledge, 1994), pp. 253–59.

13. Murray Kempton, *Part of Our Time: Some Ruins and Monuments of the Thirties* (1955; New York: Modern Library, 1998), p. 184.

14. Daniel Aaron, *Writers on the Left* (New York: Avon, 1961), p. 248.

15. Eugene Lyons, "In Defense of Red-Baiting," *New Leader* 29, 8 (December 7, 1946): p. 8.

16. Eugene Lyons, "Is Freedom of Expression Really Threatened?," *American Mercury*, January 1953, pp. 22–33. See also George Nash, "Forgotten Godfathers: Premature Jewish Conservatives and the Rise of the *National Review*," *American Jewish History* 87, 2–3 (June and September 1999): p. 138.

17. Lisle Rose, *The Cold War Comes to Main Street: America in 1950* (Lawrence: University Press of Kansas, 1999), p. 142.

18. *New York Times*, January 7, 1947, p. 25.

19. P. E. B. Canny, "Nineteen-thirty-seven," *Poetry Review* 41, 2 (1950): p. 64.

20. Eugene Lyons, "A Tour of the Leftist Press," *Nation's Business* 34 (August 1946): 48.

21. E. Merrill Root, *Collectivism on the Campus* (New York: Devin-Adair, 1955), pp. 28–30; emphasis added.

22. "Poets Here Scorn Soviet Attack on Work; Versifier with 'Cure' Held 'Bore, Charlatan,'" *New York Times*, January 7, 1947, p. 25.

23. Arthur Schlesinger Jr., *The Vital Center: The Politics of Freedom* (Boston: Houghton Mifflin, 1949), p. 122.

24. [Ray B. West], "On Beginnings, Middles, and Ends," *Western Review* 23, 1 (Autumn 1958): p. 4.

25. Peter Viereck, *The Unadjusted Man: A New Hero for Americans* (Boston: Beacon, 1956), p. 110.

26. George H. Nash, *The Conservative Intellectual Movement in America since 1945* (Wilmington, Del.: Intercollegiate Studies Institute, 1998), p. 87.

27. Owen Lattimore, "Mr. Lattimore Takes Exception," *New Leader* 35, 22 (June 2, 1952): p. 16.

28. Norman Podhoretz, "The New Nihilism and the Novel" (1958), in *Doings and Undoings: The Fifties and After in American Writing* (New York: Farrar, Straus, 1964), p. 175.

29. Leslie Fiedler, "Hiss, Chambers, and the Age of Innocence," in *An End to Innocence: Essays on Culture and Politics* (Boston: Beacon, 1952). See also Ronald Radosh, "The Legacy of the Anti-Communist Liberal Intellectuals," *Partisan Review* 67, 4 (October 2000): p. 555.

30. M. L. Rosenthal, "Poet in Spite of Himself," *New Republic*, April 24, 1950, p. 30.

31. Peter Viereck, "Symbols: Hiss and Pound," *Commonweal* 55, 25 (March 28, 1952): p. 608. Viereck's political reading of the New Deal is a good deal more complicated than this phrase suggests; it narrowly focused on the communists' betrayals, about which Viereck sensed no ambiguity. But about the New Deal generally, he contended that 1933 would come to occupy for American *conservatives* the same "sacred aura" that 1688 occupied for British conservatives—not a revolution but "a revolution aborted." He did not subscribe to the "the shared Republican and New Deal view" that the New Deal was anti-conservative (*Unadjusted Man*, pp. 235–36).

32. Daniel Bell, *The End of Ideology: On the Exhaustion of Political Ideas in the Fifties*, rev. ed. (New York: Collier, 1961), p. 305. This section of the book was first published in the *Saturday Review of Literature* in 1955.

33. Louise Bogan, "The Situation in American Writing," *Partisan Review* 6, 4 (1939): p. 107.

34. William Van O'Connor, "The Isolation of the Poet," *Poetry* 70, 1 (April 1947): p. 36.

35. Leslie A. Fiedler, *American Quarterly* 1, 2 (Summer 1949): p. 176.

36. Leo Gurko, *The Angry Decade* (New York: Dodd, Mead, 1947), is actually at points sympathetic to 1930s writing, but not to the poetry of the period. Moreover, Gurko's critical specialty was modern fiction. He published critical and scholarly articles in the 1950s on Hemingway, Conrad, Lawrence, and Sinclair Lewis (some twenty-five in all) but not a one on poetry. His views on poetry in *The Angry Decade* represent the stereotypical views of the decade by an educated nonspecialist.

37. Ben Hecht, *A Child of the Century* (New York: Fine, 1954), p. 159.

38. Dan Smoot, "Centralism," *Dan Smoot Report*, November 28, 1960, p. 380 (Dan Smoot Vertical File, TL). I have also read Smoot's master's thesis on playwright Maxwell Anderson (housed in Fondren Library, Southern Methodist University, Dallas).

39. "Practically all influential 'liberals' in America, although regarding themselves as anticommunists, want the same kind of society that communists are after" (Smoot, "Centralism," p. 381). "The philosophy of communism is closely similar to that philosophy of 'liberalism' which has dominated the intellectual and political life of America since 1933" (qtd. in Harry and Bonaro Overstreet, *The Strange Tactics of Extremism* [New York: Norton, 1964], p. 129).

40. Frank S. Meyer, *In Defense of Freedom: A Conservative Credo* (Chicago: Regnery, 1962), p. 108.

41. R[obert]. F[riedman]., "Valuable Survey of the Radical Novel in U.S.," *Daily Worker*, October 10, 1956, p. 6.

42. Richard Weaver, *The Ethics of Rhetoric* (Chicago: Regnery, 1953), pp. 228–29.

43. Ralph de Toledano, *Lament for a Generation* (New York: Farrar, Straus, and Cudahy, 1960), p. 11.

44. Edwin Rolfe, *Collected Poems*, ed. Cary Nelson and Jefferson Hendricks (Urbana: University of Illinois Press, 1993), p. 110.

45. Langston Hughes, *Selected Poems* (New York: Random House, 1959), p. 201. The poem was first published in *Negro Story*, October 1944.

46. John Chamberlain, "A Reviewer's Notebook," *Freeman*, August 11, 1952, p. 777.

47. Alfred Kazin to Granville Hicks, July 2, 1953, Granville Hicks Papers, b30, SUSCRC.

48. See Leo Marx, "The Teacher," *Monthly Review* 2, 6 (October 1950): pp. 210–11. Matthiessen's name had been included in a *Life* magazine spread that identified communist "dupes" ("Dupes and Fellow Travelers Dress Up Communist Fronts," *Life*, April 4, 1949, pp. 42–43).

49. Barrows Dunham in the *Monthly Review* 2, 6 (October 1950): p. 270.

50. Harry Levin, "The Private Life of F. O. Matthiessen," *New York Review of Books* 25, 12 (July 20, 1978): p. 42.

51. On the Harvard Hall speech, see Brad Gooch, *City Poet: The Life and Times of Frank O'Hara* (New York: Knopf, 1993), p. 129.

52. F. O. Matthiessen, "The Education of a Socialist," *Monthly Review* 2, 6 (October 1950): p. 177.

53. M. L. Rosenthal, "Confessions," typescript, n.d., MLR/F, s6, f6.

54. Stanley Burnshaw, interview by Alan Filreis and Harvey Teres, May 18, 1989, New York City.

55. William Phillips, "What Happened in the 30's," *Commentary* 30, 3 (September 1962): pp. 204, 205. Phillips's answer to this question was that it was both marginal and central.

56. See Theodore Draper, *The Roots of American Communism* (New York: Viking, 1957); Theodore Draper, *American Communism and Soviet Russia* (New York: Viking, 1960).

57. Nathan Glazer, *The Social Basis of American Communism* (New York: Harcourt, Brace, and World, 1961), p. 166.

58. Daniel Bell, "Marxian Socialism in the United States," in *Socialism and American Life*, ed. Donald Drew Egbert and Stow Persons (Princeton: Princeton University Press, 1952), vol. 1, p. 228.

59. Bell, *End of Ideology*, p. 302.

60. See Alan Filreis, "Words 'With All the Effects of Force': Cold War Interpretation," *American Quarterly* 39, 2 (Summer 1987): p. 310.

61. "An Interview with Paul Sweezy," *Monthly Review* 51, 1 (May 1999): pp. 42–43, 35.

62. "What is encouraging is that [communism] seemed highly unattractive to all but a handful" during the 1930s (Granville Hicks, "How Red Was the Red Decade," *Harper's Magazine*, July 1953, p. 61).

63. His point was that it had not nearly got us, and he referred his readers to a new book by Frederick Lewis Allen, *The Big Change: America Transforms Itself, 1900–1950* (New York: Harper, 1952), which argued the same point from a nonpartisan view.

64. Qtd. in Hicks, "How Red Was the Red Decade," p. 61.

65. Vivienne Koch to Karl Shapiro, November 11, 1951, PMP 1936–53, s1, b14, f9.

66. Alfred Kazin, statement in *Monthly Review* 2, 6 (October 1950): pp. 282–83.

67. See esp. s11, b12, f11–34A, Counterattack Papers, TL. Typical is a typewritten memo prepared for the Counterattack files summarizing Matthiessen's involvement as a sponsor of fund-raising efforts for the *Daily Worker* in the mid-1940s.

68. Billy James Hargis, *If Our Foundations Be Destroyed*, qtd. in John Harold Redekop, *The American Far Right: A Case Study of Billy James Hargis and Christian Crusade* (Grand Rapids, Mich.: Eerdmans, 1968), p. 50.

69. E. Merrill Root to Rolfe Humphries, August 20, 1944, Rolfe Humphries Papers, b1, f6, Amherst College, Amherst, Massachusetts.

70. Chamberlain, "Reviewer's Notebook," p. 777.

71. "Taming of the Muse," *News from Behind the Iron Curtain* 2, 4 (April 1953): p. 37.

72. Fulton Lewis Jr., *Top of the News*, radio broadcast transcript, July 16, 1959, Fulton Lewis Jr. Papers, vol. 1, p. 14, SUSCRC.

73. E. Merrill Root, "Trapped in Our Armor," *Freeman* 5, 7 (January 1955): p. 281.

74. Lewis, *Top of the News*, p. 14.

75. Gabriel Almond, *The Appeals of Communism* (Princeton: Princeton University Press, 1954), pp. 74–75.

76. Viereck, *Unadjusted Man*, p. 43.

77. One conservative attack on Hollywood produced a poster featuring the arm of a well-dressed man, shirt cuff adorned with a hammer-and-sickle cufflink, strong hand grasping an Oscar statuette: "To the American Amusement Industry . . . AN OSCAR (RED) . . . FOR MURDERING THE ENGLISH LANGUAGE . . . following the communist line . . . Un-American activities." The poster is in the collection of the Museum of American Political Life in West Hartford, Connecticut, and has been reproduced in Paul Buhle and Edmund B. Sullivan, *Images of American Radicalism* (Hanover, Mass.: Christopher, 1998), p. 292.

78. Kazin's "amnesia" in this respect is discussed briefly but well in Graham Barnfield's essay on rhetoric about prolecult, "The Novel as Propaganda: Revisiting the Debate," in *Propaganda: Political Rhetoric and Identity, 1300–2000,* ed. Bertrand Taithe and Tim Thornton (Phoenix Mill, U.K.: Sutton, 1999), pp. 288–89. Yet Hilton Kramer essentially accuses Kazin of falling under the sway of the communists by ignoring Faulkner's greatness and that of other writers who "resisted the blight of the Popular Front mentality." "If you doubt this," Kramer wrote, "go back and see how Faulkner fared in the pages of . . . *On Native Grounds* (1942). That [Kazin and Malcolm Cowley] afterwards lavished all sorts of praise on Faulkner is beside the point. While the communists and their fellow travelers were still a power on the literary scene, such critics could be counted on to fall into line" ("Arthur M. Schlesinger Jr.'s 'Innocent Beginnings,'" *New Criterion* 19, 7 [March 2001]: p. 60).

79. Alfred Kazin, *On Native Grounds: An Interpretation of Modern American Prose Literature* (New York: Reynal and Hitchcock, 1942), pp. 401, 407, 408, 409, 415.

80. Isidor Schneider, "Background to Error," *New Masses* 58, 7 (February 12, 1946): p. 23.

81. Kempton, *Part of Our Time*, p. 161.

82. Norman F. Cantor, *The Age of Protest: Dissent and Rebellion in the Twentieth Century* (New York: Hawthorn, 1969), p. 118.

83. David Carpenter, "Books," *Daily Worker*, December 3, 1948, p. 12.

84. Isidor Schneider, "Probing Writers' Problems," *New Masses* 57, 4 [October 23, 1945]: p. 23. Schneider's view was, indeed, a minority among cultural leadership in the party. A few months later, in "Says Full Discussion Necessary," *Daily Worker*, March 1, 1946 (p. 14), Schneider continued to hold such a view but had become more defensive. This was the time of the controversy stirred by Albert Maltz's article, "What Shall We Ask of Writers?" (*New Masses* 58, 7 [February 12, 1946], pp. 19–20). Schneider's "Says Full Discussion Necessary" is mostly a rejoinder to Samuel Sillen's attack on Maltz. See also Schneider, "Background to Error," pp. 23–25; Aaron, *Writers on the Left*, pp. 386–89.

85. Wallace Phelps [William Phillips], "The Methods of Joyce," *New Masses* 10, 8 (April 3, 1934): p. 26. Phillips would soon break away to join the dissident *Partisan Review*.

86. "Taming of the Muse," p. 41.

87. Solon Barber, "Nocturne in the Modern Manner," *Janus* 1, 1 (Autumn 1929): p. 24.

88. Rolfe Humphries to E. Merrill Root, November 15, 1936, July 11, 1938, Humphries Papers, b2, f15d.

89. Malcolm Cowley, "In Memory of Harriet Monroe," *Poetry* 49, 3 (December 1936): p. 158.

90. Eda Lou Walton to George Dillon, February 12, 1938, PMP 1936–53, s1, b26, f15.

91. Herbert Aptheker to the author, April 22, 1999.

92. Eda Lou Walton to George Dillon, February 12, 1938, PMP 1936–53, s1, b26, f15.

93. The disconnection of 1930s from 1960s radicalisms has been itself one of the legacies of the 1950s, as Maurice Isserman and other historians have shown. Isserman's *If I Had a Hammer: The Death of the Old Left and the Birth of the New Left* (New York: Basic Books, 1987) is a book-length attempt to reattach the severed connections between the Old and New Left—to find strands of continuity through the 1950s. Andrew Jamison and Ron Eyerman, *Seeds of the Sixties* (Berkeley: University of California Press, 1994), a study of intellectuals who served as a preservers of the Old Left narrative, also connects the 1930s to the 1960s. Among scholars of the literary left, Alan Wald has most persuasively demonstrated continuity through studies of radical careers that superseded the flat categorization as "1930s art." See esp. Alan Wald, "The 1930s Left in U.S. Literature Reconsidered," in *Radical Revisions: Rereading 1930s Culture*, ed. Bill Mullen and Sherry Lee Linkon (Urbana: University of Illinois Press, 1996), pp. 13–28; Wald, "Communist Writers Fight Back"; Alan Wald, "Culture and Commitment: U.S. Communist Writers Reconsidered," in *New Studies in the Politics and Culture of U.S. Communism*, ed. Michael E. Brown, Randy Martin, Frank Rosengarten, and George Snedeker. (New York: Monthly Review Press, 1993), pp. 281–305. For an example of a critic who argued that there ought not to be a connection made between 1930s and 1960s radicalism, see Phillips, "What Happened in the 30's," pp. 204–12, esp. 210.

94. Warren French, "The Thirties—Poetry," in *The Thirties: Fiction, Poetry, Drama*, ed. Warren French (Deland, Fla.: Edwards, 1967), p. 121.

95. E.g., by Mark Royden Winchell in his biography of the antimodernist poet Donald Davidson. Winchell's assertion that "although some memorable verse was written in the thirties, no major figures or important movements originated during the decade" is documented only by citation to French. Winchell goes on to call Kenneth Fearing, as representative of American poets of the thirties, a "talented propagandist . . . whose work seems curiously dated" (*Where No Flag Flies: Donald Davidson and the Southern Resistance* [Columbia: University of Missouri Press, 2000], p. 168).

96. See Alan Filreis, *Modernism from Right to Left* (New York: Cambridge University Press, 1994), esp. pp. 139–290. On Stevens's relationship to the liberal-left state of the 1930s, see also Michael Szalay, *New Deal Modernism: American Literature and the Invention of the Welfare State* (Durham: Duke University Press, 2000), pp. 120–61.

97. See Filreis, *Modernism from Right to Left*, pp. 180–247.

98. See Victor Navasky, *Naming Names* (New York: Viking, 1980), chapter 10, "Degradation Ceremonies," pp. 314–29.

99. Sister Mary Julian Baird, "Why Modern Poets Have Failed," *Catholic World*, December 1958, pp. 208–18.

100. Peter Viereck, "The Dignity of Lyricism II," *New Republic*, June 7, 1954, pp. 18–19.

101. John Chamberlain not only admired Viereck but paired him with Kirk. Both men admirably "work[ed] in defiance of critical fashions" (John Chamberlain, "The Literary Market, 1952–1953," *Human Events* 10, 33 [August 19, 1953]: p. [4]).

102. See, e.g., Kirk's review of *The Unadjusted Man* in *Annals of the American Academy of Political and Social Science* 309 (January 1957): pp. 181–82.

103. For Meyer, Viereck was a "counterfeit at a popular price." He "pass[ed] off his unexceptionably Liberal sentiments as conservatism," and his prose was full of "preposterous masquerades," typically involving "a speculative flutter on the long side in Metternich or Burke" yet "always well hedged with short commitments in whatever is particularly obnoxious to the Liberals on the contemporary scene." Viereck's was a "game" that "has to be played if one wants success upon the terms within which the Establishment is prepared to grant success" (Frank S. Meyer, "Counterfeit at a Popular Price," *National Review* 2, 12 [August 11, 1956]: p. 18). Meyer's general case against New Conservatism is presented in *In Defense of Freedom*.

104. When Viereck was given a central role in George Nash's *The Conservative Intellectual Movement in America, since 1945* (New York: Basic Books, 1976), Regnery took exception, noting that Viereck's "rather pale epigrammatic formulation would never have brought about a vigorous intellectual movement" (Henry Regnery, "The Picture of a Remnant," *Modern Age* 21, 1 [Winter 1977]: p. 93). Although Regnery felt that Viereck was finally "on the right side," especially in his view that William F. Buckley would "become a real force," Regnery felt that Viereck "went too far in his criticisms" (Henry Regnery to William F. Buckley, Henry Regnery Papers, b10, Buckley f, HI).

105. See Samuel Sillen, "Van Wyck Brooks and the Literary Crisis," *Masses & Mainstream*, October 1953, p. 21. "Nor . . . is the world inspired by the current mess of warmed-over mystical and anti-liberal creeds, such as . . . Peter Viereck's 'Conservatism Revisited.' "

106. Kenneth Rexroth to Babette Deutsch, October 17, 1952, Babette Deutsch Papers, WU.

107. John Frederick Nims to Henry Rago, November 8, 1956, PMP 1954–61, b25, f15.

108. Root, "Trapped in Our Armor," p. 281.

109. Viereck, "Symbols," p. 607.

110. The theme is struck throughout Bell's writings about culture. E.g., "Traditional modernism, no matter how daring, played out its impulses in the imagination, within the constraints of art" (Daniel Bell, *The Cultural Contradictions of Capitalism* [New York: Basic Books, 1976], p. 51).

111. Selden Rodman in the *Saturday Review of Literature*, qtd. on the dustjacket of Viereck's *Strike through the Mask!: New Lyrical Poems* (New York: Scribner's, 1950); emphasis added.

112. Kissinger's prose style evinced the qualities he admired in Bismarck: he "could never accept the good faith of any opponent," which "accounts for his mastery in adapting

to the requirements of the moment" (Walter Isaacson, *Kissinger: A Biography* [New York: Simon and Schuster, 1992], pp. 107–8).

113. Peter Viereck, "New Views on Metternich," *Review of Politics* 13, 2 (April 1951): pp. 211–28. On Kissinger and Metternich, see Isaacson, *Kissinger*, pp. 74–77.

114. Peter Viereck, " 'Bloody-Minded Professors': The Anti-Social Role of Some Intellectuals," *Confluence* 1, 3 (September 1952): pp. 29–45. Some of the letters to Kissinger were published in vol. 2, no. 1 (March 1953): pp. 123–24; vol. 1, no. 4 (December 1952): pp. 101–2.

115. Viereck, " 'Bloody-Minded Professors,' " pp. 38, 39.

116. Ibid., p. 38.

117. Shaemas O'Sheel to Rolfe Humphries, September 6, 1937, Humphries Papers. O'Sheel, a fellow traveler, had gone during the summer of 1937 to New York to make communist literary connections, and Rovere was his guide, introducing the older writer to contacts at the *Daily Worker*, at *New Masses*, and in the League of American Writers. By 1939, Rovere had joined a group of intellectuals disenchanted with the CPUSA (Aaron, *Writers on the Left*, p. 376).

118. See Richard Rovere, *Final Reports: Reflections on Politics and History in Our Time* (Garden City, N.Y.: Doubleday, 1984), pp. 42–57.

119. Richard Rovere, "Return from Utopia," *Partisan Review* 18, 4 (July–August 1951): pp. 474–76; Richard Rovere, "Communists in a Free Society," *Partisan Review* 19, 3 (May–June 1952): pp. 339–46. "Senator McCarthy," he wrote, "is as contemptuous of the truth as any Communist" ("Communists in a Free Society," p. 340). Rovere's liberal anticommunist position is well described in his review of Clair Wilcox's *Civil Liberties under Attack* (*American Quarterly* 3, 4 [Winter 1951]: pp. 366–68). Rovere later claimed that he had "never been an anti-Communist," although he conceded, "I am against a good many things, Communism among them" (contribution to a symposium on "Liberal Anti-Communism Revisited," *Commentary* 44, 3 [September 1967]: p. 68).

120. Richard H. Rovere, "Bloody-Minded Professors: A Reply to Mr. Viereck," *Confluence* 1, 4 (December 1952): pp. 77–85.

121. Viereck, *Unadjusted Man*, p. 11.

122. Richard Rovere, "Two New Conservatives," *New Yorker*, March 21, 1953, pp. 126–34. See also Richard Rovere, "Books Are News," *United Nations World* 7, 5 (May 1953): pp. 48–49.

123. Hilton Kramer, "To Hell with Culture," *Dissent*, Spring 1959, pp. 164–65.

124. In the fall of 1949, Frank O'Hara attended Poggioli's course on "Theory of the Advance-Guard Art" at Harvard, which formed the basis of his study (Gooch, *City Poet*, p. 150).

125. Renato Poggioli, *The Theory of the Avant-Garde*, trans. Gerald Fitzgerald (1962; Cambridge: Harvard University Press, 1968), p. 168; emphasis added.

126. Ibid., p. 95.

127. See Peter Bürger, *Theory of the Avant-Garde*, trans. Michael Shaw (1974; Minneapolis: University of Minnesota Press, 1984), p. 95.

128. Ibid., p. 49.

129. Under Calverton's editorship, the *Modern Quarterly* maintained a link between communism (to which he was then sympathetic) and modernism; see Alan Wald, *Exiles from a Future Time: The Forging of the Mid-Twentieth-Century Literary Left* (Chapel Hill: University of North Carolina Press, 2002), p. 26.

130. This is Arthur M. Schlesinger Jr.'s phrase, used when he summarized Lincoln Steffens's point of view as a supporter of the Soviet Union (*The Age of Roosevelt: The Politics of Upheaval* [Boston: Houghton Mifflin, 1960], vol. 3, p. 185).

131. V. F. Calverton to Max Eastman, n.d., V. F. Calverton Papers, b5, Rare Books and Manuscripts Division, New York Public Library, New York, Astor, Lenox, and Tilden Foundations.

132. Stephen Spender, "The New Orthodoxies," in *The Arts at Mid-Century*, ed. Robert Richman (New York: Horizon, 1954), p. 6.

133. Eliseo Vivas, "Allen Tate as Man of Letters," *Sewanee Review* 62 (1954): pp. 131, 135.

134. Eliseo Vivas, "Art, Morals, and Propaganda," *International Journal of Ethics* 46, 1 (October 1935): pp. 91–92, 92 n. 6. The note read, in part, "My formulation of their position, however, is still valid for many Marxists and was valid for most of them until, say, 1933–34." Vivas was a favorite of conservative antimodernists; see Henry Regnery, ed., *Viva Vivas!: Essays in Honor of Eliseo Vivas* (Indianapolis: Liberty, 1976).

135. Kempton, *Part of Our Time*, pp. 178–79; emphasis added.

136. Diana Trilling, "The Other Night at Columbia: A Report from the Academy," *Partisan Review* 26, 2 (Spring 1959): p. 214.

137. Funaroff's "What the Thunder Said" (1932) was a revolutionary "answer" to Eliot.

138. Kempton, *Part of Our Time*, pp. 178–79.

139. Kerker Quinn, untitled review of Willard Maas's *Fire Testament*, *New Republic*, November 20, 1935, p. 55. For more about Maas's admiration of Stevens, see Filreis, *Modernism from Right to Left*, pp. 126–27.

140. George Dillon to H. H. Lewis, November 2, 1938, PMP 1936–53, b15, f4. See also Douglas Wixon, *Worker-Writer in America* (Urbana: University of Illinois Press, 1994), p. 455.

141. Ruth Lechlitner, "Edna Millay Writes a Long Drama of Ideas," *New York Herald Tribune Books*, July 25, 1937, p. 3.

142. See Herman Spector, *Bastard in the Ragged Suit: Writings of, with Drawings by, Herman Spector*, comp., ed., and intro. Bud Johns and Judith S. Clancy (San Francisco: Synergistic, 1977).

143. Walter Lowenfels, "Three Decades of Poems," *Mainstream* 10, 3 (May 1957): p. 52.

144. Eda Lou Walton, "The Death of Yeats," in *So Many Daughters* (New York: Bookman, 1952), p. 19.

145. Henry Roth, "On Being Blocked and Other Literary Matters," *Commentary* 64, 2 (August 1977): p. 31.

146. See *Rebel Poet* 1, 9 (March 1931): p. 1.

147. John Edgar Tidwell seems certain that Davis joined CPUSA. Alan Wald writes that Davis was "close to the Communist Left, perhaps even a member in the 1940s"

(Wald, "Radical Poetry, 1930s–1960s," in *Encyclopedia of the American Left*, 2d ed., ed. Mari Jo Buhle, Paul Buhle, and Dan Georgakas [New York: Oxford University Press, 1998], p. 674).

148. John Edgar Tidwell, ed., *Frank Marshall Davis: Black Moods, Collected Poems* (Chicago: University of Chicago Pres, 2002), pp. xxvi–xxvii.

149. "Artist and laborer," Kreymborg wrote to CPUSA's chief cultural commissar, V. J. Jerome, "were never divorced in the greatest ages of human culture and the divorce that holds them apart now through a common slavery to the bourgeoisie must be destroyed" (Kreymborg to Jerome, December 15, 1940, V. J. Jerome Papers, b589, Yale University Library, New Haven, Connecticut). See also Filreis, *Modernism from Right to Left*, pp. 189, 194–98, 229.

150. Alfred Kreymborg to Henry Rago, November 1, 195[6] (Kreymborg misdated it 1954), PMP 1954–61, b19, f24.

151. See, e.g., "Social Worker," which was published in the November 1931 issue (reprinted in Jack Conroy, ed., *Writers in Revolt: The "Anvil" Anthology* [New York: Hill, 1973], pp. 224–25): "Several young social workers who had radical tendencies, caused by reading Bolshevik books at universities, / Have been brought to see the errors of their ways and now appreciate the benevolent goodness of our men of great wealth" (p. 225).

152. Nina Singleton, "Poet of the Thirties Regains Stronger Voice in the Seventies," in Walter Snow, *The Glory and the Shame, Poems* (Coventry, Conn.: Pequot, 1973), p. xiii.

153. Isidor Schneider to Amy Bonner, December 4, 1941, Amy Bonner Papers, b1, f15, Regenstein Library, University of Chicago.

154. See Filreis, *Modernism from Right to Left*, pp. 194–98.

155. Spector, *Bastard in the Ragged Suit*, p. 15.

156. Roger Seamon to the author (e-mail), November 12, 1997. Seamon is Walton's nephew.

157. Alan Filreis and Harvey Teres, "An Interview with Stanley Burnshaw," *Wallace Stevens Journal* 13, 2 (Fall 1989): p. 111.

158. Stanley Edgar Hyman, "The Marxist Criticism of Literature," *Antioch Review* 7, 4 (December 1947): p. 547.

159. Leslie Fiedler, "Images of Walt Whitman," in *An End to Innocence*, p. 165.

160. Meyer refers to "Bertolt Brecht, the only poet of stature Western Communism has produced" (*The Moulding of Communists: The Training of the Communist Cadre* [New York: Harcourt, Brace, and World, 1961], p. 25).

161. Kempton, *Part of Our Time*, p. 170.

162. [West], "On Beginnings, Middles, and Ends," p. 4.

163. Kempton, *Part of Our Time*, p. 183.

164. Rovere, "Two New Conservatives," p. 127.

165. Rovere, "Bloody-Minded Professors," pp. 77–85.

166. The essay, in somewhat revised form, appeared as a section of chapter 7 ("Christopher Caudwell and Marxist Criticism") in Stanley Edgar Hyman, *The Armed Vision: A Study in the Methods of Modern Literary Criticism* (New York: Knopf, 1948), pp. 168–208.

167. F. O. Matthiessen, "Marxism and Literature," *Monthly Review* 4, 11 (March 1953): p. 399.

168. This was especially clear to those who had been privy to Hyman's strict readings of class in popular leftist literature. His line on Steinbeck, for instance, stood well to the left of Isidor Schneider, who at the time (1942) followed the Popular Front position of broadly defining cultural proletarianism. "History, I am afraid," wrote Hyman to Schneider, "will not see John Steinbeck as the author of a great proletarian novel, but as a rather tragic character of the type of Wordsworth, a man who sold out the class he once assumed to speak for" (Hyman to Schneider, June 10, 1942, Isidor Schneider Papers, b "correspondence A–L," Rare Books and Manuscript Library, Columbia University, New York).

169. Marx's daughters caught their father in a game of "confessions" in the early 1860s; Tupper was his response when asked to name his "pet aversion" (published as "The Confessions of Karl Marx," *Monthly Review* 4, 11 [March 1953], p. 401).

170. Hyman, "Marxist Criticism of Literature," pp. 553–54.

171. Ibid., pp. 566–68.

172. Karl Shapiro, "T. S. Eliot: The Death of Literary Judgment," in *In Defense of Ignorance* (New York: Random House, 1960), p. 41.

173. F. O. Matthiessen, *The Achievement of T. S. Eliot: An Essay on the Nature of Poetry*, 3d ed. (New York: Oxford University Press, 1959), p. ix. Here Matthiessen wrote of "my growing divergence from [Eliot's] view of life is that I believe that it is possible to accept the 'radical imperfection' of man, and yet to be a political radical as well" (p. ix).

174. William E. Cain, *F. O. Matthiessen and the Politics of Criticism* (Madison: University of Wisconsin Press, 1988), p. 62.

175. Matthiessen, *Achievement of T. S. Eliot* (1959), p. 110.

176. Ibid.

177. Cid Corman to the author (e-mail), December 1, 2001.

178. Corman's personal copy of F. O. Matthiessen, *The Achievement of T. S. Eliot: An Essay on the Nature of Poetry*, 2d ed. (New York: Oxford University Press, 1947), bound in blue-green cloth, stamped in gold, with dust jacket, from the library of Cid Corman, with his annotations. Laid into the book is the December 9, 1950, review published in the *Nation* (pp. 531–34). Special Collections, Kent State University Library, Kent, Ohio. I have referred to and quoted from pp. 29, 68, 43, 86.

179. Irving Howe, "The Critic as Stuffed Head," *Nation*, July 3, 1948, pp. 22–24; Giles B. Gunn, *F. O. Matthiessen: The Critical Achievement* (Seattle: University of Washington Press, 1975), pp. 46–58, esp. 56–57.

180. This statement, of course, by no means signified Matthiessen's willingness to separate his politics from the critical subjectivity of the study, and he also wrote, "My growing divergence from [Eliot's] view of life is that I believe that it is possible to accept the 'radical imperfection' of man, and yet to be a political radical as well" (Matthiessen, *Achievement of T. S. Eliot* [1959], p. ix).

181. The article, in the August 1947 issue of the *Anti-Communist* (p. 2), was based on Walter Steele's testimony before HUAC. Steele served as chair of the Security Coalition,

representing eighty-five patriotic groups. Matthiessen was mentioned as a member of the faculty at the Samuel Adams School in Boston (Counterattack Papers).

182. Corman's copy of Matthiessen, *Achievement of T. S. Eliot* (1947), p. 195, Special Collections, Kent State University Library, Kent, Ohio.

Chapter 3

1. Herbert A. Bloch, review of *The Radical Novel in the United States, 1900–1954: Some Interrelations of Literature and Society*, by Walter B. Rideout, *American Sociological Review* 22, 2 (April 1957): pp. 235–36; emphasis added.

2. Robert Richman, untitled review, *Accent* 5, 1 (Autumn 1944): pp. 249, 252.

3. Malcolm Cowley, *And I Worked at the Writer's Trade* (New York: Viking, 1978), pp. 136–37.

4. Kenneth Allott, ed., *The Penguin Book of Contemporary Verse, 1918–60* (London: Penguin, 1960), p. 27.

5. Donald Hall, "The New Poetry: Notes on the Past Fifteen Years in America," *New World Writing* 7 (1955): p. 231.

6. Cowley, *And I Worked at the Writer's Trade*, pp. 136–37.

7. Matthew Josephson to Kenneth Burke, April 1, 1947, Matthew Josephson Papers, Beinecke Library, Yale University, New Haven, Connecticut.

8. Daniel Aaron, "The Treachery of Recollection," *Carleton Miscellany* 6, 3 (Summer 1965): pp. 4–5.

9. Cowley, *And I Worked at the Writer's Trade*, pp. 136–37.

10. Harold Rosenberg, "The End of the World," *Poetry* 52, 4 (July 1938): pp. 206–7.

11. Kenneth Burke, "Thirty Years Later: Memories of the First American Writers' Congress," *American Scholar* 35, 3 (Summer 1966): p. 507. With Isidor Schneider and a few others, Rosenberg in the mid-1930s "kept alive" the League of American Writers, which was closely affiliated with the CPUSA (Burke, "Thirty Years Later, p. 513). In 1939, Rosenberg joined with poets Harry Roskolenko, Clark Mills, Parker Tyler, James Laughlin, Sherry Mangan, and others, led by Dwight MacDonald, to form the League for Cultural Freedom and Socialism. The league was openly anti-Stalinist, but its members retained the radical "scepticism in respect to bourgeois values in art and life" and hailed the cultural achievements of the 1920s *and* the "radicalisation of a significant part of the intelligentsia" during the 1930s (untitled pamphlet published by the League for Cultural Freedom and Socialism, "Statement to American Writers and Artists," 1939, enclosed with Dwight MacDonald to George Dillon, June 5, 1939, PMP 1936–53, s2, b6, f13).

12. George Dillon qtd. in Harold Rosenberg to Dillon, July 26, 1938, PMP 1936–53, s1, b22, f1.

13. Harold Rosenberg, "The God in the Car," *Poetry* 52, 6 (September 1938): p. 339. He was responding to Archibald MacLeish, "In Challenge Not Defense," *Poetry* 52, 4 (July 1938): pp. 212–19 (the quoted phrase is on p. 218).

14. Harold Rosenberg, "Couch Liberalism and the Guilty Past," in *Voices of "Dissent": A Collection of Articles from "Dissent" Magazine* (New York: Grove, 1958), p. 225.

15. Indeed, Dan Wakefield, who admired and befriended Kempton in the fifties, recalls that *Part of Our Time* gave him "a sense of the passion and excitement of [the thirties, of] what had always seemed to me a drab and dreary decade, the hangover after the Roaring Twenties" (Wakefield, *New York in the Fifties* [New York: St. Martin's, 1992], p. 61).

16. Murray Kempton, "The U.S. as Pickpocket" (December 21, 1955), in *America Comes of Middle Age: Columns, 1950–1962* (Boston: Little, Brown, 1963), pp. 7–10.

17. Murray Kempton, contribution to a symposium on "Liberal Anti-Communism Revisited," *Commentary* 44, 3 (September 1967): p. 52.

18. Murray Kempton to Granville Hicks, May 17, 1955, Granville Hicks Papers, b30, SUSCRC.

19. Murray Kempton, *Part of Our Time: Some Ruins and Monuments of the Thirties* (1955; New York: Modern Library, 1998), pp. 4–5.

20. Summaries of Kael's anticommunist film criticism for KPFA, where she was a regular film reviewer for years, can be found in Leah Brummer, "Pauline Kael's Berkeley Days," *Berkeley Insider*, July–August 1995, p. 15; Matthew Lasar, *Pacifica Radio: The Rise of an Alternative Network* (Philadelphia: Temple University Press, 1999), p. 125.

21. Qtd. in Brummer, "Pauline Kael's Berkeley Days," p. 15.

22. Rosenberg, "Couch Liberalism and the Guilty Past," p. 236.

23. Ibid., p. 225.

24. Ibid., pp. 233, 227; emphasis added.

25. Joseph Freeman to Granville Hicks, May 17, 1958, Hicks Papers, b21.

26. Rosenberg, "Couch Liberalism and the Guilty Past," esp. p. 228, 228n.

27. Ibid., p. 227.

28. James T. Farrell to Granville Hicks, "Strike Bulletin" and "Open Letter," n.d., "James Farrell I: 1934–63" file, Hicks Papers.

29. Angus Cameron to Eve Merriam, January 6, 1956, TL.

30. Samuel Sillen, "Van Wyck Brooks and the Literary Critics," *Masses & Mainstream*, October 1953, p. 25. See also Samuel Sillen, "The Living Emerson," *Masses & Mainstream*, May 1953, pp. 28–35; Perry Miller, "Emersonian Genius and the American Democracy," *New England Quarterly* 26, 1 (March 1953): pp. 27–44.

31. Alfred Kazin, *On Native Grounds: An Interpretation of Modern American Prose Literature* (New York: Reynal and Hitchcock, 1942), p. 420.

32. Joseph Freeman to Granville Hicks, May 4, 1958, Hicks Papers, b21.

33. Joseph Freeman to Floyd Dell, April 30, 1953, Floyd Dell Papers, "De Reserve Box," Newberry Library, Chicago.

34. Joseph North, "The Thirties! The Thirties!," *Sunday Worker*, May 17, 1964, p. 6.

35. Philip Frankfeld, "The Thunderous Thirties, and Granville Hicks," *Daily Worker*[?] clipping, n.d. [May–June 1964], Hicks Papers, b21, Philip Frankfeld file.

36. Daniel Bell, *The End of Ideology: On the Exhaustion of Political Ideas in the Fifties*, rev. ed. (New York: Collier, 1961), pp. 404–5.

37. Dennis Wrong, "Reflections on the End of Ideology," in *The End of Ideology Debate*, ed. Chaim I. Waxman (New York: Funk and Wagnalls, 1968), p. 118.

38. Robert Duncan, typescript sent to M. L. Rosenthal, n.d. [August 1957], MLR/F, b10, f10.

39. A line from a poem, "At a Bach Concert," published in Rich's first collection, *A Change of World* (1951); see Adrienne Rich, *The Fact of a Doorframe: Selected Poems, 1950–2001* (New York: Norton, 2002), p. 5.

40. Bell, *End of Ideology*, pp. 404–5.

41. Murray Kempton, contribution to a symposium on "Liberal Anti-Communism Revisited," *Commentary* 44, 3 (September 1967): p. 52.

42. See the chapter on "Politics and the Individual" in Philip Rieff, *Freud: The Mind of the Moralist* (Chicago: University of Chicago Press, 1959), pp. 220–56.

43. See Lionel Trilling, "Freud: Within and Beyond Culture" (1955), in *Beyond Culture* (London: Penguin, 1965), pp. 87–110.

44. Alfred Kazin to Granville Hicks, July 2, 1953, Hicks Papers, b30, Alfred Kazin file.

45. A condensation of the latter chapter had been published under the same title in the *New Republic*, October 19, 1942, pp. 492–95.

46. J. Malcolm Brinnin, "Observatory Hill," in *No Arch, No Triumph* (New York: Knopf, 1945), p. 72.

47. S.A.C. [Stanton Coblentz], *Wings* 5, 8 (Winter 1943): pp. 21–22.

48. Brinnin, "Observatory Hill," p. 73.

49. Henry Roth, "On Being Blocked and Other Literary Matters," *Commentary* 64, 2 (August 1977): pp. 29–34.

50. Leonie Adams, "Spinning Singular," *Poetry* 85, 2 (November 1954): p. 116.

51. Ibid.

52. Ibid.

53. Eda Lou Walton, "Wreath for a Congressman (W.B.W.)," in *So Many Daughters* (New York: Bookman, 1952), p. 29.

54. Robert Lowell, "Memories of West Street and Lepke," in *Life Studies / For the Union Dead* (New York: Farrar, Straus, and Giroux, 1964), p. 85.

55. J. Malcolm Brinnin, "For My Pupils in the War Years," in *No Arch, No Triumph*, p. 5.

56. Eda Lou Walton, "Poet as Teacher," in *So Many Daughters*, p. 61.

57. Leo Gurko, *The Angry Decade* (New York: Dodd, Mead, 1947), pp. 63, 69, 127.

58. Adams, "Spinning Singular," pp. 114–15; emphasis added.

59. Gurko, *Angry Decade*, pp. 13, 127, 173, 63, 69.

60. Adams had been a member of the League of Professional Groups for Foster and Ford (the national Communist Party candidates in the 1932 election) and was one of the signers of *Culture and Crisis: An Open Letter*, urging artists to vote communist (Daniel Aaron, *Writers on the Left* [New York: Avon, 1961], p. 437 n. 73).

61. Adams, "Spinning Singular," p. 116.

62. Eugene Lyons, *The Red Decade: The Stalinist Penetration of America* (Indianapolis: Bobbs-Merrill, 1941), p. 148.

63. Kazin, *On Native Grounds*, p. 415.

64. Ibid., p. 417; emphasis added.

65. Ibid., p. 409.

66. Ibid., p. 421; emphasis added.

67. Louis Francis Budenz, *Men without Faces: The Communist Conspiracy in the U.S.A.* (New York: Harper, 1948), p. 246. This has remained the anticommunist position on the treachery of many anticommunist liberal intellectuals. Although *all* had "been aware since the 1930s of the reality of Stalinism," some liberals clung to claims of innocence about the decade and gave "comfort to Stalinist tyranny" (Ronald Radosh, "The Legacy of the Anticommunist Liberal Intellectual," *Partisan Review* 67, 4 [October 2000], pp. 551, 562 [the latter phrase is quoted from Irving Kristol]).

68. Peter Viereck, " 'Bloody-Minded Professors': The Anti-Social Role of Some Intellectuals," *Confluence* 1, 3 (September 1952): p. 38 n. 4.

69. Kazin, *On Native Grounds*, p. 420.

70. See Alan Wald, "Radical Poetry," in *Encyclopedia of the American Left*, 2d ed., ed. Mari Jo Buhle, Paul Buhle, and Dan Georgakas (New York: Oxford University Press, 1998), p. 676. When the CPUSA-affiliated Jefferson School of New York City created a card index of poems published in periodicals by radical poets, Humphries's work was included (Jefferson School Card Index, TL). See also "Melody for the Virginals," *New Masses* 35, 9 (May 21, 1940): p. 18. Humphries's interest in communism dates back to at least 1924, when "theoretically and rather fatalistically I endorse the revolution" (Humphries to E. Merrill Root, July 15, 1924, Rolfe Humphries Papers, b2, f15d, Amherst College, Amherst, Massachusetts). By 1947 he paid "as little attention . . . [t]o politics . . . as possible" (Humphries to Root, December 21, 1947, Humphries Papers, b2, f15d, Amherst College).

71. Louise Bogan, "Verse," *New Yorker*, March 7, 1942, p. 62.

72. Sophia Molk, "A Word in Your Hand," *Talaria* 14, 3 (Autumn 1949): p. 18.

73. Vivienne Koch to Karl Shapiro, November 11, 1951, PMP 1936–53, s1, b14, f9.

74. Kazin, *On Native Grounds*, pp. 415, 421, 424, 407.

75. Ibid., p. 409.

76. Evidence indicates that Kazin brought these views to bear on the new poetry that emerged in the early 1950s. He was, for instance, a member of the committee that reviewed applications from poets for residency fellowships at the Yaddo artists' retreat. Both Granville Hicks and Malcolm Cowley were also members of the committee during the difficult months just after Yaddo's leadership had been red-baited (an attack that was initiated by Robert Lowell). At least from Hicks's and Cowley's point of view, board members who had been tainted as part of the "Yaddo left wing" had difficulty contending against the evaluations of poets put forward by members who had sided with or at least accepted the anticommunist critique leveled at Yaddo's administration. Hicks saw Kazin as part of the group urging safe choices. Hicks wrote to Cowley to describe how Kazin's preference for certain poets could not be countered (Hicks to Cowley, April 4, 1950, Malcolm Cowley Papers, Newberry Library, Chicago).

77. Kazin, *On Native Grounds*, pp. 407–8.

78. "Poets Here Scorn Soviet Attack on Work; Versifier with 'Cure' Held 'Bore, Charlatan,' " *New York Times*, January 7, 1947, p. 25.

79. Nelson Algren, "We Thank You with Reservations," *Poetry* 59, 4 (January 1942): p. 221.

80. Harry Roskolenko to Peter de Vries, n.d. [1942], PMP 1936–53, s1, b22, f5.

81. Kazin, *On Native Grounds*, p. 414.

82. Granville Hicks to Alfred Kazin, September 26, [1941], Hicks Papers, b30, Alfred Kazin file.

83. Alfred Kazin to Granville Hicks, October 16, 1941, Hicks Papers, b30, Alfred Kazin file.

84. Alan Wald, "In Retrospect," *Reviews in American History* 20, 2 (June 1992): p. 280; the phrase from Kazin is quoted by Wald from p. 382 of the 1982 edition published by Harcourt, Brace, Jovanovich.

85. Ibid., p. 281.

86. For "very accurately located," see Kenneth Burke, "Recent Poetry," *Southern Review* 1 (1935–36): p. 177. See also Edward Dahlberg, introduction to *Poems by Kenneth Fearing* (New York: Dynamo, 1935), pp. 11–14.

87. Paul Carroll, "An Introduction to Edward Dahlberg: 'After Intercourse Every Animal Is Depressed,' " in *The Edward Dahlberg Reader*, ed. Paul Carroll (New York: New Directions, 1967), pp. xi, xii, xviii.

88. Robert Duncan, draft of a review of H.D.'s *Selected Poems*, ca. August 1957, from a paragraph cut from the published review (typescript in PMP 1954–61, b10, f9). See "In the Sight of a Lyre, a Little Spear, a Chair," *Poetry* 91, 4 (January 1958): pp. 256–60.

89. Robert Duncan, "Against Nature," typescript draft, ca. 1957, PMP 1953–61, b10, f10.

90. E.g., in Edward Dahlberg to Robert Creeley, October 22, 1955, Robert Creeley Papers, b31, f16, Manuscripts Division, Stanford University Library, Stanford, California.

91. Robert Creeley, talk at the Louis Zukofsky Centennial Conference, Columbia University and Barnard College, September 17, 2004, recorded for PENNsound, <http://writing.upenn.edu/pennsound/x/Zukofsky-Conference-2004.html>.

92. Edward Dahlberg to Robert Creeley, November 3, 1955, Creeley Papers, b31, f16. He had read *Call Me Ishmael* as a manuscript.

93. Ibid., March 14, 1958. On Lowenfels's conviction under the Smith Act, see "9 Red Leaders Get Jail Terms," *Philadelphia Inquirer*, June 21, 1955, p. 1; Walter Lowenfels, *The Prisoners: Poems for Amnesty* (Philadelphia: Whittier, 1954).

94. Kempton, *Part of Our Time*, p. 181.

95. See Abe C. Ravitz, *Leane Zugsmith: Thunder on the Left* (New York: International, 1992), pp. 119–20, 102–8.

96. Louise Bogan, "Verse," *New Yorker*, December 16, 1939, p. 120.

97. Louise Bogan, "The Situation in American Writing," *Partisan Review* 6, 4 (Summer 1939): p. 107.

98. Kempton, *Part of Our Time*, p. 184; emphasis added.

99. See, e.g., Isidor Schneider to Paul Goch, June 14, 1935, Harry Roskolenko Papers, SUSCRC. In the letter, Schneider, then the poetry editor at the *New Masses*, responded to poems Roskolenko had submitted to the magazine. Roskolenko's later wrote on the letter, "Pseudonyms [*sic*] of Harry Roskolenkier" (his given surname).

100. Harvey Breit to Harry Roskolenko, May 5, 1938, Roskolenko Papers.

101. Roskolenko signed the league's inaugural manifesto, "Statement to American Writers and Artists," in May–June 1939.

102. Harry Roskolenko, "A Question of Governance," *Poetry* 89, 2 (November 1956): pp. 118–19.

103. See Alvah Bessie, *Alvah Bessie's Spanish Civil War Notebooks*, ed. Dan Bessie (Lexington: University Press of Kentucky, 2001).

104. Alvah Bessie, "Edwin Rolfe Says Farewell in a Moving Book of Poems," *Daily Worker*, November 10, 1955, p. 7; reprinted from the *Daily People's World*, November 3, 1955, p. 7. In the latter version, the title was ". . . Moving 'First' Book of Poems."

105. On this point, see Susan Sontag's 1961 essay on Norman O. Brown in *Against Interpretation* (New York: Farrar, Strauss, and Giroux, 1966), p. 257.

106. Wrong, "Reflections on the End of Ideology," p. 123.

107. Kazin, *On Native Grounds*, p. 407.

108. Ibid., p. 428.

109. Ibid., p. 407.

110. Ibid., pp. 429, 433.

111. Ibid., p. 451; emphasis added.

112. Alfred Kazin, "Criticism at the Poles," *New Republic*, October 19, 1943, p. 407.

113. Allen Tate to John Peale Bishop, November 2, 1942, in *The Republic of Letters in America: The Correspondence of John Peale Bishop and Allen Tate*, ed. Thomas Daniel Young and John J. Hindle (Lexington: University Press of Kentucky, 1981), p. 195.

Chapter 4

1. A phrase that appears on the dust jacket of the first 1961 hardback edition, Harcourt, Brace, and World.

2. Daniel Aaron, "The Treachery of Recollection," *Carleton Miscellany* 6, 3 (Summer 1965): pp. 4–5.

3. J. Donald Adams, *The Shape of Books to Come* (New York: Viking, 1944), p. 147.

4. Don J. Hager, "The Rhetoric of Intergroup Liberalism" (1954), in *The Scene before You: A New Approach to American Culture*, ed. Chandler Brossard (New York: Rinehart, 1955), pp. 43, 48.

5. Aaron, "Treachery of Recollection," p. 4.

6. Milton Howard, "Hemingway and Heroism," *Masses & Mainstream* 5, 10 (October 1952): pp. 1–8.

7. Milton Howard, "New Realities for the Intellectuals," *Masses & Mainstream* 8, 2 (February 1955): p. 36.

8. Aaron, "Treachery of Recollection," p. 5.

9. Robert Warshow, "The Legacy of the '30's," *Commentary* 4, 6 (December 1947): pp. 541–42.

10. In 1935, Joseph Freeman introduced Hayes to a fellow communist as "one of our best revolutionary poets" ("J. F. Evans" [Joseph Freeman] to Nancy [Reed], June 7, 1935,

Joseph Freeman Papers, b25, f43, HI). Hayes was a member of the editorial board of *Partisan Review* before it turned away from the Communist Party. His poem, "In a Coffee Pot," widely anthologized in the 1930s (and still today used when editors seek a representative "proletarian poem"), appeared in the first issue of *Partisan Review* (February–March 1934) and was praised for its presentation of "the depression generation." Hayes was a member of the John Reed Club and the Young Communist League. "In Madrid," a blank-verse celebration of the Spanish republic before its cause was popular even among leftists, was published in the September 30, 1934, issue of the *New Masses*. "Success Story," appearing in the *New Masses* on January 24, 1939, satirizes rhyme, the rich, and the ambivalent Eliotic figure: "I'll leave. I must get away. What shall I do? / do you think I would like it in Mexico?"

11. Ann Winslow, ed., *Trial Balances: An Anthology of New Poetry* (New York: Macmillan, 1935), p. 214.

12. Alfred Hayes, "Welcome to the Castle," in *Welcome to the Castle* (New York: Harper, 1950), pp. 66–67.

13. E.g., Jessie Wilmore Murton initiated an organized campaign of protest letters directed at Houghton Mifflin in anticipation of bias against traditional poets in the annual one thousand dollar poetry contest hosted by that publishing house in part because Horace Gregory was to be one of the judges (Murton to Lilith Lorraine, January 21, 1945, Jessie Wilmore Murton Papers, b9, f7, KSA/WKU).

14. Horace Gregory to Selden Rodman, n.d. [1934], Horace Gregory Papers, SUSCRC. For a further sense of Gregory's antifascist commitment through the CPUSA, see "Against the Fascist Terror in Germany: Noted American Writers Join United Front," *New Masses* 8, 6 (April 1933): p. 11.

15. J. Malcolm Brinnin, "Observatory Hill," in *No Arch, No Triumph* (New York: Knopf, 1945), pp. 72–73. Although he was "politically somewhat chastened," in 1943 he was still arguing strongly for the centrality of the "social poet," by which he mean the procommunist poet (J. Malcolm Brinnin, "Muriel Rukeyser: The Social Poet and the Problem of Communication," *Poetry* 61, 5 [January 1943]: pp. 554–75). On Brinnin's radical involvements generally, see Alan Wald, *Exiles from a Future Time: The Forging of the Mid-Twentieth-Century Literary Left* (Chapel Hill: University of North Carolina Press, 2002), pp. 306–7.

16. Leslie Fiedler, "Hiss, Chambers, and the Age of Innocence," in *An End to Innocence: Essays on Culture and Politics* (Boston: Beacon, 1952), pp. 6, 5.

17. J. Malcolm Brinnin, "For My Pupils in the War Years," in *No Arch, No Triumph*, pp. 5–6.

18. Stephen Spender, "Thoughts during an Air Raid," in *Collected Poems, 1928–1985* (New York: Random House, 1986), p. 74.

19. See Alan Filreis, *Modernism from Right to Left* (New York: Cambridge University Press, 1994), pp. 31–45.

20. Wallace Stevens, "The Men That Are Falling," in *The Collected Poems* (New York: Knopf, 1954), pp. 187–88.

21. Joseph Warren Beach, *Obsessive Images: Symbolism in Poetry of the 1930's and 1940's*, ed. William Van O'Connor (Minneapolis: University of Minnesota Press, 1960), p. 333.

22. William Phillips, "What Happened in the 30's," *Commentary* 30, 3 (September 1962): p. 205.

23. Hayes, "Welcome to the Castle," pp. 66–67.

24. Horace Gregory to Selden Rodman, n.d. [1934], Gregory Papers.

25. O'Connor wrote frequently about the 1920s in the 1950s and in 1959 hosted a series on the reputation of the 1920s, which he discussed in a correspondence with Malcolm Cowley (Cowley to O'Connor, [1959], William Van O'Connor Papers, SUSCRC). O'Connor's work on Stevens focused on *Harmonium* (1923) and the relation of the High Modern Stevens to the later philosophical style and on the politics of Stevens's work in the 1930s, especially *Owl's Clover*, with respect to the 1920s.

26. Dagmar Beach to Henry Rago, September 5, 1957, PMP 1954–61, b2, f18. The same file includes a typescript of O'Connor's remembrance of Beach.

27. William Van O'Connor, "The Politics of a Poet," *Perspective* 1 (Summer 1948): p. 205. See also Alan Filreis, *Wallace Stevens and the Actual World* (Princeton: Princeton University Press, 1991), pp. 273–74.

28. William Van O'Connor, "Lionel Trilling's Critical Realism," *Sewanee Review* 58 (1950): pp. 494, 485.

29. William Van O'Connor, "The Isolation of the Poet," *Poetry* 70, 1 (April 1947): p. 33.

30. William Van O'Connor, *The Age of Criticism, 1900–1950* (Chicago: Regnery, 1952), p. 131 (in a chapter that had been published separately in 1951); W. K. Wimsatt, "Exhuming the Recent Past," *Sewanee Review* 62 (1954): pp. 352–53.

31. Karl Shapiro to William Van O'Connor, May 31, 1949, O'Connor Papers.

32. O'Connor, "Isolation of the Poet," p. 36.

33. Stanton Coblentz, *New Poetic Lamps and Old* (Mill Valley, Calif.: Wings, 1950), pp. 54–55.

34. William Van O'Connor f, PMP 1954–61, b26, f3; Henry Rago to William Van O'Connor, August 18, 1957, and other materials, PMP 1954–61, b26, f3.

35. E.g., Edward Dahlberg to Joseph Warren Beach, September 22, 1934, Waldo Frank to Beach, November 5, 1932, Joseph Warren Beach Papers, University Archives, University of Minnesota, Minneapolis.

36. Joseph Warren Beach to Robert Penn Warren, August 18, [1953], Beach Papers.

37. Joseph Warren Beach, "May Day in Colmar 1952," *University of Kansas City Review* 24, 3 (March 1958): p. 240: "old and young in every lane and street / Across the land, out of the coil and smother of beating hearts." Joseph Warren Beach to Karl Shapiro, July 18, 1952, PMP 1954–61, b2, f18.

38. Joseph Warren Beach to Robert Penn Warren, July 29, [1956], Beach Papers.

39. E.g., when describing the ongoing *Obsessive Images* project to Robert Penn Warren in private correspondence, he half jokingly dubbed one section "Our Poets Report on Their World" while saying that his next task was "How They Say It." To get to that point he would need to provide "an abbreviated glossary of poetic clichés in the thirties and

forties," an undertaking that in itself took up some two hundred manuscript pages (Joseph Warren Beach to Robert Penn Warren, n.d. [1956?], Beach Papers).

40. Leo Gurko, *The Angry Decade* (New York: Dodd, Mead, 1947), p. 258.

41. Joseph Warren Beach, *Obsessive Images*, p. xi.

42. Joseph Warren Beach to Robert Penn Warren, October 27, 1956, Beach Papers.

43. Leonard Unger, *South Atlantic Quarterly*, Summer 1961, p. 355.

44. Alfred Hayes, "Heine: A Biography of a Night," in *Welcome to the Castle*, p. 73.

45. For a detailed account of Cowley's revisions, see John D. Hazlett, "Conversion, Revisionism, and Revision in Malcolm Cowley's *Exile's Return*," *South Atlantic Quarterly*, Spring 1983, pp. 179–88.

46. Eugene Lyons, *The Red Decade: The Stalinist Penetration of America* (Indianapolis: Bobbs-Merrill, 1941), p. 134.

47. Malcolm Cowley, "1930: The Year That Was the New Year's Eve: The Great Binge and Its Leftist Aftermath," *Commentary* 11, 6 (June 1951): pp. 567–71.

48. Murray Kempton, *Part of Our Time: Some Ruins and Monuments of the Thirties* (New York: Modern Library, 1998), p. 151.

49. Hans Bak, *Malcolm Cowley: The Formative Years* (Athens: University of Georgia Press, 1993), p. 470.

50. Robert Spiller to Malcolm Cowley, March 13, 1945, Malcolm Cowley Papers, Newberry Library, Chicago.

51. Robert E. Spiller, review of *Exile's Return: A Literary Odyssey of the Nineteen-twenties*, by Malcolm Cowley, *American Quarterly* 3, 3 (Autumn 1951): pp. 273–75.

52. Louise Bogan, *Achievement in American Poetry, 1900–1950* (Chicago: Regnery, 1951), p. 63.

53. Willard Thorp, "American Writers on the Left," in *Socialism and American Life*, ed. Donald Drew Egbert and Stow Persons (Princeton: Princeton University Press, 1952), vol. 1, pp. 604–5.

54. Edward Dahlberg, "The Art of Concealment" (1952), in Dahlberg, *Samuel Beckett's Wake and Other Uncollected Prose*, ed. Steven Moore (Elmwood Park, Ill.: Dalkey, 1989), p. 278.

55. Lewis Leary, *South Atlantic Quarterly*, January 1952, p. 172. See also John W. Aldridge, "The Case of Malcolm Cowley," *Nation*, February 19, 1955, pp. 162–64. Although Aldridge did not take Cowley's historical method seriously, he praised *Exile's Return* as "a work of personal history conceived poetically." Since *Exile's Return* had attained the status of lyric, "It was the poet in Cowley who was responsible for the lucid prose" of the book (p. 162).

56. *New York Times Book Review*, June 17, 1951, p. 18.

57. Arthur Mizener, "Home Was the Stranger," *New York Times Magazine*, June 10, 1951, p. BR5.

58. Robert E. Spiller, review of *Exile's Return: A Literary Odyssey of the Nineteen-twenties*, by Malcolm Cowley, *American Quarterly* 3, 3 (Autumn 1951): p. 274.

59. Cowley, "1930," p. 567.

60. John Wheelwright, *Collected Poems of John Wheelwright*, ed. Alvin H. Rosenfeld (New York: New Directions, 1972), p. 59.

61. In the late 1960s critics sought to repoliticize the use of Crosby as an instance of modernist social excess. See, e.g., Hugh Fox, "Harry Crosby: A Heliograph," *Books at Brown* 23 (1969): pp. 95–100.

62. On Crosby's affiliation with the Rebel Poets, see Wald, *Exiles from a Future Time*, pp. 26–27.

63. Richard Davidson, "Death of a Poet," *Mainstream* 12, 4 (April 1959): p. 35.

64. Joseph Warren Beach, *Obsessive Images*, pp. 156–58; emphasis added.

65. Hayes, *Welcome to the Castle*, p. 55.

66. Alfred Hayes, "—As a Young Man," in ibid., pp. 42–43.

67. Beach once joked that the " 'project' [was] guaranteed to last me till at least 1970" (Joseph Warren Beach to Robert Penn Warren, n.d. [1956?], Beach Papers).

68. Leonard Unger speculated that *Obsessive Images* is a book too easily taken for granted because its political independence makes its leftist viewpoint seem not fresh but outmoded. "So much of our 'best' criticism has been partisan and programmatic [so] that some readers may mistake for old-fashioned what is essentially independent and refreshing" (*South Atlantic Quarterly*, Summer 1961, pp. 354–55).

Chapter 5

1. T. R. Fyvel, "Reflections on Manifest Destiny," *New Republic*, January 7, 1952, p. 10.

2. See H. F. Peters, "American Culture and the State Department," *American Scholar* 21, 2 (Spring 1952): pp. 265–74; Jacob Epstein, "The CIA and the Intellectuals," *New York Review of Books* 8, 7 (April 20, 1967): pp. 16–21; Frances Stoner Saunders, *The Cultural Cold War: The CIA and the World of Arts and Letters* (New York: New Press, 1999); Volker R. Berghahn, *America and the Intellectual Cold Wars in Europe* (Princeton: Princeton University Press, 2001); (with relevance to poetry and painting) Alan Filreis, " 'Beyond the Rhetorician's Touch': Stevens' Painterly Abstractions," *American Literary History* 4, 1 (Spring 1992): pp. 230–63.

3. David Daiches, "American Culture in Britain," *New Republic*, January 28, 1952, p. 16.

4. Peter Viereck to Robert Hillyer, May 4, 1950, Robert Hillyer Papers, b5, f28, SUSCRC.

5. Hugh Kenner, "Whitman's Multitudes," *Poetry* 87, 3 (December 1955): p. 183.

6. "Poems by Whitman," *Daily Worker*, July 4, 1955, p. 7.

7. David Daiches, "Walt Whitman's Philosophy," in *Literary Essays* (Chicago: University of Chicago Press, 1956), pp. 62–87. The original recording, on a preservation master made in 1973, is available at the Library of Congress.

8. S.A.C. [Stanton Coblentz], *Wings* 12, 4 (Winter 1956): p. 23.

9. Winfield Townley Scott, *"A Dirty Hand": The Literary Notebooks of Winfield Townley Scott* (Austin: University of Texas Press, 1969), p. 57.

10. Qtd. in Malcolm Cowley, "Walt Whitman, Champion of America," *New York Times Book Review*, February 6, 1955, pp. 1, 22.

11. Kenner, "Whitman's Multitudes," p. 184.

12. The quintessential leftist reading of Whitman in the 1930s was Newton Arvin's *Walt Whitman* (New York: Macmillan, 1938). For a summary, see Michel Fabre, "Walt Whitman and the Rebel Poets: A Note on Whitman's Reputation among Radical Writers during the Depression," *Walt Whitman Review* 12 (1966): pp. 88–93.

13. David Daiches, "Notes for a History of Poetry," *Poetry* 98, 2 (May 1961): pp. 80–81.

14. Daiches, "Walt Whitman's Philosophy," p. 67.

15. Ibid.

16. Ralph de Toledano, *Lament for a Generation* (New York: Farrar, Straus, 1960), pp. 196, 194.

17. Richard Chase, "Walt Whitman as American Spokesman," *Commentary* 19, 3 (March 1955): p. 261.

18. E. Merrill Root, "Trapped in Our Armor," *Freeman* 5, 7 (January 1955): p. 281.

19. E. Merrill Root, *Collectivism on the Campus* (New York: Devin-Adair, 1955), p. 3.

20. Samuel Sillen, "Van Wyck Brooks and the Literary Crisis," *Masses & Mainstream* 6, 10 (October 1953): p. 26.

21. Isidor Schneider, "Background to Error," *New Masses* 58, 7 (February 12, 1946): p. 24.

22. David Platt, "Outpouring of Peoples [*sic*] Poetry," *Sunday Worker*, August 2, 1953, p. 8.

23. Leo Marx, "The Careful Young Men: Tomorrow's Leaders Analyzed by Today's Teachers," *Nation*, March 9, 1957, p. 203.

24. Ray Smith, "Whitman: The Leaves of Grass Centennial, 2055," *Approach* 18 (November 1955): p. 7.

25. For "British communists," see, e.g., Sam Aaronovitch, "The American Threat to British Culture," *Agenda* 2, 6 (February–March 1951): p. 3: "There are two ways of life, two cultures in the United States. The one is that which represents the struggle of the American people, the America of . . . Whitman . . . Paul Robeson and Howard Fast. *This* America does not seek to impose its way of life on other people."

26. Whitman centennial issue f, PMP 1954–61, b42, f17. *Poetry* ran, instead, a translation of Lorca's "Ode to Walt Whitman" by Ben Belitt (85, 4 [January 1955]: pp. 187–92). The Whitman issue was to coincide with the Library of Congress program (Ray Basler to Karl Shapiro, December 8, 1954, PMP 1954–61, b42, f17).

27. Jerome Rothenberg, "Poetry in the 1950s as a Global Awakening: A Recollection and Reconstruction," paper presented at the American Poetry in the 1950s Conference, University of Maine, Orono, June 1996 <http://www.txt.de/spress/reader/stateside/one/essays/awakening/text.htm>.

28. Harold Norse, preface to William Carlos Williams and Harold Norse, *The American Idiom: A Correspondence*, ed. John J. Wilson (San Francisco: Bright Tyger, 1990), p. v; Harold Norse, *Memoirs of a Bastard Angel* (New York: Morrow, 1989), esp. pp. 40–43.

29. Karl Shapiro, "Why Out-Russia Russia?," *New Republic*, June 9, 1958, p. 11.

30. Root, "Trapped in Our Armor," p. 281.

31. Kenneth Rexroth to Malcolm Cowley, n.d. [postmarked April 15, 1955], Malcolm Cowley Papers, Newberry Library, Chicago.

32. Leslie Fiedler, "Images of Walt Whitman," in *An End to Innocence: Essays on Culture and Politics* (Boston: Beacon, 1955), p. 166.

33. Walt Whitman, *Leaves of Grass* (1892; New York: Modern Library, 2001), pp. 698–99.

34. Sillen, "Van Wyck Brooks," p. 23.

35. Fiedler, "Images of Walt Whitman," p. 162.

36. Shapiro, "Why Out-Russia Russia?," p. 11.

37. Stephen Vincent Benét, "Ode to Walt Whitman," *Saturday Review of Literature*, May 4, 1935, pp. 7–10.

38. Arvin, *Walt Whitman*, pp. 10–26.

39. Ray Smith, "Whitman," pp. 10, 9.

40. Fiedler, "Images of Walt Whitman," p. 162.

41. F. O. Matthiessen, "The Education of a Socialist," *Monthly Review* 2, 6 (October 1950): pp. 181, 186–87.

42. Joseph Freeman dissented from this view, writing in 1953, "The Monthly Review calls itself 'an independent socialist magazine,' but is actually a Stalinite magazine" (Freeman to Floyd Dell, April 15, 1953, Floyd Dell Papers, "De Reserve Box," Newberry Library, Chicago).

43. R. W. B. Lewis, *The American Adam* (Chicago: University of Chicago Press, 1955), p. 44.

44. M. L. Rosenthal, "A Note on Tradition in Poetry," *Nation*, May 11, 1957, p. 419.

45. Fiedler, "Images of Walt Whitman," p. 163.

46. *New Masses* 11, 13 (June 26, 1933): p. 16.

47. Joseph Kalar, "Pamphlet Poetry," *New Masses* 16, 6 (August 6, 1935): p. 24.

48. Kenneth Patchen, *Before the Brave* (New York: Random House, 1936), pp. 116–20. It was published a year earlier in Granville Hicks, Joseph North, Michael Gold, Paul Peters, Isidor Schneider, and Alan Calmer, eds., *Proletarian Literature in the United States* (New York: International, 1935), and has been reprinted in Jack Salzman, ed., *Years of Protest: A Collection of American Writings of the 1930's* (New York: Pegasus, 1967), pp. 366–71. The poem first appeared in the *New Masses* and received such a response from readers that the editors introduced the twenty-two-year-old Patchen in a biographical profile ("Between Ourselves," *New Masses* 13, 10 [December 4, 1934]: p. 30).

49. Patchen, *Before the Brave*, p. 117.

50. Lola Ridge, *Dance of Fire* (New York: Smith and Haas, 1935), pp. 56–58.

51. Louise Jeffers, "My Thoughts Are Free," *Daily Worker*, October 19, 1952, p. 7.

52. Frank Marshall Davis, "War Quiz for America," *Crisis* 51, 4 (April 1944): 113–14, 122.

53. See Alan Wald, *Exiles from a Future Time: The Forging of the Mid-Twentieth-Century Literary Left* (Chapel Hill: University of North Carolina Press, 2002), pp. 20–21.

54. Allen Ginsberg, *Journals Mid-Fifties, 1954–1958* (New York: HarperCollins, 1995), p. 221.

55. Fiedler, "Images of Walt Whitman," p. 163.

56. Allen Ginsberg, interview by the author, Poetry of the Thirties Conference sponsored by the National Poetry Foundation, Orono, Maine, June 26, 1993.

57. Fiedler, "Images of Walt Whitman," p. 163.

58. The program, organized by Roy P. Basler, associate director of the Library of Congress, also featured lectures by Mark Van Doren, Gay Allen, and (to open the Whitman exhibition in the library's gallery) Charles Feinberg.

59. David Daiches, *Poetry and the Modern World* (Chicago: University of Chicago Press, 1940), p. 69.

60. Ibid., p. 85; emphasis added.

61. Ibid., p. 74.

62. Ibid., pp. 74, 84. Daiches's ideas about Whitman were somewhat changed by 1958, when his thirty-two-page pamphlet, *Two Studies*, appeared. There Whitman was presented as a prophet of impressionism.

63. Daiches, *Poetry and the Modern World*, p. 210.

64. Ibid., p. 213.

65. Ibid., p. 191.

66. Babette Deutsch, *Poetry in Our Time* (New York: Columbia University Press, 1956), p. 360.

67. She joined communist poets in protesting the executions of Sacco and Vanzetti and contributed to *America Arraigned!*, edited by Lucia Trent and Ralph Cheyney (New York: Dean, 1928). In 1936, E. Merrill Root bitterly joked that "if the Communists triumphed, [Isidor Schneider] and Babette Deutsch were to have their books published[,] which I think would scarcely justify the revolution" (Root to Rolfe Humphries, December 3, 1936, Rolfe Humphries Papers, b1, f6, Amherst College, Amherst, Massachusetts). Looking back on the between-wars generation of poets in the winter of 1940–41, Deutsch wrote, "The idea most frequently found in contemporary verse is that society is sick and only a radical cure will save it. Some time ago a sonneteer wrote: 'The Muse of Darwin, next the Muse of Freud.' He might have said: 'The Muse of Freud, and then the Muse of Marx' " ("Understanding Poetry," *American Scholar* 10, 1 [Winter 1940–41]: p. 70). See also Deutsch's poem, "Of Sacco and Vanzetti," *New Republic*, August 24, 1927, p. 16. She seems to have broken with the communists at the time of the third League of American Writers Congress in 1939.

68. For an instance of Macleod's contributions to the *New Masses*, see his "Hoover Dam Remembered from El Tovar," *New Masses* 8, 5 (December 1932): p. 28. On his experience with the *Front*, see Norman Macleod to Jack Conroy, October 22, 1969, Jack Conroy Papers, Newberry Library, Chicago. For the call for the American Writers Congress, see "Between Ourselves," *New Masses* 14, 10A (March 12, 1935): p. 30.

69. Kenneth Rexroth, "Poetry in Our Time," *New York Herald Tribune Books*, October 26, 1952, p. 4.

70. "The only trouble w/the '3rd Period' is it stopped. Left Social Fascist is a more accurate term. I have been a life long anti Bolshevik—but incidentally or concomitantly I grew up on the IWW soapbox in Chicago & the Far West. The Wobblies are gone—but I am still there." He was sure to distinguish himself from typical anticommunism, however. He "believe[d] I am close to being permanently defeated. . . . However—if I didn't know

better—after reading anything from the Chicago Tribute to the Kenyon Review—or listening to the radio—or just taking a walk down Market Street—I would join the Communist Party" (Kenneth Rexroth to Babette Deutsch, September 17, 1952, Babette Deutsch Papers, WU).

71. Kenneth Rexroth to Babette Deutsch, June 16, 1952, Deutsch Papers.

72. Raymond Nelson, *Kenneth Patchen and American Mysticism* (Chapel Hill: University of North Carolina Press, 1984), p. 160.

73. Daiches, *Poetry and the Modern World*, p. 211.

74. Ibid., p. 239.

75. Deutsch, *Poetry in Our Time*, p. 360. In her section on the Auden group, Deutsch concluded that the "devotees of the Social Muse in Great Britain were young men whose social sympathies did not destroy a lively interest in their craft." Earlier parts of the book on American poets of the 1930s drew the opposite conclusion about them.

76. Louise Bogan, *Achievement in American Poetry, 1900–1950* (Chicago: Regnery, 1951), pp. 82–93.

77. Ibid., pp. 105, 106.

78. Louise Bogan, "The Situation in American Writing," *Partisan Review* 6, 4 (Summer 1939): p. 107.

79. Louise Bogan, "Verse," *New Yorker*, December 16, 1939, p. 120.

80. Louise Bogan, "Yvor Winters," in *Selected Criticism: Prose Poetry* (New York: Noonday Press, 1955), p. 270; a review of *The Giant Weapon* by Winters was first published in 1944.

81. Fred Dupee to Louise Bogan, July 10, 1939, Louise Bogan Papers, b1, f8, Amherst College, Amherst, Massachusetts.

82. Bogan, "Situation in American Writing," p. 106.

83. Ibid., p. 105.

84. Ruth Lechlitner to Louise Bogan, June 28, 1937, Bogan Papers, b2, f8.

85. See Alan Filreis, *Modernism from Right to Left* (New York: Cambridge University Press, 1994), pp. 121–36.

86. Ruth Lechlitner to Louise Bogan, August 14, 1937, Bogan Papers, b2, f8.

87. Louise Bogan, "Verse," *New Yorker*, December 16, 1939, p. 120.

88. Marjorie Fischer to Louise Bogan, January 13, 1938, Bogan Papers, b3, f13.

89. Humphries was at this time trying to recruit E. Merrill Root back into the party. "Don't be a rebel; be a revolutionist," he urged. "Come in. . . . You have a world to gain!" (Humphries to Root, February 4, 1937, January 12, 1937, Humphries Papers, b2, f15d).

90. Louise Bogan to Rolfe Humphries, July 8, 1938, in Bogan, *What the Woman Lived: Selected Letters of Louise Bogan, 1920–1970*, ed. Ruth Limmer (New York: Harcourt Brace Jovanovich), pp. 172–73.

91. Frederick Morgan, "Six Poets," *Hudson Review* 6, 1 (Spring 1953): pp. 131–32.

92. Peter Viereck made this point clearest in "A Middle Ground for Poetry" (*New Leader* 34, 47 [November 19, 1951]: pp. 22–23), a review of Max Eastman's *Enjoyment of Poetry*. "Those of us who sympathize with Eastman's distrust of the modernist Pound-

Eliot and New Critics schools will wish there had in addition been a lot more explicit recognition of their positive accomplishments" (p. 23).

93. Conrad Aiken, "Back to Poetry," *Atlantic Monthly*, August 1940, p. 219.

94. James Burnham, "The Calculus of Diffusion," *Confluence* 2, 2 (June 1953): pp. 100–101.

95. Morgan, "Six Poets," 132.

96. Peter Viereck, "Beyond Revolt: The Education of a Poet," in *The Arts in Renewal*, ed. Scully Bradley (Philadelphia: University of Pennsylvania Press, 1950), p. 56.

97. Morgan, "Six Poets," p. 135.

98. Burnham, "Calculus of Diffusion," pp. 103, 105, 107.

99. Aiken, "Back to Poetry," p. 217.

100. M. L. Rosenthal, "The Unconsenting Spirit," *Nation*, November 10, 1956, p. 414; emphasis added.

101. Daniel Bell, *The End of Ideology: On the Exhaustion of Political Ideas in the Fifties*, rev. ed. (New York: Collier, 1961), p. 405.

102. Muriel Rukeyser to Louis Untermeyer, June 25, 1940, Louis Untermeyer Collection, b7, f142, Special Collections, University of Delaware, Newark.

103. Louise Bogan, "Verse," *New Yorker*, December 16, 1939, pp. 120–21.

104. Louise Bogan, "Modernism in American Literature," *American Quarterly* 2, 2 (Summer 1950): p. 109.

105. Peter Viereck, "Poets versus Readers," *Atlantic Monthly*, July 1947, p. 109.

106. Bogan, *Achievement in American Poetry*, p. 92; emphasis added.

107. Ibid., p. 110.

108. John Ciardi, "An Ulcer, Gentleman, Is an Unwritten Poem," *Canadian Business*, June 1955, p. 36.

109. John Ciardi, "What Does It Take to Enjoy a Poem?," *Saturday Review of Literature*, December 10, 1949, p. 26.

110. Stephen Spender, "Can't We Do without the Poets?," *New York Times Book Review*, September 2, 1951, pp. 1, 11.

111. Peter Viereck, "The Mob within the Heart: The New Russian Revolution," *TriQuarterly*, Spring 1965, p. 25.

112. Louise Bogan to Rolfe Humphries, July 8, 1938, in Bogan, *What the Woman Lived*, pp. 172–73.

Chapter 6

1. See Harvey Klehr, "Reflections on Anti-Anticommunism," *Continuity* 26 (Spring 2003): pp. 27–37; Ronald Radosh, "The Persistence of Anti-Anti-Communism," *FrontPageMagazine.com*, July 11, 2001, <http://www.frontpagemag.com/columnists/radosh/2001/rr07-11-01p.htm>. For a summary of the extent to which scholars of communism in the United States still disagree, see John Earl Haynes and Harvey Klehr, "The Historiography of American Communism: An Unsettled Field," *Labour History Review* 68, 1 (April 2003): pp. 61–78.

2. Ronald Radosh implicitly contends that the anti-anticommunists began espousing that position in the person of the young socialist Michael Harrington ("The Legacy of the Anti-Communist Liberal Intellectuals," *Partisan Review* 67, 4 [October 2000]: p. 565). By the end of the 1950s, red-baiting clipping services—such as the clipping service of the Counterattack project—routinely culled U.S. daily newspapers for the term (see Counterattack Papers, b1, s9, f "9–0 subversive activities misc. 1–100," TL; e.g., a *Miami Herald* article reporting Edward Hunt's criticism of liberal opposition to the 1958 Pentagon directive to teach the military about radicalism; the article quotes Hunt referring to "the anti-antis" [n.d.]).

3. E. Merrill Root, *Collectivism on the Campus* (New York: Devin-Adair, 1955), pp. 197–99.

4. Richard Gid Powers, *Not without Honor: The History of American Anticommunism* (New York: Free Press, 1995), p. 232.

5. William Henry Chamberlin, "Exit Party-Liner, Enter the AAC," *New Leader* 33, 24 (June 17, 1950): p. 20.

6. Alfred Kazin, "Ideology vs. the Novel," *Commentary* 11, 4 (April 1951): 398–400.

7. Ignazio Silone, *Bread and Wine*, trans. David Gwenda and Eric Mosbacher (New York: Penguin, 1946). In 1946, too, Silone wrote and published a new play, *And He Did Himself*, based on a subplot of *Bread and Wine*, featuring "the revolution of our epoch, promoted by politicians and economists" (qtd. in Paolo Milano, "Inspired Martyrs," *New York Times Book Review*, May 19, 1946, p. 5).

8. Murray Kempton, *Part of Our Time: Some Ruins and Monuments of the Thirties* (New York: Modern Library, 1998), p. 175.

9. Kazin, "Ideology vs. the Novel."

10. Ibid.

11. See, e.g., Daniel Bell, *The End of Ideology: On the Exhaustion of Political Ideas in the Fifties*, rev. ed. (New York: Collier, 1961), pp. 300, 393, 406.

12. Kazin, "Ideology vs. the Novel," 398–400. For more on the anticommunist view on communist novelistic "types," see "The Iron Tower," *News from behind the Iron Curtain* 2, 11 (November 1953): pp. 24–31.

13. Louise Bogan, *Achievement in American Poetry, 1900–1950* (Chicago: Regnery, 1951), p. 92.

14. Qtd. in Walter and Miriam Schneir, *Invitation to an Inquest* (Garden City, N.Y.: Doubleday, 1965), p. 170.

15. Frank Meyer, *The Moulding of Communists* (New York: Harcourt, Brace, and World, 1961), pp. 130, 46.

16. The fact was indicated in Taggard's file at *Poetry* (she had reported this in a 1937 biographical summary of herself for *Poetry* editor Amy Bonner) (Genevieve Taggard to Amy Bonner, "1937" [in Bonner's hand], Amy Bonner Papers, b1, f17, Regenstein Library, University of Chicago).

17. Genevieve Taggard, notes, n.d. [1947], Genevieve Taggard Papers, b4, f36, Rauner Special Collections Library, Dartmouth College, Hanover, New Hampshire.

18. Henry Rago, "The Immediate Is the Irrelevant," *Poetry* 69, 5 (February 1947): pp. 289–91.

19. Genevieve Taggard, notes, n.d., Taggard Papers, b2, f8. Taggard here was quoting Herbert Read's introduction to *English Prose Style* (New York: Holt, 1928), p. x.

20. T[heodore] Weiss, "A Neutral Platter," *Saturday Review of Literature*, June 16, 1956, p. 52.

21. The phrases are Manifold's from the poem "A Hat in the Ring" (*Selected Verse* [New York: Day, 1946], pp. 46–47). In a rejoinder, Gene Frumkin acknowledged that Rolfe's poems revealed "a man very pained and incensed at some roughshod congressional investigations" but wondered whether either Weiss or Harry Roskolenko (who had defended Weiss's review against leftist complaints) would exclude right-wing poet Roy Campbell on the same grounds: poems "highly political" and of "fixed ideas." Weiss's response remains unknown; Frumkin's comment was never published (Gene Frumkin, "To the Editor of *Poetry*," tearsheet marked "HOLDOVER," PMP 1954–61, b21, f21.)

22. Winfield Townley Scott, "Light Poignancy," *Poetry* 69, 1 (October 1946): pp. 43–45. By 1953, Manifold attempted to anticipate this critical assumption that paired his Australian primitive "nature" and his left-wing poetry by writing radical *sonnets*. See, e.g., John Manifold, "Birthday Sonnet for a New China," *Masses & Mainstream* 6, 10 (October 1953): p. 17.

23. Scott, "Light Poignancy," pp. 43–45. See also Manifold, "Birthday Sonnet for a New China," p. 17.

24. M. L. Rosenthal, "Hard Cores and Soft," *Poetry* 68, 2 (May 1946): p. 107. In an anthology of war poems, Rosenthal admired the inclusion of Berryman's "Farewell to Miles" but found its "poetry of frustration" a keynote in a book that otherwise left out any indication that among modern poets writing about the war against Germany, Japan, and Italy were at least some who produced "excellent antifascist writing, tragic but by no means desperate" (p. 109).

25. William Meredith, "Alcan Epic," *Poetry* 69, 2 (November 1946): p. 101.

26. Daniel Aaron, "The Treachery of Recollection," *Carleton Miscellany* 6, 3 (Summer 1965): p. 5.

27. Rukeyser pushed hard for Meredith with the editors of *Poetry* (letters in PMP 1936–53, s1, b22, f7).

28. Meredith, "Alcan Epic," p. 101.

29. Ibid.

30. Angus Cameron to Florence Becker Lennon, n.d. [September 1957], Eve Merriam to Angus Cameron, September 10, 1957, Eve Merriam Papers, TL.

31. Eve Merriam, "A.W.O.L.," *Poetry* 51, 3 (December 1942): pp. 471–72.

32. Michael Davidson, *Ghostlier Demarcations: Modern Poetry and the Material Word* (Berkeley: University of California Press, 1997), p. 138.

33. Meredith, "Alcan Epic," pp. 101–3.

34. See Davidson, *Ghostlier Demarcations*, pp. 135–70. With "Discursive 'excrescences,'" Davidson picks up Philip Wheelwright's negative term in a review of Rukeyser (p. 143).

35. Bell, *End of Ideology*, p. 508.

36. R. P. Blackmur, "Notes on Eleven Poets," *Kenyon Review* 7, 2 (Spring 1945): pp. 346–47.

37. Muriel Rukeyser, *Beast in View* (Garden City, N.Y.: Doubleday, Doran, 1944), p. 34.

38. Blackmur, "Notes on Eleven Poets," p. 347.

39. Robert Duncan, "The Homosexual in Society," *Politics* 1, 7 (August 1944): pp. 209–11.

40. Muriel Rukeyser, typescript of a review of Duncan she wrote for *Poetry*, PMP 1936–53, s1, b22, f7. The review was published as "Myth and Torment," *Poetry* 72, 1 (April 1948): p. 49.

41. Blackmur, "Notes on Eleven Poets," p. 346.

42. R. P. Blackmur to Allen Tate, May 4, 1934, Allen Tate Collection, b12, f6, Princeton University Library, Princeton, New Jersey.

43. Edward Said, "The Horizon of R. P. Blackmur," *Raritan* 6, 2 (Fall 1986): p. 39.

44. Rukeyser, *Beast in View*, p. 16.

45. Blackmur, "Notes on Eleven Poets," pp. 346–47.

46. Rukeyser, *Beast in View*, p. 37.

47. Meredith, "Alcan Epic," pp. 101–3.

48. Norman Friedman, "Poem vs. Slogan," *Reconstructionist* 18, 1 (February 22, 1952): pp. 19–20.

49. Meredith, "Alcan Epic," pp. 101–3.

50. Norman Rosten, introduction to Alfred Levinson, *Cauldron* (Prairie City, Ill.: Decker, 1948), p. [7].

51. Ibid., pp. [7–8].

52. Levinson, *Cauldron*, p. 18; emphasis added.

53. Ibid., p. 83.

54. Ibid., p. 73.

55. Ibid., p. 72.

56. James Decker to Harry Roskolenko, November 24, 1938, Harry Roskolenko Papers, SUSCRC.

57. He also published a play, *Socrates Wounded*, in the collection *New American Plays*, edited by Robert W. Corrigan (New York: Hill and Wang, 1965).

58. Alfred Levinson, "The Kiss," *Outposts* 77 (Summer 1968): p. 10.

59. Alfred Levinson, "The Middle East," *Commentary* 73, 6 (June 1982): p. 16.

60. "Only the Lions Remained," *Soviet Russia Today*, March 1944, p. 30.

61. Norman Rosten to Aaron Kramer, n.d. [1951], Aaron Kramer Papers, University of Michigan Special Collections, Ann Arbor.

62. F. O. Matthiessen, "Poetry," in *Literary History of the United States*, ed. Robert Spiller, Willard Thorp, Thomas H. Johnson, and Henry Seidel Canby (New York: Macmillan, 1948), p. 1350.

63. Benét prepared six "Dear Adolf" shows for the Council of Democracy as well as the "This Is War" series. He had deferred the completion of *Western Star* to devote all his time to the war effort.

64. Norman Rosten, "*Western Star* by Stephen Vincent Benét" (New York: National

Broadcasting Company/Council for Democracy, 1944), typescript, n.p., Norman Rosten Papers, Harlan Hatcher Graduate Library, University of Michigan, Ann Arbor.

65. See Stanton Coblentz's review of *Western Star* in *Wings* 6, 5 (Spring 1944): p. 23.

66. Stephen Vincent Benét, *The Devil and Daniel Webster* (New York: Holt, Rinehart, and Winston, 1937), p. 49.

67. As late as the early 1950s, Untermeyer joined Howard Fast, Albert Kahn, Eve Merriam, and other communist literary figures as part of the Arts, Sciences, and Professions contingent in the May Day demonstration. "Can you write while the books are being banned? Can you toss aside the ethics of your profession and accept instead the dictates of the Un-American Committee?" (n.d. [1952?], broadside copy in the Eve Merriam Papers, carton 1, f3, Schlesinger Library, Radcliffe College, Cambridge, Massachusetts).

68. Stephen Vincent Benét, "The Power of the Written Word," *Yale Review*, n.s., 30, 3 (March 1940): pp. 522–30; the deconstruction is on pp. 523–25: "Let us take some of the rest of the sentence—the mere words 'United States.' Well, of course, we know what the United States means—we know it so well that we do not even have to think about it. And yet do we? For it took five years of active revolution to make the one word, 'States'—and twelve years of confederation and argument and, later on, four years of Civil War to make the word 'United' an effective word."

69. In a December 21, 1946, article by Vladimir Rubin qtd. in Deming Brown, *Soviet Attitudes toward American Writing* (Princeton: Princeton University Press, 1962), p. 142.

70. New York: Council for Democracy, 1941. It is a broadside measuring twenty-seven by twenty-six centimeters, with illustrations.

71. E.g. with Lewis Mumford, who carried on a correspondence with the council for a decade (Lewis Mumford Papers, f1067, Van Pelt Library Special Collections, University of Pennsylvania, Philadelphia).

72. Alan Wald, *Exiles from a Future Time: The Forging of the Mid-Twentieth-Century Literary Left* (Chapel Hill: University of North Carolina Press, 2002), p. 307.

73. His first produced play seems to have been *Labor for the Wind*; a hand-corrected typescript of this apparently unpublished production (n.d. [early 1930s]) is in the Student Play Collection at the University of Michigan, Ann Arbor.

74. Norman Rosten to Aaron Kramer, n.d. [1949 or 1950?], Kramer Papers.

75. As he was not yet successfully shopping around the manuscript for *The Plane and the Shadow*, Rosten reported to Aaron Kramer that his "play" was "still a-begging" (Rosten to Kramer, July 16, 1952, Kramer Papers). Whatever play in draft this was, it was not produced, and it has apparently been lost. In 1983, Rosten excised "playwright" from a biographical profile, noting that he had "lost the playwright along the way" (Rosten to Kramer, February 13, 198[3?], Kramer Papers).

76. Alan Wald, "Science Fiction," "Popular Fiction," and "Radical Poetry," in *Encyclopedia of the American Left*, 2d ed., ed. Mary Jo Buhle, Paul Buhle, and Dan Georgakas (New York: Oxford University Press, 1998), pp. 724–26, 620–27, 671–79; "The Urban Landscape of Marxist Noir: An Interview with Alan Wald," *Crime Time: The Journal of Crime Fiction* 27 (2002): pp. 81–89.

77. George Oppen, *The Selected Letters of George Oppen*, ed. Rachel Blau DuPlessis (Durham: Duke University Press, 1990), p. xiv. For more on Oppen in Mexico, see Diana Anhalt, *A Gathering of Fugitives: American Political Expatriates in Mexico, 1948–1965* (Santa Maria, Calif.: Archer, 2001).

78. See Alan Wald, *Trinity of Passion: The Literary Left and the Antifascist Crusade* (Chapel Hill: University of North Carolina Press), pp. 82–83.

79. Alan Wald, "American Writers on the Left," in *The Gay and Lesbian Literary Heritage: A Reader's Companion to the Writers and Their Works, from Antiquity to the Present*, ed. Claude J. Summers (New York: Holt, 1995), p. 54.

80. Frank Marshall Davis, *Black Moods: Collected Poems*, ed. John Edgar Tidwell (Urbana: University of Illinois Press, 2002), pp. xxviii, xxx, xxxvi.

81. Dudley Randall, " 'Mystery Poet': An Interview with Frank Marshall Davis," *Black World* 23, 3 (January 1974): p. 40; Frank Marshall Davis, *Livin' the Blues: Memoirs of a Black Journalist and Poet*, ed. John Edgar Tidwell (Madison: University of Wisconsin Press, 1992), p. 304.

82. Norman Macleod, "Generation of Anger: A Writer in the Twentieth Century," typescript, pp. 1–2, Norman Macleod Papers, Princeton University Library, Princeton, New Jersey.

83. I am grateful to Alan Wald for helping me characterize the Taggard archive.

84. Alfred Kreymborg, "Remembering Genevieve Taggard," *Masses & Mainstream* 2, 1 (January 1949): pp. 48–49.

85. Millen Brand file, Counterattack Papers, s14.1, b28, f14–178.

86. See Alan Filreis, *Modernism from Right to Left* (New York: Cambridge University Press, 1994), pp. 113–28.

87. Ira Wolfert, interview by Alan Wald and the author, June 21, 1993.

88. Cary Nelson, *Revolutionary Memory: Recovering the Poetry of the American Left* (New York: Routledge, 2001), pp. 48, 58.

89. Ibid., p. 58.

90. Felix Wittmer, *Conquest of the American Mind: Comments on Collectivism in Education* (Boston: Meador, 1956), p. 215.

91. Louis Francis Budenz, "Do Colleges *Have* to Hire Red Professors?," *American Legion Magazine*, November 1951, p. 40. See also William Moore, "Charges Reds Turn Out Books for State Dept.; Budenz Says 75 Writers Are Communists," *Chicago Daily Tribune*, March 26, 1953, sec. 1, p. 6, *National Republic* Papers, b54, HI.

92. *Official Report of the Proceedings before the Subversive Activities Control Board, Herbert Brownell, Attorney General of the United States, Petitioner, v. the Jefferson School of Social Science, Respondent*, docket no. 107-53, December 10, 1953, pp. 720–21 (transcript no. 8, copy no. 5 is a holding of the Subversive Activities Control Board Papers, b31, HI).

93. Wittmer, *Conquest of the American Mind*, p. 266.

94. Fulton Lewis Jr., *Top of the News*, radio broadcast transcript, July 21, 1959, Fulton Lewis Jr. Papers, vol. 1, SUSCRC.

95. *Official Report of the Proceedings before the Subversive Activities Control Board,*

January 5, 1954, p. 1193 (transcript no. 13, copy no. 6 is a holding of the Subversive Activities Control Board Papers, b31).

96. See Marvin Gettleman, "No Varsity Teams: New York's Jefferson School of Social Science," *Science and Society* 66, 3 (Fall 2002): pp. 336–59; Marvin Gettleman, "The Lost World of United States Labor Education: Curricula at East and West Coast Communist Schools, 1944–1957," in *American Labor and the Cold War: Grassroots Politics and Postwar Political Culture*, ed. Robert W. Cherny, William Issel, and Kieran Walsh Taylor (New Brunswick: Rutgers University Press, 2004), pp. 205–15.

97. Roger Seamon to the author, November 12, 1997.

98. Myrtle G. Hance, *REaD-READING: A Report on Our San Antonio Public Libraries, Communist Front Authors and Their Books Therein* (San Antonio, Texas, 1952), copy in the Wisconsin Historical Society, Madison. See also Oliver Carlson, "A Slanted Guide to Library Selections," *Freeman* 2, 8 (January 14, 1952): pp. 239–42.

99. Of the thirty libraries reporting copies of *So Many Daughters* through WorldCat, none are in Texas. Nor are any copies of the book to be found today in the public libraries of Abilene, Austin, Brownsville, Bryan, College Station, Dallas, Denton, El Paso, Fort Worth, Galveston, Houston, Midland, Odessa, San Angelo, San Antonio, Tyler, and Waco.

100. Leonie Adams, "Spinning Singular," *Poetry* 85, 2 (November 1954): p. 114.

101. Roger Seamon to the author, November 12, 1997.

102. Eda Lou Walton to the editors of *Poetry*, July 30, 1961, PMP 1954–61, b36, f9.

103. Eda Lou Walton, "Our Daily Death," in *So Many Daughters* (New York: Bookman, 1952), p. 26. For more about Walton's life and ideas in the late 1920s and 1930s, see Alan Wald's account of her relationship with Henry Roth in *Trinity of Passion*, pp. 147, 149, 150–53.

104. Alfred Kreymborg to Henry Rago, November 1, 195[6] (Kreymborg misdated it 1954), PMP 1954–61, b19, f24.

105. Although Kreymborg was personally on good terms with CPUSA cultural commissar (and novelist) V. J. Jerome, some difficult moments arose, such as the time in 1942 (the communist line then was to support the Allies against fascism) when Jerome wanted Kreymborg to omit from *Ten American Ballads* "one or two of the poems because of their pacifist implications, and in their place to have some of those weapon-like poems you read for us at our house." Kreymborg took exception to this, although apologetically (V. J. Jerome to Alfred Kreymborg, June 15, 1942, Kreymborg to Jerome, June 18, 1942, V. J. Jerome Papers, b589, Yale University Library, New Haven, Connecticut).

106. Alfred Kreymborg to Isidor Schneider, March 4, 1946, Isidor Schneider Papers, Rare Books and Manuscript Library, Columbia University, New York. This was the time of the controversy stirred by Albert Maltz's article, "What Shall We Ask of Writers?" (*New Masses* 58, 7 [February 12, 1946], pp. 19–20).

107. Note written by Aaron Kramer (1965[?]) on materials given to the University of Michigan's Norman Rosten Papers pertaining to Rosten's plan to do a new edition of *Seven Poets in Search of an Answer*.

108. Arthur Miller, *Timebends—A Life* (New York: Grove, 1987), pp. 263–64.

109. E. San Juan Jr., "Carlos Bulosan," in *The American Radical*, ed. Mari Jo Buhle, Paul Buhle, and Harvey J. Kaye (New York: Routledge, 1994), pp. 253–54.

110. Carlos Bulosan, "Freedom from Want," *Saturday Evening Post*, March 6, 1943, p. 12.

111. Alvaro Cardona-Hine to the author, September 20, 1998; Alan Wald, "From Old Left to New to U.S. Literary Radicalism," in *Writing from the Left: New Essays on Radical Culture and Politics* (London: Verso, 1994), pp. 114–15. This essay offers a brief overview of Cardona-Hine's life and work.

112. Alvaro Cardona-Hine, "Bulosan Now," *Mainstream* 11, 7 (July 1958): pp. 53–55.

113. John Hagan, "Ben Maddow," in *Writers and Production Artists*, ed. Samantha Cook (Detroit: St. James, 1993), pp. 485–86.

114. Isidor Schneider to Malcolm Cowley, August 29, 1946, January 30, 1947, Malcolm Cowley Papers, Newberry Library, Chicago. For more on Schneider's experiences in the immediate postwar period, see Wald, *Trinity of Passion*, pp. 219–26.

115. Malcolm Cowley to Isidor Schneider, August 30, 1946, Schneider Papers.

116. Isidor Schneider to Malcolm Cowley, August 29, 1946, January 30, 1947, Cowley Papers.

117. Herman Spector, *Bastard in the Ragged Suit: Writings of, with drawings by, Herman Spector*, comp., ed., and intro. Bud Johns and Judith S. Clancy (San Francisco: Synergistic, 1977), p. 13.

118. Ibid., pp. 3, 15.

119. "Between Ourselves," *New Masses* 14, 10A (March 12, 1935): p. 30.

120. Counterattack files on the *Daily Worker* included negative photostatic copies of subscriber addresses and phone numbers. Also in these files was a set of addressograph labels, n.d. ("CPUSA—Daily Worker," Counterattack Papers, b12).

121. Myra Neugass, telephone interview with the author, June 30, 1994. "James Neugass," biographical profile for *Story Magazine*, n.d. (*Story* Archives, b26, f33, Princeton University Libraries, Princeton, New Jersey). A series of never-completed experimental verse projects was outlined in notes Neugass made in April 1937 while serving with an ambulance corps in Spain (privately held manuscripts provided by Myra Neugass to the author, first page dated April 24, 1937). In 1963, when Walter Lowenfels asked communist critic V. J. Jerome to search through his personal library, Jerome wrote back, "I have nothing by Neugass" (V. J. Jerome to Walter Lowenfels, May 27, 1963, V. J. Jerome Papers, b5, f98, Manuscripts and Archives, Yale University Library). Neugass's poem, "Give Us This Day," has been republished in *The Wound and the Dream: Sixty Years of American Poems about the Spanish Civil War*, ed. Cary Nelson (Urbana: University of Illinois Press, 2002), pp. 124–34.

122. FBI file on Muriel Rukeyser, a portion available at <http://foia.fbi.gov/foiaindex/rukeyser.htm>.

123. Merrill Folsom, "Sarah Lawrence Again under Fire," *New York Times*, November 14, 1958, p. 11. Nearly 120 pages of Rukeyser's FBI file is now available under the Freedom of Information Act at <http://foia.fbi.gov/foiaindex/rukeyser.htm>.

124. Aaron Kramer, *Wicked Times: Selected Poems*, ed. Cary Nelson and Donald Gilzinger Jr. (Urbana: University of Illinois Press, 2004), p. xxxvii.

125. Aaron Kramer to the author, June 26, 1994.

126. Nothing then came of this plan, but later, after the blacklisting era was finished and Cameron was again a senior editor at a major New York firm, he expressed interest in publishing Kramer's dissertation, "The Prophetic Tradition in American Poetry, 1835–1900" (Ph.D. diss., New York University, 1966).

127. Aaron Kramer's notes to his correspondence with Norman Rosten; Rosten's letter, which Kramer dated "mid-1950," asks about his friend's illness (Kramer Papers).

128. E.g., three poems for the April 1933 issue (pp. 20–21).

129. Eugene Lyons, *The Red Decade: The Stalinist Penetration of America* (Indianapolis: Bobbs-Merrill, 1941), p. 248. In another of the many instances, during the Judith Coplon spy trial, the defendant's attorney demanded that the judge force the FBI to produce its intelligence-gathering materials. When the judge issued the order, federal agents came to court bearing names of communists. Brand was one of those named, exposure that cascaded from report to report, blacklist to blacklist ("Millen Brand," p. 2, Counterattack Papers, s14.1, b28, f14–178).

130. Hance, *REaD-READING*, p. 3.

131. E.g., John Logan to Isabella Gardner, October 13, 1953, Isabella Gardner Papers, WU. Logan knew that Brand was an editor at Crown and had tried to follow Brand's new poems, noting "An Old Man toward the End," which had found its way into *Accent* into 1953. As Ron Silliman (at http://ronsilliman.blogspot.com/) has pointed out, today Logan would not be considered an aesthetic rebel, yet in the late 1950s and early 1960s he was gathered into a group of anti-establishmentarians, e.g., in David Ossman's *The Sullen Art* (New York: Corinth, 1963).

132. Millen Brand, "Local Lives," in *Cross Section 1945: A Collection of New American Writing*, ed. Edwin Seaver (New York: Fischer, 1945), pp. 67–68.

133. Millen Brand, "The Lute," *Masses & Mainstream* 2, 6 (June 1949): p. 53. At this point, according to the note published with this poem, Brand was already planning a book of "Local Lives" lyrics.

134. "For Whom Do You Write?—Replies from Forty American Writers," *New Quarterly* 1, 2 (Summer 1934): pp. 7, 5. The other statement was that of Joseph Freeman.

135. Brand, "Local Lives," pp. 67–68.

136. He published "Joe Heimbacher—The Start" and "Dinner" in *Poetry* 70, 3 (June 1947): p. 136.

137. "Morning" had been published in the December 1941 issue (59, 3; p. 140).

138. Millen Brand, "The Old Man toward the End," *Accent*, Winter 1953, pp. 34–39.

139. Millen Brand to Henry Rago, December 19, 1955, PMP 1954–61, b4, f25.

140. Millen Brand to Karl Shapiro, May 15, 1952, PMP 1936–53, s2, b2, f1.

141. Henry Rago to Millen Brand, December 28, 1955, PMP 1954–61, b4, f25.

142. Millen Brand to Henry Rago, December 19, 1955, PMP 1954–61, b4, f25.

143. Millen Brand to Karl Shapiro, June 3, 1952, PMP 1936–53, s2, b2, f1.

144. See Filreis, *Modernism from Right to Left*, pp. 186–94.

145. His story, "Can I Play with Your Little Girl?," was published in the fourth issue of the book-length paperback *Discovery* (1954), pp. 1–13.

146. Norman Rosten to Aaron Kramer, n.d. [1951], Kramer Papers.

147. For the Crawford project, see notes by Aaron Kramer, attached to ibid; for Arthur Miller, see Kramer's notes to Rosten's letter dated February 13, 198[3?], which confirm a long-standing friendship that ended with a break only in the early 1980s. Rosten knew Miller when he was married to Marilyn Monroe; years later, he published a memoir of Monroe, *Marilyn: An Untold Story* (New York: New American Library, 1973).

148. Norman Rosten to Aaron Kramer, March 20, [1951?], Kramer Papers.

149. Norman Rosten, *The Plane and the Shadow* (New York: Bookman, 1953), p. 13.

150. Ruth Lechlitner, "Lines for an Abortionist's Office," in *Tomorrow's Phoenix* (New York: Alcestis, 1937), p. 33.

151. Rosten, *Plane and the Shadow*, p. 12.

152. "Gloucester Port," typescript draft, sent to Aaron Kramer, probably with an undated letter from Rosten to Kramer which Kramer's notes for the archivist indicated was sent in mid-1950 (Kramer Papers).

153. Rosten, *Plane and the Shadow*, p. 15.

154. Ibid., p. 29.

155. Norman Rosten, *The Big Road* (New York: Rinehart, 1946), pp. 7, 35, 162, 47, 48, 62, 74, 81, 87, 98, 103, 120, 123, 195, 139, 147, 146, 195, 162, 163, 165, 184, 185, 148.

156. Michael Thurston, *Making Something Happen: American Political Poetry between the World Wars* (Chapel Hill: University of North Carolina Press, 2001), pp. 169–210; Davidson, *Ghostlier Demarcations*, pp. 8–9, 135–70.

157. Harvey Breit, "Who Are We?," *Poetry* 58, 3 (June 1941): p. 156. This was a review of Rosten's *Return Again, Traveler* (New Haven: Yale University Press, 1940).

158. Mona Van Duyn, "What People?," *Poetry* 68, 1 (April 1946): pp. 49–51.

Chapter 7

1. John Chamberlain, "A Reviewer's Notebook," *Freeman* 2, 23 (August 11, 1952): p. 777.

2. B. Y. [Williams], "By 3 A.M.," *Talaria* 15, 2 (Summer 1950): p. 2.

3. Read Bain, "Poetry and the Cult of Incomprehensibility," *Humanist* 15, 3 (May–June 1955): p. 127. He had begun as poetry editor with the March–April 1954 issue.

4. Stanton Coblentz, *New Poetic Lamps and Old* (Mill Valley, Calif.: Wings, 1950), p. 9; Stanton Coblentz, "What Are They?—Poems or Puzzles?," *New York Times Magazine*, October 13, 1946, p. 24.

5. This man, Carl Edwin Burklund, was the brother-in-law of Peter DeVries, one-time editor of *Poetry*, and might thus be considered somewhat of a poetry insider (*The Moment in Time: Collected Poems of Carl Edwin Burklund* [Unadila, Mich.: Burklund, 1973], p. v). For Burklund's antimodernism, see "The Treason of 'Modern' Poetry," *Lyric* 28, 3 (1949): p. 142.

6. See Marnix Gijsen, *Belgian Letters: A Short Survey of Creative Writing in the French and Dutch Languages in Belgium* (New York: Belgian Government Information Center, 1950), esp. p. [2]; Jan-Albert Goris, *Belgium in Bondage* (New York: Fischer, 1943); Jan-Albert Goris, "The Belgian Congo," *Journal of International Affairs* 7, 2 (Winter 1953): p. 181.

7. Goris was doubtless referring to the political poetry movement founded by Ayukawa Nobuo and Tamura Ryūichi after the war. In that period even haiku, such as those by Kaneko Tōta, freely treated topics such as the atomic bombing and the United States–Japan Mutual Security Treaty. *The Waste Land*, founded in 1947, was one venue for such verse.

8. Jan-Albert Goris, "Tradition and Controversy in Poetry: The Elements That Constitute the Basis of Poetry," speech, St. Bonaventure University, New York, September 24, 1958, published in *Vital Speeches*, October 15, 1958, pp. 28–32.

9. William Terry Couch, director of the University of Chicago Press in the late 1940s and early 1950s, was deeply impressed by *Faith and Force* and encouraged Lalley to finish the large work of which *Faith and Force* was to be an introduction (it was called "An Inquiry into the Nature of Authority" and was never completed). "Biographical Sketch," Finding Aid, p. 2, J. M. Lalley Papers, ms. 199, Milton S. Eisenhower Library, Johns Hopkins University, Baltimore, Maryland.

10. Joseph M. Lalley, *Faith and Force: An Inquiry into the Nature of Authority* (Washington, D.C.: Human Events, [1946]), pp. 17, 5.

11. Stanton Coblentz, "Literary Decadence and World Decay," *Wings* 12, 8 (Winter 1947): pp. 3–6.

12. Mary O'Connor, "Lord Dunsany, an American Memory," *Poetry Review* 51, 1 (January–February 1960): p. 51.

13. R. B. Beaman, "The Cubist Witch," *South Atlantic Quarterly*, June 1949, p. 211.

14. Jacob Hauser, "Academies of the Perverse," *Lyric*, 31, 2 (Spring 1951): p. 64.

15. Stanton Coblentz, *The Literary Revolution* (1927; New York: AMS, 1969), pp. 187–88.

16. Robert Hillyer, "Poetry's New Priesthood," *Saturday Review of Literature*, June 18, 1949, pp. 7, 38.

17. Robert Hillyer to Leigh Hanes, April 4, 1949, b6, f dated 1948, Leigh Hanes Papers, 7689-a, Albert and Shirley Small Special Collections Library, University of Virginia, Charlottesville.

18. Stanton Coblentz to Robert Hillyer, June 3, 1949, Robert Hillyer Papers, b1, f40, SUSCRC.

19. Robert Hillyer in the *Bulletin of the Poetry Society of America*, qtd. in Coblentz, *New Poetic Lamps and Old*, p. 9.

20. Gilbert Malcolm Fess, "Thank God for Existentialism!," *Books Abroad* 26, 3 (Summer 1952): pp. 252–53.

21. Stanton Coblentz, "Will the Current Change?," *Wings* 12, 3 (Autumn 1955): p. 3.

22. Stanton Coblentz, "The Poet, the Politician, and the Press Agent," *Wings* 11, 2 (Summer 1953): p. 4.

23. Coblentz, *New Poetic Lamps and Old*, p. 129.

24. Stanton Coblentz, "The New Caste System in Poetry," *Wings* 12, 7 (Autumn 1956): p. 5.

25. "Must Poets Be Exterminated?," *Pinnacle: Bulletin of the League for Sanity in Poetry* (May 1945): p. 2.

26. Hauser, "Academies of the Perverse," p. 64.

27. Leigh Hanes to "Harry," October 15, 1956, b2, f "Poetry Society of Va. (Efforts to Have School Children Read Poetry Orally)," Hanes Papers; emphasis added.

28. Stanton Coblentz, "Truth Is Beauty, Beauty Is Truth," *Wings* 12, 1 (Spring 1955): p. 6.

29. Alice Hunt Bartlett, "Dynamics of American Poetry: CXVI," *Poetry Review* 38, 2 (March–April 1947): p. 147.

30. See Alice Hunt Bartlett, "Dynamics of American Poetry: CXV," *Poetry Review* 38, 1 (January–February 1947): p. 63.

31. Coblentz, *New Poetic Lamps and Old*, pp. 9, 12.

32. Robert M. La Follette Jr., "Turn the Light on Communism," *Collier's*, February 8, 1947, p. 22.

33. Hillyer, "Poetry's New Priesthood," p. 7.

34. See John Timberman Newcomb, "The Footprint of Twentieth Century American Skyscrapers and Modernist Poems," *Modernism/Modernity* 10, 1 (January 2003): pp. 97–125. Horace Gregory, in his 1958 biography of Amy Lowell, noted that in 1917, *Poetry Journal* was banned from the mails because of the final two lines in Scudder Middleton's poem "Interlude": "Dark arms pull her down to a face seeking kisses— / A whore again, serving her master" (*Poetry Journal* 6, 3 [January 1917]: p. 99; Horace Gregory, *Amy Lowell: Portrait of the Poet in Her Time* [Edinburgh: Nelson, 1958], p. 223).

35. See Edward Bok, *The Americanization of Edward Bok* (New York: Scribner's, 1920), p. 296. Bok insisted that even in poetry, "the message itself is of greater import than the manner in which it is said."

36. Conrad Aiken, "The Place of Imagism," *New Republic*, May 22, 1915, pp. 75–76. "Of organic movement there is practically none" in imagism, he wrote (p. 75). Early anti-modernism is typified by Oscar W. Firkins, "Poetry and Prose in Life and Art," *Poet-Lore* 15, (July 1904): pp. 78–79.

37. Bok, *Americanization of Edward Bok*, p. 295.

38. The fullest account is in Irene Gammel, *Baroness Elsa: Gender, Dada, and Everyday Modernity: A Cultural Biography* (Cambridge: MIT Press, 2002), pp. 248–60.

39. Stanton Coblentz, *An Editor Looks at Poetry* (Mill Valley, Calif.: Wings, 1947), p. 102.

40. "Taming of the Muse," *News from behind the Iron Curtain* 2, 4 (April 1953): p. 37. The communist phrase is Kazimierz Wyka's (*Nowa Kultura*, September 7, 1952).

41. Here I am following the lines of Peter Bürger's argument in *The Theory of the Avant-Garde*, trans. Michael Shaw (Minneapolis: University of Minnesota Press, 1984).

42. Richard M. Weaver, *Ideas Have Consequences* (Chicago: University of Chicago Press, 1948), pp. 44, 165, 129.

43. John Livingston Lowes, "An Unacknowledged Imagist," *Nation*, February 24, 1916,

pp. 217–19. The phrase is from George Meredith's prose fiction; Lowes created "imagist" poems out of passages from Meredith's novels to argue that modern poetry was nothing new. The title of the "poem" in which the phrase "a species / of mad metaphor" appears was given by Lowes himself; it is called "Imagists" (p. 219). For the League for Sanity in Poetry, see chapters 11 and 13.

44. Qtd. from a letter written to the officers of the League for Sanity in Poetry in Stanton Coblentz, in *My Life in Poetry* (New York: Bookman, 1959), p. 177.

45. "Appeal to the Great," *Pinnacle: Bulletin of the League for Sanity in Poetry* 5 (August–September 1945): p. 2.

46. Padriac Colum, "Egoism in Poetry," *New Republic*, November 20, 1915, p. 6.

47. Coblentz, *New Poetic Lamps and Old*, p. 64.

48. Colum, "Egoism in Poetry," p. 6.

49. Aiken, "Place of Imagism," p. 75.

50. Ibid., p. 75.

51. Howard Devree, "Modernism under Fire," *New York Times*, September 11, 1949, sec. 10, p. 6.

52. Beaman, "Cubist Witch," pp. 204, 211.

53. Geoffrey Wagner, "The Organized Heresy: Abstract Art in the United States," *Modern Age* 4, 3 (Summer 1960): pp. 264, 260. Wagner quoted Hans Hoffmann ("Imitation should not be permitted to have even the slightest part in the creative process") and cited a section of Xavier Gonzalez's *Notes about Painting* (Cleveland: World, 1955) on "The Sterility of Composition."

54. Qtd. in Alfred H. Barr Jr., "Is Modern Art Communistic?," *New York Times Magazine*, December 14, 1952, p. 22.

55. Welford Inge, "The Poetry of Fear," *Catholic World*, May 1956, p. 136.

56. Joseph Auslander to Archer M. Huntington, April 16, 1953, Archer M. Huntington Papers, SUSCRC.

57. Maxwell Anderson to Archer Huntington, April 14, 1949, Huntington Papers.

58. Arthur U. Pope, *Archer Milton Huntington: Last of the Titans* (n.p., n.d. [1955?]), pp. 7–8.

59. Archer M. Huntington to Maxwell Anderson, April 20, 1949, Huntington Papers.

60. A. Hyatt Mayor, *A. Hyatt Mayor: Selected Writings and a Bibliography* (New York: Metropolitan Museum of Art, 1983), pp. 9–22. For "editing by juxtaposition," see Lincoln Kirstein, *A. Hyatt Mayor* (New York: Metropolitan Museum of Art, 1980), n.p.

61. Archer Huntington to Nicholas Murray Butler, undated second page, Huntington Papers. See also Beatrice Gilman Proske, *Archer Milton Huntington* (New York: Hispanic Society of America, 1963); James Thorpe, *Henry Edwards Huntington: A Biography* (Berkeley: University of California Press, 1994); Pope, *Archer Milton Huntington*.

62. Alice Hunt Bartlett, "Dynamics of American Poetry: CIX," *Poetry Review* 36, 5–6 (November–December 1945): p. 322.

63. Cullen Jones, " 'To Him,' " *Pinnacle: Bulletin of the League for Sanity in Poetry* 5 (August–September 1945): p. 2.

64. Cullen Jones, "Abnormal Poets and Abnormal Poetry," *Poet Lore* 56, 3 (Autumn 1951): pp. 234, 235.

65. Donald Jenks to Karl Shapiro, August 5, 1949, PMP 1936–1953, s1, b2, f4.

66. Jones, "Abnormal Poets," pp. 234–35.

67. Karl Shapiro, "The Critic in Spite of Himself," in *In Defense of Poetry* (New York: Random House, 1960), p. 27.

68. Alfred Ralph Korn, "Extremists in Modern Poetry," *Christian Poet*, April 1945, p. 5.

69. "The League for Sanity in Poetry Believes That . . . ," *Pinnacle: Bulletin of the League for Sanity in Poetry* 2 (May–July 1945): p. [1].

70. Stanton Coblentz, "Poetry, Progress and Prose," *Wings* 5, 8 (Winter 1943): p. 3.

71. Stanton Coblentz to Robert Hillyer, June 3, 1939, Hillyer Papers, b1, f40.

72. Stanton Coblentz, "The Walls of Freedom," *Wings* 10, 2 (Summer 1951): p. 3, collected in *The Rise of the Anti-Poets: Selected Editorials from "Wings: A Quarterly of Verse"* (Mill Valley, Calif.: Wings, 1955), p. 17.

73. Ibid., p. 18.

74. Ibid., pp. 17–18.

75. See the chapter "Some Dogmas of the Modernists" in Coblentz, *Literary Revolution*, esp. pp. 154–57; phrase quoted appears on p. 156.

76. Coblentz, "Walls of Freedom," p. 19.

77. Coblentz, *My Life in Poetry*, p. 113.

78. Stanton Coblentz, "The Poet, the Politician, and the Press-Agent," *Wings* 11, 2 (Summer 1953): pp. 5–6; emphasis added.

79. Stanton Coblentz and Jeffrey M. Elliot, *Adventures of a Freelancer: The Literary Exploits and Autobiography of Stanton A. Coblentz* (San Bernardino, Calif.: Borgo, 1993), pp. 136–37. For more on Coblentz, see Velma West Sykes, "Coblentz Gave Readable Poets a Forum," *Kansas City Times*, August 11, 1960, p. 44.

80. Eric Hoffer, *The True Believer: Thoughts on the Nature of Mass Movements* (New York: Harper and Row, 1951), p. 31.

81. Robert Hillyer, "Escape the Dark Destructive Force," in *This I Believe*, ed. Edward R. Murrow (New York: Simon and Schuster, 1952), pp. 71–72; Robert Hillyer, "Speaking of Books," *New York Times Book Review*, February 3, 1957, p. 2.

82. Robert Hillyer, *In Pursuit of Poetry* (New York: McGraw-Hill, 1960), p. 190.

83. See, e.g., Robert Hillyer, "Modern Poetry versus the Common Reader," *Saturday Review of Literature*, March 24, 1945, pp. 5–7.

84. Robert Hillyer to Phyllis McGinley, January 6, 1952, Phyllis McGinley Papers, SUSCRC. *The Suburb by the Sea* was Robert Hillyer's major work of the 1950s. He lived with his family in Greenwich, Connecticut, a place that provided the setting of many of his poems. His paeans to suburbia are never so vexed and ambivalent as Stevens's final cantos in *The Man with the Blue Guitar* or "An Ordinary Evening in New Haven." A poem, "Above Clustered Suburban Roofs," published in the *New Yorker* in 1950, confirms this:

> If now, with lesser members of my race,
>
> I sip the coffee of the commonplace,

yet would I boast how I have quaffed with you

The vanished distillation of the dewe,

And, with superior smile and stifled yawn,

Be known as one who rises with the dawn. (*New Yorker*, September 9, 1950, p. 80)
See also Phyllis McGinley, "Suburbia, of Thee I Sing," in *The Province of the Heart* (New York: Viking, 1959), pp. 121–33.

85. Karl Shapiro, "Poets and Psychologists," *Poetry* 80, 3 (June 1952): p. 182.

86. Robert Hillyer to Leigh Hanes, March 15, 1948, b6, f dated 1948, Hanes Papers.

87. Harold R. Medina to Sonia Levinthal, November 14, 1960, Hillyer Papers.

88. Hawthorne Daniel, *Judge Medina* (New York: Funk, 1952), p. 134.

89. Phrases taken from two editorials—from the *New Orleans Item* and the *Elizabeth City (N.C.) Independent*—excerpted in a document titled "Editorials," part of a file kept by Medina's office on press responses to the Foley Square trial (Harold R. Medina Papers, b215, Seeley Mudd Library, Princeton University, Princeton, New Jersey).

90. Harold R. Medina, "The Judge and His God," speech, Church Club of New York, February 5, 1951, published in *Vital Speeches*, April 15, 1951, pp. 388–89.

91. Robert Hillyer, "The Crisis in American Poetry," *American Mercury*, January 1950, p. 65.

92. Lawrence Lipton, "Poetry and the Vocal Tradition," *Nation*, April 18, 1956, p. 323.

93. Ibid., p. 323.

94. Nettie Lipton, "Lawrence Lipton," in *The Beats: Literary Bohemians in Postwar America*, ed. Ann Charters (Storrs, Conn.: University of Connecticut/Gale Research, 1983), pp. 352–56.

95. Lawrence Lipton, "Poetry and the Vocal Tradition," p. 323.

96. Ibid., p. 321.

97. Leigh Hanes to "Harry," October 16, 1956, b2, Hanes Papers.

98. Lawrence Lipton, "Vocal Poetry and Vocal Poets" and "Mr. Lipton's Answer," *Nation*, June 9, 1956, p. 481.

99. Stanton Coblentz to Jessie Wilmore Murton, February 26, 1949, Jessie Wilmore Murton Papers, b1, f14, KSA/WKU.

100. Stanton Coblentz, "Poetry in the Hour of Need," *Wings* 11, 3 (Autumn 1953): pp. 3–6.

101. Ibid., p. 20.

102. Coblentz, *Editor Looks at Poetry*, pp. 110–12.

Chapter 8

1. "Mr. Hoagland," "Back to Sunsets!," July 31, 1940. Lee Anderson retained a proof copy of this otherwise unidentified letter to an editor (Lee Anderson Papers, WU).

2. Robert Hillyer, "Poetry's New Priesthood," *Saturday Review of Literature*, June 18, 1949, p. 8. For an instance of the identification of the term "modern" with the term "ideological," see Karl Shapiro, "The Critic in Spite of Himself," in *In Defense of Ignorance* (New York: Random House, 1960), pp. 31–32.

3. R. B. Beaman, "The Cubist Witch," *South Atlantic Quarterly*, April 1949, pp. 204–12.

4. Howard Devree, "Modernism under Fire," *New York Times*, September 11, 1949, sec. 10, p. 6.

5. Lawrence Lipton, "Poetry and the Vocal Tradition," *Nation*, April 18, 1956, pp. 319–24. He attacked Stanton Coblentz and *Wings* in particular (p. 323).

6. William Rose Benét to Hayden Carruth, December 3, 1949, PMP 1936–53, s1, b2, f3.

7. William Phillips, "What Happened in the 30's," *Commentary* 30, 3 (September 1962): p. 212.

8. *Wings* 9, 5 (Spring 1950): p. 21.

9. Mary Stack McNiff, "Poets in Action," *America*, September 23, 1950, p. 648. This was a summary of the conference.

10. Typewritten transcript, Harvard Summer School Conference on the Defense of Poetry, August 14–17, 1950, Harvard University Archives, Pusey Library, Cambridge, Massachusetts, HUE 83.550.14, p. 5.

11. Ibid., p. 13.

12. Ibid., pp. 29–31.

13. Richard Wirtz Emerson and Frederick Eckman, "Editorial Report on the Crisis," *Golden Goose Chapbook* 9 (1950): pp. 5, 6, 11.

14. Carruth might have counted among these enemies his editorial colleague at *Poetry*, Marion Strobel. When Carruth took over as editor in 1949, he was considered too young to be trusted with complete editorial control and was forced to share this function with Strobel and John F. Nims. Strobel was a traditionalist, disliked the internationalist modern school, preferred intuitive lyrics, and felt that Carruth was in the pocket of the New Critics. Carruth's editorial on the Pound controversy must have confirmed Strobel's view. By the end of 1949, she had gathered enough votes on the *Poetry* board to demand Carruth's resignation. Karl Shapiro, whose opposition to Pound's Bollingen Prize was well known, was appointed editor. Frank A. Ninkovich has pointed out that during these years, *Poetry* depended on a three-year grant from the Bollingen Foundation that ran out in October 1949 ("The New Criticism and Cold War America," *Southern Quarterly* 20, 1 [Fall 1981]: pp. 5–8).

15. Hayden Carruth, "The Anti-Poet All Told," *Poetry* 74, 5 (August 1949): pp. 280–81.

16. Ibid., p. 280.

17. Virginia Kent Cummins, "What Is Traditional Poetry?," *Lyric* 29, 2–3 (1949): p. 193.

18. Harry Roskolenko, "The Cant in Pound's Cantos," *Congress Weekly*, April 11, 1949, p. 7.

19. The Robert Hillyer Papers at SUSCRC contain numerous such letters. Several, such as Burton Frye to Robert Hillyer, September 2, 1949 (b3, f1), respond specifically to Carruth's *Poetry* editorial. Louis Kent wrote to assure Hillyer that he could not "be destroyed as poet" by his detractors (Kent to Hillyer, October 23, 1949, Hillyer Papers, b3, f24).

20. Hilton Kramer, "T. S. Eliot in New York: Notes on the End of Something," *Western Review*, 14, 4 (Summer 1950): p. 305.

21. Compare J[ames] B. Sheerin, "Pound Affair," *Catholic World*, August 1949, pp. 322–23, with, e.g., Sheerin's "Korea, Communists, Corruption," *Catholic World*, November 1952, pp. 81–85.

22. Sheerin, "Pound Affair," pp. 322–23.

23. Devree, "Modernism under Fire," sec. 10, p. 6.

24. Hillyer, "Poetry's New Priesthood," p. 8.

25. Sheerin, "Pound Affair," pp. 322–23.

26. Roskolenko, "Cant in Pound's Cantos," p. 7.

27. Harry Roskolenko, draft version of "The Cant in Pound's Cantos," p. 5, Harry Roskolenko Papers, b30, SUSCRC.

28. Although Burt was a Wyoming rancher, he had worked for some years as a reporter on the *Philadelphia Times* and wrote regularly about Philadelphia. His most recent book was *Philadelphia: Holy Experiment* (Garden City, N.Y.: Doubleday, Doran, 1945). *Along These Streets* (New York: Scribner's, 1942) is a volume of travel writing.

29. Struthers Burt, "Pro Bollingen Bosh," *Saturday Review of Literature*, August 27, 1949, p. 21.

30. Hellman had recommended to Cousins "that when you are invited to dinner, you wait until you get home before you talk about your hosts" (qtd. in Jim Tuck, *The Liberal Civil War: Fraternity and Fratricide on the Left* [Lanham, Md.: University Press of America, 1998], p. 213).

31. Qtd. in Ingrid Winther Scobie, "Jack B. Tenney and the 'Parasitic Menace': Anti-Communist Legislation in California, 1940–1949," *Pacific Historical Review* 43, 2 (May 1974): p. 197.

32. *Official Report of the Proceedings before the Subversive Activities Control Board, Herbert Brownell, Attorney General of the United States, Petitioner, v. the Jefferson School of Social Science*, Docket no. 107-33, December 11, 1953, p. 812, Subversive Activities Control Board Papers, b31, HI.

33. W. Cleon Skousen, *The Naked Communist* (Salt Lake City: Ensign, 1958), pp. [i], 279–80.

34. Harry Overstreet and Bonaro Overstreet, *The Strange Tactics of Extremism* (New York: Norton, 1964), p. 42.

35. Hillyer, "Poetry's New Priesthood," pp. 7–9, 38.

36. Welford Inge, "The Poetry of Fear," *Catholic World*, May 1956, pp. 132, 133; emphasis added.

37. Geoffrey Parsons, *Peter's Progress* (Aldington, Kent: Hand and Flower, 1953), p. 34.

38. Read Bain, "Poetry and the Cult of Incomprehensibility," *Humanist* 15, 3 (May–June 1955): p. 127; George H. Fathauer, John E. Dolibois, Johanne Fathauer, Mildred Seltzer, Delbert Snider, and John A. Weigel, "A Memorial to Read Bain" (1979), unpublished essay, University Archives, Miami University, Miami, Ohio.

39. Stanton Coblentz, *An Editor Looks at Poetry* (Mill Valley, Calif.: Wings, 1947), p. 26.

40. Stanton Coblentz, "Will the Current Change?," *Wings* 12, 3 (Autumn 1955): pp. 3, 5.

41. Stanton Coblentz, *The Literary Revolution* (1927; New York: AMS, 1969), p. 156.

42. Cullen Jones, "The One Poet of the Generation," *Poetry Review* 35, 4 (July–September 1944): pp. 189, 190.

43. See, e.g., Werner Cohn, " 'A Clear Provocation': Esoteric Elements in Communist Language," *Encounter* 64, 5 (May 1985): pp. 75–78.

44. Gerhart Neimeyer, *An Inquiry into Soviet Mentality* (New York: Praeger, 1956), pp. 38–39.

45. Geoffrey Wagner, "The Organized Heresy: Abstract Art in the United States," *Modern Age* 4, 3 (Summer 1960): pp. 264, 265.

46. For an example of Russell Kirk on tactical confusion, see his *The American Cause* (Chicago: Regnery, 1957), pp. 127–31.

47. Cullen Jones, "Abnormal Poets and Abnormal Poetry," *Poet Lore* 56, 3 (Autumn 1951): pp. 228, 230.

48. *Firing Line* 1, 8 (May 1, 1952): p. 1; typescript, Brenda Putnam Papers, SUSCRC.

49. Stefan T. Possony, *Language as a Communist Weapon* (Washington, D.C.: U.S. House Committee on Un-American Activities, 1959). See also Alan Filreis, "Words with 'All the Effects of Force': Cold-War Interpretation," *American Quarterly* 39, 2 (Summer 1987): p. 312. See also Overstreet and Overstreet, "A Reading Lesson," in *Strange Tactics of Extremism*, pp. 54–65.

50. See, e.g., J. Edgar Hoover, *Masters of Deceit* (New York: Simon and Schuster/Pocket Books, 1958), pp. 265–66.

51. See Filreis, "Words with 'All the Effects of Force,' " pp. 306–12; Julia M. Allen, " 'That Accursed Aesopian Language': Prosecutorial Framing of Linguistic Evidence in U.S. v. Foster, 1949," *Rhetoric and Public Affairs* 4, 1 (2001): pp. 109–34.

52. Harry Hodgkinson, *Doubletalk: The Language of Communism* (London: Allen and Unwin, 1955), p. v.

53. Jessie Wilmore Murton, "Report to Mr. Olmstead," n.d. [1948], Jessie Wilmore Murton Papers, b1, f14, KSA/WKU.

54. [Jessie Wilmore Murton,] "Horrible Examples," n.d., Murton Papers, b9, f7; Louis Zukofsky, *All the Collected Short Poems, 1923–1958* (New York: Norton, 1965), p. 58.

55. Virginia Kent Cummins, untitled editorial, *Lyric* 31, 2 (Spring 1951): p. 62.

56. Jones, "Abnormal Poets and Abnormal Poetry," p. 235.

57. Robert M. La Follette Jr., "Turn the Light on Communism," *Collier's*, February 8, 1947, p. 22.

58. Stanton Coblentz, "The Weed and the Wheat," in *The Rise of the Anti-Poets: Selected Editorials from "Wings: A Quarterly of Verse"* (Mill Valley, Calif.: Wings, 1955), p. 26.

59. Lilith Lorraine to Jessie Wilmore Murton, January 21, 1945, b9, f7, Murton Papers.

60. League for Sanity in Poetry, *Making Treason Pay* (Rogers, Ark.: League for Sanity in Poetry, [1949]), p. [1].

61. Hillyer, "Poetry's New Priesthood," p. 38.

62. Robert Hillyer, "The Crisis in American Poetry," *American Mercury*, January 1950, p. 65.

63. Stanton Coblentz, *My Life in Poetry* (New York: Bookman, 1959), p. 48.

64. Stanton Coblentz, "The Break in the Dike," *Wings* 9, 7 (Autumn 1950): pp. 3–4.

65. Edward John Dunsany, "How to Conquer America," *Wings* 10, 3 (1951): pp. 8–9.

66. Lilith Lorraine to Jessie Wilmore Murton, January 21, 1945, Murton Papers, b9, f7.

67. *The Avalon National Poetry Shrine* (brochure), Murton Papers, b9.

68. The first clear articulation of this centrist perspective—later dubbed "the end of ideology"—came in Arthur M. Schlesinger Jr.'s *The Vital Center* (Boston: Houghton Mifflin, 1949).

69. Henry Regnery to Roy Cullen, March 19, 1953, Robert E. Wood Papers, s "Regnery, Henry," HI.

70. Clarke Beach, "A Tardy Muse at College Park," June 28, 1936, University of Maryland alumni magazine [?] clipping, Susan E. Harman Papers, University of Maryland Archives, Hornbake Library, College Park.

71. See Coblentz, *My Life in Poetry*, p. 175; Stanton Coblentz and Jeffrey M. Elliot, *Adventures of a Freelancer: The Literary Exploits and Autobiography of Stanton A. Coblentz* (San Bernardino, Calif.: Borgo, 1993), p. 140.

72. B. Y. [Williams], "By 3 A.M.," *Talaria* 13, 1 (Spring 1948): p. 2.

73. J. Donald Adams, "The Right to Be Conservative," *Freeman* 3, 8 (January 12, 1953): p. 273.

74. J. Donald Adams, *The Shape of Books to Come* (New York: Viking, 1944), p. 114.

75. J. Donald Adams, "The Arraignment," *Poetry* 68, 5 (August 1946): p. 262.

76. "A Hard Look at Criticism," *Poetry* 68, 5 (August 1946): p. 262; emphasis added.

77. Adams, *Shape of Books to Come*, p. xiv.

78. Daniel Bell, *The Cultural Contradictions of Capitalism* (New York: Basic Books, 1976), p. xxix.

79. Robert Avrett, "What Is Happening to Poetry?," *Writer's Digest* 40, 10 (October 1960): pp. 28, 29.

80. Robert Avrett, "Lest Fools Remind," *Wings* 12, 3 (Autumn 1955): p. 9.

81. Avrett, "What Is Happening to Poetry?," p. 29.

82. Robert Avrett, "Meter, Rhyme, and Wit," *Writer's Digest* 37, 12 (November 1957): p. 39.

83. Stanton Coblentz, "Pegasus Shorn: The Outlook for Poetry in America," *Wings* 5, 3 (Autumn 1941): pp. 5–6.

84. Frank S. Meyer, "Counterfeit at a Popular Price," *National Review* 2, 12 (August 11, 1956): p. 18.

85. Stanton Coblentz, " 'Why Do You Not Compromise?,' " in *Rise of the Anti-Poets*, p. 21.

86. Jacob Hauser, "Academies of the Perverse," *Lyric* 31, 2 (Spring 1951): p. 63.

87. Burklund was a *Rebel Poet* contributor in the early 1930s. See, e.g., his Whitmanian "A Chant for America," *Rebel Poet* 17, 8 (October 1932): p. 8: "Let us sing America, / the greatest nation on earth; / Greatest in everything—radios, automobiles, and soup lines."

88. Carl Edwin Burklund, "The Treason of 'Modern' Poetry," *Lyric* 28, 3 (1949): p. 142.

89. Coblentz, " 'Why Do You Not Compromise?,' " p. 21.

90. Robert Hillyer, "Other Years, Other Lyrics," *Lyric* 17, 2 (1937–38): pp. 79–80.

91. Hayden Carruth to John Frederick Nims, July 16, 1961, PMP 1954–61, b6, f15.

92. Gilbert Neiman to Karl Shapiro, September 15, 1951, PMP 1936–53, s2, b7, f12.

93. As he reported to *Poetry* editor George Dillon in a September 1, 1941, letter (PMP 1936–53, s2, b7, f12).

94. Gilbert Neiman, "To Write Poetry Nowadays You Have to Have One Foot in the Grave," *Poetry* 74 (April 1949): p. 32.

95. Viereck's phrase for himself (Peter Viereck to Robert Hillyer, May 4, 1950, Hillyer Papers, b5, f28).

96. Neiman, "To Write Poetry Nowadays," p. 33.

97. Hillyer, "Crisis in American Poetry," p. 65.

98. "The Iron Tower," *News from behind the Iron Curtain* 2, 11 (November 1953): p. 30.

99. Chad Walsh and Robert H. Glauber, "Why Another 'Little Magazine'?," *Beloit Poetry Journal* 1, 1 (Fall 1950): p. 1.

100. Cartoon by Trent, *Saturday Review of Literature*, August 6, 1949, p. 48, reprinted from *Saturday Review of Literature*, August 14, 1943, p. 13.

101. Eve Merriam, "Said Prose to Verse," n.d., typescript sent to Angus Cameron, Cameron-Merriam Correspondence, f3, TL.

102. Peter Viereck, "Four Notes on Values," in *The Unadjusted Man: A New Hero for Americans* (Boston: Beacon, 1956), p. 299.

103. Robert Creeley to John Frederick Nims, January 18, 1961, PMP 1954–61, b8, f6; Robert Creeley to the author (e-mail), June 2, 2000.

104. Harold Norse to William Carlos Williams, June 1, 1960, in *The American Idiom: A Correspondence*, ed. John J. Wilson (San Francisco: Bright Tyger), p. 139.

105. Neiman, "To Write Poetry Nowadays," p. 30.

106. See Peter Biskind, *Seeing Is Believing: How Hollywood Taught Us to Stop Worrying and Love the Fifties* (New York: Pantheon, 1983), pp. 102–22, 145–59.

107. Qtd. in ibid., p. 137.

108. Joseph Freeman to Floyd Dell, April 15, 1953, Floyd Dell Papers, "De Reserve Box," Newberry Library, Chicago.

109. Stanton Coblentz, "Walls of Freedom," *Wings* 10, 2 (Summer 1951): p. 5.

110. Douglas V. Kane, "Poetry Seminar," *Wings* 5, 1 (Spring 1941): p. 21.

111. William Carlos Williams, introduction to *The Wedge*, in *Selected Essays of William Carlos Williams* (New York: New Directions, 1969), p. 256; Frank S. Meyer, *The Moulding of Communists* (New York: Harcourt, Brace, and World, 1961), pp. 170, 130, 129; Louis Francis Budenz, "Communists Are Made—Not Born," n.d. [1952?], clipping in J. B. Matthews Papers, b595, Perkins Library, Duke University, Durham, North Carolina.

112. Daniel Bell, "Modernism and Capitalism," in *Writers and Politics: A "Partisan Review" Reader*, ed. Edith Kurzweil and William Phillips (Boston: Routledge and Kegan Paul, 1983), p. 125.

113. Adams's *New York Times Book Review* column was retitled "The Arraignment" and published in *Poetry* 68, 5 (August 1946): pp. 262–65; the quoted phrases appear on p. 264.

114. Ben Lucien Burman, "The 'Little Men' of Literature," *Saturday Review of Literature*, January 17, 1948, p. 6.

115. Phillips, "What Happened in the 30's," p. 206.

116. E. Merrill Root, *Collectivism on the Campus* (New York: Devin-Adair, 1955), pp. 30–31.

117. Phillips, "What Happened in the 30's," p. 212.

118. See Coblentz and Elliot, *Adventures of a Freelancer*, pp. 6–8.

119. Stanton Coblentz, *New Poetic Lamps and Old* (Mill Valley, Calif.: Wings, 1950), p. 11.

120. Gilbert Neiman to George Dillon, August 21, [1948?], PMP 1936–53, s2, b7, f12.

121. Jan Kujawa to the editors of *Poetry*, October 9, 1947, PMP 1936–53, s2, b6, f4; emphasis added.

122. Jones, "Abnormal Poets and Abnormal Poetry," pp. 230, 228, 232.

123. Hauser, "Academies of the Perverse," p. 63.

124. Stanton Coblentz, "The New Caste System in Poetry," *Wings* 12, 7 (Autumn 1956): p. 5.

125. Neiman, "To Write Poetry Nowadays," p. 31.

126. George Dondero, "Modern Art Shackled to Communism," 81st Cong., 1st sess., *Congressional Record*, p. 11584.

127. Truly Nolen, "Termite-ism Compared to Communism," undated newspaper clipping, Counterattack Papers, TL.

128. Edward John Dunsany, "The Leaden Bells of Modern Poetry," *Saturday Review of Literature*, February 6, 1954, p. 22.

129. "Wing Beats," p. 32.

130. E. Merrill Root, "Consider the Lilies," *Freeman* 2, 25 (September 8, 1952): p. 840.

131. Coblentz, *Rise of the Anti-Poets*, pp. 26–27.

132. Coblentz, *New Poetic Lamps and Old*, p. 32.

133. For a sample of Burman's regionalism, see "Kentucky: Where Men Die Standing," *Nation*, July 25, 1923, pp. 83–85.

134. *Firing Line*, 1, 8 (May 1, 1952): p. 2.

135. Ben Lucien Burman, typescript speech, n.d. [ca. 1949?], Ben Lucien Burman Papers, Manuscripts Collection 529, Manuscripts Department, Howard-Tilton Library, Tulane University, New Orleans.

136. Ben Lucien Burman, "An Open Letter to Comrade Ivan," typescript, n.d. [ca. 1950–51], Burman Papers.

137. Burman, " 'Little Men' of Literature," p. 6. "Homespun" is from a *Newsweek* feature on Burman; see "Grass Roots," *Newsweek*, November 9, 1953, p. 100.

138. John K. Hutchins, introduction to *Three from Catfish Bend: High Water at Catfish Bend, Seven Stars for Catfish Bend, The Owl Hoots Twice at Catfish Bend* (New York: Taplinger, 1967), p. xi.

139. Burman Papers, b7, f7, "Fear of Totalitarianism."

140. Qtd. in ibid.

141. J. Donald Adams, "Speaking of Books," *New York Times Book Review*, January 12, 1947, p. 2.

142. Richard M. Weaver, "Reflections of Modernity" (1961), in *Life without Prejudice* (Chicago: Regnery, 1965), pp. 110, 112.

143. Ben Lucien Burman, "The Cult of Unintelligibility," *Saturday Review of Literature*, November 1, 1952, p. 38.

144. Dondero, "Modern Art Shackled to Communism," p. 11587.

145. Esther Julia Pels, "Art for Whose Sake?," *American Legion Magazine*, October 1955, pp. 16–17, 54–55.

146. Norma S. Steinberg, "William Gropper: Art and Censorship from the 1930s through the Cold War Era," Ph.D. diss., Boston University, 1994, p. 175 n. 47.

147. Hillyer, "Poetry's New Priesthood," p. 7.

148. Richard M. Weaver, *Relativism and the Crisis of Our Times* (Philadelphia: Intercollegiate Society of Individualists, n.d.), p. 5, in Henry Regnery Papers, b81, f16a, HI.

149. Ibid., p. 12.

150. Frederick Fraley, "Dunsany—'Three Cheers,'" *Saturday Review of Literature*, February 27, 1954, p. 23.

151. Coblentz, "'Why Do You Not Compromise?,'" pp. 21–22.

152. Coblentz, "Break in the Dike," p. 3.

153. Richard M. Weaver, *Relativism and the Crisis*, p. 6.

154. Mary O'Connor, "Lord Dunsany, an American Memory," *Poetry Review* 51, 1 (January–February 1960): p. 51.

155. See an interview with Dunsany conducted during one of these tours, published in *Fortnight*, April 13, 1953, qtd. in Coblentz, *My Life in Poetry*, p. 179.

156. Dunsany and Coblentz were correspondents and mutual admirers. See Coblentz and Elliot, *Adventures of a Freelancer*, pp. 125–27.

157. Edward John Dunsany, "The Fall of the Muses," *Poetry Review* 43, 4 (October–November 1952): p. 201.

Chapter 9

1. Edward John Dunsany, "The Leaden Bells of Modern Poetry," *Saturday Review of Literature*, February 6, 1954, p. 22.

2. William McFee to Malcolm Cowley, January 8, 1952, April 9, 1956, Malcolm Cowley Papers, Newberry Library, Chicago.

3. William McFee, "Modern Poetry," *New Republic*, October 15, 1951, p. 4.

4. Geoffrey Wagner, "The Organized Heresy: Abstract Art in the United States," *Modern Age* 4, 3 (Summer 1960): p. 266.

5. Dunsany, "Leaden Bells," p. 22.

6. Stanton Coblentz, *My Life in Poetry* (New York: Bookman, 1959), p. 80.

7. B. Y. [Williams], "By 3 A.M.," *Talaria* 13, 4 (Winter 1948): p. 2.

8. Ben Lucien Burman, "The 'Little Men' of Literature," *Saturday Review of Literature*, January 17, 1948, pp. 6, 28.

9. Stanton Coblentz to Charles Wharton Stork, September 20, 1947, Charles Wharton Stork Papers, SUSCRC.

10. Ibid., February 14, 1948.

11. Charles Wharton Stork, *A Vision of Misjudgment: An Adventure among the Latest Poets* (New York: Fine Editions, 1958), pp. 18, 17, 11, 13. Stork had once been a player among modern poets. A 1923 cartoon in the *New York Times Book Review* depicting poets gathered around a table of literary conversation included Stork along with William Rose Benét, Elinor Wylie, Maxwell Bodenheim, and other leading New York avant-garde figures (May 13, 1923, p. 7). And he published his poetry widely in those years. But more recent books of verse, *On Board Old Ironsides, 1812–1815: A Rope-Yarn Epic* (Mill Valley, Calif.: Wings, 1948), *Hearts and Voices* (Boston: Christopher, 1949), and *Navpac* (New York: Bookman, 1952), received scant critical attention. Stork was part of the family that founded the Wharton School at the University of Pennsylvania, where Stork had an unhappy career on the English department faculty. The Charles Wharton Stork papers are housed at the SUSCRC. See also "Charles Wharton Stork," in *The Vineyard and the Sea: Poems by Charles Wharton Stork* (Philadelphia: Atheneum, 1977), pp. 6–15; "Dr. C. W. Stork Dies, Poet, Writer, Was 90," *Philadelphia Inquirer*, May 24, 1971, p. 32.

12. John Lydenberg, "Mobilizing Our Novelists," *American Quarterly* 4, 1 (Spring 1952): pp. 35–36.

13. "Fiction in the U.S.," *Life*, August 16, 1948, p. 24.

14. Lewis Dabney, "The American Novel in the Age of Conformity," *Nation*, February 23, 1957, p. 167. See also John Chamberlain, "The Businessman in Fiction," *Fortune* 38, 5 (November 1948): pp. 134–48.

15. "Fiction in the U.S.," p. 24.

16. Charles E. Plant to W. E. Reynolds, August 28, 1950, copy retained by George Dondero (George A. Dondero Papers, Archives of American Art, Washington, D.C.).

17. Burton Frye to Robert Hillyer, September 2, 1949, Robert Hillyer Papers, b3, f1, SUSCRC.

18. The same line was quoted and criticized by Stanton Coblentz, as he rhetorically asked in "Poetry in the Hour of Need," "Could I find a balm for my pain in a typical modernism such as that of Kenneth Fearing?" (*Wings* 11, 3 [Autumn 1953]: p. 4).

19. In *Wings*, Fearing is probably the poet most often cited as committing modernist sins. See, e.g., Stanton Coblentz, "The Unmemorable Moderns," *Wings* 7, 2 (Summer 1945): pp. 4–5. The document printed to attract the founding members of the League for Sanity in Poetry featured first and foremost an extended attack on several of Fearing's poems (*The Need for Sanity in Poetry* [Dallas, n.d.], Jessie Wilmore Murton Papers, KSA/WKU).

20. William Gibson, "POD," *Poetry* 74, 6 (September 1949): p. 311.

21. E.g., in Stanton Coblentz, *New Poetic Lamps and Old* (Mill Valley, Calif.: Wings, 1950), p. 57. See also Stanton Coblentz, "The Spark That Holds the Future," *Wings* 11, 5 (Spring 1954): p. 5.

22. Reuel Denney, "The Honest Retired Lodger on the Porch," *Poetry* 86, 5 (August 1955): p. 255.

23. Stanton Coblentz, *The Rise of the Anti-Poets: Selected Editorials from "Wings: A Quarterly of Verse"* (Mill Valley, Calif.: Wings, 1955), p. 27.

24. Dunsany, "Leaden Bells," p. 2.

25. Edward John Dunsany, "Prose or Poetry," *Atlantic Monthly*, May 1945, p. 94.

26. Dunsany, "Leaden Bells," p. 2.

27. Dunsany, "Prose or Poetry," p. 94.

28. Alfred Noyes, foreword to Donald Parson, *Surely the Author* (Boston: Luce, 1944), pp. viii–xi.

29. Carl Edwin Burklund, "The Treason of 'Modern' Poetry," *Lyric* 28, 3 (1949): p. 141.

30. So Dunsany was described in the author's note accompanying "Prose or Poetry," p. 92.

31. Robert Hillyer, "The Crisis in American Poetry," *American Mercury*, January 1950, p. 65.

32. Richard Rovere used this term in a review that nicely describes the difference between liberal anticommunism (his position) and the "rampant" anti-ism-ism of "McCarthyism, McCarranism" (*American Quarterly* 3, 4 [Winter 1951]: p. 366).

33. Willard Thorp, "American Writers on the Left," in *Socialism in American Life*, ed. Donald Drew Egbert and Stow Persons (Princeton: Princeton University Press, 1952), vol. 1, p. 606.

34. S. B. Lush, "Modern Poetry," *New Republic*, October 22, 1951, p. 2.

35. [Leigh Hanes], "Note on a Birthday," *Lyric* 25, 1 (Spring 1945): n.p.

36. Geoffrey Wagner, "The Organized Heresy: Abstract Art in the United States," *Modern Age* 4, 3 (Summer 1960): p. 260.

37. Hillyer, "Crisis in American Poetry," p. 67.

38. Peter Viereck, "Four Notes on Values," in *The Unadjusted Man: A New Hero for Americans* (Boston: Beacon, 1956), p. 299.

39. Mrs. John W. Garrett to Robert Hillyer, June 18, 1949, Hillyer Papers, b3, f2.

40. Qtd. in Jane De Hart Mathews, "Art and Politics in Cold War America," *American Historical Review* 81, 4 (October 1976): p. 778.

41. Richard Rovere, *Final Reports: Reflections on Politics and History in Our Time* (Garden City, N.Y.: Doubleday, 1984), p. 54.

42. Herbert Read, "What Is Revolutionary Art?," in *Five on Revolutionary Art*, ed. B. Rea (London: Wishart, 1935), p. 13. This was a speech delivered at the Revolutionary Art symposium hosted by the Artists' International Association in London in 1935.

43. George A. Dondero, "Modern Art Shackled to Communism," *Congressional Record*, 81st Cong., 1st sess., August 16, 1949, p. 11584.

44. The McCarthyite rhetoric has been italicized. A copy of Williams's summary of these "notes" was sent to Dondero and is now part of the Dondero Papers at the Archives of American Art. The material is undated but follows closely on other material dated May 1958.

45. "Dondero's Warning," *Roanoke World-News*, June 28, 1947, p. 4.

46. Lewis Mumford to George Dondero, July 16, 1952, Lewis Mumford Papers, Van Pelt Library Special Collections, University of Pennsylvania, Philadelphia. Dondero's speech had been reprinted in the *Congressional Record*, March 17, 1952, pp. 2458–60.

47. Archer M. Huntington to A. Hyatt Mayor, October 9, 1945, Archer M. Huntington Papers, SUSCRC.

48. Ibid., April 25, 1939.

49. Ibid.

50. Daniel Bell, *The End of Ideology: On the Exhaustion of Political Ideas in the Fifties*, rev. ed. (New York: Collier, 1961), p. 404.

51. Archer Huntington to His Excellency Generalissimo Franco, May 25, 1955, Anna Hyatt Huntington Papers, SUSCRC.

52. Archer M. Huntington to A. Hyatt Mayor, April 25, 1939, Archer M. Huntington Papers.

53. Ibid., October 9, 1945.

54. Ibid., April 25, 1939.

55. George Dondero to Martha Wilson, April 27, 1966, George A. Dondero Papers, Burton Historical Collections, Detroit Public Library.

56. Telephone message for George A. Dondero, February 24, 1955, Anna Hyatt Huntington Papers.

57. "A Former OSS Agent Meets the Press," *American Mercury*, August 1950, pp. 199–207; transcription of an NBC telecast of *Meet the Press*, May 21, 1950, Fulton Lewis Jr. Papers, SUSCRC.

58. "Pew Admits Fight to Crush New Deal," *New York Times*, June 13, 1949, p. 9.

59. "Frank Bielaski, O.S.S. Aide, Dead," *New York Times*, April 6, 1961, p. 26; "Bielaski Demands Amerasia Hearing," *New York Times*, August 8, 1950, p. 17; "President Opens 81 Loyalty Files to Senate Inquiry," *New York Times*, May 5, 1950, p. 1. On Ruth Shipley, see David Caute, *The Great Fear* (New York: Simon and Schuster, 1978), pp. 246–47.

60. Dorothy Drew to Anna Hyatt Huntington, November 29, 1949, Anna Hyatt Huntington Papers.

61. Frank B. Bielaski to Archer M. Huntington, July 19, 1949, Anna Hyatt Huntington Papers.

62. Dorothy Drew to Anna Huntington, November 29, 1949, Anna Hyatt Huntington Papers.

63. Frank B. Bielaski to Archer M. Huntington, September 6, 1949, Anna Hyatt Huntington Papers.

64. Frank B. Bielaski to Archer M. Huntington, invoice, September 1, 1949, Anna Hyatt Huntington Papers.

65. Frank B. Bielaski to Archer Huntington, August 26, 1949, Anna Hyatt Huntington Papers.

66. In June 1961, Dorothy Drew and Anna Hyatt Huntington were still corresponding about the Huntingtons' financing publication and distribution of Dondero's speeches (Drew to Anna Huntington, June 18, 1961, Dondero Papers, Archives of American Art).

67. Lilith Lorraine to Joseph Lalley, May 3, 1946, J. M. Lalley Papers, ms. 199, Milton S. Eisenhower Library, Johns Hopkins University, Baltimore, Maryland.

68. A. M. Sullivan to Phyllis McGinley, October 7, 1953, February 12, 1954, Phyllis McGinley Papers, SUSCRC.

69. William F. Buckley, *Up from Liberalism* (New Rochelle, N.Y.: Arlington House, 1968), p. 51.

70. Murray Kempton, *Part of Our Time: Some Ruins and Monuments of the Thirties* (New York: Modern Library, 1998), p. 6.

71. J. B. Matthews to Frank Bielaski, April 16, 1958, April 11, 1958 (concerning other anticommunist investigations), J. B. Matthews Papers, s "Persons Files," b593, Perkins Library, Duke University, Durham, North Carolina.

72. Frank Bielaski to Archer Huntington, August 26, 1949, Archer M. Huntington Papers.

73. Lilith Lorraine to Joseph Lalley, May 8, 1946, Joseph Lalley Papers.

74. C. O. Garshwiler to Anna Hyatt Huntington, August 10, 1961, Anna Hyatt Huntington Papers.

75. Ibid., October 28, 1960.

76. Anna Huntington to C. O. Garshwiler, October 15, 1960, Anna Hyatt Huntington Papers.

77. C. O. Garshwiler to Anna Huntington, June 21, 1963, in Anna Hyatt Huntington Papers.

78. See, e.g., *How Red Is the Federal [sic] Council of Churches?* (Madison, Wis.: American Council of Christian Laymen, 1959) and *The National Council of Churches Speaks, for Whom?: Council's Own Statistical Reports Show That NCC Represents Only 36 Per Cent of American Protestants* (Madison, Wis.: American Council of Christian Laymen, 1953).

79. *2000 BC: The Bruce Conner Story Part II* (Minneapolis: Walker Art Center, 1999), pp. 174, 28, 160.

80. C. O. Garshwiler to Anna Huntington, December 28, 1960, Anna Hyatt Huntington Papers.

81. "Art Week to Be Celebrated in Local Scarsdale Schools," *Scarsdale Inquirer*, May 2, 1958, pp. 1, 12; "The Weapon of Art in Scarsdale Schools," *Westchester Spotlight*, November 1958, p. 2.

82. Brenda Putnam, typescript draft of protest letter, January 21, 1952[?], Brenda Putnam Papers, SUSCRC.

83. Ibid.

84. Jean de Marco, Edmondo Quattrocchi, Katherine Thayer Hobson, Wheeler Williams, and Donald De Lue to members of the National Sculpture Society, January 21, 1952, Putnam Papers.

85. Alan Filreis, " 'Beyond the Rhetorician's Touch': Stevens' Painterly Abstractions," *American Literary History* 4, 2 (Spring 1992): pp. 230–63.

86. Vladimir Prosorov, "The Ills of Limitation and the Evils of Disorientation: Perceptions of Post-WWII American Literature in the USSR/Russia," *American Studies International* 39, 3 (October 2001): pp. 41–50. See also Alfred Frankfurter's direct response to Dondero, making the same point: "Abstract Red Herring," *Art News* 48, 4 (Summer 1949): p. 15.

87. Peter Viereck, "The Mob within the Heart," *TriQuarterly*, Spring 1965, p. 21.

88. James Thrall Soby, "A Letter from the National Sculpture Society," *Saturday Review of Literature*, March 1, 1952, p. 52.

89. Harry Cohen to George Dondero, November 8, 1956, Dondero Papers, Archives of American Art.

90. Ibid.

91. Wagner, "Organized Heresy," pp. 267, 260, 268.

92. Harry Cohen to George Dondero, November 8, 1956, Dondero Papers, Archives of American Art. Cohen wrote to Dondero that although he was "not 'conscious' of politics, communist leanings, or the mild left-wingers, for being so purely art minded as to concentrate principally on art to the exclusion of all else in determ[in]ing quality and craftsmanship, we have nevertheless been rather rudely awakened to a great deal of this subversive stuff. . . . Even as we prepare now to draw up the conclusion for the nominations . . . we are filled with all kinds of apprehension as to 'who' might be 'what.' "

93. "Reds Use 'Culture' as a Weapon," *Westchester Spotlight*, November 1958, p. 1. The *Spotlight* was quoting J. Edgar Hoover, who also wrote in this passage, "Every facet of the member's life, even when he plays the piano, sings, goes to a movie, sees a painting, or reads a book, must be saturated with communism."

94. Robert Hillyer, "Modern Poetry versus the Common Reader," *Saturday Review of Literature*, March 24, 1945, pp. 5–7.

95. Earl Byrd, review of *The Auroras of Autumn*, *Wings* 10, 2 (Summer 1951): pp. 25–26.

96. Gerald Kennedy, "Poets, Politicians, and Preachers," *Christian Century* 69, 14 (April 2, 1952): pp. 394–95.

97. Richard M. Weaver, *Visions of Order* (Baton Rouge: Louisiana State University Press, 1964), pp. 22–24.

98. Ben Lucien Burman, "The Cult of Unintelligibility," *Saturday Review of Literature*, November 1, 1952, p. 9. See also Robert Hillyer, "An American's Merry Way through Darkest Africa," review of Burman's *The Street of the Laughing Camel*, New York Times Book Review, September 13, 1959, p. 5.

99. Stanton Coblentz, *An Editor Looks at Poetry* (Mill Valley, Calif.: Wings, 1947), pp. 109–10.

100. Richard Ashman to Henry Rago, May 17, 1955, PMP 1953–61, b2, f2.

101. Burman, "Cult of Unintelligibility," pp. 9, 10, 38.

Chapter 10

1. Gerald Kennedy, "Seventy Five Years of American Preaching," *Christendom* 7, 2 (Spring 1942): p. 214; Gerald Kennedy, "Using Preaching as Teaching," *Religious Education* 44 (1949): p. 229.

2. See Amos N. Wilder, "Revolutionary and Proletarian Poetry: Kenneth Patchen" (1940), in *Kenneth Patchen: A Collection of Essays*, ed. Richard G. Morgan (New York: AMS, 1977), pp. 127–35. The phrase ("we have the Marxian version . . .") is quoted from this essay, p. 131.

3. Gerald Kennedy, "Poets, Politicians, and Preachers," *Christian Century* 69, 14 (April 2, 1952): pp. 394–95.

4. Stanton Coblentz, *The Rise of the Anti-Poets: Selected Editorials from "Wings: A Quarterly of Verse"* (Mill Valley, Calif.: Wings, 1955), pp. 23, 22.

5. Ibid., pp. 22–23.

6. Kennedy, "Poets, Politicians, and Preachers," pp. 394–95.

7. Robert Langbaum, "The New Nature Poetry," *American Scholar*, Summer 1959, pp. 323–40.

8. Russell Baker, "When the Muse Presides in Congress," *New York Times Magazine*, August 23, 1959, pp. 27, 30.

9. Selden Rodman, "Orozco Evaluated: An Artist of Expressive Content in a Formalist World," *Chicago Review* 9, 3 (Fall 1955): p. 50.

10. Qtd. in Alfred H. Barr, "Is Modern Art Communistic?," *New York Times Magazine*, December 14, 1932, p. 22.

11. S. B. Lush, "Modern Poetry," *New Republic*, October 22, 1951, p. 2.

12. Stanton Coblentz, "Everyman's Art—And No Man's Art," *Wings* 13, 4 (Winter 1958): p. 3.

13. H. L. Brock, "Favorite White House Poems," *New York Times Magazine*, December 9, 1945, p. 14; Alfred Tennyson, *The Poems of Tennyson*, 2d ed., ed. Christopher Ricks (Berkeley: University of California Press, 1987), vol. 2, p. 126. A hobbyist painter in oils, Dwight Eisenhower acted on his assumption that art is not merely "realistic" but can serve as a pattern for tracing the day's every mundane activity, and he ventured so far into mimeticism as to seek Bobby Jones's approval of his putting stance in a portrait of the golfer the president had just painted from a press photograph (Rodman, "Orozco Evaluated," p. 50). When radical modernists' works were among those shown in a U.S. Information Agency–sponsored exhibit in Moscow, Eisenhower was asked at a press conference for his opinion. He refused to get involved in censoring the show post facto, although the president suggested that "there ought to be [on the review committee] one or two people that . . . say we are not too certain exactly what art is but we know what we like, and what America likes" and that "what America likes is after all some of the things that ought to be shown" ("Transcript of President's News Conference on Foreign and Domestic Matters," *New York Times*, July 2, 1959, p. 10). Eisenhower added that in this exhibit for cultural exchange, "artistic representation is only a minor part of this business" (p. 10). Modernism's arrival at the gates of the executive branch of the national government awaited the Kennedys' arrival in 1961. The first gathering of poets ever sponsored by the U.S. government—"which clearly was as uncertain as any of its citizens about how to deal with poets," quipped *Newsweek*—occurred in 1962 ("A Poet's Lot," *Newsweek*, November 5, 1962, p. 96).

14. Both were published in Phyllis McGinley, *Sixpence in Her Shoe* (New York: Macmillan, 1964); the pieces had previously been published in *Ladies Home Journal* in the late 1950s and in 1960.

15. Morris Bishop, "The Case for Light Verse," *Harper's Magazine*, March 1954, p. 34.

16. M. L. Rosenthal, "Hard Times in Xanadu," *Nation*, February 6, 1950, p. 20.

17. Douglas Bush, "Scholars, Critics and Readers," *Virginia Quarterly Review* 22, 2 (Spring 1946): p. 247.

18. J. Donald Adams, "Speaking of Books," *New York Times*, November 11, 1956, p. 2.

19. Peter Viereck, *The Unadjusted Man: A New Hero for Americans* (Boston: Beacon, 1956), p. 20.

20. Douglas Bush, "Education for All Is Education for None," *New York Times Magazine*, January 9, 1955, p. 3.

21. Bush, "Scholars, Critics, and Readers," p. 247.

22. Douglas Bush, "Sex in the Modern Novel," *Atlantic Monthly*, January 1959, p. 73–75; Douglas Bush, "Education and the Humanities," *Daedalus* 88, 1 (Winter 1959): pp. 40–55; Douglas Bush, "The New Use of the Word," *Centennial Review* 1, 1 (Winter 1957): pp. 70–92.

23. Douglas Bush to M. L. Rosenthal, October 16, 1960, March 4, 1962, MLR/F, s1, b1, f12.

24. Qtd. in S. I. Hayakawa, "Poetry and Advertising," *Poetry* 67, 4 (January 1946): p. 208.

25. Ralph Gustafson, "Poetry Can't Wind Clocks, but . . . ," *Saturday Review of Literature*, March 19, 1949, p. 10.

26. Ibid.

27. Donald Jenks to [editor of *Poetry*], August 5, 1949, PMP 1936–53, s1, b20, f4 (correspondence pertaining to the Bollingen controversy).

28. "What's Wrong with the Nobel Prize?," *Books Abroad* 25, 3 (Summer 1951): pp. 213–19.

29. In the late 1950s, Clancy served as chair of the English department at Marymount College. For a sampling of Clancy's traditionalist poems, see "A Villanelle for Paul," *Chicago Review* 8, 3 (Fall 1954): p. 57; "Paris," *Epoch*, Spring 1955, pp. 202–4. Unlike most anticommunist antimodernists, Clancy published in some of the mainstream modern poetry magazines.

30. Joseph P. Clancy, "Lament for the Readers," *America*, February 8, 1958, pp. 539–40.

31. Robert Hillyer, "Modern Poetry versus the Common Reader," *Saturday Review of Literature*, March 24, 1945, pp. 5–7. For a similar antimodernist view of heroism, see Richard M. Weaver, *Ideas Have Consequences* (Chicago: University of Chicago Press, 1948), pp. 116–22.

32. Donald Davidson, "In Memory of John Gould Fletcher," *Poetry* 77, 3 (December 1950): pp. 154–61.

33. Mark Royden Winchell, *Where No Flag Flies: Donald Davidson and the Southern Resistance* (Columbia: University of Missouri Press, 2000), pp. 221–22.

34. "The Pulitzer Prizes," *New York Times*, May 2, 1939, p. 22; "How to Win a Pulitzer Prize," *New Republic*, May 10, 1939, p. 2; "The Pulitzer Prize Winners," *Saturday Review*, May 6, 1939, p. 7.

35. In Fletcher's complaint to Scott, he offered a quarrel between Karl Shapiro and Delmore Schwartz as an example of what's wrong with contemporary poetry: "Whenever

two Jews quarrel, they really do quarrel masterly" (John Gould Fletcher, *Selected Letters of John Gould Fletcher*, ed. Leighton Rudolph, Lucas Carpenter, and Ethel Simpson [Fayetteville: University of Arkansas Press, 1996], pp. 222–24).

36. Jackson Mac Low, "Three Books and a Marvel," *Western Review* 11, 3 (Spring 1947): p. 190. Mac Low's reference to "symphonies" was meant to recall Fletcher's breakthrough "Symphonies" series written during 1914 and early 1915, especially "The Blue Symphony," which was collected in John Gould Fletcher, *Goblins and Pagodas* (Boston: Houghton Mifflin, 1916) and famously anthologized in Harriet Monroe and Alice Corbin Henderson, *The New Poetry: An Anthology* (New York: Macmillan, 1917).

37. Mac Low, "Three Books and a Marvel," p. 191.

38. Fletcher, *Selected Letters*, p. 223. The source of Patchen's phrase was Scott's previous letter to Fletcher.

39. Karl Shapiro, "Why Out-Russia Russia?," *New Republic*, June 9, 1958, p. 11.

40. Louis Kent to Robert Hillyer, October 23, 1949, Robert Hillyer Papers, b3, f24, SUSCRC; Robert Hillyer to Howard Nemerov, February 25, 1959, March 5, 1959, October 24, 1959, Howard Nemerov Papers, WU. "Ciardiism" appears in the October 24, 1959, letter.

41. In April 1952, Eastman unabashedly defended Joseph McCarthy, causing Richard Rovere, a liberal anticommunist, to assert that Eastman did not "give a damn about cultural freedom" (qtd. in Ronald Radosh, "The Legacy of the Anti-Communist Liberal Intellectuals," *Partisan Review* 67, 4 [October 2000]: p. 559).

42. Robert Hillyer, "Elizabethan Pastoral Landscape," *American Scholar*, Summer 1951, pp. 277–78. Hillyer was a scholar of Elizabethan literature as well as a lecturer on modern poetry.

43. Robert Hillyer, "A Voice in the Night," *Poetry* 71, 1 (October 1947): p. 23.

44. Stanton Coblentz, "Communication at the People," in *Rise of the Anti-Poets*, p. 80.

Chapter 11

1. Robert Graves, *The Crowning Privilege* (Garden City, N.Y.: Doubleday, 1956), pp. 136, 126.

2. Ibid., p. 122.

3. Robert Graves, "Wordsworth by Cable," *New Republic*, September 9, 1957, pp. 10–13.

4. Ibid.

5. Graves, *Crowning Privilege*, pp. 119, 121.

6. Horace Gregory to M. L. Rosenthal, March 18, 1965, MLR/F, b1, f41.

7. Max Eastman, *The Literary Mind* (New York: Scribner's, 1931), p. 105.

8. Unsigned review, *New Masses* 12, 7 (August 14, 1934): p. 28.

9. Leo Marx, "The Careful Young Men: Tomorrow's Leaders Analyzed by Today's Teachers," *Nation*, March 9, 1957, p. 206.

10. Graves, "Wordsworth by Cable," pp. 10–13. See chapter 13. See also *Wings* 12, 7 (Autumn 1956): pp. 22–23.

11. Stanton Coblentz to Charles Wharton Stork, July 23, 1956, Charles Wharton Stork Papers, SUSCRC.

12. Robert Creeley to Henry Rago, September 7, 1958, PMP 1954–61, b8, f6; emphasis added. In a 1959 review, Creeley elaborated, "Graves' forms are primarily traditional, which fact may blur them for a careless reader; but he both uses and informs them in a manner unlike our own current 'traditionalists.' By which I mean that he is at home in them, thinks with them, and shapes the content of his obligation to their pattern with a good grace" (Robert Creeley, "His Service Is Perfect Freedom," *Poetry* 93, 6 [March 1959]: pp. 387–98).

13. Horace Gregory to M. L. Rosenthal, March 18, 1965, MLR/F, b1, f41.

14. Creeley, "His Service Is Perfect Freedom," p. 398.

15. Scott's observations were entered in his notebook, later published as Winfield Townley Scott, *"A Dirty Hand": The Literary Notebooks of Winfield Townley Scott* (Austin: University of Texas Press, 1969), p. 100.

16. [Leigh Hanes], "Note on a Birthday," *Lyric* 25, 1 (Spring 1945): n.p. John Aldridge contended that Malcolm Cowley's status as a lyric poet—"it was the poet in Cowley" who wrote the prose, and the prose "lyricize[d] his historical subject"—permitted him to remain "free of the defects inherent in his essentially historical method." The less lyrically Cowley wrote, the more visible were the defects of his historicizing. Cowley's decline into mere literary politics was marked by a change in Cowley's language "from the lyric to the avuncular" (John Aldridge, "The Case of Malcolm Cowley," *Nation*, February 19, 1955, p. 162).

17. Melville Cane, "Are Poets Returning to Lyricism?," *Saturday Review*, January 16, 1954, pp. 8–10, 40–41.

18. Gilbert Neiman to George Dillon, August 21, [1948?], PMP 1936–53, s2, b7, f12.

19. Peter Viereck, *The Unadjusted Man: A New Hero for Americans* (Boston: Beacon, 1956), p. 290.

20. Cullen Jones, "Abnormal Poets and Abnormal Poetry," *Poet Lore* 56, 3 (Autumn 1951): pp. 231, 234.

21. Cullen Jones, "A Defense of a Non-Defense of Poetry," *Poetry Review* 35, 1 (January–February 1944): p. 59.

22. Viereck, *Unadjusted Man*, p. 272.

23. "How to Dislike Poetry," *Time*, September 15, 1947, p. 73.

24. "Back to School," *Time*, September 15, 1947, p. 73.

25. "How to Dislike Poetry," *Time*, September 15, 1947, pp. 73–74. I have consulted Strong's report, appearing under the title "Poetry in the School," in *The Teaching of English in Schools: A Symposium Edited for the English Association*, ed. Vivian De Sola Pinto (London: Macmillan, 1947), pp. 1–16.

26. Jacob Hauser, "Academies of the Perverse," *Lyric* 31, 2 (Spring 1951): p. 63.

27. Peter Viereck, "The Dignity of Lyricism," *New Republic*, May 31, 1954, p. 18.

28. Peter Viereck, "Meter Is Time in Leotards," *New York Quarterly* 32, 1 (Spring 1987): p. 113.

29. Louis Harap, untitled review of Herbert Read's *Art and Society*, *Science and Society* 1, 3 (Spring 1937): p. 423.

30. Herbert Read, *Poetry and Anarchism* (London: Freedom, 1941), p. 45.

31. Herbert Read, *Phases of English Poetry* (1928), *Direction* 19 (1951): pp. 175–77.

32. Herbert Read, preface to Richard Ott, *The Art of Children* (New York: Pantheon, 1952), p. 3.

33. Peter Viereck, "A Middle Ground for Poetry," *New Leader* 34, 47 (November 19, 1951): p. 22.

34. Richard M. Weaver, "Gnostics of Education," in *Visions of Order* (Baton Rouge: Louisiana State University Press, 1964), pp. 114, 115, 116.

35. Richard M. Weaver, "Language Is Sermonic," in ibid., p. 215.

36. Richard Avrett, "Broad Is the Way," *Pinnacle* 1 (May 1945): p. 2.

37. Stanton Coblentz, *An Editor Looks at Poetry* (Mill Valley, Calif.: Wings, 1947), p. 109.

38. E. Merrill Root, "Untying Knots in Nothing," *Freeman* 5, 12 (June 1955): p. 531.

39. Russell Kirk, *The Conservative Mind, from Burke to Santayana* (1953; Chicago: Regnery, 1985), p. 493. Kirk is quoting *The Idea of a Christian Society*. On Kirk's relationship with Eliot, I consulted the Kirk-Eliot letters in the Russell Kirk Collection, Clarke Historical Library, Central Michigan University, Mount Pleasant.

40. Henry Regnery, *Memoirs of a Dissident Publisher* (New York: Harcourt, Brace, Jovanovich, 1979), p. 190.

41. Richard M. Weaver, *Ideas Have Consequences* (Chicago: University of Chicago Press, 1948), pp. 155, 163, 162. On "infinite-valued orientation," see Richard M. Weaver, "To Write the Truth," *College English* 10, 1 (October 1948): pp. 25–30.

42. Gilbert Malcolm Fess, "Thank God for Existentialism!," *Books Abroad* 26, 3 (Summer 1952): pp. 252, 253; emphasis added.

43. Daniel Bell, *The Cultural Contradictions of Capitalism* (New York: Basic Books, 1976), p. xxv.

44. Root, "Untying Knots in Nothing," p. 531.

45. Geoffrey Wagner, "The Organized Heresy: Abstract Art in the United States," *Modern Age* 4, 3 (Summer 1960): p. 267.

46. Peter Viereck, "The Revolution in Values: Roots of the European Catastrophe, 1870–1952," *Political Science Quarterly* 67, 3 (September 1952): p. 349.

47. Daniel Bell, "Modernism and Capitalism," in *Writers and Politics: A "Partisan Review" Reader*, ed. Edith Kurzweil and William Phillips (Boston: Routledge and Kegan Paul, 1983), pp. 131, 132.

48. Alice Hunt Bartlett, "Dynamics of American Poetry: CXVIII," *Poetry Review* 38, 4 (July–August 1947): p. 287.

49. A. M. Sullivan to Phyllis McGinley, May 2, 1961, Phyllis McGinley Papers, SUSCRC.

50. A. M. Sullivan, "The Three Dimensional Man—The Humanities in Management," typescript of speech, College of Business Administration Forum, Lehigh University, April 18, 1961, A. M. Sullivan Papers, b6, SUSCRC.

51. A. M. Sullivan to Phyllis McGinley, June 17, 1955, Phyllis McGinley Papers.

52. A. M. Sullivan, "The Poets of Little Faith," proofs of essay to be published in the *Saturday Review of Literature*, ca. February 13, 1947, filed in Sullivan Papers, b5, with Sullivan–Robert Hillyer correspondence.

53. A. M. Sullivan, "Poet in Search of His Audience," *Saturday Review of Literature*, July 21, 1947, pp. 18–19.

54. Francis Grant Bartlett and Claude C. Crawford, *Art for All: Art Appreciation as Related to Dress, Home, School, and Work*, ed. Ray Faulkner (New York: Harper, 1942), pp. xi, 1.

55. Stanley Edgar Hyman, *The Armed Vision: A Study in the Methods of Modern Literary Criticism* (New York: Knopf, 1948), p. 207. Hyman purported to be *defending* Caudwell against what he considered Gregory's unthinking comparison, in a chapter that while praising Caudwell condemns almost all aspects of Marxist literary criticism.

56. Harap, untitled review of *Art and Society*, p. 422.

57. Herbert Read, *Education through Art* (1943; London: Faber and Faber, 1950), p. 109.

58. Ibid., p. 300.

59. Ibid., p. 97.

60. Great Britain, Board of Education, Consultative Committee, *Report of the Consultative Committee on Secondary Education with Special Reference to Grammar Schools and Technical High Schools* (London: H. M. Stationery Office, 1938). Sir Will Spens (1882–1962), master of Corpus Christi College, Cambridge, served as chair of the committee that prepared the groundbreaking report.

61. Georges-Henri Luquet, *Children's Drawings* (*Le Dessin Enfantin*), trans. Alan Costall (1927; London: Free Association, 2001), pp. 93–101. See also Great Britain, Board of Education, Consultative Committee, *Report of the Consultative Committee on Secondary Education*, p. 159; emphasis added.

62. Read, *Education through Art*, pp. 210–11.

63. Kurt Koffka, *Principles of Gestalt Psychology* (New York: Harcourt, Brace, 1935); Arthur J. Jersild, "Platform for Psychology," *New Republic*, September 4, 1935, pp. 110–11.

64. H. Teasdale, "A Quantitative Study of Eidetic Imagery," *British Journal of Educational Psychology* 4, 1 (February 1934): p. 56. See Read, *Education through Art*, p. 312.

65. See Read, *Education through Art*, e.g., p. 268.

66. Arthur Lismer, "Education through Art," *American Journal of Psychiatry* 107 (July 1950): pp. 76–77.

67. See Hans Syz, "The Social Neurosis," *American Journal of Sociology* 42, 6 (May 1937): pp. 895–97.

68. Ibid., p. 104.

69. Read, *Education through Art*, p. 211.

70. Ibid., p. 107.

71. Herbert Read, *Art and Society* (New York: Macmillan, 1937), p. 253.

72. Hans Syz, *Psychiatry* 10, 1 (February 1947): p. 104 (a review of the first edition of *Art and Society*).

73. In 1951–52, Richman corresponded with Malcolm Cowley, his predecessor at the *New Republic*, about the problems of literary editorship. Among the issues they discussed was the difficulty of finding suitable young writers who could offer political criticism (Malcolm Cowley Papers, Newberry Library, Chicago).

74. "In Richard Ott's view, as in mine," Herbert Read wrote, "we are not concerned here with a reform in one branch of education: it is the educational system itself, as it has so far existed, that is challenged by these methods and discoveries. . . . We believe that the prevailing methods, which are exclusively logical and discursive, lead to a disintegration of the personality" (Read, preface to Ott, *Art of Children*, p. 4).

75. Robert Richman, "Museums by Children," *New Republic*, April 21, 1952, p. 20.

76. Francis Grant Bartlett and Crawford, *Art for All*, p. 153.

77. J. D. Lindquist, "Children and Poetry," *Hornbook Magazine*, June 1954, p. 157.

78. Herbert Read, "George Lukacs," *New Statements and Nation*, n.s., 53, 1351 (February 2, 1957): p. 127.

79. Robert Richman, "A Theory of Everyday Art," *Kenyon Review* 17, 1 (Winter 1955): pp. 152–59.

80. Robert Richman, ed., *The Arts at Mid-Century* (New York: Horizon, 1954), p. xi.

81. Stephen Spender, "The New Orthodoxies," in ibid., pp. 23, 9, 21–22, 5; emphasis added.

82. Ibid., p. 6.

83. Eric Hoffer, *The True Believer: Thoughts on the Nature of Mass Movements* (New York: Harper and Row, 1951), pp. 32–33.

84. Milton Klonsky, "Greenwich Village: Decline and Fall," *Commentary* 6, 5 (November 1948): p. 458.

85. Richard Rovere, "Two New Conservatives," *New Yorker*, March 21, 1953, pp. 126–34.

86. William Carlos Williams, *Imaginations* (New York: New Directions, 1970), pp. 100, 91.

87. Herbert Read, *The Education of Free Men* (London: Freedom, 1944); Herbert Read, *Poetry and Anarchism*, 2d ed., (London: Freedom, 1947). Freedom Press also published Herbert Read, *The Philosophy of Anarchism* (1940), one of the group's most sought-after pamphlets; by 1947 it was in a seventh printing. The now-rare pamphlets are in Herbert Read Author File, Vertical File Collection, TL.

88. Read, *Poetry and Anarchism* (1941), p. 40.

89. Qtd. in Read, *Education through Art*, p. 296 (Forster on Woolf from a 1942 Cambridge lecture).

90. Richard M. Weaver, "Gnostics of Education," pp. 130, 132.

91. Read, *Education through Art*, p. 211.

92. Great Britain, Board of Education, Consultative Committee, *Report of the Consultative Committee on Secondary Education*, pp. 172, 225, 229, 171, 153, 152, 159, 153.

93. John M. Aitkenhead, "Poetry for Children," *Commonweal* 51 (November 1949): p. 154.

94. Read, *Education through Art*, p. 99; emphasis added.

95. Wagner, "Organized Heresy," p. 264.

96. Eliseo Vivas, *The Moral Life and the Ethical Life* (Chicago: University of Chicago Press, 1950), pp. 128–37.

97. Richard M. Weaver, "Gnostics of Education," p. 127.

98. Read, *Education through Art*, p. 187n. The girl's drawing was given the title "Snake round the World and a Boat," reproduced in Read's book above the caption, "Abstract symbolic drawing, entirely spontaneous in origin" (figure 1b/g5).

99. Qtd. in Jane DeHart Mathews, "Art and Politics in Cold War America," *American Historical Review* 81, 4 (October 1976): p. 777.

100. Harry Roskolenko, "Satire, Nonsense, and Worship," *Poetry* 84, 4 (July 1954): p. 233.

101. Harry Roskolenko, "On Kenneth Koch Again: A Rebuttal," *Poetry* 86, 3 (June 1955): p. 178; Kenneth Koch, "Where Am I Kenneth?," in *The Collected Poems of Kenneth Koch* (New York: Knopf, 2005), p. 25. A version of this sentence from Roskolenko's rebuttal was in the first typescript draft of the review (and was cut by an editor at *Poetry*): "Children have a way of working up some verbal magic out of nonsense, but infantile gurglings in the mature, whether *avant-garde* or not, are hogwash served with soda" (PMP 1954–61, b29, f21).

102. Frank O'Hara, "Another Word on Kenneth Koch," *Poetry* 85, 6 (March 1955): p. 349.

103. This paper was published in *Commentary* 22, 1 (July 1956): pp. 75–83) and later became the first chapter of Daniel Bell, *The End of Ideology: On the Exhaustion of Political Ideas in the Fifties*, rev. ed. (New York: Collier, 1961) . The redaction of Ortega appears in that book on p. 23.

104. Max Eastman, "Non-Communicative Art," *American Artist*, December 1954, p. 18.

105. Read Bain, "Poetry and the Cult of Incomprehensibility," *Humanist* 15, 3 (May–June 1955): p. 127.

106. J. M. Lalley, "The Road to Unreason," *Washington Post*, May 31, 1948, unpaginated clipping enclosed with Joseph M. Lalley to W. T. Couch, June 9, 1948, Richard Weaver Papers, University of Chicago Archives, Regenstein Library.

107. Stanton Coblentz, "Lunacy Enthroned," *Wings* 5, 1 (Spring 1941): pp. 3, 5, 6–7.

108. Eastman, "Non-Communicative Art," pp. 18, 20, 61, 65.

109. See Max Eastman, "What to Call Yourself," *Freeman* 3, 24 (August 24, 1953): pp. 839–43.

110. Joseph Kamp, *We Must Abolish the United States: The Hidden Facts behind the Crusade for World Government* (New York: Constitutional Educational League/Hallmark, 1950), p. 148.

111. Regnery, *Memoirs of a Dissident Publisher*, pp. 202, 194–95, 205–6; Winfield Townley Scott, "Has Anyone Seen a Trend?," *Saturday Review of Literature*, January 3, 1959, p. 12.

112. Russell Kirk, "That Man and Enemy," *National Review* 3, 20 (May 18, 1957): p. 481.

113. Neville Braybrooke, "Roy Campbell: Soldier-Poet," *America*, December 9, 1950, p. 309.

114. William J. Casey to Henry Regnery, September 4, 1952, Henry Regnery Papers, b13, HI.

115. Henry Regnery to William F. Buckley, March 9, 1953, Regnery Papers, b10. Regnery met up again with Hunt when Regnery accompanied Buckley on a lecture tour (Regnery to H. L. Hunt, February 8, 1954, Regnery Papers, b32).

116. Sister Mary Julian Baird, "Why Modern Poets Have Failed," *Catholic World*, December 1958, pp. 208–18.

Chapter 12

1. Mary Faith Schuster, "Poets Have Always Failed," *Catholic World*, September 1959, pp. 253–56.

2. Daniel J. Berrigan, "Domes," *America*, October 10, 1957, p. 72. See Rita Brady Kiefer, "The 'Fragile Unkillable Flower' of Daniel Berrigan's Poetry," *Christian Century* 93, 38 (November 24, 1976): pp. 1038–42, 1047.

3. Daniel Berrigan to the author, March 12, 2005.

4. Schuster, "Poets Have Always Failed," pp. 253–56.

5. Alice Hunt Bartlett, "Dynamics of American Poetry," *Poetry Review* 38, 2 (March–April 1947): p. 147.

6. Sister M. Maura, "In Praise of Loneliness," in *Initiate the Heart* (New York: Macmillan, 1946), p. 3; Alice Hunt Bartlett, "Dynamics of American Poetry: CXVI," *Poetry Review* 37, 5–6 (November–December 1946): p. 379.

7. Alice Hunt Bartlett, "Dynamics of American Poetry: CXVI," p. 147.

8. Maura, *Initiate the Heart*, p. 12.

9. J. Donald Adams, *The Shape of Books to Come* (New York: Viking, 1944), p. xiii.

10. J. Donald Adams, "The Right to Be Conservative," *Freeman* 3, 8 (January 12, 1953): p. 273.

11. J. Donald Adams, "The Arraignment," *Poetry* 68, 5 (August 1946): p. 264.

12. Adams, "Right to Be Conservative," p. 273.

13. J. Donald Adams, *Literary Frontiers* (New York: Duell, Sloan, and Pearce, 1951), p. 10.

14. Adams, "Arraignment," pp. 263, 262, 264.

15. Peter Viereck, *Dream and Responsibility: Four Test Cases of the Tension between Poetry and Society* (Washington, D.C.: University Press of Washington, 1953), p. 53.

16. Stanton Coblentz, "Everyman's Art—And No Man's Art," *Wings* 13, 4 (Winter 1958): p. 3.

17. Adams, "Arraignment," pp. 263, 262, 264. Kenneth Burke had been one of the signers of the "Call" to "American revolutionary writers" to attend the first League of American Writers Congress (*New Masses: An Anthology of the Rebel Thirties*, ed. Joseph North [New York: International, 1969], p. 349).

18. Lorraine claimed that the Avalon National Poetry Shrine had three thousand participating members worldwide (Lilith Lorraine to Jessie Wilmore Murton, January 21, 1945, Jessie Wilmore Murton Papers, b9, f7, KSA/WKU). She was also the editor and publisher of *Different*, the official organ of Avalon.

19. Lilith Lorraine to Joseph Lalley, May 8, 1946, J. M. Lalley Papers, ms. 199, Milton S. Eisenhower Library, Johns Hopkins University, Baltimore, Maryland.

20. Michael F. Moloney, "Modern Literature: Darkness at Dawn," *America*, August 11, 1951, p. 461.

21. Michael F. Moloney, *John Donne: His Flight from Mediaevalism* (New York: Russell and Russell, 1965), pp. 15, 19. For more of Moloney's anticommunist literary criticism, see "Half-Faiths in Modern Fiction," *Catholic World*, August 1950, pp. 344–50.

22. Peter Viereck, *The Unadjusted Man: A New Hero for Americans* (Boston: Beacon, 1956), pp. 248–49.

23. Chad Walsh, "Christianity and the Arts," *Theology Today* 6, 4 (January 1952): pp. 514–23; Beloit College News Service, "Chad Walsh," July 1959, Beloit College Archive, Beloit, Wisconsin. For the clearest expression of Walsh's anticommunism, see chapter 3 ("Mostly Isms") of Chad Walsh, *Campus Gods on Trial* (New York: Macmillan, 1953).

24. Chad Walsh, *From Utopia to Nightmare* (New York: Harper and Row, 1962), p. 18.

25. Chad Walsh, "Flat Minds, Kind Hearts, and Fine Arts," *Christian Scholar* 36, 2 (June 1953): pp. 104–5.

26. E.g., he credited the "beatniks" for loosening "the 'image' of the poet" for undergraduates (Chad Walsh, "When a Poem Confronts an Undergraduate," *College English* 24, 5 [February 1963]: p. 384).

27. Jacob Hauser qtd. in Virginia Kent Cummins, untitled editorial, *Lyric* 31, 2 (Spring 1951): p. 62.

28. Edward John Dunsany, "How to Conquer America," *Wings* 10, 3 (1951): p. 9. W. Cleon Skousen urged ministers to "resist the erosion of the Modernists who seek to discredit the Bible" (*The Naked Communist* [Salt Lake City: Ensign, 1958], p. 286).

29. Stanton Coblentz, "Beauty Is Truth, Truth Is Beauty," *Wings* 12, 1 (Spring 1955): p. 4.

30. Although Coblentz attacked the New American Poets frequently after 1960, his offered his most sustained critique in *The Poetry Circus* (New York: Hawthorn, 1967), esp. pp. 37–40.

31. Peter Viereck to Robert Hillyer, May 5, 1950, Robert Hillyer Papers, b5, f28, SUSCRC.

32. The ACCL Papers are at the Wisconsin Historical Society as are issue of the ACCL's newsletter, *Challenge*. I thank Travis Koplow for her help with my research into Christian antimodernism. The "Christian Americanism" of Billy James Hargis (Christian Crusade leader) favored letter-of-the-law antirelativism and equated interpretive change and social dynamism (or progress) with materialism and un-Christian acquisitiveness (John Harold Redekop, *The American Far Right: A Case Study of Billy James Hargis and Christian Crusade* [Grand Rapids, Mich.: Eerdmans, 1968], pp. 91, 71, 121). See also Vincent P. DeSantis, "American Catholics and McCarthyism," *Catholic Historical Review* 51, 1 (April 1965): pp. 1–30. For a summary of the historical legacy of Catholic antiradicalism, see Donald F. Crosby, "The Politics of Religion: American Catholics and the Anti-Communist Impulse," in *The Specter: Original Essays on the Cold War and the Origins of McCarthyism*, ed. Robert Griffith and Athan G. Theoharis (New York: New Viewpoints, 1974), pp. 20–38.

33. As noted earlier, Viereck was a critic of McCarthy.

34. William F. Buckley, *Up from Liberalism* (New Rochelle, N.Y.: Arlington House, 1968), pp. 50–55.

35. Peter Viereck, *Terror and Decorum: Poems, 1940–48* (New York: Scribner's, 1950), dustjacket.

36. Ibid., p. 34.

37. J. Anthony Marcus to Robert Hillyer, July 4, 1949, Hillyer Papers, b4, f11.

38. David Crosby, *God, Church, and Flag: Senator Joseph R. McCarthy and the Catholic Church, 1950–1957* (Chapel Hill: University of North Carolina Press, 1978), pp. 18, 20–21; Crosby, "Politics of Religion," *Specter*, pp. 22, 24.

39. Qtd. in Crosby, "Politics of Religion," p. 12.

40. Richard M. Weaver to Henry Regnery, July 11, 1955, Henry Regnery Papers, b77, f17 ("Weaver"), HI.

41. Russell Kirk, "Richard M. Weaver, RIP," *Individualist* 2, 2 (September 1963): p. 2.

42. Charles Frankel, "Property, Language, and Piety," *Nation*, May 29, 1948, pp. 609–10. The phrase "music to go with empiricism" is Weaver's, qtd. in Frankel, p. 609.

43. See James Powell, "The Foundations of Weaver's Traditionalism," *New Individualist Review* 3, 3 (1964): pp. 3–6.

44. See, e.g., Morris U. Schappes, "Historic and Contemporary Particulars," *Poetry* 41, 6 (March 1933): pp. 340–43. "There must be trees (particulars)," Schappes wrote, "but you must able to discern a wood" (p. 341).

45. Susan Sontag, "Piety without Content" (1961), in *Against Interpretation, and Other Essays* (New York: Farrar, Straus, and Giroux, 1966), p. 250.

46. Viereck, *Unadjusted Man*, pp. 297–300, 313–14.

47. Peter Viereck, *Strike through the Mask!: New Lyrical Poems* (New York: Scribner's, 1950), p. 21.

48. Peter Viereck, "The Dignity of Lyricism," *New Republic*, May 31, 1954, p. 18.

49. Ibid., p. 17.

50. Viereck, *Strike through the Mask!*, p. 38.

51. Ibid., p. 39.

52. E. Merrill Root to Rolfe Humphries, n.d. [1948], Rolfe Humphries Papers, b1, f6, Amherst College, Amherst, Massachusetts.

53. Randall Jarrell, "A Literary Tornado," *New York Times Book Review*, April 17, 1955, p. 4; Henry Regnery to Allen Tate, July 21, 1955, Regnery Papers, b72, Tate f.

54. Cullen Jones, "Rhythm Is in Disgrace," *Lyric* 29, 2–3 (1949): p. 192.

55. Frank O'Hara, "A Poem about Russia," in *The Collected Poems of Frank O'Hara*, ed. Donald Allen (Berkeley: University of California Press, 1971), pp. 51–52.

56. Jones, "Rhythm Is in Disgrace," p. 192.

57. Jones's anticommunist antimodernist poetry of the postwar period is almost all metapoetic. The antimodernist culture war forced such self-reference on him. His prewar poetry—such as "On Returning to the Western Desert" (*Catholic World*, April 1939, p. 69)—is straightforwardly (and apolitically) traditional:

O vast and rolling land that dims the eye
With seeing: canyoned, sentineled with buttes,
And pinnacled with jagged, rim-rock peaks,
Your silence speaks eternal meditation—
Eternal changeless Silence brooding Truth.

See also Cullen Jones, "Of 'Modern' Art," *Wings* 12, 2 (Summer 1955): p. 6:

Thus in the book I read the single page:

Here beauty passes away as the summer rose . . .

Here beauty passed away.

58. Arthur M. Schlesinger Jr., "The Politics of Nostalgia" (1955), reprinted in *The Politics of Hope* (Boston: Houghton Mifflin, 1962), p. 72.

59. Viereck, *Unadjusted Man*, p. 14; Jack Scherting, "An Approach to the Western Poetry of Thomas Hornsby Ferril," *Western American Literature* 7, 3 (Fall 1972): pp. 179–90; Robert C. Baron, Stephen Leonard, and Thomas J. Noel, eds., *Thomas Hornsby Ferril and the American West* (Golden, Colo.: Fulcrum, Center for the American West, 1996), pp. 165–66.

60. Viereck, *Unadjusted Man*, p. 272.

61. Ibid., p. 272.

62. Stanton Coblentz to Florence Keene, May 6, 1944, Florence Keene Papers, Huntington Library, San Marino, California.

63. Gladys Lawrence Payne, "Heart Tasks," *Westward* 13, 5 (1946): p. [1].

64. Viereck, *Strike through the Mask!*, p. 25.

65. Ibid.

66. Ibid., p. 272.

67. Ibid., p. 25.

68. Richard M. Weaver, *Relativism and the Crisis of Our Times* (Philadelphia: Intercollegiate Society of Individualists, n.d.), p. 7, copy in Regnery Papers, b81, f16a.

69. Viereck, *Unadjusted Man*, p. 297.

70. Stanton Coblentz, "Parnassus—And Parlor Games," *Wings* 5, 6 (Summer 1942): pp. 4–6.

71. Stanton Coblentz, "The Broad-Minded Fallacy," *Wings* 9, 5 (Spring 1950): pp. 4–5.

72. Frederick Wilhelmsen, "The Conservative Vision," *Commonweal* 62, 12 (June 24, 1955): pp. 295, 298, 299.

73. E. Merrill Root to Rolfe Humphries, July 6, 1938, Humphries Papers, b1, f6.

74. Viereck, *Strike through the Mask!*, p. [23].

75. See Susan Sontag, *Illness as Metaphor* (New York: Farrar, Straus, and Giroux, 1978), pp. 69–70.

76. Cartoon by Lloyd, *Saturday Review of Literature*, August 6, 1949, p. 50.

Chapter 13

1. Peter Viereck, "Pure Poetry, Impure Politics: The Implications of Ezra Pound and the Bollingen Controversy," in *Dream and Responsibility: Four Test Cases of the Tension between Poetry and Society* (Washington, D.C.: University Press of Washington, 1953), p. 12.

2. Ibid., pp. 12–13.

3. Peter Viereck, "Meter Is Time in Leotards," *New York Quarterly* 32, 2 (Spring 1987): p. 113.

4. Ibid., p. 115. For a full argument for the iamb as part of the natural order (part of the

"binary code"), see Peter Viereck, "Strict Form in Poetry: Would Jacob Wrestle with a Flabby Angel?," *Critical Inquiry* 5, 2 (Winter 1978): pp. 203–22. This essay is, in passing, another attack on Williams (pp. 210–11).

5. Robert Hillyer to Leigh Hanes, March 15, 1948, b6, f dated 1948, Leigh Hanes Papers, 7689-a, Albert and Shirley Small Special Collections Library, University of Virginia, Charlottesville.

6. S. B. Lush, "Modern Poetry," *New Republic*, October 22, 1951, p. 2.

7. Louise Bogan, "Young Poets: 1944–1954," in *Selected Criticism: Prose, Poetry* (New York: Noonday, 1955), pp. 385–86, 387. The review of Warren's *Selected Poems, 1923–1943* and Fitzgerald's *A Wreath for the Sea* was originally published in 1944.

8. Stanton Coblentz, "Do We Know What Poetry Is?," *Wings* 12, 4 (Winter 1956): p. 3. A passage from Williams's "Sonnet in Search of an Author" (*Nation*, April 14, 1956, p. 313) came in for special excoriation in the Autumn 1956 issue of *Wings* (p. 21). "The Desert Music" was featured in the Summer 1953 issue (p. 21). For more on "This Is Poetry" and "This Is NOT Poetry," see "Wing Beats," *Wings* 11, 2 (Summer 1953): p. 32.

9. Robert Hillyer in the *Bulletin of the Poetry Society of America*, qtd. in Stanton Coblentz, *New Poetic Lamps and Old* (Mill Valley, Calif.: Wings, 1950), p. 9.

10. Richard M. Weaver, *Ideas Have Consequences* (Chicago: University of Chicago Press, 1948), p. 87.

11. Richard M. Weaver, *Visions of Order* (Baton Rouge: Louisiana State University Press, 1964), p. 19.

12. These summaries are drawn from Weaver's arguments in *Ideas Have Consequences* and *Visions of Order* (in particular, chapters 1 and 3, "The Image of Culture" and "The Attack on Memory") and especially from "Reflections of Modernity" and "Aspects of Grammatical Categories" in *Ethics of Rhetoric* (Chicago: Regnery, 1953). For "the fallacy of presentism" and "the impulse to . . . present," see "Reflection of Modernity" (1961), in *Life without Prejudice* (Chicago: Regnery, 1965), pp. 107, 108.

13. Richard M. Weaver, *Ideas Have Consequences*, pp. 52, 53, 57, 58. This is chapter 3, "Fragmentation and Obsession."

14. Viereck, "Pure Poetry, Impure Politics," p. 7.

15. Peter Viereck to Robert Hillyer, May 4, [1950], Robert Hillyer Papers, b5, f28, SUSCRC.

16. Robert Hillyer to Leigh Hanes, February 1, 1949, b6, f dated 1948, Hanes Papers.

17. Viereck, "Pure Poetry, Impure Politics," p. 12. Responses to Roethke help distinguish between moderate and extreme antimodernists. For an instance of the latter, see Coblentz, *New Poetic Lamps and Old*, pp. 48–49. For Viereck's distinctions between and among lefts and rights, see, e.g., chapter 4 of *The Unadjusted Man: A New Hero for Americans* (Boston: Beacon, 1956), pp. 35–41.

18. Even Henry Regnery, who in 1959 acquired the firm that published Edgar Guest and profited from sales of Guest's books, was not a fan of the poetry (Henry Regnery to Joseph Lalley, April 27, 1959, J. M. Lalley Papers, ms. 199, Milton S. Eisenhower Library, Johns Hopkins University, Baltimore, Maryland).

19. Viereck, *Unadjusted Man*, p. 14.

20. Leigh Hanes, "Poetic Doodles," typescript, b4, f dated 1946, Hanes Papers. He sent this essay to the *Atlantic Monthly*; it was never published.

21. Ernest Hemingway, *In Our Time* (New York: Scribner's, 1925), p. 11.

22. Ernest Hemingway, *The Old Man and the Sea* (New York: Scribner's, 1952), p. 9.

23. Hemingway, *In Our Time*, p. 11.

24. Donald Davidson, "Grammar and Rhetoric: The Teacher's Problem," *Quarterly Journal of Speech* 39, 4 (December 1953): p. 425.

25. Richard M. Weaver, "Language Is Sermonic," first published in *Dimensions of Rhetorical Scholarship*, ed. Roger E. Nebergall (Norman: University of Oklahoma Department of Speech, 1963), reprinted in *Language Is Sermonic: Richard M. Weaver and the Nature of Rhetoric* (Baton Rouge: Louisiana State University Press, 1970), p. 214.

26. "Lenin" was published in the October 1932 issue of *Rebel Poet* (reprinted in Jack Conroy, ed., *Writers in Revolt: The "Anvil" Anthology* [New York: Hill, 1973], p. 222).

27. Kenneth Patchen, "And a Man Went Out Alone," originally published in *Red Wine and Yellow Hair* (New York: New Directions, 1949), in *The Collected Poems of Kenneth Patchen* (New York: New Directions, 1968), pp. 366–67; qtd. in Stanton Coblentz, "This is NOT Poetry," *Wings* 11, 3 (Autumn 1953): p. 21. See also Stanton Coblentz and Jeffrey M. Elliot, *Adventures of a Freelancer: The Literary Exploits and Autobiography of Stanton A. Coblentz* (San Bernardino, Calif.: Borgo, 1993), pp. 151–52; Stanton Coblentz, *The Poetry Circus* (New York: Hawthorn, 1967), pp. 39–40.

28. Coblentz and Elliot, *Adventures of a Freelancer*, p. 152.

29. Karl Shapiro to William Van O'Connor, April 30, 1946, William Van O'Connor Papers, SUSCRC.

30. Donald Jenks, "Tell Me No More," *Humanist* 11, 5 (October–November 1951): p. 227.

31. Richard M. Weaver, *Ideas Have Consequences*, pp. 55, 59.

32. Donald Davidson, "Grammar and Rhetoric," p. 425.

33. "Must Poets Be Exterminated?," *Pinnacle* 1 (May 1945): p. 2; emphasis added.

34. J. Donald Adams, *The Shape of Books to Come* (New York: Viking, 1944), p. 149.

35. Robert Hillyer, "Poetry's New Priesthood," *Saturday Review of Literature*, June 18, 1949, p. 8.

36. Joseph M. Lalley, *Faith and Force: An Inquiry into the Nature of Authority* (Washington, D.C.: Human Events, [1946]), pp. 16–17.

37. See Henry Regnery, *Memoirs of a Dissident Publisher* (New York: Harcourt, Brace, Jovanovich, 1979), p. 204.

38. Joseph M. Lalley, introduction to Roy Campbell, *Selected Poetry*, ed. Joseph M. Lalley (Chicago: Regnery, 1968), p. [2].

39. Lalley, *Faith and Force*, p. 16.

40. Welford Inge, "The Poetry of Fear," *Catholic World*, May 1956, pp. 134–35.

41. Sidney A. Cooley to Karl Shapiro, [May 1952?], PMP 1936–53, s2, b2, f14.

42. W. Cleon Skousen, *The Naked Communist* (Salt Lake City: Ensign, 1958), p. 276.

43. "J. Anthony Marcus Dead at 68; Lecturer against Communism," *New York Times*, November 24, 1960, p. 29; J. Anthony Marcus, "Soviet-American Relations," *New York Times*, July 30, 1947, p. 20.

44. J. Anthony Marcus to Robert Hillyer, July 4, 1949, Hillyer Papers, b4, f11.

45. Richard M. Weaver, *Ideas Have Consequences*, p. 44.

46. David Antin and Charles Bernstein, *A Conversation with David Antin* (New York: Granary, 2002), pp. 14–15.

47. Gillian G. Gaar, *She's a Rebel: The History of Women in Rock and Roll* (Seattle: Seal, 1992), p. 231. For an example of the antimodernist case against the convergence of poetry and prose, see Coblentz, *New Poetry Lamps and Old*, pp. 35–44.

48. Michael F. Moloney, "Modern Literature: Darkness at Dawn," *America*, August 11, 1951, p. 461.

49. Stanton Coblentz, *My Life in Poetry* (New York: Bookman, 1959), p. 37.

50. Daniel Bell, "Modernism and Capitalism," in *Writers and Politics: A "Partisan Review" Reader*, ed. Edith Kurzweil and William Phillips (Boston: Routledge and Kegan Paul, 1983), p. 125.

51. Herbert Read, *The Phases of English Poetry* (1928), *Direction* 19 (1951): p. 179.

52. Richard M. Weaver, "Etiology of the Image," *Poetry* 72, 3 (June 1948): pp. 160, 158.

53. Cleanth Brooks, University of Chicago Press—Manuscript Report, April 28, 1947, University of Chicago Press Papers, Regenstein Library, University of Chicago. At the time Brooks read the manuscript, the provisional title of the book was *The Adverse Descent*.

54. Inge, "Poetry of Fear," pp. 134–35.

55. Qtd. in Howard Devree, "Modernism under Fire," *New York Times*, September 11, 1949, sec. 10, p. 6.

56. E. Merrill Root, "Our Left-Handed Colleges," *Freeman* 3, 2 (October 20, 1952): p. 51.

57. Ben Ray Redman, "T. S. Eliot on Sight of Posterity," *Saturday Review of Literature*, March 12, 1949, p. 31.

58. Robert Hillyer, "Poetry's New Priesthood," *Saturday Review of Literature*, June 18, 1949, p. 8, 9.

59. Richard M. Weaver, *Ideas Have Consequences*, pp. 44, 42.

60. Ibid., p. 159.

61. League for Sanity in Poetry, *Making Treason Pay* (Rogers, Ark.: League for Sanity in Poetry, [1949]); the summary of this pamphlet appears in Stanton Coblentz to Robert Hillyer, June 3, 1949, Hillyer Papers.

62. Inge, "Poetry of Fear," pp. 134–35.

63. League for Sanity in Poetry, *Making Treason Pay*, [1]; Ezra Pound, *The Pisan Cantos* (New York: New Directions, 1948), p. 8.

64. Stanton Coblentz, "The Unmemorable Moderns," *Wings* 7, 2 (Summer 1945): p. 6.

65. Susan Sontag, "The Imagination of Disaster" (1965), in *Against Interpretation, and Other Essays* (New York: Farrar, Straus, and Giroux, 1966), p. 213.

66. Neville Braybrooke, "Roy Campbell: Soldier-Poet," *America*, December 9, 1950, p. 309.

67. Leigh Hanes to "Harry," October 15, 1956, b2, Hanes Papers.

68. Stanton Coblentz, "Poetry, Progress, and Prose," *Wings* 5, 8 (Winter 1943): pp. 4, 5.

69. Stanton Coblentz, "Everyman's Art—And No Man's Art," *Wings* 13, 4 (Winter 1958): p. 5.

70. It was first published privately in 1922 and subsequently published in a trade edition by B. W. Huebsch in 1925.

71. Glenn Hughes, *Imagism and the Imagists: A Study in Modern Poetry* (Stanford: Stanford University Press, 1931), 54–59, analyzes Leonard's charges.

72. Renato Poggioli, *The Theory of the Avant-Garde*, trans. Gerald Fitzgerald (1962; Cambridge: Harvard University Press, 1968), p. 157.

73. Right-wing critics of modern poetry often merged their complaints against pro-pagandistic poetry and against the modernist urge to move poetry out of its autonomous sphere and into the world of functional language. The first clear articulation of this point of view is in Kemp Malone's "What Is Poetry For?" (*Poetry Forum* 1, 1–2 [Summer 1941]: pp. 14–15): "Current didacticism is concerned less with eternal verities and more with immediate issues. . . . Our poets . . . seem curiously indifferent to their . . . duty . . . to mak[e] this propaganda interesting to the general [reader. Poets'] functional approach has led us to a sorry conclusion. . . . Poetry . . . is a thing apart" (14–15).

74. Harry Hodgkinson, "Formalism," in *Doubletalk: The Language of Communism* (London: Allen and Unwin, 1955), p. 51; on "Cosmopolitanism," see pp. 37–38.

75. For "strangely hybrid critics" and "dynamized dialectic," see J. Donald Adams, "A Hard Look at Criticism," *Poetry* 68, 5 (August 1946): p. 264, 263; for "poverty of method," see J. Donald Adams, *The Shape of Books to Come* (New York: Viking, 1944), p. xiv.

76. E. Merrill Root, *Collectivism on the Campus: The Battle for the Mind in American Colleges* (New York: Devin-Adair, 1955), p. 29.

77. See Coblentz, *Poetry Circus*, p. 38; Donald Allen, ed., *The New American Poetry, 1945–1960* (New York: Grove, 1960), pp. 352–54.

78. Cullen Jones, "A Defense of a Non-Defense of Poetry," *Poetry Review* 35, 1 (January–February 1944): p. 59. Poets' "continuous revolt against the work-a-day world" is *good* because it removes them still further from reality, to a place where they can sing of "something finer" (p. 59).

79. See Viereck, *Unadjusted Man*, p. 272.

80. Joe Scotchie, "The Patron Saint of Southern Traditionalists," *Southern Events* 5, 4 (2002): p. 6.

81. Donald Davidson, "The Southern Writer and the Modern University," *Georgia Review* 12, 1 (Spring 1958): p. 23.

82. Lee Richard Hayman, "Free Verse for Sale," *Writer* 62, 9 (September 1949): p. 302.

83. William Meredith, "A Good Modern Poet and a Modern Tradition," *Poetry* 70, 4 (July 1947): p. 209.

84. Hayman, "Free Verse for Sale," p. 302.

85. See David Ogilvy, *Confessions of an Advertising Man* (1963; New York: Ballantine, 1971), see esp. chapters 6 and 7.

86. Coblentz, *New Poetic Lamps and Old*, pp. 10, 9. Coblentz quoted the phrase "the cold conformity of intellectualism" from Robert Hillyer.

87. Ralph Gustafson, "For William Carlos Williams," *Poetry New York* 2 (1950): p. 11.

88. Coblentz, *New Poetic Lamps and Old*, p. 9.

89. See Jane De Hart Mathews, "Art and Politics in Cold War America," *American Historical Review* 81, 4 (October 1976): pp. 770–71; R. B. Beaman, "The Cubist Witch," *South Atlantic Quarterly*, June 1949, p. 204.

90. Howard Sparber, drawing for Stanton A. Coblentz's "What Are They?—Poems or Puzzles?," *New York Times Magazine*, October 13, 1946, p. 24.

91. Paul Scott Mowrer, "In Praise of Rhyme," typescript, n.d., Hillyer Papers, b4, f27.

92. William Carlos Williams, *Paterson* (New York: New Directions, 1958), p. 182.

93. M. L. Rosenthal, "The Unconsenting Spirit," *Nation*, November 10, 1956, p. 414.

94. William Carlos Williams, *Collected Poems of William Carlos Williams*, ed. A. Walton Litz and Christopher MacGowan (New York: New Directions, 1986), vol. 1, p. 129.

95. William Carlos Williams, *Paterson*, p. 182.

96. Ibid., p. 183.

97. Ibid., pp. 182–83.

98. See Alexander Cowie, untitled essay, *American Literature* 27, 3 (November 1955): p. 443.

99. J. Donald Adams, "Speaking of Books," *New York Times*, November 11, 1956, p. 322.

100. William Carlos Williams, *Paterson*, p. 185.

101. Adams, "Speaking of Books," p. 322.

102. Galway Kinnell, " 'Only Meaning Is Truly Interesting . . .' " *Beloit Poetry Journal* 2 (1953): pp. 1–2; emphasis added.

103. Florence Williams to Conrad Aiken, January 14, 1953, AIK915, Conrad Aiken Papers, Huntington Library, San Marino, California.

104. Merrill Moore to Florence Williams, January 30, 1953, Merrill Moore Papers, Poetry/Rare Books Collection, SUNY Buffalo.

105. Florence Williams to Norman Holmes Pearson, December 14, 1952, Norman Holmes Pearson Papers, Yale University Library, New Haven, Connecticut.

106. Sidney Hook to Michael Weaver, December 6, 1966, Sidney Hook Papers, b171, f16, HI.

107. E.g. *Lyric* 33, 4 (Autumn 1952): unpaginated insert.

108. Sidney Hook to Michael Weaver, December 6, 1966, Hook Papers, b171, f16.

109. Michael Weaver to Sidney Hook, December 2, 1966, Hook Papers, b171, f16.

110. Sidney Hook to Michael Weaver, December 6, 1966, Hook Papers, b171, f16.

111. Stanton Coblentz to Luther H. Evans, July 7, 1949, carbon copy sent to Robert Hillyer, Hillyer Papers.

112. Stanton Coblentz to Robert Hillyer, July 5, 1949, Hillyer Papers.

113. Ibid., June 3, 1949.

114. Vivienne Koch, "The Necessary Angels of Earth," *Sewanee Review* 59 (1951): pp. 9–10.

115. Vivienne Koch, "The Man and the Poet," *Kenyon Review* 14, 3 (Summer 1952): pp. 507–8.

116. Mike Weaver, *William Carlos Williams: The American Background* (Cambridge: Cambridge University Press, 1971), p. 102.

117. William Carlos Williams, *Collected Poems*, vol. 2, p. 68.

118. M. L. Rosenthal, "Chief Poets of the American Depression," Ph.D. diss., New York University, 1945. See also M. L. Rosenthal, "The Meaning of Kenneth Fearing's Poetry," *Poetry* 66, 4 (July 1944): pp. 208–23.

119. M. L. Rosenthal, "Confessions," typescript drafts, n.d., MLR/F, s6, f6; John T. Frederick to M. L. Rosenthal, April 10, 1939, October 16, 1939, MLR/F, s6, f8.

120. Rosenthal, "Meaning of Kenneth Fearing's Poetry," p. 215.

121. M. L. Rosenthal, "Hard Cores and Soft," *Poetry* 68, 2 (May 1946): pp. 112, 113. This was a review of Coblentz's *The Music Makers*.

122. This is nowhere more evident than in Rosenthal's correspondence with Kenneth Fearing during Rosenthal's time at the *Nation* (MLR/F, s1, f31).

123. M. L. Rosenthal, "A Note on Tradition in Poetry," *Nation*, May 11, 1957, p. 420.

124. Ibid.

125. Rosenthal, "Unconsenting Spirit," p. 414.

126. Ibid., p. 415.

127. See, e.g., M. L. Rosenthal, "Paul Blackburn, Poet," *New York Times Book Review*, August 11, 1974, section 7, p. 27.

128. See M. L. Rosenthal materials, PMP 1936–53, s1, b22, f3.

129. M. L. Rosenthal, "In the Roar of the Present," *New Republic*, August 27, 1951, p. 18–19.

130. Barbara Nauer Folk, calling it a "landslide" ("Modern Verse: Not Blank but Not Free," *Catholic World*, September 1955, pp. 438–44), offered a summary of the responses. See William McFee, "Modern Poetry," *New Republic*, October 15, 1951, p. 4; Lush, "Modern Poetry," p. 2.

131. Leo Gurko, *The Angry Decade* (New York: Dodd, Mead, 1947), p. 65.

132. Upton Sinclair, "The Riddle of Modern Poetry," *New Republic*, September 24, 1951, p. 2.

133. *New Masses* and *Daily Worker* reviews of Sinclair's writing in the 1940s indicate how poorly he was received by communist literary critics. See Samuel Sillen's review of the 1946 edition of *The Jungle* (*Sunday Worker Magazine*, September 22, 1946, p. 5); Robert Friedman's review of *O Shepherd Speak!* (*Daily Worker*, October 6, 1949, p. 12); and Sally Alford's review of *Dragon Harvest* (*New Masses* 56, 6 [August 7, 1945]: p. 25). Sinclair, according to Alford, subscribed to the notion that "Nazism was caused by Bolshevism," and she dubbed Sinclair a red-baiter (p. 25). Friedman lamented Sinclair's decline from *The Jungle*, and Sillen observed that weaknesses of that novel were "more discernible today than in 1906" (p. 12).

134. Stanton Coblentz, "Modern Poetry," *New Republic*, October 8, 1951, p. 2.

135. Stanton Coblentz, *An Editor Looks at Poetry* (Mill Valley, Calif.: Wings, 1947), p. 111.

136. See chapter 8. See also *Brief to Establish the Illegal Status of the Communist Party of the United States of America*, part 1, *Origin and Continuity*, February 3, 1948, John McGohey Papers, Harry S. Truman Library, Independence, Missouri; *Official Report of the Proceedings before the Subversive Activities Control Board, Herbert Brownell, Attorney General of the United States, Petitioner, v. the Jefferson School of Social Science, Respondent*, docket no. 107-53, December 11, 1953, pp. 763–820, Subversive Activities Control Board Papers, box 31, HI; Peter L. Steinberg, *The Great "Red Menace": United States Prosecution of American Communists, 1947–1952* (Westport, Conn.: Greenwood, 1984).

137. Werner Cohn, "Esoteric Elements in Communist Language," *Encounter* 64, 5 (May 1985): p. 77.

138. Richard Weaver, *Ethics of Rhetoric*, p. 142.

139. Joseph Freeman to Floyd Dell, April 15, 1953, Floyd Dell Papers, "De Reserve Box," Newberry Library, Chicago.

140. Viereck, *Unadjusted Man*, p. 80.

141. Richard Weaver, *Ethics of Rhetoric*, p. 142. Eliseo Vivas made a similar point about grammar and citizenship in "Allen Tate as a Man of Letters," *Sewanee Review* 62 (1954): pp. 131–43.

142. Ray Smith, "Whitman: The Leaves of Grass Centennial, 2055," *Approach* 18 (November 1955): pp. 7, 10.

143. Ron Silliman, "The Desert Modernism," paper presented at the Modernist Studies Association, University of Pennsylvania, October 12, 2000, <http://www.epoetry.org/iss ues/issue4/text/prose/silliman1.htm>. Silliman encountered *The Desert Music* as a sixteen-year-old in 1963. Its sense of isolation gave him the notion that he would be or perhaps already was a poet.

144. Karl Shapiro, "Modern Poetry as Religion," *American Scholar* 28, 3 (Summer 1959): p. 298.

145. Randall Jarrell, "Fifty Years of American Poetry," in *The Third Book of Criticism* (New York: Farrar, Straus, and Giroux, 1965), p. 511. The lecture was first published in *Prairie Schooner* 37, 1 (Spring 1963): pp. 1–27. See also "A Poet's Lot," *Newsweek*, November 5, 1962, p. 96.

146. Robert Graves, "Wordsworth by Cable," *New Republic*, September 9, 1957, pp. 11–12

147. Beaman, "Cubist Witch," p. 204. For more on the official Soviet critique of modernism, see "Planned Culture," *News from behind the Iron Curtain* 2, 9 (September 1953): pp. 30–39.

148. Ray Smith, "Whitman," p. 7.

149. William Jay Smith, "Wordsworth by Cable," *New Republic*, September 23, 1957, p. 23.

150. Mark Van Doren, introduction to *William Wordsworth: Selected Poetry*, ed. Mark Van Doren (New York: Modern Library, 1950), p. xiv.

151. John Crowe Ransom, "Wordsworth's Scrapbook," *New Republic*, September 23, 1957, p. 23.

152. Graves, "Wordsworth by Cable," pp. 11–12.

153. Anna T. Harding, "The Conventions of Poetry," *Pinnacle* 6 (October–November 1945): p. 3.

154. Viereck, *Unadjusted Man*, p. 285.

155. Kenneth Patchen, "Hell Gate Bridge," in *The Teeth of the Lion* (Norfolk, Conn.: New Directions, 1942), n.p., qtd. in Raymond Nelson, *Kenneth Patchen and American Mysticism* (Chapel Hill: University of North Carolina Press, 1984), pp. 159–60.

156. Jonathan Williams, "Out of Sight, Out of Conscience," *Contact* 2 (February 1961), reprinted in *Kenneth Patchen: A Collection of Essays*, ed. Richard G. Morgan (New York: AMS, 1977), pp. 59–62.

157. Raymond Nelson, *Kenneth Patchen*, pp. 156, 160, 1–2. Nelson wrote a 1971 Stanford University dissertation on Patchen. He began writing on Patchen in the late 1960s. For more on Patchen's proletarianism, see Amos N. Wilder, "Revolutionary and Proletarian Poetry: Kenneth Patchen," in *Kenneth Patchen*, ed. Morgan, pp. 127–35.

158. Douglas Manson, "What Is a Prepoetics?: Some Views on Kenneth Patchen and bpNichol," *Celery Flute* 1, 1 (June 2006): pp. 16, 18. The best overview of Patchen's political phases can be found in Larry Smith, *Kenneth Patchen: Rebel Poet in America* (Huron, Ohio: Bottom Dog, 2000).

159. Although he was included in Jed Rasula and Steve McCaffrey, *Imagining Language: An Anthology* (Cambridge: MIT Press, 1998). See also Craig Dworkin, "'Seeing Words Machinewise': Technology and Visual Prosody," *Sagetrieb* 18, 1 (Spring 1999): pp. 59–86.

160. Manson, "What Is a Prepoetics?," pp. 16, 18.

161. A scholar-critic who has explored this continuity is Walter Kaladjian. See his *American Culture between the Wars: Revisionary Modernism and Postmodern Critique* (New York: Columbia University Press, 1993).

162. See, e.g., "Dropping Leaflets" and "The Astounding Complex," in *An Essay in Asterisks* (New York: Roof, 2004), pp. 28–29, 35–56; "Court Reports—Working Notes," published in *How2* 1, 2 (1999), (www.scc.rutgers.edu/however/v1_2_1999). Osman has already acknowledged her connection to Reznikoff—in a symposium hosted by the author, Kelly Writers House, Philadelphia, October 2000, where she also read some of her own works under this influence (writing.upenn.edu/wh/9poets.html).

163. Lyn Hejinian, *My Life* (Los Angeles: Sun and Moon, 1987).

164. Lyn Hejinian, *My Life in the Nineties* (New York: Shark, 2003).

165. Lyn Hejinian, "Strangeness," in *The Language of Inquiry* (Berkeley: University of California Press, 2000), pp. 324, 325.

Permissions

Alfred Hayes: verse from *Welcome to the Castle* © 1950 by Alfred Hayes and Harper & Brothers, reprinted with the consent of the poet's daughter, Josephine Hayes Dean.

George Hitchcock: "War" from *The Wounded Alphabet: Poems Collected & New, 1953–1983* © 1984 by George Hitchcock. Used by permission of the author.

Alfred Kazin: unpublished correspondence to Granville Hicks is quoted with permission of The Wyle Agency; © 1953 by Alfred Kazin.

Kenneth Koch: several lines are quoted from *The Collected Poems of Kenneth Koch* © 2005 by The Kenneth Koch Literary Estate. Used by permission of Alfred A. Knopf, a division of Random House, Inc.

Kenneth Patchen: lines from "Joe Hill Listens to the Praying" by Kenneth Patchen, from *The Collected Poems of Kenneth Patchen* © 1939 by New Directions Publishing Corporation are reprinted by permission of New Directions. The quotation from "And a Man Went Out Alone" is used by permission of Special Collections, University Library, University of California at Santa Cruz, Kenneth Patchen Archive.

Ezra Pound: lines from "Canto LXXIV" by Ezra Pound from *The Cantos of Ezra Pound* © 1934, 1937, 1940, 1948, 1956, 1959, 1962, 1963, 1966, and 1968 by Ezra Pound are reprinted by permission of New Directions Publishing Corporation.

Carl Rakosi: "Surrealists (1930)," first collected in *Selected Poems* © 1941 by New Directions and Carl Rakosi, and reprinted in Andrew Crozier's Sun & Moon Press edition of *Poems 1923–1941* © 1995, 1967 by Callman Rawley [Rakosi]. Quoted by permission of Marilyn Kane, Carl Rakosi's literary executor.

Norman Rosten: verse passages from *The Big Road* © 1946 by Rinehart and Norman Rosten, *The Plane and The Shadow* © 1953 by Bookman Associates and Norman Rosten, are quoted by permission of Patricia Rosten Filan.

Wallace Stevens: passages from Wallace Stevens's "The Men That Are Falling" and "A Dish of Peaches in Russia," from *The Collected Poems of Wallace Stevens* by Wallace Stevens, © 1954 by Wallace Stevens and renewed 1982 by Holly Stevens, used by permission of Alfred A. Knopf, a division of Random House, Inc.

Peter Viereck: "Is Mary Everybody?" in *Tide and Continuities: Last and First Poems, 1995–1938* © 1995 by Peter Viereck; "Big Crash Out West" in *New and Selected Poems* © 1967 by Bobbs-Merrill and Peter Viereck; and "Love Song of J. Smith" and "A Masque of Tears" in *Strike through the Mask!* © 1950 by Peter Viereck; "Is Mary Everybody" is also quoted with permission of the University of Arkansas Press.

William Carlos Williams: excerpt from "Portrait of a Lady" by William Carlos Williams from *Collected Poems 1909–1939*, volume 1, © 1938 by New Directions Publishing Corporation is reprinted by permission of New Directions. Lines from "To All

Gentleness" by William Carlos Williams from *Collected Poems 1939–1962*, volume 2, © 1953 by William Carlos Williams are reprinted by permission of New Directions. A page from book 4 of *Paterson* by William Carlos Williams is reproduced in facsimile from *Paterson* © 1951 by William Carlos Williams; used by permission of New Directions Publishing Corporation.

Louis Zukofsky: lines from "Song 27-¾ Time" from *The Collected Short Poems* (New York: W. W. Norton, 1965) are used by permission of Paul Zukofsky; all Zukofsky material © Paul Zukofsky; the material may not reproduced, quoted, or used in any manner whatsoever without the explicit and specific permission of the copyright holder.

Index

Ashman, Richard, 229
Auden, W. H., 43, 104, 108, 109, 202, 231;
    satire of, 33
Augusta Chronicle, 196
Auslander, Joseph, 169–70
Authors' Club (London), 209
Avalon National Poetry Shrine, 192, 223–
    24, 272, 298, 394 (n. 18)
Avrett, Robert, 193, 194, 195, 248

Baarslag, Karl, 206
Bain, Read, 161, 187, 265
Baird, Mary Julian, 41, 43, 267, 268
Baker, Russell, 193, 232–33
Barber, Solon, 8, 42
Barnes, Djuna, 211
Bartlett, Alice Hunt, 166–67, 179, 196, 271
Beach, Joseph Warren, 11–12, 84–93, 314,
    330 (n. 95)
Beckett, Samuel, 122
Beecher, John, 142
Bell, Daniel, 34, 38, 39, 65, 77, 122, 127, 193,
    194, 200–201, 203, 219, 249–50
Beloit Poetry Journal, 13, 198, 273, 309, 312
Benét, Stephen Vincent, 22, 100, 136–37
Benjt, William Rose, 180, 381 (n. 11)
Berding, A. H., 216
Berrigan, Daniel, 268–71
Bessie, Alvah, 77
Between Worlds, 199
Bielaski, A. Bruce, 221
Bielaski, Frank B., 221–22, 223
Big Table, 74
Bishop, Elizabeth, 107, 109
Bishop, John Peale, 79
Bishop, Morris, 234
Biskind, Peter, 284
Blackburn, Paul, 274, 314
Black Mountain Review, 74
Blackmur, Richard P., 128–29
Blaser, Robin, 107, 141, 182
Blume, Peter, 221

Bodenheim, Maxwell, 22, 23–24, 80, 107,
    223, 258–59, 381 (n. 11)
Bogan, Louise, 34–35, 51, 70, 71, 75, 89, 99,
    115; *Achievement in American Poetry*,
    108–10, 112, 116; end of experimental-
    ism, according to, 288, 289; and
    Humphries, 111, 117–18; and Lechlitner,
    110–11; on MacLeish, 111; on Rukeyser,
    114–15, 117
Bollingen Prize. *See* Pound, Ezra
Brand, Millen, 141, 147–50
Braque, Georges, 261–62
Bratt, George, 107
Brecht, Bertolt, 50
Bremser, Ray, 299
Brinnin, J. Malcolm, 10, 22, 66, 68, 83–84,
    107
Brooks, Cleanth, 176
Broom, 23
Browder, Earl, 50
Brown, Bob, 8, 10, 107, 259, 321
Brown, Malcolm, 244
Buckley, William F., 223, 266, 275
Budenz, Louis, 69, 143, 188–89, 316. *See
    also* Aesopian Language Thesis
Bulosan, Carlos, 32, 107, 145
Bürger, Peter, 47
Burke, Fielding, 75
Burke, Kenneth, 8, 56–57, 181, 272
Burkland, Carl Edwin, 193, 195, 215
Burman, Ben Lucien, x, 192, 201, 204–5,
    210, 227–30, 286
Burnham, James, 112–14
Burnshaw, Stanley, 10, 17, 38, 47–48, 107,
    142, 327 (n. 48); *Poetry*, closely followed
    by, 49; on Stevens, 43
Burt, Struthers, 185
Bush, Douglas, 193, 235–37
Butler, Nicolas Murray, 170–71

Cain, William, 53
California Quarterly, 13

Calverton, V. F., 48, 51

Cameron, Angus, 142, 147

Campbell, Roy, 241, 260, 266, 281, 294, 361 (n. 21)

Cane, Melville, 193, 243, 244–45, 248

Cantor, Norman, 41

Cantwell, Robert, 75

Cardona-Hine, Alvaro, 9, 15, 107, 145

Carroll, Paul, 74

Carruth, Hayden, 183, 185, 197, 212, 374 (n. 14)

Casey, William J., 266

Catholic Poetry Society of America, 33, 235

Catholic World, 184, 262, 276

Caudwell, Christopher, 252

Central Intelligence Agency (CIA), 95, 221, 264, 354 (n. 2)

Cezanne, Paul, 247

Chamberlain, John, 37, 75

Chamberlin, William Henry, 34, 120, 122

Chambers, Whittaker, 59, 89, 107

Chase, Richard, 98

Child-art movement, 251–56, 261–64

Ciardi, John, 14, 99, 116–17, 181

Circle, 107, 182, 289

Civil defense drills, protest against, 19

Clancy, Joseph P., 193, 238

Coastlines, 13

Coblentz, Stanton, ix, 162, 166, 172–73, 177–78, 179, 187, 194, 196, 197, 204, 209, 223, 242, 244, 248–49, 265, 289, 300, 302, 313, 398 (n. 17); attack on New American poetics, 299; on cummings, 195; as extremist, 191, 207; as fantasy and science fiction writer, 201–2; on modernist atheism, 274; on modernist fragmentation and parataxis, 292, 293; "What Are They--Poems or Puzzles?" 301, 303–5, 306; on Williams, 310–11, 314; Wings Press, 210. See also *Wings*

Colum, Padraic, 168

Commentary, 89

Committee for Cultural Freedom, 264, 310

Communism: circumlocution for, 128; disease, likened to, 204–5, 225, 286; on Emerson, 63; historiography of, 334 (n. 10); intellectuals' attraction to, 50; jargon, 188; and liberalism, 336 (n. 39); and Millet, 3–6, 21; modernism said to function like, 215–16; Old Left and New Left, 339 (n. 93); Rosenthal's early attraction to, 313; Roth's, 66; in Rukeyser's verse, 131; Soviet policy on experimentalism, 4; teaching of, 5, 365 (n. 96); on Whitman, 97–98, 102; Young Communist League, 10, 83, 100. *See also* Anticommunism; Marxism

Communist Party of the United States (CPUSA), xiv, 3–5, 136, 142, 143, 147, 174, 320, 328 (n. 57), 332 (n. 140), 342 (n. 147); Coplon spy trial, 185, 367 (n. 129); and Till case, 4. *See also* Communism

Confluence, 44–45, 112

Congressional Record, 217, 233–35

Connor, Bruce, 224

Conroy, Jack, 75, 327 (n. 51)

Cooley, Sidney, 295

Copland, Aaron, 210

Coplon, Judith, 185, 367 (n. 129)

Corman, Cid, 53–54

Counterattack, 141, 146

Cousins, Norman, 185

Cowley, Malcolm, 14, 42, 55–56, 57, 145, 209, 348 (n. 76), 391 (n. 73); *Exile's Return*, 88–93; as lyric poet, 389 (n. 16)

Crane, Hart, 24, 91, 108–9, 110, 114, 127, 154, 188, 203, 290, 313

Crane, Stephen, 211

Creeley, Robert, 14, 15, 74–75, 182, 199; on Graves, 244

Crews, Judson, 15–17

Crosby, Harry, 91

Cubism, 206, 253

Cullen, Countee, 312

cummings, e. e., 177, 195, 289, 301; satire of, 210

Cummins, Virginia Kent, x, 196, 245, 299, 309; red-baiting of Williams, 309–10, 311

Cunard, Nancy, 104

Dadaism, 23, 206, 239, 250

Dahlberg, Edward, 11, 14, 74–75, 89–90; Beach on, 86; *Understanding Poetry* omits, 176

Daiches, David, 95–97, 103–4, 107, 108

Daily Worker, 25, 96, 146, 310, 326 (n. 29)

Dalí, Salvador, 210, 219, 303

Davidman, Joy, 22, 105, 314

Davidson, Donald, 181, 239, 291, 300; on modernist parataxis, 292

Davidson, Michael, 127, 157

Davidson, Richard, 13, 91

Davis, Frank Marshall, 49–50, 103, 107, 135, 140

Davis, Stuart, 216, 221

Day, Dorothy, 19, 31

Decker, James, 132–33, 135

Dell, Floyd, 64

Dellinger, David, 269

Denney, Reuel, 213

de Toledano, Ralph, 36–37, 98

Deutsch, Babette, 9, 14, 44, 357 (n. 67); *Poetry in Our Time*, 105–6

DeVries, Peter, 18, 193

Dewey, John, 250, 254, 262

Dickinson, Emily, 11, 328 (n. 57)

Dillon, George, 6, 18, 150, 202, 325 (n. 14)

Documentary poetry, 71, 127, 150, 154–57, 295, 312, 321

Dondero, George, 204, 206, 217–18, 219, 221, 222, 225, 226–27

Donne, John, 10, 272

Doolittle, Hilda (H.D.), 23, 28; Gregory commends, 17, 20

Dorn, Ed, 141

Dos Passos, John, 13, 127, 211, 253

Doughty, LeGarde S., 196

Drew, Dorothy, 221, 222

Duchamp, Marcel, 23, 224, 250, 286; readymades, 203

Dulles, John Foster, 86

Duncan, Robert, 65, 74, 75, 107, 129, 182

Dunsany, Edward John, 191, 192, 204, 206, 207–8, 209–10, 212–14, 215, 274

Dupee, Fred, 110

DuPlessis, Rachel Blau, 140

Dynamo Poets, The, 12, 49, 127, 321

Eastman, Max, 48, 241, 244, 248, 260, 264–65, 266, 326 (n. 22)

Eberhart, Richard, 17, 109

Education Information, Inc., 218, 224

Education through art, 252–57, 261–62. *See also* Read, Herbert

Eigner, Larry, 141, 199

Eisenhower, Dwight D., 386 (n. 13)

Eliot, T. S., 9, 10, 14, 41, 47, 80, 82, 113, 114, 144, 184, 202, 231, 236, 244, 246, 247, 249, 257, 284, 311, 324 (n. 3); Beach on, 86; Bogan on, 108, 109; Christians competent to teach, 273; communist poets on, 42; Donne as influence on Eliotic mode, 273; Fletcher on, 240; Gregory influenced by, 17; Hillyer on, 179; and Kirk, 390 (n. 39); Matthiessen on, 52–54; middle-class fashion for, 300; satire of, 210; Viereck's answer to Prufrock, 278

Emerson, Ralph Waldo, 62–63

Emmanuel, Pierre, 181–82

Encounter, 316

End of ideology, 77–78, 94. *See also* Bell, Daniel

Enslin, Theodore, 182

Evergreen Review, 13

Experiment, 300

Farrell, James T., 49–50, 58, 62

Fearing, Kenneth, 12, 28, 31, 47–48, 49, 109, 152, 289, 312, 313, 339 (n. 95); Blackburn influenced by, 314; conservatives' attack on, 212–13, 381 (n. 19); Dahlberg on, 74; and Rosenthal, 403 (n. 122); Rosten, influence on discerned, 158

Federal Bureau of Investigation (FBI), 140, 146–47, 221, 269, 272, 366 (n. 123)

Federal Writers Project, 313

Ferlinghetti, Lawrence, 60

Ferril, Thomas Hornsby, 282

Fess, Gilbert Malcolm, 165–66, 249

Fiedler, Leslie, 34–35, 48, 50, 60; on Whitman, 100–103

Finkelstein, Sidney, 9, 326 (n. 29)

Fitzgerald, Robert, 289

Fletcher, John, 128

Fletcher, John Gould, 23, 104, 193, 239–41

Flint, F. S., 104

Ford, Charles Henri, 8, 106, 107

Forster, E. M., 260

Franco, Francisco, 219

Frank, Waldo, 80, 86, 107

Frankenberg, Lloyd, 235

Frankfeld, Philip, 64–65

Freeman, Joseph, 13, 61–64, 69, 200, 312, 317; and CPUSA, 329 (n. 68); Hyman on, 52

Freeman, The, 75

French, Warren, 43

Freytag-Loringhoven, Elsa von, 167

Friar, Kimon, 107

Friedman, Norman, 132

Friend, Robert, 140

Frost, Robert, 10, 11, 80, 86, 99; in Beach's book, 87; Bush on, 237; Graves praises, 319

Frumkin, Gene, 13, 15, 107, 361 (n. 21)

Funaroff, Sol, 47–48, 49–50, 106, 312

Futurism, 253

Fyvel, T. R., 94, 95

García Villa, José, 8, 177

Gardner, Isabella, 14

Garrett, Alice, 216

Gascoyne, David, 104

Gibson, William, 213

Ginsberg, Allen, 12, 99, 103, 288

Glazer, Nathan, 38

Gold, Mike, 51, 69, 78

Golden Goose, 141, 182–83

Gordon, Don, 8, 106

Goris, Jan-Albert, 162–63, 299

Graves, Robert, 99, 193, 243–44, 317, 318, 319

Greenwood, Robert, 174

Gregory, Horace, 17, 20, 28–29, 83, 85, 125, 176, 244, 252, 313, 330 (n. 95), 370 (n. 34)

Grigson, Geoffrey, 104

Gropper, William, 225

Grumbach, Doris, 14

Guest, Barbara, 141

Guest, Edgar, 291, 300

Gunn, Giles, 53

Gurko, Leo, 35, 68–69, 86, 315

Gustafson, Ralph, 237–38, 241, 302

Hall, Donald, 56

Hanes, Leigh, 174, 176, 179, 245, 288, 309, 317

Harding, Anna T., 320

Harvard Communist, 33

Harvard University, 14, 193, 253, 283; communist unit at, 64; Conference on the Defense of Poetry hosted by, 180–81

Hauser, Jacob, 165, 192, 195, 203, 246, 274

Hayes, Alfred, 82–83, 85, 87–88, 92, 146, 311

Hayman, Lee Richard, 300, 301

H.D. *See* Doolittle, Hilda

Hejinian, Lyn, 321–22

Hellman, Lillian, 185

Hemingway, Ernest, 82, 211, 212, 292, 293

Herberg, Will, 273

Hicks, Granville, xiii, 37, 39, 64–65, 68, 69–70, 78–79; *The Great Tradition*, 51–52, 61–63, 64, 65; and Kazin, 40, 73–74, 78–79; and Kempton, 58

Hillyer, Robert, x, 165, 167, 173–74, 179, 182, 191, 196, 198, 212, 215, 228, 239, 244, 276; on Burman, 205; on iamb, 288; on modernist difficulty, 186, 238–39; poetry of, 241–42, 300; *Poetry* warned by, 184–85; Pound, attack on, 184; rhyme defended by, 289; Viereck deemed an ally by, 290–91. *See also* Pound, Ezra: Bollingen Prize controversy

Hiss, Alger, 34

Hitchcock, George, 14–15, 107

Hoffer, Eric, 173, 258

Hofstadter, Richard, xii

Hollo, Anselm, 199

Holmes, Oliver Wendell, 206

Homosexuality, 203; and communism, 129; implicit in attacks on modernist effeminacy, 239, 246; Whitman's, 101

Hook, Sidney, 310, 311

Hoover, J. Edgar, 188, 203, 221, 227, 385 (n. 93)

Hopkins, Gerard Manley, 27–28, 109, 191

Hound & Horn, 170

House, Homer, 192

House Committee on Un-American Activities, 76, 206, 344 (n. 181)

Howard, Milton, 81–82

Howe, Irving, 54

Hudson Review, 112, 113

Hughes, Langston, 22–23, 26, 31, 36–37, 189

Hulme, T. E., 104, 252, 253

Humanist, The, 161

Humboldt, Charles, 9

Humphries, Rolfe, 10, 42, 70; and Bogan, 111, 117–18

Hunt, H. L., 266

Hunter, Edward, 203, 204

Huntington, Anna Hyatt, 221–22

Huntington, Archer Milton, x, 169–71, 218–19, 221, 223, 299, 318

Huntington, Collis P., 170

Hyman, Stanley Edgar, 48, 50, 51–54, 252

Imagism, 49, 87, 104, 168, 240; and children, 251–52, 253; satirized, 298–99, 371 (n. 43)

Inge, Welford, x, 179, 186, 190, 290, 291, 294, 297

International Fine Arts Council, 217, 227

Invasion of the Body Snatchers, 183, 199–200, 202

James, Henry, 41, 110; admired by communists, 13

Janus, 8

Jarrell, Randall, 109, 181, 281; on Williams, 318

Jeffers, Louise, 103

Jeffers, Robinson, 10

Jefferson School of Social Science, 143, 348 (n. 70)

Jenks, Donald, 171, 238

Jerome, V. J., 331 (n. 117), 343 (n. 149), 365 (n. 105)

John Birch Society, 186, 286

John Reed Clubs, 91, 133, 218, 351 (n. 10)

Jolas, Eugene, 106

Jones, Cullen, 161, 171, 179, 182, 188, 190, 203, 246, 281–82, 299–300; poetry of, 396 (n. 57)

Josephson, Matthew, 56

Joyce, James, 9, 10, 13, 41, 108, 197, 203, 228, 258; *Ulysses*, 42, 49

Kael, Pauline, 60

Kafka, Franz, 14; influence on Fearing, 13

Kahn, Albert, 147, 363 (n. 67)

Kaladjian, Walter, 405 (n. 161)

Kalar, Joseph, 9, 107

Kane, Daniel V., 200

Kayak, 15

Kazin, Alfred, 37, 40, 55–56, 69, 77; on
Dahlberg, 74–75; and Hicks, 73–74,
78–79; "Ideology versus the Novel,"
121–22; on Marxist critical style, 72; *On
Native Grounds*, 40, 63, 65–66, 70, 71,
73, 74, 78, 79; *A Walker in the City*, 39,
71

Keats, John, 272

Keene, Florence, 196, 282

Kellogg Company, 189

Kempton, Murray, 32, 48, 50, 76, 89, 223;
on Dahlberg, 75; and Hicks, 58–59; on
1920s, 63–64

Kennedy, Gerald, 192, 228, 231–32

Kenner, Hugh, 96

Kinnell, Galway, 309

Kirk, Russell, 188, 248, 249, 276; and Eliot,
390 (n. 39); Wyndham Lewis admired
by, 266; on Viereck, 44

Kirstein, Lincoln, 170

Kissinger, Henry, 44–45

Koch, Kenneth, 262–64

Koch, Vivienne, 310, 311

Koestler, Arthur, 120–22

Korn, Alfred Ralph, 171–72, 193

Kraepelin, Emil, 265

Kramer, Aaron, 21, 24–25, 139, 147, 153

Kramer, Hilton, 47, 184, 338 (n. 78)

Kreymborg, Alfred, 22, 23, 28, 107, 144;
supported by Eliot, 49

Kujawa, Jan, 202

Kunitz, Joshua, 52

Lalley, Joseph M., 163–64, 222, 265, 291,
294

Langbaum, Robert, 233

Larkin, Margaret, 140

Laughlin, James, 8, 10, 197, 345 (n. 11)

Latimer, J. Ronald Lane, xiv, 141, 142

Lawrence, D. H., 74, 110, 314

League of American Writers, 70, 106, 123,
146, 312, 327 (n. 45), 341 (n. 117)

League for Sanity in Poetry, ix, 166, 167–
68, 172, 190, 191, 192, 194, 222, 248, 272,
282, 294, 300, 320; Fearing attacked by,
381 (n. 19); on *The Pisan Cantos*, 297

Lechlitner, Ruth, 22, 49–50, 110–11, 135,
142, 152, 325 (n. 14)

Left, The, 8

Leite, George, 107, 289

Leonard, William Ellery, 298–99

Leslie, Kenneth, 223

Levinson, Alfred, 132–36, 139

Lewis, C. Day, 43, 104–5, 107

Lewis, Fulton Jr., 143

Lewis, H. H., 49

Lewis, R. W. B., 101

Lewis, Wyndham, 260, 266

Lieberson, Goddard, 10

Life, 211–12

Lindsay, Vachel, 80

Lipton, Lawrence, 176–77, 180

Living Theatre, 19

Logan, John, 367 (n. 131)

Lorraine, Lilith, 192, 196, 222, 223, 272, 297

Lowell, Amy, 56, 104, 167, 168, 370 (n. 34)

Lowell, Robert, 56, 60, 68, 99, 109, 181, 184

Lowenfels, Walter, xiii, 7, 9, 13, 49–50, 75,
107

Lowes, John Livingston, 167

Loy, Mina, 23, 199, 202

Lukács, George, 257

Lumpkin, Grace, 75

Luquet, Georges-Henri, 253

Lush, S. Beryl, 288, 314

Lydenberg, John, 211

Lyons, Eugene, 32, 33, 34, 69, 147

Lyric, 174, 176, 190–91, 194, 196, 274, 309

Maas, Willard, xiv, 8, 10–11, 49–50, 142,
312, 327 (n. 45); Stevens admired by, 49

MacDiarmid, Hugh, 104, 176

MacLeish, Archibald, 58, 86, 109, 110, 111, 112, 113; satire of, 210

Macleod, Norman, 7, 8, 49, 106, 107, 135, 140–41, 321; published by *Golden Goose*, 182

Mac Low, Jackson, 18–21, 25, 30, 331 (n. 111); anarchism of, 20; on Fletcher, 240–41

MacNeice, Louis, 108, 109

Maddow, Ben, 102, 107, 145

Madge, Charles, 104

Mailer, Norman, 211–12

Mainstream, 13, 91

Maltz, Albert, 140, 145, 338 (n. 84)

Manifold, John, 125

Marcus, J. Anthony, 276, 295

Markel, Lester, 303

Marshall Plan, 235

Marx, Karl, 50, 52, 110, 344 (n. 169)

Marx, Leo, 99

Marxism: and aesthetics, 8; Burke's alleged, 299; classic texts of, 188–89; Hyman on, 51–52; Manifold's, 125; polemicism, 69, 72–73; radicals' knowledge of, 11, 38; Read's, 247; in schools, 143, 186; United States, appeal in, 167. *See also* Communism

Masses, 25, 144, 315

Masses & Mainstream, 13, 15, 81, 150, 180, 301

Matthews, J. B., 223

Matthiessen, F. O., 14, 35, 39, 129; *The Achievement of T. S. Eliot*, 52–54; on Hicks, 51–52; red-baiting of, 54, 336 (n. 48); suicide of, 37; on Whitman, 100, 101

Mayakovsky, Vladimir, 49

Mayor, A. Hyatt, 170, 219

Maxham, F. B., 8

McAlmon, Robert, 182

McCarthy, Joseph, x, 22, 30, 61, 64, 137, 221, 223, 275; Cameron named by, 142; Eastman defends, 388 (n. 41); Sheerin praises, 184

McCarthy, Kevin, 183

McClure, Michael, 224

McFee, William, 209, 314

McGinley, Phyllis, 174, 223, 234

McGrath, Thomas, 13, 15, 77, 176

McKay, Claude, 107

Measure, 141

Medina, Harold R., 174

Meredith, George, 371 (n. 43)

Meredith, William, 126–27, 129, 131–32, 152, 300

Merriam, Eve, 10, 22, 126, 142, 198–99, 321, 363 (n. 67)

Merton, Thomas, 267

Metropolitan Museum of Art, 225, 226

Meyer, Frank, 36, 44, 50, 123, 143, 195, 200

Millay, Edna St. Vincent, 14, 49, 107, 110

Miller, Arthur, 144, 151

Millet, Martha, 3–7, 18, 20–21, 25–27, 31, 33, 41, 107, 333 (n. 140)

Milton, John, 209, 214, 236

Mizener, Arthur, 90

Modern Age, 210

Modernism: in American fiction assailed, 211–12; antibourgeois origins of, debated, 46–47; "anything goes" principle alleged in, 195, 207, 247, 277–78, 284, 286, 309; audience, its disconnection from, 169, 231–42; Christian arguments against, 231, 239, 268–86, 395 (n. 32); communism, functions like, 166, 173, 215–16; communist poets' interest in, 7–18, 41–43, 49–50, 107; defense of, 179–84; dehumanization alleged, 168, 200–201; difficulty, indirectness, and obscurity in, 163, 186–87, 189, 190, 205, 208, 216, 229–30, 232, 238, 247, 303–5, 329 (n. 76); disease, likened to, 205–7; disjunction and parataxis in criticized, 291–93, 315; domino theory, relation between grammar and, 292–94; early detractors of, 167–68, 298–99; effeminacy alleged, 239, 246; fragmentation in, 292–94; as genocide, 166; genre confusion in, 198–99, 295; Harvard Conference on the Defense of Poetry, 180–81; insanity, likened to, 264–65; market for, 301, 303; in post-Marxist era, 194; prewar reaction against, as compared to postwar, 167–69; satirized in allegory, 210–11; Sinclair attacks, 314–15; urbanization, coincides with, 181; Victorianism, its reaction against, 153; vision, loss of, 283–86; weeds, verse compared to, 204

Molk, Sophia, 70, 71

Moloney, Michael Francis, 272–73, 291

Mondrian, Piet, 13

Monroe, Harriet, 6, 7, 176, 196

Monthly Review, 37–38; Matthiessen memorial issue, 101

Moody, William Vaughn, 153–54

Moore, Marianne, 28, 99, 165, 181, 202, 270

Morada, The, 8

Morgan, Frederick, 112–13

Mowrer, Paul Scott, 305

Mumford, Lewis, 218

Murton, Jessie Wilmore, x, 189, 210, 351 (n. 13)

Museum of Modern Art, 224

Nation, 176, 194, 195, 301, 313

National Council of Churches, 224

National Dance Congress, 147

National Institute of Arts and Letters, 219

National Republic, 22

Neiman, Gilbert, 193, 196–99, 202, 203, 245, 298

Neimeyer, Gerhart, 188

Nelson, Cary, 60, 76

Nelson, Raymond, 320

Nemerov, Howard, 241

Neugass, James, 22, 146

New American Poetry, The (Donald Allen, ed.), 56, 274, 280, 299, 321

New Criticism, 78–79, 176, 236, 245, 259, 287, 311

New Deal: attack on, 31–46, 161, 221, 276; conservative critique of its acronyms, 36–37

New Masses, ix, 8–9, 25, 27, 31, 42, 49, 50, 123–24, 138, 217, 272; aesthetic policy, 10; Rexroth praises, 107

New Republic, 78, 79, 95, 194, 195, 255, 301, 314

New Yorker, 173

New York Times Book Review, 177, 211

New York Times Magazine, 303–4

Nichol, Barry Phillip (bpNichol), 321, 322

Niedecker, Lorine, 74, 182, 189

Nims, John Frederick, 44

Nobel Prize, 238

Norse, Harold, 99, 199

North, Joseph, 50, 64

Noyes, Alfred, 215

Objectivist poetry, 176, 277. *See also* Rakosi, Carl

O'Connor, Mary, 207

O'Connor, William Van, 35, 85–86, 87; on Stevens, 352 (n. 25)

Ogilvy, David, 301

O'Hara, Frank, 14, 264, 280–81

Olson, Charles, 74, 288, 313

Ono, Yoko, 295, 296

Oppen, George, 11, 107, 145, 146

Oral poetry, 176–77, 180

Ortega y Gasset, José, 264

Orwell, George, 122

O'Sheel, Shaemas, 22, 27, 341 (n. 117)

Osman, Jena, 321

Ostroff, Anthony, 309

335 (n. 31); "Big Crash Out West," 282–83; "Bloody-Minded Professors," 45–46, 50–51; conservatism, associates poetry with, 198–99, 216; conservatism of, doubted by Meyer, 195; on Daiches, 95–96; at Defense of Poetry conference, 181; "The Dignity of Lyricism," 245, 247, 278–79; "Don't Look Now but Mary Is Everybody," 275–76, 277; as Hillyer's student, 241; "A Masque of Tears," 279–80, 283; on Pound, 287–88, 307; *Strike through the Mask!*, 278–79; *Terror and Decorum*, 275; *The Unadjusted Man*, 236, 246, 248, 252, 277, 282, 291; on Williams, 398 (n. 4)

Vinson, Fred, 206

Vivas, Eliseo, 48, 262, 404 (n. 141)

Waggoner, Hyatt, 273

Wagner, Geoffrey, 250, 262

Wald, Alan, 60, 74, 75, 139, 148; on Freeman, 329 (n. 68); on Old and New Lefts, 339 (n. 93)

Wallace, Henry, 13, 37, 142

Walsh, Chad, 13, 198, 273, 312

Walters, August, 306–9, 311

Walton, Eda Lou, 33, 42, 50, 66, 68, 69, 107, 144; poetry of, 67–68; red-baiting of, 142–44; and Roth, 66; on Yeats, 49

Walton, William Bell, 67

Warhol, Andy, 49

Warren, Robert Penn, 17, 86, 87, 176, 289, 352 (n. 39)

War Resisters' League, 16, 18, 19

Warshow, Robert, 31–32, 82

Weaver, Mike, 310, 311, 312

Weaver, Richard, 167, 205, 206, 228, 248, 290, 291, 303; acronyms, critique of, 36–37; cause-and-effect rhetoric commended by, 292, 293; on education,

260, 262; grammar as a precondition of citizenship, belief in, 303, 316–17; *Ideas Have Consequences*, 249, 265, 276, 297, 398 (n. 12); jazz hated by, 289–90

Wechsler, James, 55

Weiners, John, 141

Weiss, George Henry, 10

Weiss, Theodore, 124–25

West, Ray B., 33–34, 50

Western Review, 33–34

Whitman, Walt, 66, 95, 104, 110, 133, 191, 228, 245, 288; Arvin's leftist reading of, 355 (n. 12); homosexuality of, 101; influence on modern poetry disdained, 317; *Leaves of Grass* centennial, 96–103

Wilbur, Richard, 99, 109, 238, 241, 291

Wilde, Oscar, 188, 246

Wilder, Amos N., 231

Wilhelmsen, Frederick, 284

William-Frederick Press, 147

Williams, B. Y., 70, 196, 210

Williams, Florence, 309–10

Williams, Jonathan, 320

Williams, Wheeler, 217, 224, 226, 262

Williams, William Carlos, x, 6, 7, 15, 23, 30, 31, 47, 99, 107, 125, 142, 154, 157, 199, 200, 259, 288, 301–3, 313, 318; attacked as communist, 184, 189, 297, 309–12, 317; Bush on, 237; deradicalized, 317–18; Fletcher on, 240–41; "Flowers by the Sea," 148; and Kreymborg, 28; *Paterson*, 295, 305–8, 311, 312, 314; poetry attacked, 177, 209–10, 289, 305, 314–15, 398 (n. 4); poetry imitated, 300; "Portrait of a Lady," 306–7; and Pound, 302, 307–9; "Red Wheelbarrow" satirized, 302–3; Rosenthal praises, 314–15; *Spring and All*, 309; "To All Gentleness," 312, 314; on Whitman, 102

Wilson, Edmund, 53, 79

Wimsatt, W. K., 85